For Quality British Coins

RODERICK RICHARDSON LTD

(S ins

For appointments in London or my latest circular, please contact me at
Old Granary Antiques Centre, Kings Staithe Lane,
King's Lynn, Norfolk, England PE30 1LZ

.co.uk

m

SELLING YOUR COINS & BANKNOTES?

Warwick and Warwick have an expanding requirement for coin and banknote collections, British and worldwide and for coins and notes of individual value. Our customer base is increasing dramatically and we need an ever larger supply of quality material to keep pace with demand. The market has never been stronger and if you are considering the sale of your collection, now is the time to act.

FREE VALUATIONS

We will provide a free, professional and without obligation valuation of your collection. Either we will make you a fair, binding private treaty offer, or we will recommend inclusion of your property in our next specialist public auction.

FREE TRANSPORTATION

We can arrange insured transportation of your collection to our Warwick offices completely free of charge. If you decline our offer, we ask you to cover the return carriage costs only.

FREE VISITS

Visits by our valuers are possible anywhere in the country or abroad, usually within 48 hours, in order to value larger collections. Please telephone for details.

ADVISORY DAYS

We are staging a series of advisory days and will be visiting all areas of England, Scotland, Wales and Ireland during the coming months. Please visit our website or telephone for further details.

EXCELLENT PRICES

Because of the strength of our customer base we are in a position to offer prices that we feel sure will exceed your expectations.

ACT NOW

Telephone or email Richard Beale today with details of your property.

Warwick & Warwick Ltd.
Auctioneers and Valuers
Chalon House, Scar Bank, Millers Road,
Warwick CV34 5DB
Tel: 01926 499031 Fax: 01926 491906
E-mail: richard.beale@warwickandwarwick.com

Warwick & Warwick

British Numismatic Trade Association

The British Numismatic Trade Association represents the foremost British coin dealers who abide by a stringent code of conduct.

Buy and sell with confidence, wherever you see the BNTA logo.

For all our members' details and much more visit us at:

www.BNTA.net

Standard Catalogue of British Coins
Volume One

COINS OF ENGLAND

& THE UNITED KINGDOM
Pre-Decimal Issues

54th Edition

LONDON

A Catalogue of the Coins of Great Britain
and Ireland
first published 1929

Standard Catalogue of British Coins
Coins of England and the United Kingdom
54th edition, 2019

© Spink & Son Ltd, 2018
69 Southampton Row, Bloomsbury
London WC1B 4ET
www.spinkbooks.com

www.spink.com

Typeset by Design to Print UK Ltd,
9 & 10 Riverview Business Park, Forest Row, East Sussex RH18 5DW
www.designtoprintuk.com
Printed and bound in Malta
by Gutenberg Press Ltd.

Cover design: Russell White
E-mail: uk47@me.com

The contents of this volume, including the numbering system and illustrations,
are protected by copyright.

ISBN 978-1-907427-93-0

CONTENTS

ACKNOWLEDGEMENTS

We wish to acknowledge the valuable contributions of the following.

Richard Abdy *(The British Museum)*
Tony Abramson
Dr Martin Allen *(Fitzwilliam Museum)*
Keith Bayford
Joe Bispham
Jon Blyth
James Booth
Ron Churchill
Nigel Clark
Chris Comber
Barrie Cook *(The British Museum)*
Simon Cope
Jonathan Cope
Dave Craddock
Joe Cribb *(The British Museum)*
Mike Cuddeford
Paul Davies
Charles Davis
Tim Everson
David Fletcher
Glen Gittoes
Eric Green
Dave Greenhalgh
David Guest
Peter Hendra

Heritage Auctions UK
Steve Hill
Peter Jackson
Richard Kelleher *(The Fizwilliam Museum)*
Geoff Kitchen
Stewart Lyon
William MacKay
Nigel Mills
Graeme Monk
Neil Paisley
Rob Pearce
Gary Poole
Nigel Prevost
Mark Rasmussen
Martin Roberts
The Schneider Family
Dr Irving Schneider
Peter D Spencer
Bob Thomas
Andrew Wayne
Tim Webb Ware
Walter Wilkinson
Gareth Williams *(The British Museum)*
Paul & Bente R. Withers

Museums/Institutions
The Trustees of the British Museum, London
The Fitzwilliam Museum, Cambridge

Photography
Richard Hodges
Paul & Bente R. Withers
Wioletta Madaj

ABBREVIATIONS

Archb.	Archbishop	laur.	laureate
Æ	bronze	mm.	mintmark
R	silver	mon.	monogram
N	gold	O., obv.	obverse
Bp.	Bishop	p.	new penny, pence
BV	bullion value	pl	plume
cuir.	cuirassed	quat.	quatrefoil
d.	penny, pence	qtr.	quarter
diad.	diademed	rad.	radiate
dr.	draped	R., rev.	reverse
ex.	exergue	r.	right
grs.	grains	s.	shillings
hd.	headstg.	stg.	standing
i.c.	inner circle	trun.	truncation
illus.	illustration	var.	variety
l.	left	wt.	weight

Welcome to the 54th edition of Coins of England and the United Kingdom.

Continuing our commemorative cover theme, this year we have chosen a striking depiction of a youthful Queen Victoria by the revered engraver William Wyon RA, to mark the bicentenary of her birth. Hindsight tells us that a record-breaking reign would follow, the global impact and duration of which was still reverberating as recently as 10th September 2015, when our current Queen Elizabeth II finally surpassed her great-great-grandmother's tenure. Christened Princess Alexandrina Victoria of Kent, she was born on 24th May 1819 at Kensington Palace, then fifth in line to the throne behind the four sons of King George III. She would later describe her childhood as rather melancholy on account of her Duchess mother's oppressive parenting style. Such domineering did not go unnoticed by the King incumbent, her uncle William IV, who publicly declared to the Duchess that he wished to live to see Victoria turn 18 so that her regency could be avoided. Fortunately for William, he achieved his ambition with a matter of weeks to spare, leaving Victoria to ascend the throne on 20th June 1837. She would go on to rule as Queen of the United Kingdom of Great Britain and Ireland, and from 1877, also Empress of India, until her death on 22nd January 1901.

It comes as no surprise that over six decades of coinage a wide variety of effigies across a multitude of denominations were produced. There would be four main portraits: the first, commonly referred to as the 'Young Head', reflected Victoria's youthfulness at time of her Coronation, and with only minor modifications would be used on all gold and silver denominations until 1887, when the 'Jubilee' head by Sir Joseph Edgar Boehm succeeded it, and on Copper and Bronze until 1895, when the 'Old Head' was introduced. Before this redesign however, radical attempts were made in Parliament and at the mint to decimalise the English monetary system. Hence in 1849, a new coin called the 'Florin' was issued at a value of 2-Shillings; clearly issued in direct competition to the currently circulating Halfcrown (2-Shillings and Sixpence). Hoping to avoid initial public disquiet, these new coins bore an explanation of value in the form of 'One Tenth of a Pound'. However alarm still followed, on account of the simple omission of two words: DEI GRATIA ('By the Grace of God'), which has forever condemned the issue to numismatic folklore as the 'Godless' or 'Graceless' type. Soon rectified, a more extensive issue of Florins followed that have come to be known as the 'Gothic' series for their stark revivalist but nevertheless attractive portraiture. While Gothic design is found earlier on the enduringly popular Proof Crown issues of 1847 and 1853 (a more famous example of Wyon's aptitude), its regular use on British currency was confined to the Florin issues, which by 1874 had begun to circulate in tandem with the more established and still popular Halfcrown and the Shilling to provide a complicated monetary system by the time of Victoria's Golden Jubilee.

Not content with an overhaul of the imagery for this national event, a further, and very short-lived denomination was also introduced at this time, again on the canon of decimalisation. The 'Double-Florin' or 4-Shillings appeared but survived only four years of issue on account of its similarity in size to the Crown (5-Shillings); as such it became colloquially known as a 'Barmaid's ruin' for in low light, one could often mistake the former with the latter which would prove very costly very quickly! Despite alteration, Boehm's Jubilee series did not prove at all popular with the public, some contemporaries describing the small crown on Victoria's head as looking precariously balanced and constantly on the verge of falling off! In 1893, Thomas Brock successfully submitted his suggestions for a redesign that would ultimately spawn the 'Old' or 'Veiled' or 'Widow' head design that would last until her death. It seems therefore only fitting that after many years of being overlooked by collectors, Victorian coinage has come to the fore in recent years, with another of Wyon's designs - his 1839 'Una and the Lion' Pattern gold Five Pounds (S.3851) proving to be a star attraction in a Spink saleroom this past year, with an example selling for almost £210,000 (HP).

As ever, 2018 has proven to be an extremely busy year for Spink as it sought to juggle both its regular calendar of general auctions with the addition of a number of exceptional single owner collections that began in March with the highly-important Williams collection of Anglo-Saxon to Anarchy period currency. It would be fair to say that such a comprehensive and detailed assemblage is unlikely to be achieved privately again this generation, if at all, and as such, it has been an immense and unique privilege to handle unquestionably some of the most important coins in the history of the British Isles. One might even think it prophetic for such an auction to have taken place given our ongoing political and international uncertainty – a situation to which the likes of Alfred the Great and Aethelred II 'the Unready' could have undoubtedly related. In October, another lifetime collection graced our saleroom; this time the Pywell-Phillips assemblage, which offered a remarkably complete run of Silver, Copper and Tin coin issued from the Protectorate of Oliver Cromwell to the present day, so comprehensive indeed that one could simply have reviewed the latter half of this volume to obtain an accurate order of sale!

Such a comprehensive corpus of coinage this past year has enabled the editorial committee to further evaluate ways in which to develop the Standard Catalogue going forward. We recognise the importance the market continues to entrust to this publication, and its increasing use for corroboration and confirmation of new discoveries. We therefore feel it is time to radically overhaul the legibility and clarity of its contents, primarily the illustrations (which have inevitably deteriorated since they were first published), and hope to see improvements being achieved as soon as the 2020 edition, with the ultimate intention being to reconnect with the catalogue's founding principle: a standardised if not necessarily complete overview of the coinage of England, from Celtic to present day, with an accurate reflection on market attainability for the 21st Century collector.

As always, thanks are due to those who have contacted us with corrections for this catalogue – the input of all who use this reference work is essential in keeping it as accurate and interesting as possible. We should again point out that we cannot guarantee to include new discoveries unless they have been verified by the Royal Mint, and all new suggestions are subject to the agreement of the editorial committee.

Gregory Edmund with Emma Howard
Editor, Coins of England

A note on bullion value in this edition: we have listed the 2019 spot price for gold quoted on page 452 onwards at £900 an ounce, but obviously this is subject to fluctuation because the price of gold has been and continues to be so volatile.

INTRODUCTION

Arrangement

The arrangement of this catalogue is not completely uniform, but generally it is divided into metals (gold, silver, copper, etc) under each reign, then into coinages, denominations and varieties. In the Celtic section the uninscribed coins are listed before the dynastic coins; under Charles II all the hammered coins precede the milled coinage; the reign of George III is divided into coins issued up to 1816 and the new coinage from 1816 to the end of the reign; and under Elizabeth II the decimal issues are separated from the pre-decimal *(£.s.d.)* coinages and listed in a separate volume of the SCBC since 2015.

Every major coin type is listed though not every variety. We have endeavoured to give rather more coverage to the varieties of relatively common coins, such as the pennies of Edward I, II and III, than to the very much rarer coins of, for instance, King Offa of Mercia.

Values

The values given represent the range of retail prices at which coins are being offered for sale at the time of going to press and **not** the price which a dealer will pay for those coins. These prices are based on our knowledge of the numismatic market, the current demand for particular coins, recent auction sale prices and, in those cases where certain coins have not appeared for sale for some years, our estimation of what they would be likely to sell at today, bearing in mind their rarity and appeal in relation to somewhat similar coins where a current value is known. Values are given for two grades of preservation from the Celtic period onwards and three to four grades of preservation for coins of the 17th to the 20th century.

Collectors normally require coins in the best condition they can afford and, except in the case of a really rare coin, a piece that is considerably worn is not wanted and has little value. The values given in the catalogue are for the exact state of preservation stated at the head of each column and bearing in mind that a score of identical coins in varying states of wear could be lined up in descending order from mint condition (FDC, *fleur de coin*), through very fine (VF) to *poor* state. It will be realized that only in certain instances will the values given apply to particular coins. A 'fine' (F) coin may be worth anything between one quarter and a half of the price quoted for a 'very fine' (VF); on the other hand, a piece in really mint condition will be valued substantially higher than the price quoted for 'extremely fine' (EF). The designation BV has been adopted for coins whose value on the market has yet to exceed its bullion value. Purchasing sovereigns, catalogued as BV, will attract a dealers' premium.

We emphasize again that the purpose of this catalogue is to give a general value for a particular class of coin in a specified state of preservation, and also to give the collector an idea of the range and value of coins in the English series. The value of any particular piece depends on three things:

Its exact design, legend, mintmark or date.

Its exact state of preservation; this is of prime importance.

The demand for it in the market at any given time.

Some minor varieties are much scarcer than others and, as the number of coins issued varies considerably from year to year, coins of certain dates and mintmarks are rarer and of more value than other pieces of similar type. The prices given for any type are for the commonest variety, mintmark or date of that type.

The Scope

Coin collecting, numismatics, is a fascinating hobby. It requires very little physical exertion and only as much mental effort as one wishes or is able to put into it at any time. There is vast scope and boundless ramifications and byways encompassing not only things historical and geographical, but also touching on economics, metallurgy, heraldry, literature, the fine arts, politics, military history and many other disciplines. This catalogue is solely concerned with British coinage from its earliest times right up to date. From the start the beginner should appreciate that the coinage of our own nation may be seen as a small but very important part of the whole story of world currency.

The first coins, made of electrum, a natural alloy of gold and silver, were issued in western Asia Minor (Lydia) in the later seventh century B.C. Over the next century or so coinage of gold and silver spread across the Aegean to mainland Greece, southwards to the eastern Mediterranean lands and eventually westward to the Greek colonies in southern Italy, Sicily (Magna Graecia) and beyond. The coins of the Greeks are noted for their beautiful, sometimes exquisite craftsmanship, with many of the coin types depicting the patron deities of their cities. Coins of Philip II of Macedon (359-336 B.C.), father of Alexander the Great, circulated amongst the Celtic peoples of the Danubian Basin and were widely copied through central Europe and by the Gauls in France. Gold Gaulish staters were reaching Britain around the beginning of the first century B.C. and the earliest gold to be struck in the island must have been produced shortly afterwards. Although their types and designs copy the Apollo head and racing charioteer of Philip II's gold coins, they are stylistically much removed from the original representation and very individually Celtic in concept.

The coins of the Romans cover some seven centuries and include an enormous number of different types that were current throughout a major part of the civilized world from Spain to Syria and from the Rhine in the north to the Sudan in the south. The Roman province of Britain was part of this vast empire for four hundred years from AD 43 until the early fifth century. Innumerable Roman coins have been recovered from sites in this country, most being made of brass or bronze. Many of these are quite inexpensive and very collectable. In recent years many hoards of gold and silver coins have been found, usually by use of metal detectors.

Following the revival of commerce after the Dark Ages, coinage in Western Europe was virtually restricted to silver until the thirteenth century, though gold was still being minted in Byzantium and in the Islamic world. In the Middle Ages many European cities had their own distinctive coinage and money was issued not only by the kings but also by nobles, bishops and abbots. From the time of the later Crusades gold returned to the West, and the artistic developments of the Renaissance in the fifteenth century brought improved portraiture and new minting techniques.

Large silver crown-size thalers were first minted at Joachimsthal in Bohemia early in the sixteenth century. The substantial shipments of silver coming to Europe from the mines of Spanish America over the next couple of centuries led to a fine series of larger coins being issued by the European states and cities. The larger size allowed greater artistic freedom in the designs and the portraits on the coins.

Both Germany and Italy became unified nation states during the later nineteenth century, thereby substantially reducing the number of mints and coin types. Balancing the reduction in European minting authorities were the new coins that were issued by the independent states of South and Central America. Since the 1950s many new nations have established their independence and their coinage provides a large field for the collector of modern coins.

It can be seen that the scope for the collector is truly vast, but besides the general run of official coinage there is also the large series of token coins—small change unofficially produced to supplement the inadequate supply of authorized currency. These tokens were issued by merchants, innkeepers and manufacturers in many towns and villages in the seventeenth, eighteenth and nineteenth centuries and many collectors specialize in their local issues.

Some coins have designs of a commemorative nature; an example being the Royal Wedding crown of 1981, but there are also large numbers of commemorative medals which, though never intended for use as coinage, are sometimes confused with coins because they are metal objects of a similar shape and sometimes a similar size to coins. This is another interesting field for collectors as these medals often have excellent portraits of famous men or women, or they may commemorate important events or scientific discoveries. Other metallic objects of coin-like appearance that can be confusing for the beginner are reckoning counters, advertising tickets, various other tickets and passes, and items such as brass coin weights.

Minting processes

From the time of the earliest Greek coins in the late seventh century BC to about the middle of the sixteenth century AD, coins were made by hand. The method of manufacture was simple. The obverse and reverse designs were engraved or punched into the prepared ends of two bars of bronze or iron, shaped or tapered to the diameter of the required coin. The obverse die, known as the *pile*, was usually spiked so that it could be anchored firmly into a block of wood or metal. The reverse die, the *trussel*, was held by hand or grasped by tongs.

The coin was struck by placing a metal blank between the two dies and striking the trussel with a hammer. Thus, all coinage struck by this method is known as 'hammered'. Some dies are known to have been hinged so there would be an exact register between the upper and lower die. Usually a 'pair of dies' consisted of one obverse die (normally the more difficult to make because it had the finer detail, such as the ruler's portrait) and two reverse dies. This was because the shaft of iron bearing the reverse design eventually split under the constant hammering; two reverse dies were usually needed to last out the life of the obverse die.

Some time toward the middle of the sixteenth century, experiments, first in Germany and later in France, resulted in the manufacture of coins by machinery.

The term 'milled', which is applied to all machine-made coins, comes from the type of machinery used – the mill and screw press. With this machinery the obverse die was fixed as the lower die and the reverse die brought down into contact with the blank by heavy vertical pressure applied by a screw or worm-drive connected to a cross bar with heavy weights at each end. These weights usually had long leather thongs attached which allowed a more powerful force to be applied by the operators who revolved the arms of the press. New blanks were placed on the lower die and the struck coins were removed by hand. The screw press brought more pressure to bear on the blanks and this pressure was evenly applied, producing a far better and sharper coin.

Various attempts were made during the reigns of Elizabeth I and Charles I to introduce this type of machinery with its vastly superior products. Unfortunately problems associated with the manufacture of blanks to a uniform weight greatly reduced the rate of striking and the hand manufacture of coins continued until the Restoration in 1660, when Charles II brought to London from Holland the Roettiers brothers and their improved screw press.

The first English coins made for circulation by this new method were the silver crowns of 1662, which bore an inscription on the edge, DECVS ET TVTAMEN, 'an ornament and a safeguard', a reference to the fact that the new coins could not be clipped, a crime made easy by the thin and often badly struck hammered coins.

The mill and screw press was used until new steam-powered machinery made by Boulton and Watt was installed in the new mint on Tower Hill in London. This machinery had been used most successfully by Boulton to strike the large 'cartwheel' two- and one- penny pieces of 1797 and other coins, including 'overstriking' Spanish *eight-reale* pieces into Bank of England 'dollars' since the old Mint presses were not able to exert sufficient power to do this. This new machinery was first used at the Mint to strike the 'new coinage' halfcrowns of 1816, and it operated at a far greater speed than the old type of mill and screw presses and achieved a greater sharpness of design.

The very latest coining presses now operating at the Royal Mint at Llantrisant in South Wales, are capable of striking at a rate of up to 800 coins a minute.

Condition

One of the more difficult problems for the beginner is to assess accurately the condition of a coin. A common fault among collectors is to overgrade and, consequently, to overvalue their coins.

Most dealers will gladly spare a few minutes to help new collectors. Many dealers issue price lists with illustrations, enabling collectors to see exactly what the coins look like and how they have been graded.

Coins cannot always be graded according to precise rules. Hammered coins often look weak or worn on the high parts of the portrait and the tops of the letters; this can be due to weak striking or worn dies and is not always attributable to wear through long use in circulation. Milled coins usually leave the Mint sharply struck so that genuine wear is easier to detect. However a x5 or x10 magnifying glass is essential, especially when grading coins of Edward VII and George V where the relief is very low on the portraits and some skill is required to distinguish between an uncirculated coin and one in EF condition.

The condition or grade of preservation of a coin is usually of greater importance than its rarity. By this we mean that a common coin in superb condition is often more desirable and more highly priced than a rarity in poor condition. Coins that have been pierced or mounted as a piece of jewellery generally have little interest to collectors.

One must also be on the lookout for coins that have been 'plugged', i.e. that have been pierced at some time and have had the hole filled in, sometimes with the missing design or letters re-engraved.

Badly cleaned coins will often display a complexity of fine interlaced lines and such coins have a greatly reduced value. It is also known for coins to be tooled or re-engraved on the high parts of the hair, in order to 'increase' the grade of coin and its value. In general it is better to have a slightly more worn coin than a better example with such damage.

In recent years professional grading services have come to exert considerable influence over the grading of coins and the subsequent prices they can command. Whilst such services can provide an accurate way to grade coins, and is well -suited to milled and machine made issues, the resulting grading remains an opinion with grading of hammered and ancient requiring different considerations to milled and machine made coins. Associated with professional grading is the practise of sealing the coin within a clear plastic container, colloquially referred to as slabbing. Whilst now a well-established practise in the US market it has had less impact in the UK where collectors prefer to handle a coin which allows for closer examination of the surfaces and the edges, a necessity for a milled coin with an inscribed edge which once enscapulated cannot be examined.

Cleaning coins

Speaking generally, *do not* clean coins. More coins are ruined by injudicious cleaning than through any other cause, and a badly cleaned coin loses much of its value. A nicely toned piece is usually considered desirable. Really dirty gold and silver can, however, be carefully washed in soap and water. Copper coins should never be cleaned or washed, they may be lightly brushed with a brush that is not too harsh.

Buying and selling coins

Exchanging coins with other collectors, searching around the antique shops, telling your relatives and friends that you are interested in coins, or even trying to find your own with a metal detector, are all ways of adding to your collection. However, the time will come when the serious collector needs to acquire specific coins or requires advice on the authenticity or value of a coin.

At this point an expert is needed, and the services of a reputable coin dealer or independent numismatic consultant are necessary. There are now a large number of coin dealers in the UK, many of whom belong to the B.N.T.A. (The British Numismatic Trade Association) or the I.A.P.N. (The International Association of Professional Numismatists) and a glance through the 'yellow pages' under 'coin dealer' or 'numismatist' will often provide local information. Many dealers publish their own lists of coins. Studying these lists is a good way for a collector to learn about coins and to classify and catalogue their own collections.

In recent years the internet has made it very much easier to locate, view and acquire coins online not just in the United Kingdom but worldwide. Many dealers now offer lists of stock online. It has also revolutionised the availability of coins at auction with printed catalogues supplemented by online catalogues and the increasing use of online bidding making the need to attend an auction on the day less critical than it once was. As a result buying and selling at auction has grown as a way to add to and dispose of collections. In buying at auction it is always advisable to examine the coin before deciding to bid and it should be borne in mind that the description given will only be as good as the expertise of the person describing the coin. It is still possible to find and acquire bargains at auction, but the chance of doing so is perhaps less these days than it once was. It should also be pointed out that auction houses charge the buyer a premium on the hammer price, generally at 20%, on which, in the United Kingdom , VAT is applicable with the total price paid generally hammer price plus 24%. Coins disposed of at auction will be subject to a vendor's commission charge made by the auction house which can be up to 15% of the price realised. An active market for buying and selling coins exists also on e-bay, however in general items offered here should be treated with caution with the onus on checking the veracity of the coin very much with the bidder.

The Standard Catalogue of Coins of England and the UK has been published since 1929. It serves as a price guide for all coin collectors. Spink also publish books on many aspects of English, Greek, Roman and Byzantine coins and on British tokens which serve as a valuable source of information for coin collectors. Our books are available directly from Spink, selected high street booksellers and online outlets such as Amazon.

Numismatic Clubs and Societies

There are over thirty numismatic societies and clubs in the British Isles. Joining one is the best way to meet fellow enthusiasts, learn about your coins and other series in a friendly and informative way. For details and contacts for a club or society near you see Appendix III, page 534 or online, www.coinclubs.org.uk. The British Association of Numismatic Societies (BANS), which acts as the national body for all Societies, holds two weekend meetings each year with a range of speakers in convivial surroundings.

Useful suggestions

Security and insurance. The careful collector should not keep valuable coins at home unless they are insured and have adequate protection. Local police and insurance companies will give advice on what precautions may be necessary.

Most insurance companies will accept a valuation based on *The Standard Catalogue*. It is usually possible to have the amount added to a householder's contents policy but particularly valuable individual coins may have to be separately listed. A 'Fire, Burglary and Theft' policy will cover loss only from the insured's address, but an 'All Risks' policy will usually cover accidental damage and loss anywhere within the U.K.

Until recently most high street banks offered safe-deposit boxes which formed a useful way for holding a collection in a secure environment. However in recent years many high street banks have stopped providing such services. The alternative is to acquire and install a safe at your home where coins can be stored. There are many options available here and most insurance companies will offer reduced premiums for coins securely stored at the home.

Keeping a record. All collectors are advised to have an up-to-date record of their collection and, if possible, photographs of the more important and more easily identifiable coins. This should be kept in a separate place from the collection so that a list and photographs can be given to the police should loss occur. Note the price paid, from whom purchased, the date of acquisition and the condition of the coin.

Storage and handling. New collectors should get into the habit of handling coins by the edge. This is especially important as far as highly polished proof coins are concerned.

Collectors may initially keep their coins in paper or plastic envelopes housed in boxes, albums or special containers. Many collectors will eventually wish to own a hardwood coin cabinet in which the collection can be properly arranged and displayed. If a home-made cabinet is being constructed avoid using oak and cedar wood; mahogany, walnut and rosewood are ideal. It is important that coins are not kept in a humid atmosphere; especial care must be taken with copper and bronze coins which are very susceptible to damp or condensation which may result in a green verdigris forming on them.

From beginner to numismatist

The new collector can best advance to becoming an experienced numismatist by examining as many coins as possible, noting their distinctive features and by learning to use the many books of reference that are available. It will be an advantage to join a local numismatic society, as this will provide an opportunity for meeting other enthusiasts and obtaining advice from more experienced collectors. Most societies have a varied programme of lectures, exhibitions and occasional auctions of members' duplicates.

Those who become members of one or both of the national societies, the Royal Numismatic Society and the British Numismatic Society, receive an annual journal containing authoritative papers and have access to the societies' library and programme of lectures.

Many museums have coin collections available for study, although they may not always be displayed, and a number of museum curators are qualified numismatists. Many collectors enjoy deepening their knowledge of the coins they collect by referring to books and articles which provide detailed study of specific coins and coinages. These provide more detail on varieties than can be included here in the Standard Catalogue. References to relevant studies and books are given within this catalogue to allow for more detailed study. Appendix 1 gives details of a selection of key works useful to the specialist collector.

SOME NUMISMATIC TERMS EXPLAINED

Obverse	That side of the coin which normally shows the monarch's head or name.
Reverse	The side opposite to the obverse, the 'Tails'.
Blank	The coin as a blank piece of metal, i.e. before it is struck.
Flan	The whole piece of metal after striking.
Type	The main, central design.
Legend	The inscription. Coins lacking a legend are called 'mute' or anepigraphic.
Field	That flat part of the coin between the main design and the inscription or edge.
Exergue	That part of the coin below the main design, usually separated by a horizontal line, and normally occupied by the date.
Die	The block of metal, with design cut into it, which actually impresses the coin blank with the design.
Die variety	Coin showing slight variation of design.
Mule	A coin with the current type on one side and the previous (and usually obsolete) type on the other side, or a piece struck from two dies that are not normally used together.
Graining or reeding	The crenellations around the edge of the coin, commonly known as'milling'.
Proof	Carefully struck coin from special dies with a mirror-like or matt surface. (In this country 'Proof' is not a term used to describe the state of preservation, but the method of striking.)
Hammered	Refers to the old craft method of striking a coin between dies hammered by hand.
Milled	Coins struck by dies worked in a coining press. The presses were hand powered from 1560-1800, powered by steam from 1790 and by electricity from 1895.

CELTIC COINAGE EXPLAINED

The Celtic or Ancient British issues are amongst the most interesting and varied of all British coins. They are our earliest coins and are the product of a society that left no historical sources of its own. It is therefore often difficult to be specific about for whom, when or where they were produced. Despite only being used for approximately a hundred and fifty years they do provide a rich variety of designs and types in gold, silver and bronze. Collectors looking for a theme to concentrate on may find the coins of one tribe, an individual ruler or a particular phase in the coinage interesting.

Grading Celtic Coins

The majority of Celtic coins were struck by hand, sometimes resulting in a loss of definition through weak striking. In addition, the design on the dies was often bigger than the blank flan employed, resulting in the loss of some of the design. Coins with full legends are generally more valuable than examples with incomplete legends. Bronze coins in good condition (VF or better) and especially toned examples attract a premium. Factors that detract from a coin's value are chips, scratches and verdigris on bronze coins. It is important to take into account these factors as well as the amount of wear on a coin when assessing its grade.

	Cunobelin Bronze Unit	Epaticcus Silver Unit	Cunobelin Gold Stater
Fine			
Very Fine			

Plated Coins

Plated gold staters, quarter staters and silver units are recorded for many known types. They vary considerably in the quality of their production and are usually priced at around a quarter of the substantive types value. Their exact purpose or relation to the type they copy is not fully understood.

References and Select Bibliography.

ABC   Rudd, C. (2010), Ancient British Coinage.
V   Van Arsdell, R.D. (1989), Celtic Coinage of Britain.
BMC   Hobbs, R. (1996), British Iron Age Coins in the British Museum.

de Jersey, P. (1996), Celtic Coinage in Britain. *A good general introduction to the series.*
Nash, D. (1987), Coinage in the Celtic World. *Sets the coinage in its social context.*

The layout of the following list is derived from the standard works by Van Arsdell and the British Museum Catalogue by Richard Hobbs. References are made to these works where possible, in the case of the last work it should be noted that the British Museum collection is not exhaustive, and therefore should not be used to assess the rarity of a coin with, for example Rudd ABC listing many more varieties than can be listed here.

IMPORTED COINAGE

The earliest coins to circulate in Britain were made in northern Gaul (Belgica) and imported into the south-east of England from around 150 B.C. onwards. They were principally the product of two tribal groups in this region, the Ambiani and Suessiones. In Britain these types are known as Gallo-Belgic A to F. The first type Gallo-Belgic A is ultimately derived from the Macedonian gold staters (M) of Philip II (359-336 B.C.)

The reasons why they were imported are not fully understood. However, the context for their importation is one of close social, political and economic ties between Britain and Gaul. Within this cross-channel relationship they undoubtedly had various functions, such as payment for military service or mercenaries, in exchanges between the elite of each society: in cementing alliances for example, or as gifts in a system of exchange.

GALLO-BELGIC ISSUES

	2	4	5	7		
					F	VF
					£	£

From c.150 B.C. – c.50 B.C.

		F	VF
1	**Gold Stater.** Gallo-Belgic (Ambiani). Good copy of Macedonian stater, large flan. Laureate head of Apollo r. R. Horse l. *ABC 1; V. 10.*	1750	8500
2	Similar, but head and horse l. *ABC 4; V. 12.*	1100	5250
3	B. (Ambiani). Somewhat similar to 1, but small flan and 'defaced' *obv.* die. R. Horse r. *ABC 7; V. 30.*	475	2000
4	— Similar, but with lyre between horse's legs. *ABC 10; V. 33.*	575	2500
5	C. (Ambiani), *Stater.* Disintegrated Apollo head. R. horse. *ABC 13; V. 44.*	275	1000
6	**Gold Quarter Stater.** Gallo-Belgic A. Similar to 1. *ABC 28; V .15.*	300	1000
7	— Similar to 2. *ABC 31; V. 20.*	275	850
8	B. Similar to 3. *ABC 34; V. 35.*	300	950
9	— Similar. R. Two horses l. with lyre between legs. *ABC 37; V. 37.*	200	525
10	D. Portions of Apollo head R. A mixture of stars, crescents, pellets, zig-zag lines; often referred to as 'Geometric' types (See also British 'O', S. 46.). *ABC 40, 43, 46, 49; V. 65/7/9/146.*	80	185

From *c.*50 B.C.

11

		F £	VF £
11	**Gold Stater.** Gallo-Belgic E. (Ambiani). Blank obv. R. Disjointed curved horse r., pellet below, zig-zag in exergue. *ABC 16; V. 52, 54.*	175	400
12	F. (Suessiones). Devolved Apollo head r. R. Disjointed horse r. With triple-tail. *ABC 22; V. 85.*	575	2000
13	Xc. Blank except for VE monogram at edge of coin, R. S below horse r. *ABC 19; V. 87-1.*	275	1000

Armorican (Channel Islands and N.W. Gaul, *c.*75-50 B.C.)

		F £	VF £
14	**Billon Stater.** Class I. Head r. R. Horse, boar below, remains of driver with Victory above, lash ends in or two loops, or 'gate'.	35	160
15	— Class II. Head r. R. Horse, boar below, remains of Victory only, lash ends in small cross of four pellets.	30	150
16	— Class III. Head r., anchor-shaped nose. R. Somewhat similar to Class I.	30	150
17	— Class IV. Head r. R. Horse with reins, lyre shape below, driver holds vertical pole, lash ends in three prongs.	35	160
18	— Class V. Head r. R. Similar to last, lash ends in long cross with four pellets.	45	200
19	— Class VI. Head r. R. Horse, boar below, lash ends in 'ladder'	50	225
20	**Billon Quarter Stater.** Similar types to above.	40	175

CELTIC COINS STRUCK IN BRITAIN

Coin production in Britain began at the very end of the second century B.C. with the cast potin coinage of Kent (Nos 62-64). Inspired by Gaulish issues and ultimately derived from the potin coins of Massalia (Marseilles) in southern Gaul, the precise function and period of use of this coinage is not fully understood. The domestic production of gold coins started around 70 B.C., these issues are traditionally known as British A-P and are derived from imported Gallo-Belgic issues. Broadly contemporary with these issues are quarter staters, silver units, and bronze units. Recent work by John Sills has further enhanced our understanding of this crucial early period with the identification of two new British staters (Insular Belgic C or Kentish A and the Ingoldisthorpe type) and their related quarters and a Westerham quarter stater. The Insular Belgic C or Kentish A type derived from Gallo-Belgic C now becomes the first British stater.

EARLY UNINSCRIBED COINAGE FROM c.65 BC

20A   20B

		F	VF
		£	£
20A	**Gold Stater.** Insular Belgic C/Kentish A type. Devolved Apollo head r. R.		
	Disjointed horse r, a rosette behind or in front, or both. *ABC 515; V. —; BMC —*	575	2250
20B	Ingoldisthorpe type. Similar to last, as illustration. *ABC 2421; V.—; BMC—*	475	1750

	21	22	23	24		
21	British A. Westerham type. Devolved Apollo head r. R.					
	Disjointed horse l. large pellet below. *ABC 482, 2430; V. 200, 202;*					
	BMC 1-32.				225	575
22	B. Chute type. Similar to 9 but crab-like object below horse.					
	ABC 746; V. 1205; BMC 35-76.				175	450
23	C. Yarmouth type. Similar to 9 but star-like object in front of horse.					
	ABC 518; V. 1220; BMC 78-85.				650	2250
24	D. Cheriton type. Similar to Chute type but with large crescent face.					
	ABC 755; V. 1215; BMC 86-128.				225	625
25	E. Waldingfield type. Annulet and pellet below horse. *ABC 2335;*					
	V. 1462; BMC — —.				400	1350

26   27

	F £	VF £
26	F. Clacton type 1. Similar to Westerham type but rosette below horse. *ABC 2332; V. 1458; BMC 137-44.*	450	1500
27	G. Clacton type 2. Similar but horse r., with pellet, or pellet with two curved lines below. *ABC 2329; V. 30, 1455; BMC 145-79.*	275	1000

28   30

28	H. North-East Coast type. Variety of 9, pellet or rosette below horse to r. *ABC 1716, 1719; V. 800; BMC 182-191.*	175	475
29	I. — Similar, horse l., pellet, rosette or star with curved rays below. *ABC 1722, 1728, 1731, 1734, 1740; BMC 193-211.*	175	475
30	J. Norfolk Wolf type. R. Crude wolf to r. *ABC 1393; V. 610-1; BMC 212-16.*	350	1250
31	— Similar but wolf to l. Usually base gold. *ABC 1396, 1399; V. 610-2/3; BMC 217-78.*	175	500

32   36

32	L. Whaddon Chase type. R. Spirited horse r. of new style, various symbols below. *ABC 2240, 2347, 2433, 2436, 2439, 2442, 2445; V. 1470-6; 1485/7/9/93; BMC 279-343.*	225	725
33	— Plain. R. Horse r. With ring ornament below or behind. *ABC 2338, 2341, 2344; V. 1498-1505; BMC 344-46.*	300	900
33A	— Climping type. Similar to Whaddon Chase type but horse left, bird-like object above, pellet in ring and crescent below. *V.-; BMC-.*	675	2250
34	Lx. North Thames group. Blank apart from reversed SS. R. Similar to last. *ABC 2237; V. 1509; BMC 350.*	700	2400
35	Lz. Weald group. Blank with some traces of Apollo head. R. Horse r., large wheel ornament below. *ABC 186; V. 1507; BMC 347-49.*	750	2750
36	Ma. Wonersh type. Crossed wreath design with crescents back to back in centre. R. Spiral above horse, wheel below. *ABC 527; V. 1520; BMC 351-56.*	475	1500

37 38

		F £	VF £
37	Mb. Savernake Forest type. Similar but *obv.* plain or almost blank. *ABC 2091; V. 1526; BMC 361-64*	175	500
38	Qa. British 'Remic' type. Crude laureate head. R. Triple-tailed horse, wheel below. *ABC 485, 494, 497; V. 210-214; BMC 445-58.*	225	725
39	Qb. — Similar, but *obv.* blank. *ABC 488; V. 216; BMC 461-76.*	200	550
39A	**Gold Quarter Stater.** Insular Belgic C/Kentish A type. Similar to Gallo-Belgic D, but with rosette in field on obverse. *ABC 530; V.—; BMC—*	250	850
39B	Ingoldisthorpe type. Similar to last but with sperm-like objects in field. *ABC 2448; V.—; BMC—*	300	975
39C	British A. Westerham type. Similar to last but of cruder style, or with L-shapes in field on rev. *ABC 2448; V.—; BMC—*	225	750
40	British D. Cheriton type. Similar to Stater, large crescent face. R. Cross motif with pellets. *ABC —; V. 143 var; BMC 129-136*	250	800
41	F/G. Clacton type. Plain, traces of pattern. R. Ornamental cross with pellets. *ABC 2356; V. 1460; BMC 180-1.*	125	400
42	H. Crescent design and pellets. R. Horse r. *ABC 2350; V. —; BMC 192* .	125	400

43 44 45

43	Lx. N.Thames group. Floral pattern on wreath. R. Horse l. or r. *ABC 2463; V. 234; BMC 365-370.*	150	525
44	Ly. N.Kent group. Blank. R. Horse l. or r. *ABC 201; V. 158; BMC 371-3.*	120	350
45	Lz. Weald group. Spiral design on wreath. R. Horse l. or r. *ABC 626; V. 250; BMC 548-50.*	150	450

46 47 48

46	O. Geometric type. Unintelligible patterns (some blank on obv.). *ABC 533, 536, 767; V. 143, 1225/27/29; BMC 410-32.*	90	250
47	P. Trophy type. Blank. R. Trophy design. *ABC 192, 2243, 195 (var.); V. 145-7; BMC 435-44.*	110	300
48	Qc. British 'Remic' type. Head or wreath pattern. R. Triple-tailed horse, l. or r. *ABC 500, 503, 512, 569, 572, 575, 611, 629, 779, 782, 2093, 2101, 2109, 2469; V. 220-32, 36, 42-6, 56; BMC 478-546.*	135	400
49	Xd. Head l. of good style, horned serpent behind ear. R. Horse l. *ABC 551; V. 78; BMC 571-575.*	325	950

51

53

		F £	VF £
50	**Silver Unit** Lx. Head l.or r. R̟. Horse l. or r. *ABC 1507, 2472, 2475, 2481, 2484; V. 80, 1546, 1549, 1555; BMC 376-382.*	90	325
51	— Head l. R. Stag r. with long horns. *ABC 2487; V. 1552; BMC 383-7.*	90	325
52	— **Silver Half Unit.** Two horses or two beasts. *M. ABC 2282, 2285, 2496, 2499, 2502; V. 474, 1626, 1643, 1948; BMC 389-400.*	80	300
53	Lz. Danebury group. Head r. with hair of long curves. R. Horse l., flower above. *ABC 1013; V. 262; BMC 580-82*	125	450

54

54A

54	— Helmeted head r. R. Horse r. wheel below. *ABC 662; V. 264; BMC 583 -592.*	90	350
54A	Cruciform pattern with ornaments in angles. R. Horse l., ear of corn between legs, crescents and pellets above, *ABC 2505; V.—; BMC—*	125	475
55	— **Silver Quarter Unit.** As last. *ABC 728; V. 268; BMC 642-43.*	50	175

56

61

56	— Head r. R. Horse r. star above, wheel below. *ABC 866; V. 280; BMC 595-601*	75	250
57	— Head l., pellet in ring in front. R. Horse l. or r. *ABC 857, 995; V. 284; BMC 610-630.*	50	175
58	— Serpent looking back. R. Horse l. *ABC 896; V. 286; BMC 631-33*	90	325
59	— **Silver Quarter Unit.** Cross pattern. R. Two-tailed horse. *ABC 1046; V. 482; BMC 654-56.* . *(Formerly attributed to Verica)*	40	135
60	**Bronze Unit.** Lx. Winged horse l. R. Winged horse l. *ABC 273; V. 1629; BMC 401*	60	250
61	Chichester Cock type. Head r. R. Head r. surmounted by cock. *ABC 737; V. — BMC 657-59*	70	275

POTIN, c.120-100 BC
(Cast copper/tin alloy, mainly Kent)

62

		F £	VF £

62   **Unit.** Thurrock type.Head l. R. Bull butting l. or r. *ABC 120, 123, 126, 129, 132; V. 1402-42; BMC 660-666.*   20   60

63   64

63   Class I type. Crude head. R. Lines representing bull *(Allen types A-L.)*   *ABC 147, 150, 153, 156, 162, 165, 168, 171; V. 104, 106, 108, 112, 114, 115, 117, 119, 120, 122, 123, 125, 127, 129, 131, 133; BMC 667-714.*   25   80

64   Class II type. Smaller flan, large central pellet. *(Allen types M-P.)*   *ABC 174; V. 135-39; BMC 715-23.*   20   70

CELTIC DYNASTIC AND LATER UNINSCRIBED COINAGE

From Julius Caesar's expeditions to Britain in 55/54 B.C. and his conquest of Gaul in 52 B.C. to the Claudian invasion in 43 A.D., southern Britain was increasingly drawn into the orbit of the Roman world. This process is reflected not only in the coins but also in what we know about their issuers and the tribes they ruled. Latin legends begin to appear for the first time and increasingly accompany objects and designs drawn from the classical world. A lot of what we know about the Celtic tribes and their rulers, beyond just their names on coins, is drawn from contemporary and slightly later Roman historical sources. A great deal however is still uncertain and almost all attributions to either tribes or historically attested individuals have to be seen as tentative.

The coin producing tribes of Britain can be divided into two groups, those of the core and those of the periphery. The tribes of the core, the Atrebates/Regni, Trinovantes/Catuvellauni and Cantii, by virtue of their geographical location controlled contact with the Roman world. Unlike the tribes of the periphery they widely employed Latin legends, classical designs and used bronze coinage in addition to gold and silver.

Following the Roman invasion of 43 A.D. it is likely that some coinage continued to be produced for a short time. However in 61 A.D. with the death of King Prasutagus and the suppression of the Boudiccan revolt that followed, it is likely that Celtic coinage came to an end.

TRIBAL/MINT MAP

ATREBATES AND REGNI

The joint tribal area of these two groups corresponds roughly with Berkshire and Sussex and parts of northern and eastern Hampshire. The Atrebatic portion being in the north of this region with its main centre at Calleva (Silchester). The Regni occupying the southern part of the region centred around Chichester.

COMMIUS
(Mid to Late 1st Century B.C.)

The first inscribed staters to appear in Britain, closely resemble British Q staters (no.38) and are inscribed 'COMMIOS'. Staters and silver units with an inscribed 'E' are also thought to be related. Traditionally this Commius was thought to be the Gaulish chieftain who Caesar refers to in De Bello Gallico, as firstly serving him in his expeditions to Britain and finally fleeing to Britain c.50 B.C. This attribution does however present chronological problems, and the appearance of a few early staters reading 'COM COMMIOS' suggests that the Commius who issued coins is more likely to have been the son of Caesar's Commius.

65

		F	VF
		£	£
65	**Gold Stater.** Devolved Apollo head r. R. COMMIOS around triple tailed horse r., wheel below. *ABC 1022; V. 350; BMC 724-29.*	275	800

66   67

66	Similar, but 'E' symbol above horse instead of legend. *ABC 1025; V. 352; BMC 730*	350	1050
67	**Gold Quarter Stater.** Blank except for digamma. R. Horse l. *ABC 1031; V. 353-5; BMC —.*	150	375

69

69	**Silver Unit.** Head l. R. Horse l. Mostly with 'E' symbol above. *ABC 1034, 1037, 1040; V. 355; BMC 731-58.*	40	150

70 (x1.5)

70	**Silver Minim.** Similar to Unit. *ABC 1043; V. 358-5; BMC 759-60*	35	120

TINCOMARUS or TINCOMMIUS
(Late 1st Century B.C. – Early 1st Century A.D.)

Successor to Commius and on his coins styled as 'COM.F' (son of Commius). Early coins of the reign like his predecessors are very obviously Celtic in their style. However later coins exhibit an increasing tendency towards Roman designs. Indeed Tincommius is recorded as a suppliant king of the Roman emperor Augustus (Res Gestae, xxxii), finally fleeing to Rome in the early 1st century A.D. The discovery of the Alton Hoard in 1996 brought to light gold staters with the new legend TINCOMARVS.

72

73

		F £	VF £
71	**Gold Stater.** *Celtic style.* Devolved Apollo head r. R. TINC COMM. F. around horse. *ABC —; V. 362; BMC —.*	675	2250
72	Similar but legend reads TINCOMARVS. *ABC 1049; V. 363; BMC 761-765.*	450	1500
73	**Gold Quarter Stater.** Spiral with pellet centre. R. Horse r. T above. *ABC 1094; V. 366; BMC 781-797.*	125	350

74

75

74	TINCOM, zig-zag ornament below. R. Horse l. *ABC 1073; V. 365; BMC 798-810.*	150	425
75	**Gold Stater.** *Classical style.* TINC(O) on a sunk tablet. R. Horseman with javelin r. often with CF in field. *ABC 1055, 1058, 1061; V. 375-76; BMC 765-769.*	425	1450

76

77

76	COM.(F). on a sunk tablet. R. Horseman with javelin r. TIN in field *ABC 1067; V. 385; BMC 770-774.*	350	1200
77	**Gold Quarter Stater.** TINC on a tablet, C above, A or B below. R. Winged head (Medusa?) facing. *ABC 1076; V. 378; BMC 811-826.*	375	1350
78	TIN on tablet. R. Boar l. *ABC 1079; V. 379; BMC 827-837.*	125	350

79

83

		F £	VF £
79	COMF on tablet. R. Horse r. TIN around. *ABC 1082; V. 387; BMC 838-841.*	135	425
80	— R. Horse l. TIC around. *ABC 1088; V. 388; BMC 842-851.*	135	425
81	COM on tablet. R. Horse l. T above. *ABC 1091; V. 389; BMC 852-3.*	150	475
82	COMF on tablet. R. Horse r. TINC around. *ABC 1085; V. 390; BMC 854-879.* 135	425	
83	**Silver Unit.** Laureate head r. TINCOM in front, V behind. R. Eagle stg. on snake. *ABC 1106; V. 397; BMC 880-905.*	40	185
84	Laureate head l. R. Bull l. TINC around. *ABC 1112; V. 396; BMC 906-910.*	45	200
85	Laureate head r. R. Bull r. TIN(C) around. *ABC 1115, 1118; V. 381; BMC 911-925.*	40	185
86	Facing head. R. Bull l. TINC around. *ABC 1109; V. 370; BMC 926-29*	45	200

87

91

87	TINC in angles of cross, R. Lion l. *ABC 1124; V. 372; BMC 930-45.*	45	200
88	Star. R. Boy riding dolphin r. TINC in field. *ABC 1127; V. 371; BMC 946-977.*	35	175
89	TINC around pellet. R. Lion l. *ABC 1121; V. 382; BMC 978-80.*	45	200
90	Head l. TINCOMMIVS in front. R. Horse l. lyre above. *ABC 1100; V. 473; BMC —-. (Formerly attributed to Verica)*	50	225
91	**Silver Minim.** CF within two interlinked squares. R. Boar? r. TINC. *ABC 1136; V. 383-1; BMC 981-82.*	35	125
92	As above but CO. R. Bull r. TI. *ABC 1139; V. 383-5; BMC —-*	40	135
93	C inside box, box above and below. R. Bull r. TIN. *ABC 1274; V. 383-7; BMC 983*	40	135
94	Cross, T? in angles. R. uncertain object. *ABC 1142; V. 483; BMC 984-85. (Formerly attributed to Verica)*	35	125

EPPILLUS
(Later 1st Century B.C. – Early 1st Century A.D.)

His reign is likely to have coincided with that of Tincommius's. Eppillus also claimed to be a son of Commius. Two coinages appear in his name, one for Kent and one minted at Calleva (Silchester, Hants.) in the northern part of the territory of the Atrebates and Regni. The coins of Calleva conform to the southern denominational structure of gold and silver with fractions of each, whilst the Kentish series is distinctly tri-metallic, replacing the silver minim with bronze. A joint coinage was issued by Eppillus and Verica. It is not understood if Eppillus held both territories simultaneously.

COINAGE STRUCK AT CALLEVA

	F £	VF £

95   96

| 95 | **Gold Stater.** Devolved Apollo head r. Ɽ. EPPI COMMI F around horse. ABC 1145; V. 405; BMC — .... | 2250 | 7500 |
| 96 | **Gold Quarter Stater.** CALLEV, star above and below. Ɽ. Hound r. EPPI. ABC 1148, 1151; V. 407-08; BMC 986-1005. .... | 140 | 450 |

97   98

| 97 | COMM F EPPILV, around crescent. Ɽ. Horse r. ABC 1157; V. 409; BMC 1006-1009. .... | 150 | 475 |
| 98 | EPPI COMF in two lines. Ɽ. Winged horse r. ABC 1154; V. 435; BMC 1010-15. .... | 140 | 450 |

99   100

99	**Silver Unit.** Crescent REX CALLE above and below. Ɽ. Eagle r. EPP. ABC 1160; V .415. BMC 1016-1060.	45	210
100	Bearded hd. r. in wreath. Ɽ. Boar r. EPPI(L) F CO(M). ABC 1163; V. 416; BMC 1061-87.	45	210
101	Bearded hd. in pellet border. Ɽ. Lion r. EPP COMF. ABC 1166; V. 417; BMC 1088-1115.	50	225
102	**Silver Minim.** Floral cross. Ɽ. Eagle r. EPPI. ABC 1169; V. 420; BMC 1116-17	45	185
103	Spiral and pellets. Ɽ. Ram r. EPP. ABC 1172; V. 421; BMC 1118-20.	45	185
104	Bulls head facing. Ɽ. Ram r. EPP. ABC 1175; V. 422; BMC 1121-24.	50	190
105	Wreath pattern. Ɽ. Boar r. EPP. ABC 1280; V. 423; BMC —-	60	225
106	Crescent cross. Ɽ. Hand holding trident. ABC 1298; V. 487; BMC —. ...	50	190

KENTISH TYPES

107

		F £	VF £
107	**Gold Stater.** COMF within wreath. ℞. Horseman l. EPPILLVS above. *ABC 384; V. 430; BMC 1125-26.*	2250	7500
108	Victory holding wreath l., within wreath. ℞. Horseman r. holding carnyx, F EPPI COM below. *ABC 387; V. 431; BMC 1127-28.*	2750	10500
109	**Gold Quarter Stater.** Crossed wreaths, EPPI in angles. ℞. Horse l. *ABC 390; V. 436; BMC 1129.*	475	1500
110	COMF in pellet border. ℞. Horse r. EPPI. *ABC 393; V. 437; BMC 1130-31.*	425	1350
111	**Silver Unit.** Head l. EPPIL in field. ℞. Horseman holding carnyx, EPPILL. *ABC 399; V. 441; BMC 1132.*	275	950
112	**Bronze Unit.** Bow cross, EPPI COMF around. ℞. Eagle facing. *ABC 408; V. 450; BMC 1137-38.*	45	240
113	Bull r., EPPI COF around. ℞. eagle facing. *ABC 411; V. 451; BMC 1139-41.*	45	240
114	Head l., EPPI in front. ℞. Victory l. holding wreath and standard. *ABC 414; V. 452; BMC 1142.*	50	250
115	Bearded hd. r., EPPI CF. ℞. Biga r. CF. *ABC 417; V. 453; BMC —*	60	300

JOINT TYPES OF EPPILUS AND VERICA

116	**Silver Unit.** Head l. CO VIR in front. ℞. Victory, EP. *ABC 432; V. 442; BMC 1133-34.*	725	2500

117

117	Head r. VIR CO in front. ℞. Capricorn l. EPPI COMF. *ABC 435; V. 443; BMC 1135-36.*	175	600

VERICA
(c.10.-c.40 A.D.)

The exact details of Verica's succession and relationship to Eppillus and Tincommius are not fully understood. However by c.10 A.D. it seems likely that Verica was the sole ruler of the southern region. His close contact with Rome, both political and economic, seen in the increasing use of classical designs on his coins, culminated in his flight to Rome in c.42 A.D. to seek assistance from Claudius.

		F £	VF £
118	**Gold Stater.** COM:F on tablet. R. Horseman r. holding spear, VIR below. *ABC 1187; V. 460; BMC 1143-44.*	350	1200
119	COM.F. on tablet, pellet in ring ornament above and below. R. Similar to last. *ABC 1184; 461; BMC 1146-53.*	350	1200

	120 121		
120	COM.F on tablet. R. Horseman r. holding spear, VIR above, REX below. *ABC 1190; V. 500; BMC 1155-58.*	300	900
121	Vine-leaf dividing VI RI. R. Horseman r. with shield and spear. COF in field. *ABC 1193; V. 520-1; BMC 1159-73.*	325	950
122	Similar, reads VE RI. *ABC 1193; V. 520-5/7; BMC 1174-76.*	350	1100
123	**Gold Quarter Stater.** COMF on tablet. R. Horse l. VIR. *ABC 1196; V. 465; BMC 1177-78.*	150	475

124

124	COMF on tablet, pellet in ring ornament above and below R. Horse r. VI. *ABC 1199; V. 466; BMC 1179-1206.*	135	375
125	COMF on tablet, pellet border. R. Horse r. VI above. *ABC 1202; V. 467; BMC 1207-16.*	135	375

	126 128		
126	COM FILI. in two lines, scroll in between. R. Horse r. VIR(I) above. *ABC 1205; V. 468; BMC 1217-22.*	150	475
127	VERI COMF, crescent above, star below. R. Horse r. REX below. *ABC 1208; V. 501; BMC 1223-36.*	150	475
128	VERI beneath vine-leaf. R. Horseman r. with sword and shield, FRX in field. *ABC 1211; V. 525; BMC 1237-38.*	375	1350
129	COM, horseman r. R. Seated figure, VERICA around. *ABC 1214; V. 526; BMC 1239.*	525	1850
130	Similar to last. R. Laureate bust r., VIRI in front. *ABC 1217; V. 527; BMC 1240.*	500	1750

	F £	VF £

131 **Silver Unit.** COMF, crescent and or pellet in ring above and below. R. Boar r. VI(RI) below. *ABC 1220, 1223; V. 470/72; BMC 1241-1331.* 45 175

132   133

132 VERICA COMMI F around pellet in ring. R. Lion r. REX below. *ABC 1229; V. 505; BMC 1332-1359.* 45 175
133 COMMI F, horseman with shield r. R. VERI CA, mounted warrior with spear r. *ABC 1238; V. 530; BMC 1360-92.* 45 175

134   137

134 Two cornucopiae, COMMI F. R. Figure seated r. VERICA. *ABC 1241; V. 531; BMC 1393-1419.* 40 165
135 Bust r. VIRI. R. Figure seated l. *ABC 1244; V. 532; BMC 1420.* 100 450
136 Naked figure l. R. Laureate bust r., COMMI F. *ABC 1250; V. 533; BMC 1421-49.* 40 165
137 VERICA REX, bull r. R. Figure stg. l., COMMI F. *ABC 1235; V. 506; BMC 1450-84.* 40 165
138 COMF, in tablet and scroll. R. Eagle facing, VI RI. *ABC 1226; V. 471; BMC 1485-1505.* 40 150
139 VIRIC across field, ornaments above and below. R. Pegasus r., star design below. *ABC 1256; V. —; BMC —.* 75 350
140 Head r. Verica. R. COMMI F., eagle l. *ABC 1253; V. 534; BMC —.* 90 400
141 **Silver Minim.** COF in tablet, R. Facing head (Medusa?), VE below. *ABC 1271; V. 384; BMC 1506.. (Formerly attributed to Tincommius)*......... 40 160
142 Head r. R. Horse r., VIRICO. *ABC 1289; V. 480; BMC —.* 40 160
143 Pellet and ring pattern. R. Lion r. VIR. *ABC 1292; V. 484; BMC 1514-17.* 35 135
144 VIRIC reversed. R. Boar r. *ABC 1283; V. 485; BMC 1518*.................... 35 135
145 Cross. R. Trident. *ABC 1295; V. 486-1; BMC —-*................................. 40 160
146 Uncertain. R. Boar r. *ABC 1280; V. 510-1; BMC —.* 30 125
147 Crescent cross. R. Boar r. *ABC 1301; V. 510-5; BMC 1521-23.* 35 140
148 VIR VAR in tablets. R. Winged horse r. CO. *ABC 1262; V. 511; BMC 1507-12.* 35 140

149 (x1.5)   150 (x1.5)

149 Vine-leaf, CFO. R. Horse r. VERI CA. *ABC 1307; V. 550; BMC 1524-25* 35 140
150 CF in torc. R. Head r. VERIC. *ABC 1310; V. 551; BMC 1526-33.* 30 135

		F	VF
		£	£
151	Altar, CF, R. Bull's head facing, VERICA. *ABC 1313; V. 552;* *BMC 1534-37.*	50	200
152	Temple, CF. R. Bull r, VER REX. *ABC 1316; V. 553; BMC 1538-41*	30	135

153   154

153	Cornucopia, VER COM. R. Lion r. *ABC 1319; V. 554; BMC 1542*	35	150
154	Two cornucopiae. R. Eagle l. *ABC 1322; V. 555; BMC 1543-58*	30	125
155	Floral pattern, CF. R. Lion r. *ABC 1325; V. 556; BMC 1559-63.*	35	140
156	Sphinx r., CF, R. dog curled up, VERI. *ABC 1328; V. 557;* *BMC 1564-68.*	30	135
157	VERI. R. Urn, COMMI F. *ABC 1286; V. 559; BMC* −-	40	160
158	A in star. R. Bird r. *ABC 1133; V. 561; BMC 1569-71*	65	275
159	Urn, Rex. R. Eagle r., VERRICA COMMI F. *ABC 1331; V. 563;* *BMC 1572-78.*	30	125
160	VIR inside tablet. R. Boars head r. *ABC 1268; V. 564; BMC 1579-81.* ..	30	130
161	Cross. R. bull l. *ABC 1334; V.* −*; BMC 1582*	35	150
162	Boars head r., CF, R. Eagle, VE. *ABC 1337; V.* −*; BMC 1583-86*	30	125
163	Head r, COMM IF., R. Sphinx, R VE. *ABC 1340; V.* −*; BMC 1587-89* .	35	150
164	A in tablet. R. Boar r. VI CO. *ABC 1277; V.* −*; BMC 1590*	50	200
	The two following coins are possibly issues of Epatticus.		
165	Bull r. R. Eagle with snake l. *ABC 1358; V. 512; BMC 2366-70*	35	150
166	Bust r. R. dog r. *ABC 1361; V. 558; BMC 2371-74*	40	160

CANTII

The Cantii, who gave their name to Kent, occupied a similar area to that of the modern county. Caesar considered this the most civilised part of Britain and the early production of potin units in Kent can be seen as indicative of this. A number of Kentish rulers for whom we have coins, appear to be dynasts from the two neighbouring kingdoms, who were involved in struggles to acquire territory. Eppillus (see Atrebates and Regni) produced coins specifically for circulation in Kent and like those of Cunobelin they circulated widely.

EARLY UNINSCRIBED

167	**Gold Stater.** Ly. Blank. R. Horse l. numerous ring ornaments in field. *ABC 183; V. 142; BMC 2472.*	700	3000
168	Blank. R. Horse r. numerous ornaments in field. *ABC 294; V. 157;* *BMC*−	700	3000

169   170

169	Lz. Blank. R. Horse l., box with cross hatching below. *ABC 177, 180;* *V. 150, 144; BMC 2466-68.*	750	3250
170	**Gold Quarter Stater.** Ly. Blank. R. Horse r., pentagram below. *ABC 309;* *V. 163; BMC 2473-74.*	145	450

171   173   176

		F £	VF £
171	Blank. R. Horse r., 'V' shape above. *ABC 312; V. 170; BMC 2475-77.*.	135	425
172	Lz. Blank. R. Horse l., 'V' shape above. *ABC 198; V. 151; BMC 2469-70.*	120	350
173	**Silver Unit.** Curved star. R. Horse r. Pentagram below. *ABC 2258; V. 164; BMC—.*	125	375
174	Serpent torc. R. Horse r., box with cross hatching below. *cf Mossop 8; ABC 243; BMC 2478*	160	550
175	**Silver Half Unit.** Spiral of three arms. R. Horse l. *ABC 2261; V. —; BMC 2479*	75	275
176	**Bronze Unit.** Various animal types, R. Various animal types. *ABC 258, 267, 270, 285, 288, 291; V. 154/167; BMC 2480-91. (80/141-44)*...................	40	200

INSCRIBED

DUBNOVELLAUNUS
(Late 1st Century B.C.)

Likely to be the same Dubnovellaunus recorded on coins in Essex (see Trinovantes / Catuvellauni). The two coinages share the same denominational structure and have some stylistic similarities. It has been suggested that Dubnovellaunus is the British king of that name mentioned along with Tincommius as a client king in the Res Gestae of the Roman emperor Augustus.

327   180

		F	VF
177	**Gold Stater.** Blank. R. Horse r., bucranium above, serpent like object below, DUBNOV[ELLAUNUS] or similar around. *ABC 303; V. 169; BMC 2492-96.*	325	950
178	— R. Horse r., but without bucranium and with wheel below. *ABC 300; V. 176; BMC 2497-98.*	425	1350
179	**Silver Unit.** Winged animal r. R. Horse l., DVBNO. *ABC 321; V. 171; BMC 2499-2501.*	125	400
180	Winged animal l. R. Seated fig. l., holding hammer, DVBNO. *ABC 324; V. 178; BMC 2502-03.*	135	450
181	**Bronze Unit.** Horse r. R. Lion l., DVBN. *ABC 342; V. 166; BMC 2504-06.*.	60	250
182	Boar l., DVBNO. R. Horseman r. *ABC 348; V. 181; BMC 2507-08.*	60	250
183	Boar r., DVBNO. R. Eagle facing. *ABC 345; V. 180; BMC 2509-10.*	55	225

VOSENOS
(Late 1st Century B.C./ Early 1st Century A.D.)
Little is known of this ruler who issued coins in a characteristically Kentish style similar to those of
Dubnovellaunus.

			F £	VF £

184 **Gold Stater.** Blank. R. Horse l., bucranium above, serpent like object below.,
[VOSE]NOS. *ABC 357; V. 184; BMC 2511-12.* 2000 6500

185

185 **Gold Quarter Stater.** Blank. R. Horse r., VOSI below. *ABC 360; V. 185;*
BMC 2514-15. .... 450 1500
186 **Silver Unit.** Horse and griffin. R. Horse r., retrograde legend. *ABC 363;*
V. 186; BMC −. 175 650

"SA" or "SAM"
(Late 1st Century B.C./ Early 1st Century A.D.)
An historically unattested individual whose coins are stylistically associated with those of
Dubnovellaunus and Vosenos. His coins have been predominantly found in north Kent

187   **Silver Unit.** Head l., R. Horse l., SA below. *ABC 369; V. −; BMC −*.... 200 700
187A **Bronze Unit.** Boar l., R. Horse l., SA below. *ABC 375; V. 187; BMC 2516-19.* 70 250

187B

187B Horse l., SAM below. R. Horse l., SAM below. *ABC 281; V. −; BMC −* 75 300

AMMINUS
(Early 1st Century A.D.)
Issued a coinage stylistically distinct from other Kentish types and with strong affinities to those of
Cunobelin. Indeed it has been suggested that he is the Adminius recorded by Suetonius, as a son of
Cunobelin. The enigmatic legend DVN or DVNO may be an unknown mint site.

189

188 **Silver Unit.** Plant, AMMINUS around. R. Winged horse r., DVN. *ABC 456;*
V. 192; BMC 2522-23. .... 125 475
189 (Last year 190). A in wreath. R. Capricorn r., S AM (I). *ABC 468; V. 194;*
BMC 2520-21. .... 110 425
190 **Bronze Unit.** (Last year 189). AM in wreath. R. Horse r., DVNO. *ABC 462; V. 193;*
BMC −−... 60 250
191 Head r. R. Hippocamp r., AM. *ABC 471; V. 195; BMC 2524.* 70 300

TRINOVANTES AND CATUVELLAUNI

Occupying the broad area of Essex, southern Suffolk, Bedfordshire, Buckinghamshire, Hertfordshire, parts of Oxfordshire, Cambridgeshire and Northamptonshire, they are likely to have been two separate tribes for most of their history. The Trinovantes were originally located in the eastern half of this area, with their main centre at Camulodunum (Colchester). The original Catuvellauni heartland was further west, with their main centre at Verulamium (St.Albans). The whole area eventually came under the control of Cunobelin at the end of the period.

TRINOVANTES

ADDEDOMAROS
(Late 1st Century B.C.)

Unknown to history, he appears to have been a contemporary of Tasciovanus. The design of his staters is based on the Whaddon Chase type (No.32) which circulated widely in this region.

200

		F £	VF £
200	**Gold Stater.** Crossed wreath. R. Horse r., wheel below, AθθIIDOM above. *ABC 2514; V. 1605; BMC 2390-94.*	275	950

201   202

201	Six armed spiral. R. Horse r., cornucopia below, AθθIIDOM above. *ABC 2517; V. 1620; BMC 2396-2404.*	250	850
202	Two opposed crescents. R. Horse r., branch below, spiral or wheel above, AθθDIIDOM. *ABC 2511; V. 1635; BMC 2405-2415.*	325	1100

203   204

203	**Gold Quarter Stater.** Circular flower pattern. R. Horse r. *ABC 2526; V. 1608; BMC 2416.*	165	475
204	Cross shaped flower pattern. R. Horse r. *ABC 2529; V. 1623; BMC 2417-21.*	150	400
205	Two opposed crescents. R. Horse r., AθθDIIDOM around. *ABC 2520, 2541; V. 1638; BMC 2422-24.*	200	650
206	**Bronze Unit.** Head l. R. Horse l. *ABC 2544; V. 1615/46 BMC 2450-60.*	35	130

DUBNOVELLAUNUS
(Late 1st Century B.C./ Early 1st Century A.D.)
Dubnovellaunus is likely to have been the successor to Addedomaros, with whom his coins are stylistically related. It is not clear if he was the same Dubnovellaunus who also issued coins in Kent (see Cantii) or if he is the same Dumnobeallaunos mentioned in the Res Gestae of the emperor Augustus c.AD14.

207

208

		F £	VF £
207	**Gold Stater.** Two crescents on wreath. R. Horse l., leaf below, pellet in ring, DVBNOVAIIAVNOS above. *ABC 2392; V. 1650; BMC 2425-40.*	350	1100
208	**Gold Quarter Stater.** Similar. *ABC 2395; V. 1660; BMC 2442.*	150	475

210

209	**Silver Unit**. Head l., DVBNO. R. Winged horse r., lattice box below. *ABC 315; V. 165; BMC 2443-44.*	130	400
210	Head l., legend ?, R. Horse l. DVB[NOV]. *ABC 2404; V. 1667; BMC 2445.*	125	375
211	**Bronze Unit.** Head l., R. Horse l., DVBNO above. *ABC 2407; V. 1669; BMC 2446-48.*	45	170
212	Head r., R. Horse l. *ABC 2410; V. 1665; BMC 2461-65.*	45	170

DIRAS
(Late 1st Century B.C./ Early 1st Century A.D.)
An historically unattested ruler, responsible for a gold stater related stylistically to Dubnovellaunus's.

213	**Gold Stater.** Blank. R. Horse r., DIRAS? above, yoke like object above. *ABC 297; V. 162; BMC 2449.*	2250	7500

CATUVELLAUNI

TASCIOVANUS

(Late 1st Century B.C./ Early 1st Century A.D.)

The early gold coins of Tasciovanus, like those of his contemporary Addedomaros, are based on the Whaddon Chase stater. Verulamium (St. Albans) appears to have been his principal mint, appearing as VER or VERL on the coinage. Staters and quarter staters inscribed CAM (Camulodunum/ Colchester) are known and perhaps suggest brief or weak control of the territory to the east. The later coins of Tasciovanus use increasingly Romanised designs. The adoption of the title RICON, perhaps a Celtic equivalent to the Latin REX (King), can be seen as a parallel move to that of his contemporary Tincommius to the south.

		F	VF
		£	£
214	**Gold Stater.** Crescents in wreath. R̄. TASCIAV and bucranium over horse r. *ABC 2553; V. 1680; BMC 1591-1603.*	425	1350
215	— R̄. Similar reads TAXCIAV. *ABC 2550; V. 1682; BMC 1604-05.*	525	1750
216	— R̄. Similar reads TASCIOVAN above, CAM below. *ABC 2559; V. 1684; BMC 1606-07.*	725	2500
217	— R̄. Horseman r. helmeted and with carnyx, TASC in field. *ABC 2562, 2565; V. 1730-32; BMC 1608-1613.*	325	1000
218	Crescents in wreath, with V or VER in design. R̄. Similar to last. *ABC 2568, 2571; V. 1734-35; BMC 1623-24.*	450	1500

219	TASCIO(V) RICON in panel. R. Horseman l., wearing armour and holding sword and shield. *ABC 2577, 2580; V. 1780; BMC 1628-36.*	475	1600
220	**Gold Quarter Stater.** Floral design. R. Horse r. *ABC 2583; V. —; BMC 1638-39*	225	725
221	Crossed Wreath. R. Horse l. *ABC 2586; V. 1688; BMC 1651-53.*	125	350
222	— R. Horse r., CAM. *ABC 2589; V. 1694; BMC 1640.*	185	600
223	Similar, TASCI in wreath. R. Horse r., TASC. *ABC 2595; V. 1692; BMC 1641.*	125	350

224	Similar, VERO in wreath. R. Horse l., TAS. *ABC 2598; V. 1690; BMC 1642-43.*	135	375
225	TASCIO on tablet. R. Horse l. *ABC 444; V. 1848; BMC 1646.*	225	725
226	TASC on tablet. R. Horse l. *ABC 2601; V. 1786; BMC 1647-50.*	135	375

		F	*VF*
		£	£
227	**Silver Unit.** Head l. R. Horse r. *ABC 2604; V. 1698; BMC 1654*	65	225
228	Cross and box. R. Horse r., VER in front. *ABC 2631; V. —; BMC 1655*.	65	250
229	Cross and crescent. R. Horse l., TASCI. *ABC 2607; V. —; BMC 1665-57*	65	225
230	Bearded head l. R. Horseman r., TASCIO. *ABC 2610; V. 1745; BMC 1667-68.*	75	325
231	Winged horse l., TAS. R. Griffin r., within circle of pellets. *ABC 2649; V. 1790; BMC 1660.*	70	275
232	Eagle stg. l., TASCIA. R. Griffin r. *ABC 2646; V. 1792; BMC 1658-59.*	75	300
233	VER in beaded circle. R. Horse r., TASCIA. *ABC 2622; V. 1699; BMC 1670-73.*	70	300
234	— R. Naked horseman. *ABC 2625; V. 1747; BMC 1674-76.*	70	300

235   238

235	Laureate hd. r., TASCIA. R. Bull l. *ABC 2643; V. 1794; BMC 1681-82.*	70	300
236	Cross and box, VERL. R. Boar r. TAS. *ABC 2628; V. 1796; BMC 1661-62.*	70	275
237	TASC in panel. R. Winged horse l. *ABC 2637; V. 1798; BMC 1664-65.*	65	260
238	— R. Horseman l., carrying long shield. *ABC 2640; V. 1800; BMC 1677-79.*	70	300
239	Two crescents. R. Winged griffin, VIR. *ABC 2619; V. —; BMC 1666*	75	325
240	Head r., TAS?. R. Horseman r. *ABC —; V. —; BMC 1669*	75	325

241

241	**Bronze Double Unit.** Head r., TASCIA, VA. R. Horseman r. *ABC 2652; V. 1818; BMC 1685-87.*	85	275

242

242	**Bronze Unit.** Two heads in profile, one bearded. R. Ram l., TASC. *ABC 2655; V. 1705; BMC 1711-13.*	30	135
243	Bearded head r. VER(L). R. Horse l., VIIR or VER. *ABC 2658; V. 1707; BMC 1714-21.*	25	135
244	Bearded head r. R. Horse l., TAS. *ABC 2661; V. 1709; BMC 1722-23.* ..	30	135
245	Head r., TASC. R. Winged horse l., VER. *ABC 2664; V. 1711; BMC 1688-89.*	25	125
246	— R. Horseman r., holding carnyx, VIR. *ABC 2676; V. 1750; BMC 1724-27.*	25	125

247

		F	VF
		£	£
247	VERLAMIO between rays of star. Ɍ. Bull l. *ABC 2679; V. 1808; BMC 1745-51.*	25	120
248	Similar without legend. Ɍ. Bull r. *ABC 2685; V. 1810; BMC 1752-55.* ..	30	135
249	Similar. Ɍ. Horse l., TASCI. *ABC 2688; V. 1812; BMC 1709-10.*	30	135
250	Head r., TASCIO. Ɍ. Lion r., TA SCI. *ABC 2691; V. 1814; BMC 1736-38.*	25	125
251	Head r. Ɍ. Figure std. l., VER below. *ABC 2751; V. 1816; BMC 1739-44.*	30	135
252	Cross and Crescents. Ɍ. Boar r., VER. *ABC 2667; V. 1713; BMC 1702-05.*	25	130
253	Laureate head r. Ɍ. Horse l., VIR. *ABC 2694; V. 1820; BMC 1706-08.* ..	25	130
254	Raised band across centre, VER or VERL below. Ɍ. Horse grazing r. *ABC 2673; V. 1717; BMC −.*	35	150
255	**Bronze Fractional Unit.** Animal r. Ɍ. Sphinx l. *ABC 2700; V. 1824; BMC 1760-61.*	30	135
256	Head l., VER. Ɍ. Goat r. *ABC 2709; V. 1715; BMC 1765-68.*	25	125
257	Head r. Ɍ. Boar r. *ABC 2712; V. 1826; BMC 1762-64.*	25	130
258	Head l. Ɍ. Animal with curved tail. *ABC 2697; V. 1822; BMC 1759.*	30	135

ASSOCIATES OF TASCIOVANUS

(Early 1st Century A.D.)

Towards the end of his reign, a number of joint issues bearing his name and the name of either Sego or Dias appear. In addition coins similar in style to those of Tasciovanus appear with either the name Andoco or Rues. It has been suggested that these issues belong to a period of struggle following the death of Tasciovanus and are all rival contestants for the throne. Another theory is that they are associates or sub-kings of Tasciovanus responsible for areas within the wider territory.

SEGO

259

| 259 | **Gold Stater.** TASCIO in tablet, annulets above. Ɍ. Horseman with carnyx r., SEGO. *ABC 441; V. 1845; BMC 1625-27.* ....:............... | 1350 | 5250 |

260

		F £	VF £

260   **Silver Unit.** SEGO on panel. R. Horseman r. *ABC 447; V. 1851; BMC 1684.*   375   1450

261   **Bronze Unit.** Star shaped pattern. R. Winged sphinx l., SEGO. *ABC 453; V. 1855; BMC 1690.*   110   450

ANDOCO

262

262   **Gold Stater.** Crescents in wreath. R. Bucranium over horse r., AND below. *ABC 2715; V. 1860; BMC 2011-14.*   725   2250

263   **Gold Quarter Stater.** Crossed wreaths, ANDO in angles. R. Horse l. *ABC 2718; V. 1863; BMC 2015-17.*   200   650

264

264   **Silver Unit.** Bearded head l. R. Winged horse l., ANDOC. *ABC 2721; V. 1868; BMC 2018.*   110   375

265

265   **Bronze Unit.** Head r., ANDOCO. R. Horse r., ANDOCO. *ABC 2727; V. 1871; BMC 2019-20.*   40   200

266   Head r., TAS ANDO. R. Horse r. *ABC 2730; V. 1873; BMC —.*   50   250

DIAS

267   268

267   **Silver Unit.** Saltire over cross within square. R. Boar r., TASC DIAS. *ABC 2742; V. —; BMC 1663.*   90   275

268   DIAS CO, in star. R. Horse l., VIR. *ABC 2739; V. 1877; BMC 1683.*   95   300

269

		F £	VF £
269	**Bronze Unit.** Bearded head r., DIAS TASC. R. Centaur r., playing pan pipes. *ABC 2748; V. 1882; BMC 1728-35.*	40	225

RUES

270	**Bronze Unit.** Lion r., RVII. R. Eagle. *ABC 2760; V. 1890; BMC 1691.* .	35	180
271	— R. Similar reads RVE. *ABC 2760; V. 1890-3; BMC 1692.*	30	165

272   273

272	Bearded head r., RVIIS. R. Horseman r., VIR. *ABC 2754; V. 1892;* *BMC 1698-1701.*	30	165
273	RVIIS on tablet. R. Winged sphinx l. *ABC 2757; V. 1895;* *BMC 1693-97.*	30	165
274	**Bronze Fractional Unit.** Annulet within square with curved sides. R. Eagle l.,RVII. *ABC 2763; V. 1903; BMC 1756-58.*	35	180

CUNOBELIN
(Early 1st Century A.D. to *c.*40 A.D.)

Styled as son of Tasciovanus on some of his coins, Cunobelin appears to have ruled over the unified territories of the Trinovantes and Catuvellauni, with additional territory in Kent. His aggressive policy of expansion that involved members of his family eventually lead to Roman concern over the extent of his power. Following his death just prior to 43 AD, the emperor Claudius took the decision to invade Britain.

During his long reign an extensive issue of gold, silver and bronze coins used ever increasingly Romanised designs. It has been estimated from a study of known dies that around one million of his gold corn ear staters were produced. His main centre and mint was at Camulodunum (Colchester) appearing as the mint signature CAMV. The names SOLIDV and AGR appear on a few coins associated with Cunobelin and are likely to represent personal names.

280   281

280	**Gold Stater.** Biga type. CAMVL on panel. R. Two horses l., wheel below, CVNOBELIN. *ABC 2771; V. 1910; BMC 1769-71.*	725	2250
281	Linear type. Corn ear dividing CA MV. R. Horse r., branch above., CVN. *ABC 2774; V. 1925; BMC 1772-76.*	325	850

		F £	VF £

282　— Similar, privy mark 'x' above a letter in *obv.* legend. *ABC 2774;*
VA 1925-3/5; BMC 1777-81. .... 450　1250

283　　　　　　　　　　　　285

283　Wild type. Corn ear dividing CA MV. R. Horse r., branch above., CVN(O).
ABC 2783; V. 1931/33; BMC 1784-92/1804-08. .... 300　800

284　— Similar, heart shaped object between horses forelegs. *ABC 2780;*
V. 1931-3; BMC 1793. .... 550　2000

285　— Similar, privy mark pellet or pellet triangle above a letter(s) in *obv.*
legend. *ABC 2777; V. 1931-5/7/9; BMC 1797-1803.* .... 325　950

286　　　　　　　　　　　　288

286　Plastic type. Corn ear dividing CA MV. R. Horse r., branch above., CVNO.
ABC 2786, 2792; V. 2010-1/3/5; BMC 1809-11/15-23. .... 300　800

287　— Similar, 'B' in front of horse. *ABC 2789; V. 2010-7; BMC 1813.* ...... 525　1850

289　　　　　　　　　　　　290

288　Classic type. Corn ear dividing CA MV. R. Horse r., branch above., CVNO.
ABC 2795, 2798; V. 2025/27; BMC 1827-31/33. .... 425　1200

289　— Similar, horse l., lis like object above. *ABC 2804; V. 2029;*
BMC 1834-35. .... 600　2000

290　**Gold Quarter Stater.** Biga type. Similar to 280. *ABC 2807; V. 1913;*
BMC 1836/A. .... 275　900

292　　　　　　　　　　　　296

292　Linear type. Similar to 281. *ABC 2810; V. 1927; BMC 1837-42.* .... 150　400

293　Wild type. Similar to 283. *ABC 2813; V. 1935; BMC 1843-44.* .... 150　400

294　Plastic type. Similar to 286. *ABC 2816; V. 2015; BMC 1846-48.* .... 135　375

295　— Similar but corn ear dividing CAM CVN. *ABC 2819; V. 2017;*
BMC 1845. .... 175　525

296　Classic type. Similar to 288. *ABC 2822; V. 2038; BMC —.* .... 200　600

299

		F £	VF £
299	**Silver Unit.** Two bull headed serpents, inter twined. R. Horse l., CVNO. *ABC 2831; V. 1947; BMC 1856.*	90	475
300	Curled serpent inside wheel. R. Winged horse l., CVN. *ABC 2834; V. —; BMC 1857*	90	475
301	CVN on panel R. Dog l., (C)M. *ABC 2846; V. 1949; BMC 1858-59.*	80	375
302	CVNO BELI on two panels. R. CVN below horseman r. *ABC 2858, 2861; V. 1951/53; BMC 1862.*	75	325
303	Head l., CAMVL. R. CVNO beneath Victory std. r. *ABC 2855; V. 2045; BMV 1863-65.*	80	350

304   305

304	Two leaves dividing CVN. R. Horseman r., CAM. *ABC 2888; V. 2047; BMC 1866-67.*	75	325
305	Flower dividing CAMV. R. CVNO below horse r. *ABC 2885; V. 2049; BMC1867A.*	85	425
306	CVNO on panel. R. CAMV on panel below griffin. *ABC 2897; V. 2051; BMC 1868-69.*	80	375
307	CAMVL on panel. R. CVNO below centaur l. carrying palm. *ABC 2828; V. 1918; BMC —.*	80	375
308	CAMVL on panel. R. Figure seated l. holding wine amphora, CVNOBE. *ABC 2849; V. —; BMC —.*	75	325
309	Plant, CVNOBELINVS. R. Figure stg. r. holding club and thunderbolt dividing CA MV. *ABC 2906; V .—; BMC 1897.*	85	425
310	Laur. hd. r., CVNOBELINVS. R. Winged horse springing l., CAMV below. *ABC 2909; V. —; BMC —.*	85	425
311	CVNO on panel, wreath around. R. Winged horse r., TASC F. *ABC 2876; V. 2053; BMC 1870.*	85	400

312   313

312	Head r., CVNOBELINI. R. Horse r., TASCIO. *M. ABC 2873; V. 2055; BMC 1871-73.*	70	300
313	Winged bust r., CVNO. R. Sphinx std. l., TASCIO. *ABC 2870; V. 2057; BMC 1874-78.*	60	240

314   316   318

		F £	VF £
314	Draped female fig. r., TASCIIOVAN. R. Figure std. r. playing lyre, tree behind. *ABC 2867; V. 2059; BMC 1879-82.*	70	300
315	Figure stg. l., holding club and lionskin., CVNO. R. Female rider r., TASCIOVA. *ABC 2864; V. 2061; BMC 1884-85.*	70	275
316	Female head r., CVNOBELINVS. R. Victory r., TASCIO(VAN). *ABC 2882; V. —; BMC 1883.*	75	300
317	Fig. r. carrying dead animal, CVNOBELINVS. R. Fig. stg. holding bow, dog at side, TASCIIOVANI. *ABC 2879; V. 2063; BMC 1886-88.*	75	325
318	CVNO on panel, horn above, dolphin below. R. Fig. stg. r. altar behind. *ABC 2900; V. 2065; BMC 1889-90.*	85	425
319	CVN on panel. R. Fig. holding club walking r., CVN. *ABC 2840; V. 2067; BMC 1891-92.*	80	400
320	CVN in wreath. R. CAM, dog? trampling on serpent r. *ABC 2891; V. 2069; BMC 1893.*	90	475
321	Winged horse l., CVN. R. Std. fig. r. *ABC 2903; V. 2071; BMC 1896.* ..	85	425
322	CVNO in angles of cross. R. Capricorn r., CVNO. *ABC 2843; V. —; BMC 1898*	80	400
323	**Bronze Unit.** Head l., CVNO. R. Boar l., branch above. *ABC 2993; V. 1969; BMC—.*	35	130
324	CVNOB ELINI in two panels. R. Victory std. l., TASC. *ABC 2918; V. 1971; BMC 1921-27.*	25	110
325	Winged horse l., CAM. R. Winged Victory stg l., CVN. *ABC 2921; V. 1973; BMC 1938-43.*	30	120

326

326	Bearded head facing R. Boar l., CVN. *ABC 2912; V.1963; BMC 1904-05.*	35	125
327	Ram-headed animal coiled up in double ornamental circle. R. Animal l., CAM. *ABC 2915; V. 1965; BMC —.*	35	125
328	Griffin r., CAMV. R. Horse r., CVN. *ABC 2945; V. 2081; BMC 1909-12.*	30	120
329	Bearded head l., CAMV. R. CVN or CVNO below horse l. *ABC 2951; V. 2085/2131; BMC 1900-01.*	30	120
330	Laureate head r., CVNO. R. CVN below bull butting l. *ABC 2948; V. 2083; BMC 1902-03.*	35	125
331	Crude head r., CVN. R. Figure stg. l., CVN. *ABC —; V. 2135; BMC —.*	35	135

332

		F £	VF £
332	CAMVL / ODVNO in two panels. R. CVNO beneath sphinx crouching l. *ABC 2924; V. 1977; BMC 1928-30.*	30	120
333	Winged horse l., CAMV. R. Victory stg. r. divides CV NO. *ABC 2927; V. 1979; BMC 1931-34.*	30	120
334	Victory walking r. R. CVN below, horseman r. *ABC 2930; V. 1981; BMC 1935.*	35	135
335	Head l., CAM. R. CVNO below eagle. *ABC 2954; V. 2087; BMC −.*	35	135

336 337

336	Head l., CVNOBELINI. R. Centaur r., TASCIOVANI.F. *ABC 2957; V. 2089; BMC 1968-71.*	25	100
337	Helmeted bust r. R. TASCIIOVANII above, sow stg. r., F below. *ABC 2960; V. 2091; BMC 1956-60.*	25	100
338	Horseman galloping r. holding dart and shield, CVNOB. R. Warrior stg. l., TASCIIOVANTIS. *ABC 2963; V. 2093; BMC 1961-67.*	25	100

339 340

339	Helmeted bust l., CVOBELINVS REX. R. TASC FIL below boar l., std. on haunches. *ABC 2933; V. 1983; BMC 1952-55.*	30	120
340	Bare head r., CVNOBELINVS REX. R. TASC below bull butting r. *ABC 2966; V. 2095; BMC 1944-51.*	25	110
341	Bare head l., CVNO. R. TASC below bull stg. r. *ABC 2996; V. 1985; BMC −.*	35	125

342 343

342	Head l., CVNOBELIN. R. Metal worker std. r. holding hammer, working on a vase, TASCIO. *ABC 2969; V. 2097; BMC 1972-83.*	30	120
343	Winged horse r., CVNO. R. Victory r. sacrificing bull, TASCI. *ABC 2972; V. 2099; BMC 1913-19.*	25	95
344	CVNO on panel within wreath. R. CAMV below horse, prancing r. *ABC 2975; V. 2101; BMC 1987-90.*	30	120

345   346

		F £	VF £

345 Bearded head of Jupiter Ammon l., CVNOBELIN. R. CAM below horseman
galloping r. *ABC 2978; V. 2103; BMC 1984-86.*   35   125

346 Janus head, CVNO below. R. CAMV on panel below, sow std. r.
beneath a tree. *ABC 2981; V. 2105; BMC 1998-2003.*   30   125

347

347 Bearded head of Jupiter Ammon r., CVNOB. R. CAM on panel below
lion crouched r. *ABC 2984; V. 2107; BMC 1991-97.*   30   125

348 Sphinx r., CVNO. R. Fig stg. l. divides CA M. *ABC 2987; V. 2109;*
BMC 2004-09.   30   125

349 Horse r. R. CVN below horseman r. *ABC 2936; V. 1987; BMC 1936-47.* ...   35   135

350 Animal l. looking back. R. CVN below horse l. *ABC 2990; V. 1967;*
BMC—   35   125

350A Ship, CVN below. R. Fig. r. dividing S E. *ABC 2939; V. 1989; BMC 2010.*   135   675

"SOLIDV"

351

351 **Silver Unit.** SOLIDV in centre of looped circle. R, Stg. fig. l., CVNO.
ABC 474; V. 2073; BMC 1894-95.   300   900

"AGR"

352   353

352 **Gold Quarter Stater**. Corn ear dividing CAM CVN. R. Horse r., branch
above., AGR below. *ABC 3002; V. —; BMC 1854*   350   1250

353 — R. Horse r., branch above., cross and A below. *ABC 2999; V. —;*
BMC 1855   375   1350

354

	F	VF
	£	£
354 Silver Unit. AGR inside wreath. R. Female dog r., AGR below. *ABC 3005; V. —;*		
BMC 1899	250	900

EPATICCUS
(1st Half 1st Century A.D.)

Epaticcus, styled as a son of Tasciovanus on his coins, was most probably a brother of Cunobelin. The corn ear employed on his staters is similar to those his brother produced at Colchester. His coins appear in northern Atrebatic territory and conform to the area's denominational structure. It seems likely that Epaticcus's coinage reflects an incursion into Atrebatic territory by the Trinovantian/Catuvellaunian dynasty.

355

| 355 Gold Stater. Corn ear dividing TAS CIF. R. Horseman r., with spear and shield. EPATI. *ABC 1343; V. 575; BMC 2021-23.* .... | 950 | 3500 |

356   357

| 356 Silver Unit. Head of Hercules r., EPAT(I). R. Eagle stg. on snake. *ABC 1346; V. 580; BMC 2024-2268/2270-76.* .... | 30 | 110 |
| 357 Victory seated r. TASCIOV. R. Boar r., EPAT. *ABC 1349; V. 581; BMC 2294-2328.* .... | 35 | 135 |

358

| 358 Bearded head l., TASCIO. R. EPATI below lion r. *ABC 1352; V. 582; BMC 2329* | 95 | 425 |
| 359 EPATI inside panel. R. Lion r. *ABC 1355; V. 583; BMC 2330.* .... | 90 | 400 |

360 (x1.5)   361 (x1.5)

360 Silver Minim. EPATI. R. Boars head r., TA. *ABC 1370; V. 585; BMC 2331-46.*	30	125
361 TA inside star. R. Winged horse r., EPA below. *ABC 1367; V. 560; BMC 2351-57.*	30	135
362 Helmeted head r. R. Horse r., E below. *ABC 1364; V. —; BMC 2358-63*	30	135
363 EPATI. R. Winged horse r., cross below. *ABC 1373; V .—; BMC 2365...*	35	150

CARATACUS
(1st Half 1st Century A.D.)

Coins inscribed CARA have been traditionally associated with the historically attested son of Cunobelin, Caratacus the leader of British resistance against Rome. His coins appear in the same area as those of Epaticcus and he may have been his successor.

364   364A (x1.5)

		F £	VF £
364	**Silver Unit.** Head of Hercules r., CARA. R. Eagle stg. on snake. *ABC 1376;* *V. 593; BMC 2376-84.*	125	450
364A	**Silver Minim.** CARA around pellet in ring. R. Winged horse r. *ABC 1379;* *V. 595; BMC 2385-89.*	85	300

DUROTRIGES
(Mid 1st Century B.C. to Mid 1st Century A.D.)

The Durotriges inhabited West Hampshire, Dorset and adjoining parts of Somerset and Wiltshire. Their coinage is one of the most distinctive in Britain due to its rapid debasement. The disappearance of precious metals from the coinage should perhaps be linked to the declining trade between the south-west and western Gaul, following the Roman conquest of the Gaul. Hengistbury Head is the probable mint site of the cast bronzes. Coins inscribed CRAB have been traditionally associated with the tribe.

UNINSCRIBED

365	**Silver Stater.** White Gold type. Derived from Westerham stater (no. 21). *ABC 2157; V. 1235, 52, 54, 55; BMC 2525-2731.*	110	350

366   368

366	Silver type. Similar. *ABC 2169; V. 1235, 52, 54, 55; BMC 2525-2731.* .	45	150
367	Billon type. Similar. *ABC 2166; V. 1235, 52, 54, 55; BMC 2525-2731.* .	20	65
368	**Silver Quarter Stater.** Geometric type. Crescent design. R. Zig-zag pattern. *ABC 2205, 2208, 2211, 2214, 2217; V. 1242/29; BMC 2734-79.* . *Quality* *of metal varies, obv.almost blank on later issues*	25	90

369 371

		F £	VF £
369	Starfish type. Spiral. R. Zig-zag pattern. *ABC 2220; V. 1270; BMC 2780-81*	50	225
370	Hampshire Thin Flan type. Crude head of lines and pellets. R. Stylised horse l. *ABC 911; V. 1280; BMC 2782-87.*	75	350
371	**Bronze Stater.** Struck Bronze type. Similar to No.365-67. *ABC 2175;* *V. 1290; BMC 2790-2859.*	20	50

372

372	Cast Bronze type. Many varities, as illustration. *ABC 2178, 2181, 2184,* *2187, 2190, 2193, 2196, 2199; V. 1322-70; BMC 2860-2936.*	25	125

INSCRIBED

"CRAB"

373

373	**Silver Unit.** CRAB in angles of cross. R. Eagle. *ABC 1385; V. 1285;* *BMC 2788.*	225	750
373A	**Silver Minim.** CRAB on tablet. R. Star shape. *ABC 1388; V. 1286;* *BMC 2789.*	125	375

DOBUNNI

(Mid 1st Century B.C. to Mid 1st Century A.D.)

Dobunnic territory stretched over Gloucestershire, Hereford and Worcester and into parts of Somerset, Wiltshire and Gwent. The earliest Dobunnic coins are developed from the British Q stater, and have the distinctive tree-like motif of the tribe on the obverse. The inscribed coinage is difficult to arrange chronologically and it may be that some of the rulers named held different parts of the territory simultaneously.

UNINSCRIBED

374
374 (variant)

375

		F £	VF £
374	**Gold Stater.** Plain except for tree-like object. R. Triple tailed horse r., wheel below. *ABC 2003; V. 1005; BMC 2937-40.*	700	2750
375	**Gold Quarter Stater.** Plain with traces of wreath pattern. R. Horse r. *ABC 2009; V. 1010-3; BMC 2942-46.*	175	475
376	Wreath pattern. R. Horse l., pellet in ring motifs in field. *ABC 2105; V. 1015; BMC 2949.*	175	500

377 378

377	**Silver Unit.** Allen types A-F/I-J. Regular series. Head r. R. Triple tailed horse l. or r. *ABC 2012, 2015, 2018, 2021, 2024, 2027, 2036; V. 1020/45/49/74/78/95/ 1135/1137; BMC 2950-3011. (63-64). Style becomes progressively more abstract, from-*	45	185
378	Allen types L-O. Irregular series. Similar to last. *ABC 2030, 2122, 2125, 2137, 2140; V. 1170-85; BMC 3012-22. (63-64)*	50	200

INSCRIBED

The following types are not arranged chronologically.

ANTED

379

379	**Gold Stater.** Dobunnic emblem. R. ANTED or ANTEDRIG over triple tailed horse r., wheel below. *ABC 2066, 2069; V. 1062-69; BMC 3023-3031.*	475	1750

		F £	VF £
380	**Silver Unit.** Crude head r. Ɽ. ANTED over horse. *ABC 2072; V. 1082; BMC 3032-38.*	35	150

EISV

381

382

381	**Gold Stater.** Dobunnic emblem. Ɽ. EISV or EISVRIG over triple tailed horse r., wheel below. *ABC 2078; V. 1105; BMC 3039-42.*	525	1850
382	**Silver Unit.** Crude head r. Ɽ. Horse l., EISV. *ABC 2081, 2084; V. 1110; BMC 3043-55.*	35	140

INAM or INARA

383	**Gold Stater.** Dobunnic emblem. Ɽ. INAM or INARA over triple tailed horse r., wheel below. *ABC 2060; V. 1140; BMC 3056.*	1350	5000

CATTI

384

384	**Gold Stater.** Dobunnic emblem. Ɽ. CATTI over triple tailed horse r., wheel below. *ABC 2057; V. 1130; BMC 3057-60.*	425	1500

COMUX

385

385	**Gold Stater.** Dobunnic emblem. Ɽ. COMVX retrograde, over triple tailed horse r., wheel below. *ABC 2054; V. 1092; BMC 3061-63.*	1250	4750

CORIO

386

387

		F £	VF £
386	**Gold Stater.** Dobunnic emblem. R. CORIO over triple tailed horse r., wheel below. *ABC 2048; V. 1035; BMC 3064-3133.*	425	1500
387	**Gold Quarter Stater.** COR in centre. R. Horse r., without legend. *ABC 2051; V. 1039; BMC 3134.*	375	1350

BODVOC

388

389

		F £	VF £
388	**Gold Stater.** BODVOC across field. R. Horse r., without legend. *ABC 2039; V. 1052; BMC 3135-42.*	825	3000
389	**Silver Unit.** Head l., BODVOC. R. Horse r., without legend. *ABC 2042; V. 1057; BMC 3143-45.*	125	400

CORIELTAUVI

The Corieltauvi, formerly known as the Coritani, occupied Lincolnshire and adjoining parts of Yorkshire, Northamptonshire, Leicestershire and Nottinghamshire. The earliest staters, the South Ferriby type, are developed from Gallo-Belgic C staters, and are associated with the silver Boar/ Horse types. The distinctive dish shaped scyphate coinages have no parallels in Britain and stand apart from the main series. The later inscribed issues present a complex system of inscriptions. It has been suggested that some of the later inscriptions refer to pairs of names, possibly joint rulers or moneyers and rulers.

EARLY UNINSCRIBED
(Mid to Late 1st Century B.C.)

390

390	**Gold Stater.** South Ferriby type. Crude laureate head. R. Disjointed horse l., rosette or star below, anchor shape and pellets above. *ABC 1737, 1743, 1746, 1752; V. 809-815/19; BMC 3146-3179.*	175	450

393 394 395

	F £	VF £
391 Wheel type. Similar, but wheel below horse. *ABC 1749; V. 817; BMC 3180*	425	1350
392 Kite type. Similar to 390, but diamond shape containing pellets above, spiral below horse. *ABC 1761; V. 825; BMC 3181-84.*	200	600
393 Domino type. Similar to last, but with rectangle containing pellets. *ABC 1758; V. 829; BMC 3185-86.*	185	500
394 Trefoil type. Trefoil with central rosette of seven pellets. R. Similar to 390. *ABC 1755; V. 821; BMC —.*	1250	5250
395 North Lincolnshire Scyphate type. Stylised boar r. or l. R. Large S symbol with pellets and rings in field. *ABC 1764, 1770, 1773; V. —; BMC 3187-93*	185	500

* chipped or cracked specimens are often encountered and are worth less

396 398 399

396 **Silver Unit.** Boar/Horse type I. Boar r., large pellet and ring motif above, reversed S below. R. Horse l. or r., pellet in ring above. *ABC 869, 1779, 1782, 1785, 1791, 1797; V. 855-60, 864, 867; BMC 3194-3214.*	50	250
397 Boar Horse type II. Vestiges of boar on obv. R. Horse l. or r. *ABC 1800; V. 875-877; BMC 3214-27.*	30	120
398 Boar Horse type III. Blank. R. Horse l.or r. *ABC 1803, 1806, 1812, 1815; BMC 3228-35.*	20	75
399 **Silver Fractional Unit.** Similar to 396-97. *ABC 1827, 1836; V. 862/66; BMC 3236-3250.*	25	80
400 Similar to 398. *ABC 1833; V. 877-81; BMC 3251-55. (70/71)*	20	70
401 Pattern/Horse. Flower pattern. R. Horse l. *ABC 1606; V. —; BMC 3256-57.*	65	300

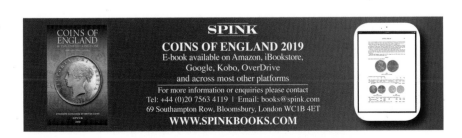

INSCRIBED
(Early to Mid 1st Century A.D.)
The following types are not arranged chronologically.

AVN COST

402   403

		F	VF
		£	£
402	**Gold Stater.** Crude wreath design. R. Disjointed horse l., AVN COST. *ABC 1929;V. 910; BMC 3258.*	325	1350
403	**Silver Unit.** Remains of wreath or blank. R. AVN COST, horse l. *ABC 1935, 1938; V. 914; BMC 3261-66.*	25	95
403A	**Silver Unit.** Inscription between three lines. R. Horse l. AVN. *ABC —; V-; BMC —.*	75	200
404	**Silver Fractional Unit.** Similar. *ABC 1953; l V. 918; BMC 3267-68.* ...	30	85

ESVP RASV

405

405	**Gold Stater.** Crude wreath design. R. Disjointed horse l., IISVP RASV. *ABC 1917; V. 920; BMC 3269.*	275	1000
406	**Silver Unit.** Similar. *ABC 1920; V. 924; BMC 3272-73.*	40	150

VEP

407

407	**Gold Stater.** Blank or with traces of wreath. R. Disjointed horse l., VEP. *ABC 1851; V. 905; BMC 3274-75.*	375	1500
408	**Silver Unit.** Blank or with traces of wreath. R. VEP, horse r. *ABC 1866; V. 963; BMC 3277-82.*	30	120
409	**Silver Half Unit.** Similar. *ABC 1887; V. 967; BMC 3283-3295.*	25	95

VEP CORF

410 412

		F £	VF £

410 **Gold Stater.** Crude wreath design. R. Disjointed horse l., VEP CORF.
ABC 1854, 1857, 1860, 1863; V. 930/40/60; BMC 3296-3304. .... 250 850
411 **Silver Unit.** Similar. ABC 1869, 1878, 1881; V. 934/50;
BMC 3305-14. .... 30 120
412 Similar but VEPOC (M)ES, pellet in ring below horse. ABC 1869; V. 955;
BMC −. 35 135
413 **Silver Half Unit.** Similar. ABC 1890, 1893, 1896, 1899, 1902, 1908;
V. 938/58; BMC 3316-24. (293/95) 30 90

DVMNO TIGIR SENO

414 415

414 **Gold Stater.** DVMN(OC) across wreath. R. Horse l., TIGIR SENO. ABC 1971;
V. 972; BMC 3325-27. .... 525 2000
415 **Silver Unit.** DVMNOC in two lines. R. Horse r., TIGIR SENO. ABC 1974;
V. 974; BMC 3328-29. .... 110 425

VOLISIOS DVMNOCOVEROS

416

416 **Gold Stater.** VOLISIOS between three lines in wreath. R. Horse r. or l.,
DVMNOCOVEROS. ABC 1980; V. 978-80; BMC 3330-3336. .... 275 1000
417 **Silver Unit.** Similar. R. Horse r., DVMNOCO. ABC 1983; V. 980;
BMC 3339. .... 125 500
418 **Silver Half Unit.** Similar. ABC 1986; V. 984; BMC 3340-41. .... 65 225

VOLISIOS DVMNOVELLAUNOS

419

		F £	VF £
419	**Gold Stater.** VOLISIOS between three lines in wreath. R. Horse r. or l., DVMNOVELAVNOS. *ABC 1995; V .988; BMC 3342-43.*	325	1350
420	**Silver Half Unit.** As last but DVMNOVE. *ABC 1998; V. 992; BMC 3344-46.*	90	350

VOLISIOS CARTIVEL

420A	**Gold Stater.** VOLISIOS between three lines in wreath. R. Horse l. CARTILLAVNOS. *ABC —; VA 933; BMC —.*	950	4000
421	**Silver Half Unit.** VOLISIOS between three lines in wreath. R. Horse r., CARTILEV. *ABC 1992; V. 994; BMC 3347-48.*	185	700

IAT ISO E

422	**Silver Unit.** IAT ISO (retrograde) on tablet, rosettes above and below. R. Horse r., E above. *ABC 1959; V. 998; BMC 3349-51.*	95	400

CAT

422A	**Silver Unit.** Boar r., pellet ring above, CAT above. R. Horse r. *ABC 1845; V. —; BMC 3352*	175	650

LAT ISON

423

423	**Gold Stater.** LAT ISO(N) in two lines retrograde. R. Horse r., ISO in box above, N below. *ABC 1956; V. —; BMC —. Only recorded as an AE/AV plated core, as illustrated.*	*Extremely rare*

ICENI

The Iceni, centred on Norfolk but also occupying neighbouring parts of Suffolk and Cambridgeshire, are well attested in the post conquest period as the tribe who under Boudicca revolted against Roman rule. Their earliest coins are likely to have been the British J staters, Norfolk Wolf type (no.30/31), replaced around the mid first century B.C. by the Snettisham, Freckenham and Irstead type gold staters and quarter staters. Contemporary with these are silver Boar/Horse and Face/Horse units and fractions. The introduction of legends around the beginning of the millennia led to the adoption of a new obverse design of back to back crescents. The continuation of the coinage after the Roman invasion is attested by the coins of King Prasutagus. Some of the Face/Horse units (no.434) have been attributed to Queen Boudicca but this attribution is uncertain.

EARLY UNINSCRIBED

(Mid to Late 1st Century B.C.)

424

		F £	VF £
424	**Gold Stater.** Snettisham type. Blank or with traces of pellet cross. R. Horse r., serpent like pellet in ring motif above. *ABC 1402, 1405; V .—; BMC 3353-59*	525	1750
425	Similar. Blank or with three short curved lines. R. Horse r., symbol above more degraded. *ABC 1408, 1411; V. —; BMC 3360-83*	300	950

426   427

426	Freckenham type. Two opposed crescents with stars or pellets in field. R. Horse r., various symbols in field. *ABC 1441, 1444, 1447, 1450; V. 620; BMC 3384-89.*	275	900
427	Similar. Blank or with traces of pellet cross. R. Horse r., wheel or arch containing pellets above. *ABC 1414, 1417, 1420; V. 624; BMC 3390-95. ...*	300	1000

428

428	Similar. Trefoil on cross design. R. Similar. *ABC 1423, 1426, 1432, 1435; V. 626; BMC 3396-3419.*	250	825

429   430

		F £	*VF* £
429	**Gold Quarter Stater.** Snettisham type. Wreath cross. R. Horse r. *ABC 1462; V. —; BMC 3420-35*	125	375
430	Irstead type. Hatched box, wreaths at sides. R. Horse r. *ABC 1474, 1480; V. 628; BMC 3436-39.*	120	350

431   432

431	**Silver Unit.** Boar / Horse type. Boar r. R. Horse r. *ABC 1576, 1579, 1582; V. 655-59; BMC 3440-3512.*	30	125
432	Bury type. Head l. or r. R. Horse l. or r. *ABC 1495, 1498, 1501; V. —; BMC 3524-35*	70	275

433   433(i)

433	Early Face / Horse type. Celticised head l. or r. R. Horse l. or r. *ABC 1522, 1525, 1531, 1537, 1540, 1546, 1549, 1552, 1555, 1558; BMC 3536-3555.*	75	325

434   435

434	Face / Horse Regular type. Head r. R. Horse r. *ABC 1564, 1567; V. 790-94; BMC 3556-3759. Attributed to Queen Boudicca by R.D. van Arsdell*	45	185
435	Early Pattern / Horse type. Cross of two opposed crescents. R. Horse l. or r. *ABC 1588, 1591; V. 675-79; BMC 3763-74.*	30	120

436

436	ECEN symbol type. Two opposed crescents. R. Horse r. *ABC 1678, 1681; V. 752; BMC 4297-4325*	25	85

	F £	VF £
437 **Silver Half Unit.** Boar / Horse type. Similar to 431. *ABC 1621, 1624; V. 661; BMC 3513-20.*	25	85
438 **Silver Fractional Unit.** Early Pattern / Horse type. Similar to 435. *ABC 1612, 1693; V. 681-83; BMC 3775-89. (76/A)*	30	110

INSCRIBED

(Early to Mid 1st Century A.D.)
The following types are not arranged chronologically.

CAN DVRO

439

439 **Silver Unit.** Boar. R. Horse r., CAN(S) above, DVRO below. *ABC 1630; V. 663; BMC 3521-23.*	75	325

ANTED

440

440 **Gold Stater.** Triple crescent design. R. Horse r., ANTED monongram below. *ABC 1639; V. 705; BMC 3790.*	525	1750

441

441 **Silver Unit.** Two opposed crescents. R. Horse r., ANTED. *ABC 1642, 1645; V. 710-11/15; BMC 3791-4025.*	25	80
442 **Silver Fractional Unit.** Similar to last. *ABC 1648; V. 720; BMC 4028-31.*	30	100

ECEN

443

		F	VF
		£	£
443	**Gold Stater.** Triple crescent design. R. Horse r., ECEN below. *ABC 1651; V. 725; BMC 4032*..............	725	2250
443A	**Silver Unit.** Two opposed crescents. R, Horse r., ECEN. *ABC 1657; V. 730; BMC 4033-4215.*	25	100
443B	**Silver Half Unit.** Similar to last. *ABC 1684; V. 736; BMC 4216-17.*	25	85

EDN

| 444 | **Silver Unit.** Two opposed crescents. R, Horse r., ED, E, EI or EDN. *ABC 1672, 1675; V. 734/40; BMC 4219-81.* .... | 25 | 100 |

ECE

| 444A | **Gold Stater** Triple crescent design R. Horse r., ECE. *ABC — ; V. — ;* .. | 850 | 3000 |

445

| 445 | **Silver Unit.** Two opposed crescents. R, Horse r., ECE. *ABC 1660, 1663, 1666, 1669; V. 761-66; BMC 4348-4538. (278-80)*................................. | 20 | 85 |

SAENU

| 446 | **Silver Unit.** Two opposed crescents. R. Horse r., SAENV. *ABC 1699; V. 770; BMC 4540-57.* .... | 30 | 125 |

AESU

447

| 447 | **Silver Unit.** Two opposed crescents. R. Horse r., AESV. *ABC 1702; V. 775; BMC 4558-72.* .... | 30 | 125 |

ALE SCA

| 448 | **Silver Unit.** Boar r., ALE. R. Horse r., SCA. *ABC 1708; V. 996; BMC 4576* | 175 | 725 |

AEDIC SIA

		F £	VF £
449	**Silver Unit.** AEDIC in two lines. ℞. Horse r., SIA? below. *ABC 1633; V.—;* *BMC 4581*	225	900

PRASUTAGUS

450

450	**Silver Unit.** Romanised head l., SUB RII PRASTO. ℞. Rearing horse r., ESICO FECIT. *ABC 1711; V. 780; BMC 4577-80.*	525	2250

This legend translates as "Under King Prasto, Esico made me", giving the name of both King and moneyer.

The systematic conquest of Britain by the Romans began in A.D. 43 when the Emperor Claudius (41-54), anxious to enhance his military reputation, authorized an invasion in which he personally participated, albeit in a purely symbolic role. The initial military contact between the two cultures had taken place almost a century before when Julius Caesar, during the course of his conquest of Celtic Gaul, led expeditions to the island in 55 and 54 B.C. Although no actual Roman occupation of Britain resulted from Caesar's reconnoitring campaigns, commercial intercourse was certainly accelerated, as evidenced by the 'Romanization' of the British Celtic coinage in the final decades of its production.

The Claudian conquest, commencing in A.D. 43, brought about a complete change in the nature of the currency circulating in Britain and ushered in a period lasting more than three and a half centuries during which Roman coinage was the only official medium of exchange. Local copies of the money brought with them by the four legions of the invasion army began to appear at a very early stage, the most popular type for imitation being the well-known Claudian copper as with reverse type fighting Minerva. Some of these copies are well-executed and of a style not much inferior to the prototype, suggesting that their local minting may have been officially sanctioned by the Roman government in order to make good a shortage of currency in the newly-conquered territory. Other examples are of much poorer style and execution and are frequently well below the normal weight of a Claudian as (usually between 10 and 11 grams). These copies must have been issued unofficially and provide evidence of the huge demand for this type of currency in a population which had never before experienced the benefits of having base metal coins available for small everyday transactions. In the decades that followed, the boundaries of the Roman province of Britannia were continually pushed further north and west until, under the celebrated Flavian governor Gnaeus Julius Agricola, the Roman army even penetrated to northern Scotland (A.D. 83/4). A few years later, under Trajan, the northern frontier was established along the Tyne-Solway line, a barrier made permanent by the construction of Hadrian's Wall following the emperor's visit to the province in 122. For a brief period in the mid-2nd century the frontier was temporarily advanced to the Forth-Clyde line with the building of the Antonine Wall, though this seems to have been abandoned early in the reign of Marcus Aurelius (ca. 163) when the Hadrianic barrier was re-commissioned and became the permanent frontier. The security thus provided to the now-peaceful province in the south facilitated urban expansion and the development of commerce. The new prosperity brought a flood of Roman coinage into the island-province and it was no longer necessary for shortages to be made good by large scale local imitation.

Until the mid-3rd century the production of Roman coinage remained the prerogative of the mint in the capital, with only occasional issues from provincial centres to serve short-term local needs. But with the deepening political and economic crisis in the third quarter of the century there was a dramatic decentralization of minting operations, with permanent establishments being set up in many important cities in the western as well as the eastern provinces. Britain, however, still remained without an official mint at this time and in the dark days of the 270s, when the separatist Gallic Empire to which Britain belonged was close to collapse, large scale production of imitative antoniniani (commonly called 'barbarous radiates') occurred in the province. The integrity and prestige of the Empire was, to some extent, restored by a rapid succession of Illyrian 'soldier emperors', until the situation was finally stabilized by Diocletian (A.D. 284-305) who established the tetrarchy system under which governmental responsibility was shared by four rulers. By the end of the 3rd century Britain had been reorganized into a civil diocese of four provinces: it had already been subdivided into Britannia Superior and Britannia Inferior almost a hundred years before, under Septimius Severus or Caracalla.

It was left to the colourful and enigmatic usurper Carausius (A.D. 287-293) to establish mints in Britain. It was, of course, vital for him to do so as his dominion was mostly confined to the island-province. Londinium (London) was his principal mint, with a secondary establishment at a place usually signing itself 'C' (probably Camulodunum, modern Colchester). After the downfall of Carausius' murderer and successor Allectus (293-296) Britain was restored to the central government, an event commemorated by the celebrated gold medallion of Constantius I showing the Caesar riding alongside the Thames approaching the gateway of the city of Londinium. At this point the mysterious 'C' mint disappears from the picture. Londinium, on the other hand, retained its status as an official mint under Diocletian's tetrarchy and its successors down to A.D. 325, when it was closed by Constantine the Great who regarded it as superfluous to his needs. In nearly four decades of existence as a Roman mint Londinium had produced a varied and extensive coinage in the names of almost all the emperors, empresses and Caesars of the period. It was destined never again to be active during Roman times, unless the extremely rare gold and silver issues of the late 4th century usurper Magnus Maximus, signed AVG, AVGOB and AVGPS, are correctly attributed to Londinium under its late Roman name of Augusta.

The termination of Roman rule in the British provinces is traditionally dated to A.D. 410 when the emperor Honorius, in response to an appeal for aid from his British subjects, told them to arrange for their own defence as best they might ('Rescript of Honorius'). In reality, the end probably came quite gradually. As the machinery of government ground to a halt and the soldiers stopped receiving their pay there would have been a steady drift of population away from the semi-ruinous cities and military installations to the countryside, where they could better provide for themselves through farming. Under these conditions the need for coinage would have been drastically reduced, as a primitive economy based on barter would largely have replaced the complex monetary economy of the late Roman period. In any case the supply of coinage from the Continent would now have dried up. The few monetary transactions which still took place were made with worn-out coins from earlier periods augmented by local imitations, production of which in Britain had resumed in the mid-4th century. Such was the pitiful end of the long tradition of Roman coinage in the remote island-province of Britannia. More than two centuries of 'Dark Ages' were to elapse before England's new rulers, the Anglo-Saxons, commenced the issue of gold thrymsas, the designs of many of which were based on late Roman types.

As Rome's Imperial coinage provided the currency needs of this country over a period of almost four centuries no representative collection of British coins is complete without some examples of these important issues. The following listing is divided into four categories: 1. Regular Roman issues, all of which would have been legal tender in Britain after A.D. 43; 2. Issues with types referring specifically to the province of Britannia, usually in commemoration of military campaigns in the north; 3. Official Roman coinage struck in Britain; 4. Imitations of Roman coins produced in Britain, all but possibly some of the earliest being of unofficial origin. The reference 'R.R.C.' is to the listing of the type in Michael Crawford's *Roman Republican Coinage* (Cambridge, 1974); and 'R.I.C.' to *The Roman Imperial Coinage* (London, 1923-1994, in ten volumes).

For more detailed collectors' information on Roman coinage, including a more comprehensive listing of types, the reader is referred to *Roman Coins and their Values Volumes 1, 2 and 3* by David R. Sear. A complete catalogue of silver issues may be found in the 5 volumes of *Roman Silver Coins* (H.A. Seaby and C.E. King) which provides a quick and convenient reference and is especially aimed at the collector. Gilbert Askew's *The Coinage of Roman Britain* (2nd edition) concentrates on those issues which are particularly associated with the Roman province of Britannia, but does not provide valuations. More recent works on this subject include R. Reece's *Coinage in Roman Britain* and *The Coinage of Roman Britain,* and also David R. Sear's *The History and Coinage of the Roman Imperators, 49—27 BC* which is devoted to the vital two decades of transition from Republic to Empire.

The standard works on the coinages of the Roman Republic and the Roman Empire have already been mentioned *(Roman Republican Coinage and Roman Imperial Coinage).* These monumental publications are essential to the advanced collector and student and their importance cannot be overstated. The British Museum Catalogues (3 volumes of Republican, 6 volumes of Imperial recently reprinted by SPINK) are also vital. They contain superb interpretive material in their introductions and are very fully illustrated. A similar work is Anne S. Robertson's *Roman Imperial Coins in the Hunter Coin Cabinet,* in 5 volumes (volume 4 is especially important for the later 3rd century coinage). For more general reading we may recommend J.P.C. Kent and M. & A. Hirmer's *Roman Coins,* undoubtedly the most lavishly illustrated book on the subject; C.H.V. Sutherland's *Roman Coins;* and R.A.G. Carson's *Coins of the Roman Empire.* Finally, for a most useful single-volume work on interpretation and background information, we would suggest A *Dictionary of Ancient Roman Coins* by John Melville Jones.

1. REGULAR ROMAN ISSUES

A token selection of the types of Roman coins which might be found on Romano-British archaeological sites. Many of the rarer emperors and empresses have been omitted and the types listed often represent only one of hundreds of variant forms which might be encountered.

		F	VF
		£	£
451	**THE REPUBLIC: P. Aelius Paetus** (moneyer), 138 B.C. ℞ *denarius*. Helmeted hd. of Roma r. Rev. The Dioscuri galloping r. R.R.C. 233/1 ...	40	110

Although dating from long before the Roman conquest many Republican coins circulated well into the Imperial period and found their way to Britain where they are often represented in early hoards.

452	**L. Thorius Balbus** (moneyer), 105 B.C. ℞ denarius. Hd. of Juno Sospita r., clad in goat's skin. Rev. Bull charging r. *R.R.C. 316/1.*	40	120
453	**Q. Antonius Balbus** (moneyer), 83-82 B.C. ℞ *denarius*. Laur. hd. of Jupiter r. Rev. Victory in quadriga r. *R.R.C. 364/1.*	40	120

454   455B

454	**C. Calpurnius Piso** (moneyer), 67 B.C. ℞ *denarius*. Laur. hd. of Apollo r. Rev. Horseman galloping r., holding palm-branch. *R.R.C. 408/1a.*	40	120
455	**Mn. Acilius Glabrio** (moneyer), 49 B.C. ℞ *denarius*. Laur. hd. of Salus r. Rev. Valetudo stg. l., holding snake and resting on column. *R.R.C. 442/1.*	40	110
455A	**Pompey the Great** (imperator) 49-48 BC. ℞ *denarius*. Diademed head of Numa r. Rev. MAGN PRO COS. Prow of galley r. *R.R.C. 446/1.*	190	480
455B	**Scipio** (imperator) 47-46 BC, ℞ *denarius*. Laureate head of Jupiter r. Rev. SCIPIO IMP. Elephant r. *R.R.C. 459/1*	110	270
455C	**Pompey Junior** (imperator) 46-45 BC. ℞ *denarius*. Helmeted head of Roma r. Rev. CN MAGNVS IMP. Hispania stg r presenting palm branch to Pompeian soldier. *RRC 469/1a.*	140	340
455D	**Sextus Pompey** (imperator) 45-36 BC. ℞ *denarius*. Bare head of Pompey. Rev. Neptune stg l between brothers Anapias and Amphinomus. *R.R.C. 511/3a.*	340	850
455E	**Julius Caesar** (dictator), visited Britain 55 and 54 B.C., died 44 B.C. ℳ *aureus*. Veiled head of Vesta r. Rev. A. HIRTIVS PR. Jug between lituus and axe. *R.R.C. 466/1.*	1300	3200

456   456B

456	℞ *denarius*. CAESAR. Elephant r. Rev. Priestly emblems. *R.R.C. 443/1.*	210	525
456A	— Wreathed hd. of Caesar r. Rev. P. SEPVLLIVS MACER. Venus stg. l., holding Victory and sceptre. *R.R.C. 480/9.*	650	1600
456B	Head of Venus. Rev CAESAR. Aeneas l bearing his father Anchises on shoulder. *R.R.C. 458/1.*	140	320

456F

		F	VF
		£	£

456C Head of Venus r. Rev. CAESAR. Trophy of Gallic arms between seated
captives. *R.R.C. 468/1*.. 150 340

456D **Brutus** (imperator) 42 BC. *Æ denarius.* Head of Apollo r. Rev. BRVTVS IMP.
Trophy. *R.R.C. 506/2.* 240 580

456E **Cassius** (imperator) 42 BC. *Æ denarius.* Head of Libertas. Rev. LENTVLVS
SPINT. Jug and lituus. *R.R.C. 500/3*... 160 400

456F **Ahenobarbus** (imperator) 41-40 BC. *Æ denarius.* Bare head r. Rev. CN
DOMITIVS IMP. Prow of galley r, surmounted by trophy. *R.R.C. 519/2.* 340 850

457 **Mark Antony** (triumvir), died 30 B.C. *Æ denarius.* Galley r. Rev. LEG. II.
Legionary eagle between two standards. *R.R.C. 544/14.* 120 300

457A Head of Antony r. Rev. CAESAR DIC. Head of Caesar r. *R.R.C. 488/2.* 340 900

457B Bare head of Antony. Rev. CAESAR IMP PONT III VIR RPC. Bare head
of Octavian. *R.R.C. 517/2.*.. 240 575

457C **Cleopatra VII** 34 BC *Æ denarius.* Bust of Cleopatra r. Rev. ANTONI
ARMENIA DEVICTA. Head of Antony r. *R.R.C. 543/1.* 2800 6500

458 459

458 **Octavian** (triumvir), named Augustus 27 B.C. *Æ denarius.* Bare hd. of
Octavian r. Rev. IMP. CAESAR. Trophy set on prow. *R.I.C. 265a*.......... 160 400

458A **THE EMPIRE: Augustus,** 27 B.C.-A.D. 14. *Æ aureus.* Rev. IMP XII ACT.
Apollo stg r, holding lyre. *R.I.C. 192a.* 1800 4400

459 *Æ denarius.* Rev. C. L. CAESARES AVGVSTI F COS DESIG PRINC IVVENT.
The emperor's grandsons, Gaius and Lucius, stg. facing, with spears and shields.
R.I.C. 207... 120 280

*Almost all the coins in the Roman Imperial series have a head or bust of the
emperor, empress or prince as their obverse type. Therefore, in most instances
only the reverses will be described in the following listings.*

459A — Rev IMP X. Bull butting r. *R.I.C. 167a.* 150 400

460 Æ *as.* ROM. ET AVG. The altar of Lugdunum. *R.I.C. 230.* 75 180

460A Æ *quadrans.* Obv. Anvil. Rev. Moneyers' inscription around large S. C.
R.I.C. 443... 22 50

461 **Augustus and Agrippa,** general and designated heir of Augustus, died
12 B.C. Æ *dupondius.* Obv. Their hds. back to back. Rev. COL. NEM.
Crocodile r., chained to palm-branch. *R.I.C. 159.* 100 240

See also no. 468.

461A **Gaius Caesar**,17 BC, grandson of Augustus. *Æ denarius.* Rev. AVGVST.
Candelabrum within floral wreath. *R.I.C. 539*............................ 380 1100

464

		F	*VF*
		£	£

462   **Divus Augustus,** deified A.D. 14. Æ as. PROVIDENT S. C. Large altar.
       R.I.C. 81.   75   180
463   **Tiberius,** A.D. 14-37. N *aureus.* PONTIF MAXIM. Livia (?) seated r.,
       holding sceptre and branch. *R.I.C. 29.*   1100   2600
464   *R denarius.* Similar. *R.I.C. 30.*   140   350
       This type is commonly referred to as the 'Tribute Penny' of the Bible (Matthew
       22, 17-21).
464A   Æ *sestertius.* Tiberius seated l. Rev Inscription around large S. C. *R.I.C. 48.*   300   800
464B   Æ *as.* Inscription around large S. C. *R.I.C. 44.*   75   180
465   **Livia,** wife of Augustus, mother of Tiberius. Æ *dupondius.* Obv. Veiled bust of
       Livia as Pietas r. Rev. Inscription of Drusus Caesar around large S. C. *R.I.C. 43.*   160   400
466   **Drusus,** son of Tiberius. Æ *as.* Inscription around large S. C. *R.I.C. 45.*   80   200
466A   **Caligula,** A.D. 37-41. N *aureus.* Rev. SPQR/PP/OBCS in three lines within
       oak wreath. R.I.C. 27.   3700   8900
466B   *R denarius,* SPQR/PP/OBCS in three lines within oak wreath, *R.I.C. 28.*   675   1950
466C   Æ *sestertius.* Rev. ADLOCVT COH. Caligula stg l on platform, haranguing
       soldiers. *R.I.C. 40.*   390   1100

467

467   Æ *as.* VESTA S. C. Vesta seated l. *R.I.C. 38.*   100   320

468

468   **Agrippa,** grandfather of Caligula, died 12 B.C. Æ *as.* S. C. Neptune stg.
       l., holding dolphin and trident. *R.I.C. 58.*   85   230
       See also no. 461 and under Category 4.

	F	VF
	£	£

469 **Germanicus,** father of Caligula, brother of Claudius, died A.D. 19. Æ *as*.
Inscription of Caligula around large S. C. *R.I.C. 35.* 80 200

470 **Agrippina Senior,** mother of Caligula, died A.D. 33. Æ *sestertius*. S.P.Q.R.
MEMORIAE AGRIPPINAE. Carpentum drawn l. by two mules. *R.I.C. 55.* 480 1600

470A **Claudius,** A.D. 41-54, initiated the conquest of Britain by his invasion in
A.D. 43. N *aureus* Rev. EX SC/OBCIVES/SERVATOS in three lines within
oak wreath. *R.I.C. 15.* 1900 5000

470B R *denarius*. PACI AVGVSTAE, winged Nemesis advancing r, snake at feet.
R.I.C. 52. .... 450 1200

470C Æ *sestertius*. Rev. SPES AVGVSTA SC. Spes walking l, holding flower.
R.I.C. 115. (see also no 744) 260 700

471   474

471 Æ *as*. LIBERTAS AVGVSTA S. C. Libertas stg. r., holding pileus.
R.I.C. 113. .... 75 200

471A Æ *quadrans*. Obv. Hand holding scales. Rev. Inscription around large
S. C. *R.I.C. 85.* 25 50
See also under Categories 2 and 4.

472 **Nero Claudius Drusus,** father of Claudius, died 9 B.C. Æ *sestertius*.
TI. CLAVDIVS CAESAR AVG. P. M. TR .P. IMP. P. P. S. C. Claudius seated
l. on curule chair amidst arms. *R.I.C. 109.* 260 950
See also under Category 4.

473 **Antonia,** mother of Claudius, died A.D. 37. Æ *dupondius*. TI. CLAVDIVS
CAESAR AVG P.M. TR. P. IMP. S. C. Claudius stg. l., holding simpulum.
R.I.C. 92. .... 120 340
See also under Category 4.

474 **Nero,** 54-68, emperor at the time of Queen Boudicca's rebellion in Britain.
N *aureus*. SALVS. Salus seated l. *R.I.C. 66.* 1200 3000

475 R *denarius*. IVPPITER CVSTOS. Jupiter seated l. *R.I.C. 53.* 140 400

476 Æ *sestertius*. ROMA S. C. Roma seated l., holding Victory and parazonium.
R.I.C. 274. .... 300 1000

476A Æ *as*. S. C. Victory hovering l., holding shield inscribed S. P. Q. R. *R.I.C. 312.* 85 230

476B **Civil Wars** (Gaul). R *denarius*. Clasped hands. Rev. FIDES PRAETOR
IANORVM. Clasped r hands. R.I.C. 121. .... 290 780

476C **Galba,** 68-69. N *aureus*. Rev. SPQR/OB CS in two lines within oak
wreath. *R.I.C. 164.* 2600 6400

477 R *denarius*. S.P.Q.R. / OB / C.S. within oak-wreath. *R.I.C. 167.* 190 500

477A **Otho,** 69. N *aureus*. Rev. SECVRITAS PR. Securitas stg l, holding wreath
and sceptre. *R.I.C. 7.* 4400 10800

478 R *denarius*. SECVRITAS P. R. Securitas stg. l. *R.I.C. 10* 340 900

478A **Vitellius,** 69. N *aureus*. Rev. CONCORDIA PR. Concordia seated l, holding
patera and cornucopiae. *R.I.C. 72.* 2800 6900

		F	VF
		£	£
479	Æ denarius. CONCORDIA P. R. Concordia seated l. *R.I.C. 90*...............	190	460
480	**Vespasian,** 69-79, commanded Legio II in the Claudian invasion of Britain (43) and appointed Agricola to governorship of the province in 77/8. *Ay aureus.* ANNONA AVG. Annona seated l. *R.I.C. 131a.*	950	2500

481

481	Æ *denarius.* VICTORIA AVGVSTI. Victory advancing r., crowning standard. *R.I.C. 52.*..	45	110
481A	Æ *sestertius.* Rev. JVDAEA CAPTA SC. Palm tree with standing Jewish captive r and female captive seated r. *R.I.C. 424*.....................................	500	1400
481B	Æ *dupondius.* FELICITAS PVBLICA S. C. Felicitas stg. l. *R.I.C. 554*...	55	140
481C	**Titus,** 79-81 (Caesar 69-79). *Ay aureus.* Rev. TRP VIIII IMP XIIII COS VII PP. Venus stg r resting on column. *R.I.C. 9.*	1400	3400
482	Æ *denarius.* TR. P. IX. IMP. XV. COS. VIII. P. P. Thunderbolt on throne. *R.I.C. 23a.*..	90	230
482A	**Julia Titi,** daughter of Titus and mistress of Domitian. Æ *denarius.* Rev. VENVS AVGVST. Venus stg r resting on column. *R.I.C. 56.*..................	340	850
482B	**Domitian,** 81-96 (Caesar 69-81), recalled Agricola in 83/4 and abandoned the conquest of northern Scotland (ca. 87). *Ay aureus.* Rev. GERMANICVS COS XV. Minerva stg l holding spear. *R.I.C. 163.*...	1300	3200

483   485

483	Æ *denarius.* IMP. XIX. COS. XIIII. CENS. P. P. P. Minerva stg. l., resting on spear. *R.I.C. 140*...	50	140
483A	Æ *sestertius.* Rev. IOVI VICTORI SC. Jupiter seated l, holding Victory and sceptre. *R.I.C. 358*..	160	425
484	Æ *dupondius.* VIRTVTI AVGVSTI S. C. Virtus stg. r. *R.I.C. 393*.............	45	130
484A	Æ *as.* MONETA AVGVSTI S. C. Moneta stg. l. *R.I.C. 354b.*	45	130
484B	**Domitia,** wife of Domitian. Æ *denarius.* Rev CONCORDIA AVGVST. Peacock stg r. *R.I.C. 212*..	575	1550
484C	**Nerva,** 96-98. *Ay aureus.* Rev. CONCORDIA EXERCITVVM. Clasped r hands. *R.I.C. 14*..	2300	5200
485	Æ *denarius.* AEQVITAS AVGVST. Aequitas stg. l. *R.I.C. 13.*................	90	230
485A	Æ *as.* LIBERTAS PVBLICA S. C. Libertas stg. l. *R.I.C. 86*....................	75	220
486	**Trajan,** 98-117, established the northern frontier in Britain along the Tyne-Solway line (ca. 100). *Ay aureus.* P. M. TR. P. COS. VI. P. P. S. P. Q. R. Genius stg. l., holding patera and corn-ears. *R.I.C. 347.*	1200	3000

487   489

	F £	VF £

487   Æ *denarius*. COS. V. P. P. S. P. Q. R. OPTIMO PRINC. Military trophy.
R.I.C. 147.   45   120

488   Æ *sestertius*. S. P. Q. R. OPTIMO PRINCIPI S. C. Spes walking l.,
holding flower. *R.I.C. 519.*   90   360

488A   Æ *dupondius*. SENATVS POPVLVSQVE ROMANVS S. C. Emperor
advancing between two trophies. *R.I.C. 676.*   65   140

489   **Hadrian,** 117-138, visited Britain in 122 and initiated the construction of
a fortified frontier line (Hadrian's Wall). Æ *aureus*. HISPANIA. Hispania
reclining l. *R.I.C. 305.*   1400   3600

490   Æ *denarius*. P. M. TR. P. COS. III. Roma stg. l., holding Victory and spear.
R.I.C. 76.   50   140

491   Æ *sestertius*. COS. III. S. C. Neptune stg. r., holding dolphin and trident,
foot on prow. *R.I.C. 632.*   95   360

491A   Æ *as*. FELICITATI AVG COS. III. P. P. S. C. Galley travelling l. over waves.
R.I.C. 719.   60   150
See also under Category 2.

492   **Sabina,** wife of Hadrian. Æ *denarius*. IVNONI REGINAE. Juno stg. l.
R.I.C. 395a.   70   175

493   **Aelius Caesar,** heir of Hadrian, 136-138. Æ *denarius*. CONCORD. TR.
POT. COS. II. Concordia seated l. *R.I.C. 436.*   120   290

493A   Æ *as*. TR. POT. COS. II. S. C. Spes walking l., holding flower. *R.I.C. 1067.*   75   190

494   **Antoninus Pius,** 138-161, ordered the expansion of the Roman province to
include southern Scotland and constructed the Antonine Wall on the Forth-Clyde
line (beginning ca. 143). An uprising in northern Britain in the 150s resulting in a
permanent withdrawal to the Hadrianic frontier early in the next reign.
Æ *aureus*. COS. IIII. Togate emperor stg. l., holding globe. *R.I.C. 233b.*   1100   2600

495   Æ *denarius*. PIETATI AVG. COS. IIII. Pietas stg. l. between two children,
holding two more in her arms. *R.I.C. 313c.*   40   100

496

496   Æ *sestertius*. SALVS AVG. S. C. Salus stg. l. at altar, feeding snake.
R.I.C. 635.   70   240

496A   Æ *dupondius*. TR. POT. XX. COS. IIII. S. C. Providentia stg. l., pointing
at globe at her feet and holding sceptre. *R.I.C. 2025.*   35   90
See also under Categories 2 and 3.

	F	VF
	£	£

497   **Antoninus Pius and Marcus Aurelius Caesar**. Æ *denarius*. Obv. Laur.
hd. of Antoninus Pius r. Rev. AVRELIVS CAESAR AVG PII F. COS. Bare
hd. of young Marcus Aurelius r. *R.I.C. 417a.* 110   260

498   501

498   **Divus Antoninus Pius,** deified 161. Æ *denarius*. CONSECRATIO.
Four-storeyed crematorium of Antoninus Pius. *R.I.C. 436.* 40   100
499   **Diva Faustina Senior,** wife of Antoninus Pius, deified 141. Æ *denarius*.
AETERNITAS. Aeternitas stg. l., holding globe and billowing veil. *R.I.C. 351.*   35   90
499A Æ *sestertius*. AVGVSTA S. C. Ceres stg. l., holding two torches. *R.I.C. 1120.*   55   170
500   **Marcus Aurelius,** 161-180 (Caesar 139-161), re-established Hadrian's Wall
as the permanent northern frontier of the province, ca. 163. A/ *aureus.*
PROV. DEOR. TR. P. XV. COS. III. Providentia stg. l., holding globe and
cornucopiae. *R.I.C. 19.* 1300   3000
501   Æ *denarius*. PIETAS AVG. Priestly emblems. *R.I.C. 424a.* 40   110
501A — SALVTI AVG. COS. III. Salus stg. l. at altar, feeding snake. *R.I.C. 222.*   40   100
502   Æ *sestertius*. CONCORD. AVGVSTOR. TR. P. XVI. COS. III. S. C. Marcus
Aurelius and Lucius Verus stg. face to face, clasping hands. *R.I.C. 826.*..   90   400
502A Æ *as*. HONOS TR. POT. II. COS. II. S. C. Honos stg. r. *R.I.C. 1271a.* ..   40   120
503   **Divus Marcus Aurelius,** deified 180. Æ *denarius*. CONSECRATIO.
Eagle stg. r. on altar. *R.I.C. 272.* 40   100

504   506A

504   **Faustina Junior,** daughter of Antoninus Pius, wife of Marcus Aurelius.
Æ *denarius*. FECVNDITAS. Fecunditas stg. r., holding sceptre and child.
R.I.C. 677... 35   90
504A Æ *sestertius*. HILARITAS S. C. Hilaritas stg. l. *R.I.C. 1642.* 60   220
505   **Diva Faustina Junior,** deified 175. Æ *as*. S. C. Crescent and seven stars.
R.I.C. 1714... 40   120
506   **Lucius Verus,** 161-169. Æ *denarius*. PAX TR. P. VI. IMP. IIII. COS. II.
Pax stg. l. *R.I.C. 561.* 60   150
506A Æ *dupondius*. TR. P. IIII. IMP. II. COS. II. S. C. Mars stg. r., resting on
spear and shield. *R.I.C. 1387.* 50   160
507   **Lucilla,** daughter of Marcus Aurelius, wife of Lucius Verus. Æ *denarius*.
IVNONI LVCINAE. Juno stg. l., holding child in swaddling clothes.
R.I.C. 771... 45   120
507A Æ *sestertius*. PIETAS S. C. Pietas stg. l., altar at feet. *R.I.C. 1756.*......... 65   240

	F	VF
	£	£

508 **Commodus,** 177-192 (Caesar 175-177), major warfare on the British
frontier early in the reign; situation restored by Ulpius Marcellus in 184/5,
followed by unrest in the British legions. Æ *denarius*. LIB. AVG. IIII. TR.
P. VI. IMP. IIII. COS. III. P. P. Liberalitas stg. l. *R.I.C. 22*...................... 50 125

509 511

509 Æ *sestertius*. IOVI VICTORI IMP. III. COS. II. P. P. S. C. Jupiter seated l.
R.I.C. 1612.. 75 330

509A Æ *as*. ANN. AVG. TR. P. VII. IMP. IIII. COS. III. P. P. S. C. Annona stg. l.,
modius at feet. *R.I.C. 339 (See also under Category 2.)*......................... 35 90

510 **Crispina,** wife of Commodus. Æ *denarius*. CONCORDIA. Clasped hands.
R.I.C. 279... 50 125

511 **Pertinax,** January-March 193, formerly governor of Britain, ca. 185-7. Æ
denarius. PROVID. DEOR. COS. II. Providentia stg l., reaching up to star.
R.I.C. 11a.. 340 850

512 513 514A

512 **Didius Julianus,** March-June 193. Æ *denarius*. CONCORD MILIT.
Concordia Militum stg. l., holding standards. *R.I.C. 1*............................ 675 1550

513 **Clodius Albinus,** 195-197 (Caesar 193-195), governor of Britain (from
191/2) at the time of his imperial proclamation by his troops. Æ *denarius*.
MINER. PACIF. COS. II. Minerva stg. l. *R.I.C. 7*.................................... 85 200

513A — FIDES LEGION. COS. II. Clasped hands holding legionary eagle. *R.I.C. 20b*. 100 240

514 **Septimius Severus,** 193-211, restored the frontier forts in northern Britain
following the downfall of Clodius Albinus; later repaired Hadrian's Wall, and
spent the years 208-11 in Britain campaigning in Scotland; divided Britannia into
two provinces, Superior and Inferior; died at York, February 211. Æ *denarius*.
VIRT AVGG. Roma stg. l., holding Victory, spear and shield. *R.I.C. 171a*. 25 65

514A — P.M. TR. P. XVIII. COS. III. P. P. Jupiter stg. l. between two children.
R.I.C. 240 (See also under Category 2.) 25 65

515 **Julia Domna,** wife of Septimius Severus, mother of Caracalla and Geta,
accompanied her husband and sons on the British expedition, 208-211, and
probably resided in London during the northern campaigns. Æ *denarius*.
VENERI VICTR. Venus stg. r., resting on column. *R.I.C. 536*............... 25 60

515A — VESTA. Vesta stg. l., holding palladium and sceptre. *R.I.C. 390*........ 25 60

516   519

	F £	VF £
516 **Caracalla,** 198-217 (Caesar 196-198), accompanied his father and brother on the British expedition, 208-211, and led the final campaign in Scotland in 210 during Severus' illness; made frontier dispositions before returning to Rome and finalized his father's arrangements for the division of Britain into two provinces. Æ *antoninianus (double denarius,* introduced in 215). VENVS VICTRIX. Venus stg. l., holding Victory and resting on shield. *R.I.C. 311c.*	55	140
517 Æ *denarius.* PART. MAX. PONT. TR. P. IIII. Trophy with two captives at base. *R.I.C. 54b.*...............	25	65
517A — P. M. TR. P. XV. COS. III. P. P. Hercules stg. l., holding olive-branch and club. *R.I.C. 192.*	25	65
See also under Category 2.		
518 **Plautilla,** wife of Caracalla. Æ *denarius.* PROPAGO IMPERI. Caracalla and Plautilla clasping hands. *R.I.C. 362.*	35	90
519 **Geta,** 209-212 (Caesar 198-209), accompanied his father and brother on the British expedition, 208-211, and took charge of the civil administration in London during the northern campaigns. Æ *denarius.* PRINC. IVVENTVTIS. Prince stg. l. beside trophy, holding branch and spear. *R.I.C. 18.*	35	90
519A — FORT RED TR. P. III. COS. II. Fortuna seated l. *R.I.C. 75.*	30	75
See also under Category 2.		
520 **Macrinus,** 217-218. Æ *denarius.* PROVIDENTIA DEORVM. Providentia stg. l., globe at feet. *R.I.C. 80.*	60	150
521 **Diadumenian,** 218 (Caesar 217-218). Æ *denarius.* PRINC. IVVENTVTIS. Prince stg. l., two standards behind. *R.I.C. 109.*	130	325

522

522 **Elagabalus,** 218-222. Æ *antoninianus.* MARS VICTOR. Mars advancing r. *R.I.C. 122.*...............	60	150
522A Æ *denarius.* P. M. TR. P. III. COS. III. P. P. Jupiter seated l., eagle at feet *R.I.C. 27.*...............	30	75
523 **Julia Paula,** first wife of Elagabalus. Æ *denarius.* CONCORDIA. Concordia seated l. *R.I.C. 211.*	55	130
524 **Aquilia Severa,** second wife of Elagabalus. Æ *denarius.* CONCORDIA. Concordia stg. l., altar at feet. *R.I.C. 226.*	65	160
525 **Julia Soaemias,** mother of Elagabalus. Æ *denarius.* VENVS CAELESTIS. Venus seated l., child at feet. *R.I.C. 243.*	40	95

	F	VF
	£	£

526 **Julia Maesa,** grandmother of Elagabalus and Severus Alexander. Æ
  denarius. SAECVLI FELICITAS. Felicitas stg. l., altar at feet. *R.I.C. 271.* | 30 | 80

527 **Severus Alexander,** 222-235 (Caesar 221-222). Æ *denarius.*
  PAX AETERNA AVG. Pax stg. l. *R.I.C. 165.* .... | 30 | 65

527A — P. M. TR. P. XIII. COS. III. P. P. Sol advancing l., holding whip. *R.I.C. 123.* | 30 | 65

528

528 *Æ sestertius.* MARS VLTOR S. C. Mars advancing r., with spear and shield.
  R.I.C. 635............... | 40 | 120

529 **Orbiana,** wife of Severus Alexander. Æ *denarius.* CONCORDIA AVGG.
  Concordia seated l. *R.I.C. 319.* .... | 80 | 200

530   531A

530 **Julia Mamaea,** mother of Severus Alexander. Æ *denarius.* VESTA.
  Vesta stg. l. *R.I.C. 362.* .... | 25 | 60

530A *Æ sestertius.* FELICITAS PVBLICA S. C. Felicitas stg. facing, hd. l.,
  resting on column. *R.I.C. 676.*...................... | 35 | 100

531 **Maximinus I,** 235-238. Æ *denarius.* PAX AVGVSTI. Pax stg. l. *R.I.C. 12.* | 30 | 70

531A *Æ sestertius.* SALVS AVGVSTI S. C. Salus seated l., feeding snake arising
  from altar. *R.I.C. 85.* .... | 40 | 110

532 **Maximus Caesar,** son of Maximinus I. Æ *denarius.* PRINC IVVENTVTIS.
  Prince stg. l., two standards behind. *R.I.C. 3.*......................... | 65 | 190

533 **Gordian I Africanus,** March-April 238, governor of Britannia Inferior
  late in the reign of Caracalla. Æ *denarius.* P. M. TR. P. COS. P. P. Togate
  emperor stg. l. *R.I.C. 1.* .... | 475 | 1150

534 **Gordian II Africanus,** March-April 238. Æ *denarius.* VIRTVS AVGG.
  Virtus stg. l., with shield and spear. *R.I.C. 3.*....................... | 475 | 1150

535 **Balbinus,** April-July 238. Æ *antoninianus.* FIDES MVTVA AVGG.
  Clasped hands. *R.I.C. 11.*............................ | 100 | 230

535A Æ *denarius.* PROVIDENTIA DEORVM. Providentia stg. l., globe at feet. *R.I.C. 7.* | 80 | 210

536 **Pupienus,** April-July 238. Æ *antoninianus.* AMOR MVTVVS AVGG.
  Clasped hands. *R.I.C. 9a.*......................... | 100 | 230

536A Æ *denarius.* PAX PVBLICA. Pax seated l. *R.I.C. 4.* .... | 75 | 200

537 539

	F £	VF £

537 **Gordian III,** 238-244 (Caesar 238). Æ *antoninianus.* LAETITIA AVG. N. Laetitia stg. l. *R.I.C. 86.* — 20 — 45

538 Æ *denarius.* DIANA LVCIFERA. Diana stg. r., holding torch. *R.I.C. 127.* — 20 — 45

538A Æ *sestertius.* AETERNITATI AVG. S.C. Sol stg. l., holding globe. *R.I.C. 297a.* — 30 — 85

539 **Philip I,** 244-249. Æ *antoninianus.* ROMAE AETERNAE. Roma seated l. *R.I.C. 65.* — 20 — 45

539A Æ *sestertius.* SECVRIT. ORBIS S. C. Securitas seated l. *R.I.C. 190.* — 35 — 95

540 **Otacilia Severa,** wife of Philip I. Æ *antoninianus.* PIETAS AVGVSTAE. Pietas stg. l. *R.I.C. 125c.* — 20 — 45

540A Æ *sestertius.* CONCORDIA AVGG. S. C. Concordia seated l. *R.I.C. 203a.* — 35 — 95

541 **Philip II,** 247-249 (Caesar 244-247). Æ *antoninianus.* PRINCIPI IVVENT. Prince stg. l., holding globe and spear. *R.I.C. 218d.* — 20 — 55

541A Æ *sestertius.* PAX AETERNA S. C. Pax stg. l. *R.I.C. 268c.* — 35 — 95

542 543

542 **Trajan Decius,** 249-251. Æ *antoninianus.* DACIA. Dacia stg. l., holding staff with ass's hd. *R.I.C. 12b.* — 20 — 50

542A Æ *sestertius.* PANNONIAE S. C. The two Pannoniae stg., each holding standard. *R.I.C. 124a.* — 40 — 110

543 **Herennia Etruscilla,** wife of Trajan Decius. Æ *antoninianus.* PVDICITIA AVG. Pudicitia stg. l. *R.I.C. 58b.* — 25 — 55

544 **Herennius Etruscus,** 251 (Caesar 250-251). Æ *antoninianus.* PIETAS AVGG. Mercury stg. l., holding purse and caduceus. *R.I.C. 142b.* — 30 — 80

545 **Hostilian,** 251 (Caesar 251). Æ *antoninianus.* PRINCIPI IVVENTVTIS. Apollo seated l., holding branch. *R.I.C. 180.* — 50 — 120

546 **Trebonianus Gallus,** 251-253. Æ *antoninianus.* FELICITAS PVBLICA. Felicitas stg. l., resting on column. *R.I.C. 34A.* — 20 — 45

546A Æ *sestertius.* SALVS AVGG S. C. Salus stg. r., feeding snake held in her arms. *R.I.C. 121a.* — 45 — 120

547 **Volusian,** 251-253 (Caesar 251). Æ *antoninianus.* VIRTVS AVGG. Virtus stg. l. *R.I.C. 186.* — 20 — 50

548 **Aemilian,** 253. Æ *antoninianus.* PACI AVG. Pax stg. l., resting on column. *R.I.C. 8.* — 85 — 200

549 **Valerian,** 253-260. Billon antoninianus. FIDES MILITVM. Fides stg. r., holding two standards. *R.I.C. 241.* — 15 — 35

		F £	VF £
550	**Diva Mariniana,** wife of Valerian, deified 253. Billon *antoninianus*. CONSECRATIO. Empress seated on peacock flying r. *R.I.C. 6*.	55	140
551	**Gallienus,** 253-268, during whose reign Rome temporarily lost control over Britain when Postumus rebelled and established the independent Gallic Empire in 260. Billon *antoninianus*. VIRT GALLIENI AVG. Emperor advancing r., captive at feet. *R.I.C. 54*.	10	30

552

552	— DIANAE CONS. AVG. Doe l. *R.I.C. 176*.	10	25
552A	— SOLI INVICTO. Sol stg. l., holding globe. *R.I.C. 658*.	10	20
553	**Salonina,** wife of Gallienus. Billon *antoninianus*. VENVS FELIX. Venus seated l., child at feet. *R.I.C. 7*.	10	25
553A	— IVNONI CONS. AVG. Doe l. *R.I.C. 16*.	10	25
554	**Valerian Junior,** son of Gallienus, Caesar 256-258. Billon *antoninianus*. IOVI CRESCENTI. Infant Jupiter seated on goat r. *R.I.C. 13*.	20	50
555	**Divus Valerian Junior,** deified 258. Billon *antoninianus*. CONSECRATIO. Large altar. *R.I.C. 24*.	20	45
556	**Saloninus,** 260 (Caesar 258-260). Billon *antoninianus*. PIETAS AVG. Priestly emblems. *R.I.C. 9*.	20	45
557	**Macrianus,** usurper in the East, 260-261. Billon *antoninianus*. SOL. INVICTO. Sol stg. l., holding globe. *R.I.C. 12*.	50	120
558	**Quietus,** usurper in the East, 260-261. Billon *antoninianus*. INDVLGENTIAE AVG. Indulgentia seated l. *R.I.C. 5*.	50	120

559

559	**Postumus,** usurper in the West, 260-268, founder of the 'Gallic Empire' which temporarily detached Britain from the rule of the central government, a state of affairs which continued until Aurelian's defeat of Tetricus in 273. Billon *antoninianus*. HERC. DEVSONIENSI. Hercules stg. r. *R.I.C. 64*.	15	35
560	— MONETA AVG. Moneta stg. l. *R.I.C. 75*.	15	30
560A	Æ *sestertius*. FIDES MILITVM. Fides stg. l., holding two standards. *R.I.C. 128*.	65	185
561	**Laelianus,** usurper in the West, 268. Billon *antoninianus*. VICTORIA AVG. Victory advancing r. *R.I.C. 9*.	350	875
562	**Marius,** usurper in the West, 268. Billon *antoninianus*. CONCORDIA MILITVM. Clasped hands. *R.I.C. 7*.	95	240

		F £	VF £
563	**Victorinus**, usurper in the West, 268-270. Billon *antoninianus*. INVICTVS. Sol advancing l. *R.I.C. 114.*	10	25
564	**Tetricus,** usurper in the West, 270-273, defeated by Aurelian, thus ending the 'Gallic Empire' and the isolation of Britain from the authority of Rome. Billon *antoninianus*. LAETITIA AVGG. Laetitia stg. l. *R.I.C. 87.* *See also under Category 4.*	10	25
565	**Tetricus Junior,** son of Tetricus, Caesar 270-273. Billon *antoninianus*. SPES PVBLICA. Spes walking l., holding flower *R.I.C. 272.* *See also under Category 4.*	10	25
566	**Claudius II Gothicus,** 268-270. Billon *antoninianus*. IOVI STATORI. Jupiter stg. r. *R.I.C. 52.*	10	25
567	**Divus Claudius II,** deified 270. Billon *antoninianus*. CONSECRATIO. Large altar. *R.I.C. 261.* *See also under Category 4.*	10	25
568	**Quintillus,** 270. Billon *antoninianus*. DIANA LVCIF. Diana stg. r., holding torch. *R.I.C. 49.*	25	70
569	**Aurelian,** 270-275, restored Britain to the rule of the central government through his defeat of Tetricus in 273; possibly began construction of the chain of 'Saxon Shore' forts on the eastern and southern coastlines. Billon *antoninianus*. ORIENS AVG. Sol stg. l. between two captives. *R.I.C. 63.*	15	35
569A	— RESTITVT. ORBIS. Female stg. r., presenting wreath to emperor stg. l. *R.I.C. 399.*	15	35
570	**Aurelian and Vabalathus,** ruler of Palmyra 267-272 and usurper in the East from 271. Billon *antoninianus*. Obv. Laur. bust of Vabalathus r. Rev. Rad. bust of Aurelian r. *R.I.C. 381*	40	100

571   574A

571	**Severina,** wife of Aurelian. Billon *antoninianus*. PROVIDEN. DEOR. Concordia (or Fides) Militum stg. r., facing Sol stg. l. *R.I.C. 9.*	20	55
572	**Tacitus,** 275-276. Billon *antoninianus*. SECVRIT. PERP. Securitas stg. l., leaning on column. *R.I.C. 163.*	20	55
573	**Florian,** 276. Billon *antoninianus*. LAETITIA FVND. Laetitia stg. l. *R.I.C. 34.*	40	100
574	**Probus,** 276-282, suppressed governor's revolt in Britain and lifted restrictions on viticulture in Britain and Gaul. Billon *antoninianus*. ADVENTVS PROBI AVG. Emperor on horseback l., captive seated before. *R.I.C. 160.*	15	35
574A	— VICTORIA GERM. Trophy between two captives. *R.I.C. 222.*	15	45
574B	**Proculus** (usurper 280-281) Billon *antoninianus*. VICTORIA AUG. Female figure stg l.	12500	36000
575	**Carus,** 282-283. Billon *antoninianus*. PAX EXERCITI. Pax stg. l., holding olive-branch and standard. *R.I.C. 75.*	25	60

		F £	VF £

576 **Divus Carus,** deified 283. Billon *antoninianus*. CONSECRATIO. Eagle
facing, hd. l. *R.I.C. 28.*.. 25 65

577 **Carinus,** 283-285 (Caesar 282-283). Billon *antoninianus*. SAECVLI
FELICITAS. Emperor stg. r. *R.I.C. 214.* 20 55

578 **Magnia Urbica,** wife of Carinus. Billon *antoninianus*. VENVS VICTRIX.
Venus stg. l., holding helmet, shield at feet. *R.I.C. 343*............................ 70 170

579 **Numerian,** 283-284 (Caesar 282-283). Billon *antoninianus*. CLEMENTIA
TEMP. Emperor stg. r., receiving globe from Jupiter stg. l. *R.I.C. 463....* 25 60

580 **Diocletian,** 284-305. Æ *argenteus*. VIRTVS MILITVM. The four tetrarchs
sacrificing before gateway of military camp. *R.I.C. 27a (Rome).*............. 130 260

581 Billon *antoninianus*. IOVI CONSERVAT AVGG. Jupiter stg. l. *R.I.C. 162.* 15 35

582 Æ *follis*. GENIO POPVLI ROMANI. Genius stg. l. R.I.C. 14a *(Alexandria).* 15 35

582A — (post-abdication coinage, after 305). PROVIDENTIA DEORVM QVIES
AVGG. Quies and Providentia stg. facing each other. *R.I.C. 676a (Treveri).* 30 75
See also under Category 3.

583 **Maximian,** 286-305 and 306-308, failed in his attempts to suppress the
usurpation of Carausius in Britain. Æ *argenteus*. VICTORIA SARMAT. The
four tetrarchs sacrificing before gateway of military camp. *R.I.C. 37b (Rome).* 120 240

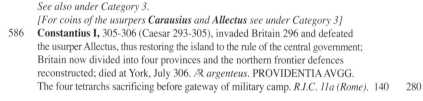

584

584 Billon *antoninianus*. SALVS AVGG. Salus stg. r., feeding snake held in
her arms. *R.I.C. 417.*.. 15 30

585 Æ *follis*. SAC. MON. VRB. AVGG. ET CAESS. NN. Moneta stg. l.
R.I.C. 105b (Rome). 15 35

585A — (second reign). CONSERVATORES VRB SVAE. Roma seated in
hexastyle temple. *R.I.C. 84b (Ticinum).* 15 35
See also under Category 3.
[For coins of the usurpers Carausius and Allectus see under Category 3]

586 **Constantius I,** 305-306 (Caesar 293-305), invaded Britain 296 and defeated
the usurper Allectus, thus restoring the island to the rule of the central government;
Britain now divided into four provinces and the northern frontier defences
reconstructed; died at York, July 306. Æ *argenteus*. PROVIDENTIA AVGG.
The four tetrarchs sacrificing before gateway of military camp. *R.I.C. 11a (Rome).* 140 280

587

587 Æ *follis*. GENIO POPVLI ROMANI. Genius stg. l. *R.I.C. 26a (Aquileia).* 15 35

| | F | VF |
| | £ | £ |

587A — SALVIS AVGG. ET CAESS. FEL. KART. Carthage stg. l., holding
fruits. *R.I.C. 30a (Carthage).* 15 40
See also under Category 3.

588 593

588 **Galerius,** 305-311 (Caesar 293-305). Æ argenteus. VIRTVS MILITVM.
The four tetrarchs sacrificing before gateway of military camp.
R.I.C. 15b (Ticinum). 130 260

588A — XC / VI in wreath. *R.I.C. 16b (Carthage).* 190 425

589 Æ *follis.* GENIO AVGG ET CAESARVM NN. Genius stg. l. *R.I.C. 11b*
(Cyzicus). 15 35

589A — GENIO IMPERATORIS. Genius stg. l. *R.I.C. 101a (Alexandria)......* 15 30
See also under Category 3.

590 **Galeria Valeria,** wife of Galerius. Æ *follis.* VENERI VICTRICI. Venus
stg. l. *R.I.C. 110 (Alexandria).* 35 90

591 **Severus II,** 306-307 (Caesar 305-306). Æ *follis.* FIDES MILITVM. Fides
seated l. *R.I.C. 73 (Ticinum).* 35 90
See also under Category 3.

592 **Maximinus II,** 310-313 (Caesar 305-310). Æ *follis.* GENIO CAESARIS.
Genius stg. l. *R.I.C. 64 (Alexandria).* 15 30

592A — GENIO POP. ROM. Genius stg. l. *R.I.C. 845a (Treveri).* 10 25
See also under Category 3.

593 **Maxentius,** 306-312 (Caesar 306). Æ *follis.* CONSERV. VRB. SVAE.
Roma seated in hexastyle temple. *R.I.C. 210 (Rome).* 15 35

594 **Romulus,** son of Maxentius, deified 309. Æ *quarter follis.* AETERNAE
MEMORIAE. Temple with domed roof. *R.I.C. 58 (Ostia).* 65 170

595 **Licinius,** 308-324. Æ *follis.* GENIO AVGVSTI. Genius stg. l. *R.I.C. 198b*
(Siscia). 10 25

595A Æ 3. IOVI CONSERVATORI AVGG. Jupiter stg. l. *R.I.C. 24 (Nicomedia).* 10 25
See also under Category 3.

596 **Licinius Junior,** son of Licinius, Caesar 317-324. Æ 3. CAESARVM
NOSTRORVM around wreath containing VOT. / V. *R.I.C. 92 (Thessalonica).* 10 25

597 **Constantine I, the Great,** 307-337 (Caesar 306-307), campaigned with
his father Constantius I against the Picts in northern Britain, summer 306,
and proclaimed emperor by the legions at York on Constantius' death
in July; closed the London mint early in 325 ending almost four decades
of operation. Æ *follis.* GENIO POP ROM. Genius stg. l. *R.I.C. 719b*
(Treveri). 15 35

598 — SOLI INVICTO COMITI. Sol stg. l. *R.I.C. 307 (Lugdunum).* 10 25

598A Æ 3. PROVIDENTIAE AVGG. Gateway of military camp. *R.I.C. 153*
(Thessalonica) 10 20

599   599B   600

	F	VF
	£	£

599 — VIRTVS EXERCIT. Trophy between two captives. *R.I.C. 280 (Treveri).* 15 35

599A Æ 3/4. GLORIA EXERCITVS. Two soldiers stg. either side of two standards.
R.I.C. 518 (Treveri).... 5 15
See also under Category 3.

599B Silver third siliqua, after 330. Obv Female bust r. Rev. K within border of
pellets. *(Constantinopolis).*... 150 400

600 **'Urbs Roma'**, after 330. Æ 3/4. Obv. Helmeted bust of Roma l. Rev.
She-wolf l., suckling twins. *R.I.C. 195 (Nicomedia).*............................. 5 20

601   604

601 **'Constantinopolis'**, after 330. Æ 3/4. Obv. Helmeted bust of
Constantinopolis l. Rev. Victory stg. l., foot on prow. *R.I.C. 339 (Rome).* 5 20

602 **Fausta,** wife of Constantine I. Æ 3. SALVS REIPVBLICAE. Empress
stg. l., holding two children. *R.I.C. 459 (Treveri)*..................................... 20 50
See also under Category 3.

603 **Helena,** mother of Constantine I. Æ 3. SECVRITAS REIPVBLICAE.
Empress stg. l., holding branch. *R.I.C. 38 (Alexandria).*........................ 20 50

603A Æ 4 (posthumous issue, 337-340). PAX PVBLICA. Pax stg. l. *R.I.C. 78*
(Treveri). 10 30
See also under Category 3.

604 **Theodora,** second wife of Constantius I. Æ 4 (posthumous issue, 337-340).
PIETAS ROMANA. Pietas stg. r., holding child. R.I.C. 43 *(Treveri).*...... 15 35

605 **Crispus,** eldest son of Constantine I, Caesar 317-326. Æ 3. CAESARVM
NOSTRORVM around wreath containing VOT. / V. *R.I.C. 68 (Aquileia).* 10 25
See also under Category 3.

606 **Delmatius,** nephew of Constantine I, Caesar 335-337. Æ 3/4. GLORIA
EXERCITVS. Two soldiers stg. either side of two standards. *R.I.C. 90*
(Antioch). 30 75

607 **Hanniballianus,** nephew of Constantine I, Rex 335-337. Æ 4. SECVRITAS
PVBLICA. River-god Euphrates reclining r. *R.I.C. 147 (Constantinople).* 140 300

608 **Constantine II,** 337-340 (Caesar 317-337). Æ 3. BEATA
TRANQVILLITAS. Altar inscribed VOT / IS / XX. *R.I.C. 312 (Treveri).* 10 25

608A Æ 3/4. GLORIA EXERCITVS. Two soldiers stg. either side of standard.
R.I.C. 392 (Rome) (See also under Category 3.)..................................... 5 15

609 **Constans,** 337-350 (Caesar 333-337), visited Britain in 343, the last
reigning emperor to do so. Æ 2. FEL. TEMP. REPARATIO. Soldier r.,
dragging barbarian from hut beneath tree. *R.I.C. 103 (Aquileia).*............ 20 45

609A   611B

		F £	VF £
609A	— FEL. TEMP. REPARATIO. Emperor stg. l. on galley steered by Victory. *R.I.C. 219 (Treveri)*.....................	20	45
609B	Æ 4. VICTORIAE DD. AVGG. Q. NN. Two Victories stg. face to face. *R.I.C. 195 (Treveri)*.....................	5	15
610	**Constantius II**, 337-361 (Caesar 324-337). Æ 3/4. GLORIA EXERCITVS. Two soldiers stg. either side of two standards. *R.I.C. 85 (Cyzicus)*..........	5	15
611	Æ *siliqua*. VOTIS / XXX. / MVLTIS / XXXX. in wreath. *R.I.C. 207 (Arelate)*.	60	160
611A	Æ 2. FEL. TEMP. REPARATIO. Emperor stg. l. on galley. *R.I.C. 218* *(Treveri)*.	20	45
611B	Æ 3. FEL. TEMP. REPARATIO. Soldier advancing l., spearing fallen horseman. *R.I.C. 189 (Lugdunum)*........................	5	15
	See also under Categories 3 and 4.		

612   616

612	**Magnentius**, usurper in the West, 350-353, temporarily detached Britain from the rule of the legitimate Constantinian dynasty. Æ 1. SALVS DD. NN. AVG. ET CAES. *Chi-Rho* Christian monogram between Alpha and Omega. *R.I.C. 34 (Ambianum)*...........................	120	280
612A	Æ 2. FELICITAS REIPVBLICAE. Emperor stg. l., holding Victory and labarum. *R.I.C. 264 (Treveri)*.................... *See also under Category 4.*	25	60
613	**Decentius**, brother of Magnentius, Caesar 351-353. Æ 2. VICTORIAE DD. NN. AVG. ET CAE. Two Victories supporting between them shield inscribed VOT. / V. / MVLT. / X. *R.I.C. 146 (Lugdunum)*. .... *See also under Category 4.*	35	80
614	**Vetranio**, 'usurper' in the Balkans, 350. Æ 2. CONCORDIA MILITVM. Emperor stg. l., holding two labara. *R.I.C. 281 (Siscia)*...........................	65	160
615	**Constantius Gallus**, Caesar under Constantius II, 351-354. Æ 2. FEL. TEMP. REPARATIO. Soldier advancing l., spearing fallen horseman. *R.I.C. 94 (Cyzicus)*...........................	20	45
615A	**Julian II**, 360-363 (Caesar 355-360). Æ *miliarense*. Rev. VIRTVS EXERCITVM. Soldier stg l, holding spear and resting on shield. *R.I.C. 290*. *(Arelate)*	380	975
616	Æ *siliqua*. VOT. / X. / MVLT. / XX. in wreath. *R.I.C. 309 (Arelate)*.	60	160

		F	VF
		£	£

617   Æ 1. SECVRITAS REIPVB. Bull stg. r. *R.I.C. 411 (Siscia).*   50   150
Beware of recent forgeries.
617A Æ 3. VOT. / X. / MVLT. / XX. in wreath. *R.I.C. 108 (Sirmium).*   10   25
618   **Jovian,** 363-364. Æ 3. VOT. / V. / MVLT. / X. in wreath. *R.I.C. 426 (Siscia).*   20   45

619   620

619   **Valentinian I,** 364-375 (in the West), during whose reign the Roman
province of Britannia was devastated by the simultaneous attack of hordes
of invaders on several fronts (the 'Barbarian Conspiracy'); order eventually
restored by Count Theodosius, father of the future emperor . *N solidus.*
RESTITVTOR REIPVBLICAE. Emperor stg. r., holding standard and
Victory. *R.I.C. 2b (Antioch).*   280   650
619A Æ *miliarense.* Rev. VICTORIA AVGVSTORVM. Victory
stg r, inscribing shield. *R.I.C. 24a. (Trier)*   360   950
619B Æ *siliqua.* Rev. VRBS ROMA. Roma seated l. *R.I.C. 27a (Trier)*   65   170
619C Æ 3. GLORIA ROMANORVM. Emperor advancing r., dragging
barbarian and holding labarum. *R.I.C. 14a (Siscia).*   10   20
619D — SECVRITAS REIPVBLICAE. Victory advancing l. *R.I.C. 32a (Treveri).*   10   20
619E **Valens,** 364-378 (in the East). *N solidus.* Rev. RESTITVTOR REIPVBLICAE.
Valens stg , holding labarum and Victory. *R.I.C. 2d (Antioch)*   280   650
619F Æ *miliarense.* Rev. VIRTVS EXERCITVS. Valens stg, holding standard.
R.I.C. 26c (Trier)   340   900
620   Æ *siliqua.* VRBS ROMA. Roma seated l. *R.I.C. 27e (Treveri).*   65   170
620A Æ 3. SECVRITAS REIPVBLICAE. Victory advancing l. *R.I.C. 42b
(Constantinople).*   10   20
621   **Procopius,** usurper in the East, 365-366. Æ 3. REPARATIO FEL. TEMP.
Emperor stg. r., holding standard and shield. *R.I.C. 17a (Constantinople).*   55   140
621A **Gratian,** 367-383 (in the West), overthrown by Magnus Maximus who had
been proclaimed emperor by the army in Britain. *N solidus.* Rev. VICTORIA
AVGG. Two Emperors enthroned holding globe, Victory behind. *R.I.C. 17g
(Trier)*   300   750
621B Æ *miliarense.* Rev. VIRTVS EXERCITVS. Gratian stg, holding standard.
R.I.C. 40 .(Lugdunum)   360   950
622   Æ *siliqua.* VRBS ROMA. Roma seated l. *R.I.C. 27f (Treveri).*   65   170
622A **Valentinian II,** 375-392 (in the West). *N solidus.* Rev. VICTORIA AVGG.
Two Emperors enthroned holding globe, Victory behind. *R.I.C. 34b
(Thessalonica)*   340   850
622B Æ *miliarense.* Rev. GLORIA ROMANORVM. Valentinian stg , holding
standard. *R.I.C. 40 (lugdunum)*   375   980
622C Æ *siliqua.* Rev. VIRTVS ROMANORVM. Roma seated l. *R.I.C. 43a.
(Lugdunum)*   70   180
623   Æ 2. REPARATIO REIPVB. Emperor stg. l., raising kneeling female figure.
R.I.C. 20c (Arelate)   15   35
623A Æ 4. SALVS REIPVBLICAE. Victory advancing l., dragging barbarian.
R.I.C. 20a (Alexandria).   10   20

	F	VF
	£	£

623B **Theodosius I,** the Great, 379-395 (in the East), son of the Count Theodosius who had cleared Britain of barbarian invaders in the reign of Valentinian I; the Emperor Theodosiua twice restored Britain to the rule of the central government, by his defeat of the usurpers Magnus Maximus (in 388) and Eugenius (in 394). *N solidus.* Rev. CONCORDIA AUGGG. Constantinopolis seated, holding sceptre and shield. *R.I.C. 71a (Constantinople)* ... 320 800

623C *R miliarense.* Rev. VIRTUS EXERCITUS. Theodosius stg , holding standard. *R.I.C. 53c (Trier)* ... 380 1000

624 *R siliqua.* CONCORDIA AVGGG. Constantinopolis enthroned facing, foot on prow. *R.I.C. 55a (Treveri).* ... 65 170

624A

624A — VIRTVS ROMANORVM. Roma enthroned facing. *R.I.C (Aquileia) 28d.* 65 170

624B Æ 2. VIRTVS EXERCIT. Emperor stg. r., foot on captive, holding labarum and globe. *R.I.C. 24b (Heraclea)* ... 20 45

625 **Aelia Flaccilla,** wife of Theodosius I. Æ 2. SALVS REIPVBLICAE. Victory seated r., inscribing Christian monogram on shield set on cippus. *R.I.C. 81 (Constantinople).* ... 25 70

625A **Magnus Maximus,** usurper in the West, 383-388, proclaimed emperor by the army in Britain, invaded Gaul, and overthrew the legitimate western emperor Gratian; possibly reopened the London mint for a brief issue of precious metal coinage (Rudyard Kipling presented a rather fanciful version of his career in "Puck of Pook's Hill"). *N solidus.* Rev. RESTITVTOR REPVBLICAE. Maximus stg, holding labarum and Victory. *R.I.C. 76 (Trier)* ... 1200 2800

625B *R miliarense.* Rev. VIRTVS EXERCITVS. Maximus stg, holding labarum. *R.I.C. 82 (Trier)* ... 725 1800

626 627

626 *R siliqua.* VIRTVS ROMANORVM. Roma enthroned facing. *R.I.C. 84b (Treveri)* *(See also under Category 3.)* ... 75 200

626A **Flavius Victor,** son of Magnus Maximus, co-emperor 387-388. *R siliqua.* VIRTVS ROMANORVM. Roma seated facing on throne. *R.I.C. 84d (Treveri)* 280 650

627 Æ 4. SPES ROMANORVM. Gateway of military camp. *RIC 55b (Aquileia).* 50 120

627A **Eugenius,** usurper in the West, 392-394, recognized in Britain until his defeat by Theodosius the Great. *N solidus.* VICTORIA AUGG. Two emperors enthroned facing holding globe. *R.I.C. 28 (Treveri)* ... 3000 8000

627B *R miliarense.* Rev. VIRTVS EXERCITVS. Eugenius stg, holding standard. *R.I.C. 105 (Trier)* ... 1600 4000

628 629

		F	VF
		£	£
628	Æ *siliqua.* VIRTVS ROMANORVM. Roma seated l. on cuirass. *R.I.C. 32c (Milan).*	300	750
629	**Arcadius,** 395-408 (in the East, co-emperor with his father Theodosius I from 383). *N solidus.* VICTORIA AVGGG. Emperor stg. r., foot on captive, holding standard and Victory. *R.I.C. 1205 (Milan).*	300	750
629A	Æ *miliarense.* Rev. GLORIA ROMANORVM. Arcadius stg, raising r hand and holding globe in l. *R.I.C. 25b (Milan)*	400	1000
629B	Æ *siliqua.* Rev. VOT V MVLT X in wreath. *R.I.C. 13 (Milan)*	70	170
629C	Æ 2. GLORIA ROMANORVM. Emperor stg. l., holding standard and shield, captive at feet. *R.I.C. 41 (Antioch).*	20	55
630	**Honorius,** 395-423 (in the West, co-emperor with his father Theodosius I and brother Arcadius from 393), this reign saw the end of Roman rule in Britain following a succession of usurpations in the province, culminating in that of Constantine III against whom the Britons rebelled in 409; Honorius' celebrated ' Rescript' of the following year instructed the provincials to look to their own defence as he was no longer able to assist them. *N solidus.* VICTORIA AVGGG. Emperor stg. r., foot on captive, holding standard and Victory. *R.I.C. 1287 (Ravenna).*	280	650
630A	Æ *miliarense.* Rev. VIRTVS EXERCITVS *(Rome)*	425	1100
630B	Æ *siliqua.* VIRTVS ROMANORVM. Roma seated l. on cuirass. *R.I.C. 1228 (Milan).*	65	170

631

631	**Constantine III,** usurper in the West, 407-411, proclaimed emperor by the army in Britain, but his authority rejected by the Romano-Britons two years later, thus effectively ending 366 years of Roman rule in Britain. Æ *siliqua.* VICTORIA AVGGG. Roma enthroned l. *R.I.C. 1532 (Treveri)*	200	450
632	**Valentinian III,** 425-455 (in the West), during whose reign the Saxon conquest of the former Roman province commenced, following the final unsuccessful appeal of the Romano-Britons for help addressed to the general Aetius in 446. *N solidus.* VICTORIA AVGGG. Emperor stg. facing, foot on human-headed serpent. *R.I.C. 2010 (Ravenna).*	300	700
632A	Æ 4. VOT. PVB. Gateway of military camp. *R.I.C. 2123 (Rome).*	30	85

2. ISSUES WITH TYPES REFERRING SPECIFICALLY TO THE PROVINCE OF BRITANNIA

Struck in Rome, unless otherwise indicated. These usually commemorate military operations in the northern frontier region of the province or beyond.

633   635

		F	VF
		£	£
633	**Claudius,** A.D. 41-54. AV aureus, celebrating the early stages of the Roman conquest of Britain which commenced in A.D. 43. DE BRITANN on architrave of triumphal arch. *R.I.C. 33.*	2600	5800
634	Æ *denarius.* Similar. *R.I.C. 34.*	650	1600
634A	Æ *didrachm* of Caesarea in Cappadocia. DE BRITANNIS. Emperor in triumphal quadriga r. *R.I.C. 122.*	550	1500
635	**Hadrian,** 117-138. Æ as, commemorating the restoration of order in the province following a serious uprising (or invasion) in the north, probably early in the governorship of Q. Pompeius Falco (118-122). BRITANNIA PONT. MAX. TR. POT. COS. III. S. C. Britannia seated facing on rock. *R.I.C. 577a.*	300	750
636	Æ *sestertius,* commemorating Hadrian's visit to the province in 122, when he planned and initiated the construction of the northern frontier system which bears his name. ADVENTVI AVG. BRITANNIAE S.C. Emperor and Britannia stg. either side of altar. *R.I.C. 882.*	6000	19000

638A

637	— BRITANNIA S. C. Britannia seated facing, foot resting on rock. *R.I.C. 845.*	6500	21000
637A	Æ *dupondius* or as. *Similar. R.I.C. 846.*	550	1600
638	Æ *sestertius,* commemorating Hadrian's attention to the legionary garrison strength of the province, principally his transfer of *VI Victrix* from Germany in 122. EXERC. BRITANNICVS S. C. Emperor on horseback r., addressing gathering of troops. *R.I.C. 912.*	6000	19000
638A	— EXERC. BRITANNICVS S.C. Emperor stg. r. on tribunal, addressing gathering of troops. *R.I.C. 913.*	6000	19000

	F £	VF £

639 **Antoninus Pius,** 138-161. A/ *aureus,* commemorating the conquests in Scotland by the governor Q. Lollius Urbicus (138/9-142/3) at which time construction of the Antonine Wall was begun. BRITAN. IMPERATOR II. Victory stg. l. on globe. *R.I.C. 113*.. 1900 4400

640

640 Æ *sestertius.* BRITANNIA S. C. Britannia seated l. on rock, holding standard. *R.I.C. 742.* 800 2000

641 — BRITAN. IMPERATOR II. S. C. Helmeted Britannia seated l., foot on rock. *R.I.C. 743*...................... 800 2000

642 — BRITAN. IMPERATOR II. S. C. Britannia seated l. on globe above waves, holding standard. *R.I.C. 744.* 900 2400

643 — BRITAN. IMPERATOR II. S. C. Victory stg. l. on globe. *R.I.C. 719.* 280 675

643A — BRITANNIA IMPERATOR II. S. C. Britannia seated l. on rock, holding standard. *R.I.C. 745.* 800 2000

644 Æ *as.* IMPERATOR II. S. C. Victory hovering l., holding shield inscribed BRI / TAN. *R.I.C. 732.* 140 325

645 Æ *dupondius,* commemorating the quelling of a serious uprising in the north, ca. 154/5, necessitating the evacuation of the recently constructed Antonine Wall in Scotland. BRITANNIA COS. IIII. S. C. Britannia seated l. on rock, shield and vexillum in background. *R.I.C. 930.* 250 600

646 Æ *as.* Similar. *R.I.C. 934.* 120 325

Many specimens of this type are carelessly struck on inadequate flans.
Moreover, they have been found in significant quantities on Romano-British
sites, notably in Coventina's Well at Carrawburgh fort on Hadrian's Wall,
raising the interesting possibility that they may have been issued from a
temporary mint in Britain. The style of the engraving is quite regular,
indicating that even if locally produced these coins would have been struck
from normal Roman dies brought to Britain especially for this purpose.
See under Category 3.

647 **Commodus,** 177-192. Æ *sestertius,* commemorating the victories in Scotland of the governor Ulpius Marcellus in 184/5. These were in retribution for a major barbarian invasion several years earlier resulting in serious damage to Hadrian's Wall, which had been temporarily overrun, and the defeat and death of an unknown governor. BRITT. P. M. TR. P. VIIII. IMP. VII. COS. IIII. P. P. S. C. Britannia stg. l., holding curved sword and helmet. *R.I.C. 437.* 5500 17000

648

		F £	VF £

648 — VICT. BRIT. P. M. TR. P. VIIII. (or X.) IMP. VII. COS. IIII. P. P. S. C.
Victory seated r., about to inscribe shield. *R.I.C. 440, 452*...................... 200 550

649

649 **Septimius Severus,** 193-211. *N aureus,* commemorating the success of
the punitive Roman campaigns in Scotland during 209 and 210 culminating
in the illness and death of Severus at York in Feb. 211. VICTORIAE BRIT.
Victory advancing l. *R.I.C. 334.* 2650 6700

650 — VICTORIAE BRIT. Victory advancing r., leading child by hand.
R.I.C. 302... 2900 6900

651 *R denarius.* VICTORIAE BRIT. Victory advancing r. *R.I.C. 332.* 60 130

651A — VICTORIAE BRIT. Victory stg. facing beside palm-tree with shield
attached. *R.I.C. 336*.. 65 140

651B — VICTORIAE BRIT. Victory stg. l. *R.I.C. 333.*.................................... 70 150

651C — VICTORIAE BRIT. Victory seated l., holding shield. *R.I.C. 335.*....... 65 140

652

652 *Æ sestertius.* VICTORIAE BRITTANNICAE S. C. Two Victories placing
shield on palm-tree with captives at base. *R.I.C. 818*................................ 450 1400

653 — P. M. TR. P. XVIII. COS. III. P. P. S. C. Similar. *R.I.C. 796.* 275 650

654 *Æ dupondius.* VICT. BRIT. P. M. TR. P. XIX. COS. III. P. P. S. C. Victory
stg. r. between two captives, holding vexillum. *R.I.C. 809.* 160 400

655 *Æ as.* VICTORIAE BRITTANNICAE S. C. Similar. *R.I.C. 837a*........... 175 425

| | F | VF |
| | £ | £ |

656   Billon *tetradrachm* of Alexandria in Egypt. NEIKH KATA BRET. Nike
       flying l. *Milne 2726.* 925 2250

657   **Caracalla,** 198-217. *N aureus,* commemorating the victories achieved
       by the Romans in Scotland during the campaigns led jointly by Severus
       and Caracalla in 209, and by Caracalla alone the following year during
       his father's illness. VICTORIAE BRIT. Victory seated l., holding shield.
       R.I.C. 174. .... 2800 6900

658   659A

658   *R denarius.* VICTORIAE BRIT. Victory advancing l. *R.I.C. 231.* 65 140
658A   — VICTORIAE BRIT. Victory advancing r., holding trophy. *R.I.C. 231A.* 65 140
659   Æ *sestertius.* VICTORIAE BRITTANNICAE S. C. Victory stg. r., erecting
       trophy to r. of which Britannia stands facing, captive at feet. *R.I.C. 464.* 375 950
659A   — VICT. BRIT. TR. P. XIIII. COS. III. S.C. Similar. *Cf. R.I.C. 483c.* 325 850
660   Æ *dupondius.* VICTORIAE BRITTANNICAE S. C. Victory stg. r.,
       inscribing shield set on palm-tree. *R.I.C. 467* 150 380
661   Æ *as.* VICT. BRIT. TR. P. XIIII. COS. III. S. C. Similar. *R.I.C. 490* 140 350
662   **Geta,** 209-212. *R denarius,* commemorating the victories achieved by
       his father and brother in Scotland in 209-10 while he and his mother were
       resident in London. VICTORIAE BRIT. Victory stg. l. *R.I.C. 92* 70 150
662A   — VICTORIAE BRIT. Victory advancing r. *R.I.C. 91.* 70 150

663

663   Æ *sestertius.* VICTORIAE BRITTANNICAE S. C. Victory seated r.,
       inscribing shield set on knee. *R.I.C. 166.* 450 1300
663A   — VICT. BRIT. TR. P. III. COS. II. S. C. Similar. *R.I.C. 172b.* 380 1000
664   Æ *as.* VICTORIAE BRITTANNICAE S. C. Victory seated l., balancing
       shield on knee. *R.I.C. 191a* 160 425
665   Billon *tetradrachm* of Alexandria in Egypt. NEIKH KATA BRETAN.
       Nike advancing l. *B.M.C. (Alexandria) 1481.* 1000 2500

3. OFFICIAL ROMAN COINAGE STRUCK IN BRITAIN

The London mint, and the associated 'C' mint (new research indicates that this was a secondary mint that operated initially in North London and subsequently moved around the country with Carausius), were created by the usurper Carausius soon after his seizure of Britain in 287. Prior to this, in the mid-2nd century, there may have been minting of 'Britannia' asses of Antoninus Pius in the province using dies brought from Rome, though this has not been firmly established. After the downfall of the rebel British regime in 296 the minting establishment in London (though not the subsidiary mint) was retained by the tetrarchal government and the succeeding Constantinian administration. Early in 325, however, Constantine the Great closed the London mint after almost four decades of operation. A possible brief revival under the usurper Magnus Maximus has been postulated for gold and silver coins marked 'AVG', 'AVGOB' and 'AVGPS', though the attribution has not received universal acceptance.

For more on the bronze coinage struck at London Mint c.296-97 to c.325 see Cloke, H.J. and Toone, L., *The London Mint of Constantius and Constantine* (Spink 2015)

		F	VF
		£	£
666	**Antoninus Pius,** 138-161. Æ *as,* struck in northern Britain (?) in 155. BRITANNIA COS. IIII. S. C. Britannia seated l. on rock, shield and vexillum in background. *R.I.C. 930.*	160	450

Many poorly struck examples of this type have been found on Romano-British sites, notably at Brocolitia (Carrawburgh) fort on Hadrian's Wall in Northumberland, where no fewer than 327 specimens were discovered in the great votive deposit in the well which formed part of the shrine of the water-nymph Coventina. There appears to be a very real possibility that many of these 'Britannia' asses had been issued from a temporary mint in Britain, most likely situated in the north. The dies, however, are quite regular, and would thus have been brought from Rome to the island province for the express purpose of supplementing the money supply at a time of crisis.

667	**Carausius,** usurper in Britain and northwestern Gaul, A.D. 287-293. N *aureus,* London. CONSERVAT. AVG. Jupiter stg. l., eagle at feet, ML in ex. *R.I.C. 1.*	30000	75000
667A	R *denarius* ADVENTVS AUG. Emperor riding l, captive before horse. *R.I.C. 1068*	1600	3600
667B	— CONCORDIA AVG. Clasped hands. RSR. *R.I.C. 545*	1200	2750
668	— EXPECTATE VENI. Britannia stg. r. and emperor l., clasping hands, RSR in ex. *R.I.C. 555.*	1500	3400

669   672A

669	— RENOVAT. ROMANO. She-wolf r., suckling twins, RSR in ex. *R.I.C. 571.*	1300	3000
669A	— Rev. VIRTVS AVG. Lion walking l. RSR in exergue. *R.I.C. 591*	1800	4000
669B	— Rev. VOTO PVBLICO, MVLTIS XX IMP in altar. RSR below. *R.I.C. 595.*	1400	3200
670	Billon *antoninianus,* London. COMES AVG. Victory stg. l., S—P in field, ML in ex. *R.I.C. 14.*	95	260
670A	— HILARITAS AVG. Hilaritas stg. l., B—E in field, MLXXI in ex. *R.I.C. 41.*	70	180

		F £	VF £
671	— LAETITIA AVG. Laetitia stg. l., F—O in field, ML in ex. *R.I.C. 50.*.	55	140
671A	— LEG. II. AVG. Capricorn l., ML in ex. *R.I.C. 58.*..............................	140	360
	Legio II Augusta was stationed at Isca (Caerleon in South Wales).		
672	— LEG. XX. V. V. Boar stg. r. *R.I.C. 82.*..	150	380
	Legio XX Valeria Victrix was stationed at Deva (Chester in the northwest Midlands).		
672A	— PAX AVG. Pax stg. l., F—O in field, ML in ex. *R.I.C. 101.*..............	45	120
673	— Similar, but without mint mark. *R.I.C. 880.*.....................................	40	110
673A	— PROVIDENT. AVG. Providentia stg. l., B—E in field, MLXXI in ex. *R.I.C. 149.*..	55	140
674	— SALVS AVGGG. Salus stg. r., feeding snake held in her arms, S—P in field, ML in ex. *R.I.C. 164.*...	70	180
	The reverse legends with triple-ending (AVGGG.) presumably are subsequent to Carausius' recognition by Diocletian and Maximian in 289 following the failure of the latter's attempt to dislodge the usurper from his island stronghold.		
674A	— TEMPORVM FELICITAS. Felicitas stg. l., B—E in field, ML in ex. *R.I.C. 172.*..	55	140
675	— VIRTVS AVGGG. Mars (or Virtus) stg. r., holding spear and shield, S—P in field, MLXXI in ex. *R.I.C. 183.*...	70	180
676	Billon *antoninianus,* Colchester (?). CONCORDIA MILIT. Emperor stg. r. and Concordia l., clasping hands, C in ex. *R.I.C. 205.*.......................	120	325
676A	— EXPECTATE VENI. Britannia stg. r. and emperor l., clasping hands, MSC in ex. *R.I.C. 216.*...	180	475
677	— FELICITAS AVG. Galley with mast and rowers, CXXI in ex. *R.I.C. 221.*	160	425
677A	— FORTVNA RAEDVX. Fortuna seated l., SPC in ex. *R.I.C. 237.*	90	240
678	— LAETITIA AVG. Laetitia stg. l., globe at feet, S—P in field, C in ex. *R.I.C. 255.*...	55	140
678A	—-MONETA AVG. Moneta stg. l., CXXI in ex. *R.I.C. 287.*	60	150
679	— ORIENS AVG. Sol stg. l., C in ex. *R.I.C. 293.*...................................	70	170
679A	— PAX AVGGG. Pax stg. l., S—P in field, MC in ex. *R.I.C. 335.*..........	50	120

680

680	— PROVID. AVG. Providentia stg. l., S—P in field, C in ex. *R.I.C. 353.*	55	140
680A	— SALVS AVG. Salus stg. l. at altar, feeding snake, S—C in field, C in ex. *R.I.C. 396.*	70	180
681	— SPES PVBLICA. Spes walking l., holding flower, S—P in field, C in ex. *R.I.C. 413.*	80	200
681A	— VICTORIA AVG. Victory advancing l., captive at feet, MC in ex. *R.I.C. 429.*	85	220
682	**Carausius, Diocletian and Maximian,** after 289. Billon *antoninianus,* Colchester (?). Obv. CARAVSIVS ET FRATRES SVI. Conjoined busts of the three emperors l. Rev. PAX AVGGG. Pax stg. l., S—P in field, C in ex. *R.I.C. 1.*	1800	4700

682A

		F	VF
		£	£

682A — MONETA AVGGG. Moneta stg. l., S—P in field, C in ex. *R.I.C.* —..   2000   5000

See also nos. 693-4 and 698-700 as well as regular Carausian types with the triple-ending 'AVGGG.' on reverse.

683   **Allectus,** usurper in Britain, 293-296. N aureus, London. ORIENS AVG. Sol stg. l. between two captives, ML in ex. *R.I.C. 4*..................................   30000   85000

684   Æ *antoninianus*, London. LAETITIA AVG. Laetitia stg. l., S—A in field, 35000MSL in ex. *R.I.C. 22*...   65   160

684A

684A — PAX AVG. Pax stg. l., S—A in field, ML in ex. *R.I.C. 28*.   55   150

685   — PROVID. AVG. Providentia stg. l., holding globe and cornucopiae, S—P in field, ML in ex. *R.I.C. 36*.   70   175

685A — SALVS AVG. Salus stg. r., feeding snake held in her arms, S—A in field, MSL in ex. *R.I.C. 42*...   75   200

686   — TEMPOR. FELICITAS. Felicitas stg. l., S—A in field, ML in ex. *R.I.C. 47*.   65   170

686A — VICTORIA AVG. Victory advancing l., S—P in field, ML in ex. *R.I.C. 48*.   85   225

687   Æ *antoninianus*, Colchester (?). AEQVITAS AVG. Aequitas stg. l., S—P in field, C in ex. *R.I.C. 63*.   65   170

687A — FIDES MILITVM. Fides stg. l., holding two standards, S—P in field, C in ex. *R.I.C. 69*.   85   200

688A

688   — LAETITIA AVG. Laetitia stg. l., S—P in field, CL in ex. *R.I.C. 79*. ..   70   190

This form of mint mark has given rise to the alternative identification of this mint as Clausentum (Bitterne, Hants.)

688A — MONETA AVG. Moneta stg. l., S—P in field, C in ex. *R.I.C. 82*.   65   170

		F	VF
		£	£
689	— PAX AVG. Pax stg. l., S—P in field, C in ex. *R.I.C. 86.*	55	150
689A	— PROVIDENTIA AVG. Providentia stg. l., globe at feet, S—P in field, C in ex. *R.I.C. 111.*	60	160
690	— TEMPORVM FELIC. Felicitas stg. l., S—P in field, CL in ex. *R.I.C. 117.*	65	170
690A	— VIRTVS AVG. Mars stg. r., holding spear and shield, S—P in field, C in ex. *R.I.C. 121.*	75	200
691	Æ *'quinarius'*, London. VIRTVS AVG. Galley l., QL in ex. *R.I.C. 55.*....	50	130

An experimental denomination issued only during this reign, the types of the so-called 'quinarius' would seem to indicate that it was in some way associated with the operations of the fleet upon which the survival of the rebel regime in Britain was totally dependent.

692   693

692	Æ *'quinarius'*, Colchester (?). LAETITIA AVG. Galley r., QC in ex. *R.I.C. 124.*	50	130
692A	— VIRTVS AVG. Galley l., QC in ex. *R.I.C. 128.*...................................	50	130
693	**Diocletian,** 284-305. Billon *antoninianus* of London, struck by Carausius between 289 and 293. PAX AVGGG. Pax stg. l., S—P in field, MLXXI in ex. *R.I.C. 9.*	70	190
694	Billon *antoninianus* of Colchester (?), same date. PROVID AVGGG. Providentia stg. l., globe at feet, S—P in field, C in ex. *R.I.C. 22*............	70	190

695

695	Æ *follis,* London. GENIO POPVLI ROMANI. Genius stg. l., LON in ex. *R.I.C. 1a.*...	200	500

By the time the central government had recovered control of Britain in 296 the antoninianus had been replaced by the larger follis under Diocletian's sweeping currency reform. London was retained as an official imperial mint, but the secondary British establishment (at Colchester?) was now abandoned. Except for its initial issue in 297 (marked 'LON') the London mint under the tetrarchic government produced only unsigned folles throughout its first decade of operation. Perhaps Constantius did not wish to draw attention to his employment of a mint which had been the creation of a rebel regime.

696	— Similar, but without mint mark. *R.I.C. 6a.*	25	55

| | *F* | *VF* |
| | £ | £ |

697 — (post-abdication coinage, after 305). PROVIDENTIA DEORVM
QVIES AVGG. Quies and Providentia stg. facing each other (no mint mark).
R.I.C. 77a. 40   90

697A   704

697A — QVIES AVGG. Quies stg. l., holding branch and sceptre, PLN in ex.
R.I.C. 98. 34   80
698 **Maximian,** 286-305 and 306-308. *N aureus* of London, struck by
Carausius between 289 and 293. SALVS AVGGG. Salus stg. r., feeding
snake held in her arms, ML in ex. *R.I.C. 32.* 34000 75000
699 Billon *antoninianus* of London, same date. PROVIDENTIA AVGGG.
Providentia stg. l., S—P in field, MLXXI in ex. *R.I.C. 37.* 60   150
700 Billon *antoninianus* of Colchester (?), same date. PAX AVGGG. Pax stg.
l., S—P in field, C in ex. *R.I.C. 42.* 60   150
701 Æ *follis,* London. GENIO POPVLI ROMANI. Genius stg. l., LON in ex.
R.I.C. 2. 180   420
702 — Similar, but without mint mark. *R.I.C. 23b.* 25   60
703 — (post-abdication coinage, after 305). PROVIDENTIA DEORVM
QVIES AVGG. Quies and Providentia stg. facing each other (no mint mark).
R.I.C. 77b. 40   85

706

704 — (second reign). GENIO POP. ROM. Genius stg. l., PLN in ex. *R.I.C. 90.* 30   70
704A — HERCVLI CONSERVATORI. Hercules stg. l., resting on club,
PLN in ex. *R.I.C. 91.* 40   100
705 **Constantius I,** 305-306 (Caesar 293-305). Æ *follis,* London (as Caesar).
GENIO POPVLI ROMANI. Genius stg. l., LON in ex. *R.I.C. 4a.* 200   500
706 — Similar, but without mint mark. *R.I.C. 30.* 20   50
707 — (as Augustus). Similar. *R.I.C. 52a.* 25   60
708 **Divus Constantius I,** deified 306. Æ *follis,* London. MEMORIA FELIX.
Altar flanked by eagles, PLN in ex. *R.I.C. 110* 30   80
709 **Galerius,** 305-311 (Caesar 293-305). Æ *follis,* London (as Caesar).
GENIO POPVLI ROMANI. Genius stg. l., LON in ex. *R.I.C. 4b.* 180   420

		F	VF
		£	£
710	— Similar, but without mint mark. *R.I.C. 15.*	20	45
711	— (as Augustus). Similar. *R.I.C. 42.*	20	45
711A	— GENIO POP. ROM. Genius stg. l., PLN in ex. *R.I.C. 86.*	25	60
712	**Severus II,** 306-307 (Caesar 305-306). Æ *follis,* London (as Caesar). GENIO POPVLI ROMANI. Genius stg. l. (no mint mark). *R.I.C. 58a* ...	45	110
713	— (as Augustus). Similar. *R.I.C. 52c.*	45	110
714	**Maximinus II,** 310-313 (Caesar 305-310). Æ *follis,* London (as Caesar). GENIO POPVLI ROMANI. Genius stg. l. (no mint mark). *R.I.C. 57.*	20	50
715	—-GENIO POP. ROM. Genius stg. l., PLN in ex. *R.I.C. 89a*	20	55
716	— (as Augustus). Similar, but with star in r. field. *R.I.C. 209b.*	20	50
717	**Licinius,** 308-324. Æ *follis,* London. GENIO POP. ROM. Genius stg. l., star in r. field, PLN in ex. *R.I.C. 209c.*	20	50
717A	— Similar, but with S—F in field. *R.I.C. 3.*	20	45
718	— SOLI INVICTO COMITI. Sol stg. l., holding globe, S—P in field, MSL in ex. *R.I.C. 79.*	20	45
719	**Constantine I, the Great,** 307-337 (Caesar 306-307). Æ *follis,* London (as Caesar). GENIO POPVLI ROMANI. Genius stg. l. (no mint mark). *R.I.C. 72.*	30	75
719A	— GENIO POP. ROM. Genius stg. l., PLN in ex. *R.I.C. 88b*	20	50
720	— PRINCIPI IVVENTVTIS. Prince stg. l., holding standards, PLN in ex. *R.I.C. 97.*	30	80
721	— (as Augustus). ADVENTVS AVG. Emperor on horseback l., captive on ground before, star in r. field, PLN in ex. *R.I.C. 133*	35	85
722	— COMITI AVGG. NN. Sol stg. l., holding globe and whip, same mint mark. *R.I.C. 155.*	25	60
723	— CONCORD. MILIT. Concordia stg. l., holding standards, same mint mark. *R.I.C. 195.*	20	55
724	— MARTI CONSERVATORI. Mars. stg. r., holding spear and shield, star in l. field, PLN in ex. *R.I.C. 254.*	20	55
724A	— SOLI INVICTO COMITI. Sol stg. l., holding globe, S—F in field, MLL in ex. *R.I.C. 27.*	15	40
725	Æ 3, London. VICTORIAE LAETAE PRINC. PERP. Two Victories supporting shield, inscribed VOT. / P. R., over altar, PLN in ex. *R.I.C. 159.*	15	35

726

726	— VIRTVS EXERCIT. Vexillum, inscribed VOT. / XX., between two captives, PLN in ex. R.I.C. 191.	15	35
727	— BEAT. TRANQLITAS. Altar, inscribed VOT / IS / XX., surmounted by globe and three stars, PLON in ex. *R.I.C. 267*	15	35
727A	— SARMATIA DEVICTA. Victory advancing r., trampling captive, PLON and crescent in ex. *R.I.C. 289.*	25	55
728	— PROVIDENTIAE AVGG. Gateway of military camp, PLON in ex. *R.I.C. 293.*	15	35

		F	VF
		£	£
729	**Fausta,** wife of Constantine I. Æ 3, London. SALVS REIPVBLICAE. Empress stg. l., holding two children, PLON in ex. *R.I.C. 300*.	110	300
730	**Helena,** mother of Constantine I. Æ 3, London. SECVRITAS REIPVBLICE. Empress stg. l., holding branch, PLON in ex. *R.I.C. 299.*	110	300
731	**Crispus,** eldest son of Constantine I, Caesar 317-326. Æ 3, London. SOLI INVICTO COMITI. Sol stg. l., holding globe, crescent in l. field, PLN in ex. *R.I.C. 144.*	20	45
731A	— VIRTVS EXERCIT. Vexillum, inscribed VOT. / XX., between two captives, PLN in ex. *R.I.C. 194.*	20	45
732	— BEATA TRANQVILLITAS. Altar, inscribed VOT / IS / XX., surmounted by globe and three stars, P—A in field, PLON in ex. *R.I.C. 211.*	15	35
733	— CAESARVM NOSTRORVM around wreath containing VOT. / X., PLON and crescent in ex. *R.I.C. 291*	15	35

734

734	— PROVIDENTIAE CAESS. Gateway of military camp, PLON in ex. *R.I.C. 295.*	15	35
735	**Constantine II,** 337-340 (Caesar 317-337). Æ 3, London (as Caesar). CLARITAS REIPVBLICAE. Sol stg. l., holding globe, crescent in l. field, PLN in ex. *R.I.C. 131.*	15	35
736	— VICTORIAE LAETAE PRINC. PERP. Two Victories supporting shield, inscribed VOT. / P. R., over altar ornamented with wreath, PLN in ex. *R.I.C. 182.*	15	35
737	— VIRTVS EXERCIT. Vexillum, inscribed VOT. / XX., between two captives, PLON in ex. *R.I.C. 190.*	15	35

737A

737A	— BEATA TRANQVILLITAS. Altar, inscribed VOT / IS / XX., surmounted by globe and three stars, PLON in ex. *R.I.C. 236*	15	35
738	— CAESARVM NOSTRORVM around wreath containing VOT. / X., PLON and crescent in ex. *R.I.C. 292*	15	35
738A	— PROVIDENTIAE CAESS. Gateway of military camp, PLON in ex. *R.I.C. 296.*	15	35
739	**Constantius II,** 337-361 (Caesar 324-337). Æ 3, London (as Caesar). PROVIDENTIAE CAESS. Gateway of military camp, PLON in ex. *R.I.C. 298.*	30	80

740   **Magnus Maximus,** usurper in the West, 383-388. *N solidus,* London (?).
       RESTITVTOR REIPVBLICAE. Emperor stg. r., holding labarum and
       Victory, AVG in ex. *R.I.C. 1.* ....   *Unique*
       The attribution to London of this rare series has not been firmly established,
       though Maximus was certainly proclaimed emperor in Britain and it is
       well attested that the principal city of the British provinces bore the name
       'Augusta' in the late Roman period (Ammianus Marcellinus XXVII, 8, 7;
       XXVIII, 3, 7).

741

741   — VICTORIA AVGG. Two emperors enthroned facing, Victory hovering
       in background between them, AVGOB in ex. *R.I.C. 2b.*   14000   45000
       Maximus appears to have struck a similar type in the name of the eastern
       emperor Theodosius I (cf. R.I.C. 2a), though it is presently known only
       from a silver-gilt specimen preserved in the British Museum.
742   *R siliqua,* London (?). VOT. / V. / MVLT. / X. within wreath, AVG below.
       R.I.C. 4.   1200   3400
742A   — VICTORIA AVGG. Victory advancing l., AVGPS in ex. *R.I.C. 3.*.......   1100   2800

4. IMITATIONS OF ROMAN COINS PRODUCED IN BRITAIN

At certain periods during the three and a half centuries of its occupation Roman Britain seems to
have been the source of much local imitation of the official imported coinage. This began soon
after the Claudian invasion in A.D. 43 when significant quantities of sestertii, dupondii and asses
(especially the last) were produced in the newly conquered territory, as evidenced by the frequency
of their occurrence in archaeological finds. The technical excellence of many of these 'copies',
together with the surprising extent of their minting, would seem to indicate that some, at least, of
these coins were produced with official sanction in order to make good an unexpected deficiency
in the currency supply. Others are much poorer and well below weight, representing the 'unofficial'
branch of this operation, some of it probably emanating from territory as yet unconquered. As
conditions in the new province settled down rapid Romanization and urbanization of British society
brought a general increase in wealth, and with it a much greater volume of currency flowing into
the country. Local imitation now virtually ceased, except for the occasional activities of criminal
counterfeiters, and this state of affairs lasted down to the great political crisis and financial collapse
of the second half of the 3rd century. At this point large scale minting of imitations of the debased
antoniniani of the late 260s and early 270s began in Britain and in the other northwestern provinces,
all of which had been serious[y affected by the political dislocation of this turbulent era. This
class of imitations is usually referred to as 'barbarous radiates', the emperor's spiky crown being
a constant and conspicuous feature of the obverses. Most frequently copied were the antoniniani
of the Gallic rulers Tetricus Senior and Tetricus Junior (ca. 270-273) and the posthumous issues
of Claudius Gothicus (died 270). The quality of the 'barbarous radiates' is variable in the extreme,
some exhibiting what appears to be a revival of Celtic art forms, others so tiny that it is virtually

impossible to see anything of the design. Their production appears to have ended abruptly with Aurelian's reconquest of the western provinces in 273. A similar phenomenon, though on a lesser scale, occurred in the middle decades of the following century when normal life in Britain was again disrupted, not only by usurpation but additionally by foreign invasion. With supplies of currency from the Continent temporarily disrupted local imitation, particularly of the 'Æ 2' and 'Æ 3' issues of Constantius II and the usurper Magnentius, began in earnest. How long this continued is difficult to determine as life in the island province was now subject to increasingly frequent episodes of dislocation. By now urban life in Britain was in serious decline and when Roman rule ended early in the 5th century, bringing a total cessation of currency supplies, the catastrophic decline in monetary commerce in the former provinces rendered it no longer necessary for the deficiency to be made good.

		F	VF
		£	£
743	**Agrippa,** died 12 B.C. Æ as, of irregular British mintage, imitating the Roman issue made under Agrippa's grandson Caligula, A.D. 37-41. S. C. Neptune stg. l., holding dolphin and trident.	55	140

The large official issue of Agrippa asses was made shortly before the Claudian invasion of Britain in A.D. 43 and would thus have comprised a significant proportion of the 'aes' in circulation at this time. In consequence, it would soon have become familiar to the new provincials providing an ideal prototype for imitation.

| 744 | **Claudius,** 41-54. Æ *sestertius,* of irregular British mintage. SPES AVGVSTA S. C. Spes walking l., holding flower. | 130 | 400 |
| 745 | Æ *dupondius,* of irregular British mintage. CERES AVGVSTA S. C. Ceres enthroned l., holding corn- ears and torch. | 50 | 130 |

746

| 746 | Æ *as,* of irregular British mintage. S. C. Minerva advancing r., brandishing spear and holding shield. | 45 | 120 |

This is by far the commonest of the Claudian imitations and the prototypes must have represented the bulk of the aes coinage carried by the legions at the time of the invasion. The martial type may well have been specially selected as a suitable theme for the initial import of coinage into the newly conquered territory.

| 747 | **Nero Claudius Drusus,** father of Claudius, died 9 B.C. Æ *sestertius,* of irregular British mintage. TI. CLAVDIVS CAESAR AVG. P. M. TR .P. IMP. S. C. Claudius seated l. on curule chair amidst arms | 150 | 450 |

This type was issued by Claudius half a century after his father's death and would thus have been prominently represented in the initial wave of coinage imported into the new province.

| 748 | **Antonia,** mother of Claudius, died A.D. 37. Æ *dupondius,* of irregular British mintage. TI. CLAVDIVS CAESAR AVG P.M. TR. P. IMP. P. P. S. C. Claudius stg. l., holding simpulum. | 90 | 300 |

Another Claudian issue for a deceased parent, this represents one of only two dupondius types struck during this reign and would have entered Britain in significant quantities at the time of the invasion in A.D. 43.

749A   749B   749C

	F £	VF £
749 **'Barbarous radiates',** ca. 270-273. British and Continental imitations of billon *antoniniani,* principally of Divus Claudius II (A), Tetricus Senior (B) and Tetricus Junior (C). The inscriptions are usually blundered and the types sometimes unrecognizable. British mintage can only be established by provenance.	5	15
750 **Barbarous 4th century,** mostly of the second half of the century, and principally imitated from 'Æ 2' and 'Æ 3' issues of the later Constantinian period, notably those of Constantius II ('soldier spearing fallen horseman' type), and the usurpers Magnentius and Decentius ('two Victories' type). The copies, especially those of Magnentius and Decentius, are often of excellent style and execution, though the legends frequently contain small errors. Those of Constantius II are sometimes very barbarous and poorly struck, occasionally over regular issues of the earlier Constantinian period. Again, the likelihood of British mintage can only be established by provenance.	10-15	15-20

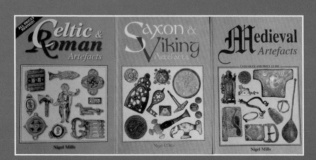

Grading of Hammered Coins

As the name suggests, hammered coins were struck by hand with a hammer. This can lead to the coin being struck off-centre, double struck, areas of the design not being struck up as well as cracks or other defects in the flan. It is important to take these factors into account along with surface wear, quality of the metal and patina when assessing the grade of this series. Value is considerably reduced if the coin is holed, pierced, plugged or mounted. Coins with proven provenance from important old collections will carry a price premium. For further detail on condition see pages ix to x.

Extremely Fine	**Very Fine**	**Fine**

William I PAXS type penny

Henry VIII 1st coinage gold Angel

Edward VI silver shilling

EARLY & MIDDLE ANGLO-SAXON KINGDOMS & MINTS (c.650-973)

Approximate extent of Danelaw

Approximate extent of Hiberno-Norse Kingdom of York

NORTHUMBRIA

York

Lincoln

Chester

Newark (?)

Derby

Nottingham

Stafford

Shrewsbury

Leicester   Stamford (?)

Norwich

Tamworth

EAST ANGLIA

MERCIA

Thetford

Northampton   Huntingdon

Warwick

Hereford

Newport   Bedford

Buckingham   Hertford   Maldon

Gloucester   Oxford

Malmesbury   Wallingford   London

Bath

Rochester

Canterbury

Wilton

Winchester

KENT

Dover

Barnstaple

Langport

Shaftesbury

Lympne

Southampton   Lewes

Exeter   Bridport

Wareham

Chichester

Totnes

WESSEX

EARLY ANGLO-SAXON PERIOD, *c.* 600-*c.* 775

The withdrawal of Roman forces from Britain early in the 5th century A.D. and the gradual decline of central administration resulted in a rapid deterioration of the money supply. The arrival of Germanic raiders and settlers, even in relatively small numbers, disrupted life and it was probably not until late in the 6th century that renewed political, cultural and commercial links with the kingdom of the Merovingian Franks led to the appearance of small quantities of Merovingian gold *tremisses* (one-third solidus) in England. A purse containing 37 such pieces (plus 3 gold blanks and 2 ingots) was found in the Sutton Hoo ship-burial; a further hoard of at least 60 Continental tremisses came to light in Norfolk in 2014. Native Anglo-Saxon gold shillings (*thrymsas*) were minted from the *c.*620s, initially in the style of their continental prototypes or copied from obsolete Roman coinage with others in pure Anglo-Saxon style. The mixed Crondall hoard of 101 gold coins (1 Byzantine, 24 Merovingian or Frankish, 69 Anglo-Saxon, 7 others) gives structure to the arrangement of thrymsas with types found in this hoard differentiated from those, some of the same date, that were not. By the middle of the 7th century the gold coinage was being increasingly debased with silver, and according to recent scientific analysis of grave goods gold had been superseded entirely by the 660s.

The silver coins, contemporary with the *deniers or denarii* of the Merovingian Franks, are the first English pennies, typically referred to as *sceats* or *sceattas* (pronounced 'skeets' or 'shatters' possibly meaning 'treasure' or 'wealth'); the singular is *sceat*. The term early-penny is now favoured. They provide important material for the student of Anglo-Saxon art. Indeed, it could be said that, until recently, the largely anonymous, anepigraphic, nature of the sceatta coinage detracted from its numismatic character, however, Anna Gannon's work on the subtle iconography of this period has elevated its status significantly.

The silver coins of the early ('primary') phase, *c.*680-710, are a transition from the gold coinage and are conservative in style. Those of the 'secondary' period, *c.*710-60, are far more diverse in design. Trading types were issued in substantial numbers (probably tens of millions) especially by the Frisians of the Low Countries ('Continental'), evidencing the significant volume of North Sea trade, and their central role in the economic resurgence. Early coins are of good silver content, though the quality deteriorates early in the 8th century, with weights then averaging around 1.00 g. The secondary types exist in numerous varieties, though the survival rate, for the non-trading types is low and for some types, extremely low. The designs on many of these mix Christian with pagan symbolism though the iconography is often, and probably intentionally, ambiguous. In this the coinage reflects the changes taking place during the period when Christianity was being adopted with the designs looking appeal to differing cultural strands in Anglo-Saxon England at the time. As well as the official issues there are mules and other varieties, which may be contemporary imitations; there is no clear line of demarcation. The 'eclectic' types are those which do not sit comfortably in the alphabetic Serial classification. However, Abramson's listing of varieties recognised here attempts to bring the eclectic issues into the general classification.

Many of the sceats were issued at the time of Aethelbald, King of Mercia, (A.D. 716-757) who was overlord of the southern English, but as few bear inscriptions it is only in recent years that research has enabled their correct dating and the attribution of certain types to specific areas. The Northumbrian issues are more literate and facilitate attribution to issuers. The Aston Rowant (Oxon.) hoard of 324 sceats, deposited *c.* 710, separates the primary and secondary phases. The sceatta 'penny' coinage came to an end *c.*780 when it was replaced by the broad flan penny initially in Kent before its wider adoption in Mercia. The Northumbrian kingdom continued to use the small flan sceatta which after 810 was increasingly a copper coinage, known as stycas, this ending with Danish conquest of York in 867.

Through recent detector finds and continued research, a definitive classification is evolving but remains fluid. The arrangement given below is informed by Michael Metcalf's work on the series, developing Rigold's alphabetical classification. In this listing, the primary sceats are followed by the Continental then the secondary and, finally, the eclectic. This is not chronologically precise as there is some overlap but has been adopted for ease of reference and identification. This list is more extensive than previously published in *Coins of England* but is not exhaustive. The reference Abr. refers to the type listing by Abramson; 'B.M.C.' to the type given in *British Museum Catalogue: Anglo-Saxon Coins*. The reference *M* is to an illustration, and *M. p.* to a page, in Metcalf (below).

Useful reference works include:

Abramson, T., *Sceatta List: An Illustrated and Priced Catalogue of Sceats for Collectors* (2017).

Abramson, T., *The Abramson Collection: Coins of Early Anglo-Saxon England and the North Sea Area*, SCBI, 69 (2018).

Gannon, A., *The Iconography of Early Anglo-Saxon Coinage* (2003).

Gannon, A., British Museum, Anglo Saxon Coins I, *SCBI* 63 (2013).

Lyon, S., 'The Lyon Collection of Anglo-Saxon Coins', *SCBI* 68, (2016).

Metcalf, D. M., *Thrymsas and Sceattas in the Ashmolean Museum*, Vols I-III.

Op den Velde, W., & Klaassen, C.J.F., *Sceattas and Merovingian Deniers from Domburg and Westenschovwen* (2004)

Rigold, S. E., '*The two primary series of sceattas*', *B.N.J.*, XXX (1960).

Sutherland, C. H. V., *Anglo-Saxon Gold Coinage in the light of the Crondall Hoard* (1948).

ᚠᚪᚦᛖᚱᚴ·ᚷᛈᚾᛏᛁᚩᛋᚳᚣᛗᛏᛒᛗᚻᚱᛉᚻᛟᚠᚠᛏᚪ

f u th o r k z w h n i j ih p x s t b e m l ng d oe a Æ ea y

Early Anglo-Saxon Runes (Futhark)

GOLD

752

		F	VF
		£	£

A. EARLY PIECES, OF UNCERTAIN MONETARY STATUS

751   Thrymsa. Name and portrait of Bishop Liudhard (chaplain to Queen Bertha of Kent). ℞. Cross. ....   *Extremely rare*

752   Solidus. Imitating solidi of Roman rulers. Blundered legends, some with runes.   *Extremely rare*

      753   754   758

B. CRONDALL TYPES, *c.* 620 – *c.* 645

Twelve different types, which are almost certainly English, were found in the Crondall hoard of 1828. All are thrysmas, containing 40-70% gold.

		F	VF
753	'Witmen' type. Bust r. with trident. ℞. Cross. Legend normally blundered. *M. 1-21*	1250	4000
754	London-derived type. Head r. with pseudo-legend. ℞. Cross. Pseudo-legend. *M. 22-32*	1350	4500
755	'Licinius' type. Elegant imitation of Roman triens. Bust l. ℞. VOT XX. *M. 33-41*	2250	8500
756	'LEMC' type. Head l. ℞. Maltese cross with letters L, E, M, C in angles, or cross on steps. *M. 42-9*	1650	6250
757	'LONDINIV' type. Facing bust, crosslets l. and r. ℞. Tall cross, LONDVNIV and pseudo-legend around. *M. 51-7*	2250	8000
758	Eadbald of Kent (616-40) London. Bust r. AVDVARLD REGES. ℞. Cross on globule, LONDENVS. Usually garbled. *M. 50*	4750	17500
758A	— Canterbury. As 758 but DOROVERNVS M. *M-*	5000	18500
759	Other crude types, usually with head or bust, ℞. Cross. *M. 58-72*	975	3250

C.   ULTRA-CRONDALL TYPES, *c*. 620 – *c*. 655

Thrymsas not represented in the Crondall hoard, but probably of the same date range.

760   761

		F £	VF £
760	'Benutigo' type. Bust r., blundered legend. R. Cross on steps, runic legend (Benutigoii?)	2000	7500
761	'Wuneetton' type. Bust r., cross before. R. Cross. Blundered legend (WVNEETON or similar). *M. 77*	1350	4750
762	'York' group, inscribed type, stylised face cross each side, lattice pattern below, R. uncertain blundered legend. *M. 76*	2500	9000

762   762B

762A	— uninscribed, similar, R., four 'faces' around central square or similar	2750	10000
762B	— uninscribed, standing facing figure facing hold long cross each side, R., cross within inner circle, symbols around	3750	15000
763	— Bishop Paulinus of York (c.625-633), as 762, rev. :PAOLIENVS EP legend some letters inverted	3500	13500

D.   POST-CRONDALL TYPES, *c*. 655 – *c*. 675

Pale gold types, visibly debased and sometimes almost silvery, containing 10-35% gold. The description "standard" is a reference to the Roman legionary ensign bearing the legend e.g. VOTIS X MVLTIS XX also carried in Anglo-Saxon episcopal processions. The legend is reduced to TOTII on the coinage and may be described as the "votive standard".

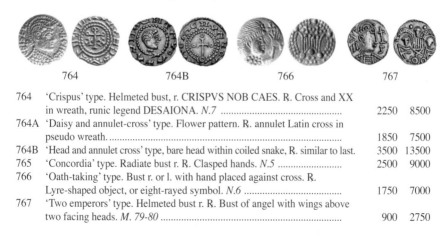

764   764B   766   767

764	'Crispus' type. Helmeted bust, r. CRISPVS NOB CAES. R. Cross and XX in wreath, runic legend DESAIONA. *N.7*	2250	8500
764A	'Daisy and annulet-cross' type. Flower pattern. R. annulet Latin cross in pseudo wreath.	1850	7500
764B	'Head and annulet cross' type, bare head within coiled snake, R. similar to last.	3500	13500
765	'Concordia' type. Radiate bust r. R. Clasped hands. *N.5*	2500	9000
766	'Oath-taking' type. Bust r. or l. with hand placed against cross. R. Lyre-shaped object, or eight-rayed symbol. *N.6*	1750	7000
767	'Two emperors' type. Helmeted bust r. R. Bust of angel with wings above two facing heads. *M. 79-80*	900	2750

768A   769   771

		F	VF
		£	£
768	'Pada', Type Ia. Helmeted bust r. R. Runic PADA on panel. *M.p.73.*	1250	4000
768A	— Type Ib. Similar. R. Standard TTXX, PADA in runes in legend. *M. 81*	850	2750
769	— Type IIa. bust r. R. PADA in runes in field, blundered legend around, *M.p.73.*	650	2000
770	— Type III. bust r. R. Cross with annulets in angles, legend includes runic PADA and other lettering *M.p.73.*	575	1750
771	'Vanimundus', Type A. bust r. holding sceptre. R. Cross, with CA in lower angles. VANIMVNDVS MONE. *M.p.82*	950	3250
772	— Type B. Similar. R. Small cross in double circle of dots. *M. 84*.........	850	3000

SILVER

773

SCEATTA COINAGE, *c.* 675 – *c.* 760

A.   EARLY TRANSITIONAL TYPES BY THRYMSA MONEYERS, c.675 – c.685

773	'Pada', Type III. As 770, but silver. *Abr. 1, M. 82, M. p. 73-9*	350	1100
773A	— , obv. as 769, rev. cross on steps (PaIIb). *Abr. 1.40*		
774	'Vanimundus', Type B. As 772, but silver. *Abr. 2, M. 85-7. M. p. 80-4* ..	400	1350

B.   PRIMARY PHASE, *c.* 680 – *c.* 710

Minted in various regions of south-eastern and eastern England.

775

775	**Series A 2a**. Radiate bust r., TIC. R. Standard, TOTII. Several varieties. *Abr. 3* 80		225

776   777

776	**Series BX**. Diademed bust r., VANTAVMA or similar. R. Bird r. above cross on steps, annulets and pellets in field vary. *Abr. 15, B.M.C. 26. M. 97-9, M. p. 99*	95	275
777	**Series BI**. Diademed head r. within serpent circle. R. Bird r. on cross. Some with symbols by bird. *Abr. 16, B.M.C. 27a. M. 100-106, M. 113-16*	50	150

777A: varieties   778

	F	VF
	£	£

777A   **Series BIIIA**, Type 27a. Diademed head r. with either protruding jaw or pointed nose,
symbols before, serpent circle. R. Full bodied or linear bird on cross within serpent
circle, annulets either side, pellets below. *Abr. 16.70-80, M. p. 158-65* .   65   200

778   **Series BZ**. Abstract facing head. R. Simplified bird on cross in linear style,
blundered legend. *Abr. 17, BMC 29a, M. 138-9. M. p. 136-7*   100   300

779 C1   779 C2

779   **Series C**. Radiate bust r., similar to 775 but runic ᚠᛗᚳᚠ replaces TIC. R. Variety C1,
standard, TOTII; variety C2, four crosses around standard, variety C2, cross abuts
standard. *Abr. 4, B.M.C. 2b. M. 117-125, 132-2. M. P. 106-13*   45   125

780   781

780   Attributed to King Aethelred of Mercia (674-704). Degenerate head. R. 'Æthiliræd'
in runes in two lines. *Abr. 92, M. 134-5, M. p. 120-4*   225   700

781   **Series F**. Bust r., with pelleted helmet, blundered legend. R. Small cross on
steps, arrangement of surrounding annulets and letters "T" and "I" varies, as
do styles. *Abr. 106, M. 136-7, M. p. 125-32*   65   225

782: various styles

782   **Series Z**. Broad facing portrait (Christ?) with forked or straight beard. R. Hound
running r., legs straight or crossed, tail curled beneath or above, erect ears
sometimes with chevrons above, various styles known. Some coarse.
Abr. 102.10-60, BMC 66, M. 140-2, M. p. 137-8   275   950

782A   783

782A   **Series Z-related**. Skeletal hound r., perhaps copy of 782. R. Saltire standard or
cross-crosslet design, various styles known. *Abr. 102.70-80, M. 143-4,
M. p. 138-9*..   125   475

783   **'Vernus' group**, Types 2b, 3b and 91. Degenerate head r., VER before,
execution deteriorates in later issues. R. Standard, various styles known.
Abr. 6, M. 146-8, M. p. 140-6   50   150

784   785   786

		F	VF
		£	£

784   **'Saroaldo'**, Type 11. Bust r. becoming increasingly stylized R. Pseudo-legend
SAROALDO(?) around standard. Some with FIT/RV inscribed (rare) or with saltire and
pellets, various styles. *Abr. 7, M. 151-3, M. p. 147-51* 80   275

785   **'Stepped cross'**, Type 53. Degenerate 'porcupine' head. R. Stepped cross,
annulet at centre. *Abr. 91, M. 258-62, M. p. 140, M. p. 243-5*................... 65   175

786   **'SEDE'**. Type 89. Quilled serpent, pellet in mouth, coiled around cross.
R. Small central saltire, S E D E in angles with saltires between.
Abr. 93, M. 263, M. p. 682 225   750

787: various styles

787   **Series W**. Half- to full-length figure, head r., holding long cross pommée or
annulet cross either side. R. Cross crosslet on saltire. *Abr. 108, BMC 54,
M. 155, M. p. 152-7* 275   950

788: Series W related

788   **Series W related**. Monogram (Marseilles?) or monster l. looking back R.
Cross crosslet on saltire. *Abr. 53* 110   375

C.   CONTINENTAL ISSUES, *c*. 695 – *c*. 740

Most Continental sceattas emanate from the former Rhine mouth area, Frisia, particularly
the emporia of Domburg and Dorestad. The obverse motif of Series E, commonly
referred to as the "porcupine", is now recognized as a degenerate diademed bust. Series
D bust takes English Series C as its prototype retaining the runic inscription ÆPA.

790   790A *VICO*

790   **Series E**. Degenerate head enclosing three bars. R. Votive standard
with TOTII design, various styles. *Abr. 94*.. 30   85

790A   —, **'Vico' type**. Degenerate head enclosing bars. R. 'Standard' with letters possibly
reading VIC (*wic*, emporium) around central annulet. *Abr. 88, M. p. 211-16*   35   100

790B

	F £	VF £
790B —, variety D. Degenerate head, various symbols in field. R. 'Standard' with four pellets around central annulet. *Dorestad. Abr. 90, M. 209-11.*	30	80

790C

790C —, variety E. Degenerate head. R. 'Standard' with four lines and central annulet. *Abr. 89, M. p. 216-19*	30	85
790D Later issues. Degenerate head. Innumerable varieties. R. 'Standard'. *Abr. 94-97, M. 214-53, M. p. 222-42.*	30	75

791

791 —, plumed bird, usually r. R. Standard with a variety of symmetrical geometric symbols. *Abr. 87, M. 190-3, M. p.206-11*	45	130

792   792 var.

792 **Series D**, Type 2c. Bust r. (types with bust l. are possibly English and imitative), runic ÆPA before bust. R. Plain cross with pellets in angles, pseudo-letters around. *Abr. 8, M. 158-80, M. p. 184-90.*	30	90

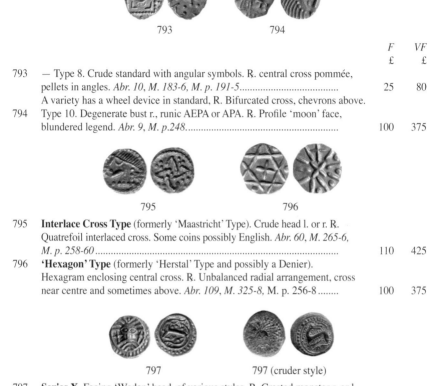

793 794

		F	VF
		£	£
793	— Type 8. Crude standard with angular symbols. R. central cross pommée, pellets in angles. *Abr. 10, M. 183-6, M. p. 191-5*.....................................	25	80
	A variety has a wheel device in standard, R. Bifurcated cross, chevrons above.		
794	Type 10. Degenerate bust r., runic AEPA or APA. R. Profile 'moon' face, blundered legend. *Abr. 9, M. p.248.*.......................................	100	375

795 796

795	**Interlace Cross Type** (formerly 'Maastricht' Type). Crude head l. or r. R. Quatrefoil interlaced cross. Some coins possibly English. *Abr. 60, M. 265-6, M. p. 258-60*	110	425
796	**'Hexagon' Type** (formerly 'Herstal' Type and possibly a Denier). Hexagram enclosing central cross. R. Unbalanced radial arrangement, cross near centre and sometimes above. *Abr. 109, M. 325-8,* M. p. 256-8	100	375

797   797 (cruder style)

797	**Series X**. Facing 'Wodan' head, of various styles. R. Crested monster r. or l., tail raised to mouth, claws below, prominent member, die mark below jaw. *Ribe, Jutland, M. 275-81, M. p. 275-86,* same cruder style possibly English. *Abr. 103-4, M. 282, M. p. 286-3*	125	475

D. SECONDARY PHASE, *c.* 710 – *c.* 760

Die duplication is the exception in this coinage, with a substantial variation of execution and fabric within each type. It is assumed that quality deteriorates over time and late issues may be of more interest monetarily than aesthetically. This coinage was issued in all the main regions of southern and eastern England. Some boundaries between Series remain indistinct e.g. K and L, C and R.

800 varieties

800	**Series G**, Type 3a. Diademed bust r., heavenward gaze, cross before. R. Standard with 3 or 4 saltires. *Abr. 21, M. 267-70, M. p. 266-72*..............................	65	185

801   801A   801B

		F	VF
		£	£

801   **Series H ('Hamwic')**, Type 39. Pecking bird. R. Celtic cross. *Abr. 46, M. 283-4,*
M. p. 324-5   90   325

801A   — Type 49. 'Wodan' head, 5-11 bosses around. R. Pecking bird in various
styles. *Abr. 48, M. 285-8, M. p. 325-32.*   125   475

801B   — Type 48. Whorl of 3 wolf heads. R. Celtic cross. *Abr. 47, M. 289-92,*
M. p. 333-40   90   325

802   802A

802   **Series J ('York')**, Type 85. Large diademed head r. R. Outline bird on cross.
Abr. 18.20, M. 293-5, M. p. 345-50   65   200

802A   — Type 37. Two diademed heads face-to-face. R. Four birds clockwise
around cross. *Abr. 19.30, M. 296-300, M. p. 351-3*   75   250

802B   — Type 60. Diademed head r. R. Two serpents coiled clockwise with
beaded bodies, heads central. *Abr. 18.10, M. p. 354-5* 125   450

802C   802D

802C   — Type 72. Two diademed heads face-to-face. R. Bird r., looking back at serpent.
Abr. 19.10-20, M. 303, M. p. 355-6. One variety has bird looking forward   100   350

802D   — Type 36. Diademed bust r., cross before. R. Two birds. *Abr. 20.10-30,*
M. 301-2, M. p. 361-4   85   300

803   803A

803   **Series K ('Kent')**, Type 33. Diademed bust r., cross before. R. Wolf's head
with long tongue, l. or r. *Abr. 38, M. 306, M. p. 388-91*   135   575

803A   — Type 42. Diademed bust r. with bird, cross or flower. R. Hound l.
looking back, plant behind, various styles. *Abr. 41, M. 311-3, M. p. 391-5*   100   400

803B   — Type 75. Roulette wheel of 11 compartments . R. Hound l. looking
back, plant behind. *Abr. 41.50*   135   575

803C

		F £	VF £

803C — Type 32a. Bust r. with cross before, cupped in hand. R. Wolf curled
head to tail or wolf headed serpent. *Abr. 39, M. 309, 310, M. p. 395-402*   125   525

803D

803D — — Similar. R. Wolf-headed serpent r. or l. *Abr. 40, M. 310, M. p. 400*   100   375

803E: Series K, Type 20   obv var.

803E — Type 20. Bust r. cross or chalice before. R. Standing figure in crescent boat
holding cross and hawk. *Abr. 33, M. 314-18, M. p. 402-5*......................   100   375

803F

803F — Type 16. Bust r. floral scroll before. R. Standing figure in crescent boat
holding cross and hawk. *Abr. 33.80, M. 314-18, M. p. 402-5*..................   100   400

804   804C   804D

804   **Series L ('London'),** Type 12. Bust r., LVNDONIA. R. Standing figure in
crescent boat holding two crosses. *Abr. 23, M. 319-22 M. p. 409-11*   120   500

804A — Type 13. Similar. R. Seated figure holding hawk and cross. *Abr. 23.20,
M. p. 409*   225   850

804B — Type 14. Similar, but bust l. R. Celtic cross. (as S.822). *Abr. 27.10, M. p. 427*   110   475

804C — Type 15. Diademed bust r. with cross, no legend. R. Standing figure
holding two crosses. *Abr. 35.20, M. 323-6*   85   300

804D — Type 16. Bust r. with floral scroll before. R. Standing figure holding
two crosses. *Abr. 35.40, M. 329-30*...   90   325

804E — Type 17. Bust l. with long cross before. R. Standing figure holding two
crosses. *Abr. 36*   95   350

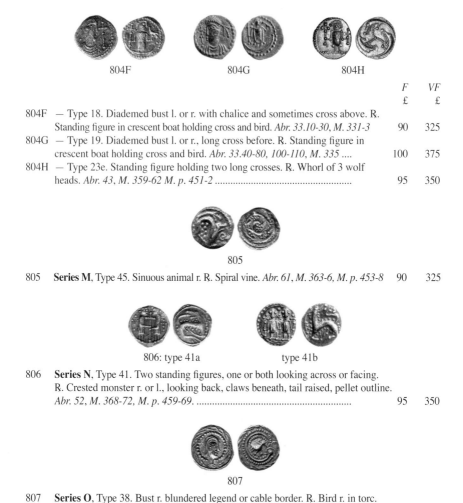

	804F	804G	804H

	F £	VF £
804F — Type 18. Diademed bust l. or r. with chalice and sometimes cross above. R. Standing figure in crescent boat holding cross and bird. *Abr. 33.10-30, M. 331-3*	90	325
804G — Type 19. Diademed bust l. or r., long cross before. R. Standing figure in crescent boat holding cross and bird. *Abr. 33.40-80, 100-110, M. 335 ....*	100	375
804H — Type 23e. Standing figure holding two long crosses. R. Whorl of 3 wolf heads. *Abr. 43, M. 359-62 M. p. 451-2*	95	350

805

805	**Series M**, Type 45. Sinuous animal r. R. Spiral vine. *Abr. 61, M. 363-6, M. p. 453-8*	90	325

806: type 41a   type 41b

806	**Series N**, Type 41. Two standing figures, one or both looking across or facing. R. Crested monster r. or l., looking back, claws beneath, tail raised, pellet outline. *Abr. 52, M. 368-72, M. p. 459-69.*	95	350

807

807	**Series O**, Type 38. Bust r. blundered legend or cable border. R. Bird r. in torc. *Abr. 58, M. 373-5, M. p. 470-2*	100	375
807A	— Type 21. Similar, but peg-nosed bust l. R. Standing figure with two crosses. *Abr. 59, M. 376, M. p. 472-4.*	135	575

807B

807C

807D various

	F £	VF £

807B — Type 40. Standing figure holding two long crosses. R. Monster l. looking back, curled tail and foreleg raised, claw beneath, "feathered" coat below. *Abr. 55, M. 379-81, M. p. 477-81, 490.* **75 250**

807C — Type 57. Peg-nosed bust r. in cable border. R. Monster looking back r. or l. curled tail and foreleg raised, claw beneath, "feathered" coat below. *Abr. 54, M. 377, M. p. 474-5.* **110 475**

807D — Type 40 variety. Monster r., looking back, tail and crest raised, foreleg raised behind head. R. Elaborate beaded standard in beaded circle, outer linear border with annulets or standard, votive or beaded. *Abr. 57, M. p. 490* ... **120 500**

808

808 **Series Q**, variety IA-D. Two Standing figures with long crosses. R. Monster r. or l., looking back, crest raised or lowered, tail raised, claws below, several varieties. *Abr. 63.10-40, M. p. 488, 489, 491.* **125 525**

808A   808B

808A —, variety IE, Type 67. Diademed bust r., cross before. R. Walking bird l., pellets in field. *Abr. 63.50-70, M. 383, M. p. 490-1* **130 550**

808B —, variety IF, Type 71. Standing facing figure with two crosses. R. Walking bird l., pellets in field. *Abr. 63.80, M. 384.* **200 750**

808C   808D

808C —, variety IG, Type 95. Facing head. R. Long-legged quadruped looking back, crest intertwines legs, tail raised. *Abr. 63.100-110, M. p. 492.* **250 950**

808D —, variety IH. Half-length profile figure holding cross r. R. Long-legged quadruped looking back, crest raised, tail intertwines legs. *Abr. 63.90, M. 385, M. p. 492* **225 900**

809

		F	VF
		£	£

809   —, variety II. Quadruped l. or r., tail intertwines legs. R. Bird l. wings spread,
cross by wing. *Abr. 64, M. p. 494*   125   525

810

810   —, variety III. Quadruped l or r. with tail ending with triquetra. R. Bird l. or r.
often with triquetra. *Abr.65, M. p. 496*..   135   550

811

811   — variety IV. Bird or lion r. or l. R. Bird or lion r. or l. *Abr. 66, M. p. 499, 501*   135   550

812 mules of Series R and Q   812 Q/R mule

812   **Series R and Q** MULES, Type 73. Crude radiate bust r. or l. blundered runes.
R. Quadruped or bird r. *M. 388, M.p.496-8 & 518,* vars. R/Q and Q/R mules.
Abr. 12, 67,...   90   350

813 (R1)   813 (R3)   813 (R4)

813   **Series R**. Varieties R1-R6, bust r. on pyramidal neck. Epa in runes, sometimes
retrograde. R. Standard, various angular symbols in and around. *Abr. 11,*
M. 391-428, M. p. 507-14   45   135

813A: Series R7, Spi   813A: Series R10, Wigræd   813A: Series R11, Tilbeorht

813A   —, varieties R7-R12, Head r. or l. with no neck. Spi, Wigræd or Tilbeorht in
runes r. or l. R. Standard with angular symbols. *Abr. 11, M. 391-428,*
M. p. 514-23   50   175

814   815

		F £	VF £
814	**Series S**, Type 47. Female centaur 1. Palm fronds either side, tail beaded or linear, with or without finial. R. Whorl of 4 wolf heads, beaded tongues meet in centre. *Abr. 68, M. 438-41, M. p. 537-44*	100	375
815	**Series T**, Type 9. Diademed bust r., +LEL or + TΛNVM. R. Degenerate 'porcupine' head l or r. *Abr. 25, M. 442-4, M. p. 545-51*	110	450

816 varieties

| 816 | **Series U**, Type 23. Standing figure facing or profile in crescent boat holding two crosses. R. Pecking bird in vine. *Abr. 45, M. 445-52, M. p. 552-569.* | 110 | 450 |

817

| 817 | **Series V**, Type 7. Wolf and twins. R. Bird in stalks of wheat. *Abr. 62, M. 453, M. p. 570-5.* | 175 | 675 |

E. ECLECTIC SCEATTAS, *c*. 710 – *c*. 760

Included here are groups of types, related often by a common reverse motif (Triquetras, Celtic cross, interlace, saltire, annulet cross groups and Type 70) that do not easily fit into the main alphabetical classification, even though there may be some features in common with or derived from the types therein. There are numerous 'mules' in this coinage, typically imitative combinations of known obverse and reverse types. Only a few of these are included.

820: C ARIP group, some varieties

| 820 | **'Carip' group.** Bust r., CARIP, often blundered. R. include pecking bird, wolf-serpent, or standing figure. *Abr. 26, M. 336-40, M. p. 416-21* | 135 | 525 |

821: Triquetras group

	F	VF
	£	£

821 **'Triquetras' group**. Man and crosses, winged figure, facing bust, or pecking
bird. R. Interlaced cross with triquetra terminals, rosettes or pellets between.
Abr. 110, M. p. 422-5. 135   525

822: Celtic cross group, some obverse varieties

822: Celtic cross group, some reverse varieties

822 **'Celtic Cross' group**. Bust r. or l. with or without legend, cross or sprig
(34a(828A)) before; one or two standing figure(s) with long crosses, cross in
torc, wolf-worm or pecking bird. R. Celtic cross, void or with superimposed
pellet cross or cross pattée, rosettes in angles. *Abr. 27-31, M. p. 426-32.*   125   475

823: Rosette type, various styles

823 **'Rosette'**, Type 68, Series L-related. Bust r., one or two rosettes in field. R.
Standing figure usually with two crosses. *Abr. 32.30-50, M. 347, M. p. 433-4*   135   525

823A

823A — Type 32b. Bust l. rosettes in field. R. Wolf-serpent within torc. *Abr. 32.10-20,*
M. 307-8, M. p. 433-4 160   625

824:Monita Scorum type   824A

824 **'(Monita) Scorum' type**. Bust r., MONITA SCORVM. R. Degenerate 'porcupine'
head l., figure with two crosses, or triquetra cross. *Abr. 24, M. p. 435-6.*   300   1100
824A —. Bust r., DE LVNDONIA. R. porcupine l., SCORVM. *Abr. 24.50, 25.50,*
M. p. 436. 325   1250

826: Hen type

	F £	VF £

825　**'Archer' group**. Kneeling archer r. R. Large bird (swan?) on branch r. or l.,
looking back. *Abr. 50, M. 349, M. p. 437-9*..　375　1500

826　**'Hen' type**. Hen r. or l. R. Large bird (swan?) on branch r. or l. looking back
and biting berries. *Abr. 51*..　225　800

827: Victory group

827　**'Victory'** Type 22. Victory standing with wreath. R. Standing figure
holding two crosses, winged figure in crescent boat, or diademed bust.
Abr. 111, M. 350-1, M. p. 440-3..　175　650

828: K/N group

828　**K/N related group**. Standing figure with two long crosses. R. Monster of Type
41 r. or l. looking back. *Abr. 37, M. p. 445.*..　100　375

829: Animal mask group

829　**'Animal mask' group**. Facing animal (feline?) with erect ears. R. Standing
figure with bird and cross, bird with cross before, segmented circle or monster.
Abr. 112, M. 354-6 , M. p. 446-8..　250　950

830: K/R mule

830　**K/R mule**. Wolf worm curled r. or l. R. Standard with annulet cross or
central Annulet. *Abr. 42, M. p. 449*...　100　375

831: Type 43

831　— Type 43. Monster of Type 40, l. looking back. R. Interlace cross.
(See also S.795.) *Abr. 54-58, M. p. 482*...　200　725

832: Fledgling type   833: Saltire standard group, varieties

	F	VF
	£	£

832 **'Fledgling' type**. Type 33 wolf head r. R. Running fledgling with fish in mouth. Style degenerates to linear style. *Abr. 44* 250   900

833 **'Saltire Standard' types**. Two standing figures or bust l. or r.. R. Saltire and pellets in square. *Abr. 13.80-90, M. 432-5, M. p. 530-2* 90   275

833A: Saltire standard group,   833B: Saltire standard group,
geometric reverses   Type 70

833A 'Saltire Standard' geometric types. Double croix ancrée or annulet cross. R. Saltire and pellets in square. *Abr. 13.150, 14.110-120, M. 432-5, M. p. 530-2*   110   400

833B **Saltire-standard and geometric symbols**, Type 70. Many varieties, typically base. R. Standard. *Abr. 13.160-170, M. 436-7, M. p. 532-4* 40   130

834: Annulets group: some varieties

834 **'Annulet cross' types**. Bust r. or l. with runic legend, 'Wodan' face, coiled serpent or saltire cross. R. Annulet cross. *Abr. 14, M. p. 534-6* 100   375

835: 'Wodan' head varieties

835 **'Wodan' Head**, Type 30. Facing 'Wodan' head various styles some coarse. R. Two standing figures, standard or Series N, type 41 monster r. *Abr. 105, M. 429-31, M. p. 527-30* 150   575

836: Flying monster type

836 **'Flying Monster'**. Monster in flight r. or l., looking back, tail erect. R. Swan-like bird r. or l., looking back, alternate with groups of pellets on limbs of central cross fourchée. *Abr. 107* 125   475

KINGS OF NORTHUMBRIA AND ARCHBISHOPS OF YORK

The issues associated with pre-Viking Northumbria comprise the York group of gold Shillings c.630-80 (S.762-763), followed by silver sceattas which became increasingly debased after c.810 becoming a copper alloy coin referred to as a Styca. There are two special presentation issues, Eanred's broad Penny and Wigmund's gold *Solidus,* for neither of which is there yet evidence of monetary use within the kingdom.

The stycas developed in two phases, becoming a robust currency of small-denomination coins, which seem to have been of great practical use. Production may have ceased early in Osberht's reign, although the old money may have continued in circulation until the Viking capture of York in 867. The official styca coinage, however, does appear to have been overwhelmed by irregular issues, which may reflect a period of civil war during the years *c.* 843 to *c.* 855.

James Booth's classification of the silver Sceatta coinage of the eighth century is used here, with newly discovered types and variants added ('Sceattas in Northumbria' in Hill and Metcalf, *Sceattas in England and on the Continent, BAR* 128 (1984), pp.71-111, and 'Coinage and Northumbrian History: *c.790-c.810,* in D.M. Metcalf, *Coinage in ninth-century Northumbria, BAR* 180 (1987), pp.57-90).

For the styca coinage of the *ninth-century* Elizabeth Pirie provides an indispensable illustrated corpus of the known material in her *Coins of the Kingdom of Northumbria c.700-867,* 1996. Her classification is however over-complex for practical use, and several aspects of it, including her division of the coins of Aethelred II between his two reigns, have not been accepted by other scholars. The division here is that which is customarily adopted in volumes in the SCBI series. Moneyers' names are shown as they appear on the coinage.

Further reading: See SCBI 68, Lyon, C.S.S., *The Lyon Collection of Anglo-Saxon Coins* (2016). The introduction to this, sections 2 and 3, provides a useful up to date assessment of the Northumbrian Sceatta and Styca coinage along with illustrations of coins in the Lyon collection; Bude, R., *The joint coinage of Ecgberht and Eadberht of Northumbria,* in BNJ 86, 2016

SILVER SCEATTA COINAGE - A: REGAL ISSUES

846: Aldfrith

846   **Aldfrith** (685-705). ALðFRIDVS in semi-uncial lettering around central boss.
R. Lion(?) l. triple tail above. *Abr. 69*   325   1100

847 vars classes

847   **Eadberht** (737-758). Classes A-F. Small cross (mainly). R. Stylized stag, to
l. or r., various ornaments. *Abr. 70*   100   325

848

F	*VF*
£	£

848   **Aethelwald Moll** (759-765) ΛD+ELΛAΓDRE (A and R inverted) around
       central boss. R. His son ΛEDILRED+R (second R reversed), around central
       cross. *Abr. 77* ....   *Extremely rare*

849   850   851

849   **Alchred** (765-774). Small cross. R. Stylized stag to l. or r., cross below. *Abr. 71*.   275   900
850   **Aethelred I** (first reign, 774-779/80). R. Stylized stag to l. or r., triquetra
       below. *Abr. 72*..   400   1350
851   **Aelfwald I** (779/80-788). R. Stylized stag to l. or r., various ornaments,
       Abr. 73..   425   1500

SILVER SCEATTA COINAGE - B: JOINT ISSUES BY KINGS OF NORTHUMBRIA AND ARCHBISHOPS OF YORK

852   854   855

852   **Eadberht** with **Abp. Ecgberht** (737-758). Small cross. R. Mitred figure
       holding two crosses. *Abr.74*..   175   475
853   **Aethelwald Moll** with **Abp. Ecgberht** (759-765). Cross each side. *Abr.76*   1750   6500
854   **Alchred** with **Abp. Ecgberht** (765-766). Cross each side. *Abr. 74*.......   325   1100
855   **Aethelred I,** with **Abp. Eanbald I** (*c.* 779-780). Various motifs. *Abr. 78*   250   850

SILVER SCEATTA COINAGE - C: REGAL ISSUES WITH NAMED MONEYERS

856

856   **Aethelred I** (second reign, 789-796). R. CEOLBALD, CVDHEARD, HNIFVLA,
       TIDVVLF, central motifs vary. *Abr.80, 82-84*..   95   325

857   858

	F	VF
	£	£
857 – Base metal. R. 'Shrine', "CVDCLS" (the moneyer Cuthgils)	325	1000
858 **Eardwulf** (first reign, 796-806). R. Small cross, CVDHEARD	2000	7500

SPECIAL ISSUES

863A

861A **Eanred**, *c*. 830. Æ *penny*. Bust right. R. Cross, part moline part crosslet	5250	22500
863A **Abp. Wigmund** (837-849/50). Æ *solidus*. Facing bust. R. Cross in wreath	37500	165000

STYCA COINAGE - A: BASE SILVER REGAL ISSUES, *c*. 810 – *c*. 830

859

859 **Aelfwald II** (806-808). R. Small cross, CVDhEARD	375	1250

860

860 **Eanred** (810-841 (total reign)). R. CVDhEARD, CYNVVLF, DAEGBERCT, EADVINI,EDILECH, HERREÐ, [HEARDVVLF, correctly VVLFHEARD], HVAETRED, TIDVINI, VILHEAH, VVLFHEARD, various central motifs	35	110

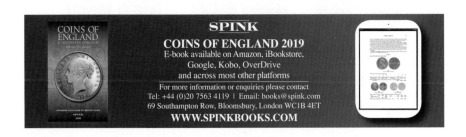

STYCA COINAGE - B: BASE SILVER ARCHIEPISCOPAL ISSUES, *c.* 830 – *c.* 867

861

		F £	VF £
861	**Abp. Eanbald II** (796-835 (total tenure)). R̃. EODWVLF or EDILWEARD	60	175

STYCA COINAGE - C: COPPER ALLOY REGAL ISSUES, *c.* 810 – *c.* 830

862

862	**Eanred.** R̃. ALDATES, BADIGILS, BROD(E)R, FORDRED, FVLCNOD, MONNE, ODILO, W(D)IHTRED, VVLFRED, various central motifs	25	75

865

865	**Aethelred II** (first reign, 841-843/4), R̃. ALGHERE, BRODER, COENRED, CVNEMVND, EANRED, FORDRED, HVNLAF, LEOFDEGN, MONNE, ODILO, VENDELBERHT, W(D)IHTRED, VVLFRED, VVLFSIG , various central motifs	20	70

866: varieties

866	– Leofdegn's 'Special' motifs, R̃. Hound 1., LEOFDEGN	475	1750

866A

866A	–various elaborate cruciform central devices, LEOFDEGN	100	375

867   868   869

867	**Redwulf** (843/4). R̃. ALGHERE, BROTHER, COENRED, CVDBEREhT, EANRED, FORDRED, HVAETNOD, MONNE	30	110
868	**Aethelred II** (second reign 843/4-849/50), R̃. EANVVLF, EARDVVLF, FORDRED, MONNE, ODILO, VVLFRED..	20	65
869	**Osberht** (849/50-867). R̃. EANVVLF, EDELHELM, MONNE, VINIBERHT, VVLFSIXT, VVLFRED	30	100

STYCA COINAGE - D: COPPER ALLOY ARCHIEPISCOPAL ISSUES, *c.* 830 – *c.* 867

870   871

		F £	VF £
870	**Abp. Wigmund** (837-849/50). Ɍ. COENRED, EDELHELM, EDILVEARD, HVNLAF..	20	70
871	**Abp. Wulfhere** (849/50-900). Ɍ. VVLFRED	60	200

STYCA COINAGE - E: IRREGULAR ISSUES IN COPPER ALLOY, *c.* 843/4 – *c.* 855

872	**Irregular Issues** (*c.*843/4-*c.*855). Various types; legends blundered.....	20	50

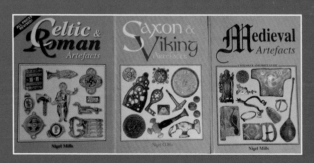

In the kingdom of the Franks a reformed coinage of good quality *deniers* struck on broad flans had been introduced by Pepin in 755 and continued by his son Charlemagne and his descendants. A new coinage of *pennies* of similar size and weighing about 20 grains (1.3 gms) was introduced into England, probably by Offa (757-96), the powerful king of Mercia, c.780, though early pennies also exist of two little known kings of Kent, Heaberht and Ecgberht, of about the same period.

The silver penny (*Lat.* 'denarius', hence the *d.* of our £ *s. d.*) remained virtually the sole denomination of English coinage for almost five centuries, with the rare exception of occasional gold coins and somewhat less rare silver halfpence. The penny reached a weight of 24 grains (c.1.55g), i.e., a 'pennyweight' during the reign of Alfred the Great. Silver pennies of this period normally bear the ruler's name, though not always his portrait, and the name of the moneyer responsible for their manufacture.

Pennies were issued by various rulers of the Heptarchy for the kingdoms of Kent, Mercia, East Anglia, Wessex and by the Danish settlers in the Danelaw and the Hiberno-Norse kings of York, and also by the Archbishops of Canterbury and a Bishop of London. Under Eadgar, who became the sole ruler of England, a uniform coinage was instituted throughout the country, and it was he who set the pattern for the 'reformed' coinage of the later Anglo-Saxon and Norman period.

Halfpence were issued by most rulers from the time of Alfred until the reform of Eadgar, c.871-973 for southern England, and although all are rare today, it is probable that reasonable quantities were made.

Nos. 873-1378 are all silver pennies except where stated.

NB. Many pennies of the early part of this period have chipped flans and prices should be reduced accordingly.

Further Reading: R. Naismith, *The Coinage of Southern England 796-865*, 2011; C.E. Blunt, B.H.I.H. Stewart & C.S.S. Lyon, *Coinage in Tenth-century England: From Edward the Elder to Edgar's Reform*, 1989.

KINGS OF KENT

874   875

876   877

		F	VF
		£	£
873	**Heaberht** (*c.* 765). Monogram for REX. R. Five annulets, each containing a pellet, joined to form a cross	7500	32500
874	**Ecgberht** (*c.* 780). Similar. R. Varied	1250	5500
875	**Eadberht Praen.** Type 1. (796-798). As illustration. R. Varied	1200	5250
875A	— Type 2. (*c.* 798). His name around, Ⓜ in centre, R. Moneyer's name in angles of a tribrach	1250	5500
876	**Cuthred** (798-807). *Canterbury*. Various types without portrait	750	2750
877	— — Portrait. R. Cross and wedges or A	975	4000

878

880 881

		F £	VF £
878	**Anonymous** (*c*. 822-823). *Canterbury*. As illustration or 'Baldred' style head	975	4000
879	**Baldred** (*c*. 823-825). *Canterbury*. diademed head r. R. DRVR CITS within inner circle	1250	5250
880	— Cross each side	800	3250
881	*Rochester*. Bust r. R. Cross moline or wheel design	1250	5250

ARCHBISHOPS OF CANTERBURY

882

881A	**Jaenberht** (765-792). New type (early). Under Ecgberht II of Kent (?). (before *c*. 780 ?) His name around small cross of pellets in centre. R. PONTIFEX in three lines	1350	5750
882	Under Offa of Mercia (*c*. 780-792) His name around central ornament or cross and wedges. R. OFFA REX in two lines	950	4000
883	— His name in three lines. R. OFFA or OFFA REX between the limbs of Celtic cross	975	4250
884	**Aethelheard** (el. 792, cons. 793, d. 805). With Offa as overlord. First issue (792-?), with title *Pontifex*...	900	3750

885 886

885	— Second issue (?-796), with title *Archiepiscopus*	800	3250
885A	— Third issue (*c*. 796-798), with title *Archiepiscopus*. His name and AR around EP in centre. R. Moneyer's name, EADGAR or CIOLHARD.....	900	3750
886	— With Coenwulf as overlord. (798-800 ?) Fourth Issue. As last. R. King's name in the angles of a tribrach	850	3500

886A   887   888 (rev.)

		F	VF
		£	£
886A	— Fifth issue (*c*. 798-805?). As last R. Coenwulf's name around Ⓜ in centre	675	2750
887	**Wulfred** (805-832). group I (805-*c*. 810). As illustration. R. Crosslet, alpha-omega........................	800	3500
888	— Group II (*c*. 810). As last. R. DOROVERNIA C monogram	750	3250
889	— Group III (pre- 823). Bust extends to edge of coin. R. As last	725	3000
890	— Groups IV and V (*c*. 822-823). Anonymous under Ecgberht. Moneyer's name in place of the Archbishop's. R. DOROBERNIA CIVITAS in three or five lines	750	3250
891	— Group VI (*c*. 823-825). Baldred type. Crude portrait. R. DRVR CITS in two lines......................	1100	5000
892	— Group VII (*c*. 832). Second monogram (Ecgberht) type. Crude portrait r., PLFRED. R. DORIB C. Monogram as 1035	900	4000

893   894

895   896

893	**Ceolnoth** (833-870). Group I with name CIALNOD. Tonsured bust facing. R. Varied	675	2750
894	— Group II. Similar but CEOLNOD. R. inscribed cross........................	725	3000
895	— Group III. Diad. bust r. R. Moneyer's name in and between lunettes .	1000	4750

898   900

896	**Aethelred** (870-889). Bust r. R. As illustration or with long cross with lozenge panel	2750	13500
897	— Cross pattée. R. ELF / STAN................	1350	5750
898	**Plegmund** (890-914). DORO in circle. R. As illustration above, various moneyers..........................	900	3500
899	— Similar, but title EPISC, and XDF in centre.....................................	900	3500
900	— Small cross pattée. R. moneyers name in two lines............................	675	2750

		F £	VF £
901	— Crosses moline and pommée on *obv.*	900	4000
901A	— Halfpenny. As 900	1250	5250

KINGS OF MERCIA

Until 825 Canterbury was the principal mint of the Kings of Mercia and some moneyers also struck coins for the Kings of Kent and Archbishops of Canterbury.

GOLD

902   903

902	**Offa** (757-796). Gold *dinar*. Copy of Arabic dinar of Caliph Al Mansur, dated 157 A.H. (A.D. 774), with OFFA REX added on *rev.*	135000	675000
903	Gold *penny*. Bust r., moneyer's name. R. Standing figure, moneyer's name	37500	200000

A copy of a solidus with a diademed bust appears to read CIOLHEARD and is probably Mercian of this or the following reign.
For further information see: *The Coinage of Offa and his Contemporaries* by Derek Chick, 2010.

SILVER

904   905

904	**Offa** (757-796). Light Coinage. (*c.* 780?-792) *London and Canterbury.* Various types without portraits. Small flans	525	1650
905	— (*c.* 780?-792) *London and Canterbury.* Various types with portraits. Small flans.	825	3500

906   908

906	— East Anglia. Various types with portraits. R. Some with runic letters, small flans	850	4000
907	— — Various types without portraits. R. often with runic letters, small flans	575	2000
908	Heavy Coinage (*c.* 792-796) *London, Canterbury and East Anglia.* Various types without portraits, large flans.	550	1850

909   911

		F	VF
		£	£
909	**Cynethryth** (wife of Offa). Coins as light coinage of Offa.With bust as illustration..	2250	8500
910	— O. without bust, as rev. of last, R, moneyers name on cross of lobes, usually EOBA...	1350	5750
911	**Eadberht** (Bishop of London, died 787/789). EADBERHT EP in three lines or ADBERHT in two lines within a beaded rectangle, EP below. R. various with name of Offa	950	4500

912   912A

912	**Coenwulf, King of Mercia** (796-821). Gold *penny* or *Mancus* of 30 pence. London, diademed bust of Coenwulf right, finely drawn with four horizontal lines on the shoulders	45000	225000
912A	Penny Group I (796-805). *London*. Without portrait, three line inscription. R. Varied	575	2000
913	— *Canterbury*. Name around Ⓜ as illus. below. R. Moneyer's name in two lines	675	2500

914   915

| 914 | — *Both mints*. Tribrach type.. | 375 | 1350 |
| 915 | — Group II (*c.* 805-810). *Canterbury*. With portrait. Small flans. R. Varied but usually cross and wedges.. | 700 | 2750 |

916   919

916	— Groups III and IV (*c.* 810-820). *Canterbury*. Similar but larger flans. R. Varied	700	2750
917	— *Rochester*. Large diad. bust of coarse style. R. Varied. (Moneyers: Dun, Ealhstan)	750	3000
918	— *London*. With portrait generally of Roman style. R. Crosslet	750	3000
919	— *E. Anglia*. Crude diad. bust r. R. Moneyer's name LVL on leaves in arms of cross	650	2500
920	— — *O.* as last. R. Various types	625	2400

921   927

		F	VF
		£	£
921	**Ceolwulf I** (821-823). *Canterbury.* Group I. Bust r. ℞. Varied. (Moneyers: Oba, Sigestef)	1350	5500
922	— — Group II. *London.* Crosslet. ℞. Varied	950	4000
923	— — Group III. Tall cross with MERCIORV̄. ℞. Crosslet. SIGESTEF DOROBERNIA	975	4500
924	— *Rochester.* Group I. Bust r. ℞. Varied	1000	4750
925	— — Group IIA. As last but head r.	1000	4750
926	— — Group IIB. Ecclesiastical issue by Bp. of Rochester. With mint name, DOROBREBIA, but no moneyer	1250	5500
927	— *East Anglia.* Crude style and lettering with coarse portrait. ℞. Varied	950	4500

928   929

928	**Beornwulf** (823-825). Group I. *East Anglia.* Bust r. ℞. Moneyer's name in three lines	1350	5750
929	— Group II. *East Anglia* or *London.* ℞. Cross crosslet in centre	1250	5250
930	Group III. *East Anglia.* Similar to 928 but moneyer's name in two lines with crosses between	1200	5500
931	**Ludica** (825-827). Bust r. ℞. Moneyer's name in three lines as 928	5250	22500

932   933

932	— Similar. ℞. Moneyer's name around cross crosslet in centre, as 929 ..	5750	25000
933	**Wiglaf,** first reign (827-829). *London.* Crude head r. ℞. Crosslet	3500	13500

934   935

		F	VF
		£	£
934	Second reign (830-840). *London*. Cross and pellets, or ⋔ R. Moneyer's name in three lines or between lunettes of pellets	2250	8000
935	**Berhtwulf** (840-852). Various types with bust	1500	6750
936	— without bust	1250	5250
937	As before. R. IAETHELWLF REX. cross pommée over cross pattée (crude die copying on obverse of Aethelwulf of Wessex)	1100	4500

938 (rev. A)   939A   939B

938	**Burgred (852-874)** Ia, 852-c.855, bust r, looks up, almond eye, r. A (MacKay P1)	675	1750
939A	Ib, c.855-c.858-60, bust r, coarse style, annulet or almond eye, two panel or triangular tunic, r. A, C, D, (MacKay P2, P4)	500	1200
939B	— — bust r, pellet in almond eye, low shoulders, high neck r. A, C (MacKay P3)	600	1500

940A (rev. D)   940B (rev. C)   940C

940A	IIa, c.858/60-c.866, bust r, almond eye, neat bust, lips sometimes omitted, r. A, C, D (MacKay H1, H2)	350	1000
940B	— —, bust r, as Aethelberht of Wessex Floreate type (S.1054), often six pellets below neck, some coarse r. C (MacKay H3-H4: coarse,H5)	700	1600
940C	— —, bust r, coarse style, large annulet eye, outward wedge lips, r. A, C, D (MacKay V1)	600	1500

941A 941B

	F £	VF £

941A IIb, c.866-868/70, bust r, various styles incl. with large annulet eye, ill-
proportioned bust, realistic pointed nose narrow tunic, r. A, C, D (MacKay H6-8)   275   750

941B — —, bust r, outward or upward wedge lips, steeply angled diadem, various
styles, incl. with wide tunic, double inner-circle, narrow diameter i.c, r. D
(MacKay V2-4)   300   800

942A 942B 942C

942A III, c.868/70-874, bust r, pellet eye, diadem cuts across eye, r. A, D (MacKay H10)   250   700

942B — —, bust r, crescent below pellet eye, r. A, D (MacKay H11)...............   250   700

942C — —, bust r, pellet eye, small crescent above and below, r. A, often with six
pellets in one angle (MacKay H12)   225   650

942D (rev. B)

942D — —, bust r, rather crude, steeply pitched diadem, outward or upward wedge
lips, r. A (MacKay V5)   220   600

*Reverse types most commonly found are listed above; type A, closed lunettes (commonly found);
B, open at base and top (very rare); C, open at sides (rare); D, 'crooks' without lunettes semi-
circles (scarce); E, as D with large M symbol added above and below dividing legend (very rare).*
    Prices for Lunettes types can vary with rare types worth more than commoner types.

		F	VF
Lunette A	....*from*	250	600
Lunette B	....*from*	600	2000
Lunette C	....*from*	400	1000
Lunette D	....*from*	300	800
Lunette E	....*from*	900	3000

For further reading see; *MacKay, The Coinage of Burgred 852-874, BNJ 85, 2015, pp 101-237.*

F	*VF*
£	£

943   **Ceolwulf II** (874-*c.* 880). Bust r. ℞. Two emperors seated. Victory above   6750   30000

944

944   — ℞. Moneyer's name in angles of long cross with lozenge centre   1750   7500
944A — Halfpenny, similar to 944   4000   12000

KINGS OF EAST ANGLIA

945   947

945   **Beonna,** King of East Anglia, *c.* 758. Æ sceat. Pellet in centre, Runic
      inscription. ℞. EFE in Roman characters around saltire cross. *Abr.113.10*   825   3250
945A — Similar. ℞. WILRED or WERFERTH in runic around pellet or cross.
      Abr. 113.20-30...   850   3500
945B — Similar. ℞. Interlace pattern (large flans). *Abr.113.40*   1750   7500
945C **Alberht** (749-?). Pellet in centre, AETHELBERT (runic) around ℞.
      Rosette in circle, TIAELRED (runic) around. *Abr. 114*...........................   3500   15000
946   **Aethelberht** (d. 794). bust r. ℞. wolf and twins.......................................   8500   35000
946A — King's name EDILBERHT around cross and pellets. ℞. Lozenge intersecting
      large cross fourchée, LVL in angles...   4500   17500
947   **Eadwald** (*c.* 798). King's name in three lines. ℞. Moneyer's name in
      quatrefoil, around cross or tribrach...   900   3750
947A — King's name around cross or Ꝋ in centre. ℞. Moneyer's name in quartrefoil   975   4500

949   950 (obv,)   951

948   **Aethelstan I** (*c.* 825-840). Bust r. or l. ℞. Crosslet or star   1350   5750
949   Bust r. ℞. Moneyer's name in three or four lines....................................   1350   5750
950   Alpha or A. ℞. Varied...   500   1750
951   *O.* and *rev.* Cross with or without wedges or pellets in angles.................   500   1750
952   — Similar, with king's name both sides..   575   2000
952A Name around ship in centre. ℞. Moneyer Eadgar, around cross of pellets
      or in two lines (Possibly the earliest of his coins.)   5750   25000

953 954

<table>
</table>

		F	VF
		£	£
953	**Aethelweard** (c. 840-c. 855), A, Omega or cross and crescents. R. Cross with pellets or wedges	950	3500
954	**Edmund** (855-870). Alpha or A. R. Cross with pellets or wedges	425	1350
955	— O. Varied. R. Similar...	425	1350

For the St. Edmund coins and the Danish issues struck in East Anglia bearing the name of Aethelred I, see Danish East Anglia.

ANGLO-VIKING COINAGES c. 885-954

DANISH EAST ANGLIA, c. 885-915

Following the treaty of Wedmore in 880 the Viking invaders were ceded control of Eastern Mercia including all territory east of Watling street. Coinage issued in this area after 880 initially imitated Wessex types of Alfred. Independent coinages were struck from early 880s in East Anglia, the east midlands and Northumbria.

956	**Aethelstan II** Guthrum (878-890), Cross pattée. R. Moneyer's name in two lines...	1750	7500
957	**Oswald** (unknown except from his coins). Alpha or A. R. Cross pattée..	2250	9500
958	— Copy of Carolingian 'temple' type. R Cross and pellets	2500	10000
959	**Aethelred** (c.870). As last, with name Aethelred. R. As last, or cross-crosslet	1750	7500
959A	— As 954	1500	6500

Oswald and Aethelred, both unattested historically, are thought to be East Anglian kings in the period after the death of Eadmund in 870 before Guthrum took control of the East Anglia c.880.

960 962

960	**St. Edmund,** memorial coinage, Æ *penny,* type as illus. above, various legends of good style	175	425
961	— Similar, but barbarous or semi-barbarous legends............................	165	400
962	*Halfpenny.* Similar...	575	2000
963	**St. Martin of Lincoln.** Sword dividing legend. R. Cross in voided cross. LINCOI A CIVIT.	3500	13500

SOUTHERN DANELAW *c.* **880-910**

965   970

		F £	VF £
964	**Alfred.** Imitation of London Monogram types- see 1061, 1062, some very barbarous, bust usually right, R. *Londonia* monogram (wt. c.1.2-1.4g) ..	2000	7500
964A	— Similar, crude bust, blundered legends, R. *Lincolla, ?Roiseng* monogram	3500	13500
965	— Similar to 1062, with moneyer's name (Aelfstan, Heawulf, Herewulf, Heremod, Winurdal)	3000	12500
966	— Imitation of two line types (1066, 1069), small cross, R. some read REX DORO	475	1350
967	— Similar. R. 'St. Edmund type' A in centre..............................	750	3500
968	— Imitation of Two Emperors type, as 943 and 964	3750	15000
969	*Halfpenny.* Imitation of London Monogram types - see 1063..................	950	3750
970	— Imitation of two line types	675	2750

971   975

971	— Imitation of Oxford type, as 1071A, ELFRED between ORSNA and FORDA, R. Moneyer's name in two lines (sometimes divided by horizontal long cross)	675	2250
972	— *Halfpenny.* Similar, of very crude appearance	675	2750
973	**Alfred/Archbishop Plegmund.** *Obv.* ELFRED REX PLEGN	1350	5750
974	**Archbishop Plegmund.** Imitative of two line type, as 900	725	2750
975	**Earl Sihtric.** Type as 971. SCELDFOR between GVNDI BERTVS. R SITRIC COMES in two lines	4500	17500

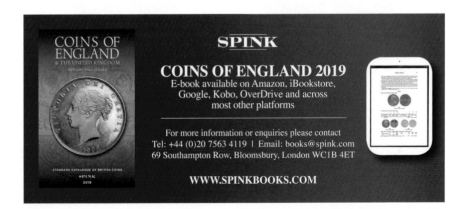

COINAGES OF THE VIKING KINGDOM OF YORK, *c.* 895-920

References are to 'The Classification of Northumbrian Viking Coins in the Cuerdale hoard', by C. S. S. Lyon and B. H. I. H. Stewart, in Numismatic Chronicle, 1964, p. 281 ff.

		F	VF
		£	£
975A	**Guthfrith.** GV DE F. RE Small cross. R̸. Moneyer's name in two lines.	3500	13500
976	**Siefred.** C. SIEFRE DIIS REX in two lines. R̸. EBRAICE CIVITAS (or contractions), small cross. *L. & S. Ia, Ie, Ii*	550	2250
977	— Cross on steps between. R̸. As last. *L. & S. If, Ij*	700	2750
978	— Long cross. R̸. As last. *L. & S. Ik*	550	2250

979

980 984

979	SIEFREDVS REX, cross crosslet within legend. R̸. As last. *L. & S. Ih...*	475	1850
980	SIEVERT REX, cross crosslet to edge of coin. R̸. As last. *L. & S. Ic, Ig, Im*	450	1750
981	— Cross on steps between. R̸. As last. *L. & S. Il*	600	2500
982	— Patriarchal cross. R̸. DNS DS REX, small cross. *L. & S. Va*	450	1750
983	— — R̸. MIRABILIA FECIT, small cross. *L. & S. VIb*	575	2250
984	REX, at ends of cross crosslet. R̸. SIEFREDVS, small cross. *L. & S. IIIa, b*	475	1850
985	— Long cross. R̸. As last. *L. & S. IIIc*	450	1750
986	*Halfpenny.* Types as 977, *L. & S. Ib;* 980, *Ic;* and 983, *VIb*	750	2750
987	**Cnut.** CNVT REX, cross crosslet to edge of coin. R̸. EBRAICE CIVITAS, small cross. *L. & S. Io, Iq*	425	1650
988	— — R̸. CVNNETTI, small cross. *L. & S. IIc*	375	1350

989 993

989	— Long cross. R̸. EBRAICE CIVITAS, small cross. *L. & S. Id, In, Ir....*	225	750
990	— — R̸. CVNNETTI, small cross. *L. & S. IIa, IId*	190	475
991	— Patriarchal cross. R̸. EBRAICE CIVITAS, small cross. *L. & S. Ip, Is*	185	450
992	— — R̸.— *Karolus* monogram in centre. *L. & S . It*	900	3250
993	— — R̸. CVNNETTI, small cross. *L. & S. IIb, IIe*	180	425

995   998

		F	VF
		£	£
994	*Halfpenny.* Types as 987, *L. & S. Iq; 989, Id; 991, Is; 992, Iu; 993, IIb and e*	650	2000
995	As 992, but CVNNETTI around *Karolus* monogram. *L. & S. IIf*	675	2250
996	**Cnut and/or Siefred.** CNVT REX, patriarchal cross. R. SIEFREDVS, small cross. *L. & S. IIId*	475	1850
997	— — R. DNS DS REX, small cross. *L. & S. Vc.*	450	1750

1000   1002

998	— — R. MIRABILIA FECIT. *L. & S. VId*	325	900
999	EBRAICE C, patriarchal cross. R. DNS DS REX, small cross. *L. & S. Vb*	450	1500
1000	— — R. MIRABILIA FECIT. *L. & S. VIc*	325	900
1001	DNS DS REX in two lines. R. ALVALDVS, small cross. *L. & S. IVa*	1350	5750
1002	DNS DS O REX, similar. R. MIRABILIA FECIT. *L. & S. VIa*	525	1850
1003	*Halfpenny.* As last. *L. & S. VIa*	750	2250

1004   1006

1004	**'Cnut'.** Name blundered around cross pattée with extended limbs. R. QVENTOVICI around small cross. *L. & S. VII*	950	3750
1005	*Halfpenny.* Similar. *L. & S. VII*	900	3000
1006	**St. Peter coinage,** *c.* 905-915. Swordless type. Early issues. SCI PETRI MO in two lines. R. Cross pattée	350	1100
1007	— similar. R. 'Karolus' monogram	950	3750
1008	*Halfpenny.* Similar. R. Cross pattée	750	2500

1009

		F £	VF £

1009 **Regnald** (blundered types). RAIENALT, head to l. or r. R. EARICE CT,
'Karolus' monogram 3500 15000

1010

1010 — Open hand. R. Similar 1750 7500
1011 — Hammer. R. Bow and arrow 2250 9500
1012 Anonymous R. Sword.. 1350 5750

ENGLISH COINS OF THE HIBERNO-NORSE VIKINGS OF YORK c. 919-954

1015   1016

EARLY PERIOD, c. 919-925

1013 **Sihtric** (921-927). SITRIC REX, sword. R. cross, hammer, mallet or T (Lincoln) 2750 10500
1014 **St. Peter coinage.** Sword type. Late issues SCI PETRI MO, sword and
hammer. R. EBORACEI, cross and pellets 900 3500
1015 — Similar. R. Voided hammer... 1050 4000
1016 — Similar. R. Solid hammer.. 1250 4500
St. Peter coins with blundered legends are rather cheaper.

LATER PERIOD, 939-954 (after the battle of Brunanburh, 937). Mostly struck at York.

1017 **Anlaf Guthfrithsson,** 939-941. Flower type. Small cross, ANLAF REX
TO D. R. Flower above moneyer's name 4500 17500
1018 — Circumscription type, with small cross each side, ANLAF CVNVNC,
M in field on reverse *(Derby)* 2250 10500
1018A — Two line type. ONLAF REX. Large letter both sides *(Lincoln?)*........ 2000 9500

1019   1020

	F	*VF*
	£	£

1019 — Raven type. As illustration, ANLAF CVNVNC.................................. 1750 7250
1020 **Anlaf Sihtricsson,** first reign, 941-944. Triquetra type, ANLAF CVNVNC.
      R̃. Danish standard.. 1650 6750

1021   1022

1021 — Circumscription type (a). Small cross each side, ANLAF CVNVNC,
      R̃. MONETR.. 1700 7250
1022 — Cross moline type, ANLAF CVNVN C. R̃. Small cross..................... 1750 7500

1024

1023 — Two line type. Small cross. R̃. ONLAF REX. R̃. Name in two lines.. 1750 7500
1024 **Regnald Guthfrithsson,** 943-944. Triquetra type. As 1020. REGNALD
      CVNVNC 4250 16500
1025 — Cross moline type. As 1022, but REGNALD CVNVNC.................... 3750 15000
1026 **Sihtric Sihtricsson,** *c.* 942. Triquetra type. As 1020, SITRIC CVNVNC 2250 10500
1027 — Circumscription type. Small cross each side 2250 10500

1027A

1027A **Anonymous?** Two line type. Small cross ELTANGERHT. R̃.
      RERNART in two lines 1100 4000
1028 **Eric Blood-Axe,** first reign, 948. Two line type. Small cross, ERICVC REX
      A; ERIC REX AL; or ERIC REX EFOR. R̃. Name in two lines 6750 27500

F	VF
£	£

1029 **Anlaf Sihtricsson,** second reign, 948-952. Circumscription type (b). Small
cross each side, ONLAF REX, R. MONE.. 1650 7000
1029A — Flower type. small cross ANLAF REX R. Flower above moneyer's
name... 2500 12500
1029B — Two line type. Small cross, ONLAF REX. R. Moneyer's name in
two lines.. 1750 8000

1030
1030 **Eric Blood-Axe,** second reign, 952-954. Sword type. ERIC REX in two
lines, sword between. R. Small cross 9500 45000

For more on the Anglo-Viking Coinages - see Blackburn M.A.S., *Viking Coinage in the British Isles
(Spink 2011)*

KINGS OF WESSEX, 786-924

BEORHTRIC, 786-802
Beorhtric was dependent on Offa of Mercia and married a daughter of Offa.

1031
1031 As illustration.. 6750 30000
1032 Alpha and omega in centre. R. Omega in centre 6500 27500

ECGBERHT, 802-839
King of Wessex only, 802-825; then also of Kent, Sussex, Surrey, Essex and East Anglia, 825-839,
and of Mercia also, 829-830.

1035
1033 *Canterbury.* Group I. Diad. hd. r. within inner circle. R. Various............. 1250 5250
1034 — II. Non-portrait types. R. Various 900   3750
1035 — III. Bust r. breaking inner circle. R. DORIB C.................................... 1100 4500
1036 *London.* Cross potent. R. LVN / DONIA / CIVIT.................................. 1500 6500
1037 — — R. REDMVND MONE around TA.. 1100 4500

1041

		F	VF
		£	£
1038	*Rochester,* royal mint. Non-portrait types with king's name ECGBEO RHT	900	3750
1039	— — Portrait types, ECGBEORHT..	1200	4750
1040	*Rochester,* bishop's mint. Bust r. R. SCS ANDREAS (APOSTOLVS)....	1350	5750
1041	*Winchester.* SAXON monogram or SAXONIORVM in three lines. R. Cross	1100	4500

AETHELWULF, 839-858

Son of Ecgberht; sub-King of Essex, Kent, Surrey and Sussex, 825-839; King of all southern England, 839-855; King of Essex, Kent and Sussex only, 855-858. No coins are known of his son Aethelbald who ruled over Wessex proper, 855-860.

1043   1045

1047

1042	*Canterbury.* Phase I (839-c. 843). Head within inner circle. R. Various. *Br. 3*	750	3000
1043	— — Larger bust breaking inner circle. R. A. *Br. 1 and 2*	800	3250
1044	— — Cross and wedges. R. SAXONIORVM in three lines in centre. *Br. 10*	625	2500
1045	— — Similar, but OCCIDENTALIVM in place of moneyer. *Br. 11*	675	2750
1046	— Phase II (*c.* 843-848?). Cross and wedges. R. Various, but chiefly a form of cross or a large A. *Br. 4*	575	2250
1047	— — New portrait, somewhat as 1043. R. As last. *Br. 7*	750	3250
1048	— — Smaller portrait. R. As last, with *Chi/Rho* monogram. *Br. 7*	800	3250

1049

1051

	F	VF
	£	£
1049 — Phase III (*c.* 848/851-*c.* 855). DORIB in centre. R. CANT mon. *Br. 5*	525	1850
1050 — — CANT mon. R. CAN M in angles of cross. *Br. 6*	700	2750
1051 — Phase IV (*c.* 855-859). Mostly Canterbury rarely Rochester. New neat		
style bust R. Large voided long cross. *Br. 8*	700	2750
1052 *Winchester.* SAXON mon. R. Cross and wedges. *Br. 9*	750	3000

AETHELBERHT, 858-865

Son of Aethelwulf; sub-King of Kent, Essex and Sussex, 858-860; King of all southern England, 860-865/6.

1053   1053A (rev.)

1053 Bust r., R large voided long cross. Mostly Canterbury, also known for		
Rochester	700	2750
1053A*O.* As 1053, R large cross pattée	1500	6500

1054

1054 *O.* Diad. bust r., R. Cross fleury over floreate cross	1100	4500

Son of Aethelwulf; succeeded his brother Aethelberht.

1055

			F	*VF*
			£	£
1055	As illustration, Wessex Lunettes, Canterbury, usually with bonnet ...		850	3500
1055A	— —, London obv. dies in style as Burgred		975	4000
1056	Similar, but moneyer's name in four lines, Canterbury or Winchester		1250	5000

For another coin with the name Aethelred see 959 under Viking coinages.
For further reading see: *Lyons & MacKay,* BNJ 2007

ALFRED THE GREAT, 871-899

Brother and successor to Aethelred, Alfred had to contend with invading Danish armies for much
of his reign. In 878 he and Guthrum the Dane divided the country, with Alfred holding all England
south and west of Watling Street. Alfred asserted over-lordship of Mercia and London from c.880.

Types with portraits

1057   1058

1057	As illustration, Wessex Lunettes, Canterbury, bust with bonnet. r. R. As			
	Aethelred I. *Br. 1 (name often* AELBRED)		900	3250
1057A	— —, London obv. dies in style as Burgred		950	3500
1058	— R. Long cross with lozenge centre, as 944, *Br. 5*		2250	9500
1059	— R. Two seated figures, as 943. *Br. 2*		8500	35000
1060	— R. As Archbp. Aethered; cross within large quatrefoil. *Br. 3*		3750	1500

1061   1062   1063

1061	*London.* Various busts. R. LONDONIA monogram, moneyer not named		3500	12500
	For contemporary Viking copies see 964.			
1062	— R. Similar, but with moneyer's name (Tilewine) added		3750	13500
1063	— *Halfpenny.* Bust r. or rarely l. R. LONDONIA monogram as 1061		975	4000
1064	*Gloucester.* R. Æ GLEAPA in angles of three limbed cross		6500	27500

<table>
<tr><td></td><td>F
£</td><td>VF
£</td></tr>
</table>

Types without portraits

1065 King's name on limbs of cross, trefoils in angles. ℞. Moneyer's name in
quatrefoil. *Br. 4.* 3500 13500

1066   1067

1066 Various styles, Cross pattée, legend in four parts. ℞. Moneyer's name in
two lines. *Br. 6* 475 1650
1067 — As last, legend in three parts. ℞ as Edward the Elder, 1087 .... 525 1750
1068 — *Halfpenny.* As 1066 .... 675 2750

1069

1069 *Canterbury.* As last but DORO added on *obv. Br. 6a* 550 1850
1070 *Exeter?* King name in four lines. ℞. EXA vertical 4750 18500
1071 *Winchester?* Similar to last, but PIN 4750 18500
1071A *Oxford.* Elfred between OHSNA and FORDA. ℞. Moneyer's name in
two lines (much commoner as a Viking Imitation - see 971) 925 3750
1072 'Offering penny'. Very large and heavy. AELFRED REX SAXORVM in
four lines. ℞. ELIMO in two lines i.e. (*Elimosina,* alms) 13500 47500

For other pieces bearing the name of Alfred see under the Viking coinages.
For further reading see: *Lyons & MacKay, The Lunettes Coinage of Alfred the Great* BNJ 2008.

EDWARD THE ELDER, 899-924

Edward, the son of Alfred, aided by his sister Aethelflaed 'Lady of the Mericians', annexed all
England south of the Humber and built many new fortified boroughs to protect the kingdom.
Rare types

1074

1073 *Br. 1. Bath?* ℞. BA 2250 9500
1074 — 2. *Canterbury.* Cross moline on cross pommée. ℞. Moneyer's name . 1350 6000

	F	VF
	£	£
1075 — 3. *Chester?* Small cross. R. Minster	3750	16500
1076 — 4. — Small cross. R. Moneyer's name in single line	1350	4500
1077 — 5. — R. Two stars	1850	9000

1078

1079

| 1078 — 6. — R. Flower above central line, name below .... | 2250 | 10500 |

1081

1083

1079 — 7. — R. Floral design with name across field	2250	10500
1080 — 8. — R. Bird holding twig	3750	17500
1081 — 9. — R. Hand of Providence, several varieties	3250	16000
1082 — 10. — R. City gate of Roman style	1850	9000
1083 — 11. — R. Anglo-Saxon burg	1650	7500

Ordinary types

1084

1087

1084 *Br. 12*. Bust l, var. styles R. Moneyer's name in two lines	800	3000
1086 — *12a*. Similar, but bust r. of crude style	1100	4500
1087 — 13. Small cross. R. Moneyers name in two lines	225	575
1087A — — As last, but in *gold*	27500	110000
1088 **Halfpenny**. Similar to 1087	900	3000
1088A — — R. Hand of Providence	1350	5750

Imitations of the types of Edward the Elder were also struck in the Danelaw territories. They are usually of lighter weight and coarser execution than the official Wessex issues of Edward the Elder.

AETHELSTAN, 924-939

Aethelstan, the eldest son of Edward, completed the re-conquest of territories controlled by the Danes with the capture of York in 927. He decreed that money should be coined only in a borough, that every borough should have one moneyer and that some of the more important boroughs should have more than one moneyer.

1089   1093

		F	VF
		£	£
1089	**Main issues.** Small cross. R. Moneyer's name in two lines....................	275	700
1090	Diad. bust r. R. As last	1000	4500
1091	— R. Small cross	950	4000
1092	Small cross both sides...	375	1200
1093	— Similar, but mint name added	425	1250
1094	Crowned bust r. As illustration. R. Small cross	750	2500

1095   1100

1095	— Similar, but mint name added	800	2650
1096	**Local Issues.** *N. Mercian mints.* Star between two pellets. R. As 1089...	900	3500
1097	— Small cross. R. Floral ornaments above and below moneyer's name .	950	4000
1098	— Rosette of pellets each side..	425	1250
1099	— Small cross one side, rosette on the other side	450	1350
1100	*N.E. mints.* Small cross. R. Tower over moneyer's name........................	1100	4500

1102

1101	Similar, but mint name added	1250	4750
1102	— Bust in high relief r. or l. R. Small cross...	975	4000
1103	— Bust r. in high relief. R. Cross-crosslet..	975	4000
1104	'Helmeted' bust or head r. R. As last or small cross...............................	900	3750
1104A	**Halfpenny.** Small cross or floral lozenge. R. Moneyer's name in two lines.	900	3000

Eadmund was a half brother of Aethelstan. At the start of his reign he lost the kingdom of York and faced renewed Viking incursions into North East England, however, by the end of his reign he had regained control of those territories.

1105   1106

	F £	VF £
1105 Small cross, rosette or annulet. R. Moneyer's name in two lines with crosses or rosettes between	275	700
1106 Crowned bust r. R. Small cross	850	3000

1107   1111

1112

1107 Similar, but with mint name	900	3250
1108 Small cross either side, or rosette on one side	475	1500
1109 Cross of five pellets. R. Moneyer's name in two lines	425	1350
1110 Small cross. R. Flower above name	1350	5750
1111 'Helmeted' bust r. R. Cross-crosslet	1000	4250
1112 **Halfpenny**. small cross, R. Moneyer's name in two lines or one line between rosettes	925	2750
1112A — Flower. R. As 1105	1100	3500

Eadred was another of the sons of Edward. He faced renewed Viking attempts to recover York whose last king, Eric Bloodaxe, he drove out in 954 to finally secure Northumbria for the English.

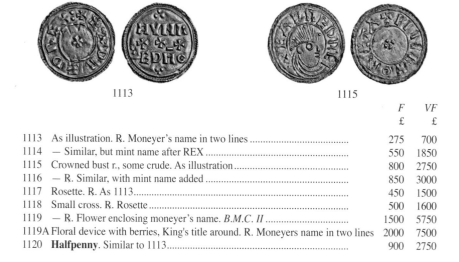

1113　　　　　　　　　　　　　　　　　　1115

	F	VF
	£	£
1113　As illustration. R. Moneyer's name in two lines	275	700
1114　— Similar, but mint name after REX	550	1850
1115　Crowned bust r., some crude. As illustration	800	2750
1116　— R. Similar, with mint name added	850	3000
1117　Rosette. R. As 1113	450	1500
1118　Small cross. R. Rosette	500	1600
1119　— R. Flower enclosing moneyer's name. *B.M.C. II*	1500	5750
1119A Floral device with berries, King's title around. R. Moneyers name in two lines	2000	7500
1120　**Halfpenny**. Similar to 1113	900	2750

HOWEL DDA, d. 949/950

Grandson of Rhodri Mawr, Howel succeeded to the kingdom of Dyfed *c*. 904, to Seisyllog *c*. 920 and became King of Gwynedd and all Wales, 942.

1121

1121　HOℲÆL REX, small cross or rosette. R. Moneyer's name in two lines . .	13500	52500

EADWIG, 955-959

Elder son of Eadmund, Eadwig lost Mercia and Northumbria to his brother Eadgar in 957.

1122　　　　　　　　　　　　　　　　1123

1122　*Br. 1*. Type as illustration	675	1850
1123　— — Similar, but mint name in place of crosses	850	2750

		F £	VF £
1124	— 2. As 1122, but moneyer's name in one line	1350	4500
1125	— 3. Similar. R. Floral design	1750	6500
1126	— 4. Similar. R. Rosette or small cross	825	2500
1127	— 5. Bust r. R. Small cross	6750	32500

1128

1128	**Halfpenny**. Small cross. R. Flower above moneyer's name	1200	4250
1128A	— Similar. R. PIN (Winchester) across field	1300	4750
1128B	— Star. R. Moneyer's name in two lines	950	3250

EADGAR, 959-975

King in Mercia and Northumbria from 957; King of all England 959-975. He was crowned King of England at Bath in 973 in the first coronation of an English King. His reign was largely free from Viking invasions, leading him to be given the sobriquet of 'The Peaceful'.

PRE-REFORM COINAGE BEFORE 973
It is now possible on the basis of the lettering to divide up the majority of Eadgar's coins into issues from the following regions: N.E. England, N.W. England, York, East Anglia, Midlands, S.E. England, Southern England, and S.W. England. (See 'Anglo-Saxon Coins', ed. R. H. M. Dolley.)

1129

1129	*Br I*. Small cross. R. Moneyer's name in two lines, crosses between, trefoils top and bottom	225	575
1130	— — R. Similar, but rosettes top and bottom (a N.W. variety)	275	700
1131	— — R. Similar, but annulets between	275	700
1132	— — R. Similar, but mint name between (a late N.W. type)	475	1500
1133	— 2. — R. Floral design	1250	4750
1133A	Voided cross, lys in angles, R. cross pattée dividing alpha and omega	1350	5000
1134	— 4. Small cross either side	240	600

1135

	F £	VF £
1135 — — Similar, with mint name	450	1500

1136   1138

		F	VF
1136	— — Rosette either side	275	850
1137	— — Similar, with mint name	475	1650
1138	— 5. Large bust to r. R. Small cross	950	3750
1139	— — Similar, with mint name	1250	5250
1140	**Halfpenny.** (8.5 grains / c.0.6 g)) *Br. 3.* Small cross. R. Flower above name	900	3000

1140A   1140B

	F	VF
1140A — — R. Mint name around cross (Chichester, Wilton)	1350	4500
1140B — Bust r. R. 'Londonia' monogram	1100	4250

For Eadgar 'reform' issues see next page.

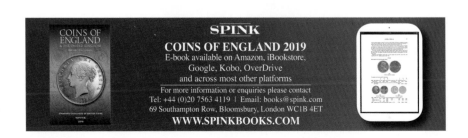

KINGS OF ENGLAND, 973-1066

In 973 Eadgar introduced a new coinage. A royal portrait now became a regular feature and the reverses normally have a cruciform pattern with the name of the mint in addition to that of the moneyer. Most fortified towns of burghal status were allowed a mint, the number of moneyers varying according to their size and importance: some royal manors also had a mint and some moneyers were allowed to certain ecclesiastical authorities. In all some seventy locations are recorded with striking coins in this period (see list of mints pp.144-46).

The control of the currency was retained firmly in the hands of the central government, unlike the situation in France and the Empire where feudal barons and bishops controlled their own coinage. Coinage types were changed at intervals to enable the Exchequer to raise revenue from new dies and periodic demonetization of old coin types helped to maintain the currency in a good state. No halfpence were minted during this period. During the latter part of this era, full pennies were sheared into 'halfpennies' and 'farthings'. They are far rarer than later 'cut' coins.

Further Reading: On the initial reform of the coinage under Eadgar see K. Jonsson, *The NewEra: The Reformation of the Late Anglo-Saxon Coinage* (London: 1987). The nature and purpose of frequent periodic recoinages is explored by I. Stewart, 'Coinage and recoinage after Edgar's reform', in *Studies in Late Anglo-Saxon Coinage*, ed. K. Jonsson (Stockholm: 1990), 455-85. References to individual types for mints and moneyers for much of the first half of the period may be found in K. Jonsson, *Viking Age Hoards and Late Anglo-Saxon Coins* (Stockholm: 1986).

EADGAR, 959-975 *(continued)*

REFORM COINAGE, 973-975

1141

	F	VF
	£	£
1141 **Penny**. Reform Small Cross type. Small diademed bust left. King's name 'Eadgar'. R. Small cross, name of moneyer and mint............................	1100	3750

EDWARD THE MARTYR, 975-978

The son of Eadgar by his first wife, Æthelflaed, Edward was murdered at Corfe in Dorset.

1142

1142 Sole type. As 1141, but reading 'Eadward'.	1500	5250

LATE ANGLO-SAXON MINTS (973-1066)

1. Gothabyrig*	16. Cadbury	31. Cricklade	46. Canterbury	61. Ipswich	76. Tamworth
2. Launceston	17. Bruton	32. Oxford	47. Rochester	62. Norwich	77. Derby
3. Lydford	18. Dorchester	33. Wallingford	48. Horndon	63. Thetford	78. Leicester
4. Barnstaple	19. Wareham	34. Reading	49. Southwark	64. Huntingdon	79. Nottingham
5. Totnes	20. Shaftesbury	35. Guildford	50. London	65. Northampton	80. Melton Mowbray
6. Exeter	21. Warminster	36. Chichester	51. Hertford	66. Warwick	81. Stamford
7. Watchet	22. Bath	37. Cissbury	52. Aylesbury	67. Worcester	82. Newark
8. Taunton	23. Bristol	38. Steyning	53. Buckingham	68. Pershore	83. Torksey
9. Langport	24. Berkeley	39. Lewes	54. Newport Pagnell	69. Winchcombe	84. Lincoln
10. Petherton	25. Malmesbury	40. Hastings	55. Bedford	70. Gloucester	85. Horncastle
11. Crewkerne	26. Wilton	41. Romney	56. Cambridge	71. Hereford	86. Caistor
12. Bridport	27. Salisbury	42. Lympne	57. Bury St Edmunds	72. Grantham*	87. York
13. Axbridge	28. Southampton	43. Hythe	58. Sudbury	73. Shrewsbury	88. Wilton. Norfolk*
14. Ilchester	29. Winchester	44. Dover	59. Maldon	74. Chester	89. Frome
15. Miborne Port	30. Bedwyn	45. Sandwich	60. Colchester	75. Stafford	90. Droitwich

Possible location of uncertain mint

Son of Eadgar by his second wife Ælfthryth, Æthelred ascended the throne on the murder of his half-brother. He is known to posterity as 'The Unready' from 'Unrede', meaning 'without counsel', an epithet gained from the weakness of his royal government. During this reign England was subjected to Viking raids of increasing frequency and strength, and a large amount of tribute was paid in order to secure peace. Large hoards have been found in Scandinavia and the Baltic region and coins are often found peck-marked. There is a high degree of regional variation in the style of dies, particularly in Last Small Cross type, for which readers are advised to consult the following paper: C.S.S. Lyon, '*Die cutting styles in the Last Small Cross issue of c.1009-1017...*', *BNJ* 68 (1998), 21-41.

1143
1144

		F £	VF £
1143	First Small Cross type. Diademed bust left, usually with three pellets before in field. No line to indicate shoulder. *B.M.C I*	800	2750
1144	First Hand type. Diademed bust right, without sceptre. R. Hand of providence between alpha and omega, issuing from cloud composed of parallel curved or angular lines. *B.M.C IIa*	175	475
1145	— —, similar but bust left. *B.M.C IIb*	675	2500

1146
1147

1146	Second Hand type. Diademed bust right, with sceptre. R. Hand of providence between alpha and omega, issuing from clouds with edges that billow outward. *B.M.C IId*	165	450
1147	Benediction Hand type. *O.* as last. R. Hand gives Latin benediction, fields without alpha and omega. *B.M.C IIf*	1250	4500

1148
1150

1148	Crux type. Bare-headed bust left, with sceptre. R. Voided short cross with letters C, R, V, X, in angles. *B.M.C IIIa*	110	285
1149	Small Crux type. Reduced weight, small flans, sceptre inclined to bust such that the base penetrates drapery.	125	325
1150	Intermediate Small Cross type. RX at end of legend separate letters. *B.M.C I*	1100	4000

1151   1152

	F	VF
	£	£
1151 Long Cross type. Bare-headed bust left. R. Voided long cross. *B.M.C IVa*	110	285
1152 Helmet type. Armoured bust left in radiate helmet. *B.M.C VIII*...............	125	325
1153 As last but struck in gold.	37500	150000

1154

1154 Last Small Cross type. Diademed bust left, RX at end of legend ligated together		
as one letter-form. *B.M.C I*	100	260
1154A — —, similar but bust right..	225	650
1155 — —, similar but bust to edge of coin..	675	2500

1156

| 1156   Agnus Dei type. As illustration. *B.M.C X*... | 8000 | 30000 |

Son of King Swein Forkbeard of Denmark, Cnut was acclaimed king by the Danish fleet in England in 1014 but was forced to leave; Cnut returned and harried Wessex in 1015. Æthelred II died in 1016 and resistance to the Danes was continued by his son Eadmund Ironside, for whom no coins are known, but upon the latter's death in 1016 Cnut became undisputed king. The following year Cnut consolidated his position by marrying Emma of Normandy, the widow of Æthelred II.

There is a high degree of regional variation in the style of dies, particularly in Quatrefoil type, for which readers are advised to consult the following paper: M.A.S. Blackburn and C.S.S. Lyon, 'Regional die production in Cnut's Quatrefoil issue' in *Anglo-Saxon Monetary History*, ed. M.A.S. Blackburn (Leicester: 1986), 223-72. Some quatrefoil coins have pellets or a cross added in the obverse or reverse fields. There is considerable weight fluctuation within and between the types.

Substantive types

1157   1158

1159

		F	VF
		£	£
1157	Quatrefoil type (c.1017-23). Crowned bust left. *B.M.C. VIII*	120	300
1158	Pointed Helmet type (1024-1030). *B.M.C. XIV*	110	240
1159	Short Cross type (c.1029-1035/6). *B.M.C. XVI*	95	220
1159A	— —, similar but sceptre replaced with a banner	750	3250

1160

Posthumous type

1160	Jewel Cross type. *B.M.C. XX*, style as 1163 in the name of Cnut.	700	2750

Type considered to have been struck under the auspices of his widow, Queen Emma of Normandy.

Harold was the illegitimate son of Cnut by Ælfgifu of Northampton and was appointed regent on behalf of his half-brother Harthacnut. Queen Emma of Normandy initially held Wessex for her son, Harthacnut, but by 1037 she had been driven from the country and Harold had been recognised as king throughout England. The principal issue was the Jewel Cross type which is also found in the name of Cnut and Harthacnut, cf. nos. 1160 and 1166.

1163   1165

		F	VF
		£	£
1162	Short Cross type (Autumn 1035). As 1159, but in the name of Harold. B.M.C. IIIa	1350	4750
1163	Jewel Cross type (c.1036-38). B.M.C. I	275	850
1164	Fleur-de-Lis type (1038-40). Armoured and diademed bust left. R. Voided long cross, trefoil of pellets in each angle. B.M.C. V	275	825
1165	— —, similar but fleur-de-lis between two pellets in each angle. B.M.C. V	250	775

HARTHACNUT, 1035-1042

Although Harthacnut was the only legitimate son of Cnut and his legitimate heir, the political situation in Denmark prevented him from leaving for England until 1040, by which time Harold had secured the kingdom. Harold's death allowed Harthacnut to reclaim England without bloodshed, but he himself died after two years of sole rule. The main variety of Harthacnut is the Arm and Sceptre type from his sole reign. The Jewel Cross type from the early period is also found in the name of Cnut and Harold I, cf. nos. 1160 and 1163.

EARLY PERIOD (DURING REGENCY) 1035–7

1166	Jewel Cross type. As 1163, but in the name of Harthacnut. Diademed bust left. B.M.C. I	1050	4000

1167

1167	— —, similar but bust right. B.M.C I	975	3500

1168

SOLE REIGN 1040–42

1168	Arm and Sceptre type. King's name given as 'Harthacnut.' Diademed bust left with sceptre in left hand, forearm visible across bust B.M.C. II	825	2750

1169

	F	VF
	£	£
1169 — —, Similar but king's name given as 'Cnut'.	600	1750

1170

1170 **Danish types.** Types exist in the name of Harthacnut other than those listed
above and are Scandinavian in origin. 300   825

EDWARD THE CONFESSOR, 1042-1066

Son of Æthelred II and Emma of Normandy, Edward spent twenty-five years in Normandy
before he was adopted into the household of his half-brother Harthacnut in 1040. On the death of
Harthacnut, Edward was acclaimed king. He is known by the title 'The Confessor' owing to his
piety and he was canonised after his death. There is considerable weight fluctuation within and
between the types, which is often unaffected by the smallness of the flan, rather the coin might be
thicker to compensate.

Further reading: P. Seaby, 'The sequence of Anglo-Saxon types 1030–1050', *BNJ* 28 (1955-7),
111–46; T. Talvio, 'The design of Edward the Confessor's coins', in *Studies in Late Anglo-Saxon
Coinage*, ed. K. Jonsson (Stockholm: 1990), 489–99. A. Freeman. *The Moneyer and the Mint in
the Reign of Edward the Confessor: Parts 1 and 2*, (BAR) 1985

1171   1172 (rev.)

1170A Arm and Sceptre type (1042). *B.M.C. IIIa*	1100	4500
1171 Pacx type (1042–4). Diademed bust left. R. Voided long cross. *B.M.C. IV*	185	525
1172 — —, Similar but R. voided short cross. *B.M.C. V*...................................	200	550

1173

	F	VF
	£	£
1173 Radiate/Small Cross type (1044–6). *B.M.C. I*	120	325

1174   1175

	F	VF
1174 Trefoil Quadrilateral type (1046–8). *B.M.C. III*	120	350
1175 Small flan type (1048–50). *B.M.C. II*	110	275
1176 Expanding Cross type (1050–53). Light issue, small flans; weight approx.		
1.10-1.30g. *B.M.C. V*	135	425

1177

	F	VF
1177 — —. Heavy issue, large flans; weight approx. 1.40-1.70g. *B.M.C. V*	135	425
1178 — —, Similar but struck in gold	42500	175000

1179

	F	VF
1179 Pointed Helmet type (1053–6). Bearded bust right in pointed helmet.		
B.M.C. VII	140	425
1180 — —, Similar but bust left.	950	3500

1181

		F	VF
		£	£
1181	Sovereign/Eagles type (1056–9). King enthroned, holding orb. R. Cross, eagles in angles *B.M.C. IX*	140	425

1182

| 1182 | Hammer Cross type (1059–62). *B.M.C. XI* | 125 | 350 |

1183

| 1183 | Facing Bust/Small Cross type (1062–5). *B.M.C. XIII* | 120 | 325 |

1184

| 1184 | Pyramids type (1065–6). *B.M.C. XV* | 125 | 375 |

1185

| 1185 | Transitional Pyramids type (c.1065). *B.M.C. XIV* | 1500 | 6250 |

Most York coins of this reign have an annulet in one quarter of the reverse.

Harold was the son of Earl Godwine of Wessex, who had dominated the royal court, and was brother-in-law to Edward the Confessor. Harold successfully repulsed an invasion of Harald Hardrada of Norway, but was himself killed in the Battle of Hastings after a reign of ten months.

Further reading: H. Pagan, 'The coinage of Harold II', in *Studies in Late Anglo-Saxon Coinage*, ed. K. Jonsson (Stockholm: 1990), 177–205.

1186   1187

		F	VF
		£	£
1186	Pax type. Crowned head left with sceptre. R. PAX across field. *B.M.C. I*	1100	3500
1187	— —, Similar but without sceptre. *B.M.C. Ia*	1350	4500
1188	— —, Similar but head right. *B.M.C. Ib*	2750	9500

Cnut, Short Cross type (S.1159) - WULNOTH ON WINC:
moneyer Wulnoth   *mint* Winchester

William, Paxs type (S.1257) - LIFINC ON WINCE
moneyer Lifinc   *mint* Winchester

Old English special letters found on Anglo-Saxon and Norman coins:

Letter	Name	Modern Equivalent
Æ	Ash	E
Đ	Eth	Th
Ᵽ (P)	Wynn	W

In late Anglo-Saxon and Norman times coins were struck in the King's name at a large number of mints distributed in centres of population, and in times of emergency in places of refuge, across England and Wales. During the 10th century the use of a mint signature was sporadic but from the Reform type of Edgar the mint name is almost invariably given, usually in conjunction with that of the moneyer responsible, e.g. EDGAR ON BERCLE. At the peak, 71 mints struck the quatrefoil type of Cnut and 65 the PAXS type of William I and they provide a valuable insight into the economic and social structures of the period.

The output of the mints varied enormously and a dozen are exceptionally rare. Approximately 100,000 pennies survive, half of which emanate from the great centres of London, Canterbury, Lincoln, Winchester and York. At the other end of the scale a mint such as Rochester is known from about 500 coins, Derby from around 250, Guildford 100, Bedwyn 25, Horncastle 4 and Pershore 1. Many of these coins, particularly those from the great Scandinavian hoards, are in museum collections and are published in the Sylloge of Coins of the British Isles (SCBI) series.

There are too many type and mint combinations, over 1500 Saxon and 1000 Norman, to price each individually and our aim is to give an indication of value for the commonest Saxon and Norman type, in VF condition, for each of the 102 attested mints (excluding Baronial of Stephen's reign), and for a further 10 mints whose location or attribution is uncertain. The threshold VF price for a Norman coin (H1 B.M.C.15 £500) exceeds that for a Saxon coin (Cnut short cross £220) accounting for the difference in starting level. Prices for coins in lower grade would be less and there is a premium for the rarer types for each mint, but for many types, e.g. in the reigns of Harthacnut or Henry I, the value of the type itself far exceeds that of many of the constituent mints and a scarce mint is only worth a modest premium over a common one.

We also give the most characteristic mint signatures (often found abbreviated) and the reigns for which the mint is known. There are many pitfalls in identifying mints, not least that Saxon and Norman spelling is no more reliable than that of other ages and that late Saxon coins were widely imitated in Scandinavia. There is extensive literature and the specialist in this fascinating series can, for further details, consult J J North, English Hammered Coinage Vol.1.

Alf	—	Alfred the Great	Hd1	—	Harold I
EdE	—	Edward the Elder	HCn	—	Harthacnut
A'stn	—	Aethelstan	EdC	—	Edward the Confessor
Edm	—	Edmund	Hd2	—	Harold II
Edw	—	Eadwig	W1	—	William I
Edg	—	Edgar	W2	—	William II
EdM	—	Edward the Martyr	H1	—	Henry I
Ae2	—	Aethelred II	St	—	Stephen
Cn	—	Cnut			

Berkeley   Hastings

	SAXON VF £	NORMAN VF £
Axbridge (AXAN, ACXEPO) Edg, Ae2, Cn, HCn	4500	—
Aylesbury (AEGEL, AEEL), Ae2, Cn, EdC	4000	—
Barnstable (BARD, BEARDA) Edw, Edg, Ae2-Hd1, EdC, W1, H1	1350	1750
Bath (BADAN) EdE-A'stn, Edw-EdC, W1-St	350	900
Bedford (BEDAN, BEDEFOR) Edw-St	450	800
Bedwyn (BEDEPIN) EdC, W1	2250	4000
Berkeley (BEORC, BERCLE) EdC	8500	—
Bramber (BRAN) St	—	3000
Bridport (BRYDI, BRIPVT) A'stn, Ae2, Cn, HCn, EdC-W1	1500	1500
Bristol (BRICSTO, BRVCSTO) Ae2-St	500	750
Bruton (BRIVT) Ae2, Cn, HCn, EdC	2250	—
Buckingham (BVCIN) Edg, EdM-Hd1, HCn, EdC	3000	—
Bury St.Edmunds (EDMVN, S.EDM) EdC, W1, H1, St	1350	850
Cadbury (CADANBY) Ae2, Cn	6500	—
Caistor (CASTR, CESTR) EdM, Ae2, Cn	5000	—
Cambridge (GRANTE) Edg-St	300	900
Canterbury (DORO, CAENTPA, CNTL) Alf, A'stn, Edr, Edg-St	220	500
Cardiff (CIVRDI, CAIERDI) W1-H1, St, Mat	—	1250
Carlisle (CARD, EDEN) H1, St	—	1250
Castle Rising (RISINGE) St (type II-VII)	—	1500
Chester (LEIGE, LEGECE, CESTRE) A'stn, Edm, Edg-St	400	750
Chichester (CISSAN, CICEST) A'stn, Edg, Ae2-St	400	600
Christchurch (orig. Twynham) (TVEHAM, TPIN) W1, H1	—	3500
Cissbury (SIDESTEB, SIDMES) Ae2, Cn	3000	—
Colchester (COLN, COLECES) Ae2-St	350	600
Crewkerne (CRVCERN) Ae2, Cn, Hd1	3500	—
Cricklade (CROCGL, CRECCELAD, CRIC) Ae2-W2	1750	1750
Derby (DEORBY, DERBI) A'stn, Edm, Edg-St	1750	1750
Dorchester (DORCE, DORECES) Ae2-H1	1500	1250
Dover (DOFERA, DOFRN) A'stn, Edg, Ae2-St	220	600
Droitwich (PICC, PICNEH) EdC, Hd2	4000	—
Dunwich (DVNE) St	—	15000
Durham (DVNE, DVRHAM, DVNHO) W1-St	—	2250
Exeter (EAXA, EAXCESTRE, IEXECE) Alf, A'stn, Edw-St	300	650
Frome (FRO) Cn, HCn, EdC	4000	—
Gloucester (GLEAP, GLEPECE, GLOPEC) Alf, A'stn, Edg-St	450	700
Grantham (GRANTHA, GRE) Ae2	6500	—
Guildford (GYLD, GILDEFRI) EdM-W2	1750	3000
Hastings (HAESTINGPOR, AESTI) Ae2-St	400	800
Hedon (HEDVN) St	—	4000
Hereford (HEREFOR, HRFRD) A'stn, Edg, Ae2-St	600	850
Hertford (HEORTF, HRTFI, RET) A'stn, Edw-EdC, W1-H1	350	1250
Horncastle (HORN) EdM, Ae2	8000	—
Horndon (HORNIDVNE) EdC	8000	—
Huntingdon (HVNTEN, HVTD) Edg, Ae2-St	350	1000
Hythe (HIÐEN, HIDI) EdC, W1, W2	3000	1250
Ilchester (GIFELCST, GIVELC, IVELCS) Edg, Ae2-St	750	1500
Ipswich (GIPESWIC, GYPES) Edg-St	350	750
Langport (LANCPORT, LAGEPOR) A'stn, Cn-EdC	2500	—
Launceston (LANSTF, LANSA, SANCTI STEFANI) Ae2, W1-H1	4000	3000
Leicester (LIHER, LEHRE, LEREC) A'stn, Edg, Ae2-St	500	750
Lewes (LAEPES, LEPEEI, LAPA) A'stn, Edg-St	350	800
Lincoln (LINCOLN, NICOLE) Edr, Edg-St	220	500
London (LVNDO, LVNDENE) Alf, A'stn, Edw-St	220	500
Lydford (LYDANFOR) Edg-EdC	450	—
Lympne (LIMENE, LIMNA) A'stn, Edg-Cn	900	—
Maldon (MAELDVN, MIEL) A'stn, Edg, Ae2-Hd1, EdC-W2	450	1500
Malmesbury (MALD, MEALDMES, MELME) Edg, Ae2-W2, H1	2000	2500
Marlborough (MAERLEBI) W1, W2	—	5000
Melton Mowbray (MEDELTV) Ae2, Cn	7000	—
Milborne Port (MYLE) Ae2, Cn, EdC	6500	—

	SAXON VF £	NORMAN VF £
Newark (NEWIR, NIWOR) Edg-Cn	6500	—
Newcastle (CAST) St	—	1750
Newport (NIPANPO, NIPEPORT) Edw, Edg, EdC	4500	—
Northampton (HAMTVN, HMTI, NORHAM) Edw, Edg-St	400	700
Norwich (NORDPIC) A'stn-Edr, Edg-St	250	500
Nottingham (SNOTING) A'stn, Ae2-St	1500	1500
Oxford (OXNA, OCXEN, OXENFO) Alf, A'stn, Edr-St	400	700
Pembroke (PEI, PAN, PAIN) H1, St	—	4000
Pershore (PERESC) EdC	8500	—
Petherton (PEDR, PEDI) Cn, EdC	7000	—
Pevensey (PEFNESE, PEVEN) W1-St	—	2250
Reading (READIN, REDN) EdC	6000	—
Rhuddlan (RVDILI) W1	—	3500
Rochester (ROFEC, ROFSC) A'stn, Edg-H1	500	1250
Romney (RVMED, RVMNE) Ae2-H1	500	900
Rye (RIE) St	—	3000
Salisbury (SEREB, SEARB, SALEB) Ae2-EdC, W1-St	500	650
Sandwich (SANDPI) EdC, W1-St	600	1000
Shaftesbury (SCEFTESB, CEFT, SAFTE) A'stn, Edg-St	500	800
Shrewsbury (SCROB, SCRVBS, SALOP) A'stn, Edg, Ae2-St	650	1000
Southampton (HAMPIC, HAMTVN) A'stn, Edw-Cn	650	1350
Southwark (SVDBY, SVDGE, SVDPERC) Ae2-St	250	500
Stafford (STAFFO, STAEF) A'stn, Edg, Ae2-Hd1, EdC, W1-St	800	1250
Stamford (STANFORD) Edg-St	220	650
Steyning (STAENIG, STENIC) Cn-W2, St	350	700
Sudbury (SVDBI, SVBR) Ae2, Cn, EdC, W1-St	600	800
Swansea (SVENSEI) St	—	2500
Tamworth (TOMPEARÐ, TAMPRD) A'stn, Edg-Hd1, EdC, W1-St	2000	1750
Taunton (TANTVNE) Ae2-St	1000	900
Thetford (ÐEOTFOR, DTF, TETFOR) Edg-St	220	500
Torksey (TVRC, TORC) EdM-Cn	2500	—
Totnes (DARENT, TOTANES, TOTNES) A'stn, Edw-HCn, W2, H1	650	1750
Wallingford (PELINGA, PALLIG) A'stn, Edm, Edg, Ae2-H1	450	650
Wareham (PERHAM, PERI) A'stn, Edg-St	600	1200
Warminster (PORIME) Ae2-Hd1, EdC	3000	—
Warwick (PAERINC, PERPIC, PAR) A'stn (?), Edg-St	800	1250
Watchet (PECED, PICEDI, WACET) Ae2-EdC, W1-St	1500	1750
Wilton (PILTVNE) Edg-St	350	650
Winchcombe (WENCLES, PINCEL, PINCL) Edg, Ae2, Cn, HCn-W1	2500	2000
Winchester (PINTONIA, PINCEST) Alf, A'stn, Edw-St	220	500
Worcester (PIGER, PIHREC, PIREC) EdM, Ae2-St	600	900
York (EBORACI, EFORPIC, EVERWIC) A'stn, Edm, Edg-St	220	700

Mints of uncertain identification or location

"Brygin" (BRYGIN) Ae2	3500	—
"Dyr/Dernt" (DYR, DERNE, DERNT) EdC (East Anglia)	1500	—
"Weardburh" (PEARDBV) A'stn, Edg	4500	—
Abergavenny (?) (FVNI) W1	—	4000
Gothabyrig (GEODA, GODABYRI, IODA) Ae2-HCn	3000	—
Eye (?) (EI, EIE) St	—	3000
Peterborough (?) (BVRI) W1, St	—	3500
Richmond, Yorks (?) (R1), St (type 1)	—	1500
St Davids (?) (DEVITVN) W1	—	3500
Wilton, Norfolk (?) (PILTV) Ae2 (LSC)	2500	—
Bamborough (BCI, CIB, OBCI) Henry of Northumberland	—	5250
Corbridge (COREB) Henry of Northumberland	—	5750

Aylesbury   Barnstaple   Cricklade   Dunwich

Exeter   Frome   Guildford   Horncastle

Ilchester   London   Milborne Port   Newark

Oxford   Pevensey   Rochester   Stafford

Torksey   Winchcombe   York

1. Launceston	13. Bath	25. Chichester	37. London	49. Huntingdon	61. Rhuddlan
2. Barnstaple	14. Marlborough	26. Steyning	38. Hertford	50. Bedford	62. Chester
3. Totnes	15. Wilton	27. Lewes	39. Maldon	51. Northampton	63. Shrewsbury
4. Exeter	16. Salisbury	28. Pevensey	40. Colchester	52. Warwick	64. Stafford
5. Watchet	17. Christchurch	29. Hastings	41. Ipswich	53. Worcester	65. Tamworth
6. Taunton	18. Abergavenny*	30. Romney	42. Sudbury	54. Winchcombe	66. Leicester
7. Bridport	19. Winchester	31. Hythe	43. Cambridge	55. Oxford	67. Derby
8. Dorchester	20. Bedwyn	32. Dover	44. Bury	56. Gloucester	68. Nottingham
9. Wareham	21. Malmesbury	33. Sandwich	45. Thetford	57. Hereford	69. Lincoln
10. Shaftesbury	22. Cricklade	34. Canterbury	46. Norwich	58. Cardiff	70. York
11. Ilchester	23. Wallingford	35. Rochester	47. Stamford	59. Pembroke	71. Durham
12. Bristol	24. Guildford	36. Southwark	48. Peterborough	60. St Davids*	72. Carlisle

Possible location of uncertain mint

William I maintained the Anglo-Saxon mint system and the practice of conducting frequent periodic recoinages by change of coin type. However, the twelfth-century witnessed a gradual transition from regional to centralised minting. Nearly seventy towns had moneyers operating under William I, but only thirty mint towns took part in the recoinage initiated by the Cross-and-Crosslets ('Tealby') coinage in 1158. Cut halfpennies and cut farthings were made during this period, but are scarce for all types up to BMC 13 of Henry I; cut coins are more frequently encountered for subsequent types.

Further reading: G.C. Brooke, *Catalogue of English Coins in the British Museum. The Norman Kings*, 2 volumes (London, 1916). (Abbr. BMC Norman Kings). I. Stewart, 'The English and Norman mints, c.600–1158', in *A New History of the Royal Mint,* ed. C.E. Challis (Cambridge, 1992), pp. 1–82.

WILLIAM I, 1066-1087

Duke William of Normandy claimed the throne of England on the death of his cousin Edward the Confessor. An important monetary reform occurred towards the close of the reign with the introduction of the *geld de moneta* assessed on boroughs. This may be seen as part of the raft of administrative reforms initiated by William I, which included the compilation of Domesday Book in 1086.

The date of the Paxs type is central to the absolute chronology of this and the subsequent reign. Currently evidence is equivocal on the matter. In BMC Norman Kings (London, 1916) it was designated the last type of the reign, an attribution maintained here, but some students regard it as having continued into the reign of William II or begun by him.

1250

1251

		F	VF
		£	£
1250 **Penny**. *B.M.C.* 1: Profile left type.		475	1500

1252

1253

1251 *B.M.C.* 2: Bonnet type.	275	900
1252 *B.M.C.* 3: Canopy type	475	1500

1254

1255

1253 *B.M.C.* 4: Two sceptres type.	325	1000
1254 *B.M.C.* 5: Two stars type.	275	900
1255 *B.M.C.* 6: Sword type.	525	1600

1256   1257

		F £	VF £
1256	*B.M.C.* 7: Profile right type (lead die struck examples exist from the Thames)	575	1850
1257	*B.M.C.* 8: Paxs type	225	550

WILLIAM II, 1087-1100

Second son of William I was killed while hunting in the New Forest. Five of the thirteen coin types in the name of 'William' have been assigned to the reign of William II, although it remains uncertain whether the Paxs type of his father continued into his reign.

1258   1259

		F	VF
1258	**Penny**. *B.M.C.* 1: Profile type.	900	2750
1259	*B.M.C.* 2: Cross in quatrefoil type.	750	2250

1260   1261

1260	*B.M.C.* 3: Voided cross type	700	2000
1261	*B.M.C.* 4: Cross pattée and fleury type.	750	2250

1262

1262	*B.M.C.* 5: Cross fleury and piles type.	850	2750

Henry was the third son of William I. Administrative reforms and military action to secure Normandy dominated the king's work. After the death of his son in 1120 Henry sought to guarantee the throne for his daughter Matilda, widow of German Emperor Henry V.

The coin types continue to be numbered according to BMC Norman Kings (London, 1916), but the order 1, 2, 3, 4, 5, 6, 9, 7, 8, 11, 10, 12, 13, 14, 15 is now accepted as a working hypothesis for the reign. Greater uncertainty pertains to the chronology of the coin types. The reign coincided with a period of monetary crisis. Scepticism concerning the quality of coinage led to the testing of coins by the public, hindering their acceptance in circulation. In response the government ordered all coins mutilated at issue to force the acceptance of damaged coins. Thus, a few coins of type 6 and all of those of types 7–14 have an official edge incision or 'snick'. Round halfpennies were produced and as some are found snicked they can be dated to the period when official mutilation of the coinage was ordered. In 1124 there was a general purge of moneyers in England as the royal government attempted to restore confidence in the coinage.

Further reading: M.A.S. Blackburn, 'Coinage and currency under Henry I; A review', *Anglo-Norman Studies* 13 (1991), 49–81. M.M. Archibald and W.J. Conte, 'Five round halfpennies of Henry I. A further case for reappraisal of the chronology of types', *Spink's Numismatic Circular* 98 (1990), 232–6, M. Allen 'Henry I Type 14', *BNJ* 79 (2009), 72-171.

1263   1263A   1264

	F	VF
	£	£
1263 **Penny**. *B.M.C.* 1: Annulets type	525	1750
1263A *B.M.C.* 2: Profile/cross fleury type	300	950

1265   1266

1264 *B.M.C.* 3: Paxs type	275	900
1265 *B.M.C.* 4: Annulets and piles type	350	1000

1267   1268

1266 *B.M.C.* 5: Voided cross and fleurs type	750	2500
1267 *B.M.C.* 6: Pointing bust and stars type	1100	4250
1268 *B.M.C.* 7: Facing bust/quatrefoil with piles type	325	1000

1269

1270

	F £	VF £
1269 B.M.C. 8: Large profile/cross and annulets type.....................................	1100	4250
1270 B.M.C. 9: Facing bust/cross in quatrefoil type	650	2000

1271

1272

1271 B.M.C. 10: Facing bust/cross fleury type	275	850
1272 B.M.C. 11: Double inscription type	575	2000

1273

1274

1273 B.M.C. 12: Small profile/cross and annulets type	375	1100
1274 B.M.C. 13: Star in lozenge fleury type	400	1250

1275

1276

1275 B.M.C. 14: Pellets in quatrefoil type...	225	700
1276 B.M.C. 15: Quadrilateral on cross fleury type	150	500

1277

1277A

1277 Round halfpenny. Facing head. R. Cross potent with pellets in angles....	1750	6000
1277A — —, As last but reverse from penny die of type 9.	2750	9500

Stephen of Blois seized the English throne on the death of his uncle, Henry I, despite his oath to support Matilda, with whom he contended for power during his reign.

Substantive types BMC 1 and BMC 7 were the only nation-wide issues, the latter introduced after the conclusion of the final political settlement in 1153. The other substantive types, BMC 2 and BMC 6, were confined to areas in the east of England under royal control. In western England coinage was issued by or on behalf of the Angevin party (q.v. below). In areas without access to new dies from London, coinage was produced from locally made dies and initially based on the designs of regular coins of BMC 1. Particular local types were produced in the midlands and the north, associated with prominent magnates, in the king's name or occasionally in the name of barons. Entries contain references to the article by Mack (M).

Further reading: R.P. Mack, 'Stephen and the Anarchy 1135-54', *British Numismatic Journal* 35 (1966), 38–112. M.A.S. Blackburn, 'Coinage and currency', in *The Anarchy of King Stephen's Reign*, ed. E. King (Oxford, 1994), 145–205.

SUBSTANTIVE ROYAL ISSUES

1278

	F	VF
	£	£
1278 **Penny**. *B.M.C*. 1: Cross Moline ('Watford') type (c.1136–45). Bust right holding sceptre.	225	850
1279 — —, Similar but obv. reads PERERIC or PERERICM	750	2750

1280

1280 *B.M.C*. 2: Voided cross and stars type (c.1145–50)	275	950

1281   1282

1281 *B.M.C*. 6: Cross and piles type (c.1150–54)	325	1000
1282 *B.M.C*. 7: Cross pommée (Awbridge) type (c.1154–58, largely posthumous) This type continued to be struck until 1158 in the reign of Henry II	275	900

The types designated BMC 3, 4 and 5 are non-substantive, listed as 1300–1302.

● = Regular mints of Stephen.

⊕ = Mints striking irregular coins including Angevin.

+ = Mints striking regular and irregular coins.

N.B. Attribution to some of the towns shown is uncertain.

Roxburgh⊕   ⊕Bamborough

Corbridge⊕   Newcastle

+ Carlisle   + Durham

York +

Hedon ●

Lincoln +

Chester ●   ⊕Newark

Derby   +Nottingham
⊕ ⊕
Stafford ●   Tutbury
Shrewsbury ●   Leicester   Stamford   ● Castle Rising
Tamworth   +   +   Norwich+

Peterborough   +Thetford
● ●
Northampton   +Huntingdon   +Bury   ⊕Eye ● Dunwich
Worcester ●   Warwick ●   ⊕ Cambridge   Ipswich
Hereford +   Bedford   Sudbury +   Colchester ●

+Gloucester

Cirencester⊕   +Oxford
Swansea   ⊕Cricklade
Pembroke ●   Cardiff +   ⊕Malmesbury   ⊕Wallingford   London
Bristol ● Bath   ⊕Marlborough   Southwark
⊕Trowbridge   Canterbury +   ● Sandwich
Watchet ●   +Ilchester   ● Wilton   Dover ●
Wivelscombe⊕   Shaftesbury ●   +Winchester   Rye ●
Taunton ●   Sherborne   Salisbury   Bramber Lewes   Hastings
Exeter ●   Dorchester   Southampton⊕   Chichester   Steyning   Pevensey
+Launceston   Wareham   ⊕Wight

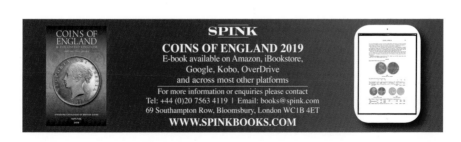

LOCAL AND IRREGULAR ISSUES OF THE CIVIL WAR

COINS STRUCK FROM ERASED DIES LATE 1130s – *c*.1145

The association of these coins with the Interdict of 1148 is erroneous. Some of the marks that disfigured the dies were probably cancellation marks, but the exigencies of the civil war required the re-use of the dies. Other defacements may well be an overtly political statement.

1283   1288

	F £	VF £
1283 As 1278, but obverse defaced with long cross. *East Anglian mints.* (M 137–47)	800	3500
1284 — —, but king's bust defaced with cross. *Nottingham (M 149)*	750	3250
1285 — —, but sceptre defaced with bar or cross. *Nottingham, Lincoln, Stamford.* (M 148, 150–54)	475	1650
1286 — —, but obverse legend erased. *Nottingham (M 157)*	575	2250
1286A — —, but with defacement other than those noted above	450	1500

SOUTH EASTERN VARIANT

1287 As 1278, but king holds mace instead of sceptre. *Canterbury (M 158)* ...	975	4000

EASTERN VARIANTS

1288 As 1278, but R. has roundels in centre, on cross limbs or in angles. *Suffolk mints (M 159–68)*	650	2250
1289 — —, but R. Plain cross, fleurs in angles. *Lincoln (M 169–73)*	625	2250
1290 — —, but R. Plain cross superimposed on cross moline *(M 174)*	600	2000
1290A — —, but R. Quadrilateral over voided cross *(M 176)*	900	3750
1290B — —, but cross penetrating legend to edge, fleurs inverted in angles. *Lincoln. (M 186–7)*	900	3500

SOUTHERN VARIANTS

1291   1295

1291 As 1278, but with large rosette of pellets at end of obverse legend *(M 184–5)*	600	2000
1292 — —, but with star at end of obverse legend *(M 187y)*	525	1650
1293 Bust r. or l., rosette in place of sceptre. R. As 1280, but solid cross. *(M 181–3)*	750	2750
1295 As 1278, but king wears collar of annulets. R. voided cross moline, annulet at centre. *Southampton. (M 207–212)*	325	1350

	F	VF
	£	£

1296 As 1278, but reverse cross penetrates legend with fleur-de-lis tips.
       Leicester (M 177–8).. 800 2750
1297 — —, but crude work. ℞. Voided cross, lis outward in angles. *Tutbury*
       (M 179) 850 3250

1298   1300

1298 — —, but crude work. ℞. Voided cross with martlets in angles. *Derby Tutbury*
       (M 175) 2250 8500
1299 — —, but ℞. plain cross with T-cross in each angle *(M 180)*.................... 850 3000
1300 *B.M.C.* 3: Facing bust. ℞. Cross pattée, fleurs inwards. *Northampton and*
       Huntingdon (?) (M 67–71).. 1000 3500

1301   1302

1301 *B.M.C.* 4: Lozenge fleury type. *Lincoln or Nottingham (M 72–5)*........... 475 1750
1302 *B.M.C.* 5: Bust half-right. ℞. Lozenge in Cross Moline with fleurs. *Leicester*
       (M 76) 1350 4750
1303 As 1280, but obverse legend ROBERTVS. *(M 269)*................................ 3250 12500

NORTH-EASTERN AND SCOTTISH BORDER VARIANTS

1304 As 1278, but star before sceptre. ℞. Annulets at tips of fleurs *(M 188)* ... 725 2750
1305 — —, but voided cross penetrating legend to edge *(M 189–92)*............... 750 3000
1306 — —, but crude style *(M 276–9, 281–2)*.. 525 2000
1307 — —, but ℞. Cross with cross pattée and crescent in angles *(M 288)* 1500 5250

King David I of Scotland

1308 As 1305, but obverse legend DAVID REX *(M 280)* 1650 5500

Earl Henry of Northumberland (son of King David I of Scotland)

1309 As 1278, but legend hENRIC ERL *(M 283–5)*...................................... 1750 5750
1310 — —, Similar but reverse cross fleury *(M 286–7)* 1750 5750
1311 As 1307, but obverse legend NENCI:COM *(M 289)* 1850 6000

YORK ISSUES: THE ORNAMENTED GROUP ATTRIBUTED TO YORK (1140s)
King Stephen

1312 As 1278, but obverse inscription NSEPEFETI, NSEPINEI or STIEFNER.
       ℞. ornamental letters WISÐGNOTA *(M 215–6)* 1100 4000

1313 1315

	F	VF
	£	£

1313 Flag type. As 1278, but lance with pennant before face, star right. R. As
 1278, letters and four ornaments in legend *(M 217)*.............................. 750 3000
1313A — —, Similar but with eight ornaments in reverse legend. *(M 217)* 750 3000
1314 As 1278, but legend STEIN and pellet lozenge for sceptre-head *(M 218)* 850 3250
1314A King standing facing, holding sceptre and standard with triple pennon. R.
 Cross pattée, crescents and quatrefoils in angles, ornaments in legend. .. 3250 12000

King Stephen and Queen Matilda
1315 Two full-length standing figures holding sceptre. R. Legend of ornaments.
 (M 220) 3500 13500

1317 1320

Eustace Fitzjohn
1316 EVSTACIVS, knight standing with sword. R. Cross in quatrefoil,
 EBORACI EDTS or EBORACI TDEFL *(M 221-222)* 2000 8250
1317 — —, Similar but reverse legend ThOMHS FILIVS VLF *(M 223)* 2250 9000
1318 — —, Similar but reverse legend of ornaments and letters. *(M 224)* 1750 6750
1319 [EVSTA]CII. FII. IOANIS, lion passant right. R. Cross moline, ornaments in
 legend *(M 225)* 2750 11000
1320 EISTAOhIVS, lion rampant right. R. Cross fleury, ornaments in legend *(M 226)* 2500 10500
William of Aumale, Earl of York
1320A WILLELMVS, Knight stg. r. holding sword. R. Cross in quatrefoil. As 1316 3000 10500

1322

Rodbert III de Stuteville
1321 ROBERTVS IESTV, knight holding sword on horse right. R. as 1314.
 (M 228) 4250 15000
1321A Type as 1312, but obverse legend RODBDS[T DE?] *(M 227)* 2750 9500
Henry Murdac, Archbishop of York
1322 HENRICVS EPC, crowned bust, crosier and star before. R. similar to 1314
 but legend STEPHANVS REX *(M 229)* 3000 10500

UNCERTAIN ISSUES

		F	VF
		£	£
1323	Obv. as 1278. R. Cross pattée with annulets in angles *(M 272)*	675	2500
1324	Obv. as 1275 (Henry I, *B.M.C.* 14), but reverse as last *(M 274 extr)*	900	3000
1325	Other miscellaneous types/varieties	650	1500

THE ANGEVIN PARTY

Matilda was the daughter of Henry I and widow of German Emperor Henry V (d.1125) and had been designated heir to the English throne by her father. Matilda was Countess of Anjou by right of her second husband Geoffrey of Anjou. Matilda arrived in England in pursuit of her inheritance in 1139 and established an Angevin court at Bristol and controlled most of south-western England. Matilda's cause was championed by her half-brother, Henry I's illegitimate son, Robert, Earl of Gloucester.

The initial phase of coinage in Matilda's name copied the designs of Stephen's BMC 1 and are dated to the early 1140s. The second type was only discovered in the Coed-y-Wenallt hoard (1980). A group of coins in the names of 'William' and 'Henry' and struck at the Angevin mints, particularly Hereford and Gloucester, are attributable, at least in part, to Earl William of Gloucester and Henry of Anjou (the future Henry II). Coins of Earl William, and his father Earl Robert, of the Lion type are now also known thanks to the discovery of the Box, Wiltshire hoard (1994). In addition to these great magnates a few minor barons placed their names on the coinage.

Further Reading: G. Boon, *Welsh Hoards 1979–81* (Cardiff, 1986). M.M. Archibald, 'The lion coinage of Robert Earl of Gloucester and William Earl of Gloucester', *British Numismatic Journal* 71 (2001), 71–86.

1326

Matilda (in England 1139–48)

1326	As 1278, but cruder style, MATILDI IMP or variant (M 230–40) *Bristol, Cardiff, Monmouth, Oxford and Wareham.*	1750	6750
1326A	— —, MATILDI IMP or IM.HE.MA. R. Cross pattée over fleury (Coed-y-Wenallt hoard). *Bristol and Cardiff.*	1850	7000
1326B	— —, as last but triple pellets at cross ends (Coed-y-Wenallt hoard). *Bristol and Cardiff.*	1850	7000

Henry de Neubourg

1326C	Similar type to 1326A but HENRICI dE NOVOB (Coed-y-Wenallt hoard) *Swansea.*	2000	7500

Issues in the name 'Henry' and 'William'

1327	As 1278, but HENRICVS or HENRICVS REX *(M 241–5). Hereford and Malmesbury.*	1200	5000
1327A	As 1295, but HENRIC *(M 246). Gloucester.*	1350	5500
1327B	As 1326A, but HENNENNVS	1350	5500
1328	Obv. as 1278, but HENRICVS. R. Cross crosslet in quatrefoil *(M 254). Gloucester.*	1500	6000

1329   1331

		F £	VF £
1329	— —, but HENRICVS or HENRICVS REX FVTVRVS R. Quadrilateral on cross fleury *(M 248–53)*. *Hereford, Cirencester (?) and Ilchester (?)*	1250	5000
1330	Facing bust and stars, HENRICVS or HENRICVS RE. R. Quadrilateral on cross botonnée *(M 255–8)*. *Bristol, Ilchester (?) and Sherborne (?)*........	1500	6000
1331	— —, Quadrilateral, on voided cross botonnée *(M 259–61)*	1500	6000
1332	As 1329, but legend [WIL]LELM *(M 262)*	1400	5500
1333	As 1330, but legend WILLELM or variant *(M 263)*. *Cirencester (?)*	1650	6500
1334	As 1331, but legend WILLELMVS *(M 264–8)*. *Dorchester and Wareham* ..	1650	6500

Earl Robert of Gloucester (1121/22–1147)

1334A	+ROB' COM' GLOC' lion passant right. R. Cross fleury	1600	6250

Earl William of Gloucester (1147-1183)

1334B	+WILLEMVS, lion passant right. R. Cross fleury	1600	6250

Brian Fitzcount, Lord of Wallingford (?)

1335	As 1330, but legend B.R:C.I.T.B.R *(M 270)*	3750	13500

1336

Earl Patrick of Salisbury (?)

1336	Helmeted bust r. with sword, star behind. R. As 1329. *(M 271)*...............	3250	11000

HENRY II, 1154-1189

CROSS-AND-CROSSLETS ('TEALBY') COINAGE, 1158-1180

Coins of Stephen's last type continued to be minted until 1158. Then a new coinage bearing Henry's name replaced the currency of the previous reign which contained a high proportion of irregular and sub-standard pennies. The new Cross and Crosslets issue is more commonly referred to as the 'Tealby' coinage, as over 6000 of these pennies were discovered at Tealby, Lincolnshire, in 1807. Twenty-nine mints were employed in this re-coinage, but once the re-minting had been completed not more than a dozen mints were kept open. The issue remained virtually unchanged for twenty-two years apart from minor variations in the king's portrait. The coins tend to be poorly struck on irregular flans.

Cut coins occur with varying degrees of frequency during this issue, according to the type and local area.

Further reading: *A Catalogue of English Coins in the British Museum. The Cross-and-Crosslet ("Tealby") Type of Henry II.* (London: 1951) by D.F. Allen.

1337   1338   1339

		F £	VF £
1337	Class A (1158-c.1163). No hair, no collar. Mantle falls from chin as two parallel lines between which is a line of pellets.	110	300
1338	Class B (c.1162-c.1163). Similar, but mantle of two folds which meet at chin (various compositions).	125	350
1339	Class C (c.1163-c.1167). Curl of hair at temple. Jewelled collar, mantle of many folds, field between sometimes jewelled, as is cuff.	110	300

1340   1341

1340	Class D (c.1167-c.1170). Jewelled collar continues down shoulder unbroken. Single curl of hair at temple, folds of mantle horizontal	120	325
1341	Class E (c.1170-c.1174). Similar to 1340. Jewelled collar only. Folds of mantle rise from hand to top of shoulder.	120	325

1342

1342	Class F (c.1174-c.1180). Similar to 1341, but hair falls in long ringlets from temple.	110	300

Mints and Moneyers for the Cross-and-Crosslets (Tealby) Coinage

From F £

London: Accard (CD), Alwin (ABCDF), Edmund (ACDE), Geffrei (ACE),
Godefrei (ACDEF), Godwin (BDE), Hunfrei (AC), Iohan (ACDEF),
Lefwine (BCEF), Martin (ABC), Pieres (ACEF), Pieres Mer. (ABD),
Pieres Sal. (AEF), Ricard (ABCD), Rodbert (AC), Swetman (ABC), Wid (A),   *110*

Canterbury: Alferg (A), Goldhavoc (ABCDEF), Goldeep (C), Lambrin (F),
Raul (CDEF), Ricard (ABCDEF), Ricard Mr. (ABCDE), Rogier (ABCDEF),
Rogier F. (A), Willem (C), Wiulf (ABCDEF),   *110*

Bedford: Arfin (A),   *Extremely Rare*

Bristol: Elaf (ACF), Rogier (ADEF), Tancard (ABD),   *250*

Bury St Edmunds: Henri (BDE), Raul (F), Willem (A),   *140*

Carlisle: Willem (ACDEF),   *140*

Chester: Andreu (A), Willem (AD),   *220*

Colchester: Alwin (AC), Pieres (CE),   *250*

Durham: Cristien (C), Iohan (B), Walter (A),   *180*

Exeter: Edwid (AC), Guncelin (AC), Rainir (BC), Ricard (A), Rogier (AD),   *220*

Gloucester: Godwin (A), Nicol (A), Rodbert (A), Sawulf (A),   *275*

Hereford: Driu (AC), Osburn (A), Stefne (A), [—]ward (A),   *250*

Ilchester: Adam (CDF), Reinard (A), Ricard (A), Rocelin (A),   *220*

Ipswich: Nicole (BCDEF), Robert (CEF), Turstain (CF),   *110*

Launceston: Willem (A),   *Extremely Rare*

Leicester: Ricard (A), Robert (A),   *250*

Lewes: uncertain (F),   *Extremely Rare*

Lincoln: Andreu (ABCDE), Godric (ABCD), Lanfram (ABCDF),
Raulf (ABCDEF), Raven (ACF), Swein (ACD),   *140*

Newcastle: Willem (ACDEF),   *150*

Northampton: Ingeram (AC), Iosep (A), Pieres (A), Reimund (AC), Stefne (A),
Waltier (AC), Warnier (AC),   *180*

Norwich: Gilebert (ABF), Herbert (ACD), Herbert R (A)., Hugo (ACF), Nicol (AC),
Picot (ABC), Reiner (AD), Ricard (A),   *180*

Oxford: Adam (ADE), Aschetil (A), Rogier (A),   *220*

Pembroke: Walter (A),   *Extremely Rare*

Salisbury: Daniel (A), Levric (A),   *220*

Shrewsbury: Warin (A),   *Extremely Rare*

Stafford: Colbrand (AC), Willem (C),   *275*

Thetford: Siwate (ACD), Turstain (ACD), Willem (ACDF), Willem Ma (A),
Willem De (A),   *140*

Wallingford: Fulke (A),   *Extremely Rare*

Wilton: Anschetil (A), Lantier (A), Willem (A),   *220*

Winchester: Herbert (AC), Hosbert (ACD), Ricard (AE), Willem (AC),   *140*

York: Cudbert (A), Gerrard (A), Godwin (AD), Griffin (AD), Herbert (ACD),
Hervi (A), Iordan (A), Norman (A), Willem (A), Wulfsi (A),   *140*

Letters in brackets after moneyer's name indicate Class known to exist for the mint and moneyer combination

'SHORT CROSS' COINAGE OF HENRY II (1180-1189)

In 1180 a coinage of new type, known as the Short Cross coinage, replaced the Tealby issue. The new coinage is remarkable in that it covers not only the latter part of the reign of Henry II, but also the reigns of his sons Richard and John and on into the reign of his grandson Henry III, and the entire issue bears the name 'hENRICVS'. There are no English coins with the names of Richard or John. The Short Cross coins can be divided chronologically into various classes: ten mints were operating under Henry II and tables of mints, moneyers and classes are given for each reign.

The Publishers acknowledge the work of the late Prof. Jeffrey Mass for re-organising and updating the shortcross series.

Further reading: *Sylloge of Coins of the British Isles Vol 56. The J.P. Mass Collection of English Short Cross Coins 1180 to 1247.* London 2002

1343 1343A

1344 1345

		F £	VF £
1343	Class 1a¹ - 1a³. Small face, square E, and/or C, and/or round M, irregular number of curls...	135	550
1343A	Class 1a⁴ and 1a⁵. Small face, seriffed X, round E and C, square M, irregular number of curls...	85	275
1344	1b. Fine portrait, curls 2 left and 5 right, stop before REX on most coins	65	200
1345	1c. Portrait less finely shaped, irregular number of curls, normally no stop before REX	60	185

RICHARD I, 1189-1199

Pennies of Short Cross type continued to be issued throughout the reign, all bearing the name hENRICVS. The coins of class 4, which have very crude portraits, continued to be issued in the early years of the next reign. The only coins bearing Richard's name are from his territories of Aquitaine and Poitou in western France.

1346 1347 1348A 1348C

1346	2. Chin whiskers made of small curls, no side whiskers, almost always 5 pearls to crown, frequently no collar, sometimes RE/X	110	375
1347	3. Large or small face, normally 7 pearls to crown, chin and side whiskers made up of small curls..	85	275

	F	VF
	£	£

1348A 4a. Normally 7 pearls to crown, chin and side whiskers made up of small
pellets, hair consisting of 2 or more non-parallel crescents left and right ... 75 ... 250

1348B 4a* Same as last, but with reverse colon stops (instead of single pellets) ... 85 ... 300

1348C 4b Normally 7 pearls to crown, chin and side whiskers made up of small
pellets, single (or parallel) crescents as hair left and right, frequent
malformed letters .... 70 ... 225

JOHN, 1199-1216

'SHORT CROSS' COINAGE *continued.* All with name hENRICVS

The Short Cross coins of class 4 continued during the early years of John's reign, but in 1205 a
re-coinage was initiated and new Short Cross coins of better style replaced the older issues. Coins of
classes 5a and 5b were issued in the re-coinage in which sixteen mints were employed. Only two of
these mints (London and Durham) were still working by the end of class 5. The only coins to bear
John's name are the pennies, halfpence and farthings issues for Ireland.

| 1349 | 1350A | 1350B |

| 1351 | 1352 | 1354 |

		F	VF
1349	4c. Reversed S, square face at bottom, 5 pearls to crown, normally single crescents as hair left and right	90	325
1350A	5a1 Reversed or regular S, irregular curved lines as hair (or circular curls containing no pellets), cross pattée as initial mark on reverse, *London and Canterbury* only..	175	600
1350B	5a2 Reversed S, circular curls left and right (2 or 3 each side) containing single pellets, cross pommée as initial mark on reverse...........................	85	275
1350C	5a/5b or 5b/5a	65	200
1351	5b. Regular S, circular pelleted curls, cross pattée as initial mark on reverse	60	175
1352	5c. Slightly rounder portrait, letter X in the form of a St. Andrew's cross	55	160
1353	6a. Smaller portrait, with smaller letter X composed of thin strokes or, later, short wedges	50	150
1354	6b. Very tall lettering and long rectangular face.......................................	45	125

For further reading and an extensive listing of the English Short Cross Coinage see:
Sylloge of Coins of the British Isles. *The J. P. Mass Collection of English Short Cross
Coins 1180-1247*

'SHORT CROSS' COINAGE *continued* (1216-47)

The Short Cross coinage continued for a further thirty years during which time the style of portraiture and workmanship deteriorated. By the 1220s minting had been concentrated at London and Canterbury, one exception being the mint of the Abbot of Bury St. Edmunds.

Halfpenny and farthing dies are recorded early in this issue; a few halfpennies and now farthings have been discovered. See nos 1357 D-E.

| | 1355 | 1355A | 1355B |

	F	VF
	£	£
1355 6c. Lettering now shorter, face narrow and triangular (also issued in the reign of John)	65	200
1355A 6c. orn. Various letters now ornamental in design, curls 3/3 left and right	90	325
1355B 6x. Canterbury mint only, RE/X, curls 2/2, nostril pellets outside nose...	475	1500
1355C 6d. Face less distinct in shape, N's containing a pellet along the crossbar	85	250

| | 1356A | 1356B | 1356C |

	F	VF
1356A 7a. Small compact face, letter A (rev. only) with top coming to a point under crossbar	35	120
1356B 7b. Letter A with square top, M appears as H (rev. only)	35	120
1356C 7c. Degraded portrait, letter A and M as in 7b, large lettering (rev. only)	30	110

| | 1357A | 1357C |

	F	VF
1357A 8a. New portrait; letter X in shape of curule; cross pattée as initial mark on reverse (early style), or cross pommée (late style)	135	450
1357B 8b. Degraded portrait, wedge-shaped X, cross pommée as initial mark ..	50	175
1357C 8c. Degraded portrait, cross pommée X, cross pommée as initial mark ..	50	175
1357D Round **Halfpenny** in style of class 7, initial mark in shape of up-turned crescent, London mint only (dated to 1222)	2750	9000
1357E Round **Farthing** in style of class 7, initial mark in shape of up-turned crescent, London mint only (dated to 1222)	2500	7500

Mints and Moneyers for the Short Cross Coinage

Fine

Henry II:

London: Aimer (1a-b), Alain (1a-b), Alain V (1a-b), Alward (1b), Davi (1b-c),
Fil Aimer (1a-b), Gefrei (1c), Gilebert (1c), Godard (1b), Henri (1a-b),
Henri Pi (1a), Iefrei (1a-b), Iohan (1a-b), Osber (1b), Pieres (1a-c),
Pieres M (1a-b), Randvl (1a-b), Ravl (1b-c), Reinald (1a-b), Willelm (1a-b) 50
Carlisle: Alain (1b-c) 85
Exeter: Asketil (1a-b), Iordan (1a-b), Osber (1a-b), Ravl (1b), Ricard (1b-c),
Roger (1a-c) 75
Lincoln: Edmvnd (1b-c), Girard (1b), Hvgo (1b), Lefwine (1b-c), Rodbert (1b),
Walter (1b), Will. D.F. (1b), Willelm (1b-c) 65
Northampton: Filip (1a-b), Hvgo (1a-b), Ravl (1a-c), Reinald (1a-c), Simvn (1b),
Walter (1a-c), Willelm (1a-b) 60
Oxford: Asketil (1b), Iefrei (1b), Owein (1b-c), Ricard (1b-c), Rodbert (1b),
Rodbt. F. B. (1b), Sagar (1b) 70
Wilton: Osber (1a-b), Rodbert (1a-b), Iohan (1a) 75
Winchester: Adam (1a-c), Clement (1a-b), Gocelm (1a-c), Henri (1a),
Osber (1a-b), Reinier (1b), Rodbert (1a-b) 60
Worcester: Edrich (1b), Godwine (1b-c), Osber (1b-c), Oslac (1b) 75
York: Alain (1a-b), Efrard (1a-c), Gerard (1a-b), Hvgo (1a-c), Hunfrei (1a-b),
Isac (1a-b), Tvrkil (1a-c), Willelm (1a-b) 60

Richard I

London: Aimer (2-4a), Fvlke (4a-b), Henri (4a-b), Ravl (2), Ricard (2-4b),
Stivene (2-4b), Willelm (2-4b) 70
Canterbury: Goldwine (3-4b), Hernavd (4b), Hve (4b), Ioan (4b), Meinir (2-4b),
Reinald/Reinavd (2-4b), Roberd (4b), Samvel (4b), Simon (4b), Vlard (2-4b) 80
Carlisle: Alein (3-4b) 125
Durham: Adam (4a), Alein (4a-b), Pires (4b) 150
Exeter: Ricard (3) 135
Lichfield: Ioan (2) 2500
Lincoln: Edmvnd (2), Lefwine (2), Willelm (2) 100
Northampton: Giferei (4a), Roberd (3), Waltir (3) 110
Northampton or Norwich: Randvl (4a-b), Willelm (4a-b) 100
Shrewsbury: Ive (4a-b), Reinald/Reinavd (4a-b), Willem (4a) 175
Winchester: Adam (3), Gocelm (3), Osbern (3-4a), Pires (4a), Willelm (3-4a) 80
Worcester: Osbern (2) 250
York: Davi (4a-b), Efrard/Everard (2-4b), Hvgo/Hve (2-4a), Nicole (4a-b),
Tvrkil (2-4a) 80

John

London: Abel (5c-6b), Adam (5b-c), Beneit (5b-c), Fvlke (4c-5b), Henri (4c-5b/5a),
Ilger (5b-6b), Ravf (5c-6b), Rener (5a/b-5c), Ricard (4c-5b), Ricard B (5b-c),
Ricard T (5a/b-5b), Walter (5c-6b), Willelm (4c-5b), Willelm B (5a/b-5c),
Willelm L (5b-c), Willelm T (5b-c) 45
Canterbury: Goldwine (4c-5c), Hernavd/Arnavd (4c-5c), Hve (4c-5c), Iohan (4c-5c),
Iohan B (5b-c), Iohan M (5b-c), Roberd (4c-5c), Samvel (4c-5c), Simon (4c-5c) 50
Bury St Edmunds: Fvlke (5b-c) 90
Carlisle: Tomas (5b) 110
Chichester: Pieres (5b/a-5b), Ravf (5b/a-5b), Simon (5b/a-5b), Willelm (5b) 80
Durham: Pieres (5a-6a) 90
Exeter: Gileberd (5a-b), Iohan (5a-b), Ricard (5a-b) 75

Ipswich: Alisandre (5b-c), Iohan (5b-c) 60
Kings Lynn: Iohan (5b), Nicole (5b), Willelm (5b) 125
Lincoln: Alain (5a), Andrev (5a-5c), Hve (5a/b-5c), Iohan (5a), Ravf (5a/b-5b),
Ricard (5a-5b/a), Tomas (5a/b-5b) 50
Northampton: Adam (5b-c), Roberd (5b), Roberd T (5b) 60
Northampton or Norwich: Randvl (4c) 80
Norwich: Gifrei (5a/b-5c), Iohan (5a-c), Renald/Renavd (5a-c) 60
Oxford: Ailwine (5b), Henri (5b), Miles (5b) 70
Rochester: Alisandre (5b), Hvnfrei (5b) 90
Winchester: Adam (5a-c), Andrev (5b-c), Bartelme (5b-c), Henri (5a), Iohan (5a-c),
Lvkas (5b-c), Miles (5a-c), Ravf (5b-c), Ricard (5a-b) 50
York: Davi (4c-5b), Nicole (4c-5c), Renavd (5b), Tomas (5a/b-5b) 50

Henry III
London: Abel (6c-7a), Adam (7b-c), Elis (7a-b), Giffrei (7b-c), Ilger (6c-7b),
Ledvlf (7b-c), Nichole (7c-8c), Ravf (6c-7b), Ricard (7b), Terri (7a-b),
Walter (6b-c) 30
Canterbury: Arnold (6c/6x, 6x), Henri (6c-6c/d, 7a-c), Hivn/Ivn (6c-7b),
Iohan (6c-7c, 8b-c), Ioan Chic (7b-c), Ioan F. R. (7b-c), Nichole (7c, 8b-c),
Osmvnd (7b-c), Robert (6c, 7b-c), Robert Vi (7c), Roger (6c-7b),
Roger of R (7a-b), Salemvn (6x, 7a-b), Samvel (6c-d, 7a), Simon (6c-d, 7a-b),
Tomas (6d, 7a-b), Walter (6c-7a), Willem (7b-c, 8b-c), Willem Ta (7b-c) 30
Bury St Edmunds: Iohan (7c-8c), Norman (7a-b), Ravf (6c-d, 7a), Simvnd (7b-c),
Willelm (7a) 35
Durham: Pieres (7a) 80
Winchester: Henri (6c) 125
York: Iohan (6c), Peres (6c), Tomas (6c), Wilam (6c) 125

Irregular Local Issue
Rhuddlan (in chronological order) 95
Group I (c. 1180 – pre 1205) Halli, Tomas, Simond
Group II (c.1205 – 1215) Simond, Henricus

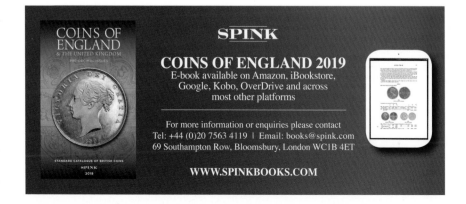

'LONG CROSS' COINAGE (1247-72)

By the middle of Henry's reign the Short Cross coinage in circulation was in a poor state and, in 1247, a new coinage was ordered with the cross on the reverse being extended to the edge of the coin in an attempt to prevent clipping. The earliest coins (1a) showed the names of the neither the mint nor the moneyer. Class 1b includes the name of the mint. From class 2 onwards all coins show the name of both the mint and the moneyer.

Following publication of the 1908 Brussels Hoard by Churchill and Thomas (2012) the classification of the Long Cross coinage was revised. This divided the Long Cross coinage into four phases: Phase I, 1247, Pre-provincial; Phase II, 1248-1250, Provincial when sixteen provincial mints, in addition to the main mints of London and Canterbury plus Bury St Edmunds were opened to facilitate the production and distribution of the new coins; Phase III, 1250-1272, The Post-provincial in which the mint of Durham re-opened operating intermittently; Phase IV, 1272-1280, Posthumous (see under Edward I on page 167) when the Long Cross coinage was continued in the name of Henry III through the first seven years of the reign of Edward I.

In Phases I and II the obverse features the King's head without a sceptre but during the Post-provincial phase, from class 4 onwards, the sceptre was re-introduced. No round Half-pennies or farthings were struck during the Long Cross coinage but cut halves and quarters were used in considerable numbers.

Mint marks feature on all coins from classes 1 to 4 inclusive and are an important aid to both chronology and identification. Five main varieties of mint mark exist.

1   2   3   4   5

Further reading: Ron Churchill and Bob Thomas, *The Brussels Hoard of 1908. The Long Cross Coinage of Henry III*. 2012.

THE LONG CROSS COINAGE, 1247-79

PHASE I, 1247 PRE-PROVINCIAL PHASE

1358   1359

		F	VF
		£	£
1358	Class 1a. Obv. hENRICVS REX. Rev. ANG LIE TER CI'. *mm* 1...........	375	1350
1359	Class 1b. Obv. hENRICVS REX ANG. Rev. LIE TER CI' LON (London),		
	CAN (Canterbury - scarce) or AED (Bury St Edmunds - very rare). *mm* 1.	60	185
1359A	Class 1a/1b and 1b/1a mules	250	950
1360	Class 1b/2a mule. (London and Canterbury only)...................................	55	175

1361

1361	Class 2a. Obv. hENRICVS REX TERCI'. *mm* 2.		
	Rev. Moneyer & mint.	35	110

PHASE II, 1248-50 PROVINCIAL PHASE

1361A

	F £	VF £
1361A Class 2b. Long, narrow bust, curly X or straight limbed X. Rev. Moneyer & mint. *mm* 3.	30	100

1362　　　　1362A　　　　1362B

1362　Class 3a1. Obv. hENRICVS REX III. Class 2 bust. *mm* 3.	25	95
1362A Class 3a2. Bust altered, eyes are round comprising pellets in crescents; often with a colon after REX. *mm* 3.	25	95
1362B Class 3ab. Neat 3a-3b transitional bust. *mm* 3.	25	85

1363　　　　1363A　　　　1364

1363　Class 3b. Neat round bust; beard is three pellets either side of a large central pellet. *mm* 3.	25	80
1363A Class 3bc. Smaller bust with necklines (sometimes vestigal). ENR usually ligated. *mm* 4.	30	90
1364　Class 3c. Similar but coarser bust usually with necklines and a colon after REX. Eyes are round comprising pellets in annulets. *mm* 4.	25	80

PHASE III, 1250-72 POST-PROVINCIAL PHASE

1364A　　　　1364B

1364A Class 3d1. Small neat bust generally with a pointed chin and neck lines. Most have a colon after REX. *mm* 4.	30	90
1364B Class 3d2. Larger more rounded bust resembling class 4 coins. Ball tailed letter R (R2). *mm* 4, with a few coins featuring *mm* 5.	30	90

| 1365 | 1365a | 1366 | 1366 detail |

	F	VF
	£	£

1365 Class 4a. Bust similar to 3d2. King holds sceptre, crown has pellet ornaments.
Legend starts at 1 o'clock. *mm* 5. .... 110 375
1365A Class 4ab. As above but crown has end pellets and true central fleur. *mm* 5. 110 375
1366 Class 4b. As above but crown has true half fleurs and central fleur. *mm* 5. 125 425

| 1367 | 1367A | 1367B | 1367B detail |

1367 Class 5a1. Legend starts at 10 o'clock. Large round bust, round eyes and
half fleur at crown ends. No *mm*... 135 475
1367A Class 5a2. As above but crown has end pellets. Some with the letter X
with one curved limb (Churchill/Thomas Class 5a3). 25 80
1367B Class 5a4. As above but with a jewelled crown.. 225 750

| 1368 | 1368A | 1368A detail |

1368 Class 5b1. Large oval bust, sometimes narrower with more pointed chin. Half
fleur crown ends. 150 525
1368A Class 5b2. As above but crown with end pellets. 25 65

| 1369 |

1369 Class 5c. Similar but with almond eyes or wedge tailed R., variety with
disjointed central fleur and/or no stalks.. 25 65

1370	1370A	1370B	1370B detail

	F	VF
	£	£

1370 Class 5d1. Completely new and very coarse bust with crude central fleur and half fleur ends often with unusual mint spellings. 100 325

1370A Class 5d2. As above but bust is more realistic and less crude................. 60 175

1370B Class 5d3. The "Beri" type; much neater and more pleasing. Central fleur has distinctly pointed ends. 60 175

1371	1372	1373	1374

1372 detail	1373 detail

1371 Class 5e. Bust similar to 5d3 (but Canterbury busts usually coarser) but with jewelled crown.. 150 525

1372 Class 5f. New large and round bust similar to those from 5a to 5c with a double banded crown and a low central fleur. 25 65

1373 Class 5g. Similar bust but crown has thick single band with low central fleur. 25 60

1374 Class 5h. Similar but coarser with 'heavier' features and a more pointed chin. Crown fleur comprises three pellets often with one or more individual stalks, possibly posthumous... 45 165

1375

1375 Gold Penny of 20 pence. As illustration. 65000 275000

Mints, Moneyers and Classes for the Long Cross Coinage

Question marks appear against certain sub classes eg Lincoln 3bc for Walter. In such cases, whilst the Brussels Hoard contained no specimens and whilst no specimen is known to Churchill and Thomas, it is thought feasible that coins of this sub-class were struck and examples may exist.

	Fine From £
London; Anonymous 1a, 1b, 1a/b, 1b/a.	
Nicole (1b/2-5c2), Henri (3a1-5g), Davi (3d1-5f), Ricard (3d1/2-5g),	
Note. Of the above four moneyers, only Nicole is known for class 4ab	
Walter (5c2-5g), Willem (5c2-5g), Ion (5c3-5g), Thomas (5g), Robert (5g),	
Renaud (5g-7), Phelip (7).	25
Note: Coins of 5a4 and 5d1 are not known for London and coins of 5d2 are excessively rare.	
Canterbury: Anonymous 1b. Nicole (1b/2-5g), Gilbert (1b/2-3ab, 3b-5c, 5d3-5g),	
Willem (1b/2, 2b-5g), Ion (4ab-5c, 5d2-5g), Robert/Roberd (5c-5d1, 5d3-5h)	
Walter (5c-5g), Ambroci (5g), Alein (5g-5h), Ricard (5h), Roger (5h).	25
Note: No coin of class 2a is known for Willem but one may exist; coins of classes 4a, 4b, 5a1 and 5b1 are not known for any Canterbury moneyer and class 5a4 is known only for Nicole and Ion.	
Bury St Edmunds: Ion (2a-3d2, 4ab, 5a2 and 5a3), Randulf (5b2-5c, 5d3, 5f), Renaud (5g),	
Stephane (5g), Ion/Iohs (5g-7), Ioce (7).	25
Durham: Ricard (5a3, 5b2 & 5c), Roger (5g), Wilelm (5g), Roberd/Robert (6, 7).	50
Bristol: Elis (3ab, b, bc, c), Henri (3ab, b), Iacob (3ab, b, bc, c), Roger (3b, bc),	
Walter (3ab, b, bc).	60
Carlisle: Adam (3ab, b, bc), Ion (3ab, b, bc, c), Robert (3ab, b, bc), Willem (3ab, b).	80
Exeter: Ion (2b, 3a, a2, ab, b), Philip (2b, 3a, a2, ab, b), Robert (2b, 3a1, a2, ab, b),	
Walter (2b2, 3a1, a2, ab, b).	50
Gloucester: Ion (2b, 3a1, a2, ab, b, c), Lucas (2b2, 3a1, a2, ab, b, c),	
Ricard (2b, 3a1, a2, ab, b, c), Roger (2b, 3a1, a2, ab, b, c).	50
Hereford: Henri (3ab, b, c), Ricard (3ab, b, c), Roger (3ab, b, c), Walter (3ab, b, c).	70
Ilchester: Huge (3a2, ab, b, bc, c), Ierveis (3a2, ab, b, bc, c), Randvlf (3a2, ab, b, bc, c),	
Stephe (3a2, ab, b, bc, c).	70
Lincoln: Ion (2b, 3a1, a2, ab, b, bc, c), Ricard (2b, 3a1, a2, ab, b, bc, c),	
Walter (2b, 3a1, a2, ab, b, bc, c), Willem (2b, 3a1, a2, ab, b, bc, c).	30
Newcastle: Adam (3ab, b, c), Henri (3ab, b, c), Ion (3ab, b, c), Roger (3ab, b, c).	40
Northampton: Lucas (2b, 3a1, a2, ab, b, bc, c), Philip (2b, 3a1, a2, ab, b, bc, c),	
Tomas (2b, 3a1, a2, ab, b, bc, c), Willem (2b, 3a1, a2, ab, b, bc, c).	40
Norwich: Huge (2b, 3a1, a2, ab, b, bc, c), Iacob (2b, 3a1, a2, ab, b, bc, c),	
Ion (2b, 3a, a2, ab, b, bc, c),Willem (2b, 3a1, a2, ab, b, bc, c).	40
Oxford: Adam (2b, 3a1, a2, ab, b, bc, c), Gefrei (2b, 3a1, a2, ab, b, bc, c),	
Henri (2b, 3a1, a2, ab, b, bc, c), Willem (2b, 3a1, a2, ab, b, bc, c).	40
Shrewsbury: Lorens (3ab, b, bc, c), Nicole (3ab, b, bc, c), Peris (3ab, b, bc, c),	
Ricard (3ab, b, bc, c).	70
Wallingford: Alisandre (3ab, b), Clement (3ab, b), Ricard (3ab, b), Robert (3ab, b).	70
Wilton: Huge (3ab, b, bc, c), Ion (3ab, b, bc, c), Willem (3ab, b, bc, c).	70
Winchester: Huge (2b, 3a1, a2, ab, b, bc, c), Iordan (2b, 3a1, a2, ab, b, bc, c),	
Nicole (2b, 3a1, a2, ab, b, bc, c), Willem (2b, 3a1, a2, ab, b, bc, c).	40
York: Alain (2b, 3a1, a2, ab, b, bc), Ieremie (2b, 3a1, a2, ab, b, bc), Ion (2b, 3a1,	
a2, ab, b, bc), Rener (2b, 3a1, a2, ab, b, bc), Tomas (3a2, ab, b, bc, c).	30

COINAGE IN THE NAME OF HENRY III 1272-1279

LONG CROSS COINAGE, 1247-79 *(continued)*

PHASE IV, POSTHUMOUS PHASE

These coins were struck between 1272 and 1279 during the reign of Edward I but they bear the name of Henry III. It is most likely that class 5h were also struck during these years but there are no means of separating the coins struck under Edward I from those struck before the death of Henry III; we have, therefore, included all coins of class 5h as being part of the Henry III Phase III.

The earliest coinage of Edward I, in the name of Henry III (Class 5i and 6), is of coarse style and was struck at London, Bury St. Edmunds and Durham only. Class 7, also only from these mints, is of neater style. In 1279 the Long Cross coinage was abandonned and a new coinage introduced.

Cut Halfpennies and Farthings also occur for this issue.

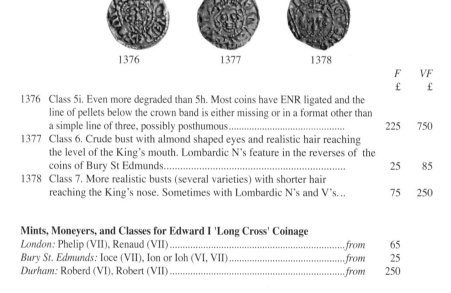

1376   1377   1378

		F	VF
		£	£
1376	Class 5i. Even more degraded than 5h. Most coins have ENR ligated and the line of pellets below the crown band is either missing or in a format other than a simple line of three, possibly posthumous	225	750
1377	Class 6. Crude bust with almond shaped eyes and realistic hair reaching the level of the King's mouth. Lombardic N's feature in the reverses of the coins of Bury St Edmunds	25	85
1378	Class 7. More realistic busts (several varieties) with shorter hair reaching the King's nose. Sometimes with Lombardic N's and V's...	75	250

Mints, Moneyers, and Classes for Edward I 'Long Cross' Coinage

London: Phelip (VII), Renaud (VII) ....*from*   65
Bury St. Edmunds: Ioce (VII), Ion or Ioh (VI, VII)...*from*   25
Durham: Roberd (VI), Robert (VII) ....*from*   250

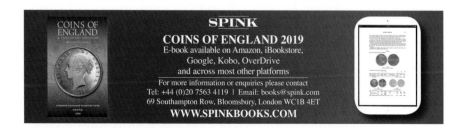

NEW COINAGE (from 1279).

A major re-coinage was embarked upon in 1279 which introduced new denominations. In addition to the penny, halfpence and farthings were also minted and, for the first time, a fourpenny piece called a 'Groat', wt. 89 grs., (from the French *Gros*).

The groats, though ultimately unsuccessful, were struck from more than thirty obverse dies and form an extensive series with affinities to the pence of classes 1c to 3g. The chronology of this series has now been definitively established (see Allen, M. The Durham Mint, pp. 172-179).

As mint administration was now very much centralized, the practice of including the moneyer's name in the coinage was abandoned (except for a few years at Bury St. Edmunds). Several provincial mints assisted with the re-coinage during 1279-81, then minting was again restricted to London, Canterbury, Durham and Bury.

The provincial mints were again employed for a subsidiary re-coinage in 1300 in order to remint lightweight coins and the many illegal *esterlings* (foreign copies of the English pennies, mainly from the Low Countries), which were usually of poorer quality than the English coins.

1379A   1379E

	F	VF
	£	£
1379A **Groat.** *London.* Variety a. (Fox 5). Small crowned bust within a quatrefoil of three lines, flowers in spandrels. Flat crown with pellet ornaments, drapery of two wedges with rosette below	2500	8500
1379B — b. (Fox 6). Larger face with flat hair. Unusual crescent crown carrying pearl ornaments, drapery with rosette in centre	2400	8250
1379C — c. (Fox 3). Similar face with bushy hair. Crown with plain band and pearl ornaments, drapery is foreshortened circle with rosette in centre ...	2750	9000
1379D — d. (Fox 7). New portrait with smaller pointed face, trefoils in spandrels. Crown with spearhead ornaments, drapery is segment of a circle with rosette in centre	2750	9000
1379E — e. (Fox 4). Larger oval face with bushy hair, flowers in spandrels. Crown with spearhead ornaments, thick curved drapery without rosette	2400	8250
1379F — f. (Fox 2). Quatrefoil of two lines. Broader face and shorter hair. Crown with spread side fleurs, drapery of two wedges, trefoil of pellets below .	2650	8500
1379G — f. (Fox 1). Quatrefoil of three lines. Drapery of two wedges, trefoil of pellets below	2850	9500
1379H — g. (Fox -). Quatrefoil of two lines. Crown with bifoliate side fleurs, drapery of two wedges with annulet (?) on breast, two annulets after ANG	3000	9750

Edward I groats were often mounted as brooches and gilt. Such specimens are worth considerably less

| | 1381 | 1382 | 1383 |

| | | F | VF |
| | | £ | £ |

1380 **Penny.** *London.* Class 1a. Crown with plain band, ЄDW RЄX; Lombardic
      Ⴖ on *obv;* pellet 'barred' S on rev. A with sloping top .... | 275 | 1100 |
1381 — 1b. — ЄD RЄX; no drapery on bust, Roman N .... | 1350 | 5750 |
1382 — 1c. — ЄDW RЄX; Roman N, normal or reversed; small lettering ..... | 30 | 135 |
1383 — 1d. — ЄDW R;—; large lettering and face .... | 25 | 120 |

| | 1384 | 1385 | 1386 |

1384 — — — Annulet below bust .... | 90 | 375 |
1385 — 2a. Crown with band shaped to ornaments; usually broken left petal
      to central fleur portrait as 1d. N usually reversed .... | 20 | 80 |
1386 — 2b. — tall bust; long neck; N reversed .... | 20 | 75 |

1388

1387 — 3a. Crescent-shaped contraction marks; pearls in crown, drapery is
      foreshortened circle with hook ends... | 25 | 100 |
1388 — 3b. — — drapery is segment of a circle, pearls in crown .... | 25 | 100 |
1389 — 3c. — normal crown; drapery in one piece, hollowed in centre.......... | 20 | 75 |

| | 1391 | 1392 | 1394 |

1390 — 3d. — — drapery in two pieces, broad face .... | 20 | 75 |
1391 — 3e. — long narrow face (Northern mints) .... | 20 | 75 |
1392 — 3f. — broad face, large nose, rougher work, late S first used............. | 25 | 100 |
1393 — 3g. — Spread crown small neat bust, narrow face .... | 20 | 70 |
1394 — 4a. Comma-shaped contraction mark, late S always used, C and Є open | 20 | 75 |

| 1395 | 1396 | 1397 | 1398 |

		F	VF
		£	£
1395	— 4b. Similar, but face and hair shorter...	20	70
1396	— 4c. Larger face with more copious hair; nick to band of crown..........	25	90
1397	— 4d. Pellet at beginning of *obv.* and *rev.* legend	20	70
1398	— 4e. Three pellets on breast, ropy hair, pellet in *rev.* legend (no pellets on Bury or Durham)..	25	80

| 1399 | 1400 |

1399	— 5a. Well spread coins, pellet on breast, face as 1398, A normally unbarred	30	110
1400	— 5b. Coins more spread, tall lettering, long narrow face, pellet on breast	25	100

| 1401 | 1402 | 1403 |

1401	— 6a. Smaller coins, smaller lettering with closed E (from now on) initial cross almost plain, crown with wide fleurs, crude appearance	90	350
1402	— 6b. Initial cross pattée...	50	175
1403	— 7a. Rose on breast (except Bury), short hair; almond-shaped eyes, double barred N	35	125

| 1404 | 1406 | 1406A |

1404	— 7b. Rose on breast (London only) longer hair, new crown..................	40	150
1405	— 8a. Crown resembling 7b with central fleur usually broken................	25	85
1406	— 8b. Similar to 1405 with wider drapery, top-tilted S	25	85
1406A	— 8c — — Crown with very arched band..	25	100

1407

		F	*VF*
		£	£

1407 — 9a. Drapery of two wedges, pellet eyes, crown of 8a-b or new flatter
one; often star on breast... 20 60

1408 — 9b. Small coins; Roman N, normal, un-barred, or usually of pot-hook
form; often star or (very rarely) pellet on breast. Some Durham coins are
from locally made dies.. 20 60

1408A – 9c. Larger crude lettering with barred A and abbreviation marks.
(only found in combination with dies of 9b or 10ab, except Bury).......... 35 125

1409 - 10ab   1409B - 10ab

1409 — 10ab. ЄDWARD. Bifoliate crown (converted 9b or new taller one).
Narrow incurved lettering... 20 50

1409A — 10ab. Similar with annulet on breast or a pellet each side of head
and on breast... 100 350

1409B — 10ab. ЄDWAR (rarely ЄDWR). Similar to 1409. A few early coins
have the trifoliate crown of 9b.. 20 50

1410   1411

Crown 1   Crown 2   Crown 3   Crown 4   Crown 5

1410 — 10cf1. Crown 1 (Axe-shaped central fleur, wedge-shaped petals).
ЄDWA from now on. Stub-tailed. R.. 20 50

1411 — 10cf2. Crown 2 (Well-shaped central lis, no spearheads). Spreading hair. 20 50

1413   1414

		F £	VF £
1412	— 10cf3. Crown 3 (Left-hand arrowhead inclines to right). Early coins have the broken lettering of 10cf2; later have new lettering with round-backed Є.	20	50
1413	— 10cf4. Crown 4 (Neat with hooked petal to right-hand side fleur)	25	80
1414	— 10cf5. Crown 5 (taller and more spread, right-hand ornament inclines to left). Later coins are on smaller flans.	20	55

Some of the coins of class 10cf3 (c.1307-9), and all of the coins of classes 10cf4 and 10cf5 (c.1309-10), were struck in the reign of Edward II.

For a more detailed classification of Class 10, see 'Sylloge of British Coins, 39, The J. J. North Collection, Edwardian English Silver Coins 1279-1351', The Classification of Class 10, c. 1301-10, by C. Wood.

Prices are for full flan, well struck coins.
The prices for the above types are for London. For coins of the other mints see following pages; types are in brackets, prices are for the commonest type of each mint.

Berwick Type 1   Type II   Type III   Type IV

1415	*Berwick-on-Tweed*. (Blunt types I-IV) Local dies	25	75
1416	*Bristol*. (2; 3b; c, d; 3f, g; 9b)	20	65
1417	*Bury St. Edmunds*. Robert de Hadelie (3c, d, g; 4a, b, c)	45	135
1418	— Villa Sci Edmundi (4e; 5b; 6b; 7a; 8ab, 9a – 10 cf 5)	20	50
1419	*Canterbury*. (2; 3b-g; 4; 5; 7a; 7b; 9;10)	20	50
1420	*Chester*. (3g; 9b)	30	90
1421	*Durham*. Plain cross *mm* (9b; 10ab; 10cf 2-3; 10cf 5)	20	50
1422	— Bishop de Insula (2; 3b, c, e, g; 4a)	20	50
1423	— Bishop Bec (4b-e; 5b; 6b; 7b; 9a, 9b, 10) with *mm*. cross moline	20	50
1424	— — (4b) cross moline in one angle of *rev*.	150	450
1425	*Exeter*. (9b)	25	80
1426	*Kingston-upon-Hull*. (9b)	30	90
1427	*Lincoln*. (3c, d, f, g)	20	50
1428	*Newcastle-upon-Tyne*. (3e; 9b; 10ab)	20	50
1429	*York*. Royal mint (2; 3b, c, d, e, f; 9b)	20	50
1430	— Archbishop's mint (3e, f; 9b). R. Quatrefoil in centre	20	50
1431	**Halfpenny**, *London*. Class 3b. ЄDWR ANGL DNS hYB, drapery composed of curved line with wedges above	40	135
1432	— 3c Drapery composed of two wedges	25	80

1434A

	F	VF
	£	£
1433 — 3g. New wide crown, thick-waisted S, drapery as 3b..........................	25	80
1433A — — 4c. Narrower crown, drapery of two unequal wedges...................	30	110
1433B — — Similar, pellet before LON	40	140
1434 — 4e. Single-piece collar with (usually) three pellets on breast.............	45	160
1434A — 6. Small face with short hair, large coarse crown, closed Є..............	50	175
1435 — 7. Larger face with square jaw, open Є, usually double-barred N.......	40	135
1436 — 8. Similar, new crown with straight sides...	45	160
1437 — 10. ЄDWAR R ANGL DNS hYB, bifoliate or trifoliate crown, new		
waisted letters	30	100

The above prices are for London; halfpence of the mints given below were also struck.

	F	VF
1438 *Berwick-on-Tweed*. (Blunt types I, II and III)...	85	275
1439 *Bristol*. Class 3c, 3g, 4c	40	125
1440 *Lincoln*. Class 3c...	45	150
1441 *Newcastle*. Class 3e, single pellet in each angle of *rev*..........................	60	175
1442 *York*. Class 3c-e...	40	125

1443A   1445

	F	VF
1443 **Farthing,** *London*. Class 1a. Base silver issue (6.65 grains), ЄDWARDVS		
RЄX. bifoliate crown with no intermediate jewels, inner circle.		
R. LONDONIЄNSIS, (rarely LONDRIЄNSIS), ...	50	175
1443A — 1c. Similar trifoliate crown	40	135
1444 — 2. Smaller face, trifoliate crown with intermediate jewels	25	90
1445 — 3c. New tapering face, wide at top, crown with curved band.............	25	100
1445A — 3de. Sterling silver issue (5.51 grains.) Є R ANGLIЄ bust (usually)		
to bottom of coin, no inner circle. R. LONDONIЄNSIS	25	110
1446 — 3g. Similar, new wide crown with curving side fleurs.	25	90
1446A — 4de. Similar to 3de. R. CIVITAS LONDON...................................	30	135
1446B — 5. Similar, crude wide crown.	30	135
1447 — 6-7. New large face with wide cheeks, pellet or almond eyes.............	25	90
1448 — 8. Similar, small rounded face, tall crude crown	30	135
1449 — 9a. Є R ANGL DN, small tapering face, (a variety has the face of		
class 6-7)...	35	150
1449A — 9b. Small ugly face, usually wide crown with outwards-sloping sides..	40	175
1450 — 10 ЄDWARDVS REX (-, A, AN or ANG,) large bust within inner circle.	25	90
Type 1450 often appears on oval flans.		

It is now thought that the order of London Farthings is class 4de, 6-7, 5, 9a, 8, 9b

1446   1452

		F	VF
		£	£
1451	*Berwick-on-Tweed.* (Blunt type I, IIIb)...	125	450
1452	*Bristol.* Class 2, 3c, 3de	35	125
1453	*Lincoln.* Class 3de...	35	125
1453A	*Newcastle.* Class 3de, ℞ NOVI CASTRI...............................	200	750
1454	*York.* Class 2, 3c, 3de	40	150

For further information see: *Farthings and Halfpennies, Edward I and II,* P. and B R Withers, 2001

EDWARD II, 1307-27

The coinage of this reign differs only in minor details from that of Edward I. No groats were issued in the years *c.* 1282-1351.

1458 (12a)   1459 (13)   1460 (14)

1461 (15a)   1462 (15b)   1463 (15c)

1455	**Penny,** *London.* Class 11a. Broken spear-head or pearl on l. side of crown; long narrow face, straight-sided N; round back to C and Є	20	75
1456	— 11b. — Є with angular back (till 15b), N with well-marked serifs (late)	25	80
1457	— 11c. — — A of special form	45	150
1458	— 12a. Central fleur of crown formed of three wedges; thick cross *mm.*	25	90
1458A	— 12b — Crown with diamond-shaped petals and cruciform central fleur; cross of four wedges *mm*	50	175
1458B	— 12c — Crown with heart-shaped petals; cross pattée *mm*	60	225
1459	— 13. Central fleur of crown as Greek double axe	25	75
1460	— 14. Crown with tall central fleur; large smiling face with leering eyes	20	75
1461	— 15a. Small flat crown with both spear-heads usually bent to l.; face of 14	25	85
1462	— 15b. — very similar, but smaller face...	25	80
1463	— 15c. — large face, large Є	25	85

| Berwick Type V | Type VI | Type VII |

	F	VF
	£	£
1464 *Berwick-on-Tweed*. (Blunt types V, VI and VII) Local dies except V	25	85
1465 *Bury St. Edmunds*. (11; 12; 13; 14; 15)...	20	75
1466 *Canterbury*. (11; 12a; 13; 14; 15)	20	75
1467 *Durham*. King's Receiver (11a), *mm*. plain cross....................................	20	75
1468 — Bishop Bec. (11a), *mm*. cross moline	20	75
1469 — Bishop Kellawe (11; 12a; 13), crozier on *rev*.	25	80
1470 — Bishop Beaumont (13; 14; 15), *mm*. lion with lis..............................	25	90
1471 *mm*. plain cross (11a, 14, 15c)	45	150

1472

| 1472 **Halfpenny,** *London*. Class 10-11, ƐDWARDVS REX (-, A, AN, ANG, ANGL or ANGLI,) bifoliate or trifoliate crown .... | 45 | 175 |
| 1473 — *Berwick-on-Tweed*. (Blunt type V).. | 150 | 525 |

1474

| 1474 **Farthing,** *London*. Class 11, 13, ƐDWARDVS REX (-, A, AN, or AG), face with pellet eyes.. | 30 | 100 |
| 1475 — *Berwick-on-Tweed*. (Blunt type V) .... | 175 | 550 |

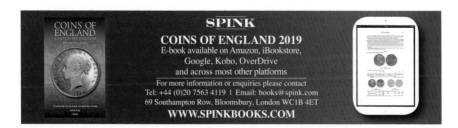

During Edward's early years small quantities of silver coins were minted following the standard of the previous two reigns, but in 1335 halfpence and farthings were produced which were well below the .925 Sterling silver standard. In 1344 an impressive gold coinage was introduced comprising the Double Florin or Double Leopard valued at six shillings, and its half and quarter, the Leopard and the Helm. The design of the Florin was based on the contemporary gold of Philip de Valois of France.

The first gold coinage was not successful and it was replaced later the same year by a heavier coinage, the Noble, valued at 6s. 8d, i.e., 80 pence, half a mark or one third of a pound, together with its fractions. The Noble was lowered in weight in two stages over the next few years, being stabilized at 120 grains in 1351. With the signing of the Treaty of Bretigny in 1360 Edward's title to the Kingdom of France was omitted from the coinage, but it was resumed again in 1369.

In 1344 the silver coinage had been re-established at the old sterling standard, but the penny was reduced in weight to just over 20 grains and in 1351 to 18 grains. Groats were minted again in 1351 and were issued regularly henceforth until the reign of Elizabeth.

Subsequent to the treaty with France which gave England a cross-channel trading base at Calais, a mint was opened there in 1363 for minting gold and silver coins of English type. In addition to coins of the regular English mints, the Abbot of Reading also minted silver pence, halfpence and farthings with a scallop shell in one quarter of the reverse while coins from Berwick display one or two boar's or bear's heads.

There is evidence of re-use of dies at later periods, e.g. 3rd coinage halfpennies.

For further study of the English Hammered Gold Coinage see: Sylloge of Coins of the British Isles, 47, the Herbert Schneider Collection Volume One, by Peter Woodhead. 1996.

Mintmarks

6	1	2	3	74	4	5	7a

1334-51	Cross pattée (6)	1356	Crown (74)
1351-2	Cross 1 (1)	1356-61	Cross 3 (4)
1351-7	Crozier on cross end (76a, *Durham*)	1361-9	Cross potent (5)
1352-3	Cross 1 broken (2)	1369-77	Cross pattée (6)
1354-5	Cross 2 (3)		Plain cross (7a)

The figures in brackets refer to the plate of mintmarks in Appendix IV.

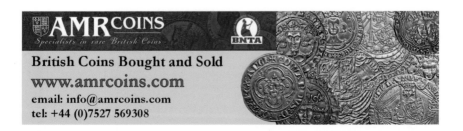

GOLD
(No gold coinage issued before 1344)

THIRD COINAGE, 1344-51, First period, 1344

	1476	1477	1478
			F VF
			£ £

1476	**Double-florin (Double Leopard).** (=6s.; wt. 108 grs., 6.99g.). King enthroned beneath canopy; crowned leopard's head each side. ℞. Cross in quatrefoil	90000	375000
1477	**Florin.** Leopard sejant with banner l. ℞. Somewhat as last	27500	135000
1478	**Half-florin.** Helmet on fleured field. ℞. Floriate cross	15000	75000

Second period, 1344-46

1479	**Noble** (=6s. 8d., wt. 138.46 grs., 8.97g.). King stg. facing in ship with sword and shield. ℞. L in centre of royal cross in tressure.................................	22500	110000
1479A	**Half-noble.** Similar	7500	27500
1480	**Quarter-noble.** Shield in tressure. ℞. As last..	2500	9500

1481

1482

Third period, 1346-51

1481	**Noble** (wt. 128.59 grs., 8.33g.). As 1479, but Є in centre; large letters ...	2750	10500
1482	**Half-noble.** Similar	2250	9000
1483	**Quarter-noble.** As 1480, but Є in centre...	325	1250

FOURTH COINAGE, 1351-77

Reference: L. A. Lawrence, *The Coinage of Edward III from 1351.*
Pre-treaty period, 1351-61. With French title.

		F £	VF £
1484	**Noble** (wt. 120 grs., 7.77g.), series B (1351). Open Є and C, Roman M; *mm.* cross 1 (1)	1100	4250
1485	— — *rev.* of series A (1351). Round lettering, Lombardic M and N; closed inverted Є in centre	1250	4500
1486	C (1351-1352). Closed Є and C, Lombardic M; *mm.* cross 1 (1)	900	3250
1487	D (1352-1353). *O.* of series C. R. *mm.* cross 1 broken (2)	1350	5250

1490   1498

1488	E (1354-1355). Broken letters, V often has a nick in r. limb; *mm.* cross 2 (3)	850	3000
1489	F (1356). *mm.* crown (74)	1050	3750
1490	G (1356-1361). *mm.* cross 3 (4). Many varieties	800	2750
1491	**Half-noble**, B. As noble with *rev.* of series A, but closed Є in centre not inverted	750	2750
1492	C. *O.* as noble. *Rev.* as last	850	3000
1493	E. As noble	1000	3500
1494	G. As noble. Many varieties	675	2250
1495	**Quarter-noble**, B. Pellet below shield. R. Closed Є in centre	350	900
1496	C. *O.* of series B. *Rev.* details as noble	400	1100
1497	E. *O.* as last. *Rev.* details as noble, pellet in centre	375	950
1498	G. *mm.* cross 3 (4). Many varieties	325	800

Transitional treaty period, 1361. French title omitted, replaced by that of Aquitaine on the noble and (rarely) on the half-noble, but not on the quarter-noble; irregular sized letters; *mm.* cross potent (5).

1499

1499	**Noble.** R. Pellets or annulets at corners of central panel	1100	4000

1504

		F £	VF £
1500	**Half-noble.** Similar	525	1750
1501	**Quarter-noble.** Similar. Many varieties. Pellet and rarely Є in centre....	275	700

Treaty period, 1361-69. Omits FRANC, new letters, usually curule-shaped X; *mm.* cross potent(5).

1502	**Noble.** *London.* Saltire or nothing before ЄDWARD...............................	950	3500
1503	— Annulet before ЄDWARD (with, rarely, crescent on forecastle).........	900	3250
1504	*Calais.* C in centre of *rev.*, flag at stern of ship	950	3500
1505	— — without flag...	975	3750

1506   1508

1506	**Half-noble.** *London.* Saltire before ЄDWARD......................................	600	2000
1507	— Annulet before ЄDWARD...	650	2250
1508	*Calais.* C in centre of *rev.*, flag at stern of ship	900	3250
1509	— — without flag..	950	3500
1510	**Quarter-noble.** *London.* As 1498. R. Lis in centre..................................	275	675
1511	— — annulet before ЄDWARD..	275	675
1512	*Calais.* R. Annulet in centre..	325	825
1513	— — cross in circle over shield	300	800
1514	— R. Quatrefoil in centre; cross over shield	400	1100
1515	— — crescent over shield...	425	1250

Post-treaty period, 1369-1377. French title resumed.

1516	**Noble.** *London.* Annulet before ЄD. R. Treaty period die......................	1350	5750
1517	— — — crescent on forecastle...	1100	4250
1518	— — post-treaty letters. R. Є and pellet in centre...............................	1050	4000
1519	— — — R. Є and saltire in centre...	1100	4250
1520	*Calais.* Flag at stern. R. Є in centre...	1050	4000

1521

		F	VF
		£	£
1521	— — *Rev.* as 1518, with Є and pellet in centre	975	3750
1522	— As 1520, but without flag. R. Є in centre	1100	4250
1523	**Half-noble.** *London. O.* Treaty die. *Rev.* as 1518	1850	6500
1524	*Calais.* Without AQT, flag at stern. R. Є in centre	1750	6250
1525	— — R. Treaty die with C in centre	1850	6500

SILVER

FIRST COINAGE, 1327-35 (0.925 fineness)

1526   1530

1526	**Penny.** *London.* As Edw. II; Fox class XVd with Lombardic n's	325	1000
1527	*Bury St. Edmunds.* Similar	425	1350
1528	*Canterbury; mm.* cross pattée with pellet centre	250	850
1529	— — three extra pellets in one quarter	225	800
1530	*Durham.* R. Small crown in centre	575	1850
1530A	*Reading.* R. Escallop in 2nd quarter	625	2000
1531	*York.* As 1526, but quatrefoil in centre of *rev;* three extra pellets in TAS quarter	175	575
1532	— — — pellet in each quarter of *mm*	175	575

1535   1537   1539

1534	— — — Roman N's on *obv.*	175	575
1535	*Berwick* (1333-1342, Blunt type VIII). Bear's head in one quarter of *rev.*	575	1750
1536	**Halfpenny.** *London.* Indistinguishable from EDWARD II (cf. 1472)	45	175
1537	*Berwick* (Bl. VIII). Bear's head in one or two quarters	85	300
1538	**Farthing.** *London.* Indistinguishable from those of EDWARD II (cf. 1474)	30	100
1539	*Berwick* (Bl. VIII). As 1537	90	325

1540   1542

| | F | VF |
| | £ | £ |

SECOND COINAGE, 1335-43 (0.833 fineness)

1540	**Halfpenny.** *London.* ЄDWARDVS RЄX AN(G). Six-pointed star after AN and before LON. Bifoliate or trifoliate crown.	25	85
1540A	— — New tall crown. Star of eight or six points after ANG and DON and before CIVI or none on rev.	25	90
1541	*Reading.* Escallop in one quarter, star before or after mint	175	575
1542	**Farthing.** *London.* A (N), six-pointed star after A (rarely omitted) and before LON, flat crown.	25	85
1542A	— ANG, star after ANG and before LON or after DON, tall crown	25	90

THIRD OR FLORIN COINAGE, 1344-51. Bust with bushy hair. (0.925 fine, 20 grs., 1.30g.)

1543   1544

Reverses: I. Lombardic n II. Roman N. III. Reversed N. IV. Reversed Double-barred N.

1543	**Penny.** Fox proposed 'Class XVI'. *London.* Class 1. ЄDW, Lombardic N. Rev. I.	25	100
1544	— — Class 2, ЄDWA, Lombardic N. Rev. I, II.	25	95
1545	— — Class 3. ЄDW. Roman N. Rev. I, II, III.	25	95
1546	— — Class 4. ЄDW. Reversed N. Rev. I, II, III, IV (doubtful)	20	95
1546A	— Unusual types designated A to E.	35	135
1547	— Canterbury. Class 2. as 1544. Rev. I.	80	275
1548	— — Class 4. as 1546 Rev. I.	65	225
1549	*Durham,* Sede Vacante (possibly 1345 issues of Bishop Richard de Bury or Bishop Hatfield). A, ЄDWR rev. No marks	30	110
1550	— — B, similar, ЄDWAR R.	45	150
1551	— Bp. Hatfield. C, similar, but pellet in centre of *rev.*	50	160
1552	— — — Crozier on *rev.*	50	160
1553	— — — — with pellet in centre of *rev.*	60	175
1554	— — D, ЄDWARDVS RЄX AIn, crozier on *rev.*	95	325

1555

1555	*Reading. obv.* as 1546. R. Escallop in one quarter	225	750
1555A	— — ЄDWARDVS RЄX AnG. Rev. as 1555.	275	1000
1556	*York. obv.* as 1546. R. Quatrefoil in centre	30	100

1557   1558

		F £	VF £
1557	**Halfpenny.** *London.* ЄDWARDVS RЄX.................................	20	90
1558	— — ЄDWARDVS RЄX AП.	25	95

1559   1561   1562

1559	— — as 1558 with pellet or small saltire each side of crown and/or in one reverse quarter......................................	35	120
1560	— *Reading.* as 1557. Rev. Escallop in one quarter..................................	200	650
1561	— — as 1558. Rev. as 1560.	225	700
1562	**Farthing.** *London.* ЄDWARDVS RЄX	25	100
1562A	*Reading.* As S.1562. Rev. as 1560..............................	275	950
1562B	— — ЄDWARDVS RЄX AП. Rev. as 1560..	300	1000

FOURTH COINAGE, 1351-77

Reference: L. A. Lawrence, *The Coinage of Edward III from 1351.*
A large variety of mules exist between styles and issue.

Pre-treaty period, 1351-61. With French title.

1563   1565

1567

1563	**Groat** (=4d., 72 grs., 4.66g.). *London,* series B (1351). Roman M, open C and Є; *mm.* cross 1	135	525
1564	— — — crown in each quarter..............................	2750	9500
1565	— C (1351-2). Lombardic М, closed Ꮯ and Є, R with wedge-shaped tail; *mm.* cross 1	45	200
1566	— D (1352-3). R with normal tail; *mm.* cross 1 or cross 1 broken (2).....	50	210
1567	— E (1354-5). Broken letters, V often with nick in r. limb; *mm.* cross 2 (3)	40	175

		F	VF
		£	£
1568	— — — lis on breast............................	45	200
1569	— F (1356). *mm.* crown (74).........................	50	220

1570   1572

1570	— G (1356-61). Usually with annulet in one quarter and sometimes under bust, *mm.* cross 3 (4). Many varieties......................	40	175
1571	*York,* series D. As London.........................	175	750
1572	— E. As London..........................	60	250

1573   1581

1573	**Halfgroat.** *London,* series B. As groat..........................	80	275
1574	— C. As groat..........................	30	110
1575	— D. As groat..........................	35	125
1576	— E. As groat..........................	35	120
1577	— F. As groat..........................	40	135
1578	— G. As groat..........................	35	125
1579	— — — annulet below bust..........................	40	140
1580	*York,* series D. As groat..........................	70	250
1581	— E. As groat..........................	50	175
1582	— — — lis on breast..........................	65	225
1583	**Penny.** *London.* Series A (1351). Round letters, Lombardic m and n, annulet in each quarter; *mm.* cross pattée..........................	80	275

1584   1585   1591

1584	— C. Details as groat, but annulet in each quarter....................	20	95
1585	— D. Details as groat, but annulet in each quarter....................	25	100
1586	— E. Sometimes annulet in each quarter....................	20	95
1587	— F. Details as groat....................	20	95
1588	— G. Details as groat....................	20	90

		F	*VF*
		£	£
1589	— — — annulet below bust	25	100
1590	— — — saltire in one quarter	30	135
1591	*Durham,* Bp. Hatfeil. Series A. As 1583, but extra pellet in each quarter,		
	VIL LA crozier DVRRЄM and VIL crozier LA DVRRЄM	70	250
1592	— C. Details as groat. R. Crozier, CIVITAS DVNЄLMIЄ	25	110
1593	— D — — —	30	125
1594	— E — — —	35	135
1595	— F — R. Crozier, CIVITAS DVRЄMЄ	30	125
1596	— G — — —	30	125
1597	— — — — — annulet below bust	35	135
1598	— — — — — saltire in one quarter	45	175
1599	— — — — — annulet on each shoulder	35	150
1600	— — — — — trefoil of pellets on breast	35	150
1601	— — — R. Crozier, CIVITAS DVRЄLMIЄ	45	175
1602	*York,* Royal Mint. Series D	30	110
1603	— — E	25	100
1604	— Archb. Thoresby. Series D. R. Quatrefoil in centre	30	120
1605	— — G —	25	100
1606	— — — annulet or saltire on breast	30	125

1607   1609   1609A

1607	**Halfpenny.** *London.* Series E. ЄDWARDVS RЄX An	60	225
1608	— G, but with *obv.* of F (*mm.* crown). Annulet in one quarter	110	400
1609	**Farthing.** *London.* Series E. ЄDWARDVS RЄX	95	375
1609A	— — Series G. Annulet in one quarter	110	450

Transitional treaty period, 1361. French title omitted, irregular sized letters; *mm.* cross potent (5).

1610	**Groat.** *London.* Annulet each side of crown	325	1250

1611   1612   1615

1611	**Halfgroat.** Similar, but only seven arches to tressure	135	525
1612	**Penny,** *London.* Omits RЄX, annulet in two upper qtrs. of *mm.*	100	375
1613	*York,* Archb. Thoresby. Similar, but quatrefoil enclosing pellet in centre		
	of *rev.*	50	175
1614	*Durham.* Bp. Hatfield. Similar. R. Crozier, CIVITAS DORЄLMЄ	60	225
1615	**Halfpenny.** Two pellets over *mm.*, ЄDWARDVS RЄX An	175	750

Treaty period, 1361-69. French title omitted, new letters, usually 'Treaty' X, rarely curule chair X *mm.* cross potent (5).

		F	VF
		£	£
1616	**Groat,** *London.* Many varieties	65	240
1617	— Annulet before ЄDWARD	70	250
1618	— Annulet on breast	110	425

1617   1618

| 1619 | *Calais.* As last | 110 | 400 |

1620   1626

1620	**Halfgroat,** *London.* As groat	50	175
1621	— — Annulet before ЄDWARDVS	50	175
1622	— — Annulet on breast	60	200
1623	*Calais.* As last	110	350
1624	**Penny,** *London.* ЄDWARD AПGL R, etc	35	125
1625	— — — pellet before ЄDWARD	40	135
1626	*Calais.* Ŗ. VILLA CALЄSIE	150	575
1627	*Durham.* Ŗ. CIVITAS DVПЄLMIS	50	175
1628	— Ŗ. Crozier, CIVITAS DVRЄMЄ	40	135
1629	*York,* Archb. Thoresby. Quatrefoil in centre of *rev.,* ЄDWARDVS DЄI G RЄX AП	40	135
1630	— — — ЄDWARDVS RЄX AПGLI	30	110
1631	— — — — quatrefoil before ЄD and on breast	35	120
1632	— — — — annulet before ЄD	35	120
1633	— — — ЄDWARD AПGL R DПS HYB	40	135
1634	**Halfpenny.** ЄDWARDVS RЄX AП, pellet stops	30	110

1635   1636

| 1635 | — Pellet before ЄD, annulet stops | 30 | 110 |
| 1636 | **Farthing.** ЄDWARDVS RЄX, pellet or no stops | 175 | 750 |

Post-treaty period, 1369-77. French title resumed, X like St. Andrew's cross; *mm.* 5, 6, 7a.

1637   1639

		F	VF
		£	£
1637	**Groat.** Various readings, *mm.* cross pattée	90	325
1638	— — row of pellets across breast (chain mail)	275	850
1639	— row of annulets below bust (chain mail); *mm.* cross potent with four pellets	375	1000
1640	**Halfgroat.** Various readings	100	300

1641

1640A	— Thin portrait of Richard II	135	475
1641	— row of pellets one side of breast (chain mail)	150	525
1642	**Penny,** *London.* No marks on breast	40	175
1643	— Pellet or annulet on breast	40	175
1644	— Cross or quatrefoil on breast	35	150
1645	*Durham,* Bp. Hatfield. *mm.* 7a, CIVITAS DVnOLM, crozier	35	140
1646	— — — — annulet on breast	40	150
1647	— — — — lis on breast	40	150
1648	*York.* Archb. Thoresby or Neville. R. Quatrefoil in centre	30	135
1649	— — — lis on breast	35	140
1650	— — — annulet on breast	30	135
1651	— — — cross on breast	40	150

1652

1652	**Farthing.** ЄDWARD RЄX ANGL, large head without neck	275	950

For further reading see:
Halfpennies and Farthings of Edward III and Richard II. *Paul and Bente R. Withers, 2002.*

There was no change in the weight standard of the coinage during this reign and the coins evolve from early issues resembling those of Edward III to late issues similar to those of Henry IV.

There is no overall, systematic classification of the coins of Richard II but a coherent scheme for the gold coinage has been worked out and is published in the Schneider Sylloge (SCBI 47). This classification has been adopted here.

Reference: *Silver coinages of Richard II, Henry IV and V.* (B.N.J. 1959-60 and 1963).

Mintmark: cross pattée (6)

GOLD

		F £	VF £
1653	**Noble,** *London.* Style of Edw. III. IA. Lis over sail	1500	5500

1654   1658

1654	— IB. Annulet over sail...	1250	4500
1655	French title omitted. IIA. Crude style, saltire over sail. IIB. Fine style, trefoil over sail. IIC. Porcine style, no mark over sail	1250	4500
1656	French title resumed. IIIA. Fine style, no marks....................................	1250	4500
1657	— IIIB. Lis on rudder. IIIC. Trefoil by shield..	1350	4750
1658	Henry IV style. IVA. Escallop on rudder. IVB. Crescent on rudder.........	1750	6500
1659	*Calais.* With altered obverse of Edw. III, Edw. III lettering....................	2250	8000
1660	Style of Edw. III. IB. New lettering. Voided quatrefoil over sail	1350	5000

1661

1661	French title omitted. IIA. Crude style, no marks. IIB. Fine style, trefoil over sail. IIC. Porcine style, no marks...	1250	4500
1662	French title resumed. IIIA. Fine style, no marks.....................................	1350	4750
1663	— IIIB. Lion on rudder. IIIC. Two pellets by shield	1500	5500

	F	VF
	£	£

1664 **Half-noble,** *London*. With altered *obv.* of Edw. III. Usually muled with *rev.* or altered *rev.* of Edw. III .... 1500 | 5250

1665   1673

1665	Style of Edw. III. IB. No marks or saltire over sail.............................	1350	4750
1666	French title omitted. IIA. New style, no marks...................................	1400	5000
1667	French title resumed. IIIA. No marks. IIIB. Lion on rudder...............	1350	4750
1668	Henry IV style. IVB. Crescent on rudder	1750	6000
1669	*Calais*. Mule with *obv.* or *rev.* of Edw. III..	1850	6500
1670	Style of Edw. III. IB. Quatrefoil over sail	1750	6000
1671	Late style. French title. IIIA. No marks. IIIB. Saltire by rudder	1600	5750
1672	**Quarter-noble,** *London*. IA. R in centre of *rev.*	525	1500
1673	IB Lis in centre of *rev.*	475	1350
1674	— lis or cross over shield	525	1500

1675   1677

1675	IIIA. Pellet in centre of *rev.*...	475	1350
1676	IIIB. Trefoil of annulets over shield or trefoils in spandrels	575	1650
1677	IVA. Escallop over shield	525	1500

SILVER

1680

	F £	VF £
1678 **Groat.** I. Style of Edw. III, F *(i.e. et)* before FRANC, etc................	425	2000
1679 II. New lettering, retrograde Z before FRANC, etc.	375	1650
1680 III. Bust with bushy hair, 'fishtail' serifs to letters............................	425	1750
1681 IV. New style bust and crown, crescent on breast.............................	1100	4500

1682

1682 **Halfgroat.** II. New lettering; with or without French title..................	225	800
1683 III. As 1680..	240	850
1684 — — with *obv.* die of Edw. III (1640A)...	275	950
1685 IV. As 1681, with or without crescent on breast................................	450	1500
1686 **Penny,** *London.* I Lettering as 1678, RICARDVS REX ANGLIE.....	175	750
1688 — II. As 1679, Z FRANC lis on breast...	185	800

1688

1689 — III. As 1680, RICARD REX AnGLIE, fish-tail letters..................	225	900
1690 *York.* I. Early style, usually with cross or lis on breast, quatrefoil in centre of *rev.*...	65	300
1691 — II. New bust and letters, no marks on breast.................................	65	300

1692

1692	— Local dies. Pellet above each shoulder, cross on breast, REX AnGLIE or AnGILIE	75	325
1693	— — — RЄX DNS ЄB	85	350
1694	— — — RЄX AnG FRAnC	80	375
1695	— III. As 1680, RЄX AnGL Z FRAnC (scallop after TAS)	75	325
1696	— IV. Very bushy hair, new letters, Ŗ. R in centre of quatrefoil	135	550
1697	*Durham.* Cross or lis on breast, DVnOLM	125	475

1698   1699

1698	**Halfpenny.** Early style. LONDON, saltire or annulet (rare) on breast	45	150
1699	Intermediate style. LOnDOn, no marks on breast	35	125
1700	Type III. Late style. Similar, but fishtail letters	35	135
1700A	Type IV. Short, stubby lettering	40	140

1701   1704A

1701	**Farthing.** Small bust and letters	110	425
1703	Similar but no neck	110	425
1704	Rose in each angle of *rev.* instead of pellets	150	575
1704A	Large head with broad face as Henry IV	225	900

For further reading see:
Halfpennies and Farthings of Edward III and Richard II. P. and B. R. Withers, 2002.

HENRY IV, 1399-1413

In 1412 the standard weights of the coinage were reduced, the noble by 12 grains and the penny by 3 grains, partly because there was a scarcity of bullion and partly to provide revenue for the king, as Parliament had not renewed the royal subsidies. As in France, the royal arms were altered, three fleur-de-lis taking the place of the four or more lis previously displayed.

Mintmark: cross pattée (6)

GOLD

HEAVY COINAGE, 1399-1412

1706   1707

		F £	VF £
1705	**Noble** (120 grs., 7.77g.), *London*. Old arms with four lis in French quarters; crescent or annulet on rudder	6500	20000
1706	— New arms with three lis; crescent, pellet or no marks on rudder	5750	17500
1707	*Calais*. Flag at stern, old arms; crown on or to l. of rudder	8000	25000

1709

1708	— — new arms; crown or saltire on rudder	6500	20000
1709	**Half-noble**, *London*. Old arms	5500	17500
1710	— new arms	5000	16500
1711	*Calais*. New arms	7000	22500
1712	**Quarter-noble**, *London*. Crescent over old arms	1350	4500
1713	— — — new arms	1250	4250
1714	*Calais*. New arms. R. *Mm.* crown	1750	5250

1715

| | F | VF |
| | £ | £ |

LIGHT COINAGE, 1412-13

1715 **Noble** (108 grs., 6.99g.). Trefoil, or trefoil and annulet, on side of ship.
R. Trefoil in one quarter.. 1850 6000
1716 **Half-noble.** Similar, but always with annulet 2500 8500

1717

1717 **Quarter-noble.** Trefoils, or trefoils and annulets beside shield, lis above. R.
Lis in centre 600   1850

SILVER

HEAVY COINAGE, 1399-1412

1718 **Halfgroat** (36 grs., 2.33g.). Star on breast 1750 5750
1718A — Muled with Edw. III (1640A) *obv.*... 700   2250
1719 **Penny,** *London.* Similar, early bust with long neck.............................. 800   2750
1720 — later bust with shorter neck, no star on breast 800   2750

1722   1723   1725

1722 *York* Bust with broad face, round chin.. 450   1350
1723 **Halfpenny.** Early small bust... 225   750
1724 — later large bust, with rounded shoulders,.. 250   800
1725 **Farthing.** Face without neck.. 900   2750

LIGHT COINAGE, 1412-13

1726

1732

		F £	VF £
1726	**Groat** (60 grs., 3.88g.). I. Pellet to l., annulet to r. of crown; altered die of Richard II	1750	8500
1727	New dies; II. Annulet to l., pellet to r. of crown, 8 or 10 arches to tressure	1600	7500
1728	— III. Similar but 9 arches to tressure	1350	6000
1729	**Halfgroat.** Pellet to l., annulet to r. of crown	975	7500
1730	Annulet to l., pellet to r. of crown	750	2750
1731	**Penny,** *London.* Annulet and pellet by crown; trefoil on breast and before CIVI	750	2750
1732	— — annulet or slipped trefoil before LON	850	3000
1733	— Pellet and annulet by crown	850	3000
1734	*York.* Annulet on breast. R. Quatrefoil in centre	425	1250
1735	*Durham.* Trefoil on breast, DVnOLM	375	1050

1737

1738

1737	**Halfpenny.** New dies; annulets by crown or neck, or no marks	250	800
1738	**Farthing.** Face, no bust; trefoil after RЄX	750	2500

For further information see:
Halfpennies and Farthings of Henry IV, V and VI. P. and B. R. Withers, 2003.

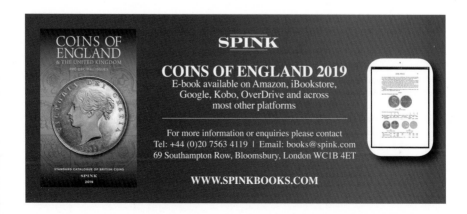

There was no change of importance in the coinage of this reign. There was, however, a considerable development in the use of privy marks which distinguished various issues, except for the last issue of the reign when most marks were removed. The Calais mint, which had closed in 1411, did not re-open until just before the end of the reign. There is now some uncertainty as to whether types A and B of Henry V should be given to Henry IV.

Mintmarks

Cross pattée (4)   Pierced cross with   Pierced cross (18).
                pellet centre (20)

GOLD

		F	VF
		£	£
1739	**Noble.** A. Quatrefoil over sail and in second quarter of *rev.* Short broad letters, no other marks	1750	7500
1740	— B. Ordinary letters; similar, or with annulet on rudder	1350	4500
1741	— C. Mullet by sword arm, annulet on rudder	1300	4250

1742   1744

1742	— — — broken annulet on side of ship	1250	4000
1743	—D. Mullet and annulet by sword arm, trefoil by shield, broken annulet on ship	1350	4500
1744	— E. Mullet, or mullet and annulet by sword arm, trefoil by shield, pellet by sword point and in one quarter, annulet on side of ship	1300	4250
1745	— — Similar, but trefoil on ship instead of by shield	1350	4500
1746	— F. Similar, but no pellet at sword point, trefoil in one quarter	1500	4750
1747	— G. No marks; annulet stops, except for mullet after first word	1750	6500
1748	**Half Noble.** B. As noble; Hen. IV *rev.* die	2250	7500
1749	— C. Broken annulet on ship, quatrefoil below sail	1050	3500
1750	— — Mullet over shield, broken annulet on *rev.*	975	3250
1751	— F. Similar, but no annulet on ship, usually trefoil by shield	1100	3750
1752	— F/E. As last, but pellet in 1st and annulet in 2nd quarter	1250	4000

1753   1756

	F £	VF £
1753 — G. As noble, but quatrefoil over sail, mullet sometimes omitted after first word of *rev*.	1100	3750
1754 **Quarter Noble.** A. Lis over shield and in centre of *rev*. Short broad letters; quatrefoil and annulet beside shield, stars at corners of centre on *rev*.	750	1850
1755 — C. Ordinary letters; quatrefoil to l., quat. and mullet to r. of shield	450	1050
1756 — — — annulet to l., mullet to r. of shield	350	750
1757 — F. Ordinary letters; trefoil to l., mullet to r. of shield	425	950
1758 — G. — no marks, except mullet after first word	450	1050

SILVER

1759

1759 **Groat.** A. Short broad letters; 'emaciated' bust	675	3000
1760 — — muled with Hen. IV *obv*	1100	4750
1761 — — muled with Hen. IV *rev*	750	3250

1762B   1767

1762 B. Ordinary letters; 'scowling' bust	325	1100
1762A — — mullet in centre of breast	375	1250
1762B — — mullet to r. of breast	525	1750
1763 — — muled with Hen. IV	650	2500
1764 C. Normal 'frowning' bust	275	950
1765 — — mullet on r. shoulder	150	575
1766 — — R muled with Hen. IV	525	2250
1767 G. Normal 'frowning' bust; no marks	325	1100
1768 **Halfgroat.** A. As groat, but usually with annulet and pellet by crown	575	2500

		F	VF
		£	£
1769	B. Ordinary letters; no marks..	325	1250
1770	− − muled with Hen. IV *obv.*..	950	3500
1771	C. Tall neck, broken annulet to l. of crown...	125	450
1772	− − − mullet on r. shoulder..	135	525

	1774 1775 1788		
1773	− − − mullet in centre of breast	120	375
1774	F. Annulet and trefoil by crown, mullet on breast	125	450
1775	G. New neat bust: no marks..	120	375
1776	**Penny.** *London.* Altered Hen. IV *obv.* with mullet added to l. of crown..	575	2250
1777	− A. Letters, bust and marks as 1768..	325	1250
1778	− C. Tall neck, mullet and broken annulet by crown	45	200
1779	− D. Similar, but whole annulet..	50	225
1780	− F. Mullet and trefoil by crown	50	225
1781	− G. New neat bust, no marks, DI GRA	60	240
1782	*Durham.* C. As 1778 but quatrefoil at end of legend............................	45	185
1783	− D. As 1779	45	185
1784	− G. Similar, but new bust. R. Annulet in one qtr.	45	200
1785	*York.* C. As 1778, but quatrefoil in centre of *rev.*...............................	40	165
1786	− D. Similar, but whole annulet by crown	40	165
1787	− E. As last, but pellet above mullet	60	240
1788	− F. Mullet and trefoil by crown	40	165
1789	− − Trefoil over mullet to l., annulet to r. of crown...............................	50	225
1790	− G. Mullet and trefoil by crown (London dies).....................................	45	185

	1791 1796 1798		
1791	− − Mullet and lis by crown, annulet in one qtr. (usually local dies)....	40	175
1792	**Halfpenny.** A. Emaciated bust, annulets by crown	175	650
1793	− altered dies of Hen. IV	225	800
1794	C. Ordinary bust, broken annulets by crown	30	110
1795	D. Annulets, sometimes broken, by hair...	35	125
1796	F. Annulet and trefoil by crown	35	125
1797	G. New bust; no marks, (usually muled with Henry VI annulet *rev.*)	50	175
1797A	**Farthing.** *London.* B. Very large head	525	1750
1798	− G. Small face with neck..	375	1250
1798A	*Calais.* G. as 1798, VILLA CALIS	475	1650

For further information see:
Halfpennies and Farthings of Henry IV, V and VI. P and B. R. Withers, 2003.

The supply of gold began to dwindle early in the reign, which accounts for the rarity of gold after 1426. The Calais mint had reopened just before the death of Henry V and for some years a large amount of coin was struck there. It soon stopped minting gold; the mint was finally closed in 1440. A royal mint at York was opened for a short time in 1423/4.

Marks used to denote various issues become more prominent in this reign and can be used to date coins to within a year or so.

Reference: C. A. Whitton, *The Heavy Coinage of Henry VI*. (B.N.J. 1938-41).

Mintmarks

⬦	✛	⚜	✚	✛	✳	✤	✢
136	7a	105	18	133	8	9	15

1422-7	Incurved pierced cross (136)	1422-34	Cross pommée (133)
1422-3	Lis (105, York)	1427-34	Cross patonce (8)
1422-60	Plain cross (7a, intermittently		Cross fleury (9)
	Lis (105, on gold)	1434-35	Voided cross (15)
1422-27	Pierced cross (18)	1435-60	Cross fleury (9)
1460	Lis (105, on rev. of some groats)		

For Henry VI (second reign 1470-71), restoration mintmarks see page 220.

GOLD

1799

		F £	VF £
Annulet issue, 1422-c.1430			
1799	**Noble.** *London.* Annulet by sword arm, and in one spandrel on *rev.;* trefoil stops on *obv.* with lis after hЄПRIC, annulets on *rev.*, with mullet after IhC	1000	3500
1800	— Similar, but *obv.* from Henry V die	1750	6500
1801	— As 1799, but Flemish imitative coinage	900	2500

1802

1802	*Calais.* As 1799, but flag at stern and C in centre of *rev*	1250	4250

		F	VF
		£	£
1803	— — with h in centre of *rev.*	1100	3750
1804	*York.* As London, but with lis over stern....................................	1350	5250

1805

1805	**Half-noble.** *London.* As 1799.................................	750	2250
1806	— Similar, but *obv.* from Henry V die........................	1250	4000
1807	*Calais.* As noble, with C in centre of *rev.*....................	1450	5000
1808	— — with h in centre of *rev.*......................................	1350	4500
1809	*York.* As noble...	1500	5250
1810	**Quarter-noble.** *London.* Lis over shield; *mm.* large lis	300	725
1811	— — — trefoil below shield	325	750
1812	— — — pellet below shield	350	825
1813	*Calais.* Three lis over shield; *mm.* large lis......................	425	1250

1814   1819

1814	— Similar but three lis around shield......................................	375	950
1815	— As 1810, but much smaller *mm*...	350	850
1816	*York.* Two lis over shield..	375	950

Rosette-mascle issue, c.1430-31

1817	**Noble.** *London.* Lis by sword arm and in *rev.* field; stops, rosettes, or		
	rosettes and mascles..	1750	6500
1818	*Calais.* Similar, with flag at stern	2000	8500
1819	**Half-noble.** *London.* Lis in *rev.* field; stops, rosettes and mascles..........	2250	9500
1820	*Calais.* Similar, flag at stern; stops, rosettes.............................	3500	12500
1821	**Quarter-noble.** *London.* As 1810; stops, as noble..........................	950	3500
1822	— without lis over shield..	1000	3750
1823	*Calais.* Lis over shield, rosettes r. and l., and rosette stops	1000	3750

Pinecone-mascle issue, c.1431-2/3

1824

		F	VF
		£	£
1824	**Noble.** Stops, pinecones and mascles.....................................	1750	6500
1825	**Half-noble.** *O.* Rosette-mascle die. Ṛ. As last	3500	13500
1826	**Quarter-noble.** As 1810, but pinecone and mascle stops........................	1000	3750

1828

Leaf-mascle issue, c.1432/3-6

1827	**Noble.** Leaf in waves; stops, saltires with two mascles and one leaf.......	3750	15000
1828	**Half-noble.** (Fishpool hoard and Reigate hoard)	3500	13500
1829	**Quarter-noble.** As 1810; stops, saltire and mascle; leaf on inner circle of *rev*.	1100	4250

Leaf-trefoil issue, c.1436-8

1830	**Noble.** Stops, leaves and trefoils	2750	11000
1830A	**Half-noble.**	3250	12500
1831	**Quarter-noble.** Similar...	1100	4250

Trefoil issue, 1438-43

1832	**Noble.** Trefoil to left of shield and in *rev.* legend....................	2750	11000

Leaf-pellet issue, 1445-54

1833	**Noble.** Annulet, lis and leaf below shield...............................	3500	13500

Cross-pellet issue, 1454-61

1834	**Noble.** Mascle at end of *obv.* legend..	3750	15000

Muling exists in Henry VI coins spanning two or three issues. Full flan coins in the smaller denominations are difficult to find.

SILVER

Annulet issue, 1422-30

1835   1836

		F	VF
		£	£
1835	**Groat.** *London.* Annulet in two quarters of *rev.*	40	150
1836	*Calais.* Annulets at neck. R. Similar..	40	145
1837	— — no annulets on *rev.*	70	275

1838

1838	*York.* Lis either side of neck. R. As 1835...............................	850	3000
1839	**Halfgroat.** *London.* As groat...	40	135

1840   1843

1840	*Calais.* As 1836..	30	110
1841	— — no annulets on *rev.*	40	135
1843	*York.* As groat...	750	2500

1845

1844	**Penny.** *London.* Annulets in two qtrs.	30	110
1845	*Calais.* Annulets at neck. R. As above.....................................	30	100

		F £	VF £
1847	*York*. As London, but lis at neck	750	2500
1848	**Halfpenny.** *London.* As penny	20	80
1849	*Calais*. Similar, but annulets at neck	20	80

1850   1852

1850	*York*. Similar, but lis at neck	575	1750
1851	**Farthing.** *London.* As penny, but *mm.* cross pommée	110	425
1852	*Calais*. Similar, but annulets at neck	135	475
1852A	*York*. Similar, but lis at neck	575	1750

Annulet-trefoil sub-issue

1854   1855

1854	**Groat.** *Calais,* as 1836 but trefoil to l. of crown, R trefoil after POSVI and only one annulet	65	210
1855	**Halfgroat.** *Calais,* similar, usually a mule with annulet issue.	55	175
1856	**Penny.** *Calais*. Similar, only one annulet on *rev*	80	275

Rosette-mascle issue, 1430-31. All with rosettes (early) or rosettes and mascles somewhere in the legends.

1858	**Groat.** *London.*	50	185

1859   1861

1859	*Calais*	45	160
1860	— mascle in two spandrels	60	175
1861	**Halfgroat.** *London.*	100	325

1862	1870	1872

		F	VF
		£	£
1862	*Calais*	40	125
1863	— mascle in two spandrels	45	130
1864	**Penny.** *London*	150	475
1865	*Calais*	30	110
1866	*York.* Archb. Kemp. Crosses by hair, no rosette	30	110
1867	— — Saltires by hair, no rosette	35	125
1868	— — Mullets by crown	30	120
1869	*Durham,* Bp. Langley. Large star to l. of crown, no rosette, DVnOLMI	65	180
1870	**Halfpenny,** *London*	25	90
1871	*Calais*	25	85
1872	**Farthing,** *London*	175	575
1873	*Calais. Mm.* cross pommée	225	750

Pinecone-mascle issue, 1431-32/3. All with pinecones and mascles in legends.

	1874	1876

1874	**Groat,** London	50	165
1875	*Calais*	45	160
1876	**Halfgroat,** *London*	60	175
1877	*Calais*	45	130
1878	**Penny,** *London*	50	175
1879	*Calais*	40	125
1880	*York,* Archb. Kemp. Mullet by crown, quatrefoil in centre of *rev.*	40	135
1881	— — rosette on breast, no quatrefoil	40	135
1882	— — mullet on breast, no quatrefoil	45	150
1883	*Durham,* Bp. Langley. DVnOLMI	45	160

1884   1886

		F £	VF £
1884	**Halfpenny,** *London*	20	90
1885	*Calais*	25	100
1886	**Farthing,** *London*	150	575
1887	*Calais. Mm.* cross pommée	225	750

Leaf-mascle issue, 1432/3-6. Usually with a mascle in the legend and a leaf somewhere in the design.

1888	**Groat.** *London*. Leaf below bust, all appear to read DONDON	375	1250
1889	— — *rev.* of last or next coinage	135	525

1890   1892

1890	*Calais.* Leaf below bust, and usually below MEVM	125	475
1891	**Halfgroat.** *London.* Leaf under bust, pellet under TAS and DON.	150	525
1892	*Calais.* Leaf below bust, and sometimes on *rev.*	135	450
1893	**Penny.** *London.* Leaf on breast, no stops on *rev.*	65	200
1894	*Calais.* Leaf on breast and below SIE	75	225
1895	**Halfpenny.** *London.* Leaf on breast and on *rev.*	35	100
1896	*Calais.* Leaf on breast and below SIE	75	225

1897   1902

Leaf-trefoil issue, 1436-8. Mostly with leaves and trefoil of pellets in the legends.

1897	**Groat.** *London.* Leaf on breast	85	250
1898	— without leaf on breast	85	250
1899	*Calais.* Leaf on breast	275	950
1900	**Halfgroat.** *London.* Leaf on breast; *mm.* plain cross	70	225
1901	— *O. mm.* cross fleury; leaf on breast	65	200
1902	— — without leaf on breast	70	225
1902A	*Calais.* leaf on breast, mule with leaf mascle *rev.*	175	600

	F	VF
	£	£
1903 **Penny.** *London*. Leaf on breast..	100	300
1903A *Calais*. Similar..	275	750
1904 *Durham,* Bp. Neville. Leaf on breast. ℞. Rings in centre, no stops, DVnOLM	110	350

1905   1907

1905 **Halfpenny.** *London*. Leaf on breast	25	90
1906 — without leaf on breast..	25	95
1906A *Calais*. leaf on breast, mule with leaf mascle rev.	100	325
1907 **Farthing.** *London*. Leaf on breast; stops, trefoil and saltire on *obv*.........	275	950

Trefoil issue, 1438-43. Trefoil of pellets either side of neck and in legend, leaf on breast.

1910

1908 **Groat.** *London*. Sometimes a leaf before LON.	80	250
1909 — Fleurs in spandrels, sometimes extra pellet in two qtrs.	85	275
1910 — Trefoils in place of fleurs at shoulders, none by neck, sometimes extra pellets..	90	300
1911 *Calais*...	225	750

1911A

1911A **Halfgroat,** *London* Similar, but trefoil after DEUM and sometimes after POSVI Mule only with leaf trefoil *obv*......................	125	425
1911B — *Calais Obv*. Similar to 1911, mule with leaf mascle *rev*.....................	250	850
1912 **Halfpenny,** *London*	25	100

1912A

1912A **Farthing,** *London*	300	1050

Trefoil pellet issue, 1443-5

1913

		F	VF
		£	£

| 1913 | **Groat.** Trefoils by neck, pellets by crown, small leaf on breast; sometimes extra pellet in two quarters .... | 110 | 375 |

1915   1917

Leaf-pellet issue, 1445-54. Leaf on breast, pellet each side of crown, except where stated.

1914	**Groat.** ANGL; extra pellet in two quarters	60	225
1915	*Similar,* but ANGLI...	60	210
1916	— — trefoil in *obv.* legend	75	275
1917	Leaf on neck, fleur on breast, R often extra pellet in two quarters...........	60	225
1918	As last, but two extra pellets by hair...	250	850
1919	**Halfgroat.** As 1914 *mm.* Cross patonce	85	300
1920	Similar, but *mm.* plain cross, some times no leaf on breast, no stops.......	70	225
1921	**Penny.** *London.* Usually extra pellets in two quarters............................	60	200
1922	— — pellets by crown omitted..	65	225
1923	— — trefoil in legend...	70	250
1924	*York,* Archb. Booth. R. Quatrefoil and pellet in centre...........................	40	135
1925	— — two extra pellets by hair (local dies)..	40	135
1926	*Durham,* Bp. Neville. Trefoil in *obv.* legend. R. Two rings in centre of cross	60	175

1928   1930

1927	— — Similar, but without trefoil..	60	175
1928	**Halfpenny.** Usually extra pellets in two quarters	20	80
1929	— *mm.* plain cross	20	80
1930	**Farthing.** As last	275	950

Unmarked issue, 1453-4

1931   1935

		F £	*VF* £
1931	**Groat.** No marks on *obv.;* two extra pellets on *rev.*	375	1350
1932	— four extra pellets on *rev.*	450	1500
1933	**Halfgroat.** As 1931	350	1250

Cross-pellet issue, 1454-61

1934	**Groat.** Saltire either side of neck, pellets by crown, leaf and fleur on breast, extra pellets on *rev.*	475	1500
1935	Saltire on neck, no leaf, pellets by crown, usually mullets in legend; extra pellets on *rev.*	110	350
1936	— Similar, but mascles in place of mullets on *obv.*	125	375
1937	— — pellets by hair instead of by crown	150	525
1938	**Halfgroat.** Saltire on neck, pellets by crown and on *rev.*, mullets in legend	275	950

1940   1943   1944

1939	**Penny.** *London.* Saltire on neck, pellets by crown and on *rev.*, mascle(s), or mullet and mascle in legend	150	475
1940	*York,* Archb. Wm. Booth. Saltires by neck, usually leaf on breast, pellets by crown. R. Cross in quatrefoil in centre.	55	175
1941	*Durham,* Bp. Laurence Booth. Saltire and B or B only at neck, pellets by crown. R. Rings in centre	65	225
1942	**Halfpenny.** Saltires by neck, usually two extra pellets on *rev.*	35	125
1943	Similar, but saltire on neck, sometimes mullet after hЄNRIC	25	90
1944	**Farthing.** Saltire on neck, usually pellets by crown and on *rev.*, but known without either.	300	1050

For further information see:
Halfpennies and Farthings of Henry IV, V and VI. P. and B. R. Withers, 2003.

Lis-pellet issue, 1456-61

1945

1945	**Groat.** Lis on neck; pellets by crown. R. Extra pellets	225	800

EDWARD IV, First Reign, 1461-70

In order to increase the supply of bullion to the mint the weight of the penny was reduced to 12 grains in 1464, and the current value of the noble was raised to 8s. 4d. Later, in 1465, a new gold coin was issued, the Ryal or 'Rose Noble', weighing 120 grains and having a value of 10s. However, as 6s. 8d. had become the standard professional fee the old noble was missed, and a new coin was issued to take its place, the Angel of 80 grains.

Royal mints were set up in Bristol, Coventry, Norwich and York to help with the recoinage. The Coventry and Norwich mints were not open for long, but the York and Bristol mints remained open until 1471 and 1472 respectively.

Reference: C. E. Blunt and C. A Whitton, *The Coinage of Edward IV and Henry VI (Restored)*, B.N.J. 1945-7.

Mintmarks

✿	✠	✚	❀	Y	✳	♔	✝
105	9	7a	33	99	28	74	11

1461-4	Lis (105)	1467-70	Lis (105, *York*)		
	Cross fleury (9)	1467-8	Crown (74)	(often	
	Plain cross (7a)		Sun (28)	combined)	
1464-5	Rose (33 and 34)	1468-9	Crown (74)	(sometimes	
1464-7	Pall (99, *Canterbury*)		Rose (33)	combined)	
1465-6	Sun (28)	1469-70	Long cross		
1466-7	Crown (74)		fitchee (l.c.f) (11)	(often	
			Sun (28)	combined)	

GOLD

HEAVY COINAGE, 1461-4

1946

		F	VF
		£	£
1946	**Noble** (=6s. 8d., wt. 108 grs., 6.99g.). Normal type, but *obv.* legend commences at top left, lis below shield; *mm.*-/lis (Spink's sale May 1993)	4750	17500
1947	— Quatrefoil below sword arm; *mm.* rose/lis	5250	20000
1948	— R. Roses in two spandrels; *mm.* rose	5500	22500
1949	**Quarter-noble**	1750	6000

1950

	F	VF
	£	£

LIGHT COINAGE, 1464-70

1950	**Ryal** or rose-noble (=10s., wt. 120 grs., 7.77g), *London*. As illustration. Large fleurs in spandrels; *mm*. 33-74	950	3250
1951	— — Small trefoils in spandrels; *mm*. 74-11	950	3250

1952

1952	— Flemish imitative coinage (mostly 16th cent. on a large flan).............	750	2500
1953	*Bristol*. B in waves, large fleurs; *mm*. sun, crown	1250	4250
1954	— — small fleurs in spandrels; *mm*. sun, crown.....................................	1350	4500
1955	*Coventry*. C in waves; *mm*. sun	1850	6000
1956	*Norwich*. ♫ in waves; *mm*. sun, rose	2000	6250
1957	*York*. Є in waves, large fleurs in spandrels, *mm*. sun, lis..........................	950	3500
1958	— — small fleurs, *mm*. sun. lis	1000	3750
1959	**Half-ryal**. *London*. As 1950	750	2250
1960	*Bristol*. B in waves; *mm*. sun, sun/crown..	1250	4750
1961	*Coventry*. C in waves; *mm*. sun..	5250	17500
1962	*Norwich*. ♫ in waves; *mm*. rose	3750	13500

1963   1965

		F	VF
		£	£
1963	*York.* € in waves; *mm.* 28, 105, 33/105	850	2750
1963A	Similar but lis instead of € in waves (probably York)............	950	3500
1964	**Quarter-ryal.** Shield in tressure of eight arcs, rose above. R. Somewhat as half ryal; *mm.* sun/rose	1350	4500
1965	Shield in quatrefoil. € above, rose on l., sun on r.; *mm.* 33/28-74/33	425	1200
1966	— — sun on l., rose on r.; *mm.* 74-11.....................	450	1250

1967

| 1967 | **Angel** (=6s. 8d., wt. 80 grs., 5.18g). St. Michael spearing dragon. R. Ship, rays of sun at masthead, large rose and sun beside mast; *mm.*-/33...................... | 10000 | 37500 |
| 1968 | — — small rose and sun at mast; *mm.*-/74... | 10500 | 40000 |

SILVER

1969   1972

HEAVY COINAGE, 1461-4

1969	**Groat** (60 grs., 3.88g.). Group I, lis on neck, pellets by crown; *mm.* 9, 7a, 105, 9/105	135	475
1970	— Lis on breast, no pellets; *mm.* plain cross, 7a/105	150	525
1971	— — with pellets at crown; *mm.* plain cross.....................	165	575
1972	II, quatrefoils by neck, crescent on breast; *mm.* rose.................	130	450
1973	III, similar but trefoil on breast; *mm.* rose	125	425

1974   1979

	F £	VF £
1974 — — — eye in *rev.* inner legend, *mm.* rose	100	325
1975 — Similar, but no quatrefoils by bust	200	675
1976 — — Similar, but no trefoil on breast	165	575
1977 IV, annulets by neck, eye after TAS; *mm.* rose	225	750
1978 **Halfgroat.** I, lis on breast, pellets by crown and extra pellets in two qtrs.; *mm.* 9, 7a	475	2000
1979 II, quatrefoils at neck, crescent on breast; *mm.* rose	325	1100
1980 III, similar, but trefoil on breast, eye on rev.; *mm.* rose	275	900
1981 — Similar, but no mark on breast	275	900
1982 IV, annulets by neck, sometimes eye on *rev.; mm.* rose	325	1100
1983 **Penny** (15 grs.), *London.* I, marks as 1978, but mascle after REX; *mm.* plain cross	375	1350
1984 II, quatrefoils by neck; *mm.* rose	250	850

1985   1991   1994

	F £	VF £
1985 III, similar, but eye after TAS; *mm.* rose	275	900
1986 IV, annulets by neck; *mm.* rose	325	1050
1987 *York,* Archb. Booth. Quatrefoils by bust, voided quatrefoil in centre of *rev.; mm.* rose	125	350
1988 *Durham. O.* of Hen. VI. R. DVnOLIn	120	325
1988A(ca.1461-c.1462). Local dies, mostly with rose in centre of rev.; *mm.* 7a, 33	35	135
1989 **Halfpenny.** I, as 1983, but no mascle	65	225
1990 II, quatrefoils by bust; *mm.* rose	35	140
1991 — saltires by bust; *mm.* rose	35	135
1992 III, no marks by bust; *mm.* rose	35	140
1992A—saltires by bust, eye after TAS, *mm.* rose	100	350
1993 IV, annulets by bust; *mm.* rose	35	140
1994 **Farthing.** I, pellets by crown, extra pellets on rev., with or without lis on breast	375	1250
1994A II. saltires by bust; *mm.* rose	400	1350
1994B III, no marks by bust; *mm.* rose	375	1250

LIGHT COINAGE, 1464-70. There is a great variety of groats and we give only a selection. Some have pellets in one quarter of the reverse, or trefoils over the crown; early coins have fleurs on the cusps of the tressure, then trefoils or no marks on the cusps, while the late coins have only trefoils.

		F	VF
		£	£
1995	**Groat** (48 grs., 3.11g), *London.* Annulets at neck, eye after TAS; *mm.* 33 (struck from heavy dies, IV)	125	450
1996	— — — Similar, but new dies, eye after TAS or DON	110	400
1997	— Quatrefoils at neck, eye; rose (heavy dies, III)	90	325
1998	— — — Similar, but new dies, eye in *rev.* legend	100	350
1999	— No marks at neck, eye; *mm* rose	135	475
2000	— Quatrefoils at neck, no eye; *mm.* 33, 74, 28, 74/28, 74/33, 11/28	40	140

2001   2002

2001	— — — rose or quatrefoil on breast; *mm.* 33, 74/28	45	165
2002	— No marks at neck; *mm.* 28, 74, 11/28, 11	50	175
2003	— Trefoils or crosses at neck; *mm.* 11/33, 11/28, 11	45	165
2004	*Bristol.* B on breast, quatrefoils at neck; *mm.* 28/33, 28, 28/74, 74, 74/28	60	185
2005	— — trefoils at neck; *mm.* sun	80	275
2006	— — no marks at neck; *mm.* sun	150	525
2007	— Without B, quatrefoils at neck; *mm.* sun	135	475

Bristol is variously rendered as BRESTOLL, BRISTOLL, BRESTOW, BRISTOW.

2008	*Coventry.* C on breast, quatrefoils at neck, COVETRE; *mm.* 28/33, 28...	135	450
2009	— — Local dies, similar; *mm.* rose	175	575
2010	— — — as last, but no C or quatrefoils	175	575
2011	Norwich. Π on breast, quatrefoils at neck, ΠORWIC or ΠORVIC, *mm.* 28/33, 28	125	350
2012	*York.* Є on breast, quatrefoils at neck, ЄBORACI; *mm.* 28, 105/74, 105, 105/28	60	185
2013	— Similar, but without Є on breast, *mm.* lis	100	325
2014	— Є on breast, trefoils at neck; *mm.* 105/28, 105	75	225
2015	**Halfgroat.** *London.* Annulets by neck (heavy dies); *mm.* 33	300	950

2016

2016	— Quatrefoils by neck; *mm.* 33/-, 28/-, 74, 74/28	60	175
2017	— Saltires by neck; *mm.* 74, 74/28	65	180
2018	— Trefoils by neck; *mm.* 74, 74/28, 11/28	65	180
2019	— No marks by neck; *mm.* 11/28	90	275

		F	*VF*
		£	£
2020	*Bristol.* Saltires or crosses by neck; *mm.* 33/28, 28, 74, 74/-....................	135	525
2021	— Quatrefoils by neck; *mm.* 28/-, 74, 74/-...	125	475
2022	— Trefoils by neck; *mm.* crown	135	525
2023	— No marks by neck; *mm.* 74/28...	165	575
2024	*Canterbury,* Archb. Bourchier (1464-7). Knot below bust; quatrefoils		
	by neck; *mm.* 99/-, 99, 99/33, 99/28..	40	150
2025	— — — quatrefoils omitted *mm.* 99	40	150
2026	— — — saltires by neck; *mm.* 99/-, 99/28...................................	50	170
2026A	— — — trefoils by neck; *mm.* 99..	55	185
2027	— — — wedges by hair and/or neck; *mm.* 99, 99/–, 99/33, 99/28	45	160
2028	— — As 2024 or 2025, but no knot..	50	170
2029	— (1467-9). Quatrefoils by neck; *mm.* 74, 74/-	50	165
2030	— — Saltires by neck; *mm.* 74/-, 74	50	165
2031	— — Trefoils by neck; *mm.* 74, 74/-, 74/28, 33...............................	45	150
2032	— No marks by neck; *mm.* sun..	75	250
2033	*Coventry.* Crosses by neck; *mm.* sun	850	2250
2034	*Norwich.* Quatrefoils or saltires by neck; *mm.* sun...............................	750	2000

2035   2063

2035	*York.* Quatrefoils by neck; *mm.* sun, lis, lis/-	100	425
2036	— Saltires by neck; *mm.* lis...	95	400
2037	— Trefoils by neck; *mm.* lis, lis/-	135	575
2038	— Є on breast, quatrefoils by neck; *mm.* lis/-	100	425
2039	**Penny** (12 grs., 0.77g.), *London.* Annulets by neck (heavy dies); *mm.* rose	275	900
2040	— Quatrefoils by neck; *mm.* 74, sun. crown	70	250
2041	— Trefoil and quatrefoil by neck; *mm.* crown...............................	70	250
2042	— Saltires by neck; *mm.* crown..	70	250
2043	— Trefoils by neck; *mm.* crown, long cross fitchée	75	275
2044	— No marks by neck; *mm.* long cross fitchée	125	400
2045	*Bristol.* Crosses, quatrefoils or saltires by neck, BRISTOW; *mm.* crown	275	950
2046	— Quatrefoils by neck; BRI(trefoil)STOLL	300	1000
2047	— Trefoil to r. of neck BRISTOLL	300	1000
2048	*Canterbury,* Archb. Bourchier. Quatrefoils or saltires by neck, knot on		
	breast; *mm.* pall...	70	250
2049	— — Similar, but no marks by neck	70	250
2050	— — As 2048, but no knot...	75	275
2051	— — Crosses by neck, no knot	70	250
2052	— Quatrefoils by neck; *mm.* crown...	135	475
2053	— King's Receiver (1462-4). Local dies, mostly with rose in centre of rev.;		
	mm. 7a, 33..	40	150
2054	— *Durham,* Bp. Lawrence Booth (1465-70). B and D by neck, B on *rev.; mm.* 33	35	140
2055	— — Quatrefoil and B by neck; *mm.* sun	35	130
2056	— — B and quatrefoil by neck; *mm.* crown....................................	40	140
2057	— — D and quatrefoil by neck; *mm.* crown....................................	40	140
2058	— — Quatrefoils by neck; *mm.* crown..	35	130
2059	— — Trefoils by neck; *mm.* crown	40	140
2060	— Lis by neck; *mm.* crown..	35	130

		F £	VF £

2061 *York,* Sede Vacante (1464-5). Quatrefoils at neck, no quatrefoil in centre
of *rev.; mm.* sun, rose.. 40 150

2062 — Archb. Neville (1465-70). Local dies, G and key by neck, quatrefoil
on *rev.; mm.* sun, plain cross.. 35 120

2063 — — London-made dies, similar; *mm.* 28, 105, 11.............................. 40 140

2064 — — Similar, but no marks by neck; *mm.* large lis................................ 40 150

2065 — — — Quatrefoils by neck; *mm.* large lis... 40 150

2066 — — — Trefoils by neck; *mm.* large lis... 40 140

2068   2077

2067 **Halfpenny,** *London.* Saltires by neck; *mm.* 34, 28, 74........................... 30 120

2068 — Trefoils by neck; *mm.* 28, 74, 11... 25 120

2069 — No marks by neck; *mm.* 11 .... 35 135

2070 *Bristol.* Crosses by neck; *mm.* crown...................................... 125 400

2071 — Trefoils by neck; *mm.* crown 110 375

2072 *Canterbury.* Archb. Bourchier. No marks; *mm.* pall............................ 75 275

2072A — — — Trefoils by neck, *mm.* pall... 75 275

2073 — Saltires by neck; *mm.* crown... 65 200

2074 — — Trefoils by neck; *mm.* crown 65 200

2074A *Norwich.* Quatrefoils by neck., *mm.* Sun................................. 350 950

2074B — — Trefoils by neck; *mm.* crown 375 1000

2075 *York.* Royal mint. Saltires by neck; *mm.* lis/-, sun/-............................... 50 175

2076 — — Trefoils by neck; *mm.* lis/- 45 150

2077 **Farthing,** *London.* ЄDWARD DI GRA RЄX, trefoils by neck, *mm.* crown 425 1350

Full flan coins are difficult to find in the smaller denominations.

For further information see:
Halfpennies and Farthings of Edward IV to Henry VII. P. and B. R. Withers, 2004.

The coinage of this short restoration follows closely that of the previous reign. Only angel gold was issued, the ryal being discontinued. Many of the coins have the king's name reading hᏋnRICV — another distinguishing feature is an R that looks like a B.

Mintmarks

Cross pattée (6)   Rose (33, Bristol)
Restoration cross (13)   Lis (105)
Trefoil (44 and 45)   Short cross fitchée (12)

GOLD

2078

		F	*VF*
		£	£
2078	**Angel,** *London.* As illus. but no B; *mm.* -/6, 13, -/105, none	1750	5500
2079	*Bristol.* B in waves; *mm.* -/13, none...	2750	9500
2080	**Half-angel,** *London.* As 2078; *mm.* -/6, -/13, -/105.........................	4500	13500
2081	*Bristol.* B in waves; *mm.* -/13	5750	17500

SILVER

2082   2084   2089

2082	**Groat,** *London.* Usual type; *mm.* 6, 6/13, 6/105, 13, 13/6, 13/105, 13 /12	200	600
2083	*Bristol.* B on breast; *mm.* 13, 13/33, 13/44, 44, 44/13, 44/33, 44/12........	375	1250
2084	*York.* Ꭼ on breast; *mm.* lis, lis/sun...	225	625
2085	**Halfgroat,** *London.* As 2082; *mm.* 13, 13/-.................................	325	1000
2086	*York.* Ꭼ on breast; *mm.* lis	750	2500
2087	**Penny,** *London.* Usual type; *mm.* 6, 13, 12...................................	325	1050
2087A	*Bristol.* Similar; *mm.* 12...	475	1500
2088	*York.* G and key by neck; *mm.* lis	250	800
2089	**Halfpenny,** *London; mm.* 12, 13, ...	200	600
2090	*Bristol.* Similar; *mm.* cross..	325	1050

The Angel and its half were the only gold denominations issued during this reign. The main types and weight standards remained the same as those of the light coinage of Edward's first reign. The use of the 'initial mark' as a mintmark to denote the date of issue was now firmly established.

Mintmarks

| 33 | 105 | 12 | 55 | 44 | 55 | 28 | 56 | 17 |

| 30 | 37 | 6 | 18 | 19 | 20 | 31 | 11 | 38 |

1471-83	Rose (33, *York & Durham*)	1473-7	Cross pattée (6)
	Lis (105, *York*)		Pierced cross 1 (18)
1471	Short cross fitchee (12)	1477-80	Pierced cross and
1471-2	Annulet (large, 55)		pellet (19)
	Trefoil (44)		Pierced cross 2 (18)
	Rose (33, *Bristol*)		Pierced cross, central
1471-3	Pansy (30, *Durham*)		pellet (20)
1472-3	Annulet (small, 55)		Rose (33, *Canterbury*)
	Sun (28, *Bristol*)	1480-3	Heraldic cinquefoil (31)
1473-7	Pellet in annulet (56)		Long cross fitchee
	Cross and four pellets (17)		(11, *Canterbury*)
	Cross in circle (37)	1483	Halved sun and rose (38)
			(Listed under Ed. IV/V.)

GOLD

2091   2093

		F	VF
		£	£
2091	**Angel.** *London.* Type as illus.; *mm.* 12, 55, 56, 17, 18, 19, 31	850	2750
2092	*Bristol.* B in waves; *mm.* small annulet	3750	12500
2093	**Half-angel.** As illus.; *mm.* 55, cross in circle, 19, 20/19, 31	750	2400
2094	King's name and title on rev.; *mm.* 12/-	850	3000
2095	King's name and the title both sides; *mm.* 55/-	1000	3500

SILVER

2097

		F £	*VF* £
2096	**Groat,** *London.* Trefoils on cusps, no marks by bust; *mm.* 12-37	60	200
2097	— — roses by bust; *mm.* pellet in annulet...	125	450
2098	— Fleurs on cusps; no marks by bust; *mm.* 18-20...................................	65	225
2099	— — pellets by bust; *mm.* pierced cross	80	250
2100	— — rose on breast; *mm.* 31	75	240

2101   2107

		F	*VF*
2101	*Bristol.* B on breast no marks by bust; *mm.* 33, 33/55, 28/55, 55, 55/-, 28	200	650
2102	*York.* Є on breast no marks by bust; *mm.* lis...	225	700
2103	**Halfgroat,** *London.* As 2096; *mm.* 12-31	65	250
2104	*Bristol.* B on breast; *mm.* 33/12	325	1050
2105	*Canterbury.* Archb. Bourchier. As 2103; *mm.* 33, 11, 11/31, 31	45	175
2106	— C on breast; *mm.* rose..	40	160
2107	— — R. C in centre; *mm.* rose...	40	160
2108	— — R. Rose in centre; *mm.* rose	40	160
2109	*York.* No. Є on breast; *mm.* lis	200	650
2110	**Penny,** *London.* No marks by bust; *mm.* 12-31	75	250
2111	*Bristol.* Similar; *mm.* rose	300	950
2112	*Canterbury.* Archb. Bourchier. Similar; *mm.* 33, 11...............................	75	275
2113	— C on breast; *mm.* rose..	85	325
2114	*Durham,* Bp. Booth (1471-6). No marks by neck; *mm.* 12, 44.................	35	100

2115   2116

		F	*VF*
2115	— — D in centre of *rev.;* B and trefoil by neck; *mm.* 44, 33, 56.............	35	100
2116	— — — two lis at neck; *mm.* rose...	35	110
2117	— — — crosses over crown, and on breast; *mm.* rose............................	35	110
2118	— — — crosses over crown, V under CIVI; *mm.* rose, pansy.................	40	110
2119	— — — B to l. of crown, V on breast and under CIVI............................	35	100

		F	VF
		£	£
2120	— — — As last but crosses at shoulders	35	100
2121	— — — R. D in centre; *mm.* rose	35	110
2122	— Bp. Dudley (1476-83). V to r. of neck; as last	40	110

2123   2125   2131

2123	— — — D and V by neck; as last, but *mm.* 31	35	100

Nos. 2117-2123 are from locally-made dies.

2124	*York*, Archb. Neville (1471-2). Quatrefoils by neck. R. Quatrefoil; *mm.* 12 (over lis)	45	165
2125	— — Similar, but G and key by neck; *mm.* 12 (over lis)	35	110
2126	— Neville suspended (1472-5). As last, but no quatrefoil in centre of *rev.*	40	135
2126A	— — no marks by bust, similar; *mm.* annulet	45	150
2127	— — No marks by neck, quatrefoil on *rev.; mm.* 55, cross in circle, 33..	35	110
2128	— — Similar but Є and rose by neck; *mm.* rose	30	100
2129	— Archb. Neville restored (1475-6). As last, but G and rose	35	110
2130	— — Similar, but G and key by bust	30	100
2131	— Sede Vacante (1476). As 2127, but rose on breast; *mm.* rose	40	135
2132	— Archb. Lawrence Booth (1476-80). B and key by bust, quatrefoil on *rev.; mm.* 33, 31	30	100
2133	— Sede Vacante (1480). Similar, but no quatrefoil on rev.; *mm.* rose	40	120

2134   2140

2134	— Archb. Rotherham (1480-3). T and slanting key by neck, quatrefoil on *rev.; mm.* 33	35	110
2135	— — — Similar, but star on breast	45	135
2136	— — — Star on breast and to r. of crown	50	150
2137	**Halfpenny**, *London*. No marks by neck; *mm.* 12-31	25	90
2138	— Pellets at neck; *mm.* pierced cross	30	100
2139	*Canterbury* (Archbishop Bourchier). C on breast and in centre of *rev.; mm.* rose	85	275
2140	— C on breast only; *mm.* rose	75	225
2141	— Without C either side; *mm.* 11	75	225
2142	*Durham*, Bp. Booth. No marks by neck. R. DЄRА M, D in centre; *mm.* rose	225	750
2142A	— — Lis either side of neck. R. with or without D in centre	250	800
2142B	— — B to l. of crown, crosses at shoulders. R. with or without D. in centre; *mm.* rose	250	800
2143	— — — Bp. Dudley V to l. of neck; as last	225	750

Full flan coins are very difficult to find in the small denominations.

On 12th February 1483, the prolific cinquefoil coinage of Edward IV came to an end and an indenture between the king and the new master of the mint, Bartholomew Reed, saw the introduction of the sun and rose mintmark.

Edward IV died on 9th April 1483, but the sun and rose coinage continued, essentially unaltered, through the short reign of Edward V and into the reign of Richard III, ending with the indenture of 20th July 1483, with Robert Brackenbury, who had been Richard's ducal treasurer, and the introduction of the boar's head mintmark.

New dies prepared after the accession of Richard III on 26th June 1483, bear his name but coins of the sun and rose coinage struck under Edward IV and Edward V can only be distinguished by arranging the dies in sequence. This is possible for the angels (Schneider Sylloge, SCBI 47, p.41) but has not yet been achieved for the silver coinage.

Mintmark: Halved sun and rose.

GOLD

2144A

		F	VF
		£	£
2144	**Angel.** Type As 2091, reading EDWARD DEI GRA (Edward IV)..........	5250	15000
2144A	— Similar but reading EDWARD DI GRA (Edward V)..........................	13500	40000
2145	**Half-angel.** As 2093 (probably Edward IV)..	4750	15000

SILVER

2146

2146	**Groat.** *London,* pellet below bust, reading EDWARD or EDVARD.......	1100	4000
2146A	— — No pellet below, reading EDWARD or EDWRD..........................	1000	3750
2147	**Penny.** *London* As 2110	950	3750
2148	**Halfpenny.** *London* As 2137...	300	950

Richard's coinage follows the pattern of previous reigns. The portrait on the silver denominations remains stylised, though increasingly distinctive. It can be divided into three types according to mintmark. Type 1, the first sun and rose coinage, lasted 24 days to 20th July 1483. Type 2, the boar's head coinage, was issued until about June 1484. Type 3, the second sun and rose coinage, was struck until the end of the reign (Schneider Sylloge, SCBI 47, pp. 41-2).

It is evident that coin dies were stored in a 'loose-box' system which led to extensive muling between types. As an interim measure, after the indenture of 20th July 1483, at least eleven existing sun and rose obverse dies, both gold and silver, were overpunched with the boar's head mark. The seven overpunched groat dies included four Edward IV/V dies, then still in use, and three dies of Richard III type 1.

Mintmarks

| SR1 | BH1 | BH2 | SR2 | SR3 | 105 | 33 |

Halved sun and rose, 1, 2 and 3.
Boar's head, 1 (62) 2 (63).
Lis (105, *Durham*)
Rose only (33).

GOLD

2150   2152

		F	VF
		£	£
2149	**Angel.** 1. Reading RICARD. R. R and rose by mast; *mm.* sun and rose 1	5500	18500
2150	— 2a. Reading EDWARD. R. E and rose or R and rose by mast; *mm.* boar's head 1 over sun and rose 1/sun and rose 1	7500	27500
2151	— 2b. Reading RICARD. R. R and rose by mast; mm. boar's head 1 over sun and rose 1/sun and rose 1, boar's head 1, boar's head 2 (often muled)	5250	17500
2152	— 3. Reading RICARD or RICAD; *mm.* sun and rose 2	5000	16500

2153
| 2153 | **Half-angel.** 2b. R. R and rose by mast; *mm.* boar's head 1 | 9500 | 32500 |

SILVER

2154   2155

		F	VF
		£	£
2154	**Groat.** 1. *London*. Reading RICARD; *mm*. sun and rose 1	700	2000
2155	— 2a. Reading EDWARD; *mm*. boar's head 1 over sun and rose 1/sun and rose 1	1750	5250

2156 - BH2   2158 - SR3

2156	— 2b. Reading RICARD; *mm*. boar's head 1 over sun and rose 1/sun and rose 1, boar's head 1, boar's head 2 (often muled)	750	2250
2157	— 3. *mm*. sun and rose 2, sun and rose 3	700	2000
2158	— — Pellet below bust, *mm*. sun and rose 2, sun and rose 3	750	2000
2159	*York*. 3. *mm*. sun and rose 2/-	1850	6000

2161   2164   2166

2160	**Halfgroat.** *London*. 2a. Reading EDWARD; *mm*. boar's head 1 over sun and rose 1/- (the *mm*. is indistinct)	1850	6000
2161	— 2b. Reading RICARD; *mm*. boar's head 2/-	1500	4500
2162	— 3. *mm*. sun and rose 2, sun and rose 2/-	1350	4250
2163	— — Pellet below bust; *mm*. sun and rose 2	1500	4500
2164	**Penny.** *London*. 2a. Reading EDWARD; *mm*. boar's head 1 over sun and rose 1/-	1850	6000
2165	— 2b. Reading RICARD; *mm*. boar's head 1/-	2000	6500
2166	*York*. Archb. Rotherham. T and upright key at neck. R. Quatrefoil in centre; *mm*. boar's head 1/-	375	1250
2167	— — *mm*. rose/-	325	1100
2168	— No marks at neck; *mm*. sun and rose 2/-	425	1500

2169   2171

2169	*Durham*. Bp. Sherwood. S on breast. R. D in centre; *mm*. lis/-................	275	900
2170	**Halfpenny.** *London*. 2b. No marks by neck; *mm*. boar's head 1/-	325	1100
2171	— 3. *mm*. sun and rose 2/-	300	1000
2171A	**Farthing.** *London*. 3. *mm*. sun and rose 2/-...	1750	4500

HENRY VII, 1485-1509

For the first four years of his reign Henry's coins differ only in name and mintmark from those of his predecessors, but from 1489 radical changes were made in the coinage. On the Groat and subsequently on the lesser denominations the traditional open crown was replaced with an arched imperial crown. Though the pound sterling had been a denomination of account for centuries, a pound coin had never been minted. Now a magnificent gold pound was issued, and, from the design of the king enthroned in majesty, was called a 'Sovereign'. A small simplified version of the Sovereign portrait was at the same time introduced on the silver pence. The reverse of the gold 'Sovereign' had the royal arms set in the centre of a Tudor rose. A few years later the angel was restyled and St. Michael, who is depicted about to thrust Satan into the Pit with a cross-topped lance, is no longer a feathered figure but is clad in armour of Renaissance style. A gold ryal of ten shillings was also minted again for a brief period.

The other major innovation was the introduction of the shilling (testoon) in the opening years of the 16th century. It is remarkable for the very fine profile portrait of the king which replaces the representational image of a monarch that had served on the coinage for the past couple of centuries. This new portrait was also used on groats and halfgroats but not on the smaller denominations.

Mintmarks

| 39 | 41 | 40 | 42 | 33 | 11 | 7a | 123 |

| 105 | 76b | 31 | 78 | 30 | 91 | 43 | 57 |

| 85 | 94 | 118 | 21 | 33 | 53 |

1485-7	Halved sun and rose (39)	1495-8	Pansy (30)
	Lis upon sun and rose (41)		Tun (123, *Canterbury*)
	Lis upon half rose (40)		Lis (105, York)
	Lis-rose dimidiated (42)	1498-9	Crowned leopard's head (91)
	Rose (33, *York*)		Lis issuant from rose (43)
1487	Lis (105)		Tun (123, *Canterbury*)
	Cross fitchée (11)	1499-1502	Anchor (57)
1487-8	Rose (33)	1502-4	Greyhound's head (85)
	Plain cross (7a, *Durham*)		Lis (105, profile issue only)
1488-9	No marks		Martlet (94, *York*)
1489-93	Cinquefoil (31)	1504-5	Cross-crosslet (21)
	Crozier (76b, *Durham*)	1504-9	Martlet (94, (*York, Canterbury*)
1492	Cross fitchée (11, gold only)		Rose (33, *York* and
1493-5	Escallop (78)		*Canterbury*)
	Dragon (118, gold only)	1505-9	Pheon (53)
	Lis (105, *Canterbury and York*)		
	Tun (123, *Canterbury*)		

GOLD

	F £	VF £
2172 **Sovereign** (20s; wt. 240 grs., 15.55g). Group I. Large figure of king sitting on backless throne. R. Large shield crowned on large Tudor rose. *mm.* 31 ..	125000	525000
2173 — Group II. Somewhat similar but throne has narrow back, lis in background. R. Large Tudor rose bearing small shield. *mm.* -/11	85000	350000

2174

2174 — III. King on high-backed very ornamental throne, with greyhound and dragon on side pillars. R. Shield on Tudor rose; *mm.* dragon............	32500	135000
2175 — IV. Similar but throne with high canopy breaking legend and broad seat, *mm.* 105/118, (also with no *obv.* i.c. *mm.* 105/118, very rare)..................	30000	125000
2176 — Narrow throne with a portcullis below the king's feet (like Henry VIII); *mm.* 105/21, 105/53	22500	95000
2177 **Double-sovereign** and **Treble-sovereign** from same dies as 2176. These piedforts were probably intended as presentation pieces *mm.* 105/21, 105/53	100000	450000

2178

2178 **Ryal** (10s.). As illustration: *mm.* -/11	27500	135000
2179 **Angel** (6s. 8d). I. Angel of old type with one foot on dragon. R. PER CRVCEM. etc., *mm.* 39, 40, (also muled both ways)...........................	1350	5500
2179A — With Irish title, and legend over angel head. *mm.* 33/-.......................	1500	5750
2180 — — Name altered from RICARD? and h on *rev.* from R. mm. 41/39, 41/40, 41/-, 39/?..	1650	6000

2181 2183

2187

		F	VF
		£	£
2181	II. As 2179, but *mm.* none. 31/-.	1100	4250
2181A	II/III mule. *mm.* 31/78, R. PER CRUC or AVTEM TRAnS	1250	4500
2182	As 2181. R. IhC AVTEM TRAnSIEnS etc.; *mm.* none, 31/-	1350	4750
2183	III. New dies, angel with both feet on dragons; (large straight lettering) *mm.* 78-85 except 91 (many mules exist)	750	2250
2183A	— Angel with very small wings. *mm.* escallop	850	2500
2184	— — R. IhC AVTEM TRAnSIEnS, etc.; *mm.* escallop	1100	4000
2185	IV. Small square lettering; *mm.* 85 (also muled with 2183)	800	2400
2186	— Tall thin lettering; *mm.* 21 (also muled with 2185 obv.)	800	2400
2187	V. Large crook-shaped abbreviation after hEnRIC; *mm.* 21 and 53 (combinations and mules exist)	750	2250
2188	**Half-angel or angelet.** I. *Mm.* 39, 41, (old dies RIII altered)	1750	5750
2189	III. Angel with both feet on dragon: *mm.* 30, 57/30, 30/85	800	2500
2190	IV. Small square lettering; *mm.* rose *mm.* -/85	725	2250
2191	— *Obv.* as last. R. Tall thin lettering; *mm.* 33/21	800	2500
2192	V. As angel; *mm.* pheon, cross-crosslet	700	2200

SILVER

Facing bust issues. Including 'Sovereign' type pennies.

2193	**Groat.** I. Open crown; *mm.* 40 (rose on bust), 39-42 and none (combinations)	100	350

2194 2195

2194	— — crosses or saltires by neck, 41, 40, 105-33 and none (combinations)	110	375
2195	IIa. Large bust with out-turned hair, crown with two plain arches; *mm.* none, 31, 31/-, 31/78	85	275

2198A   2199   2201

		F	VF
		£	£
2196	— — similar but crosses by neck; *mm.* none, -/105	100	350
2197	— — R. Portcullis over long cross; *mm.* -/lis	3500	11000
2198	IIIa. Bust as IIa. Crown with two jewelled arches, *mm.* 31	275	750
2198A	IIIb. Similar, but new bust with realistic hair *mm.* 78, 30	80	250
2199	IIIc. Bust as IIIb, but crown with one plain and one jewelled arch, *mm.* 30-21 and none	70	225
2199A	IIId. As last, but plainer letters. mm 57, 85, 33 and none	75	250
2200	IVa. Wide single arch crown; arch is single or double bar with 4 crockets; *mm.* 85, 85/33, 21	85	300
2201	IVb. — Similar, but arch is double bar with 6 uprights or crockets as jewels; *mm.* 85, 21/85, 21	100	350
2202	**Halfgroat,** *London.* I. Open crown, tressure unbroken; *mm.* 40/-, 40/39 (R. III mule)	375	1350
2203	— IIIa. Double arched crown, rosettes on tressure; mm. escallop	175	525
2204	— IIIb. Similar, nothing on tressure. R. Lozenge panel in centre; *mm.* lis	40	160
2205	— — Similar, but also with lis on breast; mm. lis	45	175
2206	— IIIc. Unarched crown with tressure broken. R. Lozenge panel in centre; *mm.* lis	35	150
2206A	— — — Similar but smaller dies and much smaller lettering	50	175

2208   2211

		F	VF
2207	*Canterbury,* Archb. Morton. I. Open crown, crosses by neck. R. Ṃ in centre; *mm.* tun/-	60	200
2208	— — II. Similar, but double-arched crown; no *mm.*	60	200
2209	III King and Archb. jointly. As last but without Ṃ; (a) early lettering, trefoil stops; *mm.* lis, tun and lis/lis	50	175
2210	— — (b) ornate lettering, rosette stops; *mm.* tun, lis in combinations	40	145
2211	— — (c) — saltire or no stops; *mm.* 123, 123 & 30/123	40	145
2212	*York,* Royal mint. (a) Double-arched crown, lis on breast (rarely omitted). R. Lozenge panel in centre; *mm.* lis	55	175
2213	— — (b) Similar, but unarched crown, tressure broken, *mm.* lis.	45	160

		F £	VF £
2214	— Archb. Savage. (a) Double-arched crown, keys at neck, no tressure; ornate lettering; *mm.* martlet	40	150
2215	— — (b) Similar, but fleured tressure, small square lettering; *mm.* martlet	45	160
2216	— — (c) As last, but tall thin lettering; *mm.* martlet	45	160
2217	— As last but no keys; *mm.* martlet	55	175

2221   2226

2218	**Penny.** Old type. London; *mm.* 40/-	200	750
2219	— — — crosses by bust, mm. small cross (obv.)	250	850
2220	— *Canterbury*, Archb. Morton. Open crown, *mm.* tun/- R̖. Ӎ in centre	200	750
2221	— — King and Archb. jointly, arched crown; *mm.* tun, tun/-	70	250
2222	— *Durham,* Bp. Sherwood. S on breast. R̖. D in centre; *mm.* 7a/-	100	350
2223	— *York,* Archb. Rotherham. With or without cross on breast, *mm.* 33/-, T and cross or key at neck. R̖. h in centre	55	200
2224	— — — T and trefoil at neck. R̖. Quatrefoil in centre and two extra pellets; *mm.* 39/-	50	175
2225	'Sovereign' type. *London.* Early lettering, no stops, no pillars to throne; no *mm.*	135	450
2226	— — — single pillar on king's right side, trefoil stops; no *mm.* or 31/-	45	150
2227	— — Ornate letters, rosette stops, single pillar; *mm.* lis (can be muled with above)	65	225
2228	— — saltire stops or none, two pillars; *mm.* none, -/30	45	150
2229	— — Similar, but small square lettering; no *mm.*	50	175
2230	— — Similar, but lettering as profile groats two double pillars; *mm.* 21, 53, none (sometimes on one side only)	45	150

2231   2233   2235

2231	— *Durham,* Bp. Sherwood. Crozier to r. of king, throne with one pillar. R̖. D and S beside shield	45	150
2232	— — Throne with two pillars, no crozier. R̖. As last	50	175
2233	— — Bp. Fox. Throne with one pillar. R̖. Mitre above shield, RD or DR at sides, no *mm.*	40	135
2234	— — Similar, but two pillars	45	150
2235	*York,* Archb. Rotherham. Keys below shield; early lettering, trefoil stops, no pillars to throne, no *mm.*	40	135
2236	— — — single pillar	35	125
2237	— — — — ornate lettering, rosette or no stops,	35	125
2238	— — — two pillars sometimes with crosses between legs of throne	35	125

2239

2244A

2245

2249

2250

		F £	*VF* £
2239	**Halfpenny,** *London.* I. Open crown; *mm.* 40, 42	45	150
2240	− − − trefoils at neck; no *mm.,* rose	50	175
2241	− − − crosses at neck; *mm.* rose, cross fitchée.................................	40	135
2242	− II. Double arched crown; *mm.* cinquefoil, none	30	100
2243	− − − saltires at neck; no *mm.*	30	100
2244	− IIIa. Crown with single arch, ornate lettering; no *mm.,* pansy.............	25	85
2244A	− IIIb. Similar but with rosette stops; *mm.* none, rose, lis	35	110
2245	− IIIc. Much smaller portrait; *mm.* pheon, lis, none	25	85
2246	*Canterbury,* Archb. Morton. I. Open crown, crosses by neck; R. M in centre	90	300
2247	− II. Similar, but arched crown, saltires by bust; *mm.* profile eye (82)	85	275
2247A	− − − no marks at neck	75	250
2248	− III. King and Archb. Arched crown; *mm.* lis, none............................	40	135
2249	*York,* Archb. Savage. Arched crown, key below bust to l or r. *mm.* martlet..	110	375
2250	**Farthing,** *London.* hENRIC DI GRA REX (A), arched crown..............	475	1500

*No.s 2239-49 have *mm.* on *obv.* only.

Profile issue

2251	**Testoon** (ls.). Type as groat. hENRIC (VS); *mm.* lis...........................	15000	40000
2252	− hENRIC VII; *mm.* lis	16000	45000

2253

2254

2253	− hENRIC SEPTIM; *mm.* lis	17500	52500
2254	**Groat,** *Tentative issue* (contemporary with full-face groats). Double band to crown, hENRIC VII; *mm.* none, 105/-, -/105: 105/85, 105, 85, 21	275	1000
2255	− − − tressure on *obv.; mm.* cross-crosslet..	2750	9500
2256	− − hENRIC (VS); *mm.* 105, -/105, 105/ 85, none	475	1500
2257	− − hENRIC SEPTIM; *mm.* -/105..	2250	8500

2258

		F £	VF £
2258	*Regular issue*. Triple band to crown; *mm*. 21, 53 (both *mm*.s may occur on *obv*. or *rev*. or both)	135	400
2259	**Halfgroat,** *London*. As last; *mm*. 105, 53/105, 105/53, 53	90	350
2260	— — no numeral after King's name, no *mm*., -/lis	450	1350
2261	*Canterbury*, King and Archb. As London, but *mm*. 94, 33, 94/33	80	275

2262   rev. enlarged

2262	*York*, Archb. Bainbridge. As London, but two keys below shield; *mm*. 94, 33, 33/94	65	225

2263

2263	— — XB beside shield; *mm*. rose/martlet	175	575
2263A	— — Similar but two keys below shield *mm*. rose(?)/martlet	250	750

Henry VIII is held in ill-regard by numismatists as being the author of the debasement of England's gold and silver coinage; but there were also other important numismatic innovations during his reign. For the first sixteen years the coinage closely followed the pattern of the previous issues, even to the extent of retaining the portrait of Henry VII on the larger silver coins.

In 1526, in an effort to prevent the drain of gold to continental Europe, the value of English gold was increased by 10%, the sovereign to 22s. 0d. and the angel to 7s. 4d., and a new coin valued at 4s. 6d.—the Crown of the Rose—was introduced as a competitor to the French *écu au soleil*. The new crown was not a success and within a few months it was replaced by the Crown of the Double Rose valued at 5s but made of gold of only 22 carat fineness, the first time gold had been minted below the standard 23c. At the same time the sovereign was again revalued to 22s. 6d. and the angel to 7s. 6d., with a new coin, the George Noble, valued at 6s. 8d. (one-third pound).

The royal cyphers on some of the gold crowns and half-crowns combine the initial of Henry with those of his queens: Katherine of Aragon, Anne Boleyn and Jane Seymour. The architect of this coinage reform was the chancellor, Cardinal Thomas Wolsey, who besides his other changes had minted at York a groat bearing his initials and cardinal's hat in addition to the other denominations normally authorized for the ecclesiastical mints.

When open debasement of the coinage began in 1544 to help finance Henry's wars, the right to coin of the archbishops of Canterbury and York and of the bishop of Durham was not confirmed. Instead, a second royal mint was opened in the Tower as in subsequent years were six others, at Southwark, York, Canterbury, Bristol, Dublin and Durham House in the Strand. Gold, which fell to 23c. in 1544, 22c. in 1545, and 20c. in 1546 was much less debased than silver which declined to 9oz 2dwt. in 1544, 6oz 2dwt. in 1545 and 4oz 2dwt. in 1546. At this last standard the blanched silver surface of the coins soon wore away to reveal the copper alloy beneath which earned for Henry the nickname 'Old Coppernose'.

Mintmarks

| 53 | 69 | 70 | 108 | 33 | 94 | 73 | 11 |

| 105 | 22 | 23 | 30 | 78 | 15 | 24 | 110 |

| 52 | 72a | 44 | 8 | 65a | 114 | 121 | 90 |

| 36 | 106 | 56 | S | E | 116 | 135 |

1509-26	Pheon (53)	1509-14	Martlet (94, *York*)
	Castle (69)	1509-23	Radiant star (22, *Durham & York*)
	Castle with H (70, gold)	1513-18	Crowned T (135, Tournai)
	Portcullis crowned (108)	1514-26	Star (23, *York & Durham*)
	Rose (33, *Canterbury*)		Pansy (30, *York*)
	Martlet (94, *Canterbury*)		Escallop (78, *York*)
	Pomegranate (73, but broader, *Cant.*)		Voided cross (15, *York*)
	Cross fitchée (11, *Cant.*)	1523-26	Spur rowel (24, *Durham*)
	Lis (105, *Canterbury, Durham*)		

1526-44	Rose (33)	1526-32	Cross patonce (8, *Cant.*)
	Lis (105)		T (114, *Canterbury*)
	Sunburst 110)		Uncertain mark (121,
	Arrow (52)		*Canterbury*)
	Pheon (53)	1529-44	Radiant star (22, *Durham*)
	Lis (106)	1530-44	Key (90, *York*)
	Star (23, *Durham*)	1533-44	Catherine wheel (36,
1526-9	Crescent (72a, *Durham*)		*Canterbury*)
	Trefoil (44 variety,	1544-7	Lis (105 and 106)
	Durham)		Pellet in annulet (56)
	Flower of eight petals and		S (Southwark)
	circle centre (*Durham*)		E or E (Southwark)
1526-30	Cross (7a, sometimes	1546-7	WS monogram (116, *Bristol*)
	slightly voided, *York*)		
	Acorn (65a, *York*)		

GOLD

FIRST COINAGE, 1509-26

2265

		F	VF
		£	£
2264	**Sovereign** (20s; wt. 240grs., 15.55g.). Similar to last sov. of Hen. VII; *mm.* 108	12500	45000
2264A	**Ryal** (10s.) King in ship holding sword and shield. R. Similar to 1950, *mm.*-/108	*Extremely rare*	
2265	**Angel** (6s. 8d.). As Hen. VII, but hEnRIC? VIII DI GRA REX, etc.; *mm.* 53, 69, 70, 70/69, 108, R. May omit h and rose, or rose only; *mm.* 69, 108	850	2500
2266	**Half-angel.** Similar (sometimes without VIII), *mm.* 69, 70, 108/33, 108	725	2000

SECOND COINAGE, 1526-44

2267

2267	**Sovereign** (22s. 6d; wt. 240grs., 15.55g.). As 2264, R. single or double tressure *mm.* 110, 105, 105/52	11000	42500
2268	**Angel** (7s. 6d.). As 2265, hEnRIC VIII D(I) G(RA) R(EX) etc,; *mm.* 110, 105	1100	4250

		F	*VF*
		£	£

2269 **Half-angel.** Similar; *mm.* lis.. 1250 4750

2270   2272

2270 **George-noble** (6s. 8d.). As illustration; *mm.* rose 9500 37500
2270A— Similar, but more modern ship with three masts, without initials hR. R.
       St. George brandishing sword behind head.. 10500 45000
2271 **Half-George-noble.** Similar to 2270 *mm* rose, lis.............................. 7500 35000
2272 **Crown of the rose** (4s. 6d., 23 c. 3 ¹/₂ gr.). As illustration; *mm.* rose,
       two legend varieties 6500 25000
2273 **Crown of the double-rose** (5s., 22 c). Double-rose crowned, hK (Henry and
       Katherine of Aragon) both crowned in field. R. Shield crowned; *mm.* rose 800 2750

2274   2285

2274 — hK both sides; *mm.* rose/lis, lis, arrow	800	2750
2275* — hK/hA or hA/hK; *mm.* arrow..	2250	7500
2276* — hR/hK or hI/hR; *mm.* arrow	1000	3250
2277 — hA (Anne Boleyn); *mm.* arrow...	2750	9500
2278 — hA/hR; *mm.* arrow...	2250	7500
2279 — hI (Jane Seymour); *mm.* arrow...	800	2750
2280* — hK/hI; *mm.* arrow	1200	3750
2281 — hR/hI; *mm.* arrow	1100	3500
2282 — hR (Rex); *mm.* arrow..	800	2750
2283 — — *mm.* pheon	1100	3500
2284 **Halfcrown.** Similar but king's name henric 8 on *rev.,* no initials; *mm.* rose	1350	4750
2285 — hK uncrowned on *obv.; mm.* rose..	725	2250
2286 — hK uncrowned both sides; *mm.* rose/lis, lis, arrow	725	2250
2287 — hI uncrowned both sides; *mm.* arrow	800	2500
2288 — hR uncrowned both sides; hIB RЄX; *mm.* pheon	900	3000

*The hK initials may on later coins refer to Katherine Howard (Henry's fifth wife).

THIRD COINAGE, 1544-7

2291

	F	VF
	£	£

2289 **Sovereign, I** (20s., Wt. 200 grs., 12.96g., 23 ct.). Large module, similar to 2291 but king with large head; *mm.* lis 35000 165000

2290 II (20s., wt. 200 or 192 grs., 23, 22 or 20 ct.). *Tower.* As illustration; *mm.* lis, pellet in annulet/lis 7000 27500

2291 — *Southwark.* Similar; *mm.* S, Є/S 6500 25000

2292 — — Similar but Є below shield; *mm.* S/Є 7500 30000

2293 — *Bristol.* As London but *mm.* WS/- 12500 50000

2294   2303

2294 **Half-sovereign** (wt. 100 or 96 grs., 6.22g.), *Tower.* As illus.; *mm.* lis, pellet in annulet 900 3000

2295 — Similar, but with annulet on inner circle (either or both sides) 950 3250

2296 *Southwark. mm.* S 950 3250

2297 — Є below shield; *mm.* S, Є, S/Є, Є/S, (known without sceptre; *mm.* S) 900 3000

2298 *Bristol.* Lombardic lettering; *mm.* WS, WS/- 1750 6500

2299 **Angel** (8s., 23 c). Annulet by angel's head and on ship, hЄnRIC' 8; *mm.* lis 850 2500

2300 — Similar, but annulet one side only or none 900 2650

2300A— Similar, but three annulets on ship, *mm.* lis 1350 4500

2301 **Half-angel.** Annulet on ship; *mm.* lis 750 2250

2302 — No annulet on ship; *mm.* lis 800 2500

2303 — Three annulets on ship; *mm.* lis 900 2750

2304

		F	VF
		£	£
2304	**Quarter-angel** Angel wears armour; *mm.* lis	850	2500
2304A—	Angel wears tunic; *mm.* lis	900	2750
2305	**Crown,** *London.* Similar to 2283, but hϵnRIC' 8 ; Lombardic lettering; *mm.* 56	675	2250
2306	— without RVTILAnS; *mm.* 56..	700	2400
2307	— — — with annulet on inner circle	700	2400
2307A—	King's name omitted. DEI GRA both sides, *mm.* 56	900	3000
2308	— *Southwark.* As 2306; *mm.* S, ϵ, E/S, ϵ/-, E/ϵ	800	2750
2309	*Bristol.* hϵnRIC VIII. ROSA etc. R. D G, etc.; *mm.*-/WS	675	2250
2309A—	— with initials H R transposed on rev...	800	2750
2310	— Similar but hϵnRIC(VS) 8 R. DϵI) G(RA); *mm.* -/WS, WS	675	2250
2311	**Halfcrown,** *London.* Similar to 2288; *mm.* 56, 56/-	475	1500
2312	— — with annulet on inner circle *mm.* 56..	525	1600
2313	*Southwark.* As 2311; *mm.* S	575	1750
2314	— *O.* hϵnRIC 8 ROSA SINϵ SPIn. R. DϵI GRA, etc.; *mm.* ϵ	575	1750
2315	*Bristol. O.* RVTILAnS, etc. R. hϵnRIC 8; *mm.* WS/-............................	725	2250

For other gold coins in Henry's name see page 221-2.

SILVER

FIRST COINAGE, 1509-26

2316   2322

2316	**Groat.** Portrait of Hen. VII. *London mm.* 53, 69, 108, 108 over 135.......	120	400
2317	— *Tournai; mm.* crowned T. R. CIVITAS TORnACϵn*, dated 1513 ...	975	3500
2318	**Halfgroat.** Portrait of Hen. VII. London; *mm.* 108, 108/-	125	475
2319	— *Canterbury,* Archb. Warham. POSVI *rev.; mm.* rose.....................	150	575
2320	— — — WA above shield; *mm.* martlet..	120	425
2321	— — — WA beside shield; *mm.* cross fitchee..	120	425
2322	— — CIVITAS CAnTOR *rev.,* similar; *mm.* 73, 105, 11/105................	80	225
2323	— *York,* POSVI *rev.,* Archb. Bainbridge (1508-14). Keys below shield;		
	mm. martlet	100	325
2324	— — — XB beside shield no keys; *mm.* martlet	110	400
2325	— — — Archb. Wolsey (1514-30). Keys and cardinal's hat below shield;		
	mm. 94, 22..	225	750
2326	— — CIVITAS ϵBORACI *rev.* Similar; *mm.* 22, 23, 30, 78, 15, 15/78..	75	250
2327	— — As last with TW beside shield; *mm.* voided cross...........................	125	450
2327A—	*Tournai.* As 2317...	950	3000

*Non-portrait groats and half-groats exist of this mint, captured during an invasion of France in
1513. (Restored to France in 1518.)

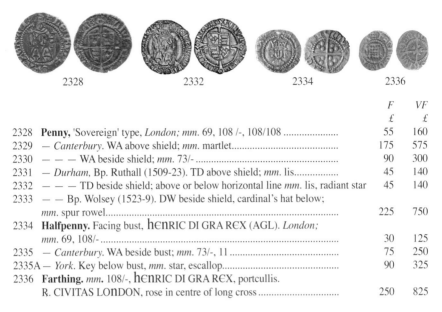

	2328	2332	2334	2336

		F	VF
		£	£
2328	**Penny,** 'Sovereign' type, *London; mm.* 69, 108 /-, 108/108	55	160
2329	— *Canterbury.* WA above shield; *mm.* martlet...	175	575
2330	— — — WA beside shield; *mm.* 73/-..	90	300
2331	— *Durham*, Bp. Ruthall (1509-23). TD above shield; *mm.* lis.................	45	140
2332	— — — TD beside shield; above or below horizontal line *mm.* lis, radiant star	45	140
2333	— — Bp. Wolsey (1523-9). DW beside shield, cardinal's hat below; *mm.* spur rowel.....	225	750
2334	**Halfpenny.** Facing bust, hℇnRIC DI GRA RℇX (AGL). *London; mm.* 69, 108/-	30	125
2335	— *Canterbury.* WA beside bust; *mm.* 73/-, 11	75	250
2335A	— *York.* Key below bust, *mm.* star, escallop..	90	325
2336	**Farthing.** *mm.* 108/-, hℇnRIC DI GRA RℇX, portcullis. R. CIVITAS LOnDON, rose in centre of long cross	250	825

SECOND COINAGE, 1526-44

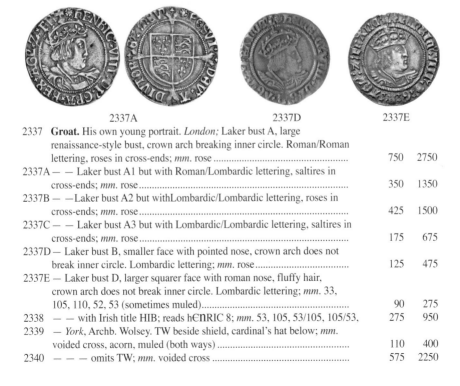

	2337A	2337D	2337E

		F	VF
2337	**Groat.** His own young portrait. *London;* Laker bust A, large renaissance-style bust, crown arch breaking inner circle. Roman/Roman lettering, roses in cross-ends; *mm.* rose	750	2750
2337A	— — Laker bust A1 but with Roman/Lombardic lettering, saltires in cross-ends; *mm.* rose......................	350	1350
2337B	— —Laker bust A2 but withLombardic/Lombardic lettering, roses in cross-ends; *mm.* rose......................	425	1500
2337C	— — Laker bust A3 but with Lombardic/Lombardic lettering, saltires in cross-ends; *mm.* rose..........................	175	675
2337D	— Laker bust B, smaller face with pointed nose, crown arch does not break inner circle. Lombardic lettering; *mm.* rose...................................	125	475
2337E	— Laker bust D, larger squarer face with roman nose, fluffy hair, crown arch does not break inner circle. Lombardic lettering; *mm.* 33, 105, 110, 52, 53 (sometimes muled)........................	90	275
2338	— — with Irish title HIB; reads hℇnRIC 8; *mm.* 53, 105, 53/105, 105/53,	275	950
2339	— *York*, Archb. Wolsey. TW beside shield, cardinal's hat below; *mm.* voided cross, acorn, muled (both ways)	110	400
2340	— — — omits TW; *mm.* voided cross	575	2250

2341   2343   2345

		F	VF
		£	£
2341	**Halfgroat.** *London;* type as groats, Lombardic lettering both sides.		
	mm. rose to arrow or none (sometimes muled)..	65	200
2341A	— — Mainly Roman letters on *obv.* or on both sides, *mm.* rose............	110	400
2342	As 2341 with Irish title HIB; *mm.* pheon..	475	1500
2343	— *Canterbury,* Archb. Warham (—1532). R. CIVITAS CAnTOR, WA		
	beside shield; *mm.* 121, 121/-, 121/33, 8, 8/T, T............................	60	180
2344	— — — nothing by shield; *mm.* 121/-	70	225
2345	— — Archb. Cranmer (1533—). TC beside shield; *mm.* 36, 36/-............	60	180
2346	— *York,* Archb. Wolsey (—1530). R. CIVITAS ЄBORACI, TW		
	beside shield, hat below; *mm.* 15/-, 15......................................	65	200
2347	— — Sede Vacante (1530/1). No marks; *mm.* key.................................	70	225
2348	— — Archb. Lee (1531-44). EL or LE beside shield; *mm.* key	60	180

2349   2358   2362

		F	VF
2349	**Penny.** 'Sovereign' type h . D . G . ROSA SINЄ SPInA, *London;*		
	mm. rose to arrow (*obv.* only), *mm.* lis both sides.................................	50	175
2350	— *Canterbury.* WA beside shield; *mm.* 121/-, 8/-, T/-............................	135	450
2351	— — TC beside shield; *mm.* 36/-	225	750
2352	— *Durham,* Bp. Wolsey (—1529). TW beside shield, hat below; *mm.* 23,		
	23/44, 23/-, 72a/-, 44, 44/-, 72a/44 (muled with 2333 *obv.,* *mm.* 24/44)..	40	125
2353	— — Sede Vacante (1529-30). No marks; *mm.* 23/-, 22/-........................	45	135
2354	— — Bp. Tunstall (1530—). CD beside shield; *mm.* 23, 23/-, 22/-, 22...	40	125
2355	— *York.* EL beside shield; *mm.* key/-......................................	475	1500
2356	**Halfpenny.** Facing bust, h D G ROSA SIЄ SPIA. *London;* sometimes		
	annulet in centre of rev. *mm.* rose to arrow, arrow/-	30	125
2357	— *Canterbury.* WA beside bust; *mm.* 121/-, 8/-, T/-............................	150	525
2358	— — TC beside bust; *mm.* 36/-...	35	135
2359	— *York.* TW beside bust; *mm.* acorn/-.......................................	80	275
2359A	— — —; key below bust...	135	450
2360	— — Sede Vacante. Key below bust; *mm.* 15/-......................................	60	175
2361	— — EL or LE beside bust; *mm.* key/-..	35	135
2362	**Farthing.** *O.* RVTILANS ROSA, portcullis; *mm.* 105/-, 110/-. R.		
	DEO GRACIAS, long cross with pellet in each angle	325	750
2363	— — *mm.* arrow/- R. DEO GRACIAS, rose on long cross	375	900
2363A	— *Canterbury.* O. Similar. R. Similar. *mm.* 36/-	900	2500

2364

	F	VF
	£	£

THIRD COINAGE, 1544-7 (Silver progressively debased. 9oz (2dwt), 6oz (2dwt) 4oz (2dwt)).

2364 **Testoon.** *Tower.* hENRIC'. VIII, etc. R. Crowned rose between crowned h
   and R.POSVI, etc.; *mm.* lis, lis and 56, lis/two lis.................................... 1500 6000

2365 — hENRIC 8, *mm.* 105 and 56, 105/56, 105 and 56/56, 56 .... 900 3500

2366 — — annulet on inner circle of rev. or both sides; *mm.* pellet in annulet 950 3750

2367

2367 — *Southwark.* As 2365. R. CIVITAS LONDON; *mm.* S, Є, S/Є, Є/S 900 3500

2368 — *Bristol. mm.*-/WS monogram. (Tower or local dies.).......................... 1750 6500

2369 Bust 1   2374 Bust 2

2369 **Groat.** *Tower.* As ill. above, busts 1, 2, 3; *mm.* lis/-, lis............................ 110 550

2369A Bust 1, R. As second coinage; i.e. saltires in forks; *mm.* lis 135 650

2370 Bust 2 or 3 annulet on inner circle, both sides or rev. only 120 600

2371 *Southwark.* As 2367, busts 1, 2, 3, 4; no *mm.* or lis/-; S or S and Є or
   Є in forks 110 550

2372 *Bristol. Mm.*-/WS monogram, Bristol bust and Tower bust 2 or 3 .... 110 550

2373 *Canterbury.* Busts 1, 2, (2 var); no *mm,* or lis/– 110 550

2374 *York.* Busts 1 var., 2, 3, no *mm*.. 110 550

2377   2384

		F	VF
		£	£
2375	**Halfgroat.** *Tower.* As 2365, bust 1; *mm.* lis, none	75	350
2376	*Southwark.* As 2367, bust 1; no *mm.*; S or Є and S in forks	100	425
2377	*Bristol. Mm.*-/WS monogram	70	325
2378	*Canterbury.* Bust 1; no *mm.*	55	250
2379	*York.* Bust 1; no *mm.*	70	325
2380	**Penny.** *Tower.* Facing bust; no *mm.* or lis/-	50	200
2381	*Southwark.* Facing bust; *mm.* S/-, Є/-, -/Є	85	300
2382	*Bristol.* Facing bust; no *mm.* (Tower dies or local but truncated at neck)	60	225
2383	*Canterbury.* Facing bust; no *mm.*	50	175
2384	*York.* Facing bust; no *mm.*	50	200

2385   2388A

		F	VF
2385	**Halfpenny.** *Tower.* Facing bust; pellet in annulet in *rev.* centre, no *mm.* or lis/-	75	225
2386	*Bristol.* Facing bust; no *mm.*	90	275
2387	*Canterbury.* Facing bust; no *mm.*, (some read H 8)	60	165
2388	*York.* Facing bust; no *mm.*	50	150
2388A	**Farthing** *obv.* Rose. R. Cross and pellets	850	2500

These coins were struck during the reign of Edward VI but bear the name and portrait of Henry VIII, except in the case of the half-sovereigns which bear the youthful head of Edward.

Mintmarks

◉	✚	𝟏	**K**	**E**	**Ⱳ**
56	105	52	K	E	116

(	**Ⲧ**	❀	ᴄᴏ	**t**	🕊
66	115	33	122	t	94

GOLD

	F	VF
	£	£
2389 **Sovereign** (20 ct.), *London*. As no. 2290, but Roman lettering; *mm*. lis..	8500	32500
2390 — *Bristol*. Similar but *mm*. WS...	12500	50000

2391

2393

2391 **Half-sovereign.** As 2294, but with youthful portrait with sceptre. *Tower*; *mm*. 52, 105, 94 (various combinations)..	750	2400
2391A — Similar but no sceptre; *mm*. 52, 52/56..	800	2500
2392 — — — K below shield; *mm*.-/K, none,. E/-	750	2400
2393 — — — grapple below shield; *mm*. 122, none, 122/-, -/122.	800	2500
2394 — *Southwark*. Mm. E, E/-, -/E, Є /E. Usually Є or E (sometimes retrograde) below shield (sceptre omitted; *mm*. -/E)..	750	2400
2394A — — — R. As 2296; *mm*.-/S...	900	2750

2395

		F	VF
		£	£
2395	**Crown.** Similar to 2305. *London; mm.* 52, 52/-, -/K, 122, 94, ...	625	2000
2396	— Similar but transposed legends without numeral; *mm.* -/arrow	675	2250
2396A	— As 2395, but omitting RVTILANS; *mm.* arrow.................................	675	2250
2396B	Similar, but RVTILANS both sides; *mm.* arrow.................................	800	2750
2397	— *Southwark.* Similar to 2396; *mm.* E.......................................	750	2500
2398	— — King's name on *obv.*; *mm.* E/-, -/E...................................	675	2250
2399	**Halfcrown.** Similar to 2311. *London; mm.* 52, K/-, 122/-, 94, -/52	600	1750
2399A	As last but E over h on *rev.*, *mm.* 56/52....................................	950	3000
2399B	As 2399 but RVTILANS etc. on both sides, *mm.* arrow	675	2250
2400	— *Southwark. mm.* E, E/-, -/E	625	2000

SILVER

AR (4oz .333)

2401	**Testoon.** *Tower.* As 2365 with lozenge stops one side; -/56, 56...........	2250	9500

2403	2403 Bust 4	2403 Bust 6

Some of the Bristol testoons, groats and halfgroats with WS monogram were struck after the death of Henry VIII but cannot easily be distinguished from those struck during his reign.

2403	**Groat.** *Tower.* Busts 4, 5, 6 (and, rarely, 2). R. POSVI, etc.; *mm.* 105-94 and none (frequently muled)....................................	95	500
2404	— *Southwark.* Busts 4, 5, 6. R. CIVITAS LONDON; no *mm.* -/E; lis/-, -/lis, K/E; roses or crescents or S and Є in forks, or rarely annulets	85	450
2405	— *Durham House.* Bust 6. R. REDDE CVIQUE QVOD SVVM EST; *mm.* bow..	250	900
2406	— *Bristol. mm.* WS on *rev.* Bristol bust B, Tower bust 2 and 3	110	525
2407	— — *mm.* TC on *rev.* Similar, Bristol bust B	125	575
2408	— *Canterbury.* Busts 5, 6; no *mm.* or rose/-	85	425
2409	— *York.* Busts 4, 5, 6; no *mm.* or lis/-, -/lis.............................	85	425

2411   2416

	F £	VF £

2410 **Halfgroat.** Bust 1. *Tower.* POSVI, etc.; *mm.* 52, 52/-, 52/K , -/K, 52/122, 122, -/122 .... 90 | 400
2411 — *Southwark.* CIVITAS LONDON; *mm.* E, -/E, none, 52/E, K/E .... 60 | 200
2412 — *Durham House.* R. REDD, etc.; *mm.* bow, -/bow .... 375 | 1500
2413 — *Bristol.* Mm. WS on *rev.*... 70 | 325
2414 — — *mm.* TC on *rev.*... 90 | 400
2415 — *Canterbury.* No *mm.* or t/-, -/t,... 45 | 185
2416 — *York.* No *mm.*, bust 1 and three-quarter facing .... 65 | 275

2417   2418

2417 **Penny.** *Tower.* CIVITAS LONDON. Facing bust; *mm.* 52/-, -/52, -/K, 122/-, -/122, none... 50 | 180
2418 — — three-quarter bust; no *mm.* .... 50 | 185
2419 — *Southwark.* As 2417; *mm.* E, -/E.. 55 | 200
2420 — *Durham House.* As groat but shorter legend; *mm.* -/bow .... 475 | 1500

2421   2426   2428

2421 — *Bristol.* Facing busts, as 2382 but showing more body, no *mm*........... 75 | 275
2422 — *Canterbury.* Similar to 2417 .... 50 | 185
2423 — — three-quarter facing bust; no *mm.* .... 55 | 200
2424 — *York.* Facing bust; no *mm.*... 50 | 185
2425 — — three-quarter facing bust; no *mm.* .... 60 | 225
2426 **Halfpenny.** *Tower.* mm 52?, none.. 45 | 140
2427 — *Canterbury.* No *mm.*, sometimes reads H8.............................. 50 | 150
2428 — *York.* No *mm.* .... 45 | 140

The 4 oz. 2.5dwt coins of Henry VIII and those issued under Edward in 1547 and 1548 caused much disquiet, yet at the same time government was prevented by continuing financial necessity from abandoning debasement. A stratagem was devised which entailed increasing the fineness of silver coins, thereby making them appear sound, while at the same time reducing their weight in proportion so that in practice they contained no more silver than hitherto. The first issue, ordered on 24 January 1549, at 8 oz.2 dwt. fine produced a shilling which, at 60 gr., was so light that it was rapidly discredited and had to be replaced in April by another at 6 oz. 2 dwt. Weighing 80 gr., these later shillings proved acceptable.

Between April and August 1551 the issue of silver coins was the worst ever – 3 oz. 2dwt. fine at 72s per lb. before retrenchment came in August, first by a 50% devaluation of base silver coin and then by the issue of a fine standard at 11oz. 1dwt. 'out of the fire'. This was the equivalent of 11oz.3dwt. commixture, and means that since sterling was only 11oz. 2dwt., this issue, which contained four new denominations – the crown, halfcrown, sixpence and threepence – was in effect the finest ever issued under the Tudors.

Some base 'pence' were struck in parallel with the fine silver, but at the devalued rate, they and the corresponding 'halfpence' were used as halfpence and farthings respectively.

The first dates on English coinage appear in this reign, first as Roman numerals and then on the fine issue crowns and halfcrowns of 1551-3, in Arabic numerals.

Mintmarks

66	52	35	115	E	53	122
t	T	111	Y	126	94	91A
92	105	y	97	123	78	26

1547-8	Arrow (52)			
	E (Southwark)			
1548-50	Bow (66, *Durham House*)	1550	Martlet (94)
1549	Arrow (52)	1550	Leopard's head (91A)
	Grapple (122)	1550-1	Lion (92)
	Rose (35, *Canterbury*)		Lis (105, *Southwark*)
	TC monogram (115, *Bristol*)		Rose (33)
	Pheon (53)	1551	Y or y (117, *Southwark*)
	t or T (*Canterbury*)		Ostrich's head (97, gold only)
1549-50	Swan (111)	1551-3	Tun (123)
	Roman Y (*Southwark*)		Escallop (78)
1549-50	6 (126 gold only)	1552-3	Pierced mullet (26, *York*)

GOLD

2430

		F	VF
		£	£
2429	**Half-sovereign** (20 c). As 2391, but reading EDWARD 6. Tower; *mm.* arrow	2250	9000
2430	— *Southwark* (Sometimes with E or Є below shield); *mm.* E..............	1750	6500
2431	**Crown.** RVTILANS, etc., crowned rose between ER both crowned. R. EDWARD 6, etc., crowned shield between ER both crowned; *mm.* arrow, E over arrow/-	2250	9000
2431A	— *Obv.* as last. R. As 2305, *mm.* 52/56	2000	7500
2432	**Halfcrown.** Similar to 2431, but initials not crowned; *mm.* arrow	1500	5000

Second period, Jan. 1549-Apr. 1550

2433

2433	**Sovereign** (22 ct). As illustration; *mm.* arrow, –/arrow, Y, ...	6500	18500
2434	**Half-sovereign.** Uncrowned bust. *Tower.* TIMOR etc., MDXLIX on *obv. mm.* arrow...	3500	12500

2435

| 2435 | — — SCVTVM, etc., as illustration; *mm.* arrow, **6,** Y............................ | 2000 | 7000 |

		F £	VF £

2436 — *Durham House.* Uncrowned, 1/2 length bust with MDXLVIII at end of
        obv. legend; *mm.* bow; SCVTVM etc. 7500 27500
2437 — Normal, uncrowned bust. LVCERNA, etc., on *obv.; mm.* bow 6500 22500
2437A — Normal, uncrowned bust. SCVTVM, etc. but with *rev.* as 2440, *mm.* bow 5250 17500

2438   2441

2438 — *London, Southwark.* Crowned bust. EDWARD VI, etc. ℞. SCVTVM, etc.;
        mm. 52, 122, 111/52, 111, Y, 94 .... 1850 6500
2439 — *Durham House.* Crowned, half-length bust; *mm.* bow 7500 27500
2440 — — King's name on *obv.* and *rev.; mm.* bow (mule of 2439/37) 8000 30000
2441 **Crown.** Uncrowned bust, as 2435; *mm.* 6, Y, 52/-, Y/- 2250 8500
2442 — Crowned bust, as 2438; *mm.* 52, 122, 111, Y (usually *obv.* only) 2000 7500
2443 **Halfcrown.** Uncrowned bust; ℞. As 2441, *mm.* arrow, Y, Y/-, 52/- 2250 8500
2444 — Crowned bust, as illus. above; *mm.* 52, 52/111, 111, 122, Y, Y/- 1650 5750
2445 — Similar, but king's name on *rev., mm.* 52, 122 .... 1750 6000

Third period, 1550-3, Fine Gold (23 ct.)
2446 **Sovereign** (30s., 240grs., 15.55g.). King on throne; *mm.* 97, 123 .... 30000 125000

2444   2448

2447 **Double sovereign.** From the same dies, *mm.* 97 .... 110000 450000
2448 **Angel** (10s.). As illustration; *mm.* 97, 123 .... 12500 42500
2449 **Half-angel.** Similar, *mm.* 97 .... 11000 37500

2450

	F £	VF £

Crown Gold (22 ct.)

2450 **Sovereign**. (=20s., 174.6 grs., 11.31g.). Half-length
figure of king r., crowned and holding sword and orb. R. Crowned shield
with supporters; *mm*. y, tun.. 7500 22500

2451

2451 **Half-sovereign**. As illustration above; *mm*. y, tun	2250	7500
2452 **Crown**. Similar, but *rev*. SCVTVM etc., *mm*. y, tun...............................	2500	8500
2453 **Halfcrown**. Similar, *mm*. tun, y..	2750	9500

*Small denominations often occur creased or straightened.

SILVER

First period, Apr. 1547-Jan. 1549

2454 2455

2454 **Groat**. Crowned bust r. *Tower*. R. Shield over cross, POSVI, etc.; *mm*. arrow	750	4500
2455 — As last, but EDOARD 6, *mm*. arrow...	850	5000
2456 *Southwark*. *Obv*. as 2454. R. CIVITAS LONDON; *mm*.-/E or none, sometimes S in forks..	750	4500
2457 **Halfgroat**. *Tower*. *Obv*. as 2454; *mm*. arrow .... •	650	2500
2458 *Southwark*. As 2456; *mm*. arrow, E on reverse only.................................	575	2000

2459   2462

	F	VF
	£	£
2459 *Canterbury.* Similar. No *mm.*, reads EDOARD or EDWARD (rare)	350	1350
2460 **Penny.** *Tower.* As halfgroat, but E.D.G. etc. R. CIVITAS LONDON; *mm.* arrow	450	1500
2461 *Southwark.* As last, but *mm.* -/E...	500	1650
2462 *Bristol.* Similar, but reads ED6DG or E6DG no *mm.*...............................	450	1500
2463 **Halfpenny.** *Tower. O.* As 2460, *mm.* E (?). R. Cross and pellets	575	1750
2464 *Bristol.* Similar, no *mm.* but reads E6DG or EDG....................................	650	2000

Second period, Jan. 1549-Apr. 1550

At all mints except Bristol, the earliest shillings of 1549 were issued at only 60 grains but of 8 oz. 2 dwt standard. This weight and size were soon increased to 80 grains, (S.2466 onwards), but the fineness was reduced to 6 oz. 2 dwt so the silver content remained the same. Dies, mm G were prepared for a coinage of 80gr shillings at York, but were not used. Coins from the *mm* are found suitably overmarked, from other mints, S.2466-8. The shilling bust types are set out in *J. Bispham 'The Base Silver Shillings of Edward VI; BNJ 1985.*

Bust 1   2465A   Bust 2

First Issue, 60 grs., 3.88g., 8oz. 2 dwt.

2465 **Shilling.** *Tower.* Broad bust with large crown. *Obv.* TIMOR etc. MDXLIX. R. Small, oval garnished shield dividing ER. EDWARD VI etc., *mm.* 52, no *mm*, Bust 1; *mm*, –/52, Bust 2 (very rare)	275	1350
2465A *Southwark.* As last, Bust 1, *mm.* Y, EY/Y	250	1250
2465B *Canterbury.* As last, Bust 1, *mm.* -/rose..	275	1500

2465C

2465C *Durham House.* Bust with elaborate tunic and collar TIMOR etc. MDXLIX. R. Oval shield, very heavily garnished in different style. EDWARD VI etc., *mm.* bow (2469)	275	1500

Second Issue, debased, 80 grs., 5.18g., 6oz. 2 dwt.

Bust 3   Bust 4

Bust 5   2466C   2468

2472

		F £	VF £
2466	*Tower.* Tall, narrow bust with small crown. *Obv.* EDWARD VI etc. MDXLIX or MDL. R. As 2465 but TIMOR etc., Busts 3, 4 and 5, *mm.* 52-91a (frequently muled)	175	950
2466A	— *Obv.* as last, MDXLIX. R. Heavily garnished shield, Durham House style, Bust 3 *mm.* grapple	425	1750
2466B	*Southwark.* As 2466, Busts 3, 4 and 5 *mm.* Y, Y/swan	175	950
2466C	— — — Bust 4; R. as 2466A. *mm.* Y	425	1750
2467	*Bristol. Obv.* similar to 2466, Bust 3 or local die R. Shield with heavy curved garniture or as 2466, *mm.* TC, or TC over G	1050	4500
2468	*Canterbury.* As 2466, Bust 3 and 4 *mm.* T, T/t, t/T, t or t over G	225	1200
2470	*Durham House.* Bust as 2465C. INIMICOS etc., no date. R. EDWARD etc.	225	1200
2472	— Bust similar to 2466. EDWARD VI etc. R. INIMICOS etc.	200	1000
2472A	— As last but legends transposed	325	1650
2472B	*Tower.* Elegant bust with extremely thin neck. Bust 6, R. As 2466, *mm.* martlet	475	2250
2472C	*Southwark.* As last, Bust 6, *mm.* Y	225	1250

For coins of Edward VI countermarked, see p. 236

Third period, 1550-3

Very base issue (1551) ca. 70grs., ca. 4.88g., 3oz. 2 dwt.

2473 Bust 6   2474   2476

	F	VF
	£	£
2473 **Shilling**, *Tower*. As 2472B. MDL or MDLI, *mm*. lion, rose, lion/rose	175	950
2473A *Southwark*. As last, *mm*. lis/Y, Y/lis, lis	175	950
2474 **Base Penny**. *London. O*. Rose. R. Shield; *mm*. escallop (*obv.*)...............	55	250
2475 — — *York. Mm*. mullet (*obv.*) as illustration..	50	225
2476 **Base Halfpenny**. As penny, but single rose	275	1350

* The base penny and halfpenny were used as halfpenny and farthing respectively.

Note: Irish very base shillings exist which are all dated MDLII, a date that does not occur for English issued shillings.

Fine silver issue, (1551-3) 460grs., 30g., 11oz. 3 dwt.

2478

2478 **Crown**. King on horseback with date below horse. R. Shield on cross;		
mm. y. 1551; tun, 1551-3 (1553, wire line inner circle may be missing) .	850	3250

2479

2479 **Halfcrown**. Walking horse with plume; *mm*. y, 1551	600	2000
2480 Galloping horse without plume; *mm*. tun, 1551-3	625	2250

2482

2483

2484

		F £	VF £
2481	Large walking horse without plume; *mm.* tun, 1553	950	3750
2482	**Shilling**. Facing bust, rose l., value XII r. *mm.* y, tun (several bust varieties)	110	450
2483	**Sixpence**. *London*. Similar value VI, as illustration; *mm.* y/-, -/y, y, tun (bust varieties)	125	500
2484	*York*. As last, but rev. reads CIVITAS ЄBORACI; *mm.* mullet	225	1250

2485

2486

2485	**Threepence**. *London*. As sixpence, but value III; *mm.* tun	185	1000
2486	*York*. As 2484, but III by bust	475	2250

2487

2487A

2487	**Penny**. 'Sovereign' type; *mm.* tun	1250	4500
2487A	**Farthing**. *O*. Portcullis, R Cross and Pellets	1350	4750

Mary brought English coins back to the sterling standard and struck all her gold coins at the traditional fineness of 0.995. The mintmarks usually appear at the end of the first or second word of the legends.

Pomegranate   Halved rose and castle

GOLD

2488

	F	VF
	£	£
2488 **'Fine' Sovereign** (30s.). Queen enthroned. R. Shield on rose, MDLIII, MDLIIII and undated, *mm.* pomegranate, half-rose (or mule)	8500	27500

2489

| 2489   **Ryal** (15s.). As illus, MDLIII. R. As 1950 but A DNO etc. *mm.* pomegranate/- | 27500 | 100000 |

2490

	F	VF
	£	£
2490 **Angel** (10s.). Class I, annulet stops; *mm.* pomegranate..........................	2000	5500
2490A — Class II, pellet stops, *mm.* pomegranate (often muled with class I reverse)	2100	6000
2490B — Class III, pellet stops, large Roman letters, *mm.* half-rose and castle .	2250	6500
2491 **Half-angel**. Similar; *mm.* pomegranate, pomegranate/-..........................	6500	17500

SILVER

2492

2492 **Groat**. Crowned bust l. R̃. VЄRITAS, etc.; *mm.* pomegranate,		
pomegranate/-	125	525
2493 **Halfgroat**. Similar..	750	2500
2494 **Penny**. Similar, but M. D. G. ROSA, etc.	575	2250

2495

| 2495 — As last. R̃. CIVITAS LONDON; no *mm*... | 575 | 2250 |

The groats and smaller silver coins of this period have Mary's portrait only, but the shillings and sixpences show the bust of the queen's husband, Philip of Spain.

Mintmarks

Lis (105

Half-rose and castle

GOLD

2496A

		F	VF
		£	£
2496	**Angel.** As illustration; wire line inner circles, calm sea, *mm.* lis	5500	20000
2496A	— — New-style, large wings, wire line i.c.	5750	21000
2496B	— — As above but beaded i.c.	6250	22500
2497	**Half-angel.** Similar to 2496	13500	40000

SILVER

2497A

2497A	**Halfcrown (Pattern).** As illustration. Bust of Philip r., crown above, date 1554 below. R. Bust of Mary l. crown and date 1554 above, without mark of value, no *mm*...	13500	47500
2498	**Shilling.** Busts face-to-face, full titles, undated, no *mm*.	400	1800
2499	— — — also without mark of value	450	2000

2500

	F £	VF £
2500 — — 1554	400	1800
2501 — English titles only 1554, 1555	425	1850
2501A — — undated	525	2250
2502 — — without mark of value, 1554, 1555 (rare)	450	2000
2503 — — date below bust, 1554, 1555	3500	12500
2504 — — As last, but without ANG., 1555	4000	13500

2505   2506

2505 **Sixpence**. Similar. Full titles, 1554 (and undated?)	400	1750
2506 — English titles only, 1555 (no *mm.*, rare), 1557 (*mm.* lis, rounder garnishing)	400	1650
2506A — As last but heavy beaded i.c. on obv. 1555. (Irish 4d. obv. mule)	425	1850
2507 — — date below bust, 1554, 1557 (very rare)	1250	5250

2508   2510A

2508 **Groat**. Crowned bust of Mary 1. ℞. POSVIMVS etc. (several legend vars.); *mm.* lis	110	475
2509 **Halfgroat**. Similar, but POSVIM, *mm.* lis	475	1850
2510 **Penny**. Similar to 2495, but P. Z. M. etc.; *mm.* lis	425	1650
2510A **Base penny**, but P. Z. M . etc.; *mm.* halved rose and castle or castle/–, (used as a halfpenny)	60	225

Elizabeth's coinage is particularly interesting on account of the large number of different denominations issued. 'Crown' gold coins were again issued as well as the 'fine' gold denominations. In 1560 the base shillings of Edward VI's second and third coinages were called in and countermarked for recirculation at reduced values. Smaller debased coins were also devalued but not countermarked. The old debased groat became a three halfpence and other coins in proportion. The normal silver coinage was initially struck at 0.916 fineness as in the previous reign but between 1560 and 1577 and after 1582 the old sterling standard of 0.925 was restored. Between 1578 and 1582 the standard was slightly reduced and the weights were reduced by 1/32nd in 1601. Gold was similarly reduced slightly in quality 1578-82, and there was a slight weight reduction in 1601.

To help alleviate the shortage of small change, and to avoid the expense of minting an impossibly small silver farthing, a threefarthing piece was introduced to provide change if a penny was tendered for a farthing purchase. The sixpence, threepence, threehalfpence and threefarthings were marked with a rose behind the queen's head to distinguish them from the shilling, groat, half-groat and penny.

Coins of exceedingly fine workmanship were produced in a screw press introduced by Eloye Mestrelle, a French moneyer, in 1561. With parts of the machinery powered by a horse-drawn mill, the coins produced came to be known as 'mill money'. Despite the superior quality of the coins produced, the machinery was slow and inefficient compared to striking by hand. Mestrelle's dismissal was engineered in 1572 and six years later he was hanged for counterfeiting.

Mintmarks

1ST ISSUE	2ND ISSUE		3RD & 4TH ISSUES				
106	21	94	23	53	33	107	92
			74	71	77	65b	27

5TH ISSUE			6TH ISSUE				
7	14	113	60	54	79	72b	86

7TH ISSUE							
1	2		123	124	90	57	0

First Issue
1558-60 Lis (106)
Second Issue
1560-1 Cross crosslet (21)
        Martlet (94)
Third & Fourth Issue
1560-6 Star (23, milled)
1561-5 Pheon (53)
1565 Rose (33)
1566 Portcullis (107)
1566-7 Lion (92)
1567-70 Coronet (74)

Lis (106, milled)
1569-71 Castle (71)
1572-3 Ermine (77)
1573-4 Acorn (65b)
1573-8 Eglantine (27)
Fifth Issue
1578-9 Greek cross (7)
1580-1 Latin cross (14)
1582 Sword (113)
Sixth Issue
1582-3 Bell (60)
1582-4 A (54)

1584-6 Escallop (79)
1587-9 Crescent (72b)
1590-2 Hand (86)
1592-5 Tun (123)
1594-6 Woolpack (124)
1595-8 Key (90)
1598-1600 Anchor (57)
1600 0
Seventh Issue
1601-2 1
1602 2

N.B. *The dates for* mms *sometimes overlap. This is a result of using up old dies, onto which the new mark was punched.*

GOLD

HAMMERED COINAGE
First to Fourth issues, 1559-78. ('Fine' gold of 0.994. 'Crown' gold of 0 .916 fineness. Sovereigns of 240 grs., 15.55g.). Mintmarks; lis to eglantine.

	F £	VF £
2511 **'Fine' Sovereign** (30 s.) Queen enthroned, tressure broken by throne, reads Z not ET, no chains to portcullis. R. Arms on rose; *mm.* lis............	10500	35000

2512

2512 — — Similar but ET, chains on portcullis; *mm.* crosslet	8000	25000

2513

2513 **Angel**. St. Michael. R. Ship. Wire line inner circles; *mm.* lis..................	1750	6000
2513A — Similar, but beaded i.c. on *obv.*, *mm.* lis	2000	7500
2514 — — Similar, but beaded inner circles; ship to r.; *mm.* 106, 21, 74, 27,..	1100	3500
2515 — — — Similar, but ship to l.; *mm.* 77-27	1200	3750
2516 **Half Angel**. As 2513, wire line inner circles; *mm.* lis	2500	9000
2516A — As last, but beaded i.c.s, legend ends. Z.HIB	1750	6000

2517

2517 — As 2514, beaded inner circles; *mm.* 106, 21, 74, 77-27	1000	3250
2518 **Quarter Angel**. Similar; *mm.* 74, 77-27..	950	3000
2519 **Half Pound** (10 s.) Young crowned bust l. R. Arms. Wire line inner circles; *mm.* lis	5750	20000

2520   2524

	F	VF
	£	£
2520 — Similar, but beaded inner circles; *mm.* 21, 33-107	1750	5250
2520A — — Smaller bust; *mm.* lion	2000	6500
2520B — — Broad bust, ear visible; *mm.* 92, 74, 71	1750	5250
2521 **Crown**. As 2519; *mm.* lis.............................	3000	10000
2522 — Similar to 2520; *mm.* 21, 33-107	1100	3500
2522A — Similar to 2520B; *mm.* 74, 71, 92.....................	1250	3750
2523 **Half Crown**. As 2519; *mm.* lis.........................	2250	7500
2524 — Similar to 2520; *mm.* 21, 33-107 (2 busts).............	1050	3250
2524A — Similar to 2520B; *mm.* 107-71	1100	3500

Fifth Issue, 1578-82 (`Fine' gold only of 0.992). *Mms* Greek cross, Latin cross and sword.

	F	VF
2525 **Angel**. As 2514; *mm.* 7, 14, 113	1000	3250
2526 **Half Angel**. As 2517; *mm.* 7, 14, 113.................	950	3000
2527 — Similar, but without E and rose above ship; *mm.* latin cross..........	1100	3500
2528 **Quarter Angel**. As last; *mm.* 7, 14, 113...............	950	3000

Sixth Issue, 1583-1600 (`Fine' gold of 0.995, `crown' gold of 0.916; pound of 174.5 grs. wt.). Mintmarks: bell to **O**.

2529

	F	VF
2529 **Sovereign** (30 s:). As 2512, but tressure not normally broken by back of throne; *mm.* 54-123.................	7000	21000

2530

		F	VF
		£	£

2530   **Ryal** (15 s.). Queen in ship. R. Similar to 1950; *mm*. 54-86 (*rev*. only) ..   20000   65000

Note: Contemporary imitations of the Elizabeth Ryal are known for the Low Countries.

2531

2531	**Angel**. As 2514; *mm*. 60-123, 90-**O**	1000	3250
2532	**Half Angel**. As 2517; *mm*. 60-86, 90-57	1000	3250

2535

2533	**Quarter Angel**. As 2518; *mm*. 60-123, 90-57/–	900	2750
2534	**Pound** (20 s.). Old bust l., with elaborate dress and profusion of hair; *mm*., lion and tun/tun, 123-**O**	3000	10500
2535	**Half Pound**. Similar; *mm*. tun..	2400	7500
2535A	— Similar but smaller bust with less hair; *mm*. 123-**O**	2250	7000

2536

2536	**Crown**. Similar to 2534; *mm*. 123-90. **O**	2250	7000
2537	**Half Crown**. Similar; *mm*. -/123, 123-0, **O**	1350	4500

Seventh Issue, 1601-3 ('Fine' gold of 0.994, 'crown' gold of 0.916; Pound of 172 gr.). Mintmarks: **1** and **2**

		F	VF
		£	£
2538	**Angel**. As 2531; *mm.* **1, 2**	1850	6000
2539	**Pound**. As 2534; *mm.* **1, 2**	3250	11000
2540	**Half Pound**. As 2535A; *mm.* **1, 2**	3500	12500
2541	**Crown**. As 2536; *mm.* **1, 2**	2500	8500
2542	**Half Crown**. As 2537; *mm.* **1, 2**	2250	7500

MILLED COINAGE, 1561-70

2543

2543	**Half Pound**. Crowned bust l.; *mm.* star, lis	3000	9000
2544	**Crown**. Similar; *mm.* star, lis	3250	9500
2545	**Half Crown**. Similar; *mm.* star, lis	4500	13500

For further details on the Gold milled coinage, *see* D. G. Borden & I.D. Brown *'The milled coinage of Elizabeth I'*. BNJ 53, 1983

SILVER

HAMMERED COINAGE
Countermarked Edward VI base shillings (1560)

2546   2547

		Fair	F
		£	£
2546	**Fourpence-halfpenny**. Edward VI 2nd period 6oz and 8oz shillings .... cmkd on obv. with a portcullis; *mm*. 66, –/33, 52, t, 111, Y and 122	1100	4250
2547	**Twopence-farthing**. Edward VI 3rd period 3 oz. shillings .... countermarked on obverse with a seated greyhound; *mm*. 92. 105, 35 and 87	1500	5750
N.B.	*Occasionally the wrong countermark was used*		

First Issue, 1559-60 (.916 fine, shillings of 96 grs., 6.22g.)

2549   2551

1A   1B   1D   2A   2B

		F	VF
		£	£
2548	**Shilling**. Without rose or date. ELIZABET(H), wire line inner circles, pearls on bodice, busts 1A, and 1B; *mm*. lis.	575	2750
2549	— Similar, ELIZABETH, wire line and beaded inner circles, busts 1A, 1D, 2A and 2B; *mm*. lis..	185	1050

1F   1E 2550 only   1G

	F £	VF £
2550 **Groat**. Without rose or date, wire line or no inner circle, (busts 1F and 1E); *mm.* lis	135	675
2551 — Similar, wire line and beaded inner circles, bust 1F; *mm.* lis...........	85	450
2551A— — Small bust 1G and shield (from halfgroat punches); *mm.* lis......	100	575

2551A   2552   2553

2552 **Halfgroat**. Without rose or date, wire line inner circles; *mm.* lis.........	175	850
2553 **Penny**. Without rose or date, wire line inner circles; *mm.* lis...............	375	1500
2554 — Similar but dated 1558 on *obv.*; *mm.* lis...	675	2500
2554A— Similar to 2553, but wire line and beaded inner circles.; *mm.* lis....	475	1750

Second Issue, 1560-1 (0.925 fineness, shilling of 96 grs., 6.22g.)

2557

2555   2558

3A   3B   3C   3J

2555 **Shilling**. Without rose or date, beaded inner circles. ET instead of Z busts 3A, 3B, 3C and 3J; *mm.* 21, 94	110	525
2555A— large bust with pearls on bodice as 2548; *mm.* 21, bust 1A, 94, bust 1B	150	850
2556 **Groat**. Without rose or date, bust as 2551; *mm.* 21, 94	75	300
2557 **Halfgroat**. Without rose or date; *mm.* 21, 94.......................................	35	150
2558 **Penny**. Without rose or date (three bust varieties); *mm.* 21, 94............	35	135

Third and Fourth Issues, 1561-77 (Same fineness and weight as last)

2559   2561   2561B

		F £	VF £
2559	**Sixpence**. With rose and date, large flan (inner beaded circle 19mm), large bust 3D with hair swept back, 1561; *mm.* pheon	135	650
2560	— Similar, small bust 1F, 1561; *mm.* pheon	75	325

3D 2559 only   1F 2560   3E 2561B only

2562   4B 2562

2561	— Smaller flan (inner beaded circle 17.5mm). Small bust 1F, 1561-6; *mm.* 53-107	65	275
2561B	— Similar, very large bust 3E, 1563-5; *mm.* pheon	95	425
2562	— Intermediate bust 4B, ear shows, 1566-73; *mm.* 92-77	55	240
2562A	— Similar, without date; *mm.* lion, coronet, ermine	750	2250

2563   5A 2563   2565

2563	— Larger bust 5A, 1573-7; *mm.* 77-27	55	240
2564	**Threepence**. With rose and date 1561, large flan (inner circle 15mm.); *mm.* pheon	50	225
2565	— smaller flan (inner circle 14mm.). Regular bust, 1561-7; *mm.* 53-92 .	40	185

2566   2567

2570   2571

		F	VF
		£	£
2566	— taller bust, ear shows, 1567-77; *mm.* 74-27	40	175
2566A	— Similar, without rose, 1568; *mm.* coronet	325	1050
2567	**Halfgroat**. Without rose or date; *mm.* 107-71	45	185
2568	**Threehalfpence**. With rose and date 1561, large flan (inner circle 12.5mm.) *mm.* pheon	45	200
2569	— — Smaller flan (inner circle 10.5-11.5mm.); 1561-2, 1564-78; *mm.* 53-27	40	175
2570	**Penny**. Without rose or date; *mm.* 33-71, 65b, 27	35	135
2571	**Threefarthings**. With rose and date 1561-2, 1564, 1567, 1568, 1572-7; *mm.* 53, 74, 77-27	70	225

Fifth Issue, 1578-82 (0.921 fineness, "shilling" of 95.6 grs., 6.19g.)

2572   2573

| 2572 | **Sixpence**. As 2563, 1578-82; *mm.* 7-113 | 50 | 225 |
| 2573 | **Threepence**. As 2566, 1578-82; *mm.* 7-113 | 40 | 185 |

2574   2575

2574	**Threehalfpence**. As 2569, 1578-9, 1581-2; *mm.* 7-113	45	200
2575	**Penny**. As 2570; *mm.* 7-113	35	135
2576	**Threefarthings**. As 2571, 1578-9, 1581-2; *mm.* 7-113	75	250

Sixth Issue, 1582-1600 (0.925 fineness, shilling of 96 grs., 6.22g.)

2577   2578

2581   6A   6B   6C

		F	VF
		£	£

2577	**Shilling**. Without rose or date, ELIZAB; busts 3B and 6A ear concealed, *mm*. 60-72b. Bust 6B. Ear shows, *mm*. 79-**0** (mules occur)	100	475
2578	**Sixpence**. As 2572, ELIZABETH, 1582, 1583 *mm*. bell	75	300
2578A	— Similar, ELIZAB, 1582-1589; *mm*. 60-72b	55	240
2578B	— Similar, but bust 6C 1589-1600, *mm*. 72b-**0**	55	240
2579	**Halfgroat**. Without rose or date, two pellets behind bust. R. CIVITAS LONDON; *mm*. 60-**0** (*mm*. bell sometimes without pellets or with ··/II).	25	95
2580	**Penny**. Without rose or date. R. CIVITAS LONDON; *mm*. 60-**0**; 90-**0** on obv only	35	135
2581	**Halfpenny**. Portcullis. R. Cross and pellets; *mm*. none, 54-**0**	35	125

Seventh Issue, 1601-2 (0.925 fineness, shilling of 92.9 grs., 6.02)

2582

2582	**Crown**. As illustration, *mm*. **1**	1750	4500
2582A	– Similar, *mm*. **2**	3250	12500

2583

2588

	F	VF
	£	£
2583 **Halfcrown**. As illustration, *mm*. **1**	900	2750
2583A – Similar, *mm*. **2**	3250	12500
2584 **Shilling**. As 2577; bust 6B *mm*. **1, 2**	100	475
2585 **Sixpence**. As 2578B, 1601-2; *mm*. **1, 2**	60	250
2586 **Halfgroat**. As 2579, *mm*. **1, 2**	25	95
2587 **Penny**. As 2580, *mm*. **1, 2**	35	135
2588 **Halfpenny**. As 2581, *mm*. **1, 2**	35	135

MILLED COINAGE 1561-71

2589 **Shilling**. Without rose or date; *mm*. star. Plain dress, large size (over 31 *mm*.)	900	3500
2590 — decorated dress, large size	375	1650
2591 — — intermediate size (30-31 *mm*.)	300	1200
2592 — — small size (under 30 *mm*.)	275	950

2593

2594

2593 **Sixpence**. Small bust, large rose. R. Cross fourchee, 1561 *mm*. star	135	475
2594 Tall narrow bust with plain dress, large rose, 1561-2; *mm*. star	125	450

2595

2596

2595 — similar, but decorated dress, 1562	110	425
2596 Large broad bust, elaborately decorated dress, small rose, 1562; *mm*. star	125	450
2597 — — cross pattée on *rev*., 1562, 64 *mm*. star	135	475

2599

		F	*VF*
		£	£
2598	— similar, pellet border, 1562-4...	150	525
2598A	Bust with low ruff, raised rim, 1564, 1566 (both overdates)...................	175	575
2599	Small bust, 1567-8, R. As 2593; *mm.* lis	110	425

2600   2601

2600	Large crude bust breaking legend; 1570, *mm.* lis; 1571/0, *mm.* castle		
	(over lis)..	375	1350
2601	**Groat**. As illustration..	200	750
2602	**Threepence**. With rose, small bust with plain dress, 1561	200	850
2603	Tall narrow decorated bust with medium rose, 1562............................	135	675
2604	Broad bust with very small rose, 1562	150	750
2605	Cross pattée on *rev.*, 1563, 1564/3..	225	900

2606

2606	**Halfgroat**. As groat	175	750
2607	**Threefarthings**. E . D . G . ROSA, etc., with rose. R. CIVITAS LONDON,		
	shield with 1563 above	3500	9000

Further reading:

The Hammered Silver Coins produced at the Tower Mint during the reign of Elizabeth I.
I. D. Brown, C. H. Comber and W. Wilkinson. 2006.

The Milled Coinage of Elizabeth I. D. G. Borden and I. D. Brown. *BNJ* 53, 1983

EAST INDIA COMPANY TRADE COINAGE - 'Portcullis money'
Trade coins of 8, 4, 2, and 1 Testerns were coined at the Tower Mint in 1600/1 for the first voyage
of the incorporated 'Company of Merchants of London Trading into the East Indies'. The coins bear
the royal arms on the obverse and a portcullis on the reverse and have the *mm.* **O**. They were struck
to the weights of the equivalent Spanish silver 8, 4, 2 and 1 reales.

2607A

	F	*VF*
	£	£
2607A Eight testerns	6250	18500

2607B

2607B Four testerns	3000	9500

2607C

2607D

2607C Two testerns	2500	7500
2607D One testern	1750	5500

JAMES I, 1603-25

With the accession of James VI of Scotland to the English throne, the royal titles and coat of arms are altered on the coinage; on the latter the Scottish rampant lion and the Irish harp now appear in the second and third quarters. In 1604 the weight of the gold pound was reduced and the new coin became known as the 'Unite'. Fine gold of 0·979 and crown gold of 0·916 fineness were both issued, and a gold four-shilling piece was struck 1604-19. In 1612 all the gold coins had their values raised by 10%; but in 1619 the Unite was replaced by a new, lighter 20s. piece, the 'Laurel', and a lighter rose-ryal, spur-ryal and angel were minted.

In 1613 the king granted Lord Harington a licence to coin farthings of copper as a result of repeated public demands for a low value coinage; this was later taken over by the Duke of Lennox. Towards the end of the reign coins made from silver sent to the mint from the Welsh mines had the Prince of Wales's plumes inserted over the royal arms.

Mintmarks

125	105	33	79	84	74	90
60	25	71	45	32	123	132
72b	7a	16	24	125	105	46

First coinage
1603-4　Thistle (125)
1604-5　Lis (105)

Second coinage
1604-5　Lis (105)
1605-6　Rose (33)
1606-7　Escallop (79)
1607　　Grapes (84)
1607-9　Coronet (74)

1609-10　Key (90)
1610-11　Bell (60)
1611-12　Mullet (25)
1612-13　Tower (71)
1613　　Trefoil (45)
1613-15　Cinquefoil (32)
1615-16　Tun (123)
1616-17　Book on lectern (132)

1617-18　Crescent (72b, gold)

1618-19　Plain cross (7a)
1619　　Saltire cross (16, gold)

Third coinage
1619-20　Spur rowel (24)
1620-1　Rose (33)
1621-3　Thistle (125)
1623-4　Lis (105)
1624　　Trefoil (46)

GOLD

FIRST COINAGE, 1603-4 (Obverse legend reads D' . G' . ANG : SCO : etc.)

		F	VF
		£	£
2608	**Sovereign** (20s; 171.9 grs., 11.14g.). King crowned r., half-length, first bust with plain armour. R. EXVRGAT, etc.; *mm.* thistle	3250	13000
2609	— second bust with decorated armour; *mm.* thistle, lis...........................	3500	13500

2610   2611

2610	**Half-sovereign**. Crowned bust r. R. EXVRGAT, etc.; *mm.* thistle	5000	18500
2611	**Crown**. Similar. R. TVEATVR, etc.; *mm.* 125, 105/125	2500	9500
2612	**Halfcrown**. Similar; *mm.* thistle, lis.......................................	900	3000

N.B. *The Quarter-Angel of this coinage is considered to be a pattern (possibly a later strike), although coin weights are known.*

SECOND COINAGE, 1604-19 (Obverse legend reads D' G' MAG : BRIT : etc.)

2613

2613	**Rose-ryal** (30s., 33s. from 1612; 213.3 grs., 13.83g.) (Fine gold, 23 ct.). King enthroned. R. Shield on rose; *mm.* 33-90, 25-132	3250	12000

2614

		F £	VF £
2614	**Spur ryal** (15s., 16s. 6d. from 1612). King in ship; *mm.* 33, 79, 74, 25-32, 132	7500	27500
2615	**Angel** (10s., 11s. from 1612). Old type but larger shield; *mm.* 33-74, 60-16	1350	4500
2616	— — pierced for use as touch-piece	675	2250
2617	**Half-angel** (5s., 5s. 6d. from 1612; 154.8 grs., 10.03 g.) (Crown gold, 22 ct.). Similar; *mm.* 71-132, 7a, 16	3250	12500
2618	**Unite** (20s., 22s. from 1612). Half-length second bust r. R̶. FACIAM etc.; *mm.* lis or rose	800	2250

2619

2619	— fourth bust; *mm.* rose to cinquefoil	675	1750
2620	— fifth bust; *mm.* cinquefoil to saltire	675	1750
2621	**Double-crown.** Third bust r. R̶. HENRICVS, etc.; *mm.* lis or rose	525	1650

2623

2622	Fourth bust; *mm.* rose to bell	475	1500
2623	Fifth bust; *mm.* key, mullet to saltire	475	1500

2624   2627

		F	VF
		£	£
2624	**Britain crown**. First bust r.; *mm.* lis to coronet	300	750
2625	Third bust; *mm.* key to cinquefoil	300	750
2626	Fifth bust; *mm.* cinquefoil to saltire	275	700
2627	**Thistle crown** (4s.). As illus.; *mm.* lis to plain cross	275	700
2628	— IR on only one side or absent both sides; *mm.* 79, 74, 71-123	300	750
2629	**Halfcrown**. I' D' G' ROSA SINE SPINA. First bust; *mm.* lis to key	225	475
2630	Third bust; *mm.* key to trefoil, trefoil/tower	225	475
2631	Fifth bust; *mm.* cinquefoil to plain cross	225	475

THIRD COINAGE, 1619-25

2632	**Rose-ryal** (30s.; 194.2 grs., 12.58 g.) (Fine gold, 23 ct.). King enthroned. R. XXX above shield; lis, lion and rose emblems around; *mm.* 24, 125, 105	4250	15000
2633	Similar but plain back to throne; *mm.* trefoil	4750	16500

2634

2634	**Spur-ryal** (15s.). As illus. R. Somewhat like 2614, but lis are also crowned. *mm.* 24-125, 46	7500	27500

2635

2635	**Angel** (10s.) of new type; *mm.* 24-46	1750	5500
2636	— pierced for use as touch-piece	575	1850

2637 2638

	F	VF
	£	£

2637 **Laurel** (20s.; 140.5 grs., 9.10 g.) (Crown gold, 22 ct.). First (large) laur,
bust l.; *mm.* 24, 24/- 1000 3750

2638 Second, medium, square headed bust, `SS' tie ends; *mm.* 24, 33 .... 700 2000

2638A Third, small rounded head, ties wider apart; *mm.* 33, 105, 125................ 675 1850

2638B Fourth head, very small ties; *mm.* 105, 46 .... 650 1750

2638C Fourth head variety, tie ends form a bracket to value; *mm.* lis 675 1750

2639

2639 Fifth, small rather crude bust; *mm.* trefoil 2250 8500

2641A 2642A

2640 **Half-laurel**. First bust; *mm.* spur rowel... 575 1750

2641 — As 2638A; *mm.* rose.. 525 1650

2641A — As 2638B; *mm.* 33-46, 105/-.. 425 1350

2642 **Quarter-laurel**. Bust with two loose tie ends; *mm.* 24-105.................... 275 700

2642A Bust as 2638C; *mm.* 105, 46, 105/46 .... 250 675

2642B As last but beaded, i.c. on *rev.* or both sides; *mm.* 105, 46...................... 275 700

Rev. mm. on $^1/_2$ *and* $^1/_4$ *laurels normally follows REGNA.*

SILVER

2644

	F	VF
	£	£

FIRST COINAGE, 1603-4

		F	VF
2643	**Crown**. King on horseback. R. EXVRGAT, etc., shield; *mm*. thistle, lis.	1250	3750
2644	**Halfcrown**. Similar	1100	5250

2645   2646

		F	VF
2645	**Shilling**. First bust, square-cut beard. R. EXVRGAT, etc.; *mm*. thistle ...	100	525
2645A	— transitional bust, nape of neck shows above broad collar, crown similar to first bust, shoulder armour as second bust, *mm*. thistle	125	650
2646	— Second bust, beard appears to merge with collar; *mm*. thistle, lis	75	300

2647   2648

		F	VF
2647	**Sixpence**. First bust; 1603; *mm*. thistle	75	375
2648	Second bust; 1603-4; *mm*. thistle, lis...	55	275

2649   2650   2651

		F	VF
2649	**Halfgroat**. First bust, II behind head; *mm*. thistle, lis	30	125
2650	**Penny**. First bust I behind head; *mm*. thistle	50	250
2650A	— Second bust; *mm*. thistle, lis	25	85
2651	**Halfpenny**. As illustration; *mm*. thistle, lis	20	80

SECOND COINAGE, 1604-19

2652

		F	VF
		£	£
2652	**Crown**. King on horseback. R. QVAE DEVS, etc. *rev.* stops; *mm.* 105-84	950	3250
2653	**Halfcrown**. Similar; *mm.* 105-79	1750	6250
2654	**Shilling**. Third bust, beard cut square and stands out (*cf.* illus. 2657); *mm.* lis, rose	70	300
2655	— Fourth bust, armour plainer (*cf.* 2658); *mm.* 33-74, 90 over 74, or 60 over 74	70	300

2656

| 2656 | — Fifth bust, similar, but hair longer; single-arched crown, *mm.* 74; higher double-arched crown, *mm.* 74 (rare), 90-7a... | 85 | 350 |

2657   2658

2657	**Sixpence**. Third bust; 1604-6; *mm.* lis, rose, escallop...............................	60	240
2658	— Fourth bust; 1605-16; *mm.* rose to book, 90/60, 25/60........................	65	250
2658A	— Fifth bust, 1618; *mm.* plain cross..	750	2750

2659

	F	VF
	£	£
2659 **Halfgroat**. As illus. but larger crown on *obv.*; *mm.* lis to coronet............	20	70
2660 — — Similar, but smaller crown on *obv.*; *mm.* coronet to plain cross......	20	70
2660A As before, but TVEATVR legend both sides; *mm.* plain cross over book	35	110
2661 **Penny**. As halfgroat but no crowns; *mm.* 105-32,7a and none, -/84, 32/-	20	70
2662 — As before but TVEATVR legend both sides; *mm.* mullet....................	35	100
2663 **Halfpenny**. Rose, R Thistle (with *mm.*) 105-25, 32; all *mm*s on rev. only	15	65

THIRD COINAGE, 1619-25

| 2664 **Crown**. As 2652, with plain or grass ground line, colon stops on *obv.*, no stops on *rev.*; *mm.* 33-46.. | 750 | 1850 |

2665

| 2665 — — plume over shield; *mm.* 125-46 .... | 1100 | 3500 |

2667

| 2666 **Halfcrown**. As 2664 with plain or grass ground line; all have bird-headed harp; *mm.* 33-46.. | 250 | 800 |
| 2666A — — Similar but no ground line; *mm.* rose... | 675 | 2500 |

2668   2669

		F	VF
		£	£
2667	— — Plume over shield; groundline *mm*. 125-46	375	1500
2668	**Shilling**. Sixth (large) bust, hair longer and very curly; *mm*. 24-46	80	350
2669	— — plume over shield; *mm*. 125-46	200	900

2670   2672   2673

		F	VF
2670	**Sixpence**. Sixth bust; 1621-4; *mm*. 33-46; 1621/0, *mm*. rose	70	275
2671	**Halfgroat**. As 2660 but no stops on *rev*.; *mm*. 24-46 and none, 105 and 46, 46/- *mm*. 24 with *rev*. stops known	20	60
2671A	Similar but no inner circles; *mm*. lis, trefoil over lis	25	70
2672	**Penny**. As illus.; *mm*. 24, 105, two pellets, none, trefoil,	20	60
2672A	— Similar but without inner circles on one or both sides; *mm*. lis, two pellets	20	60
2673	**Halfpenny**. As 2663, but no *mm*.	15	50

COPPER

For further details see Tim Everson, *The Galata Guide to the Farthing Tokens of James I and Charles I*

Farthings

2674   2675

		F	VF
2674	Harington Type 1a small size, (originally tinned surface). Mintmark on cushion of crown, *Mintmarks*: A, B, C, D, F, S, Ermine, Millrind, Pellet.	40	100
2675	— — 1b small size. Mintmark replaces central jewel on circlet of crown mm: Trefoil, Crescent, Mullet, or omitted (unmodified)	30	50
2675A	— — 1c small size. Mintmark below crown, *mm*: :<	40	100

2676

		F	VF
		£	£
2676	— — 2 normal size. Mintmark on reverse only, *mm*: Cinquefoil, Cross saltire, Lis, Mullet, Trefoil..	20	40
2676A	— — 3, large crown and harp, mintmark on reverse only, *mm* Martlet...	30	70
2677	Lennox Type 1, mintmark on reverse only; *mm*: Bell, Tower.................	35	70

2678   2679

2678	— — 2, mintmark both sides, *mm*: Flower, Fusil.....................................	10	30
2679	— — 3, mintmark on obverse only, *mm*: Annulet, Coronet, Cross flory fitchée, Cross patée fourchée, Dagger, Eagle's head, Fusil, Key (horizontal), Lion passant, Quatrefoil, Rose (double), Roundel, Thistlehead, Trefoil, Tun, Turtle, Woolpack..	10	30
2679A	Contemporary counterfeits of Lennox Type 3, *mm*: A, Annulet, Coronet, Crescent, Cross (plain or patée), Dagger, Fusil, Key, Mascle, Roundel, Star (pierced), Stirrup, Trefoil, Triangle, Triangle with pellet below, Tun	10	25

2680

2680	— — 4, as 3 but with larger, 9 jewel, crowns, *mm*: A, Dagger, Fusil, Lion rampant, Lis (three), Mascle, Stirrup, Trefoil, Triangle............................	10	30
2680A	Contemporary forgeries of Lennox Type 4, *mm* A, Annulet, Dagger, Fusil, Lis, Mascle, Pellets (four), Tun, ...	10	25
2681	— — 5, oval flan, legend starts at bottom left, *mm* Cross patée.............	60	120

Lennox Type 5, the oval farthings, were issued for use in Ireland

Numismatically, this reign is one of the most interesting. Some outstanding machine-made coins were produced by Nicholas Briot, a French die-sinker, but they could not be struck at sufficient speed to supplant hand-hammering methods, and the weights often had to be adjusted by blank filing. In 1637 a branch mint was set up at Aberystwyth to coin silver extracted from the Welsh mines and dies supplied from Tower Mint. After the king's final breach with Parliament the parliamentary government continued to issue coins at London with Charles's name and portrait until the king's trial and execution. The coinage of copper farthings continued to be manufactured privately under licences held first by the Duchess of Richmond and, lastly, by Lord Maltravers. Parliament took control of the Token House in 1643, and production ceased the following year.

During the Civil War coins were struck at a number of towns to supply coinage for those areas of the country under Royalist control. Many of these coins have an abbreviated form of the 'Declaration' made at Wellington, Shropshire, Sept., 1642, in which Charles promised to uphold the Protestant Religion, the Laws of England and the Liberty of Parliament. Amongst the more spectacular pieces are the gold triple unites and the silver pounds and half-pounds struck at Shrewsbury and Oxford, and the emergency coins, some made from odd-shaped pieces of silver plate during the sieges of Newark, Scarborough, Carlisle and Pontefract.

Mintmarks

105	10	96	71	57	88	101	35
87	107	60	70	123	57	119a	23
	119b	98	112	81	120	109	

Tower Mint under Charles I

1625	Lis (105)	1633-4	Portcullis (107)
1625-6	Cross Calvary (10)	1634-5	Bell (60)
1626-7	Negro's head (96)	1635-6	Crown (75)
1627-8	Castle (71)	1636-8	Tun (123)
1628-9	Anchor (57)	1638-9	Anchor (57)
1629-30	Heart (88)	1639-40	Triangle (119a)
1630-1	Plume (101)	1640-1	Star (23)
1631-2	Rose (35)	1641-3	Triangle in circle
1632-3	Harp (87)		(119b)

Tower Mint under Parliament

1643-4	P in brackets (98)
1644-5	R in brackets (112)
1645	Eye (81)
1645-6	Sun (120)
1646-8	Sceptre (109)

Mint mark no. 57 maybe upright, inverted, or horizontal to left or right.

59	B	58*var*	58

Briot's Mint

1631-2	Flower and B (59)	1638-9	Anchor (57)
1632	**B**		Anchor and B (58)
			(B upright or on side)
			Anchor and Mullet (58v)

61	104	35	92	103	6	65b	71
89	91*var*	131	84	94*var*	64	93	34
102	67	127	128	129	25	83	100

134	71	A	B	75

Provincial and Civil War Mints

1638-42	Book (61, *Aberystwyth*)
1642	Plume (104, *Shrewsbury*)
	Pellets or pellet (*Shrewsbury*)
1642-3	Rose (35, *Truro*)
	Bugle (134, *Truro*)
1642-4	Lion (92, *York*)
1642-6	Plume (103, *Oxford*)
	Pellet or pellets (*Oxford*)
	Lis (105, *Oxford*)
1643	Cross pattee (6, *Bristol*)
	Acorn (65b, *Bristol*)
	Castle (71, *Worcester* or *Shrewsbury*)
	Helmet (89, *Worcester* and *Shrewsbury*)
1643-4	Leopard's head (91 *var. Worcester*)
	Two lions (131, *Worcester*)
	Lis (105, *Worcs.* or *Shrews.*)
	Bunch of grapes (84, *Worcs.* or *Shrews.*)
	Bird (94 var., *Worcs.* or *Shrews.*)

1643-4	Boar's head (64 *Worcs.* or *Shrews.*)
	Lion rampant (93, *Worcs.* or *Shrews.*)
	Rosette (34, *Worcs.* or *Shrews.*)
1643-5	Plume (102, *Bristol*)
	Br. (67, *Bristol*)
	Pellets (*Bristol*)
	Rose (35, *Exeter*)
	Rosette (34, *Oxford*)
1643-6	Floriated cross (127, *Oxford*)
1644	Cross pattee (6, *Oxford*)
	Lozenge (128, *Oxford*)
	Billet (129, *Oxford*)
	Mullet (25, *Oxford*)
1644-5	Gerb (83, *Chester*)
	Pear (100, *Worcester*)
	Lis (105, *Hereford?*)
	Castle (71, *Exeter*)
1645-6	Plume (102, *Ashby, Bridgnorth*)
1645	A (*Ashby*)
1646	B (*Bridgnorth*)
1648-9	Crown (75, *Aberystwyth Furnace*)

GOLD COINAGE

TOWER, UNDER THE KING (1625-42), AND UNDER PARLIAMENT (1642-9)

For bust varieties on Tower Mint Gold see H. Schneider BNJ 1955-61
Numbers in brackets following each entry refer to numbers employed in previous editions of this catalogue

		F	VF
		£	£
2682	**Angel**. St. Michael slaying dragon, no mark of value. R. Three masted ship, royal arms on mainsail; mm. lis, cross calvary	3750	15000
2682A	— — — pierced for use as touch-piece (2683)	1250	4500
2683	— X in field to right of St. Michael; m.m. negro's head, castle, anchor, heart, castle and negro's head/castle, anchor and castle/anchor (2684)	2500	10000
2683A	— — — pierced for use as touch-piece (2685)	800	2750
2684	— X in field to left of St. Michael; mm. negro's head, heart, rose, harp, portcullis, bell, crown, tun, anchor, triangle, star, triangle-in-circle (2686)	2250	9000

2684A   2685

2684A	— — — pierced for use as touch-piece (2687)	750	2500
2685	**Unite**. Group A, first bust, in coronation robes, bust 1, high double-arched crown. R. Square-topped shield, plain or elaborate garnishing; mm. lis (2688, 2688A)	800	2250
2686	— — bust 1a, flatter single-arched crown; mm. lis, cross calvary (2689, 2689A)	850	2500
2687	Group B, second bust, in ruff, armour and mantle. R. Square-topped shield; m.m. cross calvary, negro's head, castle, anchor, heart (2690)	750	2250

2688

2688	— — more elongated bust, usually dividing legend, mm. anchor, heart, plume (2690A)	750	2250
2689	— — — anchor below bust; mm. (2691)	2250	7500
2689A	Group B/C mule. R. Oval shield with CR at sides; mm. plume (2691A)	1000	3500
2690	Group C, third bust, shorter with heavier armour. R. Oval shield with CR at sides; mm. plume, rose (2692)	750	2250
2691	Group D, fourth bust, with falling lace collar, bust 4, large bust with jewelled crown.R. Oval shield with CR at sides; mm. harp, portcullis (2693)	725	2000

	F £	VF £

2692   — — bust 5, smaller bust, unjewelled crown; mm. portcullis, bell, crown,
       tun, anchor, triangle, star (2693A)   725   2000
2693   — — — (under Parliament); mm. (P), (P)/- (2710)   1350   5000
2694   Group F, sixth 'Briot's' bust, with stellate lace collar. R. Oval shield with
       CR at sides, mm. triangle, star, triangle-in-circle (2694)   850   2500
2695   — — (under Parliament); mm. (P), (R) (2711)...................................... 1500   5250

2696

2696   Group G, (under Parliament), seventh bust, smaller collar; mm. eye, sun, sceptre
       (2712)... 1850   6500

2697

2697   **Double-crown**. Group A, first bust, in coronation robes, bust 1, high double-
       arched crown, both arches jewelled. R. Square-topped shield; mm. lis (2696)   525   1650

2698   — — bust 1a, flatter crown, outer arch only jewelled; m.m. lis, cross calvary
       (2696A)... 475   1500

2699

2699   Group B, second bust, in ruff, armour and mantle, bust 2. R. Square-topped
       shield; mm. cross calvary, negro's head, castle, anchor (2697)................ 425   1250
2700   — — busts 3-4, more elongated bust, usually dividing legend; mm.
       anchor, heart, plume (2697A)... 450   1400
2700A Group B/C mule, elongated bust dividing legend. R. oval shield, *mm.* plume   650   2000
2701   Group C, third bust, bust 5. R. Oval shield with CR at sides; mm. plume, rose
       (2698).. 525   1650

		F	VF
		£	£
2702	Group D, fourth bust, with falling lace collar, bust 6, large bust with jewelled crown. R. Oval shield with CR at sides; mm. harp, crown (2699)	500	1500
2703	— — bust 7, smaller head, inner or both arches of crown unjewelled; mm. harp, portcullis, bell, crown, tun, anchor (2699A-C)	475	1400
2703A	— — — Group Da, (under Parliament), re-cut Group D bust punches; m.m. eye (2713)	1250	4000
2704	Group E, fifth bust, 'Aberystwyth' bust, bust 8, double-arched crown. R. Oval shield with CR at sides; m.m. anchor (2700)	750	2500
2705	— — bust 9, smaller 'Aberystwyth' bust, single-arched crown; m.m. anchor, triangle (2700A)	700	2250
2705A	— — — Group Ea, (under Parliament), re-cut bust 9; m.m. sun, sceptre (2714)	1050	3500
2706	Group F, sixth 'Briot's' bust, with stellate lace collar, bust 10. R. Oval shield with CR at sides; mm. triangle, star, triangle-in-circle (2701)	575	1750
2707	— — (under Parliament); mm. (P), (R) (2715)	700	2250
2708	Group H, (under Parliament), bust 11, dumpy crude bust, single flat-arched crown; mm. sun (2716)	1350	4500

2710   2715

2709	**Crown.** Group A, first bust, in coronation robes, bust 1 var, tall narrow bust, double-arched crown. R. Square-topped shield; mm. lis (2703)	300	825
2710	— bust 1, broader, less angular bust; m.m. lis, cross calvary (2703A)	325	850
2711	Group B, second bust, in ruff, armour and mantle, bust 2. R. Square-topped shield; mm. cross calvary, negro's head, castle (2704)	275	750
2712	— — bust 3, narrower; more elongated bust; m.m. anchor, heart, plume (2704A)	275	750
2713	— — — anchor below bust; mm. anchor (2704B)	700	2250
2713A	Group B/C mule. R. Oval shield with CR at sides; mm. plume, rose (2705)	325	850
2714	Group C, third bust, bust 4. R. Oval shield with CR at sides; mm. plume (2706)	375	1000
2715	Group D, fourth bust, with falling lace collar, busts 5, 7. R. Oval shield with CR at sides; m.m. harp, -/harp, portcullis, portcullis/bell, bell, crown, tun, anchor, triangle, star/triangle, star, triangle-in-circle (2707)	250	650
2716	— — (under Parliament), bust 5, jewelled crown; m.m. (P), (R), eye, sun (2717)	350	950
2716A	— — (under Parliament), bust 6, unjewelled crown; m.m. eye, sun, sceptre (2717A)	400	1050
2717	Group E, fifth bust, small 'Aberystwyth' bust, bust 8. R. Oval shield with CR at sides; mm. anchor (2708)	450	1250
2721C	— Group F, sixth 'Briot's' bust, bust 9, only known as Briot/hammered mule (see 2721C below)	1250	4500

	F	VF
	£	£

NICHOLAS BRIOT'S COINAGES, 1631-2 and 1638-9
MILLED ISSUES, 1631-2

2718 **Angel**. Type somewhat as Tower but smaller and neater; *mm.* -/B 9500 35000

2719

2719	**Unite**. As illustration. R. FLORENT etc.; *mm.* flower and B/B...............	4250	12500
2720	**Double-crown**. Similar but X. R. CVLTORES, etc. *mm.* flower and B/B	2250	7500
2720A	Similar but King's crown unjewelled: *mm.* flower and B/B, B	2500	8000
2721	**Crown**. Similar; *mm.* B	5500	17500

BRIOT'S HAMMERED ISSUES, 1638-9

2721A **Unite**. Briot's (sixth) bust, large lace collar. R. FLORENT etc., Briot's
square-topped shield dividing crowned C R; *mm.* anchor........................ 7500 25000

2721B **Double-crown**. Briot's bust, similar. R. CVLTORES etc., square-topped
shield dividing crowned C R; *mm.* anchor.. 2000 7500

2721C **Crown**. Briot's bust, similar. R. CVLTORES etc., oval shield dividing
crowned C R (a Briot hammered issue/Tower mule); *mm.* anchor........... 1250 4500

GOLD COINAGES

PROVINCIAL ISSUES AND COINAGES OF THE ENGLISH CIVIL WAR, 1642-9
CHESTER, 1644

2722 **Unite**. As Tower. Somewhat like a crude Tower sixth bust. R. Crowned,
oval shield, crowned CR, *mm.* plume 22500 85000

SHREWSBURY, 1642 (See also 2749)

2723 **Triple unite**, 1642. Half-length figure l holding sword and olive-branch;
mm.: R. EXVRGAT, etc., around RELIG PROT, etc., in two wavy lines.
III and three plumes above, date below 75000 250000

2727

		F £	*VF* £

OXFORD, 1642-6

2724	**Triple unite**. As last, but *mm*. plume, tall narrow bust, 1642	9500	30000
2725	Similar, 1643	15000	52500
2725A	Large bust of fine style. King holds short olive branch; *mm*. small lis	45000	175000
2726	As last, but taller bust, with scarf behind shoulder, 1643, *mm*. plume	10000	32500
2727	Similar, but without scarf, longer olive branch, 1643	9500	30000
2728	Similar, but OXON below 1643, rosette stops	22500	75000
2729	Smaller size, olive branch varies, bust size varies, 1644 OXON	10000	32500
2730	— Obv. as 2729, 1644 / OX	12500	37500
2731	**Unite**. Tall thin bust. R. 'Declaration' in two wavy lines, 1642; *no mm*.	3250	10000
2732	— R. 'Declaration' in three lines on continuous scroll, 1642-3	3500	10500
2733	Tall, well-proportioned bust. R. Similar, 1643, no *mm*	4250	13500
2734	Shorter bust, king's elbow not visible. R. Similar, 1643; *mm*. plume/-	3000	9000

2735

2735	Similar but longer olive branch curving to l. 1644 / OX; *mm*. plume	3250	10000
2735A	Similar, but dumpy bust breaking lower i.c., small flan	3250	10000
2736	Tall bust to edge of coin. R. Similar, 1643	7500	25000
2737	As 2734. R. 'Declaration' in three straight lines, 1644 / OX (as shilling *rev*. S2971)	5750	17500
2738	Similar to 2734, but smaller size; small bust, low olive branch. 1645	4500	15000
2739	— R. Single plume above 'Declaration', 1645-6 / OX; *mm*. plume, rosette, none	4000	12500
2740	**Half-unite**. 'Declaration' in three straight lines, 1642	3250	10000
2741	'Declaration' on scroll; *mm*. plume; 1642-3	3000	9500

2742

	F £	VF £
2742 Bust to bottom of coin, 1643; Oxford plumes	2500	7500
2743 — 1644 / OX. Three Shrewsbury plumes (neater work)	3750	12000

BRISTOL, 1643-5

2744 **Unite**. Somewhat as 2734; Two busts known. *mm*. Br. or Br/ plumelet.; 1645	22500	80000
2745 **Half-unite**. Similar 1645	12500	37500

TRURO, 1642–3

2745A **Half-Unite**. Crowned bust l. (similar to Tower 4th bust). R. CVLT, etc., crowned shield	13500	40000

EXETER, 1643–5

2746 **Unite**. *obv*. sim. to early Oxford bust. R. FLORENT, etc., crowned oval shield between crowned CR, *mm*. rose	25000	85000
2747 — R. CVLTORES, etc., similar but no CR	25000	85000

WORCESTER, 1643-4

2748 **Unite**. Crude bust R. FLORENT, etc., double annulet stops, crowned oval shield, lion's paws on either side of garniture, no *mm*	22500	80000

SALOPIA (SHREWSBURY) , 1644

2749 **Unite**. *Obv*. bust in armour. R. Cr. shield, crowned CR. *mm*. lis/-	27500	90000

COLCHESTER BESIEGED, 1648

2750 **Ten Shillings** Gateway of castle between CR; below OBS COL 16 S/X 48. Uniface – now considered a later concoction		

PONTEFRACT BESIEGED, 1648-9. After the death of Charles I, in the name of Charles II

2751 **Unite**. DVM : SPIRO : SPERO around CR crowned. CAROLVS : SECVИDVS : 16 48, castle, OBS on l., PC above.	75000	250000
2752 **Unite**. CAROL : II, etc., around HANC : DEVS, etc. R. POST : MORTEM, etc.,around castle. *Octagonal*	65000	225000

SILVER COINAGES

TOWER, UNDER THE KING (1625-42), AND UNDER PARLIAMENT (1642-9)

2753 **Crown**. Group I, first horseman, type 1a, king on horseback left, horse caparisoned with plume on head and crupper. R. Square-topped shield over long cross fourchee; mm. lis, cross calvary	700	2250
2754 — — 1b. R. Plume above shield, no cross fourchee; mm. lis, cross calvary, castle	1750	6250
2755 Group II, second horseman, type 2a, smaller horse, plume on head only, cross on housing. R. Oval shield over cross fourchee, CR above; mm. harp	650	2000
2756 — — 2b1. R. Plume between CR above shield, no cross fourchee; mm. plume, rose	850	3000
2757 — — 2b2. R. Plume between CR, cross fourchee; mm. harp	950	3500

2758

		F	VF
		£	£
2758	Group III, third horseman, type 3a, horse without caparisons, sword upright. R. Oval shield without CR; mm. bell, crown, tun, anchor, triangle, star..	725	2400
2759	— — 3b. R. Plume above shield; mm. portcullis, crown, tun.................	900	3250
2760	'Briot's' horseman with groundline, lozenge stops on obverse; mm. triangle in circle	7500	25000
2761	Group IV, (under Parliament), fourth horseman, type 4, foreshortened horse R. Oval shield; mm. (P), (R), eye, sun (2838)	750	2500
2762	Group V, (under Parliament), fifth horseman, type 5, tall spirited horse; mm. sun (2839)...	950	3500

2763

2763	**Halfcrown.** Group I, first horseman, type 1a1, horse caparisoned with plume on head and crupper, rose on housings, ground-line. R. Square-topped shield over long cross fourchee; mm. lis (2761)	400	1750
2764	— — 1a2. No rose on housings, no ground-line; mm. lis, cross calvary (2762)	200	900
2765	— — — ground-line; mm. lis (2762A)..	375	1500
2766	— — 1a3. No rose on housings, no ground-line. R. No long cross, heavy or light garnishing to shield; mm. cross calvary*, negro's head, castle (2763-2763B)	200	900
2767	— — — R. Plume above shield, heavy or light garnishing; mm. lis, cross calvary*, negro's head, castle, anchor (2765, 2765A)..................................	575	2250
2768	Group II, second horseman, type 2/1b, plume on horse's head only, rose on housings. R. Plume over shield; mm. heart, plume (2766).......................	950	3500
2769	— — 2a. Smaller horse, cross on housings. R. Oval shield with CR above (CR divided by rose (very rare), lis over rose (rare), or lis); mm. plume, rose, plume/rose (2767)	90	375
2770	— — — 2b. R. Plume between CR above shield; mm. plume, rose (2768)	225	900

2773

		F	VF
		£	£
2771	— — 2c. R. Oval draped shield with CR at sides; mm. harp, portcullis, portcullis/harp (2769)	90	375
2772	— — — 2d. R. Plume above shield; mm. harp (2770)	1500	5250
2773	Group III, third horseman, type 3a1, no caparisons on horse, scarf flying from king's waist. R. Oval garnished shield; mm. bell, bell/crown, crown, tun, triangle (2771)	70	275
2774	— — — 3b. R. Plume above shield; mm. portcullis, bell, crown, tun (2772)	135	575
2775	— — 3a2. King wears cloak flying from shoulder. R. Oval garnished shield; mm. tun, anchor, triangle, star, triangle-in-circle (2773)...........................	65	250

2776   2779

		F	VF
2776	— — — — rough ground under horse; mm. triangle, star (2774)...........	65	250
2777	— — horseman of finer style, short busy tail, cloak like arrowhead behind shoulder, no ground below; mm. triangle, star (2773 var.).......................	110	475
2778	— — 3a3, (under Parliament), no ground, cruder workmanship; mm. (P), (R), eye, sun (2840)	60	200
2779	Group IV, fourth horseman, type 4, foreshortened horse. R. Oval garnished shield; mm. star, triangle in circle (2775)	60	225
2779A	— — (under Parliament); mm. (P) (2841)	125	575
2779B	— —, transitional type 4/5, mm. sun.......................	110	525
2780	Group V, (under Parliament), fifth horseman, type 5, tall spirited horse. R. Oval garnished shield; mm. sun, sceptre (2842)..........................	70	250

* Light weight half crowns (204 grains) exist of No. 2766 and 2767, mm. cross calvary

2781   2783

		F	VF
		£	£
2781	**Shilling**. Group A, first bust, type 1, in coronation robes, bust 1, high double-arched crown, both arches jewelled. R. Square-topped shield over cross fourchee (Sharp A1/1); mm. lis (2776)	95	475
2782	— — bust 2, larger crown, outer arch only jewelled (Sharp A2/1-2); mm. lis*, cross calvary* (2776A, 2777)...	90	450
2783	— — — 1b1. R. Plume above shield, no cross fourchee (Sharp A2/3); mm. lis, cross calvary (2778)..	750	3500
2784	Group B, second bust, type 1a, in ruff, armour and mantle. R. Square-topped shield over cross fourchee (Sharp B1-5/1); mm. cross calvary*, negro's head, castle (2779, 2780)..	90	375
2785	— — 1b2. R. Plume above shield, no cross fourchee (Sharp B1-5/2); mm. cross calvary*, negro's head, castle, anchor, heart, plume (2781, 2781A)	150	675
2786	— — 1b3. R. Plume above shield, cross fourchee (Sharp B2/3); mm. negro's head (2782)..	1750	5750
2787	Group C, third bust, type 2a, with more visible armour. R. Oval garnished shield with CR above (Sharp C1/1, C2/1-3); mm. plume, rose (2783)	65	275
2788	— — 2b. R. Plume above shield (Sharp C1/4, C2/4-6, C3/5); mm. plume, rose (2784)...	150	675
2789	Group D, fourth bust, type 3.1, with falling lace collar, inner circles. R. Garnished oval shield with CR at sides (Sharp D1-6/1); mm. harp, portcullis (2785)	65	275
2790	— — — 3.2. R. Plume above shield (Sharp D1- 3/2); mm. harp (2786)	750	2750

2791

2791	— — 3a, no inner circles. R. Round garnished shield, no CR (Sharp E1/1-2, E2/1-2; E3/2); mm. bell, crown, tun (2787)	50	185
2792	— — — rare bust varieties, no inner circles: (a) large crude bust (Sharp E4/2); mm. tun; (b) neat 'Aberystwyth' bust (Sharp E5/2); mm. tun (2787 var.)	60	250
2793	— — 3b. R. Plume above shield (Sharp E1-2/3); mm. bell, crown, tun (2788)	90	425

* Light weight shillings (81.75 grains) exist of No. 2782, mm. lis, cross calvary over lis; No. 2784, mm. cross calvary; and No. 2785 mm. cross calvary
See Sharp BNJ 1977 for shilling bust varieties including fine work coins. See also Holt, Hulett and Lyle, BNJ 2014.

2794   2797

		F £	VF £
2794	Group E, fifth "Aberystwyth' bust, type 4.2, double-arched crown, small or large XII. R. Square-topped shield over cross moline (Sharp F1/1); mm. tun, anchor (2791)...	70	275
2795	— — 4.1, larger bust, single-arched crown, small or large XII (Sharp F2/1); mm. tun, anchor (2789)	70	300
2796	— — 4.3, smaller bust, single-arched crown, large XII (Sharp F3/1-2); mm. tun, anchor, triangle (2792)	50	200
2797	— — 4.1var., larger bust with rounded shoulder, large XII (Sharp F5/1-2); mm. anchor, triangle (2790)	50	225
2798	— — rare bust varieties : (a) small 'Aberystwyth' bust, double-arched crown (Sharp F4/1); mm. anchor (to right); (b) small 'Briot's' bust, with stellate lace collar, single-arched crown (Sharp F6/1-2); mm. triangle; (c) small 'Aberystwyth' bust, single-arched crown (Sharp F7/2); mm. triangle-in-circle (2790 var.)...	100	475
2799	Group F, sixth large 'Briot's' bust, type 4.4, with stellate lace collar, double-arched crown. R. Square-topped shield over cross moline (Sharp G 1/1-2); mm. triangle, star, triangle-in-circle (2793)..................................	40	135

2800   2803

		F £	VF £
2800	— — — (under Parliament) (Sharp G1-2/2); mm. (P), (R), eye, sun (2843)	40	135
2801	— — 4.4 var., (under Parliament), small thin bust, 'nick' below truncation (Sharp G3/2); mm. sun (2843A)...	325	1250
2802	Group G, (under Parliament), seventh bust, type 4.5, tall coarse narrow bust. R. Square-topped shield over cross moline (Sharp H1/1); mm. sun, sceptre (2844)	65	275
2803	— — 4.6, shorter slim better proportioned bust (Sharp H2/2); mm. sceptre (2845)...	70	300
2804	— — — short broad bust (Sharp H3/2); mm. sceptre (2845A)	85	375

2805   2810

| | | F | VF |
|-------| | £ | £ |

2805 **Sixpence**. Group A, first bust, in coronation robes, type 1, small bust,
double-arched crown. R. Square-topped shield over cross fourchee, date
above; 1625, mm. lis (2794) 100 425

2806 — — broader bust, larger crown; 1625, mm. lis, cross calvary*; 1626, mm.
cross calvary* (2794, 2794A) 135 525

2807 Group B, second bust (several varieties), type 1a1, in ruff, armour and mantle.
R. Square-topped shield over cross fourchee, date above; 1625, mm. cross
calvary; 1626, mm. cross calvary*, negro's head; 1627, mm. negro's head,
castle; 1628, mm. castle, anchor; 1629, mm. anchor, heart (2795, 2795A) 125 500

2808 — — 1a2. R. No cross fourchee; 1630, mm. heart, plume (2796) 300 1250

2809 Group C, third bust, type 2a. R. Oval garnished shield with CR above; mm.
plume, rose (2797) 85 325

2810 — — 2b. R. Plume above shield; mm. plume, rose, plume/rose (2798) 125 500

2811   2814   2819

2811 Group D, fourth bust, type 3, with falling lace collar, inner circles, (medium,
large and small bust). R. Oval garnished shield with CR at sides; mm. harp,
portcullis (2799) 60 275

2812 — — — omits C R by shield; mm. portcullis (2799A) 175 750

2813 — — 3a, no inner circles (type 3/3a mules exist); mm. bell, crown, tun (2800) 50 200

2814 Group E, fifth 'Aberystwyth' bust, type 4.1, double-arched crown, small or large
VI. R. Square-topped shield over cross moline; mm. tun, anchor (2801, 2802) 60 225

2815 — — — R. Lyre cross-ends; mm. tun (2801A) 150 675

2816 — — 4.2, single-arched crown; mm. tun, anchor, triangle (2803, 2804) 45 185

2817 Group F, sixth 'Briot's' bust, type 4.3, with stellate lace collar. R. Square-
topped shield over cross moline; mm. triangle, star, triangle-in-circle (2805) 40 165

2818 — — (under Parliament); mm. (P), (R) (2846) 70 275

2819 Group G, (under Parliament), late 'Aberystwyth' bust with riveted shoulder,
type 4.4. R. Square-topped shield over cross moline; mm. (P), (R), eye,
sun, sceptre (2847) 60 250

*Light weight sixpences (40.85 grains) exist of No. 2806, 1625, mm. cross calvary, 1626, mm. cross
calvary; and No. 2807, 1626, mm. cross calvary*

		F £	*VF* £

2820 — — 4.5, squat bust of crude style; mm. eye, sun (over eye) (2848)..... 110 450

2821 — — 4.5 var., small 3a type bust, double-arched crown, inner circle both sides; mm. sun (over eye) (2848A).. 225 850

2822   2824   2832

2822 **Halfgroat**. Group A, without bust, crowned rose each side, type 1, inner circles on one or both sides;mm. lis, lis/-, cross calvary, castle, none (2806) 25 100

2823 — — 1a, without inner circles; mm. negro's head, castle, anchor, heart, plume (2807).. 25 100

2824 Group B, second bust, type 2a, in ruff and mantle. R. Oval shield; mm. plume, rose (2808).. 25 110

2825 — — 2b. R. plume above shield; mm. plume, plume/-, rose (2809) 35 150

2826 Group C, third bust, more armour, crown breaks inner circle; mm. plume, rose (2809A)... 25 110

2827 — — R. Plume above shield; mm. plume (2809B)................................... 35 150

2828 Group D, fourth bust, type 3.1, no inner circles. R. Oval shield dividing C R; mm. harp, portcullis crown (2810).. 20 80

2829 — — — — 3.2-4, inner circle on one or both sides; mm. harp, portcullis, ../harp (2811-13) 20 80

2830 — — — — 3.5-6. R. Oval shield, no C R, no inner circle or obv. only; mm. harp, portcullis (2814-15) 25 90

2831 — — 3a1. R. Rounder shield, no inner circles; mm. bell, crown, tun, anchor, triangle (2816) 20 80

2832 — — 3a2-3, inner circles on obverse or both sides; mm. anchor, triangle, star, triangle-in-circle (2817-18) 25 85

2833 — — — (under Parliament), type 3a3, inner circles both sides; mm. (P)/triangle-in-circle, (P), (R), eye, sun, sceptre (2849)... 20 80

2834 Group E, fifth 'Aberystwyth' bust, types 3a4-5, no inner circles or on reverse only; mm. anchor (2819-20).. 35 135

2835 — — 3a6, very small bust (from penny puncheon), no inner circles; mm. anchor (2821).. 40 150

2836 Group G, (under Parliament), seventh bust, type 3a7, older bust with pointed beard; mm. eye, sun, sceptre (2850).. 20 80

2838

2837 **Penny**. Group A, without bust, rose each side, type 1, inner circles; mm. lis, negro's head, one or two pellets (2822)... 20 80

2838 — — 1a, no inner circles; mm. lis, anchor, one or two pellets (2823).... 20 80

2839 — — 1b, inner circle on reverse; mm. negro's head/two pellets (2824). 35 135

2840 Group B, second bust, type 2, in ruff and mantle. R. Oval shield, inner circles; mm. plume, plume/rose, rose (2825) 30 120

2841 — — 2.1, no inner circles; mm. plume, rose (2826)............................... 30 110

2842 Group C, third bust, type 2a1, more armour visible, no inner circles; mm. plume, plume/rose, rose (2827).. 25 95

	F £	VF £
2843 — — 2a2-4, inner circles on obverse, both sides or reverse; mm. plume, rose (2828-30)	25	95
2844 Group D, fourth bust, type 3.1, with falling lace collar. R. CR by shield, no inner circles; mm. harp, one or two pellets (2831)	20	75

2845

	F £	VF £
2845 — — — 3.2, no C R by shield, no inner circles; mm. harp, portcullis, pellets, none (2832)	20	75
2846 — — — — 3.3-4, inner circles on obverse or reverse; mm. harp, two pellets (2833-34)	20	80
2847 — — 3a1, shield almost round with scroll garniture, no inner circles; mm. bell, triangle, one to four pellets, none (2835)	20	70
2848 — — 3a1 var., inner circle on one or both sides; mm. triangle/two pellets (2835A)	25	90
2849 Group E, fifth 'Aberystwyth' bust, type 3a3, inner circle on obverse or none; mm. triangle, anchor, one or two pellets, none (2836)	20	80
2850 Group G, (under Parliament), seventh bust, type 3a2, older bust, inner circle on obverse only; mm. one or two pellets (2851)	25	85

2851

	F £	VF £
2851 **Halfpenny**. Rose each side, no legend or mm (2837)	15	50

NICHOLAS BRIOT'S COINAGE, 1631-9

FIRST MILLED ISSUE, 1631-2

	F £	VF £
2852 **Crown**. King on horseback. R. Crowned shield between CR crowned; *mm.* flower and B / B	1250	3000

2853   2855

	F £	VF £
2853 **Halfcrown**. Similar	625	1750
2854 **Shilling**. Briot's early bust with falling lace collar. R. Square-topped shield over long cross fourchee; R. Legend starts at top or bottom (extr. rare) *mm.* flower and B/B, B	475	1350
2855 **Sixpence**. Similar, but VI behind bust; *mm.* flower and B/B, flower and B/-	175	475

2856 2856A

	F £	VF £
2856 **Halfgroat**. Briot's bust, B below, II behind. R. IVSTITIA, etc., square-topped shield over long cross fourchee	75	225
2856A Pattern halfgroat. Uncrowned bust in ruff r. R. crowned, interlocked Cs. (North 2687). (Included because of its relatively regular appearance.) ...	70	175
2857 **Penny**. Similar, but I behind bust, B below bust; position of legend may vary	80	225

SECOND MILLED ISSUE, 1638-9

2859

2858 **Halfcrown**. As 2853, but *mm.* anchor and B..	475	1350
2859 **Shilling**. Briot's late bust, the falling lace collar is plain with broad lace border, no scarf. R. As 2854 but cross only to inner circle; *mm.* anchor and B, anchor or muled	200	600
2860 **Sixpence**. Similar, but VI; *mm.* anchor, anchor and mullet/anchor..........	85	275

The last two often exhibit flan reduction marks.

HAMMERED ISSUE, 1638-9

2861 **Halfcrown**. King on Briot's style horse with ground line. R. Square-topped shield; *mm.* anchor, triangle over anchor. Also muled with Tower *rev.*.....	400	1250
2862 **Shilling**. Briot's first hammered issue, Sim. to 2859; R. Square-topped shield over short cross fleury, contraction stops on *obv.*, pellet stops *rev. mm.* anchor	750	3250
2862A — Briot's second hammered issue. As 2862 but lozenge stops both sides. *mm.* anchor, triangle over anchor or triangle	275	900
2862B Tower, Group E, obv. type 4.1 var. (S.2797) above R. as Briot's 1st or 2nd hammered issue; mm. Δ over anchor...	525	1750
2862C Tower, Group F, obv. type 4.4 (S.2799 above) R. as Briot's 2nd hammered issue; mm Δ/Δ over anchor.	300	1000

YORK, 1643-4. *Mm. Lion*

2867

		F	VF
		£	£
2863	**Halfcrown**. 1. Ground-line below horse. R. Square-topped shield between CR	525	2000
2864	— 2. — R. Oval shield as Tower 3a, groundline grass or dotted	475	1850
2865	— 3. No ground-line. R. Similar	475	1850
2866	— 4. As last, but EBOR below horse with head held low. Base metal, often very base (*These pieces are contemporary forgeries*)	100	350
2867	— 5. Tall horse, mane in front of chest, EBOR below. R. Crowned square-topped shield between CR, floral spray in legend	350	1250

2868

	F £	VF £
2868 — 6. As last, but shield is oval, garnished (*rev.* detail variations)............	325	1100
2869 — 7. Similar, but horse's tail shows between legs. R. Shield as last, but with lion's skin garniture, no CR or floral spray	300	950

2870   2872

2870 **Shilling**. 1. Bust in scalloped lace collar similar to 3¹. R. EBOR above square-topped shield over cross fleury..	200	700
2871 — 2. Similar, but bust in plain armour, mantle; coarse work...................	225	750
2872 — 3. Similar R. EBOR below oval shield..	225	750
2873 — 4. — Similar, but crowned oval shield (*obv.* finer style)....................	185	625
2874 — 5. — As last, but lion's skin garniture	185	625
2875 **Sixpence**. *Obv.* Sim. to 2870. Crowned oval shield	275	900

2876   2877

2876 — — Crowned CR at sides	250	800
2877 **Threepence**. As type 1 shilling, but III behind bust. R. As 2870............	75	225

ABERYSTWYTH, 1638/9-42. *Mm.* book.
Plume 1=with coronet and band. Plume 2=with coronet only

2878

	F £	*VF* £
2878 **Halfcrown**. Horseman similar to 2773, but plume 2 behind. ℞. Oval garnished shield with large plume above. *Obv.* plume 2, *rev.* plume 1.....	1000	4750
2879 — Similar to 2774, plume 1 behind King, ground below horse. *Obv.* squat plume 1, *rev.* plume 1	1100	5250
2880 As 2773 but more spirited horse, no ground. FRAN ET HIB, plume 2/1	950	4500

2881

2881 **Shilling**. Bust with large square lace collar, plume 2 before, small XII. ℞. As Tower 3b..	500	1750
2882 — inner circle on *rev.*	425	1500
2883 As 2881, but large plume 1 or 2, large XII, inner circles, large or small shield	425	1500

2884   2886

2884 As last, but small narrow head, square lace collar, large or square plume	450	1600
2885 Small Briot style face, small crown, plume 2, large shield	525	1850
2885A **Sixpence**. *Obv.* as Tower bust 3a, plume before. ℞. as 2889; inner circles both sides, *mm.* book (*obv.* only)..	450	1350
2886 Somewhat as 2881, but double-arched crown, small VI; no inner circles	275	850
2887 Similar to 2886, but single arched crown, plume 2, inner circle *obv.* Large VI	300	900
2888 Similar, but with inner circles both sides...	325	950
2889 — — *Rev.* with small squat-shaped plume above, sometimes no *rev. mm.*	300	900

		F	*VF*
		£	£
2890	Bust as the first Oxford sixpence; with crown cutting inner circle	350	1100

2891

2891	**Groat**. Large bust, lace collar, no armour on shoulder. Crown breaks or touches inner circle. R. Shield, plume 1 or 2..	70	185
2892	— Similar, armour on shoulder, shorter collar. R. Similar......................	75	225
2893	— Smaller, neater bust well within circle. R. Similar.............................	70	200

2894

2894	**Threepence**. Small bust, plume 2 before. R. Shield, plume 1 or 2 above, *obv*. legend variations..	55	160
2895	— Similar, but crown cuts i.c. squat pl. on *obv*., R. Pl. 2, *obv*. legend variations..	60	175
2900	**Halfgroat**. Bust as Tower type 3. R. Large plume. No inner circles, *mm*. pellet/book,book	75	225
2900A	Bust as 2886. R. As last, no inner circle....................................	60	185

2901   2903

2901	Bust with round lace collar; single arch crown, inner circles, colon stops	60	175
2902	After Briot's bust, square lace collar: inner circles.................................	55	160
2903	**Penny**. As 2901; CARO; no inner circles	75	275
2904	As 2901; CARO; inner circles..	70	250
2905	As last but reads CAROLVS; inner circles...	80	300
2906	*Obv*. similar to 2890, tall narrow bust, crown touches inner circle	85	325

2907

2907	**Halfpenny**. No legend. *O*. Rose. R. Plume...	275	950

ABERYSTWYTH-FURNACE, 1648/9. *Mm.* crown

		F	VF
		£	£
2908	**Halfcrown**. King on horseback. R. Sim. to 2878..................................	1750	7500
2909	**Shilling**. Aberystwyth type, but *mm.* crown...................................	3250	13500
2910	**Sixpence**. Similar	1350	4500

2911   2913

2911	**Groat**. Similar	225	800
2912	**Threepence**. Similar..	250	850
2913	**Halfgroat**. Similar. R. Large plume	275	950
2914	**Penny**. Similar..	750	2500

UNCERTAIN MINTS

2915

2915	**Halfcrown**. As illustration, (Hereford?) dated 1645 or undated	3250	12500
2915A	**Halfcrown**. (Compton House) Scarf with long sash ends. CH (Chirk castle?) below horse. R. Oval shield 1644...	3750	15000
2915B	− − R. Crowned oval shield, lion paws	3500	13500

SHREWSBURY, 1642. Plume without band used as *mm.* or in field.

2917	**Pound**. King on horseback, plume behind, from the puncheon of Tower grp. 3 crowns. R. Declaration between two straight lines, XX and three Shrewsbury plumes above, 1642 below; *mm.* pellets, pellets/-	4500	12500
2918	Similar, but Shrewsbury horse walking over pile of arms; no *mm.*, pellets	3500	9500
2919	As last, but cannon amongst arms and only single plume and XX above Declaration, no *mm.*..	5750	18500
2920	**Half-pound**. As 2917, but X; *mm.* pellets.....................................	2250	6000
2921	Similar, but only two plumes on *rev.*; *mm.*, pellets..................................	3750	10500
2922	Shrewsbury horseman with ground-line, three plumes on *rev.*; *mm.*, none, pellets/-	1750	5250
2923	− with cannon and arms or arms below horse; *mm.* pellets/-..................	1850	5750

			F	*VF*
			£	£
2924	— no cannon in arms, no plume in *obv.* field; *mm.* plume/pellets, plume/-		1350	3500
2925	**Crown**. Aberystwyth horseman from the puncheon of a Tower halfcrown no ground line		17500	65000

2926

2926	Shrewsbury horseman with ground-line; *mm.* -/pellets, pellets/-, none ...	1350	3500
2927	**Halfcrown**. *O*. From Aberystwyth die; (S2880); *mm.* book. R. Single plume above Declaration, 1642	3750	12500
2928	Sim. to Aberystwyth die, fat plume behind. R. Three plumes above Declaration; *mm.* pellets, pellets/-	950	3500
2929	Shrewsbury horseman, no ground line. R. As 2927, single plume, no *mm.*	1250	4500
2929A	— — R. As 2933	1050	4000

2930

2930	— R. 2: plume; 6, above Declaration	2250	9000
2931	— with ground-line. R. Similar	2250	9000
2932	— — R. As 2927, single plume...	1250	4500
2933	— — R. Three plumes above Declaration; *mm.* none or pellets	950	3500
2933A	— — R. Aberystwyth die, plume over shield; *mm.* -/book......................	3750	12500
2934	As 2933 but no plume behind king; *mm.* plume/pellets	850	3250

2935

		F	*VF*
		£	£
2935	**Shilling**. *O*. From Aberystwyth die; S2885 *mm*. book. R. Declaration type	1850	6500
2936	*O*. From Shrewsbury die. R. Similar	3250	12500

OXFORD, 1642-6. *Mm.* usually plume with band, except on the smaller denominations when it is lis or pellets. There were so many dies used at this mint that we can give only a selection of the more easily identifiable varieties.

For many years Oxford Halfcrowns and Shillings have been catalogued according to Morrieson obverse die varieties. In many cases, these are very small and difficult to identify. We have, therefore, simplified the obverse classification and used the available space to expand the listing of the more interesting reverse varieties.

2943

2937	**Pound**. Large horseman over arms, no exergual line, fine workmanship. R. Three Shrewsbury plumes and XX above Declaration, 1642 below; *mm*. plume/pellets..	8500	25000
2938	— Similar, but three Oxford plumes, 1643; *mm*. as last............................	7500	22500
2939	Shrewsbury horseman trampling on arms, exergual line. R. As last, 1642	3000	9000
2940	— — cannon amongst arms, 1642-3; *mm*. similar	2750	8500
2941	— as last but exergue is chequered, 1642; *mm*. similar............................	5250	15000
2942	Briot's horseman, 1643; *mm*. similar...	7500	22500
2943	*O*. As 2937. R. Declaration in cartouche, single large plume above, 1644 OX below..	17500	55000

		F	*VF*
		£	£
2944	**Half-pound**. Shrewsbury horseman over arms, Oxford plume behind. R. Shrewsbury die, 1642; mm. plume/-	1350	3500
2945	— R. Three Oxford plumes above, 1642; mm. plume/-	1250	3250
2945A	— — 1643; *mm*. plume/-	1250	3250
2946	**Crown**. Shrewsbury die with groundline. R. Three Oxford plumes, 1642; no mm.	1250	3750
2946A	— — 1643; no *mm*.	1250	3750
2947	Oxford horseman, grass below. R. Three Oxford plumes, 1643; *mm*. plume/-	1500	4500

2948

2948	Rawlins' crown. King riding over a view of the city. R. Floral scrolls above and below Declaration, date in script, 1644 OXON; *mm*. floriated cross/- *(Electrotypes and copies of this coin are common)*	32500	110000
2949	**Halfcrown**. *O*. Shrewsbury die with groundline, plume behind. R. Oxford die, declaration in two lines, three Oxford plumes above, 1642 below; no *mm*.	950	3500
2950	— no plume behind. R. as last, 1642; *mm*. plume/-	525	2000
2951	Shrewsbury horseman with groundline, Oxford plume behind. R. Shrewsbury die, 1642; *mm*. plume/-	525	2000
2952	— R. Three Oxford plumes, 1642; *mm*. plume/-	300	950
2953	— — without groundline, 1642; *mm*. plume/-	275	900

2954   2955

2954	Oxford horseman without groundline, 1643; *mm*. plume/-	250	850
2954A	— — R. Shrewsbury die, 1642; *mm*. plume/- or no *mm*.	575	2250
2955	— with groundline. R. Three Oxford plumes, 1643; *mm*. plume/-	250	850
2956	Briot horseman, grassy, rocky or uneven ground. R. Three Oxford plumes, 1643; *mm*. plume/-, plume & rosette/-	225	750
2957	— — 1643 OX; *mm*. plume/rosette, rosette	225	750

2961   2965A

		F	VF
		£	£
2958	— — 1644 OX; *mm.* plume/-	240	800
2958A	— — lozenges by OX, 1644 OX; *mm.* plume/-	250	825
2959	— — 1645 OX; *mm.* plume/-, plume/rosette	240	800
2959A	— — pellets by date, 1645 OX; *mm.* plume/-	275	850
2960	— — 1646 OX; *mm.* plume/-	240	800
2961	— — pellets or annulets by plumes and date, 1646 OX; *mm.* plume/- ...	300	950
2962	— R. Large central plume and two Oxford plumes, 1643; *mm.* plume/-	240	800
2963	— — 1643 OX; *mm.* plume/-, rosette/-, plume & rosette/rosette, plume & rosette/-	225	750
2964	— — rosettes by OX, 1643 OX; *mm.* rosette/-, plume & rosette/-	300	900
2965	— — plain, pellets or lozenges by plumes and/or OX, 1644 OX; *mm.* plume/- plume/rosette, rosette	210	700
2965A	— — date in script, 1644 OX; *mm.* plume/-	225	750
2966	— — rosettes by plumes and date, 1644 OX; *mm.* plume & rosette/rosette	350	1100
2967	— — small plumes by date, 1644 OX; *mm.* plume & rosette/-, rosette ..	425	1350
2968	— R. Large central plume and two small Shrewsbury plumes, lozenges in field, date in script, 1644 OX; *mm.* plume/rosette	375	1250
2969	— — small plumes by date, pellets by OX, 1644 OX; *mm.* plume/-	450	1500

2971

2970	**Shilling.** *O.* Shrewsbury die. R. Declaration in three lines, three Oxford plumes above, 1642; *mm.* plume/-	1350	5250
2971	Oxford bust (small). R. Three Oxford plumes, 1642; *mm.* Oxford plume/-,	250	800
2972	Oxford bust (small or large). R. Three Oxford plumes, 1643; *mm.* Oxford plume/-, Oxford plume/rosette	250	800
2972A	— — pellets by date, 1644; *mm.* plume/-	300	950
2972B	— — 1644 OX; mm. plume/rosette	300	950
2973	— R. Oxford and two Shrewsbury plumes, lozenges by date, 1644 OX; *mm.* plume/-	350	1100
2974	— R. Three Shrewsbury plumes, 1643; *mm.* plume/-	275	925

	F	VF
	£	£

2975 Fine Oxford bust. R. Three Oxford plumes, lozenges in field, 1644
OX; *mm.* Shrewsbury plume/- 275 900

2975A — — large date in script, 1644 OX; *mm.* plume/- 325 1050

2976 — 1645 OX; *mm.* plume/- 2250 7500

2976A — R. Oxford and two Shrewsbury plumes, 1644 OX; *mm.* plume/- 350 1100

2977 — R. Three Shrewsbury plumes, 1644 OX; *mm.* plume/- 300 950

2978 — — annulets or pellets at date, 1646; *mm.* plume/floriated cross,
plume/- 300 950

2979

2979 Rawlins' die. Fine bust with R. on truncation. R. Three Oxford plumes,
rosettes or lozenges by plumes, lozenges by date, 1644 OX; *mm.*
Shrewsbury plume/rosette, Shrewsbury plume/- 950 3750

2979A — — pellets by date, no OX, 1644; *mm.* plume/- 1000 4000

2979B — R. Oxford and two Shrewsbury plumes, 1644 OX; *mm.* plume/- 1100 4250

2980A

2980 **Sixpence.** O. Aberystwyth die R. Three Oxford plumes, 1642; *mm.* book/- 325 900

2980A — — 1643; *mm.* book/- 275 850

2981 — R. Three Shrewsbury plumes, 1643; *mm.* book/- 250 800

2982 — R. Shrewsbury plume and two lis, 1644 OX (groat rev. die); *mm.* book/- 575 2000

2983 **Groat.** O. Aberystwyth die. R. Shrewsbury plume and two lis, 1644 OX;
mm. book/- 250 800

2984 — R. Three Shrewsbury plumes, 1644 OX; mm. book/- 275 850

2985

2985 Oxford bust within inner circle. R. As 2983, 1644 OX; *mm.* floriated cross/- 175 575

2988   2990

	F	VF
	£	£
2985A — ℞. Three Shrewsbury plumes, 1644 OX; *mm.* floriated cross/-	275	900
2985B — ℞. Single plume, 2 scrolls and OX monogram over Decl, 1645; *mm.* floriated cross/-	350	1050
2986 Large bust to top of coin. ℞. As 2983, 1644 OX; *mm.* lis/-	250	800
2987 Large bust to bottom of coin. ℞. As 2983, 1644 OX; no *mm.*	250	800
2988 — ℞. Single plume, 2 scrolls and OX monogram over Decl, 1645; *mm.*	185	675
2989 Rawlins' die, no inner circle, R on shoulder. ℞. As 2983, 1644 OX; no *mm.*	425	1250
2990 — ℞. Single plume, Declaration in cartouche, 1645; no *mm.*	275	850
2991 — — 1646/5; no mm.	250	800
2992 **Threepence.** *O.* Aberystwyth die. ℞. Three lis over Declaration, 1644 OX; *mm.* book/-	225	650
2993 Rawlins; die, R below shoulder. ℞. Aberystwyth die, oval shield; *mm.* lis/book	250	725
2994 — ℞. Three lis over Declaration, 1644; *mm.* lis/-	110	350

2994   3000

2995 Crown breaks inner circle, no R. ℞. Three lis, 1646/4; *mm.* lis/-	125	375
2996 **Halfgroat.** Small bust, beaded or wireline inner circle. ℞. Large plume in field; *mm.* mullet/lis, lis, -/lis, plain cross/-, plain cross/lis	120	350
2997 — ℞. Three lis over Delcaration, 1644 OX; *mm.* lis	125	375
2998 **Penny.** *O.* Aberystwyth die, CARO. ℞. Small plume in field; *mm.* book/-	135	525
2999 Aberystwyth die, CAROLVS; ℞. Large plume; *mm.* book/-	150	575
3000 Rawlins' die, CARO. ℞. Small plume; *mm.* lis/mullet, lis/-	200	750
3001 Broad bust, CAROL. ℞. Small plume; *mm.* lis	175	650
3002 — ℞. Three lis over Declaration, 1644; *mm.* lis	750	2750

BRISTOL, 1643-5. *Mm.* usually plume or Br., except on small denominations

3003 **Halfcrown.** *O.* Oxford die with or without ground-line. ℞. Declaration, three Bristol plumes above, 1643 below, *mm.* plume/- or plume/cross....	475	1650
3004 — Obv. as above. ℞ as above, but *mm.* Br. 1643	575	1850
3005 King wears unusual flat crown, *obv. mm.* acorn? between four pellets. ℞. As 3003, 1643	575	1650
3006 — Obv. as above. ℞ as 3004, *mm.* Br., 1643-4	425	1400
3007 Shrewsbury plume behind king. ℞. As last	350	1100
3008 — Obv. as above. ℞ as 3004 but Br below date instead of as *mm* . 1644	375	1200

3009

	F	VF
	£	£
3009 — Obv. as 3007 but Br below horse. R̅ as above but 1644-5...................	350	1100
3010 — Obv. as above. R̅ as 3004, *mm*. Br. and Br. below date, 1644-5.........	400	1250
3011 **Shilling**. *O*. Oxford die. R̅. Declaration, 1643, 3 crude plumes above, no *mm*.	550	1750

3012   3014

3012 — — R̅ Similar, but *mm*. Br., 1643-4, less crude plumes........................	400	1350
3013 —Obv. Coarse bust. R̅. As 3011, no *mm*., 1643	950	3500
3014 — — Coarse bust, R̅. as 3012, *mm*. Br, but 1644....................................	525	1650

3016A   3017

3015 Obv. Bust of good style, plumelet before face. R̅. As 3012 *mm*. Br. but 1644-5	375	1250
3016 — — R̅.as 3012, 1644, but Br below date instead of *mm*.	425	1350
3016A — — R̅ as 3012, 1644 but plume and plumelet either side.....................	350	1250
3017 —Obv. Taller bust with high crown, no plumelets before, *mm*. Br. on its side. R̅ As 3016 Br.below 1644-5...	500	1650
3018 —Obv. As 3017 but no *mm*. R̅ as above but *mm*. Br., no Br. below 1644-5	525	1750
3018A — — R̅ as above but plume and plumelets, 1645	675	2250
3019 **Sixpence**. Small bust, nothing before. R̅. Declaration surrounded by CHRISTO etc., 1643; *mm*. ./Br...	525	1750

3020   3022

		F	VF
		£	£
3020	Fine style bust. Plumelet before face, 1644; *mm.* ./Br. (on its side)	325	975
3021	**Groat**. Bust l. R. Declaration, 1644	250	725
3022	— Plumelet before face, 1644	225	625
3023	— Br. below date, 1644	210	575
3023A	— Similar, but larger bust and more spread plume before. Mm. pellet/Br;		
	nothing below 1644	240	650

3024   3026   3027

3024	**Threepence**. *O.* As 2992. Aberystwyth die; *mm.* book. R. Declaration, 1644	250	750
3025	Bristol die, plume before face, no *mm.*, 1644...	325	1000
3026	**Halfgroat**. Br. in place of date below Declaration..................................	250	850
3027	**Penny**. Similar bust, I behind. R. Large plume with bands......................	400	1350

This penny may belong to the late declaration issue. It has the same reverse plume punch as 3044.

LATE 'DECLARATION' ISSUES, 1645-6

After Bristol surrendered on 11 September 1645, many of the Royalist garrison returned unsearched to Oxford and the Bristol moneyers appear to have continued work, using altered Bristol dies and others of similar type bearing the marks A, B and plume. Ashby de la Zouch was reinforced from Oxford in September 1645 and, following its fall on 28 February 1646, Royalist forces marched to Bridgnorth-on-Severn, holding out until 26 April 1646. Mr Boon suggested (cf. SCBI 33, p. xli) that Ashby and Bridgnorth are plausible mint sites and the most likely candidates for the A and B marked issues, if these do indeed represent fixed mint locations.

ASHBY DE LA ZOUCH, 1645

3028	**Halfcrown**. Horseman of Bristol type, A below. R. Altered Bristol die. A		
	(over Br) below date, 1645; *mm.* plume/A (over Br)	3250	10500
3029	- - R. A below date (new die), 1645; *mm.* plume/A	3250	10500
3030	- - R. Nothing below date 1645; *mm.* plume/A...	2750	9000
3031	**Shilling**. Crowned bust left. R. Declaration type, A below date, 1645; mm.		
	plume/A	1350	4750

3032

	F	VF
	£	£
3032 - plumelet before face, 1645; *mm.* plume/A	1500	5000
3033 **Sixpence.** Bust of Bristol style, plumelet before face. R. Declaration type, 1645; *mm.* A (on its side)/-	1350	4750
3034 **Groat.** Similar, plumelet before face, 1645; *mm.* A (on its side)/-	1100	3250
3035 **Threepence.** Similar, plumelet before face. R. Single plumelet above Declaration, 1645; no *mm.*	750	2250

BRIDGNORTH-ON-SEVERN, 1646

3036 **Halfcrown.** Horseman of Bristol type, A below (same die as 3028-30). R. Scroll above Declaration, B below, 1646; *mm.* plume/A	3750	12500
3036A - - R. Nothing below date, 1646; *mm.* plume/-	2750	9000

3037

3037 - plumelet (over A) below horse (same die as 3028-30 recut). R. Nothing below date, 1646; *mm.* plume, plume/-	1500	4750
3038 - - plumelet below date, 1646; *mm.* plume	1500	4750
3039 **Shilling.** Crowned bust left, plumelet before face (same die as 3032). R. Scroll above Declaration, 1646; *mm.* plume/plumelet	575	2000
3039A - Bristol obverse die, nothing before face. R. Scroll above Declaration, 1646; 2000 *mm.* Br/-	750	2500
3040 - - plume before face (altered die of 3039A), 1646; *mm.* plumelet (over Br)/-	575	2000

3041   3042

		F	VF
		£	£
3041	**Sixpence.** Crowned bust left, plume before face. R. Scroll above Declaration, 1646; *mm.* B/-	250	900
3042	**Groat**. Similar, plumelet before face, 1646; *mm.* plumelet, plumelet/-	185	575
3043	**Threepence.** Similar, plumelet before face. R. Single plume above Declaration, 1646; *mm.* plumelet/-	225	650
3044	**Halfgroat.** Crowned bust left, II behind. R. Large plume with bands dividing date, 1646; no *mm.*	425	1250

3045   3047

TRURO, 1642-3. *Mm.* rose except where stated

3045	**Crown.** King on horseback, head in profile, sash flies out in two ends. R. CHRISTO, etc., round garnished shield	450	1250
3046	**Halfcrown.** King on walking horse, groundline below, R. Oblong shield, CR above, *mm.* bugle/–	3250	12500
3047	Galloping horse, king holds baton. R. Oblong shield, CR at sides	3250	12500
3048	Walking horse, king holds sword. R. Similar	850	3000
3049	— R. Similar, but CR above	900	3250
3050	Galloping horse, king holds sword. R. Similar, but CR at sides	1100	4250
3051	— R. Similar, but CR above	1200	4500
3052	Trotting horse. R. Similar, but CR at sides	900	3250
3053	**Shilling**. Small bust of good style. R. Oblong shield	4500	13500

EXETER, 1643-6. Undated or dated 1644-5 *Mm.* rose except where stated

3054	**Half-pound.** King on horseback, face towards viewer, sash in large bow. R. CHRISTO, etc., round garnished shield. Struck from crown dies of 3055 on a thick flan	7500	18500
3055	**Crown.** King on horseback, sash in large bow. R. Round garnished shield	450	1350

	F	VF
	£	£

3056 — Shield garnished with twelve even scrolls 575 1850

3057 As 3055, ℞ Date divided by *mm.* 16 rose 44 .... 525 1650

3058 — ℞ Date to l. of *mm.* 1644 .... 450 1350

3059 — *mm*: rose/Ex, 1645 .... 525 1650

3060 King's sash flies out in two ends; *mm.* castle/rose, 1645 .... 600 1850

3061 — *mm.* castle/Ex, 1645 .... 475 1500

3062 — *mm.* castle, 1645 .... 375 1000

3063 **Halfcrown**. King on horseback, sash tied in bow. ℞. Oblong shield
  CR at sides 900 3500

3064 — ℞. Round shield with eight even scrolls 350 1100

3065

3065 — ℞. Round shield with five short and two long scrolls 250 750

3066 — ℞. Oval shield with angular garnish of triple lines 750 2750

3067

3067 Briot's horseman with lumpy ground. ℞. As 3064 .... 400 1350

3068 — ℞. As 3065 .... 375 1250

3069 — ℞. As 3066 .... 675 2500

3070 — ℞. As 3065, date to l. of *mm.* 1644 .... 575 2250

3071

3071 King on spirited horse galloping over arms. ℞. Oval garnished
  shield, 1642 in cartouche below 5750 17500

		F	*VF*
		£	£
3072	— R. As 3070, date to 1. of *mm.* 1644-5	6250	18500
3073	— R. *mm.* castle, 1645	6750	20000
3074	Short portly king, leaning backwards on ill-proportioned horse, 1644, 16 rose 44	1350	5250
3075	Horse with twisted tail, sash flies out in two ends R. As 3064	600	1850

3076

3076	— R. As 3070, date divided by *mm.* 16 rose 44, or date to 1. of *mm.* 1644-5	525	1650
3077	— R. *mm.* castle, 1645	575	1800
3078	— R. *mm.* Ex, 1645	550	1750
3079	— R. Declaration type; *mm.* Ex. 1644-5	3500	10500
3080	— R. Similar, Ex also below declaration, 1644	3250	10000
3081	**Shilling.** Large Oxford style bust. R. Round shield with eight even scrolls	1250	4500
3082	— R. Oval shield with CR at sides	1500	5750
3083	Normal bust with lank hair. R. As 3081	750	2250
3083A	— R. As 3082	1500	4750
3084	— R. Round shield with six scrolls	575	1650

3085

3085	— R. Similar, date 1644, 45 to left of rose *mm.* 16 rose 44 (rare), 1644 to right of rose (very rare)...	350	1000
3086	— R. Declaration type, 1645	2250	6750

3087A

3087	**Sixpence.** Similar to 3085, large bust and letters 1644 rose...................	300	900
3087A	— Smaller bust and letters from punches used on 3088, small or large VI, 16 rose 44	300	900

		F	VF
		£	£
3088	**Groat**. Somewhat similar but 1644 at beginning of *obv.* legend..............	135	425

	3089 3092		
3089	**Threepence**. Similar. R. Square shield, 1644 above...............................	125	375
3090	**Halfgroat**. Similar, but II. R. Oval shield, 1644	225	700
3091	— R. Large rose, 1644..	250	750
3092	**Penny**. As last but I behind head...	275	800

WORCESTER, 1644-45

		F	VF
3093	**Halfcrown**. King on horseback l., W below; *mm.* two lions. R. Declaration type 1644 altered from 1643 Bristol die; *mm.* pellets..............................	1350	5750
3094	— R. Square-topped shield; *mm.* helmet, castle.....................................	1000	4250
3095	— R. Oval shield; *mm.* helmet...	1050	4500

3096

		F	VF
3096	Similar but grass indicated; *mm.* castle. R. Square-topped shield; *mm.* helmet or pellets...	825	3500
3097	— R. Oval draped shield, lis or lions in legend..	850	3750
3098	— R. Oval shield CR at sides, roses in legend	900	4000
3099	— R. FLORENT etc., oval garnished shield with lion's paws each side.	1000	4500
3100	Tall king, no W or *mm.* R. Oval shield, lis, roses, lions or stars in legend	825	3500
3101	— R. Square-topped shield; *mm.* helmet.................................	850	3750
3102	— R. FLORENT, etc., oval shield; no *mm.*...................................	1000	4500
3103	Briot type horse, sword slopes forward, ground-line. R. Oval shield, roses in legend; *mm.* 91v, 105, none (combinations)....................................	850	3750
3104	— Similar, but CR at sides, 91v/-...	900	4000
3105	Dumpy, portly king, crude horse. R. As 3100; *mm.* 91v, 105, none	850	3750

3106

		F £	VF £
3106	Thin king and horse. R. Oval shield, stars in legend; *mm.* 91v, none......	825	3500

WORCESTER OR SALOPIA (SHREWSBURY), 1643-4

3107	**Shilling**. Bust of king l., adequately rendered. R. Square-topped shield; *mm.* castle	2000	7500
3108	— R. CR above shield; *mm.* helmet and lion	2000	7500
3109	— R. Oval shield; *mm.* lion, pear	1500	6500
3110	— Bust a somewhat crude copy of last (two varieties); *mm.* bird, lis. R. Square-topped shield with lion's paws above and at sides; *mm.* boar's head, helmet..	1750	7000

3108

3111	— — CR above	1650	7000
3112	— R. Oval shield, lis in legend; *mm.* lis...	1350	5250
3113	— R. Round shield; *mm.* lis, 3 lis..	1350	5250
3114	Bust r.; *mm.* pear/-, pear/lis. R. draped oval shield with or without CR. (Halfcrown reverse dies)..	3250	13500
3115	**Sixpence**. As 3110; *mm.* castle, castle/boar's hd	1100	4250

3116   3117

3116	**Groat**. As 3112; *mm.* lis/helmet, rose/helmet..	575	1650
3117	**Threepence**. Similar; *mm.* lis...	275	850
3118	**Halfgroat**. Similar; *mm.* lis (*O.*) various (*R.*)...	300	900

	F £	VF £

SALOPIA (SHREWSBURY), 1644

3119 **Halfcrown**. King on horseback l. SA below; *mm*. lis. R. (*mm*. lis, helmet, lion rampant, none). Cr. oval shield; CHRISTO etc. *mm*. helmet 4500 15000
3120 — R. FLORENT, etc., crowned oval shield, no *mm*. 4500 15000
3121 — SA erased or replaced by large pellet or cannon ball; *mm*. lis in legend, helmet. R. As 3119.. 2250 7500
3122 Tall horse with mane blown forward, nothing below; *mm*. lis. R. Large round shield with crude garniture; *mm*. helmet.............................. 1000 4500
3123 — R. Uncrowned square-topped shield with lion's paw above and at sides; *mm*. helmet.. 1250 5000
3124 — R. Small crowned oval shield; *mm*. various 900 4000

3125

3125 — R. As 3120 .... 950 4250
3126 Finer work with little or no mane before horse. R. Cr. round or oval shield 1000 4500
3127 Grass beneath horse. R. Similar; *mm*. lis or rose 1250 5250
3128 Ground below horse. R. As 3120... 2250 7500

HARTLEBURY CASTLE (WORCS.), 1646

3129

3129 **Halfcrown**. *O. Mm*. pear. R. HC (Hartlebury Castle) in garniture below shield; *mm*. three pears 1250 4750

CHESTER, 1644

3130

		F	*VF*
		£	£
3130	**Halfcrown**. As illus. ℞. Oval shield; *mm.* three gerbs and sword............	950	3750
3131	— Similar, but without plume or CHST; ℞. Cr. oval shield with lion skin; *mm.* prostrate gerb; -/cinquefoil, ⁻/⁝	850	3500
3132	— ℞. Crowned square-topped shield with CR at sides both crowned *rev.*; *mm.* cinquefoil (these dies were later crudely recut)	1350	5250
3133	As 3130, but without plume or CHST. ℞. Declaration type, 1644 *rev.*; *mm.* plume	1250	4750
3133A	**Shilling**. Bust l. ℞. Oval garnished shield; *mm.* ∴ (obv. only)	4250	13500
3133B	— ℞. Square-topped shield; *mm.* as last..	3750	11000
3133C	— ℞ . Shield over long cross..	3250	9500
3134	**Threepence**. ℞. Square-topped shield; *mm.*-/ prostrate gerb	900	3000

WELSH MARCHES? 1644

3135

| 3135 | **Halfcrown**. Crude horseman, l. ℞. Declaration of Bristol style divided by a dotted line, 3 plumes above, 1644 below .... | 1350 | 4500 |

CARLISLE, 1644-5

3137   3139

		F £	VF £
3136	**Three shillings**. Large crown above C R between rosettes III. S below. rev. OBS . CARL / . 1645, rosette below	12500	30000
3137	Similar but :- OBS :/-: CARL :./.1645, rosette above and below	11000	27500
3138	**Shilling**. Large crown above C R between trefoil of pellets, XII below. *rev.* as 3137	7500	17500
3139	Ŗ. Legend and date in two lines..	8000	18500

Note. *(3136-39) Round or Octagonal pieces exist.*

NEWARK, 1645-6

3140   3142

3140	**Halfcrown**. Large crown between CR ; below, XXX. *rev.* OBS / NEWARK / 1645	975	2750
3140A	— Similar 1646..	900	2500
3141	**Shilling**. Similar but crude flat shaped crown, NEWARKE, 1645	900	2500
3142	Similar but normal arched crown, 1645	750	1750
3143	— NEWARK, 1645 or 1646...	725	1650

3144   3146

	F £	VF £
3144 **Ninepence**. As halfcrown but IX, 1645 or 1646	650	1500
3145 — NEWARKE, 1645..	700	1650
3146 **Sixpence**. As halfcrown but VI, 1646.......................................	800	1850

PONTEFRACT, June 1648-March 1649. Before execution of Charles I

| 3147 **Two shillings** (lozenge shaped). DVM : SPIRO : SPERO around CR crowned. R. Castle surrounded by OBS, PC, sword and 1648, weight: c.9-10g. ... | 7500 | 27500 |

3148

| 3148 **Shilling** (lozenge shaped, octagonal or round). Similar.......................... | 2500 | 6500 |
| 3149 — Similar but XII on r. dividing PC .... | 2400 | 6250 |

After the execution of Charles I (30 Jan. 1649), in the name of Charles II

3150

| 3150 **Shilling** (octagonal). O. As last. R. CAROLVS : SECVꟼDVS : 1648, castle gateway with flag dividing PC, OBS on l., cannon   protrudes on r. | 2500 | 6500 |
| 3151 CAROL : II : etc., around HANC : DE / VS : DEDIT 1648. R. POST : MORTEM : PATRIS : PRO : FILIO around gateway etc. as last .... | 2750 | 7500 |

SCARBOROUGH, July 1644-July 1645*

3152

3156

3166

		VF
Type I. Large Castle with gateway to left, SC and value Vs below		
3152	**Crown.** (various weights)	65000

Type II. Small Castle with gateway, no SC, value punched on flan		
3153	**Five shillings and eightpence.**	60000
3154	**Crown.** Similar..	75000
3155	**Three shillings.** Similar	45000
3156	**Two shillings and tenpence.** Similar	45000
3157	**Two shillings and sevenpence.** Similar	45000
3158	**Halfcrown.** Similar......................................	50000
3159	**Two shillings and fourpence.** Similar	45000
3162	**One shilling and sixpence.** Similar to 3159........	40000
3163	**One shilling and fourpence.** Similar	40000
3164	**One shilling and threepence.** Similar...............	40000
3165	**Shilling.** Similar..	50000
3166	**Sixpence.** Similar......................................	35000
3167	**Groat.** Similar..	30000

*No research has been done on this complicated series for many years but a detailed overview was set out in the 'Slaney' catalogue, Spink auction 229, 14 May 2015.

VF

UNCERTAIN CASTLE
Type III. Castle gateway with two turrets, value punched below

3168	**Two shillings and twopence**	17500
3169	**Two shillings.** Castle punched twice......................................	17500
3170	**One shilling and sixpence.** Similar to 3168...........................	15000
3171	**One shilling and fourpence.** Similar.....................................	15000
3172	**One shilling and threepence.** Similar....................................	15000
3173	**One shilling and twopence.** Similar	14500
3174	**One shilling and one penny.** Similar.....................................	14500
3175	**Shilling.** Similar...	17500
3176	**Elevenpence.** Similar..	13500
3177	**Tenpence.** Similar	13500
3178	**Ninepence.** Similar...	13500
3178A	**Eightpence.** Similar	12500
3179	**Sevenpence.** Similar...	12500
3180	**Sixpence.** Similar	15000

COPPER

For further details see Tim Everson, *The Galata Guide to the Farthing Tokens of James I and Charles I*

Farthings

3182   3183

		F £	VF £
3181	Richmond 1a, colon stops, CARO over IACO, five jewel crowns on obverse, mm on obverse only; *mm*: Coronet, Crescent with mullet.	20	50
3182	— — 1b, colon stops, CARO over IACO, nine jewel crowns on obverse, *mm*: Dagger, Mascle..	20	50
3183	— — 2 CARO, colon stops, *mm* on obverse only, *mm*: Lombardic A, Lombardic A with pellet below, Annulet, Annulet with pellet within, Bell, Book, Castle, Cinquefoil, Crescent (large and small), Cross (pellets in angles), Cross calvary, Cross patée, Cross patée fitchée, Cross patonce, Cross patonce in saltire, Cross saltire, Dagger, Ermine, Estoile (pierced), Eye, Fish hook, Fleece, Fusil, Fusils (two), Halberd, Harp, Heart, Horseshoe, Key (vertical), Leaf, Lion passant, Lis (large), Lis (demi), Lis (three), Martlet, Mascle with pellet within, Nautilus, Pike-head, Rose (single), Shield, Star, Tower, Trefoil, Tun, Woolpack, Woolpack over Crescent.	10	30
3183A	— — CARA farthings (Contemporary forgeries manufactured from official punches. Usually F for E in REX), mm on obverse only; *mm*: Annulet, Coronet, Cross patée fourchée, Dagger, Fusil, Key, Mascle, Trefoil, Tun.............	150	300
3183B	— — Contemporary forgeries of Richmond Type 2, mm: Lombardic A, Annulet, Annulet with saltire within, Barbell and pellets, Cross (pellets in angles), Cross patée, Cross patonce, Cross patonce in saltire, Cross saltire, Dagger, Fusil, Heart, Horseshoe, Key (horizontal), Lis (large), Lis, Lis demi, Lis (three), Lis (two), Mascle, Mascle with pellet within, Rose, Star, Thistlehead, Tower, Triangle, Triangle (inverted), Tun..	5	15

3184   3185

		F £	VF £
3184	— — 3, apostrophe stops, eagle-headed harp, mm on obverse only; *mm*: Lion rampant, Trefoil.........	10	24
3185	— — 4, beaded harp, *mm* Rose (double) on obverse only.	15	35
3186	— — 5, scroll-fronted harp, 5 jewels on circlet, *mm* Rose (double) on obverse only.	15	35
3187	— — 6, scroll-fronted harp, 7 jewels on circlet, *mm* Rose (double) on obverse only.	15	35

3187A

3187A	Type 6 on an uncut square flan.	400	900
	— Longer strips of two to twelve farthings also exist...........................	*Extremely Rare*	

3188   3189   3193

3188	— — 7, oval flans, CARO over IACO, legend starts bottom left, *mm* Cross patée on one or both sides..	50	100
3189	— — 8, CARO, colon stops, mm on obverse only, *mm* Lis (demi)........	50	100
3190	— — 9, mm on reverse only; *mm*: Martlet, Millrind.	50	100

3195   3196

3191	— — 10a, mm on both sides; *mm*: Crescent	50	100
3192	— — 10b, upright mm both sides, *mm* Goutte..	50	100
3193	— — 10c, mm both sides, between sceptre handles on obverse, *mm* 9 ...	35	75
3194	— — 11, apostrophe stops, *mm* Rose (double) on both sides.	60	125
3194A	— — 11/10b mule, *mm* Rose (double)/Goutte	50	150
3195	— — 12, *mm* Rose (double) on obverse only..	45	90
3196	Transitional Issue Farthings, double arched crowns, mm on obverse only; *mm*: Harp, Quatrefoil.	20	50

| | | F | VF |
| | | £ | £ |

3197 Maltravers Type 1, inner circles, mm on obverse only; *mm*: Rose (double),
      Woolpack 50 100
3197A Counterfeits of Maltravers Type 1, *mm*: Bell, Lis, Tun, Woolpack 15 35
3198 — — 2, mm both sides; *mm*: Bell, Lis (large), Lis (small), Martlet, Rose
      (double), Woolpack.. 15 35
3198A Counterfeits of Maltravers Type 2, *mm*: Bell, Cross patée, Harp, Lis (small),
      Mascle, Star, Woolpack 15 35

3199   3200

3199 — — 3, different mm on each side; *mm*: Woolpack/Rose (double), Martlet/
      Bell, Woolpack/Portcullis, Lis/Portcullis, Harp/Bell, Harp/Billet............ 15 35
3199A Counterfeits of Maltravers Type 3, *mm*: Bell/Cross patée fitchée, Bell/
      Woolpack, Cross patée fitchée/Bell, Tun/Bell, Woolpack/Lis.................. 15 35
3200 Maltravers Oval Type 4, no inner circles, legend starts bottom left, mm Lis
      (large) on both sides... 75 150

*Richmond Types 7 to 12 and Maltravers Type 4, 3188 to 3195 and 3200, the oval farthings, were
issued for use in Ireland.*

3201   3202   3203

(There is frequent muling between types in the Rose Farthing sequence)
3201 Rose Type 1, large double-arched crowns, sceptres within inner Circle,
      BRIT, mm on obv. or rev. or both; *mm*: Lis, Martlet.............................. 45 90
3202 — — 2, similar but small crowns and sceptres just cross inner circle, BRIT,
      mm on obverse only or both sides, *mm* Lis 30 75
3203 — — 3, similar but crowns with pointed sides and sceptres almost to outer
      circle, BRIT, *mm* Lis, Cross patée, Mullet, Crescent.............................. 15 35

3204   3206   3207

3204 - - Mules of Type 3 with Types 4a and 4b, *mm* Lis, Mullet, Crescent. 15 35
3205 - - 4a Single arched crowns, Long legends with CAROLVS, MAG, FRAN
      and HIB, *mm*: Lis, Mullet, Crescent. 10 25
3206 — — 4b Single arched crowns, Short legends with CAROLV, MA, FRA
      and HI, *mm*: Mullet, Crescent.. 10 25
3206A Counterfeits of Rose type 4, *mm* Crescent.. 20 45
3207 — — 5, sceptres below crown, *mm* Mullet on both sides 35 75

The Rose farthings were also authorised for use in Ireland but do not seem to have reached there.

The coins struck during the Commonwealth have inscriptions in English instead of Latin as a truer expression of Protestantism. St. George's cross and the Irish harp take the place of the royal arms. The silver halfpenny was issued for the last time. Coins with *mm.* anchor were struck during the protectorship of Richard Cromwell.

Mintmarks

1649-57 Sun   1658-60 Anchor

GOLD

3208

	F	VF			F	VF
	£	£			£	£

3208 Unite. As illustration; *mm.* sun,

	F	VF			F	VF
1649	2750	8500	1654		2400	6000
1650	2500	6500	1655		3750	10500
1651	2250	5750	1656		2750	7500
1652	2500	6500	1657		2750	7500
1653	2250	5750				

3209 Similar, *mm.* anchor,

	F	VF			F	VF
1658	9500	25000	1660		8500	22500

3210

3210 Double-crown. Similar; but X; *mm.* sun,

	F	VF			F	VF
1649	2250	7500	1654		1850	6000
1650	1750	5750	1655		3250	10500
1651	1650	5250	1656		3000	10000
1652	1850	6000	1657		3250	10500
1653	1650	5250				
3211 Similar, *mm.* anchor, 1660					5250	17500

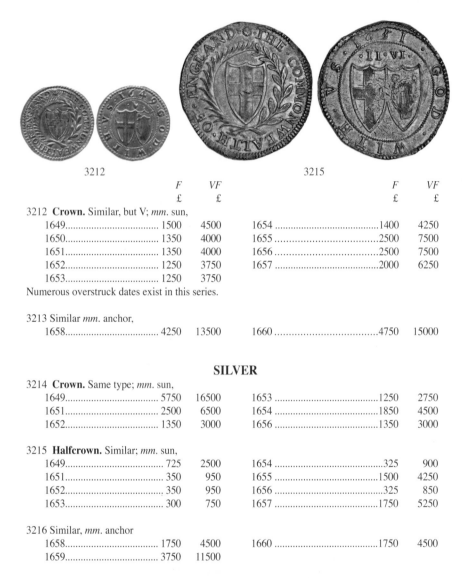

3212   3215

| | F | VF | | F | VF |
| | £ | £ | | £ | £ |

3212 Crown. Similar, but V; *mm.* sun,

1649	1500	4500	1654	1400	4250
1650	1350	4000	1655	2500	7500
1651	1350	4000	1656	2500	7500
1652	1250	3750	1657	2000	6250
1653	1250	3750			

Numerous overstruck dates exist in this series.

3213 Similar *mm.* anchor,

| 1658 | 4250 | 13500 | 1660 | 4750 | 15000 |

SILVER

3214 Crown. Same type; *mm.* sun,

1649	5750	16500	1653	1250	2750
1651	2500	6500	1654	1850	4500
1652	1350	3000	1656	1350	3000

3215 Halfcrown. Similar; *mm.* sun,

1649	725	2500	1654	325	900
1651	350	950	1655	1500	4250
1652	350	950	1656	325	850
1653	300	750	1657	1750	5250

3216 Similar, *mm.* anchor

| 1658 | 1750 | 4500 | 1660 | 1750 | 4500 |
| 1659 | 3750 | 11500 | | | |

3217 rev   3218 obv

	F	VF		F	VF
	£	£		£	£

3217 Shilling. Similar; *mm.* sun,

	F	VF		F	VF
1649	375	1050	1654	275	650
1651	250	650	1655	400	1100
1652	250	650	1656	275	650
1653	225	575	1657	800	2250

3218 Similar, *mm.* anchor

1658	975	2400	1660	975	2400
1659	3250	9000			

3219

3219 Sixpence. Similar; *mm.* sun,

1649	275	850	1654	225	625
1651	200	550	1655	650	1750
1652	200	550	1656	210	575
1653	210	575	1657	675	1850

3220 Similar; *mm.* anchor,

1658	650	1750	1660	650	1750
1659	1750	5750			

3221   3222

3221 Halfgroat. 45   125

3222 Penny. Similar, but I above shields 40   110

3223

3223 Halfpenny. 35   90

Oliver Cromwell, 'the Great Emancipator' was born on 25th April 1599 in Huntingdon. He married Elizabeth Bourchier in August 1620 and had nine children seven of whom survived infancy. The Protectorate was established on 16th December 1653, with work on the production of portrait coins authorised in 1655. Although often referred to as patterns, there is in fact nothing to suggest that the portrait coins of Oliver Cromwell were not *intended* for circulation. Authorised in 1656, the first full production came in 1657 and was followed by a second more plentiful one before Cromwell's death on 3rd September 1658. All coins were machine made, struck from dies by Thomas Simon (1618-1665) in the presses of the Frenchman, Pierre Blondeau. Later, some of Simon's puncheons were sold in the Low Countries and an imitation Crown was made there. Other Dutch dies were prepared and some found their way back to the Mint, where in 1738 it was decided to strike a set of Cromwell's coins. Shillings and Sixpences were struck from the Dutch dies, and Crowns from new dies prepared by John Tanner. Dutch and Tanner Halfbroads were also made. Oliver was succeeded as Lord Protector by his son Richard for whom no coins were struck.

GOLD

		F	VF	EF
		£	£	£
3224	**Fifty shillings**. Laur. head l. R. Crowned Shield of the Protectorate, die axis ↑↓ 1656 from the same dies as the Broad........................	27500	90000	225000
	Lettered edge PROTECTOR · LITERIS · LITERÆ · NUMMIS · CORONA · ET · SALUS			

3225
1656 gold Broad

3225	**Broad.** of Twenty Shillings. Laur. head l. R. Crowned Shield of the Protectorate, but grained edge die axis ↑↓ 1656.	6500	17500	47500

SILVER

3226
1658 Crown 8 over 7 - Die flawed drapery

3226	**Crown.** Dr. bust l. R. Crowned shield, 1658/7. Lettered edge ↑↓	1950	4250	9750
3226A	**Crown.** Dutch copy, similar with A ᴎG legend 1658	2250	6000	18500
3226B	**Crown.** Tanner's copy (struck 1738) dated 1658	2350	6250	19000

	F £	VF £	EF £

3227 **Halfcrown.** Dr. bust l. R. Crowned shield 1656 HI type
legend, lettered edge, die axis ↑↓ 2750 7500 18000

3227A
1658 Halfcrown with HIB obverse legend

3227A **Halfcrown.** Similar,1658 HIB type legend, lettered edge, die axis ↑↓   1350   2750   7000

3228
1658 Shilling

3228 **Shilling.** Dr. bust l. R. Crowned shield, grained edge, 1658 die
axis↑↓ 900 1750 5000

3229 **Sixpence.** Similar 1658 die axis↑↓ .... 25000 — —

An example in fair-fie condition sold in a USA auction in January 2017 for $38000
however Dutch copies (ESC 1506) are more often found of the sixpence   2500   6000   12500

COPPER

3230
Copper Farthing

3230 **Farthing.** Dr. bust l. R. CHARITIE AND CHANGE, shield ↑↓..   3750   8750   18500
There are also other reverse types for this coin, and an obverse with mullet on top.

CHARLES II, 1660-85

Charles II was born at St James Palace on 29th May 1630. He spent a long exile in France and returned after the fall of the Protectorate in 1660. The Restoration commenced and he married Catherine of Braganza, but he bore no legitimate successor. Charles II died on 6th February 1685.

For the first two years after the Restoration the same denominations, apart from the silver crown, were struck as were issued during the Commonwealth although the threepence and fourpence were soon added. Then, early in 1663, the ancient hand hammering process was finally superceded by the machinery of Blondeau.

For the emergency issues struck in the name of Charles II in 1648/9, see the siege pieces of Pontefract listed under Charles I, nos. 3150-1.

HAMMERED COINAGE, 1660-2

Mintmark: Crown.

GOLD

3301

3302   3303

	F	VF
	£	£

First issue. Without mark of value; *mm.* crown on *obv.* only

3301	**Unite** (20s.). Type as illustration	2250	6750
3302	**Double-crown**. As illustration	1500	4500
3303	**Crown**. Similar	1650	5250

3304   3305

Second issue. With mark of value; *mm.* crown on *obv.* only

3304	**Unite**. Type as illustration	2000	6000
3305	**Double-crown**. As illustration	1500	4500
3306	**Crown**. Similar	2250	6750

SILVER

3307

		F	*VF*
		£	£

First issue. Without inner circles or mark of value; *mm.* crown on *obv.* only

| 3307 | **Halfcrown.** Crowned bust, as 3308.. | 1500 | 5250 |

3308

| 3308 | **Shilling.** Similar. (Also known with smaller harp on reverse.)................. | 450 | 1750 |

3309

3309	**Sixpence.** Similar	350	1200
3310	**Twopence.** Similar..	50	150
3311	**Penny.** Similar..	40	120
3312	As last, but without mintmark	50	135

3313

3316

		F £	VF £

Second issue. Without inner circles, but with mark of value; *mm.* crown on *obv.* only

3313	**Halfcrown**. Crowned bust	1350	4500
3314	**Shilling**. Similar	750	2500
3315	**Sixpence**. Similar	1250	3750
3316	**Twopence**. Similar, but mm. on obv. only	90	300
3317	Similar, but mm. both sides (machine made)	20	80
3318	Bust to edge of coin, legend starts at bottom l. (machine made, single arch crown)	20	75
3319	**Penny**. As 3317	25	90
3320	As 3318 (single arch crown)	20	80

3321

3326

Third issue. With inner circles and mark of value; *mm.* crown on both sides

3321	**Halfcrown**. Crowned bust to i.c. (and rarely to edge of coin)	225	700
3322	**Shilling**. Similar, rarely *mm.* crown on *obv.* only. (Also known with smaller harp on reverse.)	135	575
3323	**Sixpence**. Similar	125	475
3324	**Fourpence**. Similar	40	125
3325	**Threepence**. Similar	25	90
3326	**Twopence**. Similar	20	70
3327	**Penny**. Similar	20	75

Knightsbridge Coins

Essential art and antiques coverage...

- ✓ Breaking news on the stories that matter
- ✓ Weekly editions delivered to your door
- ✓ Online exclusives for subscribers
- ✓ An archive of all Gazettes since January 2017
- ✓ Privileged access to our constantly updated auction and fairs calendars

Plus: you can download our app to read the Gazette on your mobile or tablet.

Available on **Google play**

Download on the **App Store**

Search for: Antiques Trade Gazette

PRINT ONLINE APP

Start your subscription now from just £1 per week
Visit: antiquestradegazette.com/subscribe

Grading of Early and Later Milled Coinage

Milled coinage refers to coins that are struck by dies worked in a mechanical coining press. The early period is defined from the time of the successful installation of Peter Blondeau's hand powered machinery at the mint, initiated to strike the first portrait coins of Oliver Cromwell in 1656. The early period continuing until the advent of Matthew Boulton's steam powered presses from 1790. The coinage of this early period is therefore cruder in its execution than the latter. When pricing coins of the early peiod, we only attribute grades as high as extremely fine, and as high as uncirculated for the latter period. Most coins that occur of the early period in superior grades than those stated, in particular copper coins retaining full original lustre, will command considerably higher prices, due to their rarity. We suggest the following definitions for grades of preservation:

Milled Coinage Conditions

Proof   A very carefully struck coin from specially prepared dies, to give a superior definition to the design, with mirror-like fields. Occurs occasionally in the Early Milled Coinage, more frequently in the latter period. Some issues struck to a matt finish for Edward VII.

FDC   *Fleur-de-coin.* Absolutely flawless, untouched, without wear, scratches, marks or hairlines. Generally applied to proofs.

UNC   *Uncirculated.* A coin in as new condition as issued by the Mint, retaining full lustre or brilliance but, owing to modern mass-production methods of manufacture and storage, not necessarily perfect.

EF   *Extremely Fine.* A coin that exhibits very little sign of circulation, with only minimal marks or faint wear, which are only evident upon very close scrutiny.

VF   *Very Fine.* A coin that exhibits some wear on the raised surfaces of the design, but really has only had limited circulation.

F   *Fine.* A coin that exhibits considerable wear to the raised surfaces of the design, either through circulation, or damage perhaps due to faulty striking

Fair   *Fair.* A coin that exhibits wear, with the main features still distinguishable, and the legends, date and inscriptions still readable.

Poor   *Poor.* A coin that exhibits considerable wear, certainly with milled coinage of no value to a collector unless it is an extremely rare date or variety.

Examples of Condition Grading

Early Milled

Gold Ν   Silver ÆR   Copper Æ

Extremely Fine

Early Milled *continued*

Gold A/ Silver Æ Copper Æ

Very Fine

Fine

*George III
Guinea*

*James II
Crown*

*George II
old head Halfpenny*

Later Milled

Gold A/ Silver Æ Copper Æ

Uncirculated

Gold Ǣ̷ V   Silver Æ̷R   Copper Æ

Extremely Fine

Very Fine

Fine

Victoria
Jubilee head Sovereign

George IV
laureate bust Crown

Victoria
Young head Halfpenny

MILLED COINAGE, 1662-85

Early in 1663, the ancient hand hammering process was finally superceded by the machinery of Blondeau. John and Joseph Roettier, two brothers, engraved the dies with a safeguard against clipping, the larger coins were made with the edge inscribed DECVS ET TVTAMEN and the regnal year. The medium-sized coins were given a grained edge.

The new gold coins were current for 100s., 40s., 20s. and 10s., and they came to be called 'Guineas' as the gold from which some of them were made was imported from Guinea by the Africa Company (whose badge was the Elephant and Castle). It was not until some years later that the Guinea increased in value to 21s. and more. The Africa Co. badge is also found on some silver and so is the plume symbol indicating silver from the Welsh mines. The four smallest silver denominations, though known today as 'Maundy Money', were actually issued for general circulation: at this period the silver penny was probably the only coin distributed at the Royal Maundy ceremonies. Though never part of the original agreement, smaller coins were eventually also struck by machinery.

A good regal copper coinage was issued for the first time in 1672, but later in the reign, farthings were struck in tin (with a copper plug) in order to help the Cornish tin industry.

Engravers and designers: John Roettier (1631-1700), Thomas Simon (1618-1665)

GOLD

3328
1672 First bust type Five-Guineas

	F £	VF £	EF £		F £	VF £	EF £

3328 **Five Guineas.** First laur. bust r., pointed trun., regnal year on edge in words, die axis ↑↓ (e.g. 1669=VICESIMO PRIMO), R. Crowned cruciform shields, sceptres in angles

1668 VICESIMO	5500	17500	80000	1671 – TERTIO	6000	18500	85000
1668 V. PRIMO	6000	18500	85000	1672 – QVARTO	5750	18000	82500
1669 – PRIMO	5000	16500	80000	1673 – QVINTO	5500	17500	82500
1670 – SECVNDO	5000	15000	75000	1674 – QVINTO	6500	20000	90000
1670 – Similar proof				1674 – SEXTO	6000	18500	87500
FDC	—	—	225000				

3328A **Five Guineas.** First bust. Similar hair of different style. Shorter ties

1674 QVINTO	6500	20000	90000	1676 – OCTAVO	6000	18500	85000
1675 V. SEPTIMO	6000	18500	85000	1677 – NONO	5250	16500	80000
1676 – SEPTIMO	5750	18000	82500	1678/7– TRICESIMO	5750	18000	82500

3329 **Five Guineas.** First bust with elephant below, similar die axis ↑↓

1668 VICESIMO	4750	13500	67500	1675 V. SEPTIMO	6000	18500	85000
1669 – PRIMO	6000	18500	85000	1677/5– NONO	6500	20000	90000

3330

1676 Five-Guineas with elephant and castle provenance mark

	F	VF	EF		F	VF	EF
	£	£	£		£	£	£

3330   Five Guineas. First bust with elephant and castle below, similar die axis ↑↓

1675 – SEPTIMO ...	7000	22500	90000	1677 – NONO...........	6000	18500	85000
1676 – OCTAVO.....	5750	18000	82500	1678/7 – TRICESIMO..	6000	18500	85000

3331   Five Guineas. Second laur. bust r., rounded trun. similar die axis ↑↓

1678/7 TRICESIMO.	5000	15500	75000	1682 T. QVARTO	4750	15000	72500
1679 – PRIMO........	4750	15000	72500	1683 – QVINTO........	4750	15000	72500
1680/79– SECVNDO	5000	15500	75000	1683/2 – QVINTO.......	5000	15500	75000
1681 – TERTIO.......	5000	15500	75000	1684 – SEXTO	4750	15000	72500

3332   Five Guineas. Second laur. bust r., with elephant and castle below, similar die axis ↑↓

1680/79 T. SECVNDO	6000	18500	85000	1683 T. QVINTO.......	6000	18500	85000
1681 – TERTIO.......	6000	18500	85000	1684 – SEXTO	5000	15500	75000
1682 – QVARTO.....	5500	16500	80000				

3333

1664 First bust type Two Guineas

3333   Two Guineas. First laur. bust r., pointed trun. Ṛ. Crowned cruciform shields, sceptres in angles, die axis ↑↓

1664	 2750	6750	25000	1671	3500	8250	32500
1665	....	*Extremely rare*		1673	....	*Extremely rare*	
1669	....	*Extremely rare*					

3334

1664 Two Guineas with elephant only below

3334   Two Guineas. First bust with elephant below, similar die axis ↑↓

1664.. 2100   5500   18500

SPINK

3335
1675 Two Guineas - second bust

3339
1663 Guinea first bust, elephant below

	F	VF	EF		F	VF	EF
	£	£	£		£	£	£

3335 Two Guineas. Second laur. bust r., rounded trun, similar die axis ↑↓

1675	2600	6500	24000	1680	2750	7000	27500
1676	2500	6500	24000	1681	2500	6250	22500
1677	2500	6250	22500	1682	2500	6250	22500
1678/7	2500	6250	22500	1683	2500	6250	22500
1679	2500	6250	2250	1684	2600	6500	24000

3336 Two Guineas. Second bust with elephant and castle below, similar die axis ↑↓

1676	2750	6750	25000	1682	2750	6750	25000
1677		*Extremely rare*		1683	3000	7000	27500
1678	2750	6750	25000	1684	2750	6750	25000

3337 Two Guineas. Second bust with elephant only below, die axis ↑↓ 1678 ... *Extremely rare*

3337A Broad of 20s. Laur. and dr. bust r. R. Crowned shield of arms (approx. 3400 issued),
die axis ↑↓ 1662 . 3000   6500   15000

3338 Guinea. First laur. bust r., R. Crowned cruciform shields, die axis
↑↓ 1663 5000   17500   65000

3339 Guinea. First bust with elephant below, similar die axis ↑↓ 1663 4000   13500   50000

3340 Guinea. Second laur. bust r.,similar die axis ↑↓

| 1663 | 3750 | 12500 | 47500 | 1664 | 2750 | 10000 | 37500 |

3341
1664 Guinea second bust elephant below

3342
1666 Guinea - third bust

3341 Guinea. Second bust with elephant below, similar die axis ↑↓1664..4000   13500   52500

3342 Guinea. Third laur. bust r. similar die axis ↑↓

1664	1200	4000	16500	1669	1000	3500	15000
1665	1000	3500	15000	1670	950	3250	14500
1666	1000	3500	15000	1671	950	3250	14500
1667	1000	3500	15500	1672	1200	4250	16000
1668	950	3250	14500	1673	1200	4250	16000

3343 Guinea. Third laur. bust r., with elephant below, similar die axis ↑↓

| 1664 | 2000 | 6250 | 22500 | 1668 | | *Extremely rare* | |
| 1665 | 2000 | 6250 | 22500 | | | | |

3344   3345
1679 Guinea - Fourth bust   1682 - Fourth bust - elephant below

	F	VF	EF		F	VF	EF
	£	£	£		£	£	£

3344 Guinea. Fourth laur. bust r., rounded trun. similar die axis ↑↓

	F	VF	EF		F	VF	EF
1672	900	3250	12000	1679	800	2650	10500
1673	850	3000	11500	1679 'O' over 'o' on its side and			
1674	900	3250	12000	R of FRA over A	850	3000	11500
1675	850	3000	11500	1680	800	2750	11000
1675 CRAOLVS error	2500	6750	—	1680/79	875	3250	12500
1676	800	2750	11000	1681	850	3000	11500
1676/4	850	3000	11500	1682	800	2750	11000
1677	800	2750	11000	1682 rev.@90° axis	875	3000	12000
1677 GRATIR error	3000	—	—	1683	800	2750	11000
1677 CAROLVS error	850	3000	12500	1684	850	3000	11500
1678	800	2750	11000				

3345 Guinea. Fourth laur. bust r., with elephant and castle below, similar die axis ↑↓

	F	VF	EF		F	VF	EF
1674		*Extremely rare*		1679	1100	4500	15000
1675	1100	4500	15000	1680	1100	4500	15000
1676	975	4250	14500	1681	1100	4500	15000
1677	975	4250	14500	1682	1100	4500	15000
1677 GRATIR error	3500	—	—	1683	975	4250	14500
1678	975	4250	14500	1684	1100	4500	15000

3346 Guinea. — — with elephant below bust, similar die axis ↑↓

1677/5		*Extremely rare*	1678	4000	13500	—

3347
1669 Half-Guinea, first bust

3347 Half-Guinea. First laur. bust r., pointed trun.R. Crowned cruciform shields, sceptres in angles die axis ↑↓

1669	550	2000	7000	1671	625	2100	7500
1670	525	1850	6750	1672	600	2000	7000

3348 - 1684 Half-Guinea, second bust

	F	VF	EF		F	VF	EF
	£	£	£		£	£	£

3348 Half-Guinea. Second laur. bust r., rounded trun. similar die axis ↑↓

1672	500	1650	5500	1678/7	525	1750	5750
1673	525	1750	5750	1679	500	1650	5500
1674	550	1800	6250	1680	500	1650	5500
1675	525	1750	5750	1681	525	1750	5750
1676	500	1650	5500	1682	500	1650	5500
1676/4	525	1750	5750	1683	500	1650	5500
1677	525	1750	5750	1684	500	1650	5500
1678	525	1750	5750				

3349 Half-Guinea. Second bust with elephant and castle below, similar die axis ↑↓

1676	750	2500	9250	1681	750	2500	9250
1677	700	2250	9000	1682	700	2250	9000
1678/7	700	2250	9000	1683		*Extremely rare*	
1680	750	2500	9250	1684	700	2250	9000

SILVER

3350 - 1662 Crown, first type, rose below bust

3350 Crown. First dr. bust r., rose below, numerous varieties in length and style of hair ties. R. Crowned cruciform shields, interlinked C's in angles edge undated,
die axis ↑↓ 1662 .... 250 1350 12500

3350A Crown. — — Similar, die axis ↑↑ 1662 .... 350 1650 —

3350B Crown. — striped cloak to drapery, 1662 similar die axis ↑↓ .... 400 2000 —

3350C Crown. — — II of legend at 12 o'clock, similar die axis ↑↓ 1662 .. 2500 — —

3351 Crown. — — edge dated, similar die axis ↑↓ or ↑↑ 1662 .... 275 1650 13500

3352 Crown. — legend re-arranged no rose, edge dated, similar die
axis ↑↓ 1662 .... 300 1750 14500

3353 Crown. — — edge not dated, similar die axis ↑↓ 1662 .... 225 1250 12500

3354 Crown. — — shields altered, 1663, similar regnal year on edge in
Roman figures ANNO REGNI XV die axis ↑↓ 185 1100 10000

1663 no stops on reverse 200 1250 12500

1663 edge not dated, as 3350 .... *Extremely rare*

3354A

F	VF	EF		F	VF	EF
£	£	£		£	£	£

3354A Pattern 'Petition' Crown, 1663 by Thomas Simon. Laur. Bust r. of fine style in high relief, *Simon* below, edge inscription of Simon's 'petition': THOMAS SIMON. MOST. HVMBLY. PRAYS. YOVR MAJESTY etc., etc. 45000 150000 475000

3354B Pattern 'Reddite' Crown, 1663, by Thomas Simon, struck from the same dies, edge inscription: REDDITE. QVAE. CESARIS etc., etc. 32500 110000 375000

3355 Crown. Second dr. bust r. smaller than first bust and with curving tie to wreath. Regnal year on edge in Roman figures (e.g. 1664 = XVI), die axis ↑↓

1664 edge XVI........ 180	1100	8750	1665 XVII................ 1350	4000	—
1664 Proof *FDC*			1666 XVIII................. 300	1250	9500
Fine work .... —	—	95000	1666 XVIII RE·X 325	1300	10000
1665 XVI................ 1750	—	—	1667 XVIII................ 4000	—	—
1665/4 XVII 1450	4000	—			

3356 Crown. Second bust elephant below, similar, die axis ↑↓

1666 XVIII............... 950	3500	20000	1666 XVIII RE·X 975	3750	—

3357

1668 Crown - second bust

3357 Crown. Second bust, similar, Regnal year on edge in words (e.g. 1667= DECIMO NONO) die axis ↑↓

1667 D. NONO 225	850	9000	1669 V· PRIMO.............325	1500	—
1667 — AN.· REG.·.. 210	800	8500	1669/8 V· PRIMO..........375	1650	—
1668 VICESIMO 200	750	8500	1670 V. SECVNDO 200	750	8500
1668 — error edge			1670/69 V. SECVND......250	800	8750
inverted..................... 450	—	—	1671 V· TERTIO 200	750	8500
1668/7 VICESIMO 225	825	8750	1671 — T/R in ET 300	1100	—
1668/5 VICESIMO	*Extremely rare*		1671 — ET over FR 325	1250	—

3358
Third bust Crown

	F	VF	EF		F	VF	EF
	£	£	£		£	£	£

3358 Crown. Third dr. bust r. much larger and broader than second bust, tie nearly straight. From end of tie to top of nose is 20mm. R.Similar die axis ↑↓

1671 V. TERTIO.......	175	700	7500	1675 —	900	3500	—
1671 V. QVARTO.......	450	1500	—	1676 V. OCTAVO	175	700	7500
1672 V. QVARTO.....	175	700	7500	1676 OCCTAVO	200	750	8000
1673 V. QVARTO	*Extremely rare*			1677 V. NONO..............	175	700	7500
1673 V. QVINTO	175	700	7500	1677/6 V. NONO............	175	700	7500
1673 B/R in BR.........	250	900	—	1678/7 TRICESIMO......	225	900	8500
1673/2 V. QVINTO ...	185	750	8000	1679 T. PRIMO.............	175	700	7500
1674 V. SEXTO..............	*Extremely rare*			1680/79 T. SECVNDO.......	220	800	8250
1675/3 V. SEPTIMO .	800	3000	—	1680 T. SECVNDO	200	750	8000

3359
Fourth bust Crown

3359 Crown. Fourth dr. bust r. still larger, with older features and more pointed nose. From end of tie to tip of nose is 21mm. R.Similar die axis ↑↓

1679 T. PRIMO.........	200	700	7500	1682/1 T. QVARTO	200	700	7500
1679 HIBR·EX..........	375	1650	—	1682 T. QVARTO...........	225	800	8000
1680 T. SECVNDO...	200	700	7500	1682/1 QVRRTO error.....	225	800	8000
1680/79 T. SECVNDO .	250	800	8250	1683 T. QVINTO	325	1250	9500
1681 T. TERTIO........	200	700	7500	1684 T. SEXTO..............	250	850	8250

3360 Crown.— elephant and castle below bust, die axis ↑↓

1681 T. TERTIO.......	5500	15000	—

3361 - First bust Halfcrown   3362 - Second bust Halfcrown

	F	VF	EF		F	VF	EF
	£	£	£		£	£	£

3361 Halfcrown. First dr. bust r. R. Crowned cruciform shields, interlinked C's in angles, regnal year on edge in Roman figures die axis ↑↓

	F	VF	EF
1663 XV	225	950	4750
1663 XV V/S in CAROLVS	250	1000	5000
1663 XV A/T in GRATIA	275	1050	5000
1663 XV no stops on obverse	240	975	4750

3362 Halfcrown. Second dr. bust r., similar die axis ↑↓ 1664 XVI 350   1250   6000

3363 Halfcrown. Third dr. bust r., similar die axis ↑↓ 1666/4 XVIII 950   3750   —

3364 - Third bust, elephant below Halfcrown

3364 Halfcrown. Third bust elephant below, die axis ↑↓ 1666 XVIII.............. 900   3500   —

3365 - 1670 Halfcrown, third bust   MRG for MAG var

3365 Halfcrown. Third dr. bust r. regnal date on edge in words (eg. 1667=DECIMO NONO) ↑↓

1667/4 D. NONO	4000	—	—	1670 V. SECVNDO	150	575	4000
1668/4 VICESIMO	375	1500	—	1670 – MRG for MAG	275	900	—
1669/4 V. PRIMO	275	1100	—	1670 V/S CAROLVS	225	800	—
1669 V. PRIMO	350	1350	—	1670 E/R in ET	240	850	—
1669 — R/I in PRIMO	375	1450	—				

3366
1671 Halfcrown third bust variety

	F	VF	EF		F	VF	EF
	£	£	£		£	£	£

3366 Halfcrown. Third bust variety r. R. Similar die axis ↑↓

1671 V. TERTIO........... 140	525	4000	1672 V. TERTIO .... *Extremely rare*
1671 A/R in MAG........ 225	800	—	1672 V. QVARTO 150 550 4000
1671/0 V. TERTIO 160	575	4250	

3367
Fourth bust Halfcrown

3367 Halfcrown. Fourth dr. bust r. R. Similar die axis ↑↓

1672 V. QVARTO..........165	575	3750	1678 TRICESIMO.........225	950	5250
1673 V. QVINTO 165	575	3750	1679 T. PRIMO..............160	550	3500
1673 — A/R in FRA 185	700	—	1679 — DECNS error 185	700	—
1673 — B/R in BR........185	700	—	1679 — DNCVS error......175	650	—
1673 — FR/M in FRA...185	700	—	1679 — PRICESIMO 165	600	3750
1674 V. SEXTO.............165	600	4000	1680 T. SECVNDO........165	600	3750
1674/3 V. SEXTO..........200	750	—	1680 T. SECVNCIO error ..175	650	4000
1675 V. SEPTIMO 165	575	3750	1681 T. TERTIO.............220	825	4750
1675 — Retrograde 1 170	600	4000	1681/0 — 250	950	—
1676 V. OCTAVO..........160	550	3500	1682 T. QVARTO...........165	600	4000
1676 R/T in BR 200	800	—	1682/79 T. QVARTO 225	850	—
1676 — Retrograde 1 165	575	3750	1683 T. QVINTO 160	550	3500
1676 F/H in FRA...........185	700	—	1684/3 T. SEXTO 350	1350	—
1677 V. NONO..............160	550	3500			
1677 F/H in FRA...........200	800	—			

3369 - Plume in centre

	F	VF	EF			F	VF	EF
	£	£	£			£	£	£

3368 Halfcrown. Fourth bust plume below, R. Similar die axis ↑↓

| 1673 V. QVINTO | 6500 | 18500 | — | 1683 T. QVINTO | 7500 | 22500 | — |

3369 Halfcrown. — plume below bust and in centre of *rev.*, die axis ↑↓

| 1673 V. QVINTO | 8500 | 24000 | — |

3370 - Elephant and Castle below bust

3370 Halfcrown. — elephant and castle below bust, die axis ↑↓

| 1681 T. TERTIO | 3750 | 12500 | 32500 |

SHILLINGS

First bust   First bust variety   Second bust   Third bust

First bust   First bust variety   First and first bust   Second bust
                                               variety, double top leaf   single top leaf

3371 - First bust   3372

	F	VF	EF		F	VF	EF
	£	£	£		£	£	£

3371 Shilling. First dr. bust r.R. Crowned cruciform shields interlinked C's in angles edge milled,

1663 die axis ↑↑ (en medaille) 150   650   —

1663 die axis ↑↓ as usual... 125   450   2500

1663 GARTIA error, die axis ↑↓ 1500   —   —

1663 Transposed shields of Scotland and Ireland, die axis ↑↓ 250   800   —

1663 A over G in FRA, die axis ↑↓ 450   —   —

3374   3375 - Second bust shilling

3372 Shilling. First bust variety r. similar die axis ↑↓

1663	125	450	2500	1668	650	2250	—
1666		*Extremely rare*		1669/6		*Extremely rare*	

3373 Shilling. First bust variety r. elephant below bust, die axis ↑↓ 1666.. 800   2750   10000

3374 Shilling. Guinea head, elephant below bust, die axis ↑↓ 1666......... 3500   9000   —

3375 Shilling. Second dr. bust r. similar die axis ↑↓

1666	1850	6000	—	1676/4	200	725	2750
1668	120	450	2250	1676/5	175	700	2650
1668/7	150	550	2400	1677	160	650	2500
1669		*Extremely rare*		1678	175	700	2650
1670	175	750	2750	1678/7	240	850	3000
1671	175	750	2750	1679	160	650	2500
1672	175	750	2750	1679/7	200	725	2750
1673	175	750	2750	1680	1100	3000	7000
1673/2	200	800	3000	1680/79	1200	3250	7500
1674	200	800	3000	1681	425	1350	—
1674/3	175	750	2750	1681/0	450	1500	—
1675	240	850	3000	1682/1	1250	3500	—
1675/4	240	850	3000	1683	1250	3500	—
1676	160	650	2500				

The 1668 shilling is also known with large 6's in the date

3376 - Plume both sides shilling of 1671

	F £	VF £	EF £		F £	VF £	EF £
3376 Shilling. Second Bust — plume below bust and in centre of *rev.* similar die axis ↑↓							
1671	550	1750	4750	1676	600	1850	5250
1673	600	1850	5250	1679	575	1800	5000
1674	550	1750	4750	1680/79	1350	3750	9000
1675	600	1850	5250				

3378
1679 Shilling - plume on obverse only

3377 Shilling. — Plume *rev.* only, similar die axis ↑↓ 1674 1250   3500   8500

3378 Shilling. — Plume *obv.* only similar die axis ↑↓

1677	1250	3500	8500	1679	1100	3250	8000

3379 Shilling. — elephant and castle below bust, die axis ↑↓ 1681/0 3750   12000   —

3380
Third bust Shilling

3381
1684 Shilling - fourth bust

3380 Shilling. Third dr. (large) bust r. similar die axis ↑↓

1674	675	2250	6500	1675/3	425	1500	4500

3381 Shilling. Fourth dr. (large) bust r., older features, similar die axis ↑↓

1683	225	800	2750	1684	225	800	2750

3382
1677 Sixpence

	F	VF	EF			F	VF	EF
	£	£	£			£	£	£

3382 Sixpence. Dr. bust r. R. Crowned cruciform shields, interlinked C's in angles die axis ↑↓

	F	VF	EF			F	VF	EF
1674	75	250	800	1679		85	300	850
1675	80	275	850	1680		85	300	900
1675/4	80	275	850	1681		75	250	800
1676	95	325	950	1682		95	325	950
1676/5	90	300	900	1682/1		90	300	900
1677	75	250	800	1683		75	250	800
1678/7	80	275	850	1684		80	275	850

3383
Undated Fourpence

3384 -
1678 Fourpence

3383 Fourpence. Undated. Crowned dr. bust l. to edge of coin, value
behind. R. Shield, die axis ↑↓ 20   50   120

3384 Fourpence. Dated. Dr. bust r. R. Crowned four interlinked Cs quartered emblems die axis ↑↓

	F	VF	EF			F	VF	EF
1670	20	45	125	1678		18	45	120
1671	18	40	110	1678/6		18	40	100
1672/1	22	48	125	1678/7		18	40	100
1673	18	40	100	1679		10	20	70
1674	18	40	100	1680		12	22	80
1674/4 sideways	20	40	150	1681		15	40	95
1674 7 over 6	18	40	100	1681 B/R in HIB		18	38	150
1675	18	40	100	1681/0		15	32	115
1675/4	18	45	120	1682		18	40	110
1676	18	40	100	1682/1		18	40	115
1676 7 over 6	18	45	135	1683		18	40	110
1676/5	18	45	120	1684		20	40	120
1677	15	32	95	1684/3		20	40	110

3386 - 1678 Threepence

	F £	VF £	EF £		F £	VF £	EF £
3385 **Threepence.** Undated. As 3383, die axis ↑↓					14	35	110
3386 **Threepence.** Dated. Dr. bust r. R. Crowned three interlinked C's, die axis ↑↓							
1670	12	25	90	1678	12	25	100
1671	10	22	80	1678 on 4d flan	12	25	125
1671 GRⱯTIA	18	38	150	1679	10	20	60
1671 GRΛTIA	12	28	100	1679 O/A in CAROLVS	15	38	150
1672/1	10	22	90	1680	12	25	85
1673	10	22	80	1681	14	22	90
1674	12	25	90	1681/0	12	30	100
1675	15	30	95	1682	15	30	105
1676	10	22	85	1682/1	15	32	95
1676/5	12	28	100	1683	15	30	105
1676 ERA for FRA	12	38	175	1684	15	30	105
1677	15	30	100	1684/3	15	32	95

3388 - 1678 Twopence

	F £	VF £	EF £		F £	VF £	EF £
3387 **Twopence.** Undated. As 3383 (double arch crown) die axis ↑↓					12	30	90
3388 **Twopence.** Dated. Dr. bust r. R. Crowned pair of linked C's, die axis ↑↓							
1668 die axis ↑↑	15	30	100	1678/6	13	28	100
1670	10	22	75	1679	10	20	65
1671	10	20	65	1679 HIB over FRA	13	38	150
1672/1	10	20	65	1680	10	20	70
1672/1 GRΛTIA	13	38	165	1680/79	13	28	85
1673	12	25	80	1681	10	20	70
1674	10	20	65	1682/1	13	28	80
1675	12	25	80	1682/1 ERA for FRA	13	38	150
1676	10	20	75	1683	10	22	70
1677	12	25	75	1683/2	13	28	70
1678	15	35	95	1684	13	28	75

3390 - 1678 Penny

	F	VF	EF		F	VF	EF
	£	£	£		£	£	£
3389 **Penny.** Undated. As 3383 (double arch crown) die axis ↑↓	12	35	110				
3390 **Penny.** Dated. Dr. bust r. R. Crowned C die axis ↑↓							
1670	12	30	105	1678	24	55	145
1671	12	30	105	1678 RATIA error ...	12	50	185
1672/1	12	30	105	1679	24	55	145
1673	12	30	105	1680	12	30	105
1674	14	35	120	1680 on 2d flan		*Extremely rare*	
1674 ꓭRATIA error...	18	40	175	1681	22	65	170
1675	12	30	105	1682	22	50	140
1675 ꓭRATIA error...	18	40	175	1682/1	18	40	145
1676	22	50	145	1682 ERA for FRA	18	40	150
1676 ꓭRATIA error...	15	40	175	1683/1	13	35	110
1677	12	30	105	1684	24	50	145
1677 ꓭRATIA error...	15	40	175	1684/3	24	50	150
3391 **Maundy Set.** Undated. The four coins..	100	225	575				
3392 **Maundy Set.** Dated. The four denominations. Uniform dates							
1670	100	275	650	1678	115	300	800
1671	90	200	550	1679	90	225	650
1672	95	250	600	1680	85	200	600
1673	80	200	550	1681	100	300	650
1674	90	210	600	1682	90	250	725
1675	90	225	600	1683	80	200	750
1676	100	250	700	1684	100	275	775
1677	90	225	675				

COPPER AND TIN

3393 - 1675 Halfpenny

	F	VF	EF			F	VF	EF
	£	£	£			£	£	£

3393 Copper **Halfpenny** Cuir. bust l. R. Britannia seated l. date in ex., die axis ↑↓

	F	VF	EF		F	VF	EF
1672............................60	350	1400	1673 no rev. stop........90	500	—
1672 CRAOLVS error....	*Extremely rare*		1675 60	350	1400
1673............................50	330	1200	1675 no stops on obv. 90	500	—
1673 CRAOLVS error .225	—	—	1675/3 165	600	—
1673 no stops on obv......	*Extremely rare*				

3394 - 1672 Farthing

3394   Copper **Farthing.** Cuir. bust l. R. Britannia sealed l. date in ex., die axis ↑↓

	F	VF	EF		F	VF	EF
1672............................45	265	825	1673 no stops on obv.165	—	—
1672 Rev.			1673 no rev. stop 165	—	—
loose drapery 65	325	1000	1674............................55	300	900
1672 no stops on obv.. 65	325	1000	1674 'O' for 'C' in		
1672 RO/OL on obv... 90	450	—	CAROLVS......100	500	—
1672 die axis ↑↑.........65	325	1000	1675............................50	275	825
1673............................50	275	825	1675 no stop after		
1673 CAROLA error 150	550	—	CAROLVS........165	—	—
1673 O/sideways O 75	325	1100	1679............................55	300	900
1673 BRITINNIA error225	—	—	1679 no rev. stop 65	325	1100

3395 - Tin Farthing

Prices for tin coinage based on corrosion free examples, and in the top grades with some lustre

3395 Tin **Farthing.** Somewhat similar, but with copper plug, edge inscribed NUMMORVM FAMVLVS, and date on edge only die axis ↑↓

1684	various varieties of edge...55	250	900	3600
1685	....		*Extremely rare*	

James II, brother of Charles II, was born on 14th October 1633, he married Anne Hyde with whom he produced 8 children. He lost control of his subjects when the loyalist Tories moved against him over his many Catholic appointments. Parliament invited his protestant daughter Mary with husband William of Orange to be joint rulers. James II abdicated and died in exile in France.

During this reign the dies continued to be engraved by John Roettier (1631-1700), the only major difference in the silver coinage being the ommission of the interlinked C's in the angles of the shields on the reverses. The only provenance marked silver coin of this reign is the extremely rare plume on reverse 1685 Shilling. The elephant and castle provenance mark continues to appear on some of the gold coins of this reign. Tin halfpence and farthings provided the only base metal coinage during this short reign. All genuine tin coins of this period have a copper plug.

GOLD

	F	VF	EF		F	VF	EF
	£	£	£		£	£	£

3396 Five Guineas. First laur. bust l., R. Crowned cruciform shields sceptres misplaced in angles smaller crowns date on edge in words (e.g. 1686 = SECVNDO)
die axis ↑↓ 1686 SECVNDO 5500   16500   80000

3397 Five Guineas. First laur bust l. R. similar bust sceptres normal. die axis ↑↓
1687 TERTIO 5000   15500   75000   1688 QVARTO....... 5000   15500   75000

3397A
1687 Five Guineas, second bust

3397A Five Guineas. Second laur. bust l. R. similar die axis ↑↓
1687 TERTIO 5000   14500   70000   1688 QVARTO....... 5000   14500   70000

3398
1687 Five Guineas, first bust, elephant and castle below

3398 Five Guineas. First laur. bust l. Elephant and castle below R. Similar die axis ↑↓
1687 TERTIO 5500   16500   80000   1688 QVARTO....... 5500   16500   80000

3399 - Two Guineas

	F	VF	EF		F	VF	EF
	£	£	£		£	£	£

3399 Two Guineas. Laur. bust l. R. Crowned cruciform shields, sceptres in angles, edge milled, die axis ↑↓

1687	3250	9500	30000	1688/7	3500	10000	32500

3400 Guinea. First laur. bust l. R. Crowned cruciform shields, sceptres in angles, edge milled, die axis ↑↓

1685	1000	3500	12500	1686 B/I			
1686	1000	3500	12500	in HIB	1050	3750	13500
1686 B/I							
in HIB	1050	3600	13000				

3401 Guinea. First bust elephant and castle below R. similar die axis ↑↓

1685	1100	4250	15000	1686	1750	—	—

3402 - 1688 Guinea, second bust   3403

3402 Guinea. Second laur. bust l. R. similar die axis ↑↓

| 1686 | 950 | 3000 | 11000 | 1687/6 | 975 | 3250 | 11500 |
| 1687 | 950 | 3000 | 11000 | 1688 | 950 | 3000 | 11000 |

3404

3403 Guinea. Second bust elephant and castle below R. similar die axis ↑↓

| 1686 | 1100 | 4000 | 14000 | 1688 | 1000 | 3750 | 13500 |
| 1687 | 1100 | 4000 | 14000 | | | | |

3404 Half-Guinea. Laur. bust l. R. Crowned cruciform shields sceptres in angles, edge milled die axis ↑↓

| 1686 | 575 | 1950 | 6000 | 1687 | 575 | 1950 | 6500 |
| 1686 OBV/BVS | 600 | 2000 | 7000 | 1688 | 575 | 1950 | 6500 |

3405 Half-Guinea. Laur bust with elephant and castle below, R. similar die axis ↑↓

| 1686 | 900 | 3250 | 10000 |

SILVER

3406
1686 Crown, first bust

	F	VF	EF		F	VF	EF
	£	£	£		£	£	£

3406 Crown. First dr. bust, l. regnal year on edge in words (e.g. 1686 = SECVNDO) die axis ↑↓

1686 SECVNDO 300	1250	8250
1686 — No stops on obverse... 325	1350	8500

3407
1687 Crown, second bust

3407 Crown. Second dr. bust l. narrower than first bust. R. Crowned cruciform shields edge
inscribed in raised letters
die axis ↑↓

1687 TERTIO 250	800	7000	1688/7 QVARTO 300	925	7500
1688 QVARTO 275	850	7250			

	3408		1st bust	2nd bust	

1686 Halfcrown, first bust

Halfcrown hair ties

| F | VF | EF | | F | VF | EF |
| £ | £ | £ | | £ | £ | £ |

3408 Halfcrown. First laur and dr. bust, l. regnal year on edge in words
(e.g. 1685 = PRIMO) die axis ↑↓

1685 PRIMO............... 200	700	5250	1686 TERTIO.............. 225	725	5000
1686 SECVNDO 185	675	4750	1687 TERTIO.............. 200	700	4750
1686/5 — 240	775	5000	1687/6 — 250	825	5250
1686 TERTIO V over S or B			1687 — 6 over 8 300	975	—
in JACOBVS 240	775	5250	1687 A/R in GRATIA . 250	825	5250

3409 Halfcrown. Second laur and dr. bust l. R. Crowned cruciform shields
edge inscribed in raised letters die axis ↑↓

| 1687 TERTIO .... 225 | 775 | 5250 | 1688 QVARTO............ 225 | 775 | 5250 |

3410

1687 Shilling

3410 Shilling. Laur and Dr. bust l. R. Crowned cruciform shields die axis ↑↓

1685 240	700	3000	1687 260	750	3250
1685 no stops on rev......250	750	3250	1687 G/A in MAG 275	800	3400
1686 240	725	3000	1687/6 240	700	3000
1686/5........................... 275	800	3400	1687/6 G/A in MAG ... 250	750	3250
1686 V/S in JACOBVS . 260	750	3250	1688 275	800	3500
1686 G/A in MAG 260	750	3250	1688/7 260	750	3250

3411 Shilling. Similar, plume in centre of *rev.*, die axis ↑↓ 1685................. 9000   20000   —

3412

1686 Sixpence, early shileds, indented tops

3412 Sixpence. Laur and dr. bust l. R. Early type crowned cruciform shields die axis ↑↓

| 1686 .... 150 | 450 | 1350 | 1687/6 .... 175 | 500 | 1500 |
| 1687 .... 175 | 525 | 1600 | | | |

3413
1687 Sixpence, later shields

	F £	VF £	EF £		F £	VF £	EF £
3413 Sixpence. Similar R. Late type shields die axis ↑↓							
1687 150	450	1400		1687 Later/early shields . 175	525	1600	
1687/6 200	550	1650		1688 150	450	1400	

3414	3415	3416	3417
Fourpence	Threepence	Twopence	Penny

3414 Fourpence. Laur. head l. R. IIII Crowned die axis ↑↓

1686 15	30	100	1688 22	45	145
1686 Date over crown 18	30	110	1688 1 over 8 25	55	150
1687/6 15	25	100	1688/7 22	45	140
1687 8 over 7 18	30	110			

3415 Threepence. Laur. head l. R. III Crowned die axis- ↑↓

1685 12	30	95	1687 12	32	100
1685 Groat flan 35	80	165	1687/6 12	32	100
1686 12	35	100	1688 22	55	145
1686 4d obv. die 18	40	120	1688/7 25	55	140

3416 Twopence. Laur. head l. R. II Crowned die axis ↑↓

1686 15	35	90	1687 ERA for FRA 25	45	150
1686 IΛCOBVS 18	35	115	1688 18	40	130
1687 12	32	85	1688/7 18	40	120

3417 Penny. Laur. head l. R. I Crowned die axis ↑↓

1685 15	30	100	1687/8 25	50	130
1686 20	40	110	1688 25	55	140
1687 20	40	110	1688/7 25	55	130
1687/6 20	40	110			

3418 Maundy Set. As last four. Uniform dates

1686 100	300	575	1688 175	350	750
1687 100	300	575			

TIN

3419 Tin Halfpenny

	Fair	F	VF	EF
	£	£	£	£

Prices for tin coinage based on corrosion free examples, and in the top grades with some lustre

3419 Halfpenny. Laur. and dr. bust r. R. Britannia seated l. date on edge die axis ↑↓

1685 various varieties of edge	100	250	775	3850
1686	110	275	825	4200
1687	90	300	775	3850

3420
Cuirassed bust Tin Farthing

3420 Farthing. Laur. and Cuir. bust r. R. Britannia seated l. date on edge die axis ↑↓

1684			*Extremely rare*	
1685 various varieties of edge	65	195	700	3000
1686 two varieties of edge	80	225	775	3250
1687			*Extremely rare*	

3421 Farthing. Dr. bust r.; date on edge, 1687 various varieties of edge ↑↓

	100	250	875	3750

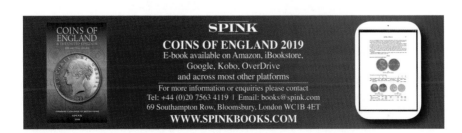

Mary Stuart was born on 30 April 1662, and married William of Orange as part of Charles II's foreign policy. She eventually became William's loyal servant but bore him no children. The Bill and the Claim of Rights were both passed in 1689 and curbed the Royal and Prerogative rights of Monarchs. Mary died from smallpox on 28 December 1694.

Due to the poor state of the silver coinage, much of it worn hammered coin, the Guinea, which was valued at 21s. 6d. at the beginning of the reign, circulated for as much as 30s. by 1694. The elephant and elephant and castle provenance marks continue on some gold coin. The tin Halfpennies and Farthings were replaced by copper coins in 1694. The rampant Lion of Nassau is now placed as an inescutcheon on the centre of the royal arms. The WM monogram appears in the angles of the silver coins of this reign.

Engravers and designers: George Bower (d.1689), Henry Harris (d.1704), John Roettier (1631-1700), James Roettier (1663-1698), Norbert Roettier (b.1665)

GOLD

3422
Five Guineas

	F £	VF £	EF £		F £	VF £	EF £
3422	**Five Guineas.** Conjoined busts r. regnal year on edge in words (e.g. 1691 = TERTIO) ↑↓						
1691 TERTIO	4500	13500	72500	1693 QVINTO	4750	13500	72500
1692 QVARTO	4750	13500	72500	1694/2 SEXTO	5750	16500	80000
1692 QVINTO	6000	17500	85000	1694 SEXTO	5250	15000	75000

3423
Elephant and castle below busts

	F	VF	EF		F	VF	EF
3423	**Five Guineas.** Conjoined busts, elephant and castle below, R. Crowned shield of arms die axis ↑↓						
1691 TERTIO	5500	15500	75000	1694/2 SEXTO	6000	17500	80000
1692 QVARTO	5500	15500	75000	1694 SEXTO	5750	16500	77500
1693 QVINTO	5750	16500	77500				

3424
1694 Two Guineas

	F	VF	EF		F	VF	EF
	£	£	£		£	£	£

3424 Two Guineas. Conjoined busts r. R. Crowned shield of arms, Lion of Nassau at centre
die axis ↑↓

l'693	2100	7000	27500	1694/3	2000	6500	25000

3425 Two Guineas. Conjoined busts, elephant and castle below, R. similar die axis ↑↓

1691	*Extremely rare*			1694/3	2100	7000	27500
1693	2250	8000	30000				

3426
1689 Guinea, later harp

3427
1689 Elephant and castle below busts

3426 Guinea. Conjoined busts r. R. Crowned shield of arms Lion of Nassau at centre die axis ↑↓

1689 Early slanting harp				1690 FT for ET obv	1050	3650	12000
with base of harp in line				1690 D/G in DEI	1050	3650	12000
with X of REX	975	3250	11000	1690 GVLIFLMVS	1050	3650	12000
1689 Later upright harp				1691	1000	3500	11500
with base of harp in line				1692	1000	3500	11500
with R of REX	975	3250	11000	1693	1000	3500	11500
1689 MVS over EL	1000	3500	11500	1694	1000	3500	11500
1690	1000	3500	11500	1694/3	1000	3500	11500

3427 Guinea. Conjoined busts elephant and castle below R. Similar die axis ↑↓

1689	975	3500	11500	1692	1100	3750	12000
1689 G of REGINA				1693	1200	4250	13500
over E	1050	3600	11750	1694	1100	3750	12000
1690	1200	4250	13500	1694/3	1150	3850	12500
1691	1050	3750	12000				

3428 Guinea. Conjoined busts elephant only below, R. Similar die axis ↑↓

1692	1100	3750	12500	1693	1200	4000	13000

3429
1689 Half-Guniea, first busts, first shield

3430
1690 Half-Guinea, second busts, second shield

	F £	VF £	EF £		F £	VF £	EF £
3429 Half-Guinea. First busts r. R. First Crowned shield of arms die axis ↑↓							
1689	675	2100	6500				
3430 Half-Guinea. Second busts r. R. Second Crowned shield of arms die axis ↑↓							
1690	650	2000	6250	1693	725	2400	7250
1691	650	2000	6250	1693/2	700	2250	7000
1692	675	2100	6500	1694	650	2000	6250
3431 Half-Guinea. Second busts elephant and castle below, R. Second shield of arms die axis ↑↓							
1691	725	2250	7000	1692	725	2250	7000
3432 Half-Guinea. Second busts elephant only below, R. Second shield of arms die axis ↑↓							
1692	825	2500	7500				

SILVER

3433
Crown

3433 Crown. Conjoined busts r. regnal year on edge in words (e.g. 1691 = TERTIO) die axis ↑↓							
1691 TERTIO	575	1850	8500	1692 QVARTO	575	1850	8500
1691 I/E in legend	650	2000	8750	1692/ℤ QVARTO	600	2250	9000
1691 TERTTIO	650	2100	9000	1692/ℤ QVINTO	575	1850	8500

The Royal Mint

Authenticity Assured

····························

Collector Services

The Royal Mint's Historic Coin Service

The Royal Mint has been striking British coins since AD 886. It's what we do. Trust us to be your source of expert advice for your next coin search and purchase, with assured authenticity.

With an extensive network of numismatic connections and in-house expert knowledge, we can source rare and special historic coins. Whether you're adding to your collection or looking for a memorable gift, our Historic Coin Finder Service can help.

If you know what you're looking for, send us the details of the coin you require and let us do the hard work sourcing it. If you are after a special coin or coins and are unsure of the exact details, or you would like some advice on the best coin to fit your requirements, get in touch with our specialist team.

Historic Coins

Authentication & Valuation

Care & Display

Secure Storage

Telephone: 0800 03 22 153
royalmint.com/historics

Follow us:

Treasure *for* Life®

Caul frosted → ← Caul not frosted

Pearls → ← No Pearls

Interior frosted

Interior not frosted

3434
1689 Halfcrown - first reverse

3435
1689 Halfcrown - second reverse

	F	VF	EF		F	VF	EF
	£	£	£		£	£	£

3434 Halfcrown. First busts, r. R. First crowned shield, 1689 PRIMO R̶. Crown with caul and interior frosted, with pearls edge inscribed die axis ↑↓ 130 350 2750

1689— 2nd L/M in GVLIELMVS 135 375 3000

1689 — 1st V/A in GVLIELMVS, only caul frosted 135 375 3000

1689 — — interior also frosted, no pearls............ 135 375 3000

1689 Caul only frosted, pearls 130 350 2750

1689 — no pearls 130 375 3000

1689 No frosting, pearls............ 130 350 2750

1689 No stops on obverse 200 575 3500

1689 FRA for FR............ 175 525 3250

3435 Halfcrown. First busts r. R. Second crowned shield die axis ↑↓

	F	VF	EF		F	VF	EF
1689 PRIMO R̶. Caul and interior frosted with pearls	120	350	2750	1689 no frosting, pearls	120	350	2750
1689 — — no pearls	130	375	3000	1689 no frosting, no pearls	120	350	2750
1689 Caul only frosted pearls	120	350	2750	1690 SECVNDO —	175	525	3250
1689 interior frosted, no pearls	130	350	2750	1690 — GRETIA error with second V of GVLIELMVS struck over S	325	850	4000
1689 Caul only frosted, no pearls	130	375	3000	1690 TERTIO	185	525	3250

3436

Halfcrown, second busts, third reverse

	F	VF	EF		F	VF	EF
	£	£	£		£	£	£

3436 Halfcrown. Second busts r. R. Crowned cruciform shields, WM monogram in angles
    die axis ↑↓

	F	VF	EF		F	VF	EF
1691 TERTIO	150	550	3500	1692 QVINTO	275	750	3750
1692 QVARTO	150	550	3500	1693 QVINTO	150	475	3000
1692 R/G in REGINA also				1693 3/inverted 3	160	550	3250
showing H/B in HI....	175	575	3650	1693 inverted 3	325	900	4000

3437 - Shilling   3438 - Sixpence

3437 Shilling. Conjoined busts r. R. Crowned cruciform shields, WM monogram in angles die axis ↑↓

1692	200	625	2850	1693 9/0......................	225	675	3000
1692 inverted 1	225	675	3000	1693	200	625	2850
1692 RE/ET on R	225	675	3000				
1692 A of GRATIA							
over T and T over I......	250	750	3250				

3438 Sixpence. Conjoined busts r. R. Crowned cruciform shields, WM monogram in angles die axis ↑↓

1693	135	425	1250	1694	145	475	1400
1693 inverted 3............	225	575	1650				

3439 - Groat, first busts

3439 Fourpence. First busts, r. no tie to wreath. R. Crowned 4 die axis ↑↓

1689 GV below bust......	15	30	80	1690	20	50	110
1689 G below bust..........	15	30	80	1690 6 over 5	20	55	120
1689 stop befor G	15	30	80	1691	20	45	130
1689 berries in wreath ...	15	30	80	1691/0	20	40	120
1689 GVLEELMVS	65	200	–	1694	20	60	160
1689 I over first E in GVLEELMVS							
corrected die for above..	65	200	–				

3440
Groat, Second busts

	F	VF	EF			F	VF	EF
	£	£	£			£	£	£

3440 Fourpence. Second busts r. tie to wreath. R. Crowned 4 die axis ↑↓

	F	VF	EF			F	VF	EF
1692	30	90	180	1693/2		35	100	280
1692/1	25	65	165	1694		30	95	200
1692 MAR•IA		*Extremely rare*		1694 small lettering		30	95	200
1693	35	100	280					

3441 Threepence. First busts, r. no tie to wreath. R. Crowned 3 die axis ↑↓

	F	VF	EF			F	VF	EF
1689	15	30	75	1690 6 over 5		20	50	105
1689 No stops on rev.	20	40	110	1690 Large lettering		20	50	105
1689 LMV over MVS	20	40	110	1690 9 over 6		20	50	105
1689 Hyphen stops on rev.	20	40	100	1691		100	220	450
1690	20	50	105					

3442 Threepence. Second busts, r. tie to wreath R. Crowned 3 die axis ↑↓

	F	VF	EF			F	VF	EF
1691	40	130	220	1693 GV below bust	20	55	140
1692 G below bust	25	65	140	1694 G below bust	20	55	140
1692 GV below bust	25	65	140	1694 — MARIA error	24	60	170
1692 GVL below bust	25	65	140	1694 GV below bust	20	55	140
1693 G below bust	20	55	140	1694 GVL below bust	20	55	140
1693/2 G below bust	20	55	140				

3443 Twopence. Conjoined busts r. R. Crowned 2 die axis ↑↓

	F	VF	EF			F	VF	EF
1689	18	40	90	1694/3	18	45	120
1691	18	45	110	1694/3 no stop after DG	18	45	120
1692	20	45	120	1694 MARLA error	35	65	275
1693	15	42	115	1694 HI for HIB	20	45	120
1693/2	18	42	115	1694 GVLI below bust	20	45	120
1693 GV below bust	18	42	115	1694 GVL below bust	20	45	120
1694	20	45	120				

3444 - Penny   3445 - Legend intruded

3444 Penny. Legend continuous over busts, R. Crowned 1 die axis ↑↓

	F	VF	EF			F	VF	EF
1689	225	425	800	1689 MARIA	250	450	850
1689 GVIELMVS error	250	525	1000				

3445 Penny. Legend broken by busts, R. Crowned 1 die axis ↑↓

	F	VF	EF			F	VF	EF
1690	28	55	125	1694 date spread	22	50	120
1691/0	35	60	135	1694 no stops on obv.	22	55	120
1692	45	85	200	1694 HI for HIB	28	60	190
1692/1	35	80	180	1694 — 9/6	25	55	135
1693	35	60	130				

3446 - Maundy Set

	F	VF	EF		F	VF	EF
	£	£	£		£	£	£

3446 Maundy Set. The four denominations. Uniform dates

	F	VF	EF		F	VF	EF
1689	375	750	1500	1693	180	475	1100
1691	175	425	1000	1694	145	375	950
1692	160	400	975				

TIN AND COPPER

3447
Tin Halfpenny first busts

	Fair	F	VF	EF
	£	£	£	£

Prices for tin coinage based on corrosion free examples, and in the top grades with some lustre

3447 Tin Halfpenny. Small dr. busts r.; date on edge ↑↓ 1689 925   1800   —   —

— — — obv. with star stops 1689 .... *Extremely rare*

3448
Tin Halfpenny cuirassed busts

3448 Tin Halfpenny. — Large cuir. busts r.; R. Britannia seated L. date only on edge, die axis ↑↓

1690 various edge varieties 80   190   800   3250

3449 Tin Halfpenny. Similar date in ex. and on edge die axis ↑↓

1691 various edge varieties 70   175   700   2750

1691 in ex. 1692 on edge... *Extremely rare*

1692 70   175   700   2750

3450 Tin Farthing. Small dr. busts r. R. Britannia seated l. die axis ↑↓

1689 275   700   2250   —

1689, in ex. 1690 on edge .... *Extremely rare*

3451
Tin Farthing

	Fair	F £	VF £	EF £
3451 Tin **Farthing.** Large cuir. busts r. R. Britannia seated l.die axis ↑↓				
1690, in ex. 1689 on edge			*Extremely rare*	
1690 various edge varieties 55		175	700	3000
1691 various edge varieties 55		175	700	3000
1692 70		190	750	3000

3452
1694 Halfpenny

3452 Copper **Halfpenny,** Conjoined busts r. R. Britannia die axis ↑↓			
1694	75	275	1150
1694 GVLIEMVS error	200	600	–
1694 MVRIA error	225	650	–
1694 MΛRIΛ error	150	525	–
1694 BRITΛNNI/Λ..	175	550	–
1694 no rev. stop	150	525	–
1694 GVLEELMVS..	250	625	–

3453
1694 Farthing

3453 Copper **Farthing,** Conjoined busts r. R. Britannia die axis ↑↓			
1694	65	275	1000
1694 MΛRIΛ error..	175	500	–
1694 no stop after MΛRIΛ..	100	415	–
1694 — BRITΛNNIΛ	125	415	–
1694 no stop on rev.	100	350	–
1694 no stop on obv.	100	350	–
1694 GVLIELMS, BRITΛNNIΛ errors	225	525	–
1694 BRITΛNNIΛ	150	475	–
1694 Broad heavier flan 25.5mm......................................	200	500	–

William of Orange was born on 4th November 1650. He married Mary Stuart under Charles II's foreign policy and was invited to England by Parliament, where he proceeded to supress the Jacobites. The Bank of England was founded during this reign, and William ruled alone and without issue after Mary's death until his own demise on 8th March 1702 following a serious fall from his horse.

In 1696 a great re-coinage was undertaken to replace the hammered silver that made up most of the coinage in circulation, much of it being clipped and badly worn. Branch mints were set up at Bristol, Chester, Exeter, Norwich and York to help with the re-coinage. For a short time before they were finally demonetized, unclipped hammered coins were allowed to circulate freely provided they were officially pierced in the centre. Silver coins with roses between the coats of arms were made from silver obtained from the West of England mines. The elephant and castle provenance mark continues on some guineas and half-guineas.

Engravers and designers: Samuel Bull (d.c.1720), John Croker (1670-1740), Henry Harris (d.1704), John Roettier (1663-1698).

GOLD

3454
1699 Five Guineas, first bust

	F	VF	EF		F	VF	EF
	£	£	£		£	£	£

3454 Five Guineas. First laur. bust r. regnal year on edge in words (e.g. 1699 = UNDECIMO) ↑↓

1699 UNDECIMO..	5500	16000	80000	1700 DVODECIMO......	5500	16000	80000

3455
Elephant and castle below first bust

3455 Five Guineas. First bust elephant and castle below, 1699 UNDECIMO...... 6250 17500 90000

3456
1701 Five Guineas 'Fine Work'

	F	VF	EF		F	VF	EF
	£	£	£		£	£	£

3456 Five Guineas. Second laur. bust r. ('fine work'), R. Crowned cruciform shields Plain or ornamental sceptres DECIMO TERTIO die axis ↑↓ 1701*......................................4750 15000 75000

3457
'Fine work' Two Guineas

3457 Two Guineas. ('fine work'), Laur. bust r. similar die axis ↑↓ 1701 2500   7000   25000

3458
1695 Guinea, first bust

3458 Guinea. First laur. bust r. R. Crowned cruciform shields, sceptres in angles die axis ↑↓
1695 large and small   1696 800   3750   11000
lis in French arms.....775   3250   10000   1697 800   3750   11000

3459 Guinea. First bust elephant and castle below R. Similar die axis ↑↓
1695 1500   6000   17500   1696 ....*Extremely rare*

* Beware of low grade counterfeits

3460
Guinea, second bust

3463
Narrow crowns

	F £	VF £	EF £		F £	VF £	EF £

3460 Guinea. Second laur. bust r. R. Similar with human-headed harp in Irish arms. die axis ↑↓

1697 800		3500	10500	1700 large or small lions			
1698 775		3000	9500	in arms 775		3000	9500
1699 800		3250	10500				

3461 Guinea. Second bust elephant and castle below. R. Similar die axis ↑↓

1697 1500		6000	–	1699		*Extremely rare*	
1698 1350		5500	16000	1700 1450		5750	–

3462 Guinea. Second laur. bust. r. R. Similar with Human headed harp. Large lettering and
large date, die axis ↑↓ 1698 .... 775 3250 10500

3463 Guinea. — R. Narrow crowns, plain or ornamented sceptres, axis ↑↓ 1701 ....775 3000 9750

3464 Guinea. Second bust elephant and castle below, die axis ↑↓ 1701 .... *Extremely rare*

3465 Guinea. Third laur. bust r. ('fine work'), R. Similar die axis ↑↓ 1701 ...... 1450 5750 17500

3466
1695 Half-Guinea, early harp

3468
Later harp

3466 Half-Guinea. Laur. bust r. R. With early harp, die axis ↑↓ 1695 .... 450 1250 4750

3467 Half-Guinea. Laur. bust elephant and castle below. R. With early harp, die axis ↑↓

1695 725		2250	7000	1696 600		1650	5750

3468 Half-Guinea. Laur. bust r. R. Crowned cruciform shields, sceptres in angles with late harp, die axis ↑↓

1697 700		2000	6750	1700 500		1350	5000
1698 450		1250	4750	1701 450		1250	4750
1699		*Extremely rare*					

3469 Half-Guinea. Laur. bust elephant and castle below, die axis ↑↓ 1698 .... 675 1950 6500

SILVER

First harp

3470
Crown - first bust - round collar

	F £	VF £	EF £		F £	VF £	EF £

3470 Crown. First dr. bust, r. with curved breast plate or drapery. R.First harp, regnal year on edge in words (e.g. 1696 = OCTAVO) ↑↓

1695 SEPTIMO..........110	400	3250		1696 G/D IN GRA 210	600	3250
1695 SEPTIMO cinquefoils				1696 — no stops........ 200	575	3100
for crosses on edge.... 200	575	—		1696/5.........................200	575	3100
1695 OCTAVO...........110	400	3000		1696 GEI for DEI.......350	1250	—
1695 TVTA·EN error 175	550	—		1696 — no stops........ 375	1350	—
1695 plain edge proof *FDC* £17500				1696 plain edge proof *FDC* £18000		
1696 OCTAVO.......... 100	350	2750				
1696 No stops on						
obverse...............225	625	3500				

Second harp

3471
1696 Crown, second bust - hair across breast

3471 Crown. Second dr. bust r. with two locks of hair across the bust and no hair below the truncation. R. Second harp (hair across breast), 1696 (two varieties) die axis ↑↓
OCTAVO .... *Each unique*

3472
Third bust, straight breastplate

	F	VF	EF
	£	£	£

3472 **Crown**. Third dr. bust, r. Easily distinguished by the straight breast plate or drapery. ℞. First harp, die axis ↑↓ 1696 OCTAVO..100 350 3000
1696 TRICESIMO .... *Extremely rare*
1696 plain edge proof *FDC* £15000

3473 **Crown.** Similar, ℞. Second harp, die axis ↑↓ 1697 NONO 2750 10000 47500

Third harp

3474
1700 Crown, third bust variety

3474 **Crown.** Third bust variety r. of same general style but dies have been recut and hair varied a little. Tie is slightly longer and thinner than normal third bust. ℞. Third harp with scroll front and back, ↑↓ 1700 DVODECIMO 110 400 3250
1700 DECIMO. TERTIO... 135 450 3500

3475 **Halfcrown.** First bust r. ℞. Small shields, 1696 die axis ↑↓ OCTAVO 80 275 2250
— — 1696 DEC∀S error 90 325 2500

3476 **Halfcrown.** B (*Bristol*) below First bust, die axis ↑↓ 1696 OCTAVO....... 90 300 2400
— 1696 B Similar proof *FDC* £16500

3477
Chester Mint

3478
Exeter Mint

3477 **Halfcrown.** C (*Chester*) below first bust, die axis ↑↓ 1696 OCTAVO 200 625 3000
3478 **Halfcrown.** E (*Exeter*) below first bust, die axis ↑↓ 1696 OCTAVO 200 625 3000

	F	VF	EF
	£	£	£
3479 Halfcrown. N (*Norwich*) below first bust, die axis ↑↓ 1696 OCTAVO	175	525	2500
3480 Halfcrown. y (*York*) below first bust, die axis ↑↓ 1696 OCTAVO	175	525	2500

3480
1696 Halfcrown - York Mint

3481
1696 Halfcrown, large shield
reverse with early harp

		F	VF	EF
3481	**Halfcrown.** First bust r. ℞. Large shield, early harp, die axis ↑↓ 1696 OCTAVO	80	275	2000
	1696 Proof plain edge *FDC*	—	—	15000
3482	**Halfcrown.** — B (*Bristol*) below bust, die axis ↑↓ 1696 OCTAVO	90	325	2250
3483	**Halfcrown.** — C (*Chester*) below bust, die axis ↑↓ 1696 OCTAVO	200	625	3000
3484	**Halfcrown.** — E (*Exeter*) below bust, die axis ↑↓ 1696 OCTAVO	150	525	2500
3485	**Halfcrown.** — N (*Norwich*) below bust, die axis ↑↓ 1696 OCTAVO	350	1200	—
3486	**Halfcrown.** — y (*York*) below bust, die axis ↑↓ 1696 OCTAVO	110	350	2250
	— — die axis ↑↓ 1696 y (*York*), Scots Arms at date	1000	—	—
	— die axis ↑↓ y over E 1696	250	850	—

3487
Large shields, ordinary harp

	F	VF	EF		F	VF	EF
	£	£	£		£	£	£
3487 Halfcrown. First bust r. ℞. Large shields, ordinary harp die axis ↑↓							
1696 OCTAVO	175	575	2750	1697 G/A in MAG	350	—	—
1697 NONO	75	250	1750	1697/6 —	150	500	2500
1697 — GRR for GRA	400	—	—	1697 Proof plain edge *FDC* £13500			
3488 Halfcrown. — B (*Bristol*) below first bust, die axis ↑↓ 1697 NONO	90	325	2250				
1697 proof on thick flan *FDC*				*Extremely rare*			
1697 — no stops on reverse	135	525	2500				

3489
Chester Mint Halfcrown, large shields

	F	VF	EF		F	VF	EF
	£	£	£		£	£	£

3489 Halfcrown. — C *(Chester)* below first bust, similar die axis ↑↓

1696 OCTAVO 200	625	3000	1697 NONO 135	525	2500

3490
Exeter Mint Halfcrown, large shields

3490 Halfcrown. — E *(Exeter)* below first bust, similar die axis ↑↓

1696 OCTAVO 150	500	2500	1697 NONO 80	275	2000
1696 NONO 450	—	—	1697 E over C or B		
1697 OCTAVO 475	—	—	under bust 200	800	—

3491
Norwich Mint Halfcrown, large shields

3491 Halfcrown. — N *(Norwich)* below first bust, similar die axis ↑↓

1696 OCTAVO 375	1350	—	1697 NONO 125	500	2500
1697 OCTAVO 250	950	—	1697 — Scots Arms at date £1000		

3492 Halfcrown. — — y *(York)* below first bust, similar die axis ↑↓

1697 NONO 85	275	2000	1697 OCTAVO 350	—	—

3493 Halfcrown. Second dr. bust r. (hair across breast), die axis ↑↓ 1696 OCTAVO *Unique*

3494

1700 Halfcrown, modified large shields

	F £	VF £	EF £		F £	VF £	EF £

3494 Halfcrown. First dr. bust R. Modified large shields die axis ↑↓

1698 OCTAVO	400	1300	—	1699 — Lion of			
1698 DECIMO	70	225	1350	Nassau inverted	525	1500	—
1698/7 —	250	800	—	1700 DVODECIMO	80	250	1500
1698 UNDECIMO	350	1000	—	1700 D. TERTIO	90	275	1600
1699 UNDECIMO	150	525	2500	1700 — DECⱯS error	90	275	1600
1699 — Inverted A's for				1701 D. TERTIO	80	250	1750
V's on edge	175	600	—	1701 — no stops			
1699 — Scots Arms at				on reverse	120	350	2250
date	900	—	—				

3495

1701 Halfcrown, elephant and castle below bust

3495 Halfcrown. – elephant and castle below bust, die axis ↑↓

1701 D. TERTIO 3250   9500   —

3496

1701 Halfcrown, plumes on reverse

3496 Halfcrown. – R. Plumes in angles, die axis ↑↓ 1701 D. TERTIO 325   1250   5750

SHILLINGS

First bust
This bust is distinctive in having
the hair turned outwards above
and below the crown of the head

Third bust
This is rather like the first bust
but the hair at the back all turns
downwards and inwards

Third bust variety,
tie thicker, more hair
below bust, more
aquiline profile and
coarser features

3498
Bristol Mint

3499
1696 Chester Mint Shilling

	F £	VF £	EF £		F £	VF £	EF £
3497 Shilling. First dr. bust r. R. Crowned cruciform shields edge milled die axis ↑↓							
1695 35	100	600		1696 GVLELMVS 575	—	—
1695 E of ET over H 50	150	750		1696 2nd L over M........125	400	—
1696 30	85	525		1696-1669 error date 800	2250	—
1696/5 and GVLICLMVS 45	135	625		1697 30	85	525
1696 no stops on reverse..100	350	—		1697 E/A in DEI............135	475	—
1696 MAB for MAG				1697 GRI for GRA error . 225	650	2500
error......................600	—	—		1697 Arms of Scot/Ireland		
1696 GVLIEMVS				transposed 650	—	—
error......................575	—	—		1697 Irish Arms at date .750	—	—
1696 GVLIELMⱯS				1697 no stops on reverse . 110	375	—
error.........................85	300	—		1697 GVLELMVS error. 525	—	—
1696 GⱯLIELMVS				1697 GVLIELMⱯS error.100	350	—
error......................110	375	—		1697 L/M in legend.......125	400	—

3498 Shilling. Similar B *(Bristol)* below bust die axis ↑↓

1696 65	225	950		1696 small x in REX................. *Scarce variety*
1696 GⱯLIELMVS error and				1697 65	225	950
large G in MAG 70	240	1000				

3499 Shilling. Similar C *(Chester)* below bust die axis ↑↓

1696 90	275	1250		1696 thick flan proof *FDC*... *Extremely rare*
1696 R/V in GRA..........110	325	1350		1697...................................85	250	1250

3500

	F	VF	EF		F	VF	EF
	£	£	£		£	£	£

3500 Shilling. Similar E (*Exeter*) below bust die axis ↑↓

1696 80   250   1100   1697 95   300   1200

1697 E over N 125   350   1350

3501 Shilling. Similar N (*Norwich*) below bust die axis ↑↓

1696 110   325   1250   1697 110   325   1250

1697 no stops on obv......125   375   1350

3502 Shilling. Similar y (*York*) below bust die axis ↑↓

1696 75   225   950   1697 Arms of France/Ireland

Also known with no stop after GVLIELMVS   transposed...........1000   —   —

1696 80   250   975   1697 Arms of Scotland/Ireland

1697 75   225   950   transposed...........1000   —   —

3503 Shilling. Similar Y (*York*) below bust die axis ↑↓

1696 100   325   1200   1697 135   500   —

1697 Y over Λ...............250   900   —

3504 Shilling. Second dr. bust r. (hair across breast), similar die axis ↑↓ 1696   *Unique*

3505 - Third bust   3513 - Chester Mint, Third bust variety

3505 Shilling. Third dr. bust r., similar die axis ↑↓ 1697.....................................40   125   650

3506 Shilling. Similar B (*Bristol*) below bust, die axis ↑↓ 1697 125   375   1350

3507 Shilling. Similar C (*Chester*) below bust die axis ↑↓

1696 125   375   1350   1697 no stops on reverse. 110   325   1350

1697 small or large   1697 Arms of Scotland

lettering 80   250   1000   at date 1000   —   —

1697 FR.A error 110   325   1350

3508 Shilling. Similar E (*Exeter*) below bust, die axis ↑↓

1696............................1750   —   —   1697 110   325   1200

3509 Shilling. Similar N (*Norwich*) below bust, die axis ↑↓ 1697....................125   350   1350

3510 Shilling. Similar y (*York*) below bust die axis ↑↓

1696 750   —   —   1697 85   275   1000

3511 Shilling. Third bust variety r. similar die axis ↑↓

1697 GVLIELMVS ....   1697 GVLIELMVS error......80   275   —

error.........................80   275   —   1698 90   300   1100

1697 40   125   650   1698 plain edge proof *FDC* £7500

	F	VF	EF		F	VF	EF
	£	£	£		£	£	£

3512 Shilling. Similar B (*Bristol*) below bust, die axis ↑↓ 1697 .... 125 | 350 | 1350
3513 Shilling. Similar C (*Chester*) below bust, die axis ↑↓ 1697.............. 135 | 450 | 1600
— — 1697 thick flan .... *Extremely rare*
3514 Shilling. Similar R. Plumes in angles, die axis ↑↓ 1698 .... 250 | 750 | 2500

Third bust   Fourth bust   Fifth bust

3515   3516
Fourth bust   Fifth bust

3515 Shilling Fourth dr. bust ('flaming hair') r. similar die axis ↑↓

1698 200	675	2750	1699 175	625	2500

1698 No stops on reverse 225   700   2850   1699 plain edge proof *FDC* £9000
1698 plain edge proof *FDC* £9000

3516 Shilling. Fifth dr. bust (hair high) r. similar die axis ↑↓

1699 125   375   1500   1700 no stop after DEI.... 50   150   650
1699 Plain edge proof .... *Extremely rare*   1700 Tall O's no stops
1700 35   110   525   on reverse.............. 45   140   600
1700 no stops on rev, also   1701 small or large lions 100   325   1250
    with larger O's....... 45 140   600   1701 DEI/GRA 300   —   —
1700 Circular small
    O's in date 35   110   525

3517
1701 Shilling, plumes on reverse

3517 Shilling. Similar R. Plumes in angles die axis ↑↓

1699 175   575   2000   1701 175   575   2000

3518
1699 Shilling, roses on reverse

3520
First bust Sixpence, French arms at date

	F	VF	EF		F	VF	EF
	£	£	£		£	£	£
3518	**Shilling.** Similar R. Roses in angles, die axis ↑↓ 1699 225				225	750	2250
3519	**Shilling.** Similar plume below bust, die axis ↑↓ 1700 3000				3000	10500	—

SIXPENCES

First bust   Third bust   Early harp.   Later harp,
large crown.   small crown.

3520   **Sixpence.** First dr. bust r. R. Crowned cruciform shields, large crowns, edge milled, early
harp, die axis ↑↓

1695 30	80	275	1696 Scots Arms		
1696 25	65	250	at date............375	—	—
1696 Heavy flan.......850	—	—	1696/5 35	100	425
1696 French Arms			1696 no stops on		
at date...............525	—	—	obverse..............45	120	475
1696 GVLIELMⱯS....35	100	425	1696 DFI for DEI.....100	—	—

3521   **Sixpence.** Similar B *(Bristol)* below bust, die axis ↑↓ 1696 30   90   375

   — — 1696 B over E 45   125   450

3522   **Sixpence.** Similar C *(Chester)* below bust, die axis ↑↓ 1696...............30   90   375

3523

3525
1696 York Mint sixpence,
early harp, first bust

3523   **Sixpence.** Similar E *(Exeter)* below bust, die axis ↑↓ 1696..................45   125   450

3524   **Sixpence.** Similar N *(Norwich)* below bust, die axis ↑↓ 1696..............45   125   450

3525   **Sixpence.** Similar y *(York)* below bust, die axis ↑↓ 1696 30   85   350

	F	VF	EF		F	VF	EF
	£	£	£		£	£	£

3526 Sixpence. Similar Y *(York)* below bust, die axis ↑↓ 1696............................30 | 90 | 375
— — — 1696 no stops on obverse...45 | 125 | 450

3527 Sixpence. Similar R. Later harp, large crowns, die axis ↑↓ 1696.................50 | 135 | 475
— — — 1696 no stops on obverse...90 | 225 | —

3528 Sixpence. — — — B *(Bristol)* below bust, similar die axis ↑↓
1696 ....70 | 175 | 575 | 1697 ....45 | 125 | 450
1696 no stops on
obv. ....90 | 225 | 650

3529 Sixpence. — — — C *(Chester)* below bust, similar die axis ↑↓ 1697 ....100 | 250 | 700

3530 Sixpence. — — — E *(Exeter)* below bust, similar die axis ↑↓ 1697 ....50 | 135 | 475

3531 Sixpence. — — R. small crowns, similar die axis ↑↓
1696 ....50 | 135 | 475 | 1697 Arms of France/Ireland
1697 ....30 | 80 | 325 | transposed ....375 | — | —
1697 GVLIELMΛS ....50 | 135 | —

3532

Bristol Mint Sixpence, small crowns

3532 Sixpence. — — — B *(Bristol)* below bust, similar die axis ↑↓
1696 ....65 | 150 | 525 | 1697 ....30 | 80 | 325
1696 no stops on O .....90 | 225 | 650 | 1697 B over E ....45 | 100 | 375

3533 Sixpence. — — — C *(Chester)* below bust, similar die axis ↑↓
1696 ....90 | 225 | 625 | 1697 Irish shield
1697 ....40 | 95 | 325 | at date......................325 | 900 | —
| | | | 1697 Plain edge ....150 | 350 | 1000

3534 Sixpence. — — — E *(Exeter)* below bust, similar die axis ↑↓
1697 ....50 | 125 | 450 | 1697 E over B ....90 | 225 | 625

3535 Sixpence. — — — N *(Norwich)* below bust, similar die axis ↑↓
1696 ....80 | 200 | 600 | 1697 ....45 | 110 | 375
1697 GVLIEMVS ..150 | 500 | —

3536 Sixpence. — — — y *(York)* below bust, similar die axis ↑↓
1697 ....50 | 125 | 450 | 1697 Irish shield at date .....250 | 700 | —

3537
Second bust Sixpence

3538
Sixpence, third bust,
later harp, large crowns

	F	VF	EF		F	VF	EF
	£	£	£		£	£	£

3537 Sixpence. Second dr. bust r. R. Similar die axis ↑↓

1696	275	800	2250	1697 GVLIEMVS	275	800	2250
1696 hair across breast				1696 GVLELMVS	325	900	2500
(as 3471) Three known examples				1697	175	650	2000
1697 GVLIELMVS	200	725	2100	1697 GR/DE in GRA	200	675	2250
1697 G/I in GRA	175	650	2000				

3537A Sixpence. Third dr. bust, r. early harp, large crowns. E *(Exeter)* below
bust, 1696 .... 525 1750 —

3537B Sixpence. — — — Y *(York)* below bust, similar die axis ↑↓ 1696 ..... 325 1000 —

3538 Sixpence. Third dr. bust, r., R. Later harp, large crowns, similar die axis ↑↓

1697 GVLIEIMVS	30	85	325	1699	90	225	650
1697	25	75	300	1700	35	90	325
1697 GVLIELMVS	35	90	350	1701	70	175	575
1698	40	100	375				

3539 Sixpence. — — B *(Bristol)* below bust, similar die axis ↑↓

1697	50	135	475	1697 IRA for FRA	90	225	—

3540
Chester Mint Sixpence, third bust

3540 Sixpence. — — C *(Chester)* below bust, similar die axis ↑↓ 1697 .... 90 225 625
3541 Sixpence. — — E *(Exeter)* below bust, similar die axis ↑↓ 1697 .... 100 250 675
3542 Sixpence. Third dr. bust, r. R. Small crowns, similar die axis ↑↓

1697	35	90	350	1697 G/D in GRA	90	225	650
1697 D/F in DEI	100	250	675				

3543 Sixpence. — — C *(Chester)* below bust, similar die axis ↑↓ 1697 .... 70 175 575
3544 Sixpence. — — E *(Exeter)* below bust, similar die axis ↑↓ 1697 .... 70 175 575

3545
York Mint Sixpence - Y provenance mark

3547
Sixpence, roses on reverse

	F	VF	EF		F	VF	EF
	£	£	£		£	£	£

3545 Sixpence.— — Y *(York)* below bust, similar die axis ↑↓ 1697............. 50   135   475
3546 Sixpence.— — R. Plumes in angles, similar die axis ↑↓
1698 100   275   750   1699 100   275   750
3547 Sixpence.— R. Roses in angles, similar die axis ↑↓
1699 110   300   825   1699 GⱯLIELMVS . 125   350   —

3548
1700 Sixpence, plume below bust

3549
1699 Groat or Fourpence

3548 Sixpence.— plume below bust, R. Similar die axis ↑↓ 1700........... 2250   —   —
3549 Fourpence. Laur. and dr. bust r. R. 4 Crowned die axis ↑↓
1697 ....   *Unique*   1700 25   50   165
1698 28   60   190   1701 30   65   190
1699 25   50   145   1702 20   45   90
3550 Threepence. Laur. and dr. bust r. R. 3 Crowned die axis ↑↓
1698 20   40   110   1701 GBA for GRA ... 24   45   150
1699 25   50   140   1701 small lettering ... 20   40   110
1700 22   45   130   1701 large lettering 20   40   110
3551 Twopence. Laur. and dr. bust r. R. Crown to edge of coin, large figure 2 die axis ↑↓
1698 25   50   135
3551A Twopence. Laur. and dr. bust r. R Crown within inner circle of legend, smaller figure 2, die axis ↑↓
1698 25   45   125   1700 18   30   95
1699 18   30   95   1701 18   30   95
3552 Penny. Laur. and dr. bust r. R. 1 Crowned die axis ↑↓
1698 25   45   135   1699 40   80   225
1698 IRA for FRA error 25   45   125   1700 35   70   165
1698 HI.BREX error... 25   45   125   1701 25   45   120

3553 - 1701 Maundy Set

	F £	VF £	EF £		F £	VF £	EF £
3553 Maundy Set. The four denominations. Uniform dates							
1698	125	300	775	1700	165	375	825
1699	175	400	925	1701	125	300	750

COPPER

3554 - Halfpenny   3556

3554 Halfpenny. First issue. Laur. and cuir. bust r. R. Britannia with r. hand raised die axis ↑↓

1695	45	210	1150	1697	35	175	950
1695 BRITANNIΛ error	200	—	—	1697 all stops omitted	225	—	—
1695 no stop on rev.	60	275	—	1697 I/E in TERTIVS	225	—	—
1695 no stops on obv.	60	275	—	1697 GVLILMVS,			
1696	35	175	1000	no rev. stop	300	—	—
1696 GVLIEMVS,				1697 no stop			
no rev. stop	300	—	—	after TERTIVS	50	275	—
1696 TERTVS error	275	—	—	1698	45	210	1150

3555 Halfpenny. Second issue. Laur. and cuir. bust r. R. Britannia, date in legend die axis ↑↓

1698 Stop after date	35	200	1050	1699 GVLIEMVS error	225	—	—
1699 no stop after date	30	165	1000	1699 BRITAN IA error	225	—	—
1699 BRITANNIΛ	225	—	—				

3556 Halfpenny. Third issue. Laur. and cuir. bust r. R. Britannia, date in exergue, die axis ↑↓

1699	35	175	950	1700 BRITANNIΛ error	40	175	950
1699 stop after date	225	—	—	1700 BRTTANNIA error	50	180	1000
1699 BRITANNIΛ error	100	380	—	1700 — no stop after	45	195	1000
1699 GVILELMVS error	275	—	—	1700 GVLIELMS	100	350	—
1699 TERTVS error	275	—	—	1700 GVLIEEMVS	65	250	1200
1699 — no rev. stop	150	—	—	1700 GVLIEEMVS	65	250	1200
1699 no stops on obv.	85	380	—	1700 TER TIVS	45	195	1000
1699 no stop after				1700 I/V in TERTIVS	225	—	—
GVLIELMVS	85	325	—	1701	40	175	950
1700	35	175	950	1701 BRITANNIΛ	50	225	1050
1700 no stops on obv.	100	350	—	1701 — no stops on obv.	225	—	—
1700 no stop after				1701 — inverted A's			
GVLIELMVS	100	350	—	for V's	60	250	1050

3557
1696 Farthing date in exergue

	F	VF	EF		F	VF	EF
	£	£	£		£	£	£

3557   Farthing. First issue Laur. and cuir. bust r. R. Britannia l. die axis ↑↓

	F	VF	EF		F	VF	EF
1695 40	250	950	1698 200	625	—
1695 GVLIELMV error . 200	—	—	1698 B/G on rev. 325	—	—
1696 35	210	900	1699 35	240	900
1697 30	175	825	1699 GVLILEMVS• 175	450	—
1697 GVLIELMS error 250	—	—	1700 30	155	775
1697 TERTIV error 250	—	—	1700 RRITANNIA........ 225	—	—

3558
1699 Farthing date in legend

3558   Farthing. Second issue. Laur. and cuir. bust r. R. Britannia date at end of legend die axis ↑↓

	F	VF	EF		F	VF	EF
1698 Stop after date 45	275	1000	1699 — No stop before or after *Extremely rare*		
1699 no stop after date.... 50	300	1050	1699 BRITANNIA........ 225	—	—
1699 no stop after			1699 BRITANNIA........ 225	—	—
GVLIELMVS 125	—	—			

Anne, the second daughter of James II, was born on 6th February 1665 and as a protestant succeeded to the throne on William III's death. Anne married Prince George of Denmark and produced 17 children, sadly none surviving to succeed to the throne. Anne died on 1st August 1714.

The Act of Union of 1707, which effected the unification of the ancient kingdoms of England and Scotland into a single realm, resulted in a change in the royal arms—on the Post-Union coinage the English lions and Scottish lion are emblazoned per pale on the top and bottom shields. After the Union the rose in the centre of the reverse of the gold coins is replaced by the Garter star.

Following a successful Anglo-Dutch expedition against Spain, bullion seized in Vigo Bay was sent to be minted into coin, and the coins made from this metal had the word VIGO placed below the Queen's bust. The elephant and castle provenance mark continues on some guineas in the Post-Union period.

Engravers and designers: Samuel Bull (d.c1720), Joseph Cave (d.c1760), James Clerk, John Croker (1670-1741), Godfrey Kneller (1646-1723)

GOLD

PRE-UNION WITH SCOTLAND 1702-07

3560
1705 Pre-Union Five Guineas

The shields on the reverse are Pre-Union type.

	F	VF	EF		F	VF	EF
	£	£	£		£	£	£

3560 Five Guineas. Dr. bust l, regnal year on edge in words (e.g. 1705 = QVARTO) die axis ↑↓

1705 QVARTO 7500	25000	110000	1706 QVINTO 7000	22500	100000

3561 Five Guineas. Similar VIGO below bust, die axis ↑↓ 1703 (Three varieties)

SECVNDO 50000 135000 400000

3562	3563
1705 Pre-Union Guinea	1703 VIGO Guinea

3562 Guinea. Dr. bust l. R. Crowned cruciform shields sceptres in angles die axis ↑↓

1702 1350	6000	17500	1706 1400	6250	17500
1702 plain edge proof... —	—	25000	1707 1400	6250	17500
1705 1500	6500	18500			

3563 Guinea. Similar with VIGO below bust, die axis ↑↓ 1703 .... 17500 50000 125000

3564
Pre-Union Half-Guinea

3565
VIGO Half-Guinea

	F	VF	EF		F	VF	EF
	£	£	£		£	£	£

3564 Half-Guinea. Dr bust l. R. Crowned cruciform shields sceptres in angles die axis ↑↓

1702 1100   3500   10500   1705 1000   3250   10000

3565 Half-Guinea. Similar with VIGO below bust, 1703 7500   22500   60000

POST UNION WITH SCOTLAND 1707-14

3566
1706 Post-Union Five Guineas

The shields on the reverse are changed to Post-Union type die axis ↑↓

3566 Five Guineas. Dr. bust l., regnal year on edge in words 1706 QVINTO 5000   15000   75000

3567
1709 - Narrow shields

3568
1711 - Broad shields

3567 Five Guineas. Similar R. Narrower shields, tall narrow crowns, larger rev. lettering, die axis ↑↓

1709 OCTAVO 5500   16000   80000

3568 Five Guineas. New bust l. R. Broader shields edge inscribed die axis ↑↓

1711 DECIMO........ 5500   16000   80000   1714/3 D. TERTIO....... 6250   18500   87500

1713 DVODECIMO 6000   17500   85000   1714 D. TERTIO.......... 6000   17500   85000

3569 - 1713 Two Guineas

	F £	VF £	EF £		F £	VF £	EF £

3569 Two Guineas. Dr. bust l.R. Crowned cruciform shields sceptres in angles edge milled die axis ↑↓

1709	1850	5750	22000	1713	1750	5500	21000
1711	1750	5500	21000	1714/3	2000	6000	22500

3570 Guinea. First dr. bust l. R. Crowned cruciform shields sceptres in angles edge milled die axis↑↓

1707	800	3250	12500	1708	800	3250	12500

3571	3574
1708 Guinea, first bust, elephant and castle below	1713 Guinea, third bust

3571 Guinea. First dr. bust l. elephant and castle below, R. Similar die axis ↑↓

1707	1450	6000	17500	1708		*Extremely rare*	

3572 Guinea. Second* dr. bust l. R. Similar die axis ↑↓

1707	825	3750	11500	1709	750	3250	9500
1708	750	3250	9500				

3573 Guinea. Second bust elephant and castle below R. Similar die axis ↑↓

1708	1250	5250	17500	1709	1100	4750	15000

3574 Guinea. Third* dr. bust l. R. Similar die axis ↑↓

1710	650	2000	8000	1713	600	1950	7500
1711	650	2000	8000	1714	600	1950	7500
1712	700	2250	8500	1714 GRΛTIΛ	625	1950	7250
1713/1	625	2000	7750				

3575 - 1710 Half-Guinea

3575 Half-Guinea. Dr. bust l. R. Crowned cruciform shields, sceptres in angles, edge milled die axis ↑↓

1707	400	1000	4500	1711	375	900	4000
1708	425	1150	4750	1712	400	1000	4500
1709	400	1000	4500	1713	375	900	4000
1710	375	950	4250	1714	375	900	4000

* There is a small difference between the 2nd and 3rd busts in the facial profile and eye.

SILVER

3576
1703 VIGO Crown

	F	VF	EF		F	VF	EF
	£	£	£		£	£	£

The shields on the reverse are Pre-Union type.

3576 Crown. VIGO below dr. bust, l., regnal year on edge in words (e.g. 1703 = TERTIO) die axis ↑↓
   1703 TERTIO 375   1500   8500

3577   3578
1705 Crown, plumes on reverse   1707 Pre-Union crown, roses and plumes

3577 Crown. Dr bust l. R. Plumes in angles, die axis ↑↓ 1705 QVINTO .. 575   2500   13500
3578 Crown. R. Similar Crowned cruciform shields Roses and plumes in angles die axis ↑↓
   1706 QVINTO 300   750   4500   1707 SEXTO 275   675   4250

3579
1703 Halfcrown, plain below bust

3579 Halfcrown . Dr. bust l. R. Similar Regnal year on edge in words die axis ↑↓
   1703 TERTIO 750   2250   9500

3580
1703 VIGO Halfcrown

	F	VF	EF		F	VF	EF
	£	£	£		£	£	£
3580	**Halfcrown.** Similar VIGO below bust, die axis ↑↓ 1703 TERTIO				150	525	2750

3581
Halfcrown, plumes on reverse

3581 Halfcrown. Dr. bust l. ℞. Plumes in angles, similar die axis ↑↓
1704 TERTIO 200   750   4250   1705 QVINTO 200   750   4250

3582
Halfcrown, Pre-Union,
roses and plumes

3583
Shilling

3582 Halfcrown. Dr. bust l. ℞. Roses and plumes in angles, similar die axis ↑↓
1706 QVINTO 135   400   2750   1707 SEXTO............ 125   375   2500

First bust   Second bust

3583 Shilling. First dr. bust l. ℞. Similar die axis ↑↓ 1702 .... 100 ·   350   1350

	F	VF	EF		F	VF	EF
	£	£	£		£	£	£

3584 Shilling. Similar R. Plumes in angles, die axis ↑↓ 1702 110   375   1750

3585 Shilling. First dr. bust VIGO below , die axis ↑↓

1702 90   300   1250   1702 :ANNA..................135   475   2000

3586
1703 VIGO Shilling

3587
'Plain' Shilling

3586 Shilling. Second dr. bust, l. VIGO below R. Similar, die axis ↑↓ 1703 85   275   1100

3587 Shilling. Similar R. Crowned cruciform shields, angles plain, die axis ↑↓

1704 475   1750   —   1705 200   675   2250

3588 Shilling. Second dr. bust l. R. Plumes in angles die axis ↑↓

1704 125   475   1850   1705 110   425   1600

3589 Shilling. Second dr. bust l. R. Roses and plumes in angles die axis ↑↓

1705 110   425   1600   1707 125   475   1850

3590 Sixpence. Dr. bust l. VIGO below dr. bust, l. die axis ↑↓ 1703..................35   125   475

3591 Sixpence. Dr bust l., R. Angles plain, die axis ↑↓ 1705 60   200   675

3592 Sixpence. Similar R. Early shields, plumes in angles, die axis ↑↓ 1705........40   150   525

3593
1705 Plumes Sixpence

Early Shield

Late Shield

3593 Sixpence. Similar R. Late shields, plumes in angles, die axis ↑↓1705..........50   185   625

3594 Sixpence. Similar R. Crowned cruciform shields Roses and plumes in angles die axis ↑↓

1705 45   175   575   1707 45   175   575

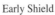

3595
Groat or fourpence, first bust

3595 Fourpence. First dr. bust l. small face, curls at back of head point downwards.

R Small crown above the figure 4 die axis ↑↓

1703 20   50   150   1704 15   30   75

3595C
Groat or Fourpence, second bust

	F £	VF £	EF £		F £	VF £	EF £

3595A Fourpence. Second dr. bust l. larger face, curls at back of head point upwards die axis ↑↓
1705 ...... 40 95 200 | 1709 ...... 15 40 100
1706 ...... 15 30 85 | 1710 ...... 12 25 70
1708 ...... 18 38 95

3595B –Fourpence. Similar R Large crown with pearls on arch, larger serifs on the figure 4 die axis ↑↓
1710 ...... 12 25 75 | 1713 ...... 15 30 80

3595C Fourpence. Second dr. bust l., but with re-engraved hair R. Crowned 4 die axis ↑↓
1710 ...... 12 25 75 | 1713 ...... 15 30 80

3596 Threepence. First dr. bust l., broader, tie riband pointing outwards. R. Crowned 3 die axis ↑↓
1703 7 above crown.... 18 45 130 | 1703 7 not above crown 18 45 130

3596A Threepence. Second dr. bust l., taller and narrow, tie riband pointing inwards die axis ↑↓
1704 ...... 18 40 100 | 1706 ...... 15 35 105
1705 ...... 18 45 130

3596B
Threepence, third bust

3596B Threepence. Third larger more finely engraved dr. bust l. R. Crowned 3, die axis ↑↓
1707 ...... 15 30 75 | 1710 ...... 12 28 85
1708 ...... 15 35 105 | 1713 ...... 15 35 100
1708/7 ...... 15 35 105 | 1713 mule with 4d obv.
1709 ...... 15 35 105 | die 20 42 150

3597 Twopence. First dr. bust l., as fourpence, R. Crown to edge of coin, small figure 2 die axis ↑↓
1703 ...... 22 50 130 | 1705 ...... 25 55 125
1704 ...... 20 40 80 | 1706 ...... 20 40 95
1704 No stops on obv. 22 50 110 | 1707 ...... 20 40 80

3597A Twopence. Second dr. bust l., as fourpence, R Crown within inner circle of legend,
large figure 2 die axis ↑↓
1708 ...... 20 40 85 | 1710 ...... 18 35 80
1709 ...... 25 50 115 | 1713 ...... 20 40 85

3598 Penny. Dr. bust l. R. Crowned 1 die axis ↑↓
1703 ...... 25 50 125 | 1709 ...... 20 40 90
1705 ...... 22 45 105 | 1710 ...... 60 120 230
1706 ...... 22 45 105 | 1713/0 ...... 30 55 135
1708 ...... 200 300 450

3599
1713 Maundy Set

	F	VF	EF		F	VF	EF
	£	£	£		£	£	£

3599 Maundy Set. The four denominations. Uniform dates

	F	VF	EF		F	VF	EF
1703	125	300	750	1709	125	250	650
1705	150	300	750	1710	150	300	750
1706	125	250	650	1713	125	250	650
1708	300	450	950				

POST UNION WITH SCOTLAND, 1707-14

The shields on the reverse are changed to the Post-Union types. The Edinburgh coins have been included here as they are now coins of Great Britain.

3600   Crown. Second dr. bust, l. E (Edinburgh) below, R. Crowned cruciform shields regnal year on edge in words, die axis ↑↓ (e.g. 1708 = SEPTIMO)

	F	VF	EF		F	VF	EF
1707 SEXTO	185	575	4000	1708 SEPTIMO	200	625	4250
1707 SEPTIMO	1850	—	—	1708/7 SEPTIMO	210	650	4250

3601
Crown, second bust, plain reverse

3601   Crown. Second dr. bust l. R. Crowned cruciform shields, angles plain die axis ↑↓

	F	VF	EF		F	VF	EF
1707 SEPTIMO	185	575	4000	1708 SEPTIMO	185	575	4000

3602   Crown. Similar R. Plumes in angles, die axis ↑↓

	F	VF	EF			
1708 SEPTIMO	210	650	4250	1708 — BR for BRI	*Extremely rare*	

3603
1713 Crown, third bust, roses and plumes

	F £	VF £	EF £		F £	VF £	EF £
3603 Crown. Third dr. bust. l. R. Roses and plumes, 1713 DVODECIMO.....	200	625	4250				

3604
1708 Halfcrown, Post-Union

3604 Halfcrown. Dr. bust R. Plain, regnal year on edge in words (e.g. 1709 = OCTAVO), die axis ↑↓

	F	VF	EF		F	VF	EF
1707 SEPTIMO	100	325	2250	1709 OCTAVO.............	100	325	2250
1707 no stops on reverse ..	150	550	—	1713 DVODECIMO	125	375	2500
1708 SEPTIMO............	100	325	2250				

3605

3605 Halfcrown. Dr. bust E below R. Crowned cruciform shields die axis ↑↓

	F	VF	EF		F	VF	EF
1707 SEXTO	100	325	2250	1708 SEPTIMO	125	375	2500
1707 SEPTIMO	475	2500	8500	1709 OCTAVO.............	275	1000	—

3606
1708 Halfcrown, plumes on reverse

3607
1714 Halfcrown, roses and plumes

	F £	VF £	EF £		F £	VF £	EF £
3606 Halfcrown. Similar R. Plumes in angles, die axis ↑↓ 1708 SEPTIMO ..	120	400	2400				

3607 Halfcrown. Similar R. Roses and plumes in angles die axis ↑↓

1710 NONO	110	325	2100	1714 D. TERTIO	110	325	2100
1712 UNDECIMO	100	300	2000	1714/3 D. TERTIO	120	350	2250
1713 DVODECIMO	100	300	2000				

3608
1707 Edinburgh Mint Shilling, second bust

3609
1708 E* Shilling

3608 Shilling. Second dr. bust, l. E *(Edinburgh)* below, R. Crowned cruciform shields die axis ↑↓

1707	125	475	1750	1707 Plain edge proof *FDC* £12500			
1707 no stops on reverse	250	850	—	1708	200	675	2400

3609 Shilling. Similar E* *(Edinburgh)* below bust die axis ↑↓

1707	175	575	2250	1708 no rays to garter star	525	—	—
1708	175	575	2250				
1708/7	350	—	—				

3609A Shilling. Similar E* *(Edinburgh)* local dies die axis ↑↓

1707	300	1000	—	1708	375	1500	—

Third bust Fourth bust

3610
Shilling, third bust

3611
Shilling, plumes on reverse

	F	VF	EF		F	VF	EF
	£	£	£		£	£	£

3610 Shilling Third dr. bust. l. R. Crowned cruciform shields, angles Plain, die axis ↑↓

1707 35   125   600   1709 30   110   550

1708 30   110   550   1711........................... 90   300   1000

3611 Shilling. Third dr. bust. l. R. Plumes in angles die axis ↑↓

1707 90   300   1000   1708 90   300   1000

3612 Shilling. Third dr. bust. E below R. angles plain die axis ↑↓

1707 100   325   1100   1708/7 120   375   1250

1708 110   350   1200

3613 Shilling. Second dr. bust l. R. Roses and plumes, die axis ↑↓ 1708... 135   525   1750

3614
1708 Shilling, roses and plumes

3614 Shilling. Third dr. bust l. R. Crowned cruciform shields Roses and plumes die axis ↑↓

1708 100   325   1100   1710 90   300   1000

	3615	3620	3623
	Edinburgh bust – E* Shilling	Edinburgh Mint Sixpence	1707 Sixpence, plumes on reverse

	F	VF	EF		F	VF	EF
	£	£	£		£	£	£

3615 Shilling. 'Edinburgh' bust, E* below, R. Crowned cruciform shields die axis ↑↓

1707	575	—	—	1709	200	700	2250
1708	225	750	2500				

3616 Shilling. — E below, R. Similar die axis ↑↓ 1709 275   1000   —

3617 Shilling. Fourth dr. bust. l. R. Roses and plumes die axis ↑↓

1710	80	225	900	1713/2	90	225	900
1710 plain edge proof *FDC*	*Extremely rare*			1714	75	200	825
1712	70	185	775	1714/3	85	250	925

3618 Shilling. Similar, R. angles plain, die axis ↑↓

1711	30	125	500	1711 plain edge proof *FDC*	*Extremely rare*		

3619 Sixpence. Normal dr. bust. l. R. angles plain die axis ↑↓

1707	35	125	450	1711	30	85	350
1707 BR. FRA error..	450	—	—	1711 Large Lis	35	90	375
1708	40	150	525				

3620 Sixpence. Normal dr. bust E *(Edinburgh)* below R. Similar die axis ↑↓

1707	45	165	550	1708/7	75	240	750
1707 Proof FDC £6750				1708	65	200	650

3621 Sixpence. Normal dr. bust E* *(Edinburgh)* below, R. Similar die axis ↑↓

1708	70	225	700	1708/7	75	240	750

3622 Sixpence. 'Edinburgh' bust, l. E* below, R. Similar die axis ↑↓ 1708.. 70   225   725

3623 Sixpence. Normal dr. bust. l. R. Plumes in angles die axis ↑↓

1707	45	150	525	1708	50	165	575

3624 Sixpence. Similar R. Roses and plumes in angles, die axis ↑↓ 1710 ... 60   200   650

COPPER

3625
1714 Pattern Farthing

3625 Farthing. Dr. bust l. R. Britannia 1714 pattern only, die axis ↑↓ 325   650   1350

GEORGE I, 1714-27

George I was born on 28th May 1660 son of Ernest, Elector of Hanover and Sophia grandaughter of James I, and inherited the English Throne as Parliament considered him a better alternative than James Edward Stuart – Anne's half-brother. He was however, thoroughly German, did not want to learn English and spent over half his reign in Germany. He brought two mistresses with him to England while his wife ironically languished in a German prison on a charge of adultery. His reign created a government that could run independently of the King. The office of Prime Minister was created in 1721. He also kept England out of war for his entire reign, and he died on 11 June 1727.

The coins of the first of the Hanoverian kings have the arms of the Duchy of Brunswick and Luneberg on one of the four shields, the object in the centre of the shield being the Crown of Charlemagne. The King's German titles also appear, in abbreviated form, and name him 'Duke of Brunswick and Luneberg. Arch-treasurer of the Holy Roman Empire, and Elector', and on the Guinea of 1714, 'Prince Elector'. A Quarter-Guinea was struck for the first time in 1718, but it was of an inconvenient size, and the issue was discontinued. The elephant and castle provenance mark continues on some guineas and half-guineas, but today are rarely seen.

Silver coined from bullion supplied to the mint by the South Sea Company in 1723 shows the Company's initials S.S.C.; similarly Welsh Copper Company bullion has the letters W.C.C. below the King's bust; and plumes and an interlinked CC in the reverse angles. Roses and plumes together on the reverse indicate silver supplied by the Company for Smelting Pit Coale and Sea Coale.

Engravers and Designers: Samuel Bull (d.c.1720), John Croker (1670-1741), John Rudulf Ochs Snr, (1673-c.1748), Norbert Roettier (b.1665)

Prime Minister: Sir Robert Walpole (1676 – 1745) –Whig, 1721-42

GOLD

3626
1717 Five Guineas

	F	VF	EF		F	VF	EF
	£	£	£		£	£	£

3626 Five Guineas. Laur. head r. regnal year on edge in words (e.g. 1717 = TERTIO) die axis ↑↓

	F	VF	EF		F	VF	EF
1716 SECVNDO	6250	16500	85000	1720 SEXTO	7000	18000	90000
1717 TERTIO	7000	18000	90000	1726 D. TERTIO....	6250	16500	85000
1717 Variety O for D on edge exits				1726 Variety Ⅵ for N on edge exists			

3627
Two Guineas

	F £	VF £	EF £		F £	VF £	EF £

3627 **Two Guineas.** Laur. head r. R. Crowned cruciform shields, sceptres in angles, edge milled, die axis ↑↓

1717	1750	5250	17500	1720/17	1850	5500	18500
1720	1750	5250	17500	1726	1650	5000	16000

3628
1714 'Prince Elector' Guinea

3630
Third bust

3631
Fourth bust

3628 **Guinea.** First laur. head r. R. Legend ends ET PR . EL (Prince Elector), die axis ↑↓

1714				1750	5250	16500

3629 **Guinea.** Second laur. head, r. tie with two ends, R. Crowned cruciform shields, sceptres in angles normal legend ↑↓ 1715 .... 900 2750 9500

3630 **Guinea.** Third laur. head, r. no hair below truncation R. Similar die axis ↑↓

1715	675	2000	7000	1716	700	2250	7500

3631 **Guinea.** Fourth laur. head, r. tie with loop at one end R. Similar die axis ↑↓

1716	675	2000	6500	1719/6	700	2100	6750
1716 Arms of Hanover				1720 large or small			
at date		*Extremely rare*		20 in date	675	2000	6500
1717	700	2200	7000	1721	700	2200	7000
1718		*Extremely rare*		1722	675	2000	6500
1718/7		*Extremely rare*		1722/0	700	2100	6750
1719	675	2000	6500	1723	700	2100	6750

3632 **Guinea.** Fourth Laur. head, elephant and castle below R. Similar die axis ↑↓

1721		*Extremely rare*		1722		*Extremely rare*

3633
Guinea, fifth bust

	F £	VF £	EF £		F £	VF £	EF £
3633 Guinea. Fifth (older) laur. head, r. tie with two ends R. Similar die axis ↑↓							
1723	650	1650	6000	1725	650	1650	6000
1723 II for H in TH	675	1750	6250	1725 large 5 in date	675	1500	6000
1724	650	1650	6000	1726	625	1500	5750
1724 R/I in GEORGIVS	675	1750	6250	1727	725	2000	7000

3634 Guinea. Fifth laur. head, elephant and castle below, die axis ↑↓ 1726 2000   7500   22500

3635 Half-Guinea. First laur. head r. R. Crowned cruciform shields, sceptres in angles die axis ↑↓

	F	VF	EF		F	VF	EF
1715	650	1650	5250	1721			*Extremely rare*
1717	400	900	4250	1722	400	900	4250
1718	375	850	4000	1722/0	425	950	4500
1718/7	400	900	4250	1723	425	950	4500
1719	375	850	4000	1724	450	1000	4750
1720	400	900	4250				

3636 Half-Guinea. First laur. head elephant and castle below, die axis ↑↓ 1721   *Extremely rare*

3637
Half-Guinea, second bust

3638
Quarter Guinea

3637 Half-Guinea. Second (older) laur. head r. R. Crowned cruciform shields, sceptres in angles die axis ↑↓

	F	VF	EF		F	VF	EF
1725	350	800	4000	1727	400	900	4250
1726	375	800	4000				

3638 Quarter-Guinea. Laur. head R. Similar die axis ↑↓ 1718 200   375   900

SILVER

3639A - 1726 Crown - small roses and plumes

	F £	VF £	EF £		F £	VF £	EF £

3639 Crown. Laur and dr. bust r. ℞. Roses and plumes in angles, regnal year on edge in words (e.g. 1716 = SECVNDO) die axis ↑↓

1716 SECVNDO	550	1600	6500	1720/18 SEXTO	575	1600	6500
1718/6 QUINTO	575	1650	6750				

3639A Crown. Similar ℞. small roses and plumes in angles

1720 SEXTO	750	2250	8500	1726 D. TERTIO	575	1650	6750

3640 Crown. Similar ℞. SSC (South Sea Company) in angles, die axis ↑↓

1723 DECIMO					575	1600	6500

3641 - 1715 Pattern Halfcrown

3641 Halfcrown. Laur and dr. bust r. ℞. Angles plain (pattern only), die axis ↑↓ 1715 *FDC* £17500

3642 - Halfcrown, roses and plumes

3642 Halfcrown. — ℞. Roses and plumes in angles, regnal year on edge in words (e.g. 1717 = TIRTIO)

1715 SECVNDO	325	900	4000	1717 TIRTIO	325	900	4000
1715 Edge wording out...				1720/17 SEXTO	325	900	4000
of order	375	1250	4500	1720 SEXTO	375	950	4250
1715 Plain edge	525	1750	—				

3643 - 1723 SSC Halfcrown

	F	VF	EF		F	VF	EF
	£	£	£		£	£	£

3643 Halfcrown. Similar R. SSC in angles, die axis ↑↓ 1723 DECIMO 300 800 3750

3644 - 1726 Halfcrown small roses and plumes

3644 Halfcrown. — R. Small roses and plumes, die axis ↑↓ 1726 D. TERTIO ...3750 12500 27500

3645	3646
Shilling, roses and plumes	1721 Shilling, plain reverse

3645 Shilling. First laur. and dr. bust. r. R. Roses and plumes in angles, die axis ↑↓

1715	85	275	1000	1721	150	500	1500
1716	150	500	1500	1721/0	110	350	1350
1717	125	375	1350	1721/19	135	450	1500
1718	80	250	950	1721/18 plumes and			
1719	150	500	1500	roses error	375	1500	—
1720	110	350	1350	1722	110	350	1350
1720/18	150	525	1650	1723	125	375	1350

3646 Shilling. First laur. and dr. bust r. R. angles plain (i.e. no marks either side) die axis ↑↓

1720	45	150	700	1721	150	575	1750
1720 large O	50	160	725	1721 O of GEORGIVS over zero			

LETTERING ERRORS:
3645 1716 V of GEORGIVS over L   1720 Large O in date
1717 Large lettering on obverse

3647   3649

1723 SSC Shilling, first bust   1727 Shilling, second bust

	F	VF	EF		F	VF	EF
	£	£	£		£	£	£

3647 **Shilling.** First laur. and dr. bust r. R. SSC in angles, die axis ↑↓

1723	30	85	350	1723 C/SS in 3rd			
1723 French Arms at				quarter	35	95	375
date	110	350	1100				

LETTERING VARIETIES:

B·RVN on Rev., Large N in BRVN and stop between E.T. after BRVN.

3648 **Shilling.** Second dr. bust, r. bow to tie. R. Similar, die axis ↑↓ 1723 ... 50   150   525

3649 **Shilling.** Similar R. Roses and plumes in angles die axis ↑↓

1723	110	375	1350	1726 no stops on obv.	750	2250	—
1724	120	400	1500	1727	575	1650	—
1725	110	375	1350	1727 no stops on obv.	500	1500	4250
1725 no stops on obv.	120	400	1500	1727 no stops on rev	600	1750	—
1725 no stops on rev	135	475	1650				

3650 - 1726 WCC Shilling

3650 **Shilling.** Second laur. and dr. bust r. W.C.C. (Welsh Copper Company) below bust die axis ↑↓

| 1723 | 750 | 2500 | 8000 | 1725 | 800 | 2750 | 8500 |
| 1724 | 750 | 2500 | 8000 | 1726 | 800 | 2750 | 8500 |

3651 **Sixpence.** Laur. and dr. bust r. R. Roses and plumes in angles, die axis ↑↓

| 1717 | 100 | 350 | 900 | 1720/17 | 90 | 300 | 800 |
| 1717 Plain edge | | *Extremely rare* | | | | | |

3652 - 1723 SSC Sixpence   3653 - 1726 Sixpence,

small roses and plumes

3652 **Sixpence.** Laur. and dr. bust r. R. SSC in angles, die axis ↑↓

| 1723 | 25 | 90 | 375 | 1723 larger lettering | 30 | 95 | 400 |

3653 **Sixpence.** Similar R. Small roses and plumes, die axis ↑↓ 1726 85   275   750

	F	VF	EF			F	VF	EF
	£	£	£			£	£	£

3654 Fourpence. Laur. and dr. bust r. R. Crowned 4, die axis ↑↓

1717	15	40	100	1723	20	50	160
1721	15	40	100	1727	22	55	160

3655 Threepence. Laur. and dr. bust r. R. Crowned 3, die axis ↑↓

1717	20	45	95	1723	20	55	160
1721	25	48	95	1727 small lettering	20	50	150

3656 Twopence. Laur. and dr. bust r. R. Crowned 2, die axis ↑↓

1717	12	32	65	1726	12	25	60
1721	12	25	60	1727 small lettering	15	32	85
1723	15	40	110				

3657 Penny. Laur. and dr. bust r. R. Crowned 1, die axis ↑↓

1716	12	32	65	1723	15	30	80
1718	12	32	65	1725	12	32	65
1720	12	32	65	1726	15	40	70
1720 HIPEX error	20	85	150	1727 BRI·FR	20	50	110

3658

3658 Maundy Set. As last four. Uniform dates

1723	150	275	800	1727	125	250	700

COPPER

3659

3659 Halfpenny. 'Dump' issue obv. legend continuous over bust, plain edge, die axis ↑↓

1717	40	250	800	1718 no stops on obv.	150	500	—
1717 no stops on obv.	100	525	—	1719	1000	—	—
1718	30	225	725	1719 grained edge	1000	—	—
1718 R/B on rev.	50	250	900	*(1719 is an extremely rare date, perhaps only 2 or 3 known to exist of each type)*			

3660

	F	VF	EF		F	VF	EF
	£	£	£		£	£	£

3660 Halfpenny. Second issue, second obverse, plain left shoulder strap,
less hair to the right of tie knot, R. Britannia plain edge, die axis ↑↓

	F	VF	EF		F	VF	EF
1719	40	210	900	1722	30	155	700
1719 grained edge	1000	—	—	1722 Ɐ for V on obv.	100	500	—
1720	30	175	825	1723	30	155	750
1721	30	165	725	1723 Thin Flan		*Extremely rare*	
1721 stop after date	40	200	800	1723 no stop on rev.	100	525	—
1721/0	40	200	800	1724	30	155	700

3660A Halfpenny. Second issue, second obverse, ornate shoulder straps, die axis ↑↓

	F	VF	EF
1719	40	195	900

3661

3662

3661 Farthing. 'Dump' issue, Similar die axis ↑↓

	F	VF	EF		
1717	200	675	1250	1718	*Unique*

3662 Farthing. Second issue laur. and cuir. bust r. R. Britannia, date in ex. die axis ↑↓

	F	VF	EF		F	VF	EF
1719 small letters	60	330	775	1720 obv. large letters	80	350	—
1719 no stop on rev.	70	380	—	1721	25	135	650
1719 large lettering				1721/0	40	165	675
on obv.	30	165	650	1721 stop after date	35	165	625
1719 — no stops on				1722	30	155	625
obv.	70	410	—	1722 obv. large letters	40	210	725
1719 — no stops on rev.	90	450	—	1723 R/≍ in REX	100	330	900
1719 last A/I on rev.	80	350	—	1723	30	165	600
1720	30	165	600	1724	30	165	625
1720 milled edge	150	500	1150				

George II was born on 30 October 1683 and was raised in Hanover, but upon his succession to the throne as George I's only son, he adapted himself to English society. His passions were the military, music and his wife – Caroline of Anspach, though he despised his eldest son Frederick as his own father despised him. George declared war on Spain in 1739 and he was the last King to have personally led his troops at the battle of Dettingen on 17 June 1743. Upon his death on 25 October 1760 the throne passed to his grandson George as Frederick had already died.

Silver was coined only spasmodically by the Mint during this reign; and no copper was struck after 1754. Gold coins made from bullion supplied by the East India Company bear the Company's E.I.C. initials. Some of the treasure seized by Admiral Anson during his circumnavigation of the globe, 1740-4, and by other privateers, was made into coin, which had the word LIMA below the king's bust to celebrate the expedition's successful harassment of the Spanish Colonies in the New World. Hammered gold was finally demonetized in 1733.

Engravers and designers: John Croker (1670-1741), John Rudolf Ochs Snr (1673-1748) and jnr (1704-88), Johann Sigismund Tanner (c.1706-75)

Prime Ministers: Sir Robert Walpole (1676-1745) Whig, 1721-43; Spencer Compton (1673-1743) Whig 1742-3; Henry Pelham (c.1695-1754) Whig 1743-54; William Cavendish (1720-1764) Whig 1756-7; Thomas Pelham-Holles (1693-1768) Whig 1754-6; 1757-62.

GOLD

3663A
1741 Five Guineas - revised shield

	F	VF	EF		F	VF	EF
	£	£	£		£	£	£

3663 Five Guineas. Young laur. head l. ℞. Crowned shield of arms, die axis ↑↓ regnal year on edge in words (e.g. 1729 = TERTIO)

1729 TERTIO	4750	14500	70000	1729 Plain edge proof *FDC* £165000			

3663A Five Guineas. Similar ℞. Revised shield garnish die axis ↑↓

1731 QVARTO	6500	18500	90000	1738 DVODECIMO	5750	16500	75000
1731 QVARTO proof *FDC* £165000				1741/38 D. QVARTO	5000	14500	72500
1735 NONO	6250	18000	85000	1741 D. QVARTO	4500	14500	70000

3664 Five Guineas. Young laur. head, E.I.C. (East India Company) below, die axis ↑↓

1729 TERTIO	4250	13500	65000

3665
1746 LIMA Five Guineas

	F	VF	EF		F	VF	EF
	£	£	£		£	£	£

3665   Five Guineas. Old laur. head, l. LIMA below, ↑↓1746 D. NONO... 4500   14500   70000

3666   Five Guineas. Old laur. head plain below, R. Crowned shield, edge inscribed die axis ↑↓

1748 V. SECVNDO.. 4500   14500   70000   1753 V. SEXTO 4500   14500   70000

3667   Two Guineas. Young laur. head l. Ɍ Crowned shield with rounded arches, die axis ↑↓

1733 Proof *FDC* £57500   1734/3 2750   7500   25000

3667A
1735 Two Guineas - new reverse

3667A Two Guineas. – Ɍ. Crown with pointed arches, new type of shield garnishing die axis ↑↓

1735 1750   4000   12500

3667B Two Guineas. Repositioned legend on obverse Ɍ. Similar

1738*........................ 900   2250   6500   1739 950   2500   6750

3668
1740 Two Guineas - Intermediate head

3668   Two Guineas. Intermediate laur. head l. R. Crowned shield of arms die axis ↑↓

1739*....................... 900   2250   6500   1740 1000   2750   6750

1740/39.................. 1000   2750   6750

3669   Two Guineas. Old laur. head l. R. Crowned shield of arms die axis ↑↓ ..

1748 1100   3250   8000   1753 1250   3500   9000

Beware recent forgeries.

		F	VF	EF			F	VF	EF
		£	£	£			£	£	£

3670 Guinea. First young laur. head, l. small lettering, die axis ↑↓ 1727. 1250   4500   15000

3671   3676
1727 Guinea - small reverse shield

3671 Guinea. Similar larger lettering, smaller shield, die axis ↑↓

1727 1350   4750   16000   1728 1350   4750   16000

3672 Guinea. Second (narrower) young laur. head l. die axis ↑↓

1729 Proof *FDC* £27500   1731 700   2750   8500

1730 775   3000   9000   1732 725   2750   8750

3673 Guinea. Second young laur. head, E.I.C. below R. Crowned shield of arms die axis ↑↓

1729 1300   5000   16000   1732 1200   4500   13500

1731 1250   4750   15000

3674 Guinea. Second young laur. head l. larger lettering R. Crowned shield of arms die axis ↑↓

1732 725   2250   7500   1736 675   2000   7000

1733 650   1850   6500   1737 675   2000   7000

1734 650   1850   6500   1738 675   2000   7000

1735 675   2000   7000

3675 Guinea. — — E.I.C. below, die axis ↑↓ 1732................................1500   4500   14500

Note: All 1739-45 Guineas read GEORGIUS

3676 Guinea. Intermediate laur. head l. r. Crowned shield of arms die axis ↑↓

1739 625   1750   6500   1741/39 825   2750   9000

1740 675   1850   6750   1743 825   2750   9000

3677 Guinea. Similar E.I.C. below, R. Similar die axis ↑↓ 1739..............1200   4500   15000

3678 Guinea. Similar larger lettering on *obv.*, GEORGIUS die axis ↑↓

1745 (also exists with small S in date) 625   1750   6000

3678A   3679
1746 Guinea - GEORGIVS legend   LIMA below bust Guinea

3678A Guinea. Similar as last but reads GEORGIVS die axis ↑↓

1746 675   1850   6750

3679 Guinea. Intermediate laur. head LIMA below, GEORGIUS die

axis ↑↓ 1745 2250   7000   20000

3680
Old head Guinea

	F	VF	EF		F	VF	EF
	£	£	£		£	£	£

3680 Guinea. Old laur. head l. R. Crowned shield of arms die axis ↑↓

1747	575	1450	6250	1753	575	1450	6250
1748	575	1450	6250	1755	575	1450	6250
1749	575	1450	6250	1756	575	1450	6250
1750	575	1450	6250	1758	525	1300	5500
1751	550	1350	6000	1759	500	1250	5250
1752	550	1350	6000	1760	525	1300	5500

3681 Half-Guinea. Young laur. head. l. R First shield of arms, die axis ↑↓

1728	550	1350	5250	1729	525	1300	5250

1728 Proof *FDC* £16500

3681A
1731 Half-Guinea - modified shield

3681A Half-Guinea. Young laur. head l. R. Modified garnished shield die axis ↑↓

1730	475	1050	4500	1736	375	950	4000
1731	350	950	4000	1737	400	1000	4250
1732	375	1000	4250	1738	350	950	4000
1734	350	950	4000	1739	350	950	4000

3682 Half-Guinea. Young laur. head l. E.I.C. below R. Similar die axis ↑↓

1729	700	1750	6000	1732		*Extremely rare*	
1730	800	1850	6750	1739		*Extremely rare*	
1731		*Extremely rare*					

3683A
Half-guinea - GEORGIVS legend

3683 Half-Guinea. Intermediate laur. head l. R. Similar die axis ↑↓

1740	350	850	4000	1745	350	1000	4250
1743		*Extremely rare*					

3683A Half-Guinea. Similar, but reads GEORGIVS, die axis ↑↓ 1746 .... 325 800 3500

3684
LIMA Half-Guinea

3685
Half-Guinea, old head

	F	VF	EF		F	VF	EF
	£	£	£		£	£	£

3684 Half-Guinea. Intermediate laur. head LIMA below, die axis ↑↓ 1745 .. 1350   3750   13500

3685 Half-Guinea. Old laur. head l. R. Similar die axis ↑↓

1747	350	850	3500	1753	300	750	3250
1748	350	850	3500	1755	285	700	3000
1749	375	950	3950	1756	275	650	2750
1750	350	850	3500	1758	300	750	3250
1751	325	825	3350	1759	250	650	2850
1751/0	350	850	3500	1759/8	275	675	3000
1752	300	750	3250	1760	275	675	3000

SILVER

3686
Crown, young head

3686 Crown. Young laur. and dr. bust. l. R. Crowned cruciform shields Roses and plumes in angles, regnal year on edge in words (e.g. 1736 = NONO), die axis ↑↓

1732 SEXTO	375	1200	5000	1735 OCTAVO	350	1100	4500
1732 Proof, plain edge *FDC* £22500				1736 NONO	350	1100	4500
1734 SEPTIMO	375	1200	5000				

3687
3687 Crown. Similar R. Roses in angles die axis ↑↓

1739 DVODECIMO	350	1000	4000	1741 D. QVARTO	350	1000	4000

3688
Crown, old head

	F	VF	EF		F	VF	EF
	£	£	£		£	£	£

3688 Crown. Old laur. and dr. bust l. ℞. Crowned cruciform shields Roses in angles, die axis ↑↓
1743 D. SEPTIMO 325 850 3500
3689 Crown. — LIMA below, die axis ↑↓ 1746 D. NONO 325 900 3750

3690
Plain reverse

3690 Crown. Old laur. and dr. bust l. ℞. angles Plain (i.e. no marks either side) die axis ↑↓
1746 Proof only, VICESIMO *FDC* £15000
1750 V. QVARTO ...... 350 1000 4500 1751 V. QVARTO 375 1100 5000

3691
1731 Pattern Halfcrown

3691 Halfcrown. Young dr. bust l. ℞. angles plain (pattern only), 1731 *FDC* £11000

3692	3693
1736 Halfcrown, roses and plumes	1741 Halfcrown, roses on reverse

	F	VF	EF		F	VF	EF
	£	£	£		£	£	£

3692 Halfcrown. Young laur. and dr. bust l. R. Roses and plumes, regnal year on edge in words
(e.g. 1732 = SEXTO), die axis ↑↓

1731 QVINTO	150	500	2500	1735 OCTAVO	165	525	2750
1732 SEXTO	150	500	2500	1736 NONO	165	525	2750
1734 SEPTIMO	165	525	2750				

3693 Halfcrown. Young laur. and dr. bust l. R. Roses in angles die axis ↑↓

1739 DVODECIMO	140	500	2500	1741 Large *obv.* letters	150	525	2600
1741 D. QVARTO	140	500	2500	1741/39 D. QVARTO	165	550	2650

3694 Halfcrown. Old dr. bust. l. GEORGIUS R. Roses in angles die axis ↑↓

1743 D. SEPTIMO	120	350	2100	1745/3 D. NONO	125	375	2200
1745 D. NONO	120	350	2100				

3695 Halfcrown. Old laur. and dr. bust LIMA below die axis ↑↓

1745 D. NONO	70	175	850	1745/3	85	225	1100

3695A Halfcrown. Old laur. and dr. bust as last LIMA below but reads GEORGIVS die axis ↑↓

1746 D. NONO	65	170	750	1746/5 D. NONO	70	175	800

3696	3697
1751 Halfcrown	1727 Plumes Shilling

3696 Halfcrown. Old laur. and dr. bust l. R. Plain angles die axis ↑↓

1746 proof only VICESIMO *FDC* £7000				1751 V. QVARTO	225	625	3000
1750 V. QVARTO	200	575	2850				

3697 Shilling. Young laur. dr. bust. l. R. Plumes in angles, die axis ↑↓

1727	150	525	2250	1731	175	625	2500

3698   3699
Shilling, young bust, small letters   Young bust Shilling, large letters

| | F | VF | EF | | | F | VF | EF |
| | £ | £ | £ | | | £ | £ | £ |

3698 Shilling. Young laur. and dr. bust l. R. Roses and plumes in angles, die axis ↑↓

1727	 100	325	1350	1731	 110	350	1500
1728	 120	375	1600	1732	 110	350	1500
1729	 120	375	1600				

3699 Shilling. Young laur. and dr. bust l. R. Plain, die axis ↑↓ 1728 95   300   1250

3700 - Shilling, plain reverse   3701 - Shilling, roses reverse

3700 Shilling. Similar larger lettering. R. Roses and plumes in angles die axis ↑↓

1734	 65	250	950	1737	 65	250	950
1735	 70	275	1000	1737 known with GRATIΛ error			
1736	 65	250	950	1737 with 3/5 exists			
1736/5	 70	275	1000				

3701 Shilling. Young laur. and dr. bust l. R. Roses in angles die axis ↑↓

1739 normal garter				1739 smaller garter star 65	250	900
star	 50	200	750	1741	 50	200	750
1739/7	 100	300	1250	1741/39	 100	300	1250

3702   3703
Shilling, old bust, roses   LIMA Shilling

3702 Shilling. Old laur. and dr. bust, l. R. Roses in angles die axis ↑↓

1743	 35	130	575	1745/3	 65	175	750
1743/1	 50	150	700	1747 only known with GEORGIVS			
1745	 60	165	725	on obv	 40	135	650

3703 Shilling. Old laur. and dr. bust LIMA below die axis ↑↓

| 1745 | .... 35 | 130 | 575 | 1746/5 | .... 90 | 300 | 1100 |
| 1746 | .... 90 | 300 | 1100 | | | | |

N.B. In and after 1746 the 'U' was changed to 'V' on old Head Shillings.

3704
1758 Shilling

	F £	VF £	EF £		F £	VF £	EF £
3704 **Shilling.** Old laur. and dr. bust R. plain angles die axis ↑↓							
1746 Proof only *FDC* £3750				1751	110	350	1350
1750	45	150	750	1758 also known with small			
1750/46	50	160	775	58 in date	20	45	225
1750 Wide O	50	160	775				

3705
1728 Sixpence, young bust

3706
1728 Sixpence, plumes
on reverse

3707
1728 Sixpence, roses
and plumes

	F £	VF £	EF £		F £	VF £	EF £
3705 **Sixpence.** Young laur. and dr. bust. l. R. Angles plain, die axis ↑↓ 1728	50	175	600				
1728 Proof *FDC* £4250							
3706 **Sixpence.** Similar R. Plumes in angles die axis ↑↓ 1728	45	150	575				
3707 **Sixpence.** Young laur. and dr. bust l. R. Roses and plumes in angles die axis ↑↓							
1728	35	125	475	1735	40	135	550
1731	35	130	525	1735/4	45	150	575
1732	35	130	525	1736	50	175	600
1734	40	135	550				

3708
Sixpence, roses

3709
Sixpence, old bust, roses

	F £	VF £	EF £		F £	VF £	EF £
3708 **Sixpence.** Young laur. and dr. bust l., R. Roses in angles, die axis ↑↓							
1739	35	125	500	1741	35	125	500
1739 O/R in legend	40	135	550				
3709 **Sixpence.** Old laur. and dr. bust. l. R. Roses in angles die axis ↑↓							
1743	25	90	375	1745/3	30	100	400
1745	25	90	375				

	F	VF	EF		F	VF	EF
	£	£	£		£	£	£

3710 Sixpence. Old laur. and dr. bust LIMA below bust R. angle plain die axis ↑↓

1745 25	85	350

3710A Sixpence. Similar as last but reads GEORGIVS die axis ↑↓

1746 20	70	300	1746/5 35	110	375

3711
Proof Sixpence

3711 Sixpence. Old laur. and dr. bust l. R. angles plain die axis ↑↓

1746 *proof only FDC* £1850

1750 30	75	350	1758 10	30	150
1751 30	85	375	1758 ÐEI error 20	40	175
1757 10	30	150	1758/7 15	35	165

3712 Fourpence. Young laur. and dr. bust l. R. Small dome-shaped crown without pearls on arch, figure 4

1729 22	48	120	1731 20	45	110

3712A Fourpence. Similar R.Double arched crown with pearls, large figure 4, die axis ↑↓

1732 22	48	120	1740 18	35	100
1735 22	48	125	1743 35	80	250
1737 22	48	125	1743/0 35	80	250
1739 20	45	110	1746 15	30	85
			1760 22	45	130

3713 Threepence. Young laur. and dr. bust l. R. Crowned 3, pearls on arch, die axis ↑↓

1729 18	38	90

3713A Threepence. Similar R. Ornate arch die axis ↑↓

1731 Smaller lettering 18	38	90	1731 18	38	90

3713B Threepence. Similar R. Double arched crown with pearls, die axis ↑↓

1732 18	38	85	1743 Large lettering... 15	30	80
1732 with stop over head 18	38	85	1743 Small lettering... 15	30	80
1735 18	38	90	1743 — stop over head 18	35	85
1737 15	35	80	1746 12	25	75
1739 15	30	80	1746/3 14	30	75
1740 15	30	80	1760 18	38	85

3714 Twopence. Young laur. and dr. bust l. R. Small crown and figure 2, die axis ↑↓

1729 15	25	70	1731 15	25	65

3714A Twopence. Young laur. and dr. bust l. R. Large crown and figure 2 die axis ↑↓

1732 15	25	70	1743/0 15	28	70
1735 15	25	65	1746 12	22	60
1737 15	25	70	1756 12	25	50
1739 15	25	70	1759 12	25	45
1740 22	35	90	1760 18	30	75
1743 15	28	70			

3715 Penny. Young laur. and dr. bust l. head. R. Date over small crown and figure 1, die axis ↑↓

1729 12	25	70	1731 12	25	70

	F £	VF £	EF £		F £	VF £	EF £

3715A Penny. Young laur. and dr. bust l. R. Large crown dividing date die axis ↑↓

	F	VF	EF		F	VF	EF
1732	12	25	65	1753/2	10	25	45
1735	15	30	60	1753	10	20	40
1737	15	30	65	1754	10	25	45
1739	12	25	60	1755	10	20	45
1740	12	25	60	1756	10	20	45
1743	10	22	60	1757	10	20	50
1746	10	20	60	1757 GRATIA:	12	35	70
1746/3	12	32	65	1758	10	20	45
1750	10	20	40	1759	10	20	50
1752	10	20	40	1760	18	30	75
1752/0	10	30	60				

3716

3716 Maundy Set. The four denominations. Uniform dates

	F	VF	EF		F	VF	EF
1729	80	225	500	1739	75	165	425
1731	80	225	500	1740	75	165	425
1732	80	200	450	1743	100	250	550
1735	80	200	450	1746	70	150	400
1737	80	200	450	1760	85	225	500

COPPER

3717

3717 Halfpenny. Young laur. and cuir. bust l. R. Britannia, date in ex. die axis ↑↓

	F	VF	EF		F	VF	EF
1729	15	100	380	1733	10	90	370
1729 rev. no stop	20	110	410	1734	10	90	370
1730	10	100	360	1734 R/O on obv	20	145	450
1730 GEOGIVS error	20	150	470	1734/3	30	210	—
1730 stop after date	20	110	380	1734 no stops on obv.	30	210	—
1730 no stop after REX on obv	25	160	470	1735	10	90	370
1731	10	90	360	1736	15	110	400
1731 rev. no stop	20	150	440	1736/0	20	130	450
1732	10	100	360	1737	15	100	400
1732 rev. no stop	20	150	440	1738	10	75	370
				1738 V/S on obv	20	145	450
				1739	10	75	370

	F	VF	EF		F	VF	EF

	£	£	£		£	£	£
3718 Halfpenny. Old laur. and cuir. bust l., GEORGIUS R. Britannia, date in ex. die axis ↑↓

1740 10	70	300	1743 10	70	300
1742 10	70	300	1744 10	70	300
1742/0 20	130	425	1745 10	70	300

3719
1746 Halfpenny

3719 Halfpenny. Old laur. and cuir. bust l. GEORGIVS, R. Britannia, date in ex. die axis ↑↓

1746 10	65	300	1751 10	65	300
1747 10	70	320	1752 10	65	300
1748 10	70	320	1753 10	65	300
1749 10	70	300	1754 10	70	320
1750 10	70	320			

3720

3720 Farthing. Young laur. and cuir. bust l. R. Britannia, date in ex. die axis ↑↓

1730 10	70	330	1735 3 over 5 20	130	425
1731 10	70	330	1736 10	70	330
1732 15	75	365	1736 triple tie ribands 30	130	425
1732/1 20	110	385	1737 small date 10	65	300
1733 10	70	330	1737 large date 15	80	375
1734 15	75	365	1739 10	65	300
1734 no stop on obv. 30	120	385	1739/5 25	100	300
1735 10	65	300			

3721 Farthing. Old laur. and cuir. bust. GEORGIUS R. Britannia, date in ex. die axis ↑↓

1741 15	80	300	1744 10	65	275

3722 Farthing. Similar R. Britannia, date in ex. die axis ↑↓

1746 8	65	240	1750 15	75	275
1746 V over U 90	250	—	1754 5	45	135
1749 15	75	275	1754/0 25	130	300

George III, grandson of George II was born on 4 June 1738. He married Charlotte of Mecklenburg and they had nine sons and six daughters. The French Revolution and the American War of Independence both happened in his long reign, the longest yet of any King. The naval battle of Trafalgar and the Battle of Waterloo also took place during his reign. Later in his reign, he was affected by what seems to be the mental disease porphyria, and the future George IV was appointed as regent. George III died at Windsor Castle on 29 January 1820.

During the second half of the 18th century very little silver or copper was minted. In 1797 Matthew Boulton's 'cartwheels', the first copper Pennies and Twopences, demonstrated the improvement gleaned from the application of steam power to the coining press.

During the Napoleonic Wars bank notes came into general use when the issue of Guineas was stopped between 1799 and 1813, but gold 7s. pieces, Third-Guineas; were minted to relieve the shortage of smaller money. As an emergency measure Spanish 'Dollars' were put into circulation for a short period after being countermarked, and in 1804 Spanish Eight Reales were overstruck and issued as Bank of England Dollars.

The transition to a 'token' silver coinage began in 1811 when the Bank of England had 3s and 1s. 6d. tokens made for general circulation. Private issues of token money in the years 1788-95 and 1811-15 helped to alleviate the shortage of regal coinage. A change over to a gold standard and a regular 'token' silver coinage came in 1816 when the Mint, which was moved from its old quarters in the Tower of London to a new site on Tower Hill, began a complete re-coinage. The Guinea was replaced by a 20s. Sovereign, and silver coins were made which had an intrinsic value lower than their face value. The St. George design used on the Sovereign and Crown was the work of Benedetto Pistrucci.

Engravers and Designers:– Conrad Heinrich Kuchler (c.1740-1810), Nathaniel Marchant (1739-1816), John Rudulf Ochs Jnr. (1704-88), Lewis Pingo (1743-1830), Thomas Pingo (d.1776) Benedetto Pistrucci (1784-1855), Johann Sigismond Tanner (c.1706-75), Thomas Wyon (1792-1817), William Wyon (1795-1851), Richard Yeo (d.1779).

GOLD

EARLY COINAGES

3723
1770 Pattern Five Guineas

3723 Five Guineas. Pattern only, young long haired bust r. R. crowned shield of
arms, die axis ↑↑ (en medaille)
1770 *FDC* £375000   1773 *FDC* £395000
3723A Five Guineas. Pattern only, young bust right, hair extends under bust similar
1777 *FDC* £350000

3724
1768 Pattern Two Guineas

3724A
1777 Pattern Two Guineas

3724   Two Guineas. Pattern only, young long haired bust r. R. crowned shield of arms, die axis ↑↑
(en medaille)
1768 *FDC* £100000   1773 *FDC* £95000
3724A Two Guineas. Pattern only, thinner young bust right, hair extends under bust similar
1777 *FDC* £90000
There are six different bust varieties for 3723 and 3724, for further details see Wilson & Rasmussen

3725   3726
1761 Guinea first head, two leaf wreath   1763 Guinea second head

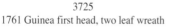

	F	VF	EF		F	VF	EF
	£	£	£		£	£	£

3725   Guinea. First laur. head r., 1761 (varieties with two or three leaves at top
of wreath). R. Crowned shield of arms die axis ↑↓ 2250   6500   15000
3726   Guinea. Second laur. head r. R. Crowned shield of arms die axis ↑↓
1763 1300   4500   11500   1764 no stop
1764 1300   4000   11000   over head........ 2250   5250   11500
*Plain edge patterns exist of 1761 Guinea by John Tanner and 1763 by Richard Yeo. Both are
extremely rare and trade too infrequently to price.*

3727	3728	3729
Guinea, third head	Guinea, fourth head	Guinea, fifth head, 'spade' type

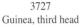

	F	VF	EF		F	VF	EF
	£	£	£		£	£	£

3727 Guinea. Third laur. head r. R. Crowned shield of arms die axis ↑↓

1765	375	750	2100	1770	1350	2850	7500
1766	375	800	2350	1771	375	700	2000
1767	475	1100	2950	1772	375	700	2100
1768	375	750	2100	1773	375	700	1900
1769	400	800	2500	1773 first 7 over 1	475	1100	—

3728 Guinea. Fourth laur. head r. Crowned shield of arms die axis ↑↓

1774	350	650	1500	1779 9/7 error *exists*			
1774 Proof *FDC* £15000				1781	350	650	1600
1775	350	650	1500	1782	350	650	1600
1776	350	850	2000	1783	350	700	1700
1777	425	650	1600	1784	350	650	1500
1778	425	1000	2850	1785	350	650	1500
1778 E over C in REX *exists*				1786	350	650	1500
1779	350	800	1850				

3729 Guinea. Fifth laur. head r. R. 'Spade'-shaped shield, die axis ↑↑

1787	300	525	1200	1794	300	575	1300
1787 Proof *FDC* £14000				1795	300	575	1300
1788	300	575	1300	1796	300	700	1600
1788 second 8/7 *exists*				1797	300	675	1650
1789	300	600	1350	1798*	300	500	1200
1790	300	625	1500	1798/2 error *exists*			
1791	300	575	1300	1798/7	300	700	1700
1792	300	575	1350	1799	350	750	1950
1793	300	600	1350	* Beware counterfeits*			

3730	3731
1813 Guinea "Military type"	Half-Guinea, first head

3730 Guinea. Sixth laur. head. r. R. Shield in Garter, known as the Military guinea, die axis ↑↑

1813	800	2250	5000

3731 Half-Guinea. First laur. head r. R. Crowned shield of arms die axis ↑↓

1762	700	2000	5500	1763	800	2650	6500

Note: All figure 1's are Roman style I's for Guineas from 1781-1799.

3732
1764 Half-Guinea, second head

3733
Half-Guinea, third head

	F £	VF £	EF £		F £	VF £	EF £

3732 Half-Guinea. Second laur. head r. R. Crowned shield of arms die axis ↑↓

	F	VF	EF			F	VF	EF
1764	250	550	1600	1772			*Extremely rare*	
1765	500	1500	4000	1773		300	750	2100
1766	250	600	1850	1774		350	800	2350
1768	250	600	1850	1775		400	1000	3250
1769	275	650	1950					

3734
Half-Guinea, fourth head

3735
Half-Guinea, fifth head

3733 Half-Guinea Third laur. head (less fine style) r. R. Crowned shield of arms die axis ↑↓

	F	VF	EF			F	VF	EF
1774	2250	4500	11000	1775		1400	3250	8500

3734 Half-Guinea Fourth laur. head r. R. Crowned shield of arms die axis ↑↓

	F	VF	EF			F	VF	EF
1775	200	500	1150	1781		200	525	1250
1775 Proof *FDC* £12500				1783		500	1750	3650
1776	275	575	1550	1784		200	525	1250
1777	200	475	1100	1785		200	450	1100
1778	200	525	1250	1786		200	425	1100
1779	200	525	1250					

3735 Half-Guinea Fifth laur. head. r. R. 'Spade' shaped shield, date below, die axis ↑↑

	F	VF	EF			F	VF	EF
1787	175	400	950	1794		175	500	1100
1787 Proof *FDC* £9500				1795		175	525	1150
1788	175	425	1050	1796		175	475	1050
1789	175	500	1100	1797		175	475	1050
1790	175	475	1050	1798		175	425	950
1791	175	475	1050	1798/7		200	550	1250
1792	1500	4000	—	1800		300	950	2300
1793	175	425	1000					

3736
Half-Guinea, sixth head

3736 Half-Guinea Sixth laur. head. r. R. Shield in Garter, date below die axis ↑↑

	F	VF	EF			F	VF	EF
1801	175	350	800	1803		225	425	900
1802	200	375	850					

3737
1813 Half-Guinea, seventh head

3738
Third-Guinea, first reverse

3739
Third-Guinea, second reverse

	F	VF	EF		F	VF	EF
	£	£	£		£	£	£

3737   Half-Guinea Seventh laur. head. r. with short hair. R. Shield in garter, date below die axis ↑↑

1804	175	325	650	1810	175	350	700
1805		*Extremely rare*		1811	400	600	1500
1806	175	425	850	1813	250	500	1150
1808	175	400	800	1813 Proof *FDC* £5500			
1809	175	400	800				

3738   Third-Guinea. First laur. head r. R. Crown, date in legend, die axis ↑↑

1797	150	300	725	1799	475	1000	2000
1798	135	275	700	1800	165	350	800

3739   Third-Guinea. First laur. head r. R. Similar but date below crown, die axis ↑↑

1801	175	400	900	1803	165	350	775
1802	165	350	775				

3740
1804 Third Guinea, second head

3741
1762 Quarter Guinea

3740   Third-Guinea. Second laur. head r. with short hair, R. Similar, die axis ↑↑

1804	125	275	625	1810	125	275	625
1806	150	325	725	1811	550	1350	3000
1808	150	325	725	1813	300	625	1350
1809	150	325	725				

3741 Quarter-Guinea. Laur. head r. R. Crowned shield die axis ↑↓ 1762 ... 250   525   900

For gold of the 'new coinage', 1816-20, see page 419.

SILVER

EARLY COINAGES

3742 - 1763 'Northumberland shilling'

3742   Shilling. Young laur. and dr. bust, r. known as the 'Northumberland' shilling, die axis ↑↓

1763* 300   575   1500

Plain edge patterns exist for 1764 and 1778. Both are extremely rare.

Beware, low grade counterfeits exist

	F	VF	EF		F	VF	EF
	£	£	£		£	£	£

3743 Shilling. Older laur. and dr. bust, R. No semée of hearts in Hanoverian shield, die axis ↑↑
1787 25   50   150
1787 Proof *FDC* .... *Extremely rare*
1787 plain edge proof *FDC* £2750
1787 plain edge pattern by Pingo, border of dots at perimeter *FDC* £1250

3744 Shilling. — No stop over head, die axis ↑↑ 1787 40   85   300

3745 - 1781 No stops at date Shilling

3745 Shilling. — No stops at date, die axis ↑↑ 1787   65 125   475

3745AShilling. — No stops on obv., die axis ↑↑ 1787................................... 450   1000   2750
3746   Shilling. — R. With semée of hearts, die axis ↑↑ 1787....................... 20   55   135
1787 1/1 retrograde 55   150   400
1787 plain edge proof *FDC (Also known on large 27mm flan.)* £2500

Hanoverian Arms

No semée of hearts   With semée of hearts   3747 - 1798 Shilling

3747   Shilling. No stop over head, 1798: known as the 'Dorrien and Magens' shilling *UNC* £30000
3748   Sixpence. Laur. and dr. bust r. R. Without semée of hearts, die axis ↑↑
1787 15   45   115   1787 Proof *FDC*............. *Extremely rare*
3749   Sixpence. Similar R. With semée of hearts, die axis ↑↑ 1787 15   45   115

3749   3750
1787 Sixpence, with hearts   1772 Fourpence

3750   Fourpence. Young laur. and dr. bust r. R. Crowned 4, die axis ↑↓

1763 12	25	75	1772/0 8	25	95
1763 Proof *FDC of highest rarity*			1776 12	25	75
1765 200	425	1100	1780 12	25	75
1766 12	25	75	1784 15	30	90
1770 10	25	55	1786 18	35	95
1772 15	30	80			

3751	3753	3755
'Wire Money' Fourpence	Young bust Threepence	Older bust Threepence

	F	VF	EF		F	VF	EF
	£	£	£		£	£	£

3751 Fourpence. Older laur. and dr. bust. R. Thin 4 ('Wire Money'), die axis ↑↑
1792 ....18 50 125

3752 Fourpence. Older laur. and dr. bust r. R. Normal Crowned 4, die axis ↑↑
1795 .... 8 25 75 1800 .... 10 20 65

3753 Threepence. Young laur. dr. bust r. R. Crowned 3, die axis ↑↓
1762 ....5 15 50 1772 small III............. 10 25 70
1763 ....5 15 50 1772 very large III 8 20 70
1763 Proof *FDC of highest rarity* 1780 .... 10 20 70
1765 .... 250 500 1150 1784 .... 12 30 75
1766 .... 10 30 70 1786 .... 10 20 65
1770 .... 10 25 65

3754 Threepence. Older laur. dr. bust. r. R. Thin 3 ('Wire Money'), die axis ↑↑
1792 ....18 55 150

3755 Threepence. Older laur. and dr. bust r. R. Normal Crowned 3, die axis ↑↑
1795 .... 10 25 65 1800 .... 8 20 45

3756 Twopence. Young laur. and dr. bust r. R. Crowned 2, die axis ↑↓
1763 .... 15 30 60 1776 .... 10 20 60
1763 Proof *FDC of highest rarity* 1780 .... 12 20 60
1765 .... 125 350 625 1784 .... 8 20 60
1766 .... 8 20 45 1786 .... 8 20 60
1772 .... 8 20 45 1786 large obv. lettering . 5 20 60
1772 second 7/6............ 6 25 70

3756
Young bust Twopence

3757 Twopence. Older laur. and dr. bust. r. R. Thin 2 ('Wire Money'), die axis ↑↑
1792 .... 18 50 115

3758 Twopence. Older laur. and dr. bust r. R. Normal Crowned 2, die axis ↑↑
1795 .... 6 15 45 1800 .... 6 15 45

3759 Penny. Young laur. and dr. bust r. R. Crowned 1, die axis ↑↓
1763 .... 15 25 60 1779 .... 8 15 60
1763 Proof *FDC* ....*Extremely rare* 1780 .... 10 20 60
1766 .... 10 20 60 1781 .... 10 18 60
1770 .... 8 15 60 1784 .... 10 18 55
1772 .... 8 20 60 1786 .... 8 15 45
1776 .... 8 15 60

3760 Penny. Older laur. and dr. bust. r. R. Thin 1 ('Wire Money'), die axis ↑↑
1792 .... 10 30 95

	F	VF	EF		F	VF	EF
	£	£	£		£	£	£

3761 Penny. Older laur. and dr. bust r. Ɍ. Normal Crowned 1, die axis ↑↑
1795 8   18   50   1800 6   18   50

3762 Maundy Set. Young laur. and dr. bust. r. Uniform dates
1763.........................115   200   425   1780.........................115   200   425
1763 Proof set *FDC* £11500   1784.........................115   200   425
1766.........................115   200   425   1786.........................115   200   425
1772.........................115   200   425

3763 Maundy Set. — Older laur. and dr. bust. r. Ɍ. Thin numerals ('Wire Money'),
1792 150   300   750

3764 Maundy Set. Older laur. and dr. bust r. Ɍ. Normal numerals. Uniform dates
1795 60   150   400   1800 60   130   375

N.B. Set prices are for matched sets, condition, toning etc.

EMERGENCY ISSUES, die axis ↑↑

3765 Dollar. Pillar type (current for 4s 9d). Spanish American 8 Reales,
oval countermark with head of George III.
    Mexico City Mint — m̥ mint mark in reverse legend 1350   3500   —
    Bolivia, Potosi Mint – PTS monogram in reverse legend 1650   4250   —
    Peru, Lima Mint – LIMÆ monogram in reverse legend 1750   4500   —

two initials of mint master

denomination

mint mark

3765A
Peru Mint Portrait type Dollar with oval countermark

3765A Dollar. Portrait type, oval countermark.
    Mexico City Mint — m̥ mint mark in reverse legend 125   375   900
    Bolivia, Potosi Mint — PTS monogram in reverse legend 175   650   1400
    Chile, Santiago Mint — s̥ mint mark in reverse legend 725   1950   —
    Guatemala Mint — NG mint mark in reverse legend......................... 900   2500   —
    Spain, Madrid Mint mint mark in reverse left field............................ 400   1600   3500
    Spain, Seville Mint mint mark in reverse left field 400   1500   3000
    Peru, Lima Mint — LIMÆ monogram in reverse legend 250   800   1650
3765B Dollar. — Oval countermark on silver French Ecu of crown size 3950   12000   —
3765C Dollar. — Oval countermark on USA Dollar...   *Of highest rarity*
3765D Dollar. — Oval countermark on silver Italian crown size coins ....   *Of highest rarity*

mint mark S

Mint Master Initials

3766

3766B

Seville Mint Portrait Dollar with octagonal countermark

	F £	VF £	EF £
3766 Dollar octagonal countermarks with head of George III			
Mexico City Mint — m̊	425	975	2500
Bolivia, Potosi Mint — PTS monogram	850	2150	4500
Guatamala Mint — NG	1250	3500	—
Peru, Lima Mint — LIME monogram	575	1650	4000
Spain, Madrid Mint M to left of reverse shield	1100	2750	—
Spain, Seville Mint S to left of reverse shield	1250	3250	—
3766A Dollar. — Octagonal countermark on French Ecu or Italian Scudi		*Of highest rarity*	
3766B Dollar. — Octagonal countermark on USA Dollar	19500	55000	—

3767

Half-Dollar with oval countermark, Madrid Mint

3767 Half-Dollar. With similar oval countermark of George III,			
Bolivia, Potosi Mint — PTS monogram	325	750	1650
Chile, Santiago Mint — s̊ mint mark	475	1250	—
Spain, Madrid Mint — Crowned M to left of shield	175	500	1150
Spain, Seville Mint — Crowned S to left of shield	175	500	1150
3767A Half Dollar. With Octagonal countermark. Similar *from* 850		1750	—

BANK OF ENGLAND ISSUE, 1804-16

3768

	F	VF	EF		F	VF	EF
	£	£	£		£	£	£

3768   Dollar. (current for 5s. until 1811, revalued at 5s. 6d. until withdrawn from circulation in
1817). laur. and dr. bust of king. r. ℞.
Britannia seated l., several varieties occur, die axis ↑↑

	F	VF	EF
1804 O. Top leaf to left side of E, ℞. Upright K to left of shield	125	300	775
1804 — —no stops in CHK on truncation	175	400	950
1804 O. Top leaf to centre of E ℞. Similar	150	350	850
1804 — —no stop after REX	125	300	800
1804 —℞. K inverted and incuse	175	475	1100
1804 O. Top leaf to right side of E, ℞. normal K	*Extremely rare*		
1804 —℞. K inverted to left of shield	175	450	1000

Various 1804 Proof strikings of varieties above *FDC from* £1950 to £4750

*These dollars were re-struck from Spanish-American 8-Reales until at least 1811. Dollars that still
show dates and Mint marks of original coin beneath are worth up to 25% more.*

3769   3770
1811 Three Shillings, first bust   Three Shillings, second head

3769   Three Shillings. Dr and laur. bust in armour r. ℞. BANK / TOKEN /
3 SHILL. / date (in oak wreath), die axis ↑↑

1811	20	75	275	1812	20	75	300

1811 Proof *FDC* £1950

3770   Three Shillings. — Laureate head r. Top leaf between I/G ℞. As before but wreath of oak
and olive, die axis ↑↑

1812	20	75	275	1813	20	75	325
1812 Proof *FDC* £2000				1814	20	75	325
1812 Proof in gold *FDC*	*Extremely rare*			1815	20	75	325
1812 Proof in platinum *FDC* £25000				1816*	375	800	2750

*Beware of counterfeits

3771   3772
Eighteenpence, first bust   Eighteenpence, second head

	F	VF	EF		F	VF	EF
	£	£	£		£	£	£

3771 Eighteenpence. Dr. and laur. bust r. in armour R BANK/TOKEN/Is. 6D./date (in oak wreath) ↑↑

| 1811 | .... | 12 | 40 | 225 | 1812 | .... | 15 | 45 | 250 |

1811 Proof *FDC* £1500

3772 Eighteenpence. Laureate head r. die axis ↑↑

1812	....	12	40	225	1813 Platinum proof *FDC of the highest rarity*			
1812 Proof *FDC* £1500				1814	....	12	45	275
1812 Platinum proof *of the highest rarity*				1815	....	12	45	275
1812 Proof R. Small letters *FDC* £3750				1816	....	12	45	275
1813	....	12	45	250				

3773
1812 Pattern Ninepence, 9D type

3773 Ninepence. Similar, Laur. head 1812, R. 9D type (pattern only) die axis ↑↑ *FDC* £3000
3773A Ninepence. — — 1812, R. 9 pence type (pattern only) die axis ↑↑ FDC £5000

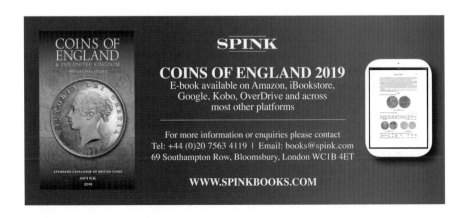

COPPER

First Issue — Tower Mint, London

3774   3775
Rev. C, leaves point between A and N

	F	VF	EF		F	VF	EF
	£	£	£		£	£	£

3774 Halfpenny. Laur. and Cuir. bust r. R. Britannia l. date in ex., die axis ↑↓

	F	VF	EF		F	VF	EF
1770 10		60	300	1772 ball below			
1770 Proof die axis ↑↑ *FDC* £2500				spear blade 10		50	225
1770 Proof in silver *FDC*	*Extremely rare*			1772 no incuse			
1770 no stop on rev. 15		65	350	hair coil 10		55	300
1771 10		50	300	1772 — no stop on rev.... 15		65	325
1771 no stop on rev........ 15		65	350	1773 12		55	300
1771 ball below				1773 no stop after REX 20		65	350
spear blade 10		50	275	1773 no stop on rev. 20		65	350
1772 incuse hair coil				1774 different obv.			
on rev. 10		55	300	profile.................. 20		80	400
1772 GEORIVS error 50		150	475	1775 — 12		75	400

3775 Farthing. Laur. and cuir. bust r. R. Britannia l. date in ex., die axis ↑↓

	F	VF	EF		F	VF	EF
1771 Proof *FDC* £1500				1773 no stop after REX . 25		75	350
1771 Rev A. leaf to r.of N.18		65	300	1774 12		50	225
1771 Rev B. leaf to N.... 18		60	275	1775 12		50	250
1771 Rev C................... 18		60	250	1775 struck en			
1771 1st 7/1 25		185	500	medaille ↑↑ 25		75	325
1773 10		50	175	1775 GEORGIVS......... 35		250	650
1773 no stop on rev........ 12		65	325				

Note: 1771 varieties refer to the direction the top leaf of olive branch points in Britannia's hand

Second Issue — Soho Mint. Birmingham 'Cartwheel' coinage, die axis ↑↓

3776

3776 Twopence. Legends incuse on raised rim,
1797 Copper proof *FDC* £2750
1797 Bronzed proof *FDC* £2500
1797 Silver proof *FDC*.......... *Extremely rare*

		F	VF	EF
1797 30			75	325
1797 Gold proof *FDC* ....*Extremely rare*				
1797 Gilt copper *FDC* £3750				

Prices for UNCIRCULATED copper coins are no longer quoted. Truly uncirculated copper coins of this period are too seldom traded on the market to fix a meaningful price. As a guide a truly uncirculated coin with full lustre or bloom should fetch 3-4 times the EF price.

3777

	F	VF	EF
	£	£	£
3777 Penny. 1797. Similar, 10 leaves in wreath on obv.	12	60	175
1797 11 leaves in wreath on obv.	15	95	250

1797 Gilt copper proof *FDC* £2250
1797 Copper proof *FDC* £1500
1797 Bronzed proof *FDC* £1250
1797 Silver proof *FDC* .... *Extremely rare*
1797 Gold proof *FDC* .... *Extremely rare*

Halfpence and Farthings of this issue are patterns.

Third Issue—Soho Mint, Birmingham, die axis ↑↓

3778   3779

	VF	EF		VF	EF
	£	£		£	£

3778 Halfpenny. Laur. and dr. bust r., R. Britannia l. date below
1799 Ship on rev. with 5 incuse gunports — 10 / 50
1799 Ship with 6 relief gunports — 10 / 100
1799 Ship with 9 relief gunports — 15 / 125

1799 Ship with plain hull — 12 / 125
1799 — raised line on hull — 15 / 125
1799 Copper proof *FDC* £750
1799 Bronzed proof *FDC* £700
1799 Gilt copper proof *FDC* £1250

3779 Farthing. Laur. and dr. bust r. date below R. Britannia l.
1799 Obv. with 3 berries in wreath — 5 / 50
1799 Copper *FDC* £550
1799 Bronzed proof *FDC* £500
1799 Copper gilt proof *FDC* £975

1799 Obv. with 4 berries in wreath — 5 / 75
1799 Gold proof *FDC of the highest rarity*
1799 Silver proof *FDC Extremely rare*

Fourth Issue—Soho Mint, Birmingham, die axis ↑↓

3780

	VF	EF		VF	EF
	£	£		£	£

3780 **Penny.** Shorter haired, laur. and dr. bust r. date below. R. Britannia l. date below

	VF	EF			
1806 incuse hair curl by tie knot	12	65	1807 Copper proof *FDC* £800		
1806 no incuse hair curl	12	95	1807 Bronzed proof *FDC* £750		
1806 Copper proof *FDC* £700			1807 Gilt copper proof *FDC* £2250		
1806 Bronzed proof *FDC* £650			1807 Silver proof *FDC* .... *Extremely rare*		
1806 Gilt copper proof *FDC* £1350			1807 Gold proof *FDC* .... *Extremely rare*		
1806 Silver proof *FDC* £6500			1807 Platinum proof *FDC* .... *Extremely rare*		
1807	20	80	1808 Proof *FDC* .... *Unique*		

3781

3782

3781 **Halfpenny.** Shorter haired laur. and dr. bust r. date below, R. Britannia l.

	VF	EF		VF	EF
1806 rev. no berries	8	35	1807	10	60
1806 rev. 3 berries	8	75	1807 Copper proof *FDC* £550		
1806 Copper proof *FDC* £550			1807 Bronzed proof *FDC* £500		
1806 Bronzed proof *FDC* £500			1807 Silver proof *FDC* £4500		
1806 Gilt proof *FDC* £950			1807 Gold proof *FDC* .... *Extremely rare*		
1806 Silver proof *FDC* .... *Extremely rare*					

3782 **Farthing.** Shorter haired laur. and dr. bust r. date below, R. Britannia l.

	VF	EF		VF	EF
1806 K. on tr.	10	57	1806 Gold proof *FDC* .... *Extremely rare*		
1806 incuse dot on tr.	30	125	1807	10	85
1806 Copper proof *FDC* £550			1807 Copper proof *FDC* £600		
1806 Bronzed proof *FDC* £500			1807 Bronzed proof *FDC* £550		
1806 Gilt copper proof *FDC* £950			1807 Silver proof *FDC* .... *Extremely rare*		
1806 Silver proof *FDC* .... *Extremely rare*			1807 Gold proof *FDC* .... *Extremely rare*		

Prices for UNCIRCULATED copper coins are no longer quoted. Truly uncirculated copper coins of this period are too seldom traded on the market to fix a meaningful price. As a guide a truly uncirculated coin with full lustre or bloom should fetch 3-4 times the EF price.

LAST OR NEW COINAGE, 1816-20

The year 1816 is a landmark in the history of our coinage. For some years at the beginning of the 19th century Mint production was virtually confined to small gold denominations, regular full production being resumed only after the Mint had been moved from the Tower of London to a new site on Tower Hill. Steam powered minting machinery made by Boulton and Watt replaced the old hand-operated presses and these produced coins which were technically much superior to the older milled coins.

In 1816 for the first time British silver coins were produced with an intrinsic value somewhat below their face value, the first official token coinage. The old Guinea was replaced by a Sovereign of twenty shillings in 1817, the standard of 22 carat (0.916) fineness still being retained.

Mint Master or Engraver's and/or designer's initials:

B.P. (Benedetto Pistrucci 1784-1855)   WWP (William Wellesley Pole)

GOLD

3783

3783   Five Pounds. 1820 LX (Pattern only) laur. head r. date below R. St George and dragon, edge inscribed die axis ↑↓ *FDC* £400000

1820 Similar plain edge proof *FDC (*only two struck) *Of highest rarity*

3784

3784   Two Pounds. 1820 LX (Pattern only) laur. head r. date below R. St George and dragon, edge inscribed die axis ↑↓ *FDC* £65000

1820 Similar plain edge proof *FDC   Extremely rare*

3785   3785A

	F	VF	EF	UNC		F	VF	EF	UNC
	£	£	£	£		£	£	£	£

3785 Sovereign. laur. head r. coarse hair, legend type A (Descending colon after BRITANNIAR, no space between REX and F:D:). R. St. George and dragon, die axis ↑↓

1817 500   900   1950   5000   1818 800   1600   4500   8750
1817 Proof *FDC* £27500   1819 45000   75000 250000   —
1817 ↑↑ die axis . 1250   —   —   —

3785ASovereign. Similar legend type B (Ascending colon after BRITANNIAR, space between REX and F:D:) ↑↓

1818 700   1400   4000   7500   1818 Proof *FDC* £37500

3785B Sovereign. laur head r. hair with tighter curls, legend type A. R. Similar die axis ↑↓

1818 ....   *Extremely rare*

3785C
Large date, open 2 variety

3785C Sovereign. Similar legend type B. (as above) die axis ↑↓

1818 .... *Extremely rare*   1820 short date height, alignment
1820 Roman I in date . *Extremely rare*   varies 450   950   2000   4750
1820 open 2, alignment of date   1820 closed 2 alignment of date
    varies 350   700   1300   4750   varies 400   800   1600   4500
1820 thin date, smaller 0 Proof *FDC* £21500

The above 1820 entries are the main variations, there do exist other subtle differences which are merely sub-varieties and therefore are not included.

3786
1817 Half-Sovereign

3786 Half-Sovereign. laur. head r. date below R. Crowned shield, edge milled die axis ↑↓

1817 175   350   700   2050   1818 250   400   800   2500
1817 Proof *FDC* £12500   1820 200   375   700   2250
*1818/7 425   900   2150   —   1820 Letter O
1818 Proof *FDC* £15000   for zero 325   500   850   2750

*Note: 7 under 8 clearly visible at top right of 8

SILVER

3787

1818 George III Crown

	F	VF	EF	UNC		F	VF	EF	UNC
	£	£	£	£		£	£	£	£

3787 Crown. Laur. head r. R. Pistrucci's St. George and dragon within Garter edge inscribed, die axis ↑↓

		F	VF	EF	UNC
1818	LVIII, edge	45	100	600	1500
1818	LVIII error edge inscription			*Extremely rare*	
1818	LVIII Proof *FDC*			*Extremely rare*	
1818	LIX	45	110	625	1650
1818	LIX TUTΛMEN error	80	350	—	
1819	LIX	40	100	525	1400
1819	LIX no stops on edge	65	200	775	1850
1819	LIX R. Thicker ruled garter	60	135	850	—
1819/8	LIX	70	250	900	—
1819	LX	50	120	550	1500
1819	LX no stop after TUTAMEN	60	150	750	—
1820	LX	45	110	575	1600
1820	LX R. S/T in SOIT	65	225	850	—
1820/19	LX	80	275	975	—

3788

1817 Halfcrown, large bust

3788 Halfcrown. Large laur. bust or 'bull' head r. date below R. Crowned garter and shield die axis ↑↑

1816	30	75	425	625	1817 E/R in DEI			*Extremely rare*	
1816 Proof *FDC* £5250					1817 S/I in PENSE	55	225	725	—
1816 Plain edge proof *FDC* £6750					1817 Proof *FDC* £5250				
1817	25	75	400	600	1817 Plain edge proof *FDC* £6250				
1817 D/T in DEI	75	300	800	—					

3789
1817 Halfcrown, small head

	F	VF	EF	UNC		F	VF	EF	UNC
	£	£	£	£		£	£	£	£

3789 Halfcrown. Small laur. head r. date below, R. Crowned garter and shield die axis ↑↑

	F	VF	EF	UNC		F	VF	EF	UNC
1817*	30	75	325	675	1818 Proof *FDC* £5750				
1817 Proof *FDC* £5250					1819 Proof *FDC* £5500				
1817 Plain edge proof *FDC* £5500					1819	30	75	400	675
1817 Reversed s's in garter		*Extremely rare*			1819/8			*Extremely rare*	
1818 Reversed s's in garter		*Extremely rare*			1820	40	100	475	775
1818**	40	100	450	775	1820 Proof *FDC* £5250				
					1820 Plain edge proof *FDC* £5750				

* *Beware recent low grade forgeries*
** *Beware of silvered base metal contemporary forgeries*

3790
1819 Shilling

3790 Shilling. laur head r. date below R. Crowned Shield in Garter edge milled, die axis ↑↑

	F	VF	EF	UNC		F	VF	EF	UNC
1816	10	18	75	150	1818	25	50	200	500
1816 Proof *FDC* £1650					1818 High 8	30	65	225	475
1816 Plain edge proof *FDC* £1850					1819/8	15	30	135	350
1816 Proof in gold *FDC*		*Extremely rare*			1819	15	25	100	200
1817	10	18	75	175	1819 9/6 exists				
1817 RRITT flaw	20	30	150	325	1820	15	25	100	200
1817 Plain edge proof *FDC* £1750					1820 I/S in HONI	35	65	250	525
1817 GEOE error	65	225	600	1100	1820 Proof *FDC* £1750				
1817 E over R in GEOR *exists*									

3791
1817 Sixpence

	F	VF	EF	UNC		F	VF	EF	UNC
	£	£	£	£		£	£	£	£

3791 Sixpence. laur head r. date below R. Crowned Shield in Garter edge milled, die axis ↑↑

	F	VF	EF	UNC		F	VF	EF	UNC
1816	7	14	65	135	1819/8	14	23	90	175
1816 Proof plain edge FDC £1350					1819	11	18	85	150
1816 Proof in gold FDC		Extremely rare			1819 small 8	11	18	78	150
1817	9	16	75	150	1820	11	18	78	135
1817 Proof plain edge FDC £1350					1820 inverted 1	70	300	575	—
1817 Proof milled edge FDC £1650					1820 I/S in HONI	70	275	525	—
1818	11	18	80	150	1820 obv. no colons	115	350	675	—
1818 Proof milled edge FDC £1800					1820 milled edge Proof FDC £1650				

3792

3792 Maundy Set. (4d., 3d., 2d. and 1d.) laur. head, date below die axis ↑↑

		F	VF	EF			F	VF	EF
1817		80	175	400	1820		75	150	375
1818		75	150	375					
3793 — **Fourpence.** 1817, 1818, 1820	from	12	25	65	100
3794 — **Threepence.** 1817, 1818, 1820	from	10	20	55	80
3795 — **Twopence.** 1817, 1818, 1820	from	10	18	35	65
3796 — **Penny.** 1817, 1818, 1820	from	8	15	35	65

Maundy pennies are always the most requested oddment, it is the smallest coin in the set and is therefore the easiest to lose. Penny collectors also dictate supply and demand for this coin.

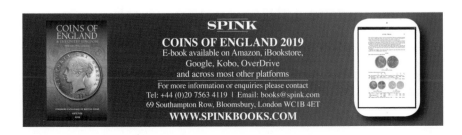

George IV, eldest son of George III, was born on 12 August 1762 and was almost a complete opposite to his father. He was very extravagant and lived in the height of luxury. He especially influenced fashion of the time which became known as the 'Regency' style. He had numerous mistresses, and had an arranged marriage with Caroline of Brunswick. She later left England and travelled Southern Europe, North Africa and the Holy Land basing herself in Naples but returned to claim her place as Queen upon George's accession. George banned her from ever being crowned, and he died without ever conceiving a son on 26 June 1830, when his younger brother William ascended the throne.

The Mint resumed the coinage of copper farthings in 1821, and pennies and halfpennies in 1825. A gold Two Pound piece was first issued for general circulation in 1823. A full cased proof set of the new bare head coinage was issued in limited quantities in 1826.

Engraver's and/or designer's initials on the coins:
B. P. (Benedetto Pistrucci)   W.W. P. (William Wellesley Pole) – Master of the Mint
J. B. M. (Jean Baptiste Merlen)

Engravers and Designers:– Francis Legett Chantrey (1781-1842) Jean Baptiste Merlen (1769-c.1850) Benedetto Pistrucci (1784-1855) William Wyon (1795-1851)

GOLD

3797
3797 Five Pounds. 1826 Bare head l. date below R. Crowned shield and mantle, inscribed edge, die axis ↑↓ Proof *FDC* £75000
1826 Piedfort proof *FDC* .... *Extremely rare*

3798   3799

	F	VF	EF	UNC
	£	£	£	£

3798 Two Pounds. 1823 Proof *FDC* £13500

1823 Proof no JBM below truncation *FDC* .... *Extremely rare*

1823 Large bare head. l. R. St. George, inscribed edge ↑↓ 700   1100   2250   4000

3799 Two Pounds. Bare head l. date below R. Crowned shield and mantle inscribed edge
   die axis ↑↓

1824 Proof *FDC* .... *Extremely rare*   1826. Piedfort proof *FDC* ...... *Extremely rare*

1825 Proof plain edge *FDC* £21500   1826. Proof *FDC* £14500

3801   3803
Sovereign, second type   Half-Sovereign, second reverse

	F	VF	EF	UNC		F	VF	EF	UNC
	£	£	£	£		£	£	£	£

3800   Sovereign. Laur. head. l. R. St. George and dragon date in ex., die axis ↑↓

1821 400	700	1850	3750	1823 1100	2750	8000	—
1821 Proof *FDC* £11500				1824 500	900	2250	4250
1822* 400	750	1850	4250	1825 750	2000	5750	9250

3801   Sovereign. Bare head. date below l. R. Crowned shield, die axis ↑↓

1825 400	750	1600	3500	1827* 425	750	1600	4000
1825 Proof 8 heart semée *FDC* £13500				1828 6000	15000	29500	—
1825 Plain edge proof 7 heart				1829 500	800	2250	4250
semée *FDC* £14500				1830 500	800	2250	4250
1826 400	700	1500	3750	1830 die axis ↑↑ *Extremely rare*			
1826 Proof *FDC* £9500				1830 Milled edge proof *Extremely rare*			

3802 Half-Sovereign. Laur. head. l. R. Ornately garnished Crowned shield. die axis ↑↓

1821 950   1800   3250   6250

1821 Proof *FDC* £9000

3803 Half-Sovereign. Laur. head l. R. Plain Crowned shield die axis ↑↓

1823 225	400	900	2350	1825 200	300	650	1800
1824 200	350	750	2000				

*Beware counterfeits

3804 -1825 Half Sovereign, bare head

	F	VF	EF	UNC		F	VF	EF	UNC
	£	£	£	£		£	£	£	£

3804 Half-Sovereign. Bare head. date below l. R. Crowned garnished shield die axis ↑↓

1826	200	325	850	1850	1827	200	350	900	2100
1826 Proof *FDC* £6000					1828	200	300	850	2000

3804A Half-Sovereign. Similar with extra tuft of hair to l. ear, much heavier border, die axis ↑↓

1826	200	300	800	1850	1827	200	350	850	2100
1826 Proof *FDC* £6000					1828	200	325	800	2000

SILVER

WWP   B.P.

3805 - 1821 Laureate bust Crown

3805 Crown. Laur. head. l. R. St. George, date in exergue, B.P. to upper right, tiny italic WWP under lance, die axis ↑↓

1821*, edge	SECUNDO	50	150	700	2000
1821	SECUNDO WWP inverted under lance	75	350	900	2250
1821	SECUNDO L - very clearly defined WWP Proof *FDC* £6000				
1821	SECUNDO Proof in copper				*Extremely rare*
1821	TERTIO Proof *FDC* £10000				
1822	SECUNDO	60	200	975	2750
1822	TERTIO	55	200	900	2250

3806 - 1826 Proof Crown, bare head

3806 Crown. Bare head. l. R. Shield with crest inscribed edge, die axis ↑↓

1825 Proof *FDC* £30000	1826 Proof *FDC* £22500

* Beware of recent counterfeits in high grade

3807   3807

Halfcrown, lightly garnished shield,   Heavy garnishing, right thistle leaf closer,
right thistle leaf further from stem   more parallel to its stem

	F	VF	EF	UNC		F	VF	EF	UNC
	£	£	£	£		£	£	£	£

3807 Halfcrown. Laur. head. l. ℞. Crowned Garnished shield, die axis ↑↓

1820	25	85	400	750	1821 Heavier shield garnishing				
1820 Proof *FDC* £3500						40	90	500	1100
1820 Plain edge proof *FDC* £4500					1823 —	1250	4500	14850	—
1821	25	85	400	750	1821 Proof *FDC* £3000				

3808   3809

Halfcrown, second reverse   1826 Halfcrown, bare head, third reverse

3808 Halfcrown. Laur. head l. ℞. Crowned Shield in garter and collar die axis ↑↓

| 1823 | 30 | 90 | 450 | 950 | 1824 | 40 | 110 | 500 | 1000 |
| 1823 Proof *FDC* £6000 | | | | | 1824 Proof *FDC* £6500 | | | | |

3809 Halfcrown. Bare head. date below l. ℞. Crowned Shield with crest die axis ↑↓

1824		*Extremely rare*			1826	35	85	375	800
1824 Proof *FDC* £12500					1826 Proof *FDC* £3500				
1825	30	80	350	750	1828	110	300	1000	2750
1825 Proof *FDC* £3500					1829	75	150	550	1100
1825 Plain edge proof *FDC* £4250									

3810 - First reverse   3811 - Second reverse

3810   Shilling. Laur. head. l. ℞. Crowned garnished shield, die axis ↑↓

| 1821 | 12 | 60 | 225 | 600 | 1821 Milled edge Proof *FDC* £1750 | | | | |

3811   Shilling. Laur. head l. ℞. Crowned shield in Garter die axis ↑↓

1823	45	125	350	950	1825	15	60	275	700
1823 Proof *FDC* £3750					1825 Milled edge Proof *FDC* £3500				
1824	8	50	250	675	1825/3		*Extremely rare*		
1824 Milled edge Proof *FDC* £3750									

3812 - Third reverse

	F	VF	EF	UNC		F	VF	EF	UNC
	£	£	£	£		£	£	£	£

3812 Shilling. Bare head l. date below R. Lion on crown die axis ↑↓

1825	8	50	175	500	1826/2		*Extremely rare*		
1825 Roman I	150	450	1100	2200	1827	45	130	450	1100
1825 Milled edge Proof *FDC* £1500					1829	25	65	350	875
1826	5	35	125	425	1829 Milled edge Proof *FDC* £4750				
1826 Proof *FDC* £1100									

3813 - First reverse   3814 - Second reverse   3815 -Third reverse

3813 Sixpence. Laur. head. l. R. Crowned Garnished shield, die axis ↑↓

| 1821 | 8 | 25 | 150 | 450 | 1821 BBITANNIAR. | 100 | 325 | 900 | — |
| 1821 Proof *FDC* £1150 | | | | | | | | | |

3814 Sixpence. Laur. head l. R. Crowned Shield in Garter die axis ↑↓

1824	8	25	175	500	1825 Proof *FDC* £1650				
1824 Proof *FDC* £1650					1826	35	100	325	775
1825	8	20	175	475	1826 Proof *FDC* £2650				

3815 Sixpence. Bare head. l. with or without tuft of hair to l. of ear date below R. Lion on crown die axis ↑↓

1826	8	30	100	450	1828	12	60	250	650
1826 Proof *FDC* £1250					1829	12	35	160	500
1827	55	125	325	775	1829 Proof *FDC* £1800				

3816 - 1822 Maundy Set

	EF	FDC		EF	FDC
	£	£		£	£

3816 Maundy Set. (4d., 3d., 2d. and 1d.) laur head l. die axis ↑↓

1822	250	450	1827	175	400
1822 Proof set *FDC*	*Extremely rare*		1828	175	400
1823	175	400	1828 Proof set *FDC*	*Extremely rare*	
1824	200	450	1829	175	400
1825	175	400	1830	165	400
1826	175	400			

			EF	FDC
3817	**Maundy Fourpence.** 1822-30	*from*	18	55
3818	— **Threepence.** small head, 1822		35	85
3819	— **Threepence.** normal head, 1823-30	*from*	15	50
3820	— **Twopence.** 1822-30	*from*	15	45
3821	— **Penny.** 1822-30	*from*	22	60

See note under 3796.

COPPER

3822 - First Issue Farthing

	F	VF	EF	BU		F	VF	EF	BU
	£	£	£	£		£	£	£	£

First Issue, 1821-6. Obv. reads GEORGIUS IIII

3822   Farthing. Laur. and dr. bust l. R. Britannia r. date in ex. die axis ↑↓

	F	VF	EF	BU		F	VF	EF	BU
1821 Proof *FDC* £1000 ...					1823 — I for 1 in date	25	85	270	—
1821 3	12	55	175		1825 — 3	12	55	175
1822 leaf ribs incuse 2	10	45	150		1825 — D/U in DEI..........20	85	295	—
1822—inv. A's legend . 30	95	340	—		1825 leaf ribs raised 5	15	60	200
1822 leaf ribs raised....... 2	10	45	150		1825 gold proof *FDC*......		*Extremely rare*	
1822 Proof *FDC* £1150					1826 —	5	18	70	225
1822 Proof die axis ↑↑ *FDC* £1400					1826 R/E in GRATIA.... 20	80	270	—
1823 — 3	12	55	175						

See 3825 for Second Issue farthings of 1826 which have die axis ↑↑

3823 - 1826 Penny - plain saltire

Second issue, 1825-30. Obv. reads GEORGIUS IV

3823   Penny. Laur. head. l. R. Britannia, with shield bearing saltire of arms die axis ↑↑

1825 10	50	375	750	1826-Proof *FDC* £975			
1825 Proof *FDC* £1750				1826 thick line on			
1826 plain saltire				saltire............. 12	70	300	825
on rev. 8	45	225	675	1826-Proof *FDC* £1100			
1826 Proof *FDC* £1200				1827 plain saltire.. 225	950	6000	18500
1826 thin line on							
saltire................8	50	375	750				

3824 - 1827 Halfpenny   3825 - 1830 Farthing

	F	VF	EF	BU		F	VF	EF	BU
	£	£	£	£		£	£	£	£

3824 Halfpenny.die axis ↑↑ Laur. head. l. R. Britannia, with shield bearing saltire of arms

1825 10	40	160	400	1826 rev. raised line				
1826 rev. two incuse				on saltire.......... 8	30	175	350
lines on saltire .. 5	15	100	350	1827 rev. two incuse lines				
1826 Proof *FDC* £825				on saltire 8	20	150	350

3825 Farthing. die axis ↑↑ Laur. head. l. R. Britannia, with shield bearing saltire of arms

1826 2	8	60	175	1828 2	8	75	185
1826 Proof *FDC* £750				1829 3	12	80	275
1826 Roman I......... 15	55	350	700	1830 2	8	75	185
1827 3	8	70	200				

3826 - 1828 Half-Farthing   3827 - 1827 Third-Farthing

3826 Half-Farthing. (for use in Ceylon). Laur. head. l. date below R.Britannia die axis ↑↑

1828 rev. helmet intrudes				1830 rev. helmet to			
legend............. 10	25	125	350	base of legend 22	70	300	—
1828 rev. helmet to base				1830 rev. helmet intrudes			
of legend 10	30	160	450	legend............ 10	30	150	425

3827 Third-Farthing. (for use in Malta). Laur. head. l. date below R.Britannia die axis ↑↑

| 1827 .... | | 12 | 60 | 275 |
| 1827 Proof *FDC* £800 | | | | |

Copper coins graded in this catalogue as BU have full mint lustre.

PROOF SET

PS1 new issue, 1826. Five pounds to Farthing (11 coins) *FDC* £150000

William IV was born on 21 August 1765, and ascended the throne on his elder brother's death. From c.1791-1811 while Duke of Clarence, he was cohabiting with the actress Dorothea Jordan (1762-1816) who bore him ten illegitimate children. After the death of George IV's daughter, William was coerced into a legitimate marriage with Adelaide of Saxe-Coburg and Saxe-Meinigen. She bore him two daughters who both died in childhood. His reign was most notable for the introduction of the Reform bill and abolition of slavery. William was the last House of Hanover King of Britain, and died on 20 June 1837 when the throne passed to his niece Victoria.

In order to prevent confusion between the Sixpence and Half-Sovereign the size of the latter was reduced in 1834, although the weight remained the same. The smaller gold piece was not acceptable to the public and in the following year it was made to the normal size. In 1836 the silver Groat was again issued for general circulation: it is the only British silver coin which has a seated Britannia as the type and was revised upon the suggestion of Mr Joseph Hume thus rendering the nickname "Joey". Crowns were not struck during this reign for general circulation; but proofs or patterns of this denomination were made and are greatly sought after. Silver Threepences and Three-Halfpence were minted for use in the Colonies.

Engraver's and/or designer's initials on the coins:
    W. W. (William Wyon)
Engravers and Designers:– Francis Legett Chantry (1781-1842) Jean Baptiste Merlen (1769-c.1850) William Wyon (1795-1851).

GOLD

3828
1831 Proof Two Pounds

3829B
Second bust with broad ear top

	F £	VF £	EF £	BU £		F £	VF £	EF £	BU £

3828 Two Pounds. bare head r. R. crowned shield and mantle, date below, edge plain. die axis ↑↓
    1831 (proof only) *FDC* £20000

3829 Sovereign. First bust. r. top of ear narrow and rounded, nose to 2nd N of BRITANNIAR, fine obv. beading. R. Crowned shield. Die axis ↑↓

1830 Proof plain edge *FDC* £26000				1832 800	1600	3750	7500
1831 600	1000	2750	5500	1832 Proof *FDC* £26500			

3829A Sovereign. Similar, WW without stops die axis ↑↓
    1831 ....900 1800 3750 8000

3829B Sovereign. Second bust. r. top of ear broad and flat, nose to 2nd I in BRITANNIAR, coarser obv. beading. ↑↓

1830 plain edge proof *FDC* 21500				1836 450	850	1850	4250
1831 ....6000 12500 — —				1836 N of ANNO struck			
1831 Proof plain edge *FDC* £10500				in shield......6000 10000 20000 —			
1832* 475 800 2000 4000				1837 ....500 900 2000 4500			
1833 ....550 950 2250 4500				1837 Tailed 8........550 1000 2750 —			
1835 ....550 950 2250 5000							

* Beware of counterfeits

3830   3831

1834 Half-sovereign   Large size Half-Sovereign

	F	VF	EF	BU		F	VF	EF	BU
	£	£	£	£		£	£	£	£

3830 Half-Sovereign. Small size (17.9mm), bare head r.R. Crowned shield and mantle. die axis ↑↓
1831 Proof plain edge *FDC* £6000   1834 350   675   1500   3250
1831 Proof milled edge *FDC* £13500

3831 Half-Sovereign. Large size (19.4mm), bare head r.R. Crowned shield and mantle.die axis ↑↓
1835 275   525   1250   2650   1837 300   575   1500   3000
1836 350   600   1500   —

3832 Half-Sovereign. *Obv.* struck from Sixpence die (19.4mm) in error,
1836 2500   5500   11000   —

SILVER

3833 - 1831 Crown. W.W. on truncation

3833 Crown. ℞. Shield on mantle, 1831 Proof only incuse W.W. on trun. struck ↑↓ *FDC* £35000
1831 Proof struck in gold of five pounds weight *FDC* £350000
1831 Bare head r. raised W. WYON on trun. struck ↑↑ en medaille (medal die axis) *FDC* £45000
1831 Bare head r. similar die axis ↑↓ *FDC* £40000
1831 Bare head r. incuse WW over W. WYON on trun. *FDC Extremely rare*
1834 Bare head r. W.W. on trun. struck die axis ↑↓ *FDC* £60000

3834   WW script

3834 Halfcrown. Bare head.WW in script on trun. ℞. Shield on mantle, die axis ↑↓

	F	VF	EF	BU			F	VF	EF	BU
	£	£	£	£			£	£	£	£
1831 Plain edge proof *FDC* £3750						1835 35		125	575	1400
1831 Milled edge proof *FDC* £4000						1836/5 45		125	850	1500
1834 25		75	475	1100		1836 25		75	450	1100
1834 Plain edge proof *FDC* £4750						1836 Proof *FDC* £4000				
1834 Milled edge proof *FDC* £3500						1837 45		175	550	1600

WW block

3834A

3834A Halfcrown. Bare head r. block WW on trun. R. Similar. die axis ↑↓

1831 Proof *FDC* £3750

1834 45   165   775   1600

3835 - 1831 Shilling   3836 - 1834 Sixpence

3835   Shilling. Bare head r. R̩. Value in wreath, date below. die axis ↑↓

1831 Plain edge Proof *FDC* £1500   1835 Proof *FDC* £4000

1831 Milled edge proof *FDC* £3500   1836 18   45   300   550

1834 12   45   300   700   1836 Proof *FDC* £4000

1834 Milled edge Proof *FDC* £3500   1837 25   75   325   725

1835 18   50   300   550   1837 Proof *FDC* £3250

3836   Sixpence. Bare head r. R̩. Value in wreath, date below. die axis ↑↓

1831 12   25   135   395   1835 Proof *FDC* Extremely rare

— Proof *FDC* die axis ↑↓ or ↑↑ £1000   1836 20   45   300   575

1831 Proof milled edge *FDC* £1250   1836 Proof *FDC* Extremely rare

1834 12   25   160   395   1837 25   60   300   575

1834 large date 18   35   200   450   1837 Proof *FDC* Extremely rare

1834 Proof *FDC* £1500   1837 B/RRITANNIAR .... Extremely rare

1835 12   25   145   400

3837 - 1836 Groat   3839 - 1835 Three-Halfpence

	F	VF	EF	BU		F	VF	EF	BU
	£	£	£	£		£	£	£	£

3837 Groat. Bare head r. R. Britannia seated, date in ex. die axis ↑↑

1836 5	18	70	150	1837 8	22	90	200

1836 Proof *FDC* £1250   1837 Type 2 obv. 'more wiry hair' *values as above*
1836 Plain edge proof *FDC* £1150   1837 Proof *FDC* £1350
1836 Proof in gold *FDC* £17500   1837 Plain edge proof *FDC* £1650

3838 Threepence. Obverse 1, small head, low hair (for use in the West Indies). As Maundy
threepence but with a dull surface, ↑↓

1834 12	25	115	275	1836 5	18	95	250
1835 5	18	85	225	1837 12	25	125	250

3838A — Obverse 2, large head, high hair

1834 8	20	95	250	1836 5	12	65	150
1835 7	15	80	195	1837 100	175	300	600

3839 Three-Halfpence (for Colonial use). Bare head r. R. Value, Crowned in wreath, die axis ↑↓

1834 4	10	50	110	1836 5	15	55	130
1835/4 5	15	55	130	1837 12	40	150	375

1835 unconfirmed without 5/4   1837 Proof *FDC* £1250

3840 - 1831 Maundy Set

	EF	FDC		EF	FDC
	£	£		£	£

3840 Maundy Set (4d., 3d., 2d. and 1d.). Bare head r. Die axis ↑↓

1831	200	475	1834	165	425
— Proof *FDC* £1000			1835	165	425
1831 Proof struck in gold *FDC* £35000			1836	200	450
1832	175	450	1837	200	450
1833	165	425			

3841	— **Fourpence,** 1831-7 ....*from*	15	40
3842	— **Threepence,** 1831-7 ....*from*	25	60
3843	— **Twopence,** 1831-7 ....*from*	12	40
3844	— **Penny,** 1831-7 ....*from*	22	50

See note on under 3796.

COPPER

3845

	F	VF	EF	UNC		F	VF	EF	UNC
	£	£	£	£		£	£	£	£

3845 Penny. Bare head r. No initials on trun. date below. R. Britannia r. die axis ↑↑

1831	....	15	65	450	1250	1834	....	18	80	450	1500
1831 Proof *FDC* ↑↓ £1250						1837	....	55	175	900	2000
1831 Proof *FDC* ↑↑ £1400											

3846 Penny. Bare head r. date below. incuse initials on trun. R. Britannia r. die axis ↑↑

1831 W.W on trun	110	475	—	—	1831 .W.W on trun.....	30	115	475	1100

3847 - 1831 Halfpenny   3848 - 1831 Farthing

3847 Halfpenny. Bare head r. date below. R. Britannia r. die axis ↑↑

1831	....	10	30	150	325	1834	....	12	35	165	375
1831 Proof *FDC* ↑↓ £825						1837	....	8	25	135	325
1831 Proof *FDC* ↑↑ £925											

3848 Farthing. Bare head r. date below. R. Britannia r. die axis ↑↑

1831 rev. incuse line					1835 die axis ↑↓	8	25	135	325
on saltire	2	12	65	150	1835 die axis ↑↑	2	12	90	250
1831 Proof *FDC* ↑↓ £800					1835 rev. incuse line				
1831 Proof *FDC* ↑↑ £850					on saltire............	2	15	85	200
1834 incuse saltire	2	12	70	165	1836 rev. raised line				
1834 rev. raised line					on saltire............	2	12	85	200
on saltire	4	15	85	200	1837 —	2	15	85	200

3849 - 1837 Half-Farthing   3850 - 1835 Third-Farthing

3849 Half-Farthing (for use in Ceylon). Bare head r. date below. R. Britannia r. die axis ↑↑

1837	....	60	225	495	—

3850 Third-Farthing (for use in Malta). Bare head r. date below. R. Britannia r. die axis ↑↑

1835	....	8	30	120	175

1835 Proof *FDC* £1100

Copper coins graded in this catalogue as UNC have full mint lustre

PROOF SET.

PS2 Coronation, 1831. Two pounds to farthing (14 coins). *FDC* £100000

Victoria was born on 24 May 1819, and enjoyed the longest reign of any Monarch so far. She marrried the German, Prince Albert with whom she enjoyed 21 years of Marriage. Upon Albert's death she descended into a lengthy period of mourning, her ecessive melancholy leading her to be nick-named 'the widow of Windsor'. She skillfully avoided conflict with other European powers, and produced connections with many Royal houses all over Europe. Victoria died on 22 January 1901 at the age of 81.

In 1849, as a first step towards decimalization, a silver Florin (1/10th pound) was introduced, but the coins of 1849 omitted the usual *Dei Gratia* and these so-called 'Godless' Florins were replaced in 1851 by the 'Gothic' issue. The Halfcrown was temporarily discontinued but was minted again from 1874 onwards. Between 1863 and 1880 reverse dies of the gold and silver coins were numbered in the course of Mint experiments into the wear of dies. The exception was the Florin where the die number is on the obverse below the bust.

The gold and silver coins were redesigned for the Queen's Golden Jubilee in 1887. The Double-Florin which was then issued was abandoned after only four years; the Jubilee Sixpence of 1887, known as the 'withdrawn' type, was changed to avoid confusion with the Half-Sovereign. Gold and silver were again redesigned in 1893 with an older portrait of the Queen, but the 'old head' was not used on the bronze coinage until 1895. The heavy copper Penny had been replaced by the lighter bronze 'bun' Penny in 1860. In 1874-6 and 1881-2 some of the bronze was made by Heaton in Birmingham, and these have a letter H below the date. From 1897 Farthings were issued with a dark surface.

Early Sovereigns had a shield-type reverse, but Pistrucci's St. George design was used again from 1871. In order to increase the output of gold coinage, branches of the Royal Mint were set up in Australia at Sydney and Melbourne and, later, at Perth for coining gold of imperial type.

Engraver's and/or designer's initials on the coins:

W. W. (William Wyon 1795-1851) T. B. (Thomas Brock 1847-1922)
L. C. W. (Leonard Charles Wyon 1826-91) B. P. (Benedetto Pistrucci, 1784-1855)
J. E. B. (Joseph Edgar Boehm 1834-90)

Engravers and Designers: George William De Saulle, (1862-1903) William Dyce (1806-64), Jean Baptiste Merlen (1769-c.1850) Edward Poynter (1836-1919)

GOLD

YOUNG HEAD COINAGE, 1838-87

3851
1839 Five Pounds - DIRIGIT reverse

3851 Five Pounds. 1839. Young filleted bust l. plain rear fillet ℞. 'Una and the lion' (proof only)

DIRIGIT legend, inscribed edge, die axis ↑↑ *FDC*	*Extremely rare*
– 1839 Similar – DIRIGIT legend, struck on thick flan	*Extremely rare*
– 1839 Similar – DIRIGIT legend, plain edge die axis ↑↑	*Extremely rare*
– 1839 –13 leaves to rear fillet, R. DIRIGE legend–proof	*FDC* £200000
– 1839 Similar – DIRIGE legend edge plain proof	*Extremely rare*
– 1839 –9 leaves to rear fillet, DIRIGE legend	*FDC* £200000
– 1839 Similar – DIRIGE legend edge plain	*Extremely rare*
– 1839 Similar – DIRIGIT legend edge plain proof	*Extremely rare*

Truly FDC 1839 Five Pound coins are hardly ever encountered.

3852
Sovereign - first smaller young head

3852C
Second large head

	F	VF	EF	BU
	£	£	£	£

3852 Sovereign. First (small) young head. l. date below. R. First shield. London mint, die axis ↑↓

	F	VF	EF	BU		F	VF	EF	BU
1838	875	1500	3500	6750	1843/2 or ᴢ	450	700	1400	2900
1838 Proof *FDC*		*Extremely rare*			1844 wider date	275	450	900	2000
1838 Plain edge proof *FDC* £27500					1844 closer date	275	450	950	2000
1839	1250	2500	4000	9500	1844 first 4/ᐁ	750	1500	2250	—
1839 die axis ↑↓ Proof *FDC* £13500					1845 wider date	225	450	900	2000
1839 die axis ↑↑ Proof *FDC* £13500					1845 closer date	300	475	925	2000
1839 Milled edge proof *FDC* £25000					1845 4/ᐁ	750	1500	2250	—
1841	5000	10000	22500	—	1845 Roman I	725	1400	—	—
1841 GRΛTIΛ	4500	9500	21000	—	1846	300	500	950	2000
1842	350	550	975	2000	1846 4/ᐁ	750	1500	—	—
1842 Open 2	600	1000	—	—	1846 Roman I	675	1250	—	—
1842 GRΛTIΛ	550	950	—	—	1847	300	500	950	2000
1843	275	450	925	2000	1847 Roman I	700	1450	—	—
1843 Roman I	675	1250	—	—	1848	1000	2250	7000	—

3852A Sovereign. Similar R similar but leaves of the wreath arranged differently with tops
of leaves closer to crown.

1838	6000	11500	25000	—

3852B Sovereign. Similar narrower shield. Considerably modified floral emblems, different leaf
     arrangement ↑↓

1843	5500	10500	22500	—

3852C Sovereign. Second (large) head. l. W W still in relief. date below R. Shield with
     repositioned legend die axis ↑↓

	F	VF	EF	BU		F	VF	EF	BU
1848	300	425	900	2500	1852 Roman I	675	1250	—	—
1849	300	425	900	2600	1852	BV	325	775	2250
1849 Roman I	675	1250	—	—	1853	BV	325	700	1950
1850	325	500	950	2400	1853 F over E				
1850 Roman I	675	1250	—	—	in DEF	750	1650	—	—
1850 ᐯICTORIA.	1250	—	—	—	1853 ᐯICTORIA.	1250	—	—	—
1850 8/5		*Extremely rare*			1854	BV	475	1350	3100
1851	BV	375	675	1750	1855	BV	375	1000	—

BV= Bullion value only (if gold price over £900 an ounce)
NB Truly BU Victorian sovereigns without any surface marks or hairlines are very rarely
encountered.

3852D
WW Incuse on truncation

3852E
Extra line in ribbon - 'Ansell' named
after Royal Mint Chemist G.F. Ansell

	F	VF	EF	BU			F	VF	EF	BU
	£	£	£	£			£	£	£	£

3852D Sovereign. Similar — WW incuse on trun. die axis ↑↓

	F	VF	EF	BU			F	VF	EF	BU
1853 300	575	1000	2300		1860 .... BV	275	500	1150
1853 Roman I.......675	1250	—	—		1860 large 0.......... BV	375	625	1300
1853 Proof *FDC* £22500					1861 .... BV	300	575	1200
1854 .... BV	375	725	1500		1861 Roman I.......500	750	3250	3250
1854 C over...............					1861 C over rotated C in			
rotated C.......750	1650	—	—		obv. leg........750	1650	—	—
1855 Roman I 650	1450	—	—		1861 T over V in			
1855 .... BV	375	725	1500		VICTORIA.. 400	750	—	—
1856 .... BV	375	725	1500		1861 F/V in DEF			
1857 .... BV	375	725	1500		narrow date . 500	1250	—	—
1857 ⱯICTORIA. 1250	—	—	—		1861 E over			
1857/5........................*Variety exists*					rotated E......750	1650	—	—
1858 small date .... BV	375	725	1600		1862 R/E in BRIT 750	1650		
1858 large date ..... BV	400	775	1600		1862 Roman I.......500	975	—	—
1858 8/7 750	—	—	—		1862 wide date ......BV	275	550	1300
1859 .... BV	375	725	1500		1862 R/Я in			
1860 O over C in					VICTORIA 1000	2500	—	—
obv. leg........450	1100	—	—		1862 F/Ɐ in DEF ... 500	1250	—	—
1860 Roman I.......650	1450	—	—		1862 narrow date BV	275	550	1300
1860 ⱯICTORIA 1250	2750	—	—		1863 .... BV	275	550	1300
1860 DEI GRⱯ ...650	1500	—	—		1863 Roman I 500	975	—	—

3852E Sovereign. Similar — As 3852D 'Ansell' ribbon. Additional raised line on the lower part of the ribbon ↑↓

				F	VF	EF	BU
1859	750	1850	8000	14500

3852F Sovereign. Similar — As 3852D with die number 827 on trun. die axis ↑↓

				F	VF	EF	BU
1863	4750	10000	18500	—

3853 - Die number location

3853   Sovereign. Similar As 3852D R. die number in space below wreath, above floral emblem, die axis ↑↓

	F	VF	EF	BU			F	VF	EF	BU
1863 ....BV	275	495	1100		1866/5 DIE 17 only... 325	450	675	1350
1864 .... BV	275	495	1100		1868 ....BV	275	495	1100
1865 .... BV	275	500	1200		1869 ....BV	275	495	1100
1866 .... BV	275	495	1100		1870 ....BV	275	495	1100

3853A Sovereign. Similar — As 3853 with die number 827 on trun. R. die number is always no. 22 die axis ↑↓

				F	VF	EF	BU
1863	3375	6300	13500	—

3853B Sovereign. Similar — WW in relief on trun. R. die number below wreath, above floral emblem die axis ↑↓

	F	VF	EF	BU			F	VF	EF	BU
1870 .... BV	285	450	1000		1872 no die number . BV	275	450	950
1871 .... BV	250	375	900		1873 ....BV	325	525	1000
1872 .... BV	275	495	1100		1874 1925	4050	9000	—

BV= Bullion value only (if gold price over £900 an ounce)

3854 - 'M' Melbourne Mint mark					3855 - 'S' Sydney Mint mark			
	F	VF	EF	BU		F	VF	EF	BU
	£	£	£	£		£	£	£	£

3854 Sovereign. Second (large) head. l. WW in relief date below R̟. M below wreath for
Melbourne Mint, Australia ↑↓

1872 M .... BV	BV	250	775	1874 M .... BV	BV	300	975
1872/1 M 180	300	750	2250	1880 M 450	1250	3000	7000

3854A Sovereign. Third young head. Similar but different hair arrangement.

1881 M .... BV	BV	300	1350	1885 M .... BV	BV	285	1100
1882 M .... BV	BV	285	1100	1886 M 1500	4000	6000	15000
1883 M .... BV	200	500	2250	1887 M 600	1100	3000	7500
1884 M .... BV	BV	285	1100				

3855 Sovereign. Similar — As 3854. R̟. with S below wreath for Sydney Mint, Australia die axis ↑↓

1871 S .... BV	BV	300	775	1878 S .... BV	BV	285	775
1872 S .... BV	BV	300	975	1879 S .... BV	BV	285	775
1873 S .... BV	BV	300	975	1880 S .... BV	BV	300	975
1875 S .... BV	BV	300	975	1880 S VICTORIA . 450	1500	2700	7500
1877 S .... BV	BV	285	775				

3855A Sovereign. Second (large) head WW incuse on trun. date below R̟. with S below wreath
for Sydney Mint die axis ↑↓

1871 S ....BV	BV	325	1400

3855B (Previously listed under 3855) as 3854A. Third head with different hair arrangements

1881 S .... BV	BV	300	900	1885 S .... BV	BV	275	900
1882 S .... BV	BV	300	900	1886 S .... BV	BV	275	900
1883 S .... BV	BV	300	900	1887 S .... BV	BV	325	1250
1884 S .... BV	BV	300	900				

*: The prices for Australian mint sovereigns are led by current trends in the Australian numismatic
market place (which moved sharply downwards in 2014) and this trend has continued, although
stabilising in 2017-2018. Being very condition conscious, it is truly UNC coins which command the
highest price, any detraction from a true UNC coin should be taken at the EF guide price. The
exchange rate of the Pound Sterling versus Australian Dollar also has an influence on price.*

3856A	3857
Horse with long tail, small BP in exergue	Melbourne Mint, WW buried in truncation

3856 Sovereign. First young head. l. WW buried in narrow trun. R̟. St. George. London mint.
Horse with short tail. Large BP and date in ex. die axis ↑↓

1871.. —	BV	300	850
1871 Proof milled edge*FDC* £18500	1871 Plain edge proof *FDC* £12500		

3856A Sovereign. — — As 3856 R̟. Horse with long tail. Small BP and date in ex.die axis ↑↓

1871........................... BV	285	850	1876 .... —	BV	285	850
1871 Proof *FDC* plain edge £11000			1878 .... —	BV	285	850
1872........................ —	BV	285	850	1879 600	1350	4750	—
1873........................ —	BV	285	850	1880 .... —	BV	285	850
1874........................ —	BV	285	850				

BV= Bullion value only. At the time of going to press the spot price for gold was £900 per oz.

Horse tails - three variations in tail length exist across Melbourne and Sydney, all are defined more accurately by the number of spurs of extra hair, or not, at tail indent on left side.
Short tail - two spurs of hair in left indent. **Medium tail** - no spurs of hair in left indent. **Long tail** - one spur of hair in left indent.

	F	VF	EF	BU		F	VF	EF	BU
	£	£	£	£		£	£	£	£

3856B Sovereign. — — As 3856 R. Horse with short tail, small BP and date in ex.die axis ↑↓

	F	VF	EF	BU		F	VF	EF	BU
1880	−	BV	295	850	1884	−	BV	295	850
1880 Second 8/7	BV	250	425	1100	1885	−	BV	295	850

3856C Sovereign. — — As 3856 R. Horse with short tail, date but no BP in ex.die axis ↑↓

	F	VF	EF	BU		F	VF	EF	BU
1880	BV	BV	385	775	1880 Second 8/7	BV	BV	425	850

3856D Sovereign. Second head. l. WW complete, on broad trun. R. Horse with long tail, small BP and date in ex.die axis ↑↓

	F	VF	EF	BU		F	VF	EF	BU
1880 Second 8/7	BV	BV	400	950	1880	BV	BV	365	775

3856E Sovereign. — — As 3856D R. Horse with short tail. Date but no BP in ex. die axis ↑↓

	F	VF	EF	BU
1880		BV	375	775

3856F Sovereign. — — As 3856E R. Horse with short tail, small BP and date in ex. die axis ↑↓

	F	VF	EF	BU		F	VF	EF	BU
1880	BV	BV	285	850	1885	BV	250	400	850
1884	BV	BV	285	850	1887 Proof *FDC* £29500				

3857 Sovereign. — — First head. l. WW buried in trun. M below head for Melbourne Mint, Australia. R. Horse with long tail, small BP and date in ex. die axis ↑↓

	F	VF	EF	BU		F	VF	EF	BU
1872 M	BV	BV	375	2250	1877 M	BV	BV	235	600
1873 M	BV	BV	250	725	1878 M	BV	BV	235	600
1874 M	BV	BV	250	725	1879 M	BV	BV	235	465
1875 M	BV	BV	250	725	1880 M	BV	BV	235	550
1876 M	BV	BV	250	725	1881 M	BV	BV	235	550

3857A Sovereign. — — As 3857 R. horse with short tail, date but no BP in ex die axis ↑↓

	F	VF	EF	BU		F	VF	EF	BU
1881 M	BV	180	235	550	1883 M	BV	BV	275	1000
1882 M	BV	BV	235	465	1885 M	BV	BV	250	700

3857B Sovereign. First head l. WW buried in trun. M below head for Melbourne Mint, Australia R. Horse with short tail, small BP and date in ex. die axis ↑↓

	F	VF	EF	BU		F	VF	EF	BU
1882 M	BV	BV	235	450	1884 M	BV	BV	235	450
1883 M	BV	BV	235	450	1885 M	BV	BV	235	595

3857C Sovereign. — — Second head. l. WW complete on broad truncation. R. Horse with short tail, small BP in ex.

	F	VF	EF	BU		F	VF	EF	BU
1882 M	BV	BV	235	675	1885 M	BV	BV	235	450
1883 M	BV	BV	235	450	1886 M	BV	BV	235	450
1884 M	BV	200	235	400	1887 M	BV	BV	250	725

3857D Sovereign. First head. l. WW buried in trun. M below R. Horse with medium tail, small BP

	F	VF	EF	BU		F	VF	EF	BU
1879 M	BV	BV	235	725	1881 M	BV	BV	250	900
1880 M	BV	BV	235	725	1882 M	BV	BV	250	900

3857E Sovereign. Second head. l. WW complete on trun. M below R. Horse with short tail, no BP in ex.

	F	VF	EF	BU		F	VF	EF	BU
1884 M			*Extremely rare*		1885 M	BV	BV	225	600

3858 Sovereign First head. l. WW buried in narrow trun. S below head for Sydney Mint, Australia, R. Horse with short tail, large BP and date in ex. die axis ↑↓

	F	VF	EF	BU
1871 S		BV	BV	500	1800

3858A Sovereign. — — As 3858 R. Horse with long tail, small BP and date in ex. die axis ↑↓

	F	VF	EF	BU		F	VF	EF	BU
1871 S	BV	BV	375	2250	1875 S	BV	BV	235	425
1872 S	BV	BV	250	900	1876 S	BV	BV	235	425
1873 S	BV	BV	250	1550	1879 S	BV	BV	850	2250
1874 S	BV	BV	250	1100	1880 S	BV	BV	235	725

BV= Bullion value only. At the time of going to press the spot price for gold was £900 per oz.

	3859 - Type A1					3859A - Type A2			
	F	*VF*	*EF*	*BU*		*F*	*VF*	*EF*	*BU*
	£	£	£	£		£	£	£	£

3858B Sovereign. First head. As 3858 ℞. Horse with short tail, date but no BP in ex. die axis ↑↓

1880 S .... BV	BV	285	975	1881 S .... BV	BV	235	675

3858C Sovereign. Second head. l. WW complete on broad trun. ℞.
   Horse with long tail, small BP and date in ex. die axis ↑↓

1880 S ....BV	BV	235	725

3858D Sovereign. — — As 3858C ℞. Horse with short tail, date but no BP in ex. die axis ↑↓

1881 S ....BV	BV	250	585	1882 S ....BV	BV	250	450

3858E Sovereign. — — As 3858D ℞. Horse with short tail small BP and date in ex. die axis ↑↓

1882 S ....BV	BV	200	450	1885 S ....BV	BV	250	450
1883 S ....BV	BV	300	1100	1886 S ....BV	BV	250	450
1884 S ....BV	BV	275	500	1887 S ....BV	BV	250	450

3858F Sovereign. Second head. Horse with long tail, no BP in ex.

1880 S ....BV	235	375	775

3859 Half-Sovereign. Type A1. First (smallest) young head. date below l. ℞. First shield, die axis ↑↓

1838...................... 185	325	1200	2500	1849...................... 175	300	850	1900
1839 die axis ↑↓ or ↑↑ Proof only *FDC* £6500				1850...................... 250	600	2250	—
1839 Milled edge proof *FDC Extremely rare*				1851...................... 175	300	700	1600
1841...................... 200	325	1350	3250	1852...................... 175	300	800	1750
1842...................... 175	300	800	1750	1853...................... 175	300	750	1600
1843...................... 175	325	850	2000	1853 Proof small date *FDC* £13000			
1844...................... 175	325	800	1900	1853 Proof large date *FDC* £16500			
1845...................... 300	800	3000	—	1855...................... 175	300	750	1700
1846...................... 175	325	800	1900	1856...................... 175	300	725	1750
1847...................... 175	325	800	1900	1856/5.................. 225	350	850	1850
1848 Close date..... 175	325	800	1900	1857...................... 175	300	750	1600
1848/7 250	500	1100	2350	1858...................... 175	300	750	1600
1848 Wide date...... 200	325	1000	2000				

3859A Half-Sovereign. Type A2, Second (larger) young head. date below. ℞. First shield die axis ↑↓

1858...................... 175	300	625	1400	1861...................... 175	300	700	1350
1859...................... 175	300	625	1400	1862...................... 850	2500	9000	—
1860...................... 175	300	600	1350	1863...................... 175	300	575	1350

3860	3860D	3860E	3860F
Die number location	Type A3	Type A4	Type A5

3860 Half-Sovereign. Type A2, second head, date below ℞. die number below shield, die axis ↑↓

1863......................175	250	700	1500	1867 ....BV	200	600	1250
1864...................... BV	200	600	1250	1869 ....BV	200	600	1250
1865...................... BV	200	600	1250	1870 ....BV	175	575	1100
1866...................... BV	200	600	1250	1871 ....BV	175	575	1150

BV= Bullion value only. At the time of going to press the spot price for gold was £900 per oz.

	F	VF	EF	BU		F	VF	EF	BU
	£	£	£	£		£	£	£	£

3860A Half-Sovereign. Second head, date below R. Re-engraved shield legend and rosettes closer to border, coarse boarder teeth both sides, with die number below shield die axis ↑↓

1870......................275	675	1500	–	1871 225	575	1350	–

3860B Half-Sovereign. Second head, date below R. As last but with normal border teeth and no die number below shield die axis ↑↓

1871... 300   750   1900   –

3860C Half-Sovereign. Second head, date below obv. with repositioned legend, nose now points to T in VICTORIA. R. Similar to last but with die number below shield die axis ↑↓

1871......................300	875	1800	–	1872 225	575	1350	–

3860DHalf-Sovereign. Type A3, Third (larger still) young head l, date below. R. As 3860A, with die number below shield die axis ↑↓

1872..................... BV	185	500	1200	1875 ....BV	175	475	1100
1873..................... BV	185	500	1200	1876 ....BV	175	475	1100
1874..................... BV	200	525	1200	1877 ....BV	175	475	1100

3860E - Half Sovereign   3861 - Type A5

3860E Half-Sovereign. Type A4. Fourth young head l. hair ribbon now narrow, date below. R. As last with die number below shield die axis ↑↓

1876..................... BV	175	475	1100	1878 ....BV	175	475	1100
1877..................... BV	175	475	1100	1879 175	225	675	1525

3860F Half-Sovereign. Type A5. Fifth young head l. in very low relief, date below. R. As last with die number below shield die axis ↑↓

1880... 175   225   675   1475

3860G Half-Sovereign. Type A4. Fourth young head, without die number below shield.

1876... *Extremely rare*

3861 Half-Sovereign. Fifth head, date below. R. Cross on crown buried in border. Legend and rosettes very close to heavy border, no die number below shield die axis ↑↓

1880..................... BV	185	500	1200	1885 ....BV	175	450	900
1883..................... BV	175	450	1000	1885/3 175	275	850	1650
1884..................... BV	175	450	1000				

3862 Half-Sovereign. Type A2, Second (larger) young head l. nose points between T and O. Date below R. First crowned shield cross clear of border with S below shield for Sydney Mint, Australia, die axis ↑↓

1871 S 125	200	800	8000	1871 S Proof ....*Extremely rare*

3862A Half-Sovereign. Similar obv. with repositioned legend, nose now points to T in VICTORIA. Date below R Re-engraved shield cross touches border, S below shield die axis ↑↓

1872 S 125   200   800   8000

3862B Half-Sovereign. Type A3. Third (larger still) young head l. I of DEI points to rear fillet. Date below R. As last die axis ↑↓

1875 S 125   200   800   8000

3862C Half-Sovereign. Type A4. Fourth young head l. front hair fillet now narrow. R. As last, die axis ↑↓

1879 S 125   200   850   7500

3862D Half-Sovereign. Type A5. Fifth young head l. in low relief wider tr. no front ear lobe. Date below R as last. die axis ↑↓

1880 S 125	175	850	1250	1882 S ....*Extremely rare*
1880 S Proof.......................... *Extremely rare*				1883 S 125	225	500	10000
1881 S 125	300	1200	14500				

* Beware recent forgeries

BV= Bullion value only. At the time of going to press the spot price for gold was £900 per oz.

	F	VF	EF	BU		F	VF	EF	BU
	£	£	£	£		£	£	£	£

3862E Half-Sovereign. Fifth head, date below Ṛ. Cross on crown buried in border. Legend and
rosettes very close to heavy border, S below shield die axis ↑↓

1880 S	125	200	500	11500	1883 S Proof				*Extremely rare*
1881 S	125	225	900	10000	1886 S	125	200	650	4750
1882 S	175	600	2250	14000	1887 S	125	200	550	3750
1883 S	125	200	650	4500					

3863 Half-Sovereign. Type A3. Third (larger still) young head l. Date below Ṛ. Re-engraved shield
with M below shield for Melbourne Mint, Australia die axis ↑↓

| 1873 M | 125 | 200 | 1100 | 8000 | 1877 M | 125 | 250 | 2750 | 9500 |

3863A Half-Sovereign. Type A4, fourth young head l. hair ribbon now narrow. R. As last die axis ↑↓

| 1877 M | 125 | 200 | 850 | 8000 | 1882 M | 125 | 200 | 2250 | 9500 |

3863B Half-Sovereign. Type A5. Fifth young head l. in low relief.Date below Ṛ. As last die axis ↑↓

1881 M	125	600	4000	12000	1885 M	150	550	5000	11000
1882 M	125	200	750	4500	1886 M	125	400	7000	12000
1884 M	125	250	2750	10000	1886 M Proof				*Extremely rare*
1884 M Proof				*Extremely rare*	1887 M	125	1250	10000	16500

JUBILEE COINAGE, 1887-93, die axis ↑↑

3864 - 1887 Five Pounds

3864* Five Pounds. Jubilee bust l. R. St. George date in ex. 1887 1350   2000   2750   3500
— Proof *FDC* £13500   — Proof no B.P. in exergue £20000
3864A* Five Pounds. Jubilee bust l. R. St George, S on ground for Sydney Mint, Australia
1887 S .... *Extremely rare*
3865* Two Pounds. Jubilee bust l. R. St George die axis ↑↑ 1887 650   875   1250   1750
1887 Proof *FDC* £3250   1887 Proof no BP in exergue FDC *Extremely rare*
3865A* Two Pounds. R. St George, S on ground for Sydney Mint, Australia ↑↑
1887 S .... *Extremely rare*

3866 - 1887 Sovereign

3866* Sovereign. Normal JEB (angled J) designer's initials fully on trun. R. St. George.
die axis ↑↑ (*DISH L7, L8*)

| 1887 | | BV | 275 | 425 | 1889 | | | | *Exists?* |
| 1888 | 325 | 750 | 1250 | 2000 | 1890 | | | | *Exists?* |

* Beware recent forgeries
BV= Bullion value only. At the time of going to press the spot price for gold was £900 per oz.
(See note on page 449 re. horse tails.)
For a detailed variety synopsis of Jubilee Head Sovereigns and their rarity see publication 'The
Jubilee Head Gold Sovereign' by David Iverson. (DISH)

	VF	EF	BU		F	VF	EF	BU
	£	£	£		£	£	£	£

3866A Sovereign. Similar with tiny JEB (hooked J) closer designer's initials at base of truncation; stops in an arc, die axis ↑↑ *(DISH L1, L4)*

1887... 325 750 1250 2000

3866B Sovereign. Similar repositioned legend. G: of D:G: now closer to crown. Normal JEB (angled J) designer's initials at base of trun. ↑↑ *(DISH L9, L11, L13, L14))*

1887 Proof *FDC* £3000				1890	BV	300	425
1888................................	BV	300	500	1891	600	1200	2000	—
1889................................	BV	300	425				

3866C Sovereign. Similar obv. as last. Ṛ. Horse with longer tail, two variations of hair strands die axis ↑↑ *(DISH L15, L16)*

| 1891................................ | BV | 300 | 425 | 1892 .... | BV | 300 | 425 |
| 1891 Proof *FDC* £19500 | | | | | | |

3866D Sovereign. First legend with tiny JEB (hooked J) with initials more spread across truncation; stops all in line ↑↑ *(DISH L2, L3)*

1887.. 350 750 1250 2000

3867
"M' Melbourne Mint on groundline above 8's in date

3867 Sovereign. Similar with small spread JEB (hooked J) designer's initials fully on trun. Ṛ. M on ground for Melbourne Mint, Australia, die axis ↑↑ *(DISH M1-M4)*

1887 M 275 650 1000 1850

3867A Sovereign. Similar with normal JEB designer's initials on trun. (angled J) die axis ↑↑ *(DISH M7, M9, M11)*

1887 M		BV	300	500
1888 M 300		600	1100	2000
1889 M		200	600	1850
1890 M				*Exists?*

3867B Sovereign. Similar repositioned legend. G: of D: G: now closer to crown. Normal JEB (angled J) initials at base of trun. die axis ↑↑ *(DISH M8, M10, M12, M14, M15)*

1887 M..............................	225	450	725	1889 M........................	BV	300	500
1888 M..............................	BV	275	500	1890 M........................	BV	300	500
1888 Proof *FDC* .... *Extremely rare*			1891 M.................	300	600	1100	2000

3867C Sovereign. Similar obv. as last. Ṛ. Horse with longer tail, two variations of hair strands die axis ↑↑ *(DISH M16-M18)*

| 1891 M.............................. | BV | 350 | 575 | 1893 M........................ | BV | 300 | 550 |
| 1892 M.............................. | BV | 275 | 450 | | | | |

3868 Sovereign. First legend with closer JEB (angled J) stops in arc on trun. Ṛ. S on ground for Sydney Mint, Australia die axis ↑↑ *(DISH S9, S11, S13)*

| 1888 S .... | BV | 350 | 600 | 1890S .... | 300 | 600 | 1350 |
| 1889S .... | BV | 350 | 625 | | | | |

3868A Sovereign. Similar with spread JEB designer's initials stop level on left side of trun. (hooked J) die axis ↑↑ *(DISH S1-S8)*

1887 S	400	750	1500	3000
1887 S Proof...			*Extremely rare*
1888 S	300	600	1100	2000

BV= Bullion value only. At the time of going to press the spot price for gold was £900 per oz.

	F	VF	EF	BU		F	VF	EF	BU
	£	£	£	£		£	£	£	£

3868B Sovereign. Similar repositioned legend. G: of D:G: now closer to crown. Normal JEB (angled J) initials on trun. die axis ↑↑ (*DISH S10, S12, S14*)

1888 S	...............BV	275	500		1890S	....	BV	300	550
1889 S	...............BV	300	550						

3868C Sovereign. Similar obv. as last. ℞. Horse with longer tail die axis ↑↑ (*DISH S15-S17*)

1891 S	...............BV	275	450		1893S	....	BV	350	575
1892 S	...............BV	300	550						

3868D Sovereign. First legend with spread JEB initials ending at right side of trun. (hooked J) ↑↑ (*DISH S2*)

1887 S 400 800 1500 3000

3869   3869D
higher shield, cross blends into border   Plain trun., lower shield, cross clear of border

3869 Half-Sovereign. Similar obv. normal JEB designer's initials. on trun. ℞. High shield die axis ↑↑

1887	..................BV	100	200	350		1890	.................BV	175	500	—
— Proof *FDC* £2000										

3869A Half-Sovereign. Similar small close JEB intitials. on trun. ℞. High shield die axis ↑↑

1887..................BV 150 450 —

3869B Half-Sovereign. Similar normal JEB initials. on trun. ℞. Lower shield, date therefore spread apart, complete cross at top, die axis ↑↑

1890	..................BV	150	475	—		1892	.................BV	150	475	—

3869C Half-Sovereign. Similar no JEB initials on trun. ℞. High Shield die axis ↑↑

1887	..................BV	150	450	—		1891	.................BV	150	450	—
1890	....	BV	240	400		1892	.................BV	150	450	—

3869D Half-Sovereign. Jubilee bust 1. ℞. Lower shield, date therefore spread apart die axis ↑↑

1890	....	BV	225	350		1892	....	BV	225	350
1891	....	BV	250	375		1893	....	BV	250	375

3870

3870 Half-Sovereign. Similar small very spread JEB initials on trun. ℞. High shield, M below for Melbourne Mint, Australia, die axis ↑↑

1887 M..................125 200 400 1600   1887 M Proof ....*Extremely rare*

3870A Half-Sovereign. Similar small close JEB initials on trun. ℞. As last die axis ↑↑

1887 M..................125 200 350 1400   1887 M Proof ....*Extremely rare*

3870B Half-Sovereign. Similar normal JEB initials on trun. ℞. Lower shield, date therefore spread part die axis ↑↑

1893 M 125 250 500 2250

3871 Half-Sovereign. Similar small very spread JEB initials on trun. (hooked J) ℞. High shield S below for Sydney Mint, Australia ↑↑

1887 S 125 200 400 1200

3871A Half-Sovereign. Similar small close JEB initials on trun. ℞ As last. die axis ↑↑

1887 S ....125 200 325 1100   1887 S Proof ....*Extremely rare*

BV= Bullion value only. At the time of going to press the spot price for gold was £900 per oz.

	EF	*BU*		*F*	*VF*	*EF*	*BU*
	£	£		£	£	£	£

3871B Half-Sovereign. Jubilee bust 1. Normal JEB initials on trun. R. Lower shield, date therefore
    spread apart, S below for Sydney Mint, Australia die axis ↑↑
1889 S 125   250   1400   4500

3871C Half-Sovereign. Jubilee bust 1. Normal JEB initials on trun. R. High shield, S below for
    Sydney Mint, Australia die axis ↑↑
1891 S 125   300   1100   3750

3871D Half-Sovereign. Jubilee bust 1. No JEB initials on trun. R. As last die axis ↑↑
1891 S 125   250   700   3000

OLD HEAD COINAGE, 1893-1901, die axis ↑↑

3872
1893 Five Pounds

3872* Five Pounds. Old veiled bust 1. R. St. George and dragon, date and BP in ex.
1893.. 1950 2750 4500 7250
1893 Proof *FDC* £16500

3873	3874
1893 Two Pounds	1893 Sovereign

3873* Two Pounds. Old veiled bust 1. R. St. George and dragon, date and BP in ex. die axis ↑↑
1893.. 750 1000 1950 2750
1893 Proof *FDC* £5250

3874 Sovereign. Old veiled bust 1. R. St. George, London Mint die axis ↑↑

1893.............................. BV	350	1898 ....BV	350
1893 Proof *FDC* £3500		1899 ....BV	350
1894.............................. BV	350	1900 ....BV	350
1895.............................. BV	350	1901 ....BV	350
1896.............................. BV	350		

3875 Sovereign. Similar R. St. George. M on ground for Melbourne Mint, Australia die axis ↑↑

1893 M .... BV	450	1898 M..........................BV	400
1894 M .... BV	400	1899 M..........................BV	375
1895 M .... BV	400	1900 M..........................BV	375
1896 M .... BV	375	1901 M..........................BV	375
1897 M .... BV	375		

* Beware recent forgeries

BV= Bullion value only. At the time of going to press the spot price for gold was £900 per oz.

*NB Truly BU old bust sovereigns are very scarce. Any surface defects will cause the value to drop
significantly.*

3876	3878
Perth Mint mark	1893 Half -Sovereign

	F	VF	EF	BU		F	VF	EF	BU
	£	£	£	£		£	£	£	£

3876 Sovereign. Similar — P on ground for Perth Mint, Australia die axis ↑↑

1899 P	BV	250	475	2250	1901 P	BV		225	450
1900 P	BV		225	450					

3877 Sovereign. Similar — S on ground for Sydney Mint, Australia die axis ↑↑

1893 S	BV			400	1898 S	BV		225	450
1894 S	BV			400	1899 S	BV			400
1895 S	BV			400	1900 S	BV			400
1896 S	BV		225	450	1901 S	BV			400
1897 S	BV		225	450					

3878 Half-Sovereign. Old veiled bust 1.R. St. George. Date in ex. (no B.P. on this issue in exergue) London Mint die axis ↑↑

1893	BV		150	300	1897	BV		150	300
— Proof *FDC* £2650					1898	BV		150	300
1894	BV		150	300	1899	BV		150	300
1895	BV		150	300	1900	BV		150	300
1896	BV		150	300	1901	BV		150	300

3879 Half-Sovereign. Similar — M on ground for Melbourne Mint, Australia die axis ↑↑

1893 M	*Extremely rare*				1900 M	125	250	650	2000
1896 M	125	250	400	2250	1900 M Proof	*Extremely rare*			
1899 M	125	250	600	2500	1896 M Proof	*Extremely rare*			
1899 M Proof	*Extremely rare*								

3880 Half-Sovereign. Similar — P on ground for Perth Mint, Australia die axis ↑↑

1899 P	Proof only *unique*				1900 P	150	300	750	4000

3881 Half-Sovereign. Similar — S on ground for Sydney Mint, Australia die axis ↑↑

1893 S	125	250	500	1650	1897 S	125	250	425	2000
1893 S Proof	*Extremely rare*				1900 S	125	300	375	1200

BV= Bullion value only. At the time of going to press the spot price for gold was £900 per oz.
NB Truly BU old bust sovereigns are very scarce. Any surface defects will cause the value to drop
significantly.

SILVER

YOUNG HEAD COINAGE, 1838-87, die axis ↑↓

Edge Stops

3882 - 1844 Crown

Cinquefoil

Star

	F	VF	EF	BU		F	VF	EF	BU
	£	£	£	£		£	£	£	£

†**3882 Crown.** Young head. l. R. Crowned shield, regnal year on edge in Roman figures (eg 1847 = XI)

					F	VF	EF	BU
1839 Proof only *FDC* £26500								
1844 Star stops, extra square of metal at tip of ponytail					225	425	2250	5400
1844 Star stops					60	200	1750	4000
1844 Cinquefoil stops					125	475	3000	5500
1844 Mistruck edge lettering					150	500	3500	–
1845 Cinquefoil stops					65	250	1750	4000
1847 XI Cinquefoil stops					125	400	2750	5000

3883

1847 Gothic Crown

3883*Crown. 'Gothic' type, bust l. R. Crowned cruciform Shields, emblems in angles. inscribed edge, mdcccxlvii=1847 Undecimo on edge die axis ↑↓ 800 1350 3000 6250

1847 Septimo on edge of highest rarity.   1847 Proof, Plain edge die axis ↑↑ *FDC* £11000

1847 Proof in gold plain edge *FDC* of highest rarity   1847 Proof in white metal plain edge *FDC* £20000

3884 Crown. Similar mdcccliii=1853. Septimo on edge die axis ↑↑ Proof *FDC* £32000

1853 plain edge proof *FDC* £42000

3885 Halfcrown. Type A^1. Young head l. with one ornate and one plain fillet binding hair. WW in relief on trun. R. Crowned shield of arms, edge milled. Die axis ↑↓

1839 Milled edge Proof *FDC Extremely rare*   1839 Proof plain edge *FDC* £5000

3886 Halfcrown. Type A^2 Similar, but two ornate fillets binding hair.die axis ↑↓

1839 Proof only *FDC* £6750

3886A Halfcrown. Type A$^{2/3}$ Similar, Two plain fillets, WW relief, die axis ↑↓ plain edge

1839 Proof *FDC* £7750

*Beware of recent forgeries.

†The Victorian young head Crowns are notoriously hard to grade. A truly BU coin must show all design elements clearly expecially on hair fillets and the reverse shield. All facial features and hair must also be present.

	F	VF	EF	BU		F	VF	EF	BU
	£	£	£	£		£	£	£	£

3887 Halfcrown. Type A³. Similar two plain fillets. WW incuse on trun. die axis ↑↓

1839....................1250	3500	10000	—		1839 Milled edge Proof *FDC* £6750				
1839 Plain edge Proof *FDC* £6750					1840 60	200	1100	2750	

3888 Halfcrown. Type A⁴. Similar but no initials on trun. die axis ↑↓

1841....................1000	2250	5250	9000	1849 large date.......65	225	1100	2500
1842....................50	150	800	1925	1849/7		*Extremely rare*	
1843....................125	450	1750	4250	1849 small date 100	350	1250	3000
1844........................45	125	775	1800	1850........................65	325	1100	2650
1844 not in edge collar		*Extremely rare*		1850 Proof *FDC* £13500			
1845........................45	125	775	1800	1853 Proof *FDC* £7500			
1845 5/3		*Extremely rare*		1862 Proof *FDC* £12500			
1846........................45	125	775	1800	1862 Plain edge Proof *FDC* £11000			
1848/6 200	600	2250	4000	1864 Proof *FDC* £12500			
1848/7		*Extremely rare*		1864 Plain edge Proof *FDC* £11000			
1848....................200	650	2450	4750				

3889
Type A5 Halfcrown

3890
1849 'Godless' Florin

3889 Halfcrown. Similar Type A⁵. As last but design of inferior workmanship ℞. Crowned shield
die axis ↑↓

1874........................20	65	375	750	1881 18	55	300	700
1874 Proof *FDC* £8000				1881 Proof *FDC* £7750			
1875........................20	55	300	700	1881 Plain edge proof *FDC* £9500			
1875 Proof *FDC* £8000				1882 20	65	375	750
1876........................20	65	375	750	1883 12	55	300	700
1876/5....................30	75	425	900	1883 Plain edge proof *FDC* £9500			
1877........................20	65	375	750	1884 15	55	300	700
1878........................25	65	375	750	1885 15	55	300	700
1878 Proof *FDC* £7750				1885 Proof *FDC* £7750			
1879........................25	65	375	750	1886 15	55	300	700
1879 Proof *FDC* £7750				1886 Plain edge proof *FDC* £8750			
1880........................18	55	300	700	1887 20	65	375	750
1880 Proof *FDC* £8500				1887 Proof *FDC* £8500			

3890 Florin. 'Godless' type A (i.e. without D.G.), WW behind bust within linear circle, die axis ↑↓

1848 Plain edge (Pattern) *FDC* £3750				1849 WW obliterated 45	75	400	800
1848 Milled edge ↑↑ or ↑↓ Proof *FDC* £5500				1849 20	55	275	575

3891 Florin. 'Gothic' type B¹. Reads brit:, WW below bust, date at end of obverse legend in gothic
numerals (1851 to 1863) Crowned cruciform Shields, emblems in angles, edge milled. die axis ↑↓

mdcccli Proof only *FDC* £32500				mdccclvii Proof *FDC* £6500			
mdccclii..................15	45	325	800	mdccclviii.............. 15	45	325	850
mdccclii Proof *FDC* £5750				mdccclviii Proof *FDC* £6500			
mdccclii, ii/i 20	55	350	900	mdccclix................ 15	45	325	850
mdccccliii.................15	45	325	825	mdccclx 20	45	350	900
mdcccliii Proof *FDC* £7000				mdccclxii............. 225	650	1750	4750
mdcccliv................850	1950	7000	—	mdccclxii Plain edge Proof *FDC* £8000			
mdccclv 25	75	325	900	mdccclxiii............. 900	2000	5500	11000
mdccclvi..................25	75	325	900	mdccclxiii Plain edge Proof *FDC* £8250			
mdccclvii	20	55	350	850				

3891   3893

1853 Florin Type B1

	F	VF	EF	BU		F	VF	EF	BU
	£	£	£	£		£	£	£	£

3892 Florin. Type B². Similar as last but die number below bust (1864 to 1867) die axis ↑↓

	F	VF	EF	BU		F	VF	EF	BU
mdccclxiv	20	60	350	850	mdccclxv	40	100	525	1025
mdccclxiv heavy flan	350	800	1750	5250	mdccclxvi	35	80	375	850
mdccclxiv heavy flan Proof *FDC* £9500					mdccclxvii	30	70	375	850
mdccclxvii Proof *FDC* £6500									

3893 Florin. Type B³. Similar reads britt:, die number below bust (1868 to 1879) die axis

	F	VF	EF	BU		F	VF	EF	BU
mdccclxviii	30	90	400	1000	mdccclxxiii	20	55	250	775
mdccclxix	25	80	400	950	mdccclxxiii Proof *FDC* £5500				
mdccclxix Proof *FDC* £6750					mdccclxxiv	25	65	350	850
mdccclxx	20	55	315	855	mdccclxxiv iv/iii	35	80	325	950
mdccclxx Proof *FDC* £6750					mdccclxxv	20	50	300	825
mdccclxxi	20	55	315	855	mdccclxxvi	20	50	300	800
mdccclxxi Proof *FDC* £6000					mdccclxxvii	25	50	300	850
mdccclxxii	15	40	250	775	mdccclxxix			*Extremely rare*	

3894 Florin. Type B⁴. Similar as last but with border of 48 arcs and no WW below bust die axis ↑↓

1877 mdccclxxvii .... *Extremely rare*

3895 Florin. Type B⁵. Similar but border of 42 arcs (1867, 1877 and 1878) die axis ↑↓

	F	VF	EF	BU		F	VF	EF	BU
mdccclxvii	2850	—	—	—	mdccclxxviii	20	50	300	775
mdccclxxvii	25	60	350	900	mdccclxxviii Proof *FDC*			*Extremely rare*	

3896 Florin. Type B⁵/⁶. Similar as last but no die number below bust (1877, 1879) die axis ↑↓

	F	VF	EF	BU		F	VF	EF	BU
mdccclxxvii	125	275	600	1400	mdccclxxix	110	275	725	1625

3897 Florin. Type B⁶. Similar reads britt:, WW; Border of 48 arcs (1879) die axis ↑↓

mdccclxxviii ....*Known to exist*

	F	VF	EF	BU
mdccclxxix	20	50	300	800

3898 Florin. Type B⁷. Similar as last but no WW, Border of 38 arcs (1879) die axis ↑↓

	F	VF	EF	BU
mdccclxxix	20	50	300	800
mdccclxxix Proof *FDC* £6000				

3899 Florin. Type B³/⁸. Similar as next but younger portrait (1880) die axis ↑↓

mdccclxxx .... *Extremely rare*

3900 Florin. Type B⁸. Similar but border of 34 arcs (1880 to 1887) die axis ↑↓

	F	VF	EF	BU		F	VF	EF	BU
mdccclxxx	15	40	300	775	mdccclxxxiii Proof *FDC* £5000				
mdccclxxx Proof *FDC* £6000					mdccclxxxiv	15	50	300	725
mdccclxxxi	15	40	300	775	mdccclxxxv	20	60	300	725
mdccclxxxi Proof *FDC* £5750					mdccclxxxv Proof *FDC* £6000				
mdccclxxxi/xxri	30	80	350	850	mdccclxxxvi	15	50	300	725
mdccclxxxiii	15	40	300	775	mdccclxxxvi Proof *FDC* £6250				

3901 Florin. Type B⁹. Similar but border of 46 arcs die axis ↑↓

	F	VF	EF	BU
1887 mdccclxxxvii	30	75	375	900
mdccclxxxvii Proof *FDC*		*Extremely rare*		

3902 Shilling. Type A¹. First head l., WW on trun.R. crowned mark of value within wreath, date below, die axis ↑↓

	F	VF	EF	BU		F	VF	EF	BU
1838	15	55	325	775	1839	45	110	425	1000
1838 Proof *FDC* £4000					1839 Proof *FDC* £3250				

3903 Shilling Type A². Second head, l. WW on trun. (proof only), 1839 die axis ↑↑ *FDC* £2000

3904 - Type A3 Shilling

	F	VF	EF	BU		F	VF	EF	BU
	£	£	£	£		£	£	£	£

3904 Shilling Type A³. Second head, l. no initials on trun. R. Similar die axis ↑↓

	F	VF	EF	BU		F	VF	EF	BU
1839	20	50	250	550	1852	10	30	225	500
1839 Proof plain edge *FDC* £1750					1853	10	25	200	500
1839 Proof plain edge en medaille ↑↑ *FDC* £3000					1853 Milled edge Proof *FDC* £3000				
1839 Proof milled edge *FDC Extremely rare*					1854	250	600	1950	4500
1840	20	50	275	650	1854/1	300	875	3750	—
1840 Proof *FDC* £4250					1855	10	25	175	500
1841	25	75	325	650	1856	10	25	175	500
1842	20	45	225	550	1857	10	25	175	500
1842 Proof *FDC* £4250					1857 REG F: Ɔ:error	215	600	1750	—
1843	25	70	300	650	1858	10	25	175	500
1844	20	40	225	550	1859	10	25	175	500
1845	30	55	250	575	1859 9/8	25	65	375	750
1846	20	40	225	550	1859 Proof *FDC* £4500				
1848 over 6	65	225	825	1750	1860	12	35	225	550
1849	25	50	275	650	1861	12	35	225	550
1850	800	1750	5000	—	1861 D/B in FD	125	325	900	—
1850/49	875	2000	5250	—	1862	45	75	275	625
1851	55	125	700	1450	1863	100	225	650	1500
1851 Proof *FDC* £5500					1863/1	120	315	950	—

3905 Shilling Type A⁴. Similar as last, R. Die number above date die axis ↑↓

	F	VF	EF	BU		F	VF	EF	BU
1864	10	30	175	500	1866 BBITANNIAR	60	300	1100	1750
1865	10	30	175	500	1867	15	35	175	500
1866	10	30	175	500					

3906 Shilling Type A⁵. Third head, l. R. Similar no die number above date die axis ↑↓

1867 Proof £4500	1879	225	500	1250	2200
1867 Proof plain edge £4750	1879 Proof, milled edge, *FDC* £4500

3906A - Type A6 Shilling   Die number location above date

3906A Shilling Type A⁶. Third head, l. R. Similar die number above date die axis ↑↓

	F	VF	EF	BU		F	VF	EF	BU
1867	200	500	1500	2600	1873	10	20	150	450
1868	10	25	150	450	1874	10	20	150	450
1869	20	40	250	500	1875	10	20	150	450
1870	15	35	225	475	1876	15	30	175	475
1871	10	20	150	450	1877	10	20	150	450
1871 Plain edge proof *FDC* £4250					1878	20	40	250	525
1871 Milled edge proof *FDC* £4000					1878 Milled edge Proof *FDC* £4250				
1872	10	20	150	450	1879 uncertain to exist as normal coin or proof?				

	F	VF	EF	BU		F	VF	EF	BU
	£	£	£	£		£	£	£	£

3907 Shilling Type A[7]. Fourth head, l. R. Similar no die number above date die axis ↑↓

1879	10	20	150	450	1883 plain edge Proof *FDC* £4750				
1879 Proof *FDC* £4250					1884	10	20	150	350
1880	10	20	175	500	1884 Proof *FDC* £3750				
1880 Proof plain edge £4000					1885	10	15	125	350
1880 Proof milled edge £3500					1885 Proof *FDC* £3750				
1881	10	20	150	350	1886	10	15	125	350
1881 Proof plain edge £4250					1886 Proof *FDC* £3750				
1881 Proof milled edge £3250					1887	10	25	150	425
1882	10	35	225	525	1887 Proof *FDC* £3250				
1883	10	20	175	450					

3907A Shilling. Type A7. Fourth head, R. Similar die number above date die axis ↑↓

| 1878 | 15 | 30 | 150 | 450 | 1879 | 10 | 35 | 175 | 425 |
| 1878 Milled edge Proof *FDC* £4000 | | | | | | | | | |

3908

Type A1 Sixpence

3908 Sixpence. Type A[1]. First head l. R. Crowned mark of value within wreath, date below die axis ↑↓

1838	10	25	150	425	1851	10	20	150	450
1838 Proof *FDC* £2750					1852	8	20	150	425
1839	10	25	150	425	1853	8	20	125	375
1839 Proof *FDC* £1500					1853 Proof *FDC* £1650				
1840	10	25	150	450	1854	200	500	1100	3150
1841	15	30	175	475	1855	8	20	150	450
1842	10	25	150	450	1855/3	10	25	175	475
1843	10	25	150	450	1855 Proof *FDC*		*Extremely rare*		
1844 Small 44	10	20	150	450	1856	8	20	150	450
1844 Large 44	15	30	175	475	1857	8	20	150	450
1845	10	20	150	450	1858	8	20	150	450
1846	10	20	125	475	1858 Proof *FDC*		*Extremely rare*		
1847 An example in fair condition sold at DNW,					1859	8	20	150	450
29/9/10, lot 1773 for £850 + premium					1859/8	10	20	150	450
1848	45	110	480	1560	1860	10	20	150	450
1848/6 or 7	45	110	575	1400	1862	100	250	750	1800
1850	10	20	130	420	1863	65	150	500	1100
1850/3	15	30	170	380	1866		*Extremely rare*		

3909

Die number location above date

3912

Type 'A5' Sixpence

3909 Sixpence. Type A[2]. First head, R. Similar die number above date die axis ↑↓

| 1864 | 8 | 20 | 150 | 475 | 1866 | 8 | 15 | 150 | 475 |
| 1865 | 8 | 25 | 175 | 450 | 1867 | 10 | 25 | 175 | 500 |

3910

	F	VF	EF	BU		F	VF	EF	BU
	£	£	£	£		£	£	£	£

3910 Sixpence. Type A³. Second head, l. R. Similar die number above date, die axis ↑↓

1867	10	20	150	450	1873	8	15	125	350
1867 Proof *FDC* £2750					1874	8	15	125	350
1868	10	20	150	450	1875	8	15	125	350
1869	10	20	175	500	1876	10	20	150	475
1869 Proof *FDC* £3000					1877	8	15	125	350
1870	10	20	175	500	1878	8	15	125	350
1870 plain edge Proof *FDC* £3000					1878 DRITANNIAR 150	420	1100	—	
1871	8	15	125	375	1878 Proof *FDC* £2500				
1871 plain edge Proof *FDC* £3000					1878/7	35	175	800	—
1872	8	15	125	375	1879	10	20	150	400

3911   3912

3911 Sixpence. Type A⁴. Second head, l. R. Similar No die number, die axis ↑↓

1871	8	15	150	400	1879 milled edge Proof *FDC* £2500
1871 Proof *FDC* £2250					1879 plain edge Proof *FDC* £3000
1877	8	15	150	400	1880 8 15 125 325
1879	8	15	150	400	

3912 Sixpence. Type A⁵. Third head l. R. Similar, die axis ↑↓

1880	8	15	100	250	1883 plain edge Proof *FDC Extremely rare*
1880 Proof *FDC* £2750					1884 8 15 90 250
1881	8	15	80	225	1885 8 15 90 250
1881 plain edge Proof *FDC Extremely rare*					1885 Proof *FDC* £2500
1881 milled edge Proof *FDC Extremely rare*					1886 8 15 90 250
1882	10	30	125	400	1886 Proof *FDC* £2500
1883	8	15	80	225	1887 8 15 80 225
1883 Small R legend 15	40	150	400	1887 Proof *FDC* £2250

3913

	F £	VF £	EF £	BU £		F £	VF £	EF £	BU £

3913 Groat (4d.). Young head 1.℞. Britannia seated r. date in ex, edge milled, die axis ↑↑

	F	VF	EF	BU		F	VF	EF	BU
1837 Plain edge Proof £13500					1846	8	15	65	150
1837 Milled edge Proof £12500					1847/6 (or 8)	30	125	360	700
1838	5	12	60	150	1848/6	10	35	90	200
1838 plain edge Proof *FDC* £1500					1848	6	15	65	150
1838 Milled edge Proof £1350					1848/7/6	10	30	110	325
1838/∞	8	20	80	175	1849	5	15	65	150
1839	7	15	70	175	1849/8	8	15	75	150
1839 die axis ↑↑ Proof plain edge *FDC* £750					1851	20	80	350	725
1839 die axis ↑↓ Proof plain edge *FDC* £800					1852	40	125	500	975
1840	7	15	65	150	1853	100	300	775	1750
1840 small round o	10	20	65	175	1853 Proof *FDC* milled edge £1350				
1841	10	25	100	250	1853 Proof *FDC* plain edge £1500				
1842	8	15	65	175	1854	5	15	60	150
1842 Proof *FDC* £1500					1855	5	15	60	150
1842/1	10	20	70	225	1855/3	10	25	75	175
1843	8	15	65	150	1857 Milled or plain edge proof *FDC* £2250				
1843 4 over 5	10	25	75	250	1857 Plain edge pattern £2750				
1844	7	15	70	150	1862 Plain or milled edge Proof *FDC* £2750				
1845	8	15	65	150	1862 Plain edge pattern *FDC* £3500				

3914 Threepence. Type A[1]. First bust, young head, high relief, ear fully visible, die axis ↑↓
℞ Crowned 3; as Maundy threepence but with a less prooflike surface.

	F	VF	EF	BU		F	VF	EF	BU
1838*	7	23	75	200	1851 reads 1551 £650				
1838 BRITANNIAB ...		*Extremely rare*			1851 5 over 8	15	40	175	325
1839*	9	35	100	250	1852*	75	200	600	950
1839 Proof (see Maundy)					1853	23	90	275	500
1840*	9	30	90	250	1854	7	18	90	225
1841*	9	35	100	250	1855	9	30	100	250
1842*	9	35	125	275	1856	7	18	90	200
1843*	7	23	75	200	1857	7	25	100	250
1844*	9	30	100	200	1858	7	14	75	200
1845	7	14	70	175	1858 BRITANNIAB ..		*Extremely rare*		
1846	27	90	275	550	1858/6	15	35	200	—
1847*	45	175	365	950	1858/5	10	30	150	—
1848*	40	150	395	900	1859	7	14	75	200
1849	9	35	100	250	1860	7	25	100	250
1850	7	18	70	150	1861	7	14	75	200
1851	7	23	75	225					

*Issued for Colonial use only.

3914A - Type A2   3914C - Type A4   3914D - Type 5

	F	VF	EF	BU		F	VF	EF	BU
	£	£	£	£		£	£	£	£

3914A Threepence. Type A^2. First bust variety, slightly older portrait with aquiline nose ↑↓

1859	7	14	75	175	1865	7	18	100	200
1860	7	14	75	175	1866	7	14	75	175
1861	7	14	75	175	1867	7	14	75	175
1862	9	23	75	175	1868	7	14	75	175
1863	14	30	100	200	1868 RRITANNIAR ..		*Extremely rare*		
1864	7	14	75	175					

3914B Threepence. Type A^3. Second Bust, slightly larger, lower relief, mouth fuller, nose more pronounced, rounded truncation, die axis ↑↓

1867	7	23	100	225

3914C Threepence. Type A^4. Obv. as last. R. Tie ribbon further from tooth border, cross on crown nearer to tooth border die axis ↑↓

1866		*Extremely rare*			1874	4	14	55	100
1867	7	25	80	200	1875	4	14	55	100
1868	7	25	80	200	1876	4	14	55	100
1869	9	25	100	275	1877	4	14	65	125
1870	4	14	70	150	1878	4	14	65	125
1871	7	18	75	175	1879	4	14	65	125
1872	7	18	75	175	1879 Proof *FDC*		*Extremely rare*		
1873	4	14	55	125	1884	4	7	55	100

3914D Threepence. Type A^5. Third bust, older features, mouth closed, hair strands leading from 'bun' vary, die axis ↑↓

1880	4	9	60	115	1885	5	8	45	100
1881	4	9	45	100	1885 Proof *FDC*		*Extremely rare*		
1882	4	9	65	175	1886	5	8	45	100
1883	4	9	45	100	1887	5	10	60	115

3914E Twopence. Young head 1. R Date divided by a crowned 2 within a wreath, die axis ↑↓

1838	4	9	30	75	1848	4	9	40	80

3915 - Three-Halfpence

3915 Three-Halfpence. (for Colonial use). Young head 1. R. Crowned value and date, die axis ↑↓

1838	4	9	45	115	1843 Proof *FDC* £1000				
1838 Proof *FDC* £1000					1843/34	4	18	75	150
1839	4	9	40	100	1843/34 Proof *FDC* £950				
1840	7	23	85	200	1860	4	18	70	175
1841	4	14	50	125	1862	4	18	70	175
1842	4	14	50	125	1862 Proof *FDC* £1250				
1843	4	7	35	115	1870 Proof only £1500				

3916 - 1880 Maundy Set

	F	VF	EF	BU			F	VF	EF	BU
	£	£	£	£			£	£	£	£

3916 Maundy Set. (4d., 3d., 2d. and 1.) Young head 1., die axis ↑↓

	F	VF	EF	BU			F	VF	EF	BU
1838			200	575		1864			125	400
1838 Proof *FDC* £1850						1865			125	400
1838 Proof in gold *FDC* £35000						1866			125	375
1839			175	550		1867			125	375
1839 Proof die axis ↑↑ *FDC* £1650						1867 Proof set *FDC* £2000				
1840			225	575		1868			125	400
1841			275	675		1869			125	425
1842			225	550		1870			125	400
1843			175	525		1871			100	375
1844			200	575		1871 Proof set *FDC* £2000				
1845			175	500		1872			100	375
1846			275	700		1873			100	375
1847			275	625		1874			100	375
1848			275	625		1875			100	375
1849			225	575		1876			100	375
1850			175	550		1877			100	375
1851			175	525		1878			125	400
1852		150	325	775		1878 Proof set *FDC* £2000				
1853			200	600		1879			100	375
1853 Proof *FDC* £1850						1880			100	375
1854			150	525		1881			100	375
1855			175	525		1881 Proof set *FDC* £2000				
1856			125	400		1882			100	375
1857			175	525		1882 Proof set *FDC* £2000				
1858			125	375		1883			100	375
1859			125	375		1884			100	375
1860			125	375		1885			100	375
1861			150	375		1886			100	375
1862			175	450		1887			125	400
1863			175	450						

			F	VF	EF	BU
3917 — **Fourpence**, 1838-87			*from*		10	35
3918 — **Threepence**, 1838-87			*from*		15	55
3919 — **Twopence**, 1838-87			*from*		10	35
3920 — **Penny**, 1838-87			*from*		15	50

Maundy Sets in good quality original cases are worth approximately £40 more than the prices quoted. Refer to footnote after 3796.

JUBILEE COINAGE 1887-93, die axis ↑↑

3921
1887 Crown

	F	VF	EF	BU		F	VF	EF	BU
	£	£	£	£		£	£	£	£

3921 Crown. Jubilee bust l. R. St. George and dragon,date in ex, edge milled, die axis ↑↑

1887....................... 25	40	95	200	1889...................... 25	40	110	300
1887 Proof *FDC* £2250				1890...................... 25	50	145	375
1888 narrow date..... 25	45	165	375	1891...................... 25	50	185	400
1888 wide date 100	250	575	1100	1892...................... 35	65	225	500

3922 Double-Florin (4s.).Jubilee bust l. R. (As Florin) Crowned cruciform shields. Sceptre in
angles. Roman I in date, die axis ↑↑

1887.. 20	40	95	200
1887 Proof *FDC* £1250			

3923
1887 Double-Florin
Arabic 1 in date

3924
1887 Halfcrown

3923 Double-Florin Jubilee bust l. R. Similar but Arabic 1 in date, die axis ↑↑

1887........................20	35	75	175	1889 20	40	100	250
1887 Proof *FDC* £1050				1889 inverted 1 for I in			
1888.......................20	40	100	250	VICTORIA.... 45	85	325	675
1888 inverted 1 for I in				1890 20	50	125	300
VICTORIA.....40	90	250	650				

3924 Halfcrown. Jubilee bust l. R. Crowned shield in garter and collar, die axis ↑↑

1887.......................15	20	45	100	1890...................... 15	30	125	275
1887 Proof *FDC* £675				1891...................... 15	30	135	375
1888.......................15	25	90	250	1892...................... 15	35	150	300
1889.......................15	30	90	250				

3925
1890 Florin reverse

	F	VF	EF	BU		F	VF	EF	BU
	£	£	£	£		£	£	£	£

3925 Florin. Jubilee bust 1. R. Crowned cruciform shields, sceptres in angles, die axis ↑↑

	F	VF	EF	BU		F	VF	EF	BU
1887............................8	12	35	75		1889........................12	35	100	225
1887 Proof *FDC* £500					1890........................15	45	185	525
1888 obverse die					1891........................25	70	325	700
of 1887...............15	45	110	225		1892........................35	110	600	1200
1888........................12	30	70	185		1892 Proof *FDC* £10000			

3926
small head Shilling

3926 Shilling. Small Jubilee head. R. Crowned shield in Garter, die axis ↑↑

	F	VF	EF	BU		F	VF	EF	BU
1887............................4	14	23	45		1888/7 7	14	55	125
1887 Proof *FDC* £425					1889 50	150	500	950
1888........................45	90	200	375					

3927 Shilling. Large Jubilee head. R. Similar as before, die axis ↑↑

	F	VF	EF	BU		F	VF	EF	BU
1889............................7	16	60	125		1891 11	18	75	175
1889 Proof *FDC* £2250					1891 Proof *FDC* £2250			
1890............................9	18	65	150		1892 11	18	75	175

3928
1887 'withdrawn type' Sixpence

3928 Sixpence. JEB designer's initials below trun. R. Shield in Garter (withdrawn type), die axis ↑↑

	F	VF	EF	BU		F	VF	EF	BU
1887............................4	9	18	35		1887 JEB on trun. ..25	70	150	375
1887 Proof *FDC* £275					1887 R/V in			
					VICTORIA....23	50	125	275

3929
Crowned value Sixpence

3930
1888 Groat

	F	VF	EF	BU		F	VF	EF	BU
	£	£	£	£		£	£	£	£

3929 Sixpence. R. Jubilee bust 1. Crowned, value in wreath, die axis ↑↑

1887...........................4	9	18	45	1890 7	14	45	125
1887 Proof *FDC* £1200				1890 Proof *FDC*.........	*Extremely rare*		
1888...........................6	13	35	100	1891 9	18	50	125
1888 Proof *FDC* £1850				1892 11	23	55	150
1889...........................6	13	35	100	1893 550	1100	3250	6500

3930 Groat (for use in British Guiana). Jubilee Bust 1. R. Britannia seated r. date in axis, die axis ↑↑

1888 Milled edge Proof *FDC* £1500			1888 11	30	75	175

3931 Threepence. As Maundy but less prooflike surface, die axis ↑↑

1887...........................–	2	11	25	1890 2	4	13	45
1887 Proof *FDC* £225				1891 2	4	16	50
1888...........................3	5	18	55	1892 3	5	18	55
1889...........................2	4	13	45	1893 20	65	200	500

3932
1889 Maundy Set

	EF	FDC		EF	FDC
	£	£		£	£

3932 Maundy Set. (4d., 3d., 2d. and 1d.) Jubilee bust 1.die axis ↑↑

1888	125	225	1890	125	225
1888 Proof set *FDC* ....*Extremely rare*			1891	125	225
1889	125	225	1892	125	225
3933 — Fourpence, 1888-92 ....*from*				12	35
3934 — Threepence, 1888-92 ....*from*				18	40
3935 — Twopence, 1888-92 ....*from*				10	30
3936 — Penny, 1888-92..*from*				15	45

Maundy Sets in the original undamaged cases are worth approximately £25 more than the prices quoted.
See footnote after 3796.

OLD HEAD COINAGE 1893-1901, die axis ↑↑

3937
1893 Old Head Crown

	F	VF	EF	BU
	£	£	£	£

3937 Crown. Old veiled bust l. R. St. George. date in ex. Regnal date on edge, die axis ↑↑

	F	VF	EF	BU
1893 edge LVI	17	25	175	425
1893 Proof *FDC* £3250				
1893 LVII	26	75	400	775
1894 LVII	17	40	275	650
1894 LVIII	17	40	275	650
1895 LVIII	17	35	225	600
1895 LIX	17	35	200	575
1896 LIX	19	60	375	725
1896 LX	17	40	225	600
1897 LX	17	35	200	550
1897 LXI	17	35	200	550
1898 LXI	26	75	450	850
1898 LXII	17	35	275	625
1899 LXII	17	35	200	600
1899 LXIII	17	35	225	650
1900 LXIII	17	35	200	600
1900 LXIV	17	35	200	550

3938
Halfcrown

	F	VF	EF	BU		F	VF	EF	BU
	£	£	£	£		£	£	£	£

3938 Halfcrown. Old veiled bust l. R. Shield in collar, edge milled, die axis ↑↑

	F	VF	EF	BU		F	VF	EF	BU
1893	10	26	55	150	1897	10	26	65	200
1893 Proof *FDC* £1150					1898	15	40	100	300
1894	13	40	125	350	1899	13	30	75	225
1895	10	35	100	275	1900	13	26	65	200
1896	10	35	100	275	1901	13	26	70	225

3938A Small reverse design with long border teeth

	F	VF	EF	BU
1896	15	35	150	300

3939
Old Head Florin

	F	VF	EF	BU		F	VF	EF	BU
	£	£	£	£		£	£	£	£

3939 Florin. Old veiled bust l. R. Three shields within garter, die axis ↑↑

	F	VF	EF	BU		F	VF	EF	BU
1893	10	20	75	150	1897	10	20	80	175
1893 Proof *FDC* £650					1898	10	25	95	250
1894	12	30	135	350	1899	10	20	90	225
1895	10	25	110	275	1900	10	20	80	175
1896	10	25	110	275	1901	10	20	85	200

3940A   3941
1901 Shilling   1897 Sixpence

3940 Shilling. Old veiled bust l. R. Three shields within Garter, small rose, die axis ↑↑

	F	VF	EF	BU		F	VF	EF	BU
1893	10	20	60	120	1894	10	20	65	160
1893 small lettering	10	15	55	110	1895	12	25	70	175
1893 Proof *FDC* £400					1896	10	20	65	165

3940A Shilling. Old veiled bust l. R. Second reverse, larger rose, die axis ↑↑

	F	VF	EF	BU		F	VF	EF	BU
1895	10	18	65	150	1899	10	18	65	150
1896	10	15	60	150	1900	10	15	55	125
1897	10	15	50	125	1901	10	15	55	125
1898	10	15	60	150					

3941 Sixpence. Old veiled bust l. R. Value in wreath, die axis ↑↑

	F	VF	EF	BU		F	VF	EF	BU
1893	7	12	40	100	1897	8	15	45	100
1893 Proof *FDC* £375					1898	8	15	50	115
1894	10	15	60	150	1899	8	15	50	115
1895	8	15	55	125	1900	8	15	50	115
1896	8	15	50	110	1901	7	12	45	100

3942 Threepence. Old veiled bust l. R. Crowned 3. As Maundy but less prooflike surface, die axis ↑↑

	F	VF	EF	BU		F	VF	EF	BU
1893	3	7	15	60	1897	3	5	15	45
1893 Proof *FDC* £225					1898	3	5	15	50
1894	3	8	22	70	1899	3	5	15	50
1895	3	8	20	60	1900	3	5	12	45
1896	3	7	20	60	1901	3	5	15	45

3943
1901 Maundy Set

	EF	FDC			EF	FDC
	£	£			£	£

3943 Maundy Set. (4d., 3d., 2d. and 1d.) Old veiled bust l., die axis ↑↑

	EF	FDC		EF	FDC
1893	120	200	1898	125	210
1894	125	215	1899	125	210
1895	125	210	1900	125	210
1896	125	210	1901	125	200
1897	125	210			

		EF	FDC
3944 — **Fourpence**. 1893-1901 ....*from*		8	30
3945 — **Threepence**. 1893-1901 ....*from*		15	40
3946 — **Twopence**. 1893-1901 ....*from*		8	30
3947 — **Penny**. 1893-1901...*from*		15	40

Maundy Sets in the original undamaged cases are worth approximately £25 more than the prices quoted. See footnote after 3796.

COPPER AND BRONZE

YOUNG HEAD COPPER COINAGE, 1838-60, die axis ↑↑

3948
Penny
Rev. with ornamental trident prongs (OT)

	F	VF	EF	BU		F	VF	EF	BU
	£	£	£	£		£	£	£	£

3948 Penny. Young head l. date below R̄. Britannia seated r.

	F	VF	EF	BU		F	VF	EF	BU
1839 Bronzed proof *FDC* £3500					1845 OT	12	35	275	825
1841 Rev. OT	10	55	275	900	1846 OT	10	25	225	725
1841 Proof *FDC* £4250					1846 OT colon close .				
1841 Silver Proof *FDC* £9000					to DEF	12	30	250	775
1841 OT. no colon					1847 — —	7	20	200	600
after REG	5	20	120	525	1847 OT DEF—:	7	20	200	600
1843 OT. —	70	275	1750	4250	1848/7 OT	5	20	170	625
1843 OT REG:	80	400	2250	4750	1848 OT	5	20	200	625
1844 OT	10	20	200	625	1848/6 OT	20	140	725	—
1844 Proof *FDC*		*Extremely rare*			1849 OT	225	600	2250	4250

Copper coins graded in this catalogue as BU have full mint lustre.

	F £	VF £	EF £	BU £		F £	VF £	EF £	BU £
3948 Penny. (Continued)									
1851 OT 15	30	225	800		1856 Proof *FDC* £4000				
1851 OT DEF:.........10	25	200	725		1856 OT DEF—:......115	400	1150	3300	
1853 OT DEF—:.......5	15	110	475		1857 OT DEF—:........7	20	130	550	
1853 Proof *FDC* £3500					1857 PT DEF: 5	15	120	525	
1853 Plain trident, (PT)					1858 OT DEF—:........5	12	110	450	
DEF: 15	35	165	625		1858/7 — — 5	15	120	525	
1854 PT 5	15	135	475		1858/3 7	30	140	525	
1854/3 PT 10	65	250	725		1858 no ww on trun 5	18	110	525	
1854 OT DEF—:.......7	20	120	500		1859 5	20	130	550	
1855 OT — 5	15	120	475		1859 Proof *FDC* £4000				
1855 PT DEF: 5	15	130	475		1860/59 850	1950	3750	6750	
1856 PT DEF: 115	300	875	3000						

3949

1845 Halfpenny

3949 Halfpenny. Young head l. date below R. Britannia seated r., die axis ↑↑   1853 Rev. incuse dots

	F	VF	EF	BU		F	VF	EF	BU
1838...........................5	15	90	325		1852 Rev. normal shield .10	20	110	350	
1839 Bronzed proof FDC £950					1853 dots on shield........3	7	55	175	
1841 5	12	65	275		1853 — Proof FDC £1350				
1841 — Proof FDC £1650					1853/2 — 15	40	165	400	
1841 Silver proof FDC		*Extremely rare*			1854 — 4	7	45	175	
1843 25	50	225	750		1855 — 4	7	45	185	
1844 12	35	175	375		1856 — 5	12	80	275	
1845 250	500	2000	—		1857 — 4	10	60	215	
1846 12	35	175	375		1857 Rev. normal				
1847 12	35	175	375		shield 4	10	55	200	
1848 25	70	225	600		1858 — 5	10	55	225	
1848/7 10	30	175	375		1858/7 — 5	10	55	225	
1851 5	15	90	325		1858/6 — 5	10	70	225	
1851 Rev. incuse dots ..					1859 — 5	10	70	225	
on shield.............5	15	100	350		1859/8 — 10	20	110	350	
1852 Similar...............7	15	95	325		1860* — 1850	3500	7000	12500	

Overstruck dates are listed only if commoner than normal date, or if no normal date is known.

*These 1860 large copper pieces are not to be confused with the smaller and commoner bronze issue with date on reverse (nos. 3954, 3956 and 3958).

Copper coins graded in this catalogue as UNC have full mint lustre.

3950 - 1849 Farthing   3950 - 1864 Proof

3950 Farthing. Young head l. date below R. Britannia seated r. die axis ↑↑

	F	VF	EF	BU		F	VF	EF	BU
	£	£	£	£		£	£	£	£
1838 WW raised on trun.	5	10	70	225	1850 5/4	10	30	110	385
1839	4	7	65	175	1851	10	20	90	285
1839 Bronzed Proof *FDC* £825					1851 D/ᗡ in DEI	80	175	525	950
1839 Silver Proof *FDC*		*Extremely rare*			1852	10	20	90	285
1839 Copper Proof *FDC* £1250					1853	5	10	50	185
1840	4	7	70	185	1853 WW incuse on trun	10	30	150	425
1841	4	7	70	185	1853 Proof *FDC* £1250				
1841 Proof *FDC*		*Extremely rare*			1854	5	10	50	165
1842	12	45	165	425	1855	5	12	85	200
1843/2	10	30	120	375	1855 WW raised	7	12	85	200
1843	4	7	45	175	1856 WW incuse	7	20	90	285
1843 I for 1 in date	85	375	825	2000	1856 R/E in VICTORIA	15	50	250	550
1844	70	225	825	2250	1857	5	10	55	185
1845	7	10	65	175	1858	5	10	55	185
1846	7	15	85	210	1859	10	20	90	315
1847	5	10	65	175	1860*	1600	3500	6250	12500
1848	5	10	65	175	1864 IWW on truncation proof *FDC* £25000				
1849	40	100	400	900					
1850	5	10	65	175					

3951 - Half-Farthing   3952 - Third-Farthing   3953 - Quarter-Farthing

3951 Half-Farthing. Young head l. R. Crowned Value and date, die axis ↑↑

	F	VF	EF	BU		F	VF	EF	BU
1839	5	10	65	175	1852	3	10	70	165
1839 Bronzed proof *FDC* £800					1853	5	15	75	215
1842	5	10	65	175	1853 Proof *FDC* £850				
1843		5	30	125	1854	7	25	125	350
1844		3	25	110	1856	7	25	125	350
1844 E/N in REGINA	10	20	95	315	1856 Large date	55	150	375	825
1847	3	7	55	175	1868 Proof *FDC* £1100				
1851 5/0	10	20	115	300	1868 Cupro nickel Proof *FDC* £1650				
1851	5	10	70	165					

3952 Third-Farthing (for use in Malta). Young head l. date below R. Britannia seated r. die axis ↑↑

	F	VF	EF	BU		F	VF	EF	BU
1844	20	45	125	375	1844 RE for REG	30	75	450	950

3953 Quarter-Farthing (for use in Ceylon). Young head l. R. Crowned Value and date, die axis ↑↑

	F	VF	EF	BU		F	VF	EF	BU
1839	20	30	90	300	1853	25	45	125	375
1851	15	25	85	275	1853 Proof *FDC* £1650				
1852	15	25	80	225	1868 Proof *FDC* £1100				
1852 Proof *FDC* £1500					1868 Cupro-nickel Proof *FDC* £1500				

Copper coins graded in this catalogue as BU have full mint lustre.
*These 1860 large copper pieces are not to be confused with the smaller and commoner bronze issue with date on reverse (nos. 3954, 3956 and 3958).

BRONZE COINAGE, "BUN HEAD" ISSUE, 1860-95, die axis ↑↑

When studying an example of the bronze coinage, if the minutiae of the variety is not evident due to wear from circulation, then the coin will not be of any individual significance. Proofs exist of most years and are generally extremely rare for all denominations.

3954 The Bronze Penny. The bronze coinage is the most complicated of the milled series from the point of view of the large number of different varieties of obverse and reverse and their combinations. Below are set out illustrations with explanations of all the varieties. The obverse and reverse types listed below reflect those as listed originally by C W Peck in his British Museum Catalogue of Copper, Tin and Bronze Coinage 1558-1958, and later in "The Bronze Coinage of Great Britain" by Michael J Freeman which gives much fuller and detailed explanations of the types. Reference can also be compared to "The British Bronze Penny" by Michael Gouby.

OBVERSES

Obverse 1 (1860) - laureate and draped bust facing left, hair tied in bun, wreath of 15 leaves and 4 berries, L C WYON raised on base of bust, **beaded border** and thin linear circle.

Obverse 1* (1860) - laureate and draped bust facing left, hair tied in bun, **more bulging lowered eye with more rounded forehead**, wreath of **15 leaves and 4 berries**, which are weaker in part, L C WYON raised on base of bust, **beaded border** and thin linear circle.

Obverse 3 (1860-61) - laureate and draped bust facing left, hair tied in bun, **complete rose to drapery**, wreath of 15 leaves and 4 berries, **two leaves have incuse outlines, L C WYON** raised on base of bust **nearly touches border**, toothed border and thin linear circle both sides.

Obverse 2 (1860-62) - laureate and draped bust facing left, hair tied in bun, wreath of 15 leaves and 4 berries, **L C WYON** raised **lower on base of bust** and clear of border, **toothed border** and thin linear circle both sides.

Obverse 4 (1860-61) - laureate and draped bust facing left, hair tied in bun, **finer hair strands at nape of neck**, wreath of 15 leaves and 4 berries, two leaves have incuse outlines, **L C WYON below bust, nearly touches border, toothed border of shorter teeth**, and thin linear circle both sides.

OBVERSES (*continued*)

Obverse 7 (1874) - laureate and draped bust facing left, hair tied in bun, finer hair strands at nape of neck, **wreath of 17 leaves, leaf veins raised, 6 berries**, no signature, toothed border and thin linear circle both sides.

Obverse 5 (1860-61) - laureate and draped bust facing left, hair tied in bun, **finer hair strands at nape of neck**, wreath of 15 leaves and 4 berries, **leaf veins incuse**, two leaves have incuse outlines, **no signature below bust**, toothed border and thin linear circle both sides.

Obverse 8 (1874-79) - laureate and draped bust facing left, hair tied in bun, with **close thicker ties to ribbons**, wreath of 17 leaves, leaf veins raised, 6 berries, no signature, toothed border and thin linear circle both sides.

Obverse 6 (1860-74) - laureate and draped bust facing left, hair tied in bun, finer hair strands at nape of neck, **wreath of 16 leaves, leaf veins raised, no signature**, toothed border and thin linear circle both sides. There is a **prominent flaw** on the **top stop of the colon after D at the end of the legend**.

Obverse 9 (1879-81) - laureate and draped bust facing left, hair tied in bun, with close thicker ties, wreath of 17 leaves, **double leaf veins incuse**, 6 berries, no signature, toothed border and thin linear circle both sides.

OBVERSES (*continued*)

Obverse 10 (1880-81) - laureate and draped bust facing left, hair tied in bun, with close thicker ties, **wreath of 15 leaves, leaf veins raised and recessed, 4 berries**, no signature, toothed border and thin linear circle both sides.

Obverse 12 (1881-94) - laureate and draped bust facing left, hair tied in bun, with close thicker ties, **no curls at nape of neck**, nose more hooked, wreath of 15 leaves, leaf veins raised, 4 berries, no signature, **toothed border, more numerous teeth**, and thin linear circle both sides, weak on obverse, **larger lettering**.

Obverse 11 (1881-83) - laureate and draped bust facing left, more **hooked nose**, hair tied in bun, with close thicker ties, nose more hooked, wreath of 15 leaves, **leaf veins raised**, 4 berries, no signature, toothed border and thin linear circle both sides, **weak circle on obverse**.

Obverse 13 (1889) - laureate and draped bust facing left, hair tied in bun, with close thicker ties, no curls at nape of neck, nose more hooked, **wreath of 14 leaves, leaf veins raised**, no signature, toothed border and thin linear circle both sides, larger lettering.

REVERSES

Reverse A (1860) - Britannia seated right on rocks with shield and trident, **crosses on shield outlined with double raised lines**, L.C.W. incuse below shield, date below in exergue, lighthouse with 4 windows to left, ship sailing to right, **beaded border** and linear circle.

Reverse C (1860) - Britannia seated right on rocks with shield and trident, **crosses on shield outlined with wider spaced thinner double raised lines, thumb touches St. George Cross**, L.C.W. incuse below shield, date below in exergue, lighthouse with 4 windows to left, rocks touch linear circle, ship sailing to right, **beaded border** and linear circle.

Reverse B (1860) - Britannia with **one incuse hemline**, seated right on rocks with shield and trident, **crosses on shield outlined with treble incuse lines**, L.C.W. incuse below shield, date below in exergue, lighthouse with 4 windows to left, ship sailing to right, **beaded border** and linear circle.

Reverse D (1860-61) - Britannia seated right on rocks with shield and trident, crosses on shield outlined with wider spaced thinner double raised lines, thumb touches St. George Cross, L.C.W. incuse below shield, date below in exergue, lighthouse with 4 windows to left, rocks touch linear circle, ship sailing to right, **toothed border**.

REVERSES *(continued)*

Reverse E (1860) - Britannia seated right on rocks with **thick rimmed shield and trident**, crosses on shield outlined with wider spaced thinner double raised lines, thumb touches St. George Cross, **L.C.W. incuse below foot**, date below in exergue, lighthouse with **sharper masonry** to left, **rocks touch linear circle**, ship sailing to right, toothed border.

Reverse G (1861-75) - Britannia seated right on rocks with **convex shield and trident**, no signature, date below in exergue, bell-topped lighthouse to left, **lamp area depicted with five vertical lines**, **no rocks to left**, **sea crosses linear circle**, ship sailing to right, toothed border.

Reverse F (1861) - Britannia seated right on rocks with thick rimmed shield and trident, **incuse lines on breastplate**, crosses on shield outlined with wider spaced thinner double raised lines, thumb touches St. George Cross, **no L.C.W. extra rocks**, date below in exergue, **lighthouse with rounded top** and sharp masonry, **three horizontal lines** between masonry and top, rocks touch linear circle, ship sailing to right, toothed border.

Reverse H (1874-75, 1877) - Britannia seated right on rocks, **smaller head, thinner neck**, with convex shield and trident, no signature, **narrow date** below in exergue, **tall thin lighthouse** to left with **6 windows**, **lamp area of four vertical lines**, close date numerals, **tiny rock to left**, **sea touches linear circle**, ship sailing to right, toothed border.

REVERSES (*continued*)

Reverse I (1874) - Britannia seated right on rocks with convex shield and trident, **thick trident shaft**, no signature, **narrow date** below in exergue, **thicker lighthouse** to left with **4 windows**, lamp area of four vertical lines, close date numerals, tiny rock to left, sea touches linear circle, ship sailing to right, toothed border.

Reverse L (1880) - Britannia seated right on rocks with shield and trident, **extra feather to helmet plume, trident with three rings above hand**, date below in exergue, lighthouse with **cluster of rocks to left**, ship sailing to right, toothed border.

Reverse J (1875-81) - **larger Britannia** seated right on rocks with shield and trident, **left leg more visible, wider date** below in deeper exergue, lighthouse to left, ship sailing to right, **sea does not meet linear circle either side**, toothed border.

Reverse M (1881-82) - larger Britannia seated right on rocks with shield and trident, **flatter shield heraldically coloured**, date and **H** below in exergue, lighthouse to left with faint masonry, ship sailing to right, **sea does not meet linear circle**, toothed border.

Reverse K (1876, 1879) - Britannia with **larger head** seated right on rocks with convex shield and trident, **thicker helmet**, no signature, **narrow date** and in exergue, **tall thin lighthouse** to left, tiny rock to left, **sea touches linear circle**, ship sailing to right, toothed border.

REVERSES (*continued*)

Reverse O (1882 - proof only) – **larger Britannia** seated right on rocks with shield and trident, flatter shield heraldically coloured, date and **H in exergue**, lighthouse to left with faint masonry, ship sailing to right, **sea meets linear circle**, toothed border with more teeth.

Reverse N (1881-94) - **thinner Britannia** seated right on rocks with shield and thinner trident, **helmet plume ends in a single strand**, shield heraldically coloured with different thickness crosses, date in exergue, thinner lighthouse to left, ship sailing to right, sea meets linear circle, toothed border with more teeth.

Beaded border

Toothed border

Shield outlined with double raised lines

Shield outlined with treble incuse lines

Normal nose

More hooked nose

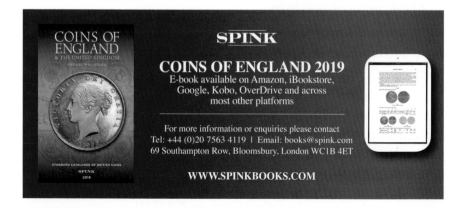

3954

	F	VF	EF	BU		F	VF	EF	BU
	£	£	£	£		£	£	£	£

3954 Penny. Laur. bust l. R. Britannia seated r. date in ex. lighthouse l. ship to r., die axis ↑↑

	F	VF	EF	BU		F	VF	EF	BU
1860 obv 1, rev A..... 70	135	650	1700		1864 Crosslet 4 25	150	1100	4000
1860 obv 1, rev B..... 15	55	350	1100		1865 obv 6, rev G........... 7	20	215	725
1860 obv 1*, rev A. 150	500	1350	2500		1865/3 obv 6, rev G 45	125	800	2000
1860 obv 1, rev C 65	125	650	2150		1866 obv 6, rev G........... 3	15	125	500
1860 obv 1*, rev C .125	475	1150	2350		1867 obv 6, rev G........... 7	30	250	1100
1860 obv 1, rev D .. 400	850	2400	4000		1868 obv 6, rev G......... 10	40	300	1150
1860 obv 2, rev B . 425	875	2750	4500		1869 obv 6, rev G...... 110	450	1850	4500
1860 obv 2, rev D....... 3	15	85	325		1870 obv 6, rev G......... 10	25	200	650
1860 — heavy flan. 2750	—	—	—		1871 obv 6, rev G......... 40	150	825	2150
1860 N/Z in ONE, 2+D 90	300	600	1250		1872 obv 6, rev G........... 3	15	100	350
1860 obv 3, rev D....... 3	15	95	500		1873 obv 6, rev G........... 3	15	100	400
1860 obv 3, rev E ... 125	375	975	2150		1874 obv 6, rev G........... 3	15	150	725
1860 obv 4, rev D 2	10	95	550		1874 obv 7, rev G........... 7	35	165	500
1860 obv 5, rev D....... 7	45	250	850		1874 obv 8, rev G......... 20	55	225	950
1860 obv 6, rev D..... 35	135	450	1000		1874 obv 8 rev H.......... 15	50	200	850
1861 obv 2, rev D..... 75	175	525	1400		1874 obv 6, rev H......... 30	85	425	975
1861 obv 2, rev F ... 125	250	950	1950		1874 obv 7, rev H........... 7	35	165	500
1861 obv 2, rev G..... 30	110	400	1100		1875 obv 8, rev G......... 15	60	300	675
1861 obv 3, rev D .. 250	600	1650	3000		1875 obv 8, rev H........... 2	10	85	350
1861 obv 4, rev D....... 2	15	100	485		1875 obv 8, rev J............ 3	15	90	400
1861 — — heavy flan....2750	—	—	—		1877 obv 8, rev J............ 2	10	95	400
1861 obv 4, rev F ... 110	350	1250	3000		1877 obv 8, rev H....... 3250	—	—	—
1861 obv 4, rev G..... 40	175	600	1850		1878 obv 8, rev J............ 2	15	135	600
1861 obv 5, rev D....... 2	10	95	425		1879 obv 8, rev J........... 7	20	165	850
1861 obv 5, rev F ... 950	—	—	—		1879 obv 9, rev J............ 1	7	85	300
1861 obv 5, rev G... 110	400	1200	2500		1879 obv 9, rev K......... 25	90	400	1500
1861 obv 6, rev D 2	10	95	350		1880 obv 9, rev J............ 2	15	165	600
1861 — — — 6 over 8 450	2150	—	—		1880 obv 9, rev L........... 2	12	135	500
1861 obv 6, rev F .. 150	600	1600	—		1881 obv 9, rev J............ 2	15	135	700
1861 obv 6, rev G....... 2	10	95	385		1881 obv 10, rev J........ 30	90	400	1000
1861 — 8 over 6..... 450	2150	—	—		1881 obv 11, rev J 60	150	600	1300
1862 obv 2, rev G... 500	1350	2950	3850		1882† obv 11, rev N. 1000	3500	—	—
1862 obv 6, rev G....... 2	10	75	285		1883 obv 12, rev N........ 2	10	80	350
1862 — 8 over 6..... 600	2150	—	—		1883 obv11, rev N.......... 2	10	85	400
1862 — Halfpenny					1884 obv 12, rev N........ 2	7	75	250
numerals...... 1250	3250	4950	—		1885 obv 12, rev N........ 2	7	75	250
1863 obv 6, rev G....... 2	10	75	300		1886 obv 12, rev N........ 2	10	85	295
1863 Die number below1500	4250	—	—		1887 obv 12, rev N........ 2	7	75	250
1863 slender 3...... 1100	2750	—	—		1888 obv 12, rev N........ 2	10	65	225
1863/1 obv 6, rev G 1000	2650	—	—		1889 obv 12, rev N........ 3	15	95	425
1864 Upper serif 20	110	925	3500					

†† *not to be confused with Heaton Mint - H - the mint letter is the first device to disappear on worn specimens*
Bronze coins graded in this catalogue as BU have full mint lustre

	F	VF	EF	BU		F	VF	EF	BU
	£	£	£	£		£	£	£	£

3954 Penny. (Continued)

1889 obv 13, rev N..........2	7	60	250	1893 obv 12, rev N..........2	7	60	250
1890 obv 12, rev N..........2	7	60	250	1893 obv 12, rev N 3			
1891 obv 12, rev N..........2	7	60	250	over 2 150	400	700	1500
1892 obv 12, rev N..........2	7	60	250	1894 obv 12, rev N..........2	15	95	325

3955 Penny. Similar R. Britannia, H Mint mark below date – (struck by Ralph Heaton & Sons, Birmingham)

1874 H obv 6, rev G......5	20	110	425	1876 H obv 8, rev K 2	15	100	400
1874 H obv 6, rev H....10	30	165	525	1876 H obv 8, rev J........10	30	190	600
1874 H obv 6, rev I ...175	1000	2500	–	1881 H obv 11, rev M.....3	15	95	450
1874 H obv 7, rev G....10	30	145	475	1881 H obv 9, rev M 475	1250	2750	–
1874 H obv 7, rev H......5	20	110	400	1882 H obv12, rev M ..10	25	165	600
1874 H obv 7, rev I ...150	480	2250	–	1882 H obv 12, rev N 2	10	75	295
1875 H obv 8, rev J.....35	100	1100	2500	1882/1 H obv 11, rev M.....10	25	135	775

3955
H Mint mark location

3956
1860 Halfpenny Beaded border

3956 Halfpenny. Laur. bust l. R. Britannia seated r. date in ex. lighthouse l. ship to r., die axis ↑↑

1860 Beaded border 1	5	35	145	1861 — R. no hemline			
1860 no tie to wreath....5	15	110	375	to drapery 2	10	100	350
1860 Toothed border ...2	10	100	325	1861 — R. door on ...			
1860 round top light house	15	110	375	lighthouse......—	4	85	250
1860 5 berries in				1861 HALP error . 300	850	–	–
wreath..................3	10	100	350	1861 6 over 8 275	800	–	–
1860 — 15 leaves,				1862 ....—	4	45	175
4 berries..............1	10	90	300	1862 Die letter to left of lighthouse			
1860 — rounded				A................600	1400	2650	4000
lighthouse...........2	10	120	350	B................900	2250	–	–
1860 — Double incuse .				C..............1000	2750	–	–
leaf veins 3	12	110	300	1863 small 3 ....—	5	70	275
1860 — 16 leaves				1863 large 3............—	5	70	250
wreath...............10	30	160	500	1864 1	10	100	350
1860 TB/BBmule 700	1400	2700	–	1865 2	12	135	550
1861 5 berries in				1865/3......................45	100	400	1200
wreath...............10	30	150	450	1866 1	10	100	350
1861 15 leaves in				1867 1	12	110	450
wreath..................5	20	110	400	1868 ....—	8	100	375
1861 — R. no hemline .				1869 25	85	450	1300
to drapery 10	30	150	400	1870 1	7	90	325
1861 — R. Door on				1871 25	90	500	1450
lighthouse...........3	12	110	400	1872 1	7	85	275
1861 4 leaves double				1873 1	10	100	325
incuse veins........1	10	90	300	1873 R. hemline to			
1861 16 leaves wreath ..3	12	100	400	drapery 1	10	100	350
1861 — R. LCW incuse				1874 4	25	165	550
on rock..............10	30	150	450	1874 narrow date....12	60	375	850

Bronze coins graded in this catalogue as BU have full mint lustre

	F	VF	EF	BU		F	VF	EF	BU
	£	£	£	£		£	£	£	£

3956 Halfpenny.

	F	VF	EF	BU		F	VF	EF	BU
1874 older features	5	25	175	550	1885	—	4	60	200
1875	—	5	85	275	1886	—	4	60	200
1877	—	5	85	275	1887	—	4	50	175
1878	4	20	150	550	1888	—	4	85	225
1878 wide date	90	200	475	1025	1889	—	4	85	225
1879	—	5	75	225	1889/8	25	60	265	550
1880	1	7	85	275	1890	—	4	50	175
1881	1	7	85	275	1891	—	4	50	175
1883	—	7	85	275	1892	1	5	95	275
1883 rose for brooch obv.	25	65	175	325	1893	—	4	85	200
1884	—	4	60	200	1894	1	6	95	250

3957 Halfpenny. Similar R. Britannia, H Mint mark below date (struck by Ralph Heaton & Sons, Birmingham)

	F	VF	EF	BU		F	VF	EF	BU
1874 H	—	4	85	275	1881 H	—	4	85	275
1875 H	1	5	90	300	1882 H	—	4	85	275
1876 H	—	4	85	275					

3958
1860 Farthing

3960
1868 Third-Farthing

3958 Farthing. Laur bust l. R. Britannia seated r. date in ex. lighthouse l. ship to r. die axis ↑↑

	F	VF	EF	BU		F	VF	EF	BU
1860 Beaded border		3	25	95	1875 —older				
1860 Toothed border		5	35	110	features	7	20	100	325
1860 — 5 berries		3	35	110	1877 Proof only £11000				
1860 TB/BB mule	175	475	1100	—	1878		3	25	100
1861 5 berries		3	45	125	1879 large 9		4	40	125
1861 4 berries		3	30	120	1879 normal 9		3	35	110
1862		3	30	110	1880		4	45	135
1862 large 8	55	175	425	—	1881		3	35	120
1863	20	50	300	650	1883	—	10	55	150
1864 4 no serif		5	50	145	1884		2	20	75
1864 4 with serif		7	55	150	1885		2	20	75
1865		3	45	125	1886		2	20	75
1865/2		10	50	175	1887		3	30	110
1866		3	40	125	1888		3	30	100
1867		3	45	135	1890		3	25	90
1868		4	45	135	1891		2	20	90
1869		10	55	175	1892	—	10	55	175
1872		3	45	125	1893		2	20	90
1873		2	30	95	1894		3	30	100
1875 large date	2	10	55	175	1895	7	25	95	275
1875 small date	10	25	150	450					

Bronze coins graded in this catalogue as BU have full mint lustre

	F	VF	EF	BU		F	VF	EF	BU
	£	£	£	£		£	£	£	£

3959 Farthing. Similar R. Britannia. H Mint mark below date (struck by Ralph Heaton & Sons, Birmingham)

	F	VF	EF	BU		F	VF	EF	BU
1874 H older features....	3	10	55	150	1876 H large 6..........	7	30	100	210
1874 H, both Gs over sideways G					1876 H normal 6.....	3	10	65	150
on obv.	125	350	900	–	1881 H...................	–	5	25	95
1875 H younger features .	80	250	400	850	1882 H...................	–	5	25	90
1875 H older features......	2	18	95						

3960 Third-Farthing (for use in Malta). Laur. head l. R. Crowned date and Value die axis ↑↑

	F	VF	EF	BU		F	VF	EF	BU
1866...........................	–	4	30	95	1881	–	5	35	100
1868...........................	–	4	30	90	1884	–	4	30	95
1876...........................	–	5	35	100	1885	–	4	30	95
1878...........................	–	4	30	95					

Old Head Issue, 1895-1901, die axis ↑↑

Proofs exist of most years and are generally extremely rare for all denominations

3961
1897 Penny

	VF	EF	BU		VF	EF	BU
	£	£	£		£	£	£

3961 Penny. Old veiled bust l. R. Britannia seated r. date in ex., die axis ↑↑

	VF	EF	BU		VF	EF	BU
1895.............................	1	30	110	1898	7	40	115
1896.............................	3	30	95	1899	3	30	85
1897.............................	3	30	95	1900	5	20	70
1897 O'NE flawed	100	385	1200	1901	1	12	50

3961 'Normal Tide'
Horizon is level with folds in robe

3961A 'Low Tide'
Horizon is level with hem line of robe

3961A Penny. Similar As last but 'Low tide' and 'P' 2mm from trident, 1895... 45   100   325   875

3961B Penny. Similar, higher tide level above two folds of robe, 1897...... 20   75   400   1500

3962 - Old Head Halfpenny

	VF	EF	BU			VF	EF	BU
	£	£	£			£	£	£

3962 Halfpenny. Old veiled bust l. R. Britannia seated r. date in ex., die axis ↑↑

1895	3	12	80	1898	3	12	80
1896	2	10	75	1899	2	10	75
1897	2	10	75	1900	2	10	70
1897 Higher tide level	5	15	80	1901	—	7	60

3963 Farthing. Old veiled bust l. R. Britannia seated r. date in ex. Bright finish, die axis ↑↑

1895	—	7	50	1897	3	12	55
1896	1	10	55				

3964 - Old Head Farthing

3964 Farthing. Similar Dark finish, die axis ↑↑

1897	—	7	35	1899	1	10	35
1897 Higher tide level.	3	12	55	1900	—	7	30
1898	1	10	45	1901		4	25

PROOF SETS

PS3 Young head, **1839.** 'Una and the Lion' Five Pounds, and Sovereign to Farthing
(15 coins) *FDC* £300000

PS4 — **1853.** Sovereign to Half-Farthing, including Gothic type Crown (16 coins) *FDC* £130000

PS5 Jubilee head. Golden Jubilee, **1887.** Five pounds to Threepence (11 coins)*FDC* £35000

PS6 — — **1887.** Crown to Threepence (7 coins) *FDC* £6750

PS7 Old head, **1893.** Five Pounds to Threepence (10 coins) *FDC* £50000

PS8 — — **1893.** Crown to Threepence (6 coins) *FDC* £8000

† *NB Truly 'FDC' proof sets are hardly ever encountered. Component coins showing any surface marks, hairlines or nicks will be worth less than the prices quoted above.*

THE HOUSE OF SAXE-COBURG-GOTHA, 1901-1917
EDWARD VII, 1901-10

'Edward the Peacemaker' was born on 9 November 1841, and married Princess Alexandra of Denmark. He indulged himself in every decadent luxury, while his wife tried to ignore his extramarital activities. Edward travelled extensively and was crucial in negotiating alliances with Russia and France. Edward VII died on 6 May 1910.

Five Pound pieces, Two Pound pieces and Crowns were only issued in 1902. A branch of the Royal Mint was opened in Canada at Ottawa and coined Sovereigns of imperial type from 1908.

Unlike the coins in most other proof sets, the proofs issued for the Coronation in 1902 have a matt surface in place of the more usual brilliant finish.

Designer's initials: De S. (G. W. De Saulles 1862-1903)
B. P. (Benedetto Pistrucci, d. 1855)
Engravers and Designers: WHJ Blakemore, George William De Saulles (1862-1903), Benedetto Pistrucci (1784-1855)

GOLD

Die axis: ↑↑

3966 - Matt Proof Five Pounds 1902

	VF	EF	BU		F	VF	EF	BU
	£	£	£		£	£	£	£

3965 Five Pounds. Bare head r. R. St. George and dragon, date in ex.
1902 .... 1350 1900 2600 3850
3966 Five Pounds. Similar Proof. 1902. *Matt surface FDC* £3250
3966A Five Pounds. Similar Proof 1902S. S on ground for Sydney Mint, Australia *Extremely rare*

3967 - 1902 Two Pounds   3969 - 1902 Sovereign

3967 Two Pounds. Bare head r. R. St George and dragon, date in ex.
1902...600 800 900 1350
3968 Two Pounds. Similar Proof. 1902. *Matt surface FDC* £2000
3968A Two Pounds. Similar Proof 1902S. S on ground for Sydney Mint, Australia *Extremely rare*
3969 Sovereign. Bare head r. R. St. George and dragon, date in ex. London mint, die axis ↑↑

1902 Matt proof *FDC* £775				1906	—	BV	400
1902...........................	—	BV	350	1907	—	BV	400
1903...........................	—	BV	400	1908	—	BV	400
1904...........................	—	BV	400	1909	—	BV	400
1905...........................	—	BV	400	1910	—	BV	400

3970 Sovereign. Similar R. C on ground for Ottawa Mint, Canada

1908 C (Satin proof only) *FDC* £12500				1909 C Satin finish			
1909 C	275	450	800	specimen *FDC* ....*Extremely rare*			
				1910 C........................	250	425	700

BV= Bullion value only. At the time of going to press the spot price for gold was £900 per oz.

	EF	BU			EF	BU
	£	£			£	£

3971 Sovereign. Similar R. St. George M on ground for Melbourne Mint, Australia, die axis ↑↑

1902 M	.... BV	425	1906 M	.... BV	450
1902 M Proof	..........................*Extremely rare*		1907 M	.... BV	450
1903 M	.... BV	450	1908 M	.... BV	450
1904 M	.... BV	450	1909 M	.... BV	450
1904 M Proof	..........................*Extremely rare*		1910 M	.... BV	450
1905 M	.... BV	450	1910 M Proof	..........................*Extremely rare*	

3972 Sovereign. Similar R. P on ground for Perth Mint, Australia die axis ↑↑

1902 P	.... BV	450	1907 P	.... BV	425
1903 P	.... BV	475	1908 P	.... BV	425
1904 P	.... BV	475	1909 P	.... BV	425
1905 P	.... BV	425	1910 P	.... BV	450
1906 P	.... BV	425			

3973 Sovereign. Similar R. S on ground for Sydney Mint, Australia die axis ↑↑

1902 S	.... BV	425	1906 S	....	425
1902 S Proof	..........................*Extremely rare*		1907 S	....	425
1903 S	.... BV	425	1908 S	....	425
1904 S	.... BV	425	1909 S	....	425
1905 S	.... BV	425	1910 S	....	425

3974A - 1902 Half-Sovereign, no BP in exergue

	F	VF	EF	BU		F	VF	EF	BU
	£	£	£	£		£	£	£	£

3974 A Half-Sovereign. Bare head r. R. St. George. London Mint no BP in exergue, die axis ↑↑

1902 Matt proof *FDC* £400					1903	..............................BV	125	235
1902	..............................BV	125		235	1904	..............................BV	125	235

3974 B Half-Sovereign. R. Similar with BP in exergue

1904	............................BV	125	235	1908	............................BV	125	235
1905	............................BV	125	235	1909	............................BV	125	235
1906	............................BV	125	235	1910	............................BV	125	235
1907	............................BV	125	235				

3975 Half-Sovereign. Similar R. M on ground for Melbourne Mint, Australia, die axis ↑↑

1906 M	.... BV	250	850	2250	1908 M	.... BV	125	250	500
1907 M	.... BV	125	225	750	1909 M	.... BV	125	275	700

3976 A Half-Sovereign. — P on ground for Perth Mint, Australia R. no BP in exergue, die axis ↑↑

1904 P	................BV	275	1250	5500

3976 B Half-Sovereign. Similar R. P on ground for Perth Mint, Australia R. with BP in exergue, die axis ↑↑

1904 P	....................................*Extremely rare*			1909 P	................BV	225	550	2000
1908 P	................BV	225	1100	4500					

3977 A Half-Sovereign. Similar R. S on ground for Sydney Mint, Australia R. No BP in exergue, die axis ↑↑

1902 S	.... BV	125	225	425	1903 S	.... BV	125	200	600
1902 S Proof	..........................*Extremely rare*								

3977 B Half-Sovereign. — S on ground for Sydney Mint, Australia R. with BP in exergue, die axis ↑↑

1906 S	............................BV	125	500	1910 S	............................BV	125	325
1908 S	............................BV	125	350				

BV= Bullion value only. At the time of going to press the spot price for gold was £900 per oz.

SILVER

3978
1902 Crown

	F	VF	EF	BU		F	VF	EF	BU
						£	£	£	£

3978 Crown. Bare head r. R̃. St. George and dragon date in ex. die axis ↑↑

1902........................65　110　200　300　　　1902 error edge inscription.... *Extremely rare*

3979 Crown. Similar Matt proof *FDC* £325

3980
1904 Halfcrown

3981
Florin

3980 Halfcrown. Bare head r. R̃. Crowned Shield in Garter, die axis ↑↑

	F	VF	EF	BU		F	VF	EF	BU
1902......................	15	40	120	275	1906......................	15	60	285	800
1902 Matt proof *FDC* £275					1907......................	15	55	275	750
1903..................	175	575	2650	5250	1908......................	20	55	475	1100
1904......................	60	300	950	2650	1909......................	15	50	325	925
1905*..................	550	1750	5250	10500	1910......................	15	40	285	800

3981 Florin. Bare head r. R̃. Britannia standing on ship's bow die axis ↑↑

	F	VF	EF	BU		F	VF	EF	BU
1902......................	7	20	80	150	1906......................	10	30	185	525
1902 Matt proof *FDC* £200					1907......................	10	40	215	550
1903..................	10	30	165	400	1908......................	15	50	350	800
1904......................	15	45	245	550	1909......................	15	50	325	700
1905......................	65	200	850	1850	1910......................	10	25	145	400

Beware of 1970's forgeries.

3982
1902 Shilling

3983
1902 Sixpence

	F £	VF £	EF £	BU £		F £	VF £	EF £	BU £

3982 Shilling. Bare head r. R. Lion passant on crown die axis ↑↑

1902	5	12	70	125	1906	5	10	85	275
1902 Matt proof *FDC* £175					1907	5	10	90	300
1903	7	20	185	525	1908	12	25	200	550
1904	7	15	165	450	1909	12	25	200	550
1905	110	350	1650	3500	1910	5	10	80	175

3983 Sixpence. Bare head r. R. Value in wreath die axis ↑↑

1902	5	10	55	100	1906	4	10	60	150
1902 Matt proof *FDC* £135					1907	5	10	65	165
1903	4	10	60	150	1908	5	12	70	175
1904	7	25	125	325	1909	4	10	65	150
1905	5	20	90	250	1910	4	7	50	100

3984 Threepence. As Maundy but dull finish die axis ↑↑

1902	2	5	15	40	1906	3	7	50	140
1902 Matt proof *FDC* £55					1907	3	7	30	65
1903	3	7	30	65	1908	2	5	15	55
1904	4	10	40	115	1909	3	7	30	65
1905	3	7	30	90	1910	2	5	15	55

3985
1903 Maundy Set

	EF £	FDC £		EF £	FDC £

3985 Maundy Set (4d., 3d., 2d. and 1d.) Bare head r. die axis ↑↑

1902	125	225	1906	125	250
1902 Matt proof *FDC* £200			1907	125	250
1903	125	250	1908	125	250
1904	125	250	1909	185	350
1905	125	250	1910	185	350

			EF	FDC
			£	£
3986 — **Fourpence.** 1902-10 ....*from*	7	30
3987 — **Threepence.** 1902-10 ....*from*	10	30
3988 — **Twopence.** 1902-10 ....*from*	7	30
3989 — **Penny.** 1902-10 ....*from*	12	35

Maundy sets in the original undamaged cases are worth approximately £25 more than the prices quoted.
See foontnote after 3796.

BRONZE

3990
1902 Penny

3990 Normal Tide   '3990A 'Low Tide'

VG	F	VF	EF	BU		F	VF	EF	BU
£	£	£	£	£		£	£	£	£

3990 Penny. Bare head r. ℞. Britannia seated r. date in ex. die axis ↑↑

	VG	F	VF	EF	BU		F	VF	EF	BU
1902		1	15	60		1906		4	30	120
1903 Normal 3 ...		2	25	110		1907		1	35	130
1903 Open 3 ... 60	150	575	—	—		1908		4	30	120
1904		7	55	160		1909		5	35	130
1905		5	50	150		1910		2	20	100

3990A Penny. Similar ℞. As last but 'Low tide', 1902,'2' has wavy
    base line .... | 7 | 50 | 150 | 300 |

3991
Halfpenny

	VF	EF	BU		F	VF	EF	BU
	£	£	£		£	£	£	£

3991 Halfpenny. Bare head r. ℞. Britannia seated r. date in ex. die axis ↑↑

	VF	EF	BU		F	VF	EF	BU
1902	1	12	45	1907	1		20	90
1903	2	20	85	1908	1		20	90
1904	2	28	125	1909	2		25	100
1905	2	25	100	1910	2		20	90
1906	2	25	95					

3991A Halfpenny. Similar ℞. As last but 'Low tide', 1902......................15   85   165   410

3992   3993
Farthing   1902 Third-Farthing

3992 Farthing. Bare head r. R. Britannia seated r. date in ex. Dark finish die axis ↑↑

	VF	EF	BU		F	VF	EF	BU
1902	—	8	25	1907		1	12	35
1903	1	12	30	1908		1	12	35
1904	2	15	35	1909		1	10	30
1905	1	12	35	1910		2	22	40
1906	1	12	35					

3993 Third-Farthing (for use in Malta) Bare head r. R. Crowned date and value die axis ↑↑.
1902 7   12   40
No proofs of the bronze coins were issued in 1902

PROOF SETS
PS9   Coronation, **1902.** Five Pounds to Maundy Penny, matt surface, (13 coins) *FDC*   £8000
PS10 — 1902. Sovereign to Maundy Penny, matt surface, (11 coins).................. *FDC*   £2500

† NB Truly 'FDC' proof sets are hardly ever encountered. Component coins showing any surface marks, hairlines or nicks will be worth less than the prices quoted above.

THE HOUSE OF WINDSOR, 1917-
GEORGE V, 1910-36

George V, the second son of Edward VII, was born on 3 June 1865 and married Mary of Teck who bore him five sons and a daughter. He was King through World War I and visited the front on several occassions. He suffered a fall breaking his pelvis on one of these visits, an injury that would pain him for the rest of his life. He watched the Empire divide; Ireland, Canada, Australia, New Zealand and India all went through changes. He died on 20th January 1936 only months after his Silver Jubilee.

Paper money issued by the Treasury during the First World War replaced gold for internal use after 1915 but the branch mints in Australia and South Africa (the main Commonwealth gold producing countries) continued striking Sovereigns until 1930-2. Owing to the steep rise in the price of silver in 1919/20 the issue of standard (.925) silver was discontinued and coins of .500 silver were minted.

In 1912, 1918 and 1919 some Pennies were made under contract by private mints in Birmingham. In 1918, as Half-Sovereigns were no longer being minted, Farthings were again issued with the ordinary bright bronze finish. Crown pieces had not been issued for general circulation but they were struck in small numbers about Christmas time for people to give as presents in the years 1927-36, and in 1935 a special commemorative Crown was issued in celebration of the Silver Jubilee.

As George V died on 20 January, it is likely that all coins dated 1936 were struck during the reign of Edward VIII.

Engravers and Designers:– George Kuger Gray (1880-1943), Bertram MacKennal (1863-1931), Benedetto Pistrucci (1784-1855) Percy Metcalfe (1895-1970)

Designer's initials:

B. M. (Bertram Mackennal)   P. M. (Percy Metcalfe)

K. G. (G. Kruger Gray)   B. P. (Benedetto Pistrucci; d. 1855)

Die axis: ↑↑

GOLD

£

3994 Five Pounds.* Bare head l. R. St. George and dragon, date in ex., 1911 (Proof only)..... 9000

3995 Two Pounds.* Bare head l. R. St. George and dragon, date in ex., 1911 (Proof only)..... 3000

3996

	VF	EF	BU		VF	EF	BU
	£	£	£		£	£	£

3996 Sovereign. Bare head l. R. St. George and dragon. London Mint die axis: ↑↑

	VF	EF	BU		VF	EF	BU
1911	BV	BV	450	1914	BV	BV	400
1911 Proof *FDC* £1750				1915	BV	BV	400
1911 Matt Proof *FDC of highest rarity*				1916	BV	350	650
1912	BV	BV	400	1917*	5500	15000	—
1913	BV	BV	400	1925	BV	BV	365

*Forgeries exist of these and of most other dates and mints.

BV= Bullion value only. At the time of going to press the spot price for gold was £900 per oz.

| | F | VF | EF | BU | | | F | VF | EF | BU |
| | £ | £ | £ | £ | | | £ | £ | £ | £ |

3997 Sovereign. Bare head l. R. St George, C on ground for the Ottawa Mint, Canada die axis: ↑↑

			F	VF	EF	BU					F	VF	EF	BU
1911 C			BV	250	550		1917 C				BV	250	450
1913 C		350	1500	—		1918 C				BV	250	450
1914 C		275	800	—		1919 C				BV	250	450
1916 C*		6500	17000	—								

* Beware of recent forgeries

3997
Canada 'c' Mint mark

3998 Sovereign. Similar R. I on ground for Bombay Mint, India 1918 ....BV   335   550
3999 Sovereign. Similar R. M on ground for Melbourne Mint, Australia die axis: ↑↑

	F	VF	EF	BU			F	VF	EF	BU
1911 M			BV	400		1920 M	800	1750	3000	5500
1912 M			BV	400		1921 M	2750	5000	7500	17000
1913 M			BV	400		1922 M	1750	4000	6500	13500
1914 M			BV	400		1923 M			250	425
1915 M			BV	400		1924 M			250	425
1916 M			BV	400		1925 M			BV	400
1917 M			BV	400		1926 M			275	425
1918 M			BV	400		1928 M	600	1000	1750	2850
1919 M			225	450						

4000 Sovereign. Similar small bare head l. die axis: ↑↑

	F	VF	EF	BU			F	VF	EF	BU
1929 M	375	850	1750	3000		1930 M		BV	225	375
1929 M Proof *FDC*				*Extremely rare*		1931 M	BV	350	550	700

4000
1930 M Sovereign, small head

4001
Perth Mint Sovereign

4001 Sovereign. Similar R. P on ground for Perth Mint, Australia die axis: ↑↑

	F	VF	EF	BU			F	VF	EF	BU
1911 P			BV	350		1920 P			BV	350
1912 P			BV	350		1921 P			BV	350
1913 P			BV	350		1922 P			BV	350
1914 P			BV	350		1923 P			BV	350
1915 P			BV	350		1924 P	—	BV	225	425
1916 P			BV	350		1925 P	BV	BV	325	600
1917 P			BV	350		1926 P	400	675	1100	2500
1918 P			BV	350		1927 P	BV	BV	375	600
1919 P			BV	350		1928 P	—	BV	225	425

BV= Bullion value only. At the time of going to press the spot price for gold was £900 per oz.

	VF	EF	BU		F	VF	EF	BU
	£	£	£		£	£	£	£

4002 Sovereign. Similar — small bare head l. die axis: ↑↑

1929 P............................BV	225	425	1931 P ....BV	350
1930 P............................BV	225	425		

4003 Sovereign. Similar R. S on ground for Sydney Mint, Australia die axis: ↑↑

1911 S................................BV	350	1919 S .... BV	400
1912 S ....BV	350	†1920 S ....*Of highest rarity*	
1913 S ....BV	350	1921 S 500 800 1700 2500	
1914 S ....BV	350	1922 S 5000 9500 14000 27500	
1915 S ....BV	350	1923 S 3500 6500 10000 25000	
1916 S ....BV	350	1924 S 400 800 1500 2750	
1917 S ....BV	350	1925 S ....BV	400
1918 S ....BV	350	1926 S 6000 12500 20000 31500	

4004 Sovereign. Similar R. SA on ground for Pretoria Mint, South Africa die axis: ↑↑

1923 SA...................1250	3000	7500	1926 SA................................. BV	350
1923 SA Proof *FDC* £1950			1927 SA................................. BV	350
1924 SA...................2250	5000	11000	1928 SA................................. BV	350
1925 SA................................. BV	350		

4005 Sovereign. Similar — small head die axis: ↑↑

1929 SA....................................BV	350	1931 SA....................................BV	350
1930 SA....................................BV	350	1932 SA....................................BV	350

† *An example of the proof 1920 S sold at a UK auction in May 2012 for £780,000*

4003
1921 Sydney 's' Sovereign

4006
1914 Half-sovereign

4006 Half-Sovereign. Bare head l. R. St. George and dragon date in ex. London Mint die axis: ↑↑

1911................................BV	125	235	1913...............................BV	125	235
1911 Proof *FDC* £1100			1914...............................BV	125	235
1911 Matt Proof *FDC of highest rarity*			1915...............................BV	125	235
1912................................BV	125	235			

4007 Half-Sovereign. Similar R. M on ground for Melbourne Mint, Australia die axis: ↑↑

1915 M..BV	BV	235

4008 Half-Sovereign. Similar R. P on ground for Perth Mint, Australia die axis: ↑↑

1911 P............................BV	125	350	1918 P 200	600	2000	3750
1915 P............................BV	125	325				

4009 Half-Sovereign. Similar R. S on ground for Sydney Mint, Australia die axis: ↑↑

1911 S............................BV	BV	185	1915 S ....BV	BV	185
1912 S ....BV	BV	185	1916 S ....BV	BV	185 V
1914 S ....BV	BV	185	250		

4010 Half-Sovereign. Similar R. SA on ground for Pretoria Mint, South Africa die axis: ↑↑

1923 SA Proof *FDC* £1500			1926 SA........................BV	BV	195
1925 SA........................BV	BV	195			

BV= Bullion value only. At the time of going to press the spot price for gold was £900 per oz.

SILVER

FIRST COINAGE, 1911-19 Sterling silver (.925 fine)

4011
1911 Halfcrown

	F	VF	EF	BU		F	VF	EF	BU
	£	£	£	£		£	£	£	£

4011 Halfcrown. Bare head l. R. Crowned shield in Garter die axis: ↑↑

	F	VF	EF	BU		F	VF	EF	BU
1911.......................8		25	85	225	1915.......................8		12	40	100
1911 Proof *FDC* £325					1916.......................8		12	40	100
1912.......................8		25	75	275	1917.......................8		15	60	150
1913.......................8		30	85	275	1918.......................8		12	45	125
1914.......................8		12	45	125	1919.......................8		15	55	150

4012
1912 Florin

4013
1911 Proof

4012 Florin. Bare head l. R. Crowned Cruciform shields sceptres in angles die axis: ↑↑

	F	VF	EF	BU		F	VF	EF	BU
1911.......................6		12	60	165	1915.......................6		20	65	200
1911 Proof *FDC* £225					1916.......................6		12	50	115
1912.......................6		15	70	225	1917.......................6		15	55	150
1913.......................8		25	85	250	1918.......................6		12	45	110
1914.......................6		12	50	115	1919.......................6		15	55	150

4013 Shilling. Bare head l. R. Lion passant on crown, within circle die axis: ↑↑

	F	VF	EF	BU		F	VF	EF	BU
1911.......................3		10	40	85	1915.......................		2	30	75
1911 Proof *FDC* £150					1916.......................		2	30	75
1912.......................3		12	45	115	1917.......................		3	40	125
1913.......................6		15	75	225	1918.......................		2	35	85
1914.......................3		10	40	90	1919.......................2		8	45	100

4014
1911 Sixpence

	F £	VF £	EF £	BU £		F £	VF £	EF £	BU £

4014 Sixpence. Bare head l. R. Lion passant on crown, within circle die axis: ↑↑

1911	1	7	30	60	1916	1	7	30	60
1911 Proof *FDC* £115					1917	4	15	55	160
1912	3	10	40	80	1918	1	7	30	65
1913	6	12	45	85	1919	3	10	35	75
1914	1	7	30	65	1920	4	12	45	90
1915	1	7	30	75					

4015 Threepence. As Maundy but dull finish die axis: ↑↑

1911	1	5	30	1916	1	5	25
1911 Proof *FDC* £55				1917	1	5	25
1912	1	5	30	1918	1	5	25
1913	1	5	30	1919	1	5	25
1914	1	5	30	1920	2	10	35
1915	1	5	35				

4016
1915 Maundy Set

	EF £	FDC £		EF £	FDC £

4016 Maundy Set (4d., 3d., 2d. and 1d.) die axis: ↑↑

1911	125	225	1916	125	225
1911 Proof *FDC* £300			1917	125	225
1912	125	225	1918	125	225
1913	125	225	1919	125	225
1914	125	225	1920	155	275
1915	125	225			

4017 — **Fourpence.** 1911-20	*from*	10	30
4018 — **Threepence.** 1911-20	*from*	12	32
4019 — **Twopence.** 1911-20	*from*	8	25
4020 — **Penny.** 1911-20	*from*	10	35

See footnote after 3796

SECOND COINAGE, 1920-27 Debased silver (.500 fine). Types as before.

	F	VF	EF	BU		F	VF	EF	BU
	£	£	£	£		£	£	£	£

4021 Halfcrown. Deeply engraved. Bare head l. R. Crowned shield in garter die axis: ↑↑

| 1920 | 3 | 12 | 60 | 185 |

4021A — recut shallow portrait

1920	5	15	75	215	1924 Specimen Finish £4250				
1921	3	12	60	160	1925	25	75	375	1000
1922	3	10	60	160	1926	3	18	85	195
1923	2	6	40	95	1926 No colon				
1924	3	10	60	160	after OMN	15	45	175	395

4022 Florin. Deeply engraved. Bare head l. R. Crowned cruciform shields, sceptres in angles die axis: ↑↑

| 1920 | 3 | 12 | 60 | 160 |

4022A — recut shallow portrait

1920	5	18	75	175	1924	2	12	65	150
1921	2	7	55	120	1924 Specimen Finish £3500				
1922	2	6	50	110	1925	25	55	275	650
1922 Proof in gold *FDC of highest rarity*				1926	2	12	65	150
1923	2	6	40	85

4023 Shilling. Deeply engraved. Bare head l. R. Lion passant on crown within circle die axis: ↑↑

| 1920 | 3 | 12 | 45 | 100 | 1921 nose to S | 12 | 30 | 90 | 225 |

4023A — recut shallow portrait

1920	4	15	65	160	1924	1	10	55	100
1921 nose to SV	3	15	65	160	1925	3	12	65	160
1922	1	4	45	95	1926	1	7	35	90
1923	1	3	35	90

Note: 1923 and 1924 Shillings exist struck in nickel and are valued at £3500 each FDC.

4024 Sixpence. Bare head l. R. Lion passant on crown within circle die axis: ↑↑

1920	1	5	30	85	1924	1	2	20	65
1921	1	2	25	80	1924 Specimen Finish *FDC* £3000				
1922	1	3	25	80	1924 Proof in gold *FDC* £28500				
1923	1	4	30	90	1925	1	2	30	70

4025 - George V Sixpence   4026 - Threepence

4025 Sixpence. Similar new beading and broader rim die axis: ↑↑

| 1925 | 1 | 2 | 30 | 60 | 1926 | 1 | 4 | 30 | 60 |

4026 Threepence. Bare head l. R. Crowned 3 die axis: ↑↑

1920		1	4	28	1924 Proof in gold *FDC* £13500				
1921		1	4	28	1925	BV	2	22	75
1922		1	20	90	1926	1	8	45	150
1924 Specimen Finish £3000				

		EF	FDC			EF	FDC
		£	£			£	£

4027 Maundy Set. (4d., 3d., 2d. and 1d.) die axis: ↑↑

1921		120	225	1925		120	225
1922		120	225	1926		120	225
1923		120	225	1927		120	225
1924		120	225

4028 — **Fourpence.** 1921-7	*from*	15	35
4029 — **Threepence.** 1921-7	*from*	12	30
4030 — **Twopence.** 1921-7	*from*	10	25
4031 — **Penny.** 1921-7	*from*	15	40

2nd coinage
BM more central on tr.

3rd coinage
Modified Effigy
BM to right of tr.

THIRD COINAGE, 1926-27. As before but modified effigy, with details of head more clearly defined. The BM on truncation is nearer to the back of the neck and without stops; beading is more pronounced.

	F	VF	EF	BU		F	VF	EF	BU
	£	£	£	£		£	£	£	£

4032 Halfcrown. Modified effigy l. R. Crowned Shield in Garter die axis: ↑↑

| 1926 | 4 | 20 | 85 | 225 | 1927 Proof in gold *FDC of highest rarity* | | | | |
| 1927 | 3 | 7 | 45 | 110 | | | | | |

4033 Shilling. Modified effigy l. R. Lion passant on crown, within circle die axis: ↑↑

| 1926 | 1 | 2 | 30 | 65 | 1927 | 1 | 5 | 40 | 75 |

4034 Sixpence. Modified effigy l. R. Lion passant on crown, within circle die axis: ↑↑

| 1926 | | 3 | 20 | 50 | 1927 | 1 | 3 | 25 | 55 |

4035 Threepence. Modified effigy l. R. Crowned 3 die axis: ↑↑

| 1926 | | | | | | 1 | 12 | 55 |

FOURTH COINAGE, 1927-36

4036
1927 'Wreath' Crown proof

4036 Crown. Modified Bare head l. R. Crown and date in wreath die axis: ↑↑

1927 –15,030 struck Proof only† *FDC* £325				1931 –4056 struck ... 95	200	350	675
1927 Matt Proof *FDC Extremely rare*				1932 –2395 struck . 150	295	525	925
1928* –9034 struck . 90	165	325	600	1933* –7132 struck . 90	185	300	575
1929 –4994 struck . 100	200	350	675	1934 –932 struck . 1350	2250	3850	5000
1930 –4847 struck ... 90	200	350	675	1936 –2473 struck . 150	300	525	925

†N.B. Proofs of other dates from 1927also exist, but are extremely rare as they were for V.I.P. issue
* Beware recent counterfeits

4037
1931 Halfcrown

4038
Florin

	F £	VF £	EF £	BU £		F £	VF £	EF £	BU £

4037 Halfcrown. Modified bare head l. R. Shield die axis: ↑↑

†1927 Proof only *FDC* £150					1932	3	6	25	85
1927 Matt Proof *FDC of highest rarity*					1933	3	4	15	75
1928	2	4	18	50	1934	3	10	75	200
1929	2	4	20	55	1935		3	15	50
1930	20	95	350	925	1936		3	12	40
1931	2	4	25	75					

4038 Florin. Modified bare head l. R. Cruciform shields, sceptre in each angle die axis: ↑↑

†1927 Proof only *FDC* £150					1931	1	4	20	70
1927 Matt Proof *FDC Extremely rare*					1932	15	70	450	1050
1928		1	14	40	1933		2	15	65
1929		1	18	55	1935		2	12	50
1930	3	7	40	95	1936		2	10	40

4039
Shilling

4040
Sixpence

4039 Shilling. Modified bare head l. R. Lion standing on crown, no inner circles die axis: ↑↑

1927	1	3	20	60	1931	1	3	15	55
†1927 Proof *FDC* £75					1932	1	3	15	55
1927 Matt Proof *FDC Extremely rare*					1933		2	15	55
1928		2	15	50	1934	1	3	20	65
1929		2	15	50	1935		1	15	50
1930	3	12	50	130	1936		1	10	40

4040 Sixpence. Modified bare head l. R. Three oak sprigs with six acorns die axis: ↑↑

†1927 Proof only *FDC* £85					1929		1	8	40
1927 Matt Proof *FDC Extremely rare*					1930		2	12	45
1928		1	8	40					

4041 Sixpence. Similar closer milling die axis: ↑↑

1931	1	3	10	45	1934	1	3	10	55
1932	1	4	18	65	1935		1	6	35
1933	1	3	10	45	1936		1	5	30

†N.B. Proofs of other dates from 1927 also exist, but are extremely rare as they were for V.I.P. issue

SILVER

4042
Threepence

4043
George V Maundy Set

	F £	VF £	EF £	BU £		EF £	BU £

4042 Threepence. Modified Bare head l. R. Three oak sprigs with three acorns die axis: ↑↑

	F £	VF £	EF £	BU £		EF £	BU £
†1927 Proof only *FDC* £150					1932	1	20
1927 Matt Proof *FDC Extremely rare*					1933	1	20
1928	1	3	15	55	1934	1	18
1930	1	5	20	65	1935	1	20
1931			1	20	1936	1	15

	EF £	FDC £		EF £	FDC £
4043 Maundy Set. As earlier sets die axis: ↑↑			1933	135	225
1928	120	225	1934	135	225
1929	120	225	1935	135	225
1930	150	250	1936	145	325
1931	120	225			
1932	120	225			

The 1936 Maundy was distributed by King Edward VIII

		EF	FDC
4044 — Fourpence. 1928-36	*from*	10	30
4045 — Threepence. 1928-36	*from*	10	30
4046 — Twopence. 1928-36	*from*	10	30
4047 — Penny. 1928-36	*from*	15	40

Silver Jubilee Commemorative issue, die axis: ↑↑

4048
1935 'Jubilee' Crown

	VF £	EF £	BU £
4048 Crown. 1935. R. St. George, incuse lettering on edge –714,769 struck ..	12	25	40
1935 — error edge		*Extremely rare*	
4049 Crown. Similar Specimen striking issued in box			65

4050 Crown. Similar raised lettering on edge 2,500 struck. Proof (.925 Æ R) *FDC* £750

     — error edge inscription Proof *FDC* £5000

     — Proof in gold –28 struck £65000

†N.B. Proofs of other dates from 1927 also exist, but are extremely rare as they were for V.I.P. issue

BRONZE

H Mint mark location – 4052

4052
1912 H Penny

KN Mint mark location
as above – 4053

	F	VF	EF	BU			F	VF	EF	BU
	£	£	£	£			£	£	£	£

4051 Penny. Bare head l. R. Britannia seated right die axis: ↑↑

	F	VF	EF	BU			F	VF	EF	BU
1911	1	15	60		1919		1	18	65	
1912	1	20	70		1920		1	18	70	
1913	3	30	95		1921		1	18	65	
1914	1	22	75		1922		3	35	135	
1915	1	25	80		1922 Rev. of 1927	4000	11500	—	—	
1916	1	22	75		1922 Specimen finish..			*Extremely rare*		
1917	1	15	65		1926		4	40	140	
1918	1	15	65							

4052 Penny. Bare head l. R. Britannia, H (Heaton Mint, Birmingham, Ltd.) to l. of date die axis: ↑↑

	F	VF	EF	BU			F	VF	EF	BU
1912 H	1	15	115	350	1919 H	1	25	375	1150	
1918 H	2	30	325	800						

4053 Penny. Bare head l. R. Britannia KN (King's Norton Metal Co.) to l. of date die axis: ↑↑

	F	VF	EF	BU			F	VF	EF	BU
1918 KN	3	75	450	1450	1919 KN	7	90	1000	2500	
1918KN Cupro-nickel . *Of the highest rarity*										

4054 Penny. Modified effigy l. R. as 4051

	F	VF	EF	BU
1926	35	350	1650	4000

4054A Penny. Modified effigy. R. Britannia sl. smaller. Shorter right thumb, date in ex. die axis ↑↑

	F	VF	EF	BU			F	VF	EF	BU
1922		*Of the highest rarity*			1927		1	12	45	
1926		*Of the highest rarity*								

4055 Penny. Small bare head l. R. Britannia Seated r. date in ex. die axis: ↑↑

	F	VF	EF	BU			F	VF	EF	BU
1928	1	12	55		1933			*Extremely rare*		
1929	1	12	65		1934*		3	25	85	
1930	3	20	85		1935		1	10	30	
1931	1	18	70		1936		1	7	25	
1932	5	45	185							

†*N.B. Proofs of other dates from 1927 also exist, but are extremely rare as they were for V.I.P. issue.*
Matt proofs also exist of some dates for most denominations and are all extremely rare.
* *Most 1934 pennies were mint darkened. Coins with original lustre are rare.*

4056
Halfpenny

4058
Small head

	VF £	EF £	BU £		VF £	EF £	BU £

4056 Halfpenny. Bare head l. R. Britannia Seated r. date in ex. die axis: ↑↑

1911	1	8	50	1919	2	12	55
1912	2	12	55	1920	2	22	65
1913	2	12	55	1921	2	12	55
1914	2	15	60	1922	2	25	100
1915	2	20	65	1923	2	12	55
1916	2	20	65	1924	2	12	55
1917	2	12	55	1924 Specimen finish.. *Extremely rare*			
1918	2	12	55	1925	2	12	55

4057 Halfpenny. Modified effigy l. R. Britannia Seated r. date in ex. die axis: ↑↑

1925	3	20	75	1927	2	8	50
1926	2	12	55				

4058 Halfpenny. Small bare head l. R. Britannia Seated r. date in ex. die axis: ↑↑

1928	1	8	40	1933	1	8	45
1929	1	8	40	1934	1	12	40
1930	4	12	50	1935	1	8	35
1931	1	8	45	1936	1	6	25
1932	1	8	45				

4059
Farthing

4059 Farthing. Bare head l. R. Britannia Seated r. date in ex. Dark finish die axis: ↑↑

1911	4	20	1915	5	25
1912	3	18	1916	3	18
1913	3	18	1917	3	14
1914	3	18	1918	10	40

	EF	BU			VF	EF	BU
	£	£			£	£	£

4060 Farthing. Similar Bright finish, die axis: ↑↑

	EF	BU			EF	BU
1918	3	18	1922		4	25
1919	3	18	1923		5	20
1920	4	20	1924		5	20
1921	4	20	1925		4	20

4061 Farthing. Modified effigy l. R. Britannia Seated r. date in ex. die axis: ↑↑

	EF	BU			EF	BU
1926	2	18	1932		2	14
1927	2	18	1933		2	18
1928	2	14	1934		2	18
1929	2	18	1935		5	30
1930	3	20	1936		2	14
1931	2	18				

4062
Third-Farthing

4062 Third-Farthing (for use in Malta). Bare head l. R. Crowned date and Value die axis: ↑↑

	VF	EF	BU
1913	3	15	40

PROOF SETS

PS11 Coronation, **1911.** Five pounds to Maundy Penny (12 coins) .... *FDC* £20000
PS12 — **1911.** Sovereign to Maundy Penny (10 coins) .... *FDC* £4250
PS13 — **1911.** Half crown to Maundy Penny (8 coins) .... *FDC* £1350
PS14 New type, **1927.** Wreath type Crown to Threepence (6 coins) .... *FDC* £675

† *NB Truly 'FDC' proof sets are hardly ever encountered. Component coins showing any surface marks, hairlines or nicks will be worth less than the prices quoted above.*

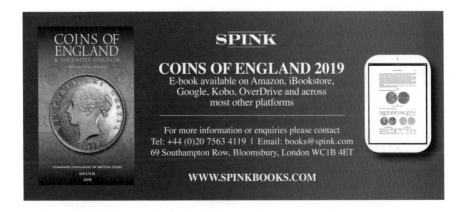

Succeeded his father on 20 January 1936. Abdicated 10 December. Edward VIII was born 23 June 1894, and was very popular as Prince of Wales. He ruled only for a short time before announcing his intended marriage to the American divorcee Wallis Simpson; a potential religious and political scandal. Edward was not a traditionalist, as evidenced on the proposed coinage, where he insisted against all advice on having his effigy face the same way as his father's, instead of opposite. He abdicated in favour of his brother, and became Edward, Duke of Windsor, marrying Mrs Simpson in France, where they lived in exile. He governed the Bahamas from 1940-45 and died on 28 May 1972.

No coins of Edward VIII were issued for currency within the United Kingdom bearing his name and portrait. The Mint had commenced work on a new coinage prior to the Abdication, and various patterns were made. No Proof Sets were issued for sale and only a small number of sets were struck.

Coins bearing Edward's name, but not his portrait, were issued for the colonial territories of British East Africa, British West Africa, Fiji and New Guinea. The projected U.K. coins were to include a Shilling of essentially `Scottish' type and a nickel brass Threepence with twelve sides which might supplement and possibly supersede the inconveniently small silver Threepence.

Engravers and Designers:– George Kruger Gray (1880-1943), Thomas Humphrey Paget (1893-1974), Benedicto Pistucci (1784-1855) Frances Madge Kitchener, Percy Metcalfe (1895-1970), H Wilson Parker (1896-1980)

Designer's initials: H. P. (T. Humphrey Paget)   B.P. (Benedetto Pistrucci, d. 1855)
                            K. G. (G. Kruger Gray)   M. K. (Madge Kitchener)
                            W. P. (H. Wilson Parker)

Die axis ↑↑

GOLD

4063
Edward VIII Proof Five Pounds

4063 Proof Set

Gold, Five Pounds, Two Pounds and Sovereign, Silver Crown, Halfcrown, Florin, Scottish Shilling, Sixpence and Threepence, Brass Threepence, Penny, Halfpenny and Farthing, 1937 *FDC. Only one complete set known in private hands..*

FDC
£

Five Pounds, Bare head 1. R St George and dragon, date in ex 650000
Two Pounds, Bare head 1. R St George and dragon, date in ex 300000
Sovereign, Bare head l. R. St George and dragon date in ex 600000
Crown, Bare head l. R. Crowned Shield of arms and supporters........................ 275000
Halfcrown, Bare head l. R. Quartered Standard of arms 135000
Florin, Bare head l. R. Crowned rose and emblems 100000
Shilling, Bare head l. R. Lion seated facing on crown....................................... 85000
Sixpence, Bare head l. R. Six interlinked rings... 55000
Threepence, Bare head l. R. three interlinked rings 42500

4064A

4064A Nickel brass. **Threepence,** 1937 Bare head l. R. Thrift plant below 55000
          Bronze. **Penny,** 1937 80000
          Halfpenny, 1937... 45000
          Farthing, 1937... 40000

Note: Matt proofs exist of most denominations

Pattern

Edward VIII Brass Threepence

UNC
£

4064B Nickel brass dodecagonal **Threepence,** 1937. Bare head l. R. Thrift plant of more
         naturalistic style than the modified proof coin. A small number of these coins were
         produced of differing thickness for experimental purposes and a few did get into
         circulation.. 57500

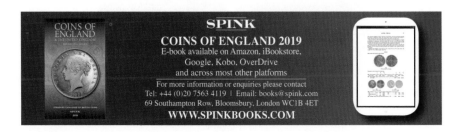

George VI was born on 14 December 1895 and never expected to be King. He suffered ill-health through much of his life and had a stammer. He married Elizabeth Bowes Lyon and together they became very popular especially through the ravages of World War II, when Buckingham Palace was bombed. The war took its toll on George, and ever a heavy smoker he succumbed to lung cancer on 6th February 1952. Elizabeth, known after his death as 'Queen Elizabeth the Queen Mother', lived on to the age of 101 dying on 30 March 2002.

Though they were at first issued concurrently, the twelve-sided nickel-brass Threepence superseded the small silver Threepence in 1942. Those dated 1943-4 were not issued for circulation in the U.K. In addition to the usual English 'lion' Shilling, a Shilling of Scottish type was issued concurrently. This depicts the Scottish lion and crown flanked by the shield of St. Andrew and a thistle. In 1947, as silver was needed to repay the bullion lent by the U.S.A. during the war, silver coins were replaced by coins of the same type and weight made of cupro-nickel. In 1949, after India had attained independence, the title IND:IMP (Indiae Imperator) was dropped from the coinage. Commemorative Crown pieces were issued for the Coronation and the 1951 Festival of Britain.

Engravers and Designers:– Frances Madge Kitchener, George Kruger Gray (1880-1943), Percy Metcalfe (1895-1970) Thomas Humphrey Paget (1893-1974), H Wilson Parker (1896-1980), Benedetto Pistrucci (1784-1855)

Designer's initials: K. G. (G. Kruger Gray) B. P. (Benedetto Pistrucci, d. 1855)
  H. P. (T. Humphrey Paget) W. P. (Wilson Parker)

Die axis ↑↑

GOLD

4074
1937 Proof Five Pounds

4076
1937 Proof Sovereign

FDC
£

4074 Five Pounds. Bare head l. R. St. George, 1937. Proof plain edge only (5001 struck).. 7500
4074-4077 Proof Struck to Matt finish *FDC of highest rarity*
4075 Two Pounds. Similar, 1937. Proof plain edge only (5001 struck)............................... 3000
4076 Sovereign. Similar, 1937. Proof plain edge only (5001 struck)................................... 3250
4077 Half-Sovereign. Similar, 1937. Proof plain edge only (5001 struck).......................... 1150

SILVER

FIRST COINAGE, 1937-46 Silver, .500 fine, with title IND:IMP

4078
1937 Crown

	VF £	EF £	BU £

4078 Crown. Coronation commemorative, 1937. R. Arms and supporters   12   30   45

4079 Crown. Similar 1937 Proof *FDC* £90

Similar 1937 Frosted 'VIP' Proof £1500

4080
Halfcrown

4081
1937 Florin

	EF £	BU £		EF £	BU £

4080 Halfcrown. Bare head l. R. Shield die axis: ↑↑

1937	5	25	1942	5	25
1937 Proof *FDC* £40			1943	5	30
1938	10	55	1944	5	25
1939	5	30	1945	5	20
1940	8	35	1946	5	20
1941	5	30			

4081 Florin. Bare head l. R. Crowned rose, etc. die axis: ↑↑

1937	4	25	1942	4	20
1937 Proof *FDC* £35			1943	4	25
1938	8	50	1944	4	25
1939	4	25	1945	4	20
1940	5	30	1946	4	20
1941	4	25			

4082
1942 'English' Shilling

4083
1945 'Scottish' Shilling

4082 Shilling. 'English' reverse. Bare head l. R. Lion standing on large crown die axis: ↑↑

1937	3	25	1942	3	25
1937 Proof *FDC* £28			1943	3	25
1938	8	50	1944	3	25
1939	3	25	1945	3	18
1940	5	30	1946		
1941	3	25			

GEORGE VI

	EF	BU		VF	EF	BU
	£	£		£	£	£

4083 Shilling. 'Scottish' reverse. Bare head l. R. Lion seated facing on crown die axis: ↑↑

	EF	BU		VF	EF	BU
1937	3	20	1942	4		30
1937 Proof *FDC* £28			1943		3	25
1938	8	45	1944		3	25
1939	3	25	1945		3	18
1940	5	30	1946		3	18
1941	4	30				

4084
1945 Sixpence

4085
1944 Threepence

4084 Sixpence. Bare head l. R. GRI crowned die axis: ↑↑

	EF	BU		EF	BU
1937	2	15	1942	2	20
1937 Proof *FDC* £25			1943	2	20
1938	6	30	1944	2	20
1939	2	25	1945	2	15
1940	5	30	1946	2	15
1941	2	25			

4085 Threepence. Bare head l. R. Shield on rose die axis: ↑↑

	EF	BU		VF	EF	BU
1937	2	15	1942*	8	20	45
1937 Proof *FDC* £20			1943*	8	25	55
1938	2	20	1944*	15	40	110
1939	6	35	1945*		*Extremely rare*	
1940	5	30	* *issued for Colonial use only*			
1941	4	30				

4086
1937 Maundy Set

	EF	FDC		EF	FDC
	£	£		£	£

4086 Maundy Set. Silver, .500 fine. Uniform dates die axis: ↑↑

	EF	FDC		EF	FDC
1937	100	175	1942	120	225
1937 Proof *FDC* £200			1943	120	225
1938	120	225	1944	120	225
1939	120	225	1945	120	225
1940	135	250	1946	120	225
1941	120	225			

	EF £	FDC £		EF £	FDC £
4087 — **Fourpence.** 1937-46 .... *from*					20
4088 — **Threepence.** 1937-46 .... *from*					22
4089 — **Twopence.** 1937-46 .... *from*					20
4090 — **Penny.** 1937-46 .... *from*					30

SECOND COINAGE, 1947-48, Silver, .925 fine, with title IND:IMP (Maundy only)
4091 Maundy Set (4d., 3d., 2d. and 1d.). Uniform dates die axis: ↑↑

1947 120	225	1948 120	225

		EF £	FDC £
4092 — **Fourpence,** 1947-8			20
4093 — **Threepence,** 1947-8			22
4094 — **Twopence,** 1947-8			20
4095 — **Penny,** 1947-8			30

THIRD COINAGE, 1949-52, Silver, .925 fine, but omitting IND:IMP. (Maundy only)
4096 Maundy Set (4d., 3d., 2d. and 1d.). Uniform dates die axis: ↑↑

1949 120	225	1952 160	275
1950 135	250	1952 Proof in copper *FDC* £7500	
1951 135	250		

The 1952 Maundy was distributed by Queen Elizabeth II.

		EF £	FDC £
4097 — **Fourpence,** 1949-52 .... *from*			20
4098 — **Threepence,** 1949-52 .... *from*			22
4099 — **Twopence,** 1949-52 .... *from*			20
4100 — **Penny,** 1949-52 .... *from*			30

See footnote re Maundy Pennies after 3796.

CUPRO-NICKEL

SECOND COINAGE, 1947-48, Types as first (silver) coinage, IND:IMP.

	EF £	BU £		EF £	BU £
4101 Halfcrown. Bare head l. ℞. Shield die axis: ↑↑					
1947	2	15	1948	2	12
4102 Florin. Bare head l. ℞. Crowned rose die axis: ↑↑					
1947	2	15	1948	2	15
4103 Shilling. 'English' reverse. Bare head l. die axis: ↑↑					
1947	2	15	1948	2	15
4104 Shilling. 'Scottish' reverse. Bare head l. die axis: ↑↑					
1947	2	15	1948	2	15
4105 Sixpence. Bare head l. ℞. GRI crowned die axis: ↑↑					
1947	2	12	1948	2	12

THIRD COINAGE, 1949-52, Types as before but title IND:IMP. omitted

4106
1949 Halfcrown

	VF	EF	BU		VF	EF	BU
	£	£	£		£	£	£

4106 Halfcrown. Bare head l. R. Shield die axis: ↑↑

1949............................		3	30	1951 Proof *FDC* £45			
1950............................		8	40	1952................................			*Unique*
1950 Proof *FDC* £45				1952 Proof *FDC* £90000			
1951............................	1	8	40				

4107 Florin. Bare head l. R. Crowned rose die axis: ↑↑

1949............................		5	35	1951	8	40
1950............................		8	35	1951 Proof *FDC* £45		
1950 Proof *FDC* £45						

4108 Shilling. 'English' reverse. Bare head l. die axis: ↑↑

1949............................	5	35	1951............................	6	35
1950............................	8	35	1951 Proof *FDC* £35		
1950 Proof *FDC* £40			1952 Proof *FDC* £47500		

4109 Shilling. 'Scottish' reverse. Bare head l. die axis: ↑↑

1949............................	5	35	1951............................	6	35
1950............................	8	35	1951 Proof *FDC* £30		
1950 Proof *FDC* £40					

4110
1952 Sixpence

4110 Sixpence. Bare head l. R. Crowned cypher die axis: ↑↑

1949............................	1	15	1951 Proof *FDC* £30		
1950............................	3	20	1951 Matt Proof *FDC* £1500		
1950 Proof *FDC* £30			1952...................... 5	45	135
1951............................	5	25			

Festival of Britain issue die axis: ↑↑

4111
Festival of Britain Crown

	EF	BU
	£	£

4111 Crown. Bare head l. R. St. George and dragon, date in ex, 1951. *Proof-like*.

Two reverse types exist	5	15

Similar — 1951 Frosted 'VIP' Proof £1750, narrow edge lettering
Similar — 1951 Matt Proof *FDC* £4000
Similar — 1951 Plain edge Proof *FDC* £2000

NICKEL BRASS

FIRST ISSUE, 1937-48, with title IND:IMP.

4112	4113
1941 Brass Threepence	Second issue obverse

	VF	EF	BU		VF	EF	BU
	£	£	£		£	£	£

4112 Threepence (dodecagonal). Bare head l. R. Thrift plant die axis: ↑↑

	VF	EF	BU		VF	EF	BU
1937............................	2		15	1942................................		2	15
1937 Proof *FDC* £22				1943................................		2	15
1938............................	6		30	1944................................		2	20
1939............................	10		50	1945................................		5	20
1940............................	6		30	1946	30	250	950
1941............................	3		20	1948................................		10	65

SECOND ISSUE, 1949-52, omitting IND:IMP.
4113 Threepence. Bare head l. R. Similar die axis: ↑↑

	VF	EF	BU		
1949	30	200	750	1951 Proof *FDC* £55	
1950		25	150	1951 Matt Proof *FDC* £1250	
1950 Proof *FDC* £50				1952............................ 5	25
1951............................3	30	150			

BRONZE

FIRST ISSUE, 1937-48, with title IND:IMP.

4114
1938 Penny

4114 Penny. Bare head l. R. Britannia Seated r. date in ex die axis: ↑↑

	EF £	BU £		EF £	BU £
1937	1	10	1944* —	6	30
1937 Proof *FDC* £28			1945* —	5	25
1938	3	12	1946* —	2	12
1939	4	20	1947 —	1	10
1940	10	60	1948 —	1	10
1940 Double exergue line	4	25	1946 ONE' die flaw	75	225

most pennies of these date were darkened at the mint.

4115
1937 Halfpenny

4116
1943 Farthing

4115 Halfpenny. Bare head l. R. Ship sailing l. date below die axis: ↑↑

1937	1	10	1943	1	10
1937 Proof *FDC* £22			1944	1	10
1938	2	15	1945	1	10
1939	3	30	1946	3	25
1940	3	30	1947	1	12
1941	2	12	1948	1	12
1942	1	10			

4116 Farthing. Bare head l. R. Wren l. date above die axis: ↑↑

1937	1	7	1943	1	7
1937 Proof *FDC* £16			1944	1	7
1938	2	15	1945	1	7
1939	1	8	1946	1	7
1940	1	8	1947	1	7
1941	1	8	1948	1	7
1942	1	7			

SECOND ISSUE, 1949-52

	VF	EF	BU		VF	EF	BU
	£	£	£		£	£	£

4117 Penny. Bare head l. R. Britannia Seated r. date in ex. die axis: ↑↑

1949		1	10	1951	12	35	60
1950	8	20	75	1951 Proof *FDC* £55			
1950 Proof *FDC* £40				1952 Proof only *FDC Unique*			

4118
Second issue Halfpenny

4119
Second issue Farthing

4118 Halfpenny. Bare head l. R. Ship Sailing l. date below die axis: ↑↑

1949		4	20	1951		5	30
1950		3	15	1951 Proof *FDC* £22			
1950 Proof *FDC* £20				1952		1	7

4119 Farthing. Bare head l. R. Wren l. date above die axis: ↑↑

1949		1	8	1951		2	9
1950		1	7	1951 Proof *FDC* £22			
1950 Proof *FDC* £20				1952		1	7

The coins dated 1952 were issued during the reign of Elizabeth II.

PROOF SETS

PS15 Coronation, **1937.** Five pounds to Half-sovereign (4 coins)	*FDC*	£15000
PS16 — 1937. Crown to Farthing, including Maundy Set (15 coins)	*FDC*	£400
PS17 Mid-Century, **1950.** Halfcrown to Farthing (9 coins)	*FDC*	£175
PS18 Festival of Britain, **1951.** Crown to Farthing (10 coins)	*FDC*	£235

Elizabeth II was born on 21 April 1926. Our current Monarch has lived a long and glorious reign celebrating her Golden Jubilee in 2002. She married Philip a distant cousin in 1947 and has four children, Charles, Anne, Andrew and Edward. Significantly she is the first Monarch to pay taxes and her coinage has been an interesting one with the change to decimal coinage and the numerous bust changes since 1953.

The earliest coins of this reign have the title BRITT:OMN, but in 1954 this was omitted from the Queen's titles owing to the changing status of so many Commonwealth territories. The minting of 'English' and 'Scottish' shillings was continued. A Coronation commemorative crown was issued in 1953, another crown was struck on the occasion of the 1960 British Exhibition in New York and a third was issued in honour of Sir Winston Churchill in 1965. A very small number of proof gold coins were struck in 1953 for the national museum collections, but between 1957 and 1968 gold sovereigns were minted again in quantity for sale in the international bullion market and to counteract the activities of counterfeiters.

Owing to inflation the farthing had now become practically valueless; production of these coins ceased after 1956 and the coins were demonetized at the end of 1960. In 1965 it was decided to change to a decimal system of coinage in the year 1971. As part of the transition to decimal coinage the halfpenny was demonetized in August 1969 and the halfcrown in January 1970. (See also introduction to Decimal Coinage.

Designer's initials:

A. V. (Avril Vaughan, 1937-2006)	M. G. (Mary Gillick, 1881-1965)
B. P. (Benedetto Pistrucci, 1784-1855)	M. M. D. (Mary Milner Dickens)
B. R. (Bruce Rushin)	M. N. (Michael Noakes)
C.D. (Clive Duncan)	M. R. (Michael Rizzello, 1926-2004)
C. T. (Cecil Thomas, 1885-1976)	N. S. (Norman Sillman, 1921-2013)
D. C. (David Cornell)	P. N. (Philip Nathan)
E. F. (Edgar Fuller)	R. D. (Ron Dutton)
G. L. (Gilbert Ledward, 1888-1960)	R. D. M. (Raphael David Maklouf)
I. R. B. (Ian Rank-Bradley)	R. E. (Robert Elderton)
J. B. (James Butler)	r. e. (Robert Evans)
J. C. (Jody Clark)	R. L. (Robert Lowe)
J. M. (Jeffrey Matthews)	T. N. (Timothy Noad)
J. M. M. (John Mills)	W. G. (William Gardner, 1914-2000)
M. B. (Matthew Bonaccorsi)	W. P. (Wilson Parker 1896-1980)

Other designers whose initials do not appear on the coins:

Christopher Ironside (1913-1992)	Leslie Durbin (1913-2005)
Arnold Machin (1911-1999)	Derek Gorringe
David Wynne (1926-2014)	Bernard Sindall (1925-1998)
Professor Richard Guyatt (1914-2007)	Tom Phillips
Eric Sewell	Edwina Ellis
Oscar Nemon (1906-1985)	David Gentleman
	Matthew Dent

PRE-DECIMAL ISSUES, 1952-71
Die axis ↑↑

GOLD

First coinage, with title BRITT.OMN, 1953. *Proof only. Originally produced for institutional collecting.*

4120 Five Pounds. Young laur. head r. R. St. George 1953..............	*of the highest rarity*
4121 Two Pounds. Young laur. head r. R. St. George 1953..............	*of the highest rarity*
4122 Sovereign. Young laur. head r. R. St. George 1953..................	£425000
4123 Half-Sovereign. Young laur. head r. R. St. George 1953.........	*of the highest rarity*

SECOND ISSUE, BRITT.OMN omitted

4125
1958 Sovereign

	EF	BU		EF	BU
	£	£		£	£

4124 Sovereign. Young laur head r. R. St. George, fine graining on edge

1957...BV   275
1957 Proof *FDC* £13500

4125 Sovereign. Similar, but coarser graining on edge

1958............................BV	275	1963 Proof *FDC* £11500	
1958 Proof *FDC* £12500		1964............................BV	275
1959............................BV	275	1965............................BV	275
1959 Proof *FDC* £12500		1966............................BV	275
1962............................BV	275	1967............................BV	275
1963............................BV	275	1968............................BV	275

SILVER

The Queen's Maundy are now the only coins struck regularly in silver.
The location of the Maundy ceremony is given for each year.

FIRST ISSUE, with title BRITT:OMN:

4126
Maundy Set

	EF	FDC		EF	FDC
	£	£		£	£

4126 Maundy Set (4d., 3d., 2d. and 1d.), 1953. *St Paul's Cathedral* 600   1150
1953 Proof struck in gold *FDC Extremely rare*
1953 Proof struck in nickel bronze *FDC Extremely rare*
4127 — Fourpence. 1953   250
4128 — Threepence. 1953..   225
4129 — Twopence. 1953..   225
4130 — Penny. 1953   375

SECOND ISSUE, with BRITT:OMN: omitted

4131 Maundy Set (4d., 3d., 2d. and 1d.). Uniform dates

1954 *Westminster* 120	250	1956 *Westminster* 120	250
1955 *Southwark*............................ 120	250	1957 *St. Albans* 120	250

BV= Bullion value only. At the time of going to press the spot price for gold was £900 per oz.

4131 Maundy Set

	EF £	FDC £		EF £	FDC £
1958 *Westminster*	120	250	1965 Canterbury	120	250
1959 *Windsor*	120	250	1966 Westminster	120	250
1960 *Westminster*	120	250	1967 Durham	120	250
1961 *Rochester*	120	250	1968 Westminster	120	250
1962 *Westminster*	125	250	1969 Selby	120	250
1963 *Chelmsford*	120	250	1970 Westminster	120	250
1964 Westminster	120	250			

For a continuation of these issues see 'Coins of England, Decimal Issues'.

4132 — Fourpence. 1954-70 ....*from*		20
4133 — Threepence. 1954-70 ....*from*		25
4134 — Twopence. 1954-70 ....*from*		20
4135 — Penny. 1954-70 ....*from*		35

See footnote after 3796

CUPRO-NICKEL

FIRST ISSUE, 1953, with title BRITT.OMN.

4136 - 1953 Coronation Crown

	EF £	BU £	Proof FDC £
4136 Crown. Queen on horseback. R. Crown in centre of emblematical cross, shield of Arms in each angle, 1953	3	8	35

Similar 1953 Frosted 'VIP' proof with more fine detail apparent £1450

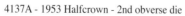

4137A - 1953 Halfcrown - 2nd obverse die   4138 - 1953 Florin

	EF	FDC
4137 Halfcrown. First obverse die, I of DEI points to a space between beads .	5	1700
4137A Halfcrown. Second obverse die, I of DEI points to a bead, with title BRITT:OMN: Young laur. head r. R. Arms, 1953	5	20
4138 Florin. Young laur. head r. R. Double rose, 1953	4	12

4139	4140	4141
1953 'English' Shilling - 1st obv. die	'Scottish' reverse	1953 Sixpence - 2nd obv. die

	BU	Proof FDC
	£	£
	£	£
4139 Shilling. 'English' reverse. Young laur. head r. R. Three lions, 1953........	2	10
4140 Shilling. '— 'Scottish' reverse. Young laur. head r. R. Lion rampant in shield, 1953	2	10
4141 Sixpence. Young laur. head r. R. Interlaced rose, thistle, shamrock and leek, 1953	1	8
4142 Set of 9 uncirculated cu-ni, ni-br and Æ coins (2/6 to 1/4d.) in Royal Mint plastic envelope	30	—

SECOND ISSUE, similar types but omitting BRITT.OMN.

4143	4144
1960 Crown	1965 Churchill Crown

	EF	UNC
	£	£
4143 Crown, 1960. Young laur. head r. R. As 4136	5	12
— — Similar, from polished dies (New York Exhibition issue)	10	35
— — 'VIP' *Proof,* frosted design *FDC* £850		
4144 Crown, Churchill commemorative, 1965. As illustration. R. Bust of Sir Winston Churchill r.		2
— — Similar, "Satin-Finish". VIP *Specimen*		2000
— — —, with 'ON' designer's initials on reverse		4000

4145 Halfcrown. Young laur. head r. R. As 4137

	EF	BU		EF	BU		EF	BU
	£	£		£	£		£	£
1954......................8		45	1960......................		20	1965......................		5
1955......................		12	1961......................		6	1966......................		3
1956......................		18	1961 Polished die ..		25	1967......................		3
1957......................		8	1962......................		6	1970 Proof *FDC* £14		
1958......................8		40	1963......................		6			
1959......................8		45	1964......................		8			

4146
1957 Florin

	EF £	*BU* £		*EF* £	*BU* £
4146 Florin. Young laur. head r. R. As 4138					
1954..8		50	1962..		5
1955..		12	1963..		4
1956..		12	1964..		4
1957..8		45	1965..		4
1958..10		50	1966..		3
1959..10		60	1967..		3
1960..		12	1970 Proof *FDC* £12		
1961..		12			

4147 Shilling. 'English' reverse. Young laur. head r. R. As 4139

	EF £	*BU* £		*EF* £	*BU* £
1954..		6	1961..		3
1955..		6	1962..		2
1956..		12	1963..		2
1957..		5	1964..		2
1958..8		65	1965..		2
1959..		5	1966..		2
1960..		8	1970 Proof *FDC* £10		

4148 Shilling. 'Scottish' reverse. Young laur. head r. R. As 4140

	EF £	*BU* £		*EF* £	*BU* £
1954..		6	1961..		20
1955..		8	1962..		5
1956..		12	1963..		2
1957..5		35	1964..		2
1958..		4	1965..		2
1959..10		110	1966..		2
1960..		8	1970 Proof *FDC* £10		

4149 Sixpence. Young laur. head r. R. As 4141

	EF £	*BU* £		*EF* £	*BU* £
1954..		8	1962..		2
1955..		4	1963..		2
1956..		5	1964..		2
1957..		4	1965..		1
1958..		10	1966..		1
1959..		3	1967..		1
1960..		7	1970 Proof *FDC* £8		
1961..		6			

NICKEL BRASS

FIRST ISSUE, with title BRITT.OMN.

4152	4153
1953 Brass Threepence - 2nd obv. die Proof	Second issue

	EF	BU	BU
	£	£	£

4152 Threepence (dodecagonal). Young laur. head r. R. Crowned portcullis, 1953 4
— Proof *FDC* £12

SECOND ISSUE (omitting BRIT.OMN)
4153 Threepence Similar type

1954	8	1962	2
1955	10	1963	2
1956	10	1964	2
1957	6	1965	2
1958	15	1966	1
1959	6	1967	1
1960	7	1970 Proof *FDC* £8	
1961	3		

BRONZE

FIRST ISSUE, with title BRITT.OMN.

4154	4155	4156
1953 Penny - 1st obv. die	1953 Halfpenny	1953 Farthing
	2nd obv. die	

	VF	EF	BU	Proof FDC
	£	£	£	£

4154 Penny. Young laur. head r. R. Britannia (only issued with Royal Mint set in plastic envelope)
1953 Beaded border 1   3   10   25
1953 Toothed border *FDC* £3250
4155 Halfpenny. Young laur. head r. R. Ship, 1953 3   12
4156 Farthing. Young laur. head r. R. Wren, 1953 2   10

	EF	BU		EF	BU
	£	£		£	£

SECOND ISSUE, omitting BRITT.OMN.

4157 Penny. Young laur. head r. R. Britannia (1954-60 *not issued*)

1954 *Unique*	77500	1965	1
1961	3	1966	1
1962	1	1967	1
1963	1	1970 Proof *FDC* £8	
1964	1		

4158 Halfpenny. Young laur. head r. R. Ship (1961 *not issued*)

1954	8	1960	2
1954 larger border teeth	10	1962	1
1955	6	1963	1
1956	8	1964	1
1957	4	1965	1
1957 calm sea	50	1966	1
1958	3	1967	1
1959	2	1970 Proof *FDC* £5	

4159 Farthing. Young laur. head r. R. Wren

1954	6	1956	3	10
1955	6			

PROOF SETS

PS19 Coronation, **1953.** Crown to Farthing (10 coins) .... *FDC*   150
PS20 'Last Sterling', **1970.** Halfcrown to Halfpenny plus medallion .... *FDC*   30

PRE-DECIMAL PROOF SETS

All prices quoted assume coins are in their original case. Issued by the Royal Mint in official case from 1887 onwards, but earlier sets were issued privately by the engraver. All pieces have a superior finish to that of the current coins.

		No. of coins	FDC £
PS1	**George IV, 1826.** New issue, Five Pounds to Farthing .... (11)		150000
PS2	**William IV, 1831.** Coronation, Two Pounds to Farthing .... (14)		100000
PS3	**Victoria, 1839.** Young head. "Una and the Lion" Five Pounds and Sovereign to Farthing .... (15)		300000
PS4	— **1853.** Sovereign to Half-Farthing, including Gothic type Crown .... (16)		130000
PS5	— **1887.** Jubilee bust for Golden Jubilee, Five Pounds to Threepence .... (11)		40000
PS6	— **1887.** Silver Crown to Threepence .... (7)		6750
PS7	— **1893.** Old bust, Five Pounds to Threepence .... (10)		50000
PS8	— **1893.** Silver Crown to Threepence .... (6)		8000
PS9	**Edward VII, 1902.** Coronation, Five Pounds to Maundy Penny. Matt finish to surfaces .... (13)		8000
PS10	— **1902.** Sovereign to Maundy Penny. Matt finish .... (11)		2500
PS11	**George V, 1911.** Coronation, Five Pounds to Maundy Penny .... (12)		20000
PS12	— **1911.** Sovereign to Maundy Penny .... (10)		4250
PS13	— **1911.** Silver Halfcrown to Maundy Penny .... (8)		1350
PS14	— **1927.** New Coinage. Wreath type Crown to Threepence .... (6)		675
PS15	**George VI, 1937.** Coronation. Five Pounds to Half-Sovereign .... (4)		15000
PS16	— **1937.** Coronation. Crown to Farthing, including Maundy Set .... (15)		400
PS17	— **1950.** Mid-Century, Halfcrown to Farthing .... (9)		175
PS18	— **1951.** Festival of Britain, Crown to Farthing .... (10)		235
PS19	**Elizabeth II, 1953.** Coronation. Crown to Farthing .... (10)		165
PS20	— **1970.** "Last Sterling" set. Halfcrown to Halfpenny plus medallion .... (8)		30

Truly flawless FDC sets of the earlier period are commanding prices in excess of catalogue values'

A SELECT NUMISMATIC BIBLIOGRAPHY

Listed below is a selection of general books on British numismatics and other works that the specialist collector will need to consult.

General Books:
BROOKE, G. C. *English Coins*. 3rd ed., 1966.
BULL, M., *English Silver Coinage since 1649* (Spink 2015)
CHALLIS, C. E. (ed.) *A New History of the Royal Mint*. 1992
GRUEBER, H. A. *Handbook of the Coins of Great Britain and Ireland*. Revised 1970
KENYON, R. Ll. *Gold Coins of England*. 1884
NORTH, J. J. *English Hammered Coinage*, Vol. I, c. 650-1272. 1994; Vol. II, 1272-1662. 1991
STEWARTBY, Lord. *English Coins 1180-1551*. 2009
SUTHERLAND, C. H. V. *English Coinage, 600-1900*. 1972

Specialist Works:
ABRAMSON, T. Sceattas, *An Illustrated Guide*. 2006
ALLEN, D. *The Origins of Coinage in Britain: A Reappraisal*. Reprint 1978
ALLEN, D. F. *The Coins of the Coritani*. (SCBI no. 3) 1963
ALLEN, D. F. *English Coins in the British Museum: The Cross-and-Crosslets* (*'Tealby'*) *type of Henry II*. 1951
ALLEN, M. *The Durham Mint*. 2003
ARCHIBALD, M. M. and BLUNT, C. E. *British Museum. Anglo-Saxon Coins. Athelstan to the reform of Edgar*. 924-c.973. 1986
ASKEW, G. *The Coinage of Roman Britain*. (1951) Reprinted 1980.
BESLY, E. M. *Coins and Medals of the English Civil War*. 1990
BIDDLE, M., with HARVEY, Y., *The Winchester Mint* (Oxford 2012)
BLACKBURN, M. A. S. *Anglo-Saxon Monetary History*. 1986
− − *Viking Coinage and Currency in the British Isles*. 2011
BLUNT, C. E. and WHITTON, C. A. *The Coinages of Edward IV and of Henry VI* (*Restored*).
BLUNT, C. E., STEWART, B.H.I.H. and LYON, C.S.S. *Coinage in Tenth-Century England. From Edward the Elder to Edgar's Reform*. 1989
BOON, G. C. *Coins of the Anarchy. 1135-54*. 1988
BRAND, J. D. *The English Coinage 1180-1247: Money, Mints and Exchanges* 1994
BROOKE, G. C. *English Coins in the British Museum: The Norman Kings*. 1916
BROWN, I. D., COMBER, C. H. & WILKINSON, W. *The Hammered Silver coins produced at the Tower Mint during the reign of Elizabeth I*. 2006
BROWN, I. D. and DOLLEY, M. *Bibliography of Coin Hoards of Great Britain and Ireland 1500-1967*. 1971
BUCK, I. *Medieval English Groats*. 2000
CARSON, R. A. G. *Mints, Dies and Currency. Essays in Memory of Albert Baldwin*. 1971
CHICK, D. *The Coinage of Offa and his Contemporaries*. 2010
CHURCHILL, R. *Mints and Moneyers during the reign of Henry III*. 2012
CHURCHILL, R. and THOMAS B. *The Brussels Hoard of 1908. The Long Cross Coinage of Henry III*. 2012
CLOKE, H.J. and TOONE, L., *The London Mint of Constantius and Constantine* (Spink 2015)
DAVIES, P. J. *British Silver Coins Since 1816 with Engravers' Patterns and Proofs and Unofficial Pieces*. 1982
DE JERSEY, P. *Coinage in Iron Age Armorica*. 1994
DOLLEY, R. H. M. (ed.). *Anglo-Saxon Coins; studies presented to Sir Frank Stenton*. 1964

EAGLEN, R.J., *The Abbey and Mint of Bury St. Edmunds,* Vol I, to 1279, Vol II, from 1279 (Spink 2006, 2014)

EVERSON, T. *The Galata Guide to The Farthing Tokens of James I & Charles I.* 2007

FREEMAN, M. J. *The Bronze Coinage of Great Britain.* 2006

GRIERSON, P. and BLACKBURN, M. A. S. *Medieval European Coinage, vol. 1, The Early Middle Ages.* 1986

HOBBS, R. *British Iron Age Coins in the British Museum.* 1996

KEARY, C. and GREUBER, H. *English Coins in the British Museum: Anglo-Saxon Series.* 1887, reprinted, 1970, 2 volumes.

LAKER, A. J. *The portrait Groats of Henry VIII.* 1978

LAWRENCE, L. A. *The Coinage of Edward III from 1351.*

LINECAR, H. W. A. *The Crown Pieces of Great Britain and the British Commonwealth.* 1962
— — *English Proof and Pattern Crown-Size Pieces.* 1968

MACK, R. P. *The R. P. Mack Collection, Ancient British, Anglo-Saxon and Norman Coins.* (SCBI no. 20) 1973

MANVILLE, H. E. *Encyclopedia of British Numismatics. Numismatic Guide to British and Irish Periodicals 1731-1991.* 1993

MANVILLE, H. E. and ROBERTSON, T. J. *An Annotated Bibliography of British Numismatic Auction Catalogues from 1710 to the Present.* 1986

MARSH, M. A. *The Gold Half Sovereign.* 2nd Edition, revised 2004

MARSH, M. A. *The Gold Sovereign.* 2nd Edition 1999

MASS, J. P. *The J. P. Mass collection of English Short Cross Coins 1180-1247. (SCBI 56).* 2001

MOSSOP H.R., *The Lincoln Mint c.890-1279* (1970)

NAISMITH, R. *The Coinage of Southern England, 796-c.865.* 2011

NORTH, J. J. *Edwardian English Silver Coins 1279-1351. (SCBI 39)* 1989

NORTH J.J., *English Hammered Coinage,* Vol I, c.600-1272, and Vol II, 1272-1662, third edition (Spink 1994, 1991)

NORTH, J. J. and PRESTON-MORLEY, P. J. *The John G. Brooker Collection: Coins of Charles I. (SCBI 33)* 1984

PECK, C. W. *English Copper, Tin and Bronze Coins in the British Museum, 1558-1958.* 1970

RAYNER, P.A. *The English Silver Coinage from 1649.* 5th ed. 1992

REECE, R. *Coinage in Roman Britain,* 1987

ROBINSON, Dr. B. *The Royal Maundy.* 1992

RUDD, C. *Ancient British Coins (ABC).* 2009

RUDING, REV. R. *Annals of the Coinage of Great Britain.* 3rd Edition 1840

SEAR, D. R. *Roman Coins and their Values. 4th Edition* (1999) Reprinted 2000

SILLS, J. *Gaulish and Early British Gold Coinage.* 2003

THOMPSON, J. D. A. *Inventory of British Coin Hoards, A.D. 600-1500.* 1956

VAN ARSDELL, R. *Celtic Coinage of Britain.* 1989

VAN ARSDELL, R. D. *The Coinage of the Dobunni.* 1994

WHITTON, C. A. *The Heavy Coinage of Henry VI.*

WILSON, A. and RASMUSSEN, M. *English Patten, Trial and Proof Coin in Gold, 1547-1968.* 2000

WITHERS, P. & B. R. *The Galata Guide to the Pennies of Edward I and II and the Coins of the mint of Berwick-upon-Tweed.* 2006

WOODHEAD, P. *English Gold Coins 1257-1603. The Herbert Schneider Collection, vol. 1 (SCBI 47)* 1996

— — *English Gold Coins 1603-20th Century. The Herbert Schneider Collection, vol. 2 (SCBI 57)* 2002

WREN, C. R. *The Short-cross coinage 1180-1247. Henry II to Henry III. An illustrated Guide to Identification.* 1992

— — *The Voided Long-Cross Coinage 1247-1279. Henry III and Edward I.* 1993

— — *The English Long-Cross Pennies 1279-1489. Edward I-Henry VII.* 1995

For further references to British hammered coinage see *Sylloge of Coins of the British Isles,* a serial publication now comprising 68 volumes cataloguing collections in private hands and institutions. For a full list of the volumes published to date in this series, please contact Spink at the address below.

Other authoritative papers are published in the *Numismatic Chronicle and British Numismatic Journal.* A complete book list is available from Spink & Son Ltd., 69 Southampton Row, Bloomsbury, London WC1B 4ET. Tel: 020 7563 4046 Fax: 020 7563 4068. Email: Books@spink.com. Spink will either have copies of newly published Numismatic books, or, if not in stock, will be able to order copies from the publishers.

Further information regarding membership of the British Numismatic Society can be found at www.britnumsoc.org

APPENDIX II

LATIN OR FOREIGN LEGENDS ON ENGLISH COINS

A DOMINO FACTUM EST ISTUD ET EST MIRABILE IN OCULIS NOSTRIS.
(This is the Lord's doing and it is marvellous in our eyes: *Psalm 118.23.*) First used on
'fine' sovereign of Mary.

AMOR POPULI PRAESIDIUM REGIS. (The love of the people is the King's
protection.) Reverse legend on angels of Charles I.

ANNO REGNI PRIMO, etc. (In the first year of the reign, etc.) Used around the edge of
many of the larger milled denominations.

CHRISTO AUSPICE REGNO. (I reign under the auspice of Christ.) Used extensively in
the reign of Charles I.

CIVIUM INDUSTRIA FLORET CIVITAS. (By the industry of its people the State
flourishes.) On the 1951 Festival Crown of George VI.

CULTORES SUI DEUS PROTEGIT. (God protects His worshippers.) On gold double
crowns and crowns of Charles I.

DECUS ET TUTAMEN. (An ornament and a safeguard: Virgil, *Aenid,* v.262.) This
inscription on the edge of all early large milled silver was suggested by Evelyn, he
having seen it on the vignette in Cardinal Richelieu's Greek Testament, and of course
refers to the device as a means to prevent clipping. This legend also appears on the
edge of U.K. and Northern Ireland one pound coins.

DIEU ET MON DROIT. (God and my right.) On halfcrowns of George IV and later monarchs

DIRIGE DEUS GRESSUS MEOS. (May God direct my steps: *Psalm 118.133.*) On the
'Una' Five pounds of Queen Victoria.

DOMINE NE IN FURORE TUO ARGUAS ME. (O Lord, rebuke me not in Thine anger:
Psalm 6, 1.). First used on the half-florin of Edward III and then on all half-nobles.

D*o*mi*N*us *Deus Omnipotens* REX. (Lord God, Almighty King.) Viking coins.

DUM SPIRO SPERO. (Whilst I live, I hope.) On the coins struck at Pontefract Castle
during the Civil War after Charles I had been imprisoned.

EXALTABITUR IN GLORIA. (He shall be exalted in glory: *Psalm 111.9.*) On all
quarter-nobles.

EXURGAT DEUS ET DISSIPENTUR INIMICI EIUS. (Let God arise and let His
enemies be scattered: *Psalm* 68, 1.) On the Scottish ducat and early English coins of
James I (VI) and was chosen by the King himself. Also on Charles I, civil war, and
Declaration coins,

FACIAM EOS IN GENTEM UNAM. (I will make them one nation: *Ezekiel, 37, 22.)* On
unites and laurels of James I.

FLORENT CONCORDIA REGNA. (Through concord kingdoms flourish.) On gold unite
of Charles I and broad of Charles II.

HANC DEUS DEDIT. (God has given this, i.e. the crown .) On siege-pieces of Pontefract
struck in the name of Charles II.

HAS NISI PERITURUS MIHI ADIMAT NEMO. (Let no one remove these [letters] from
me under penalty of death.) On the edge of crowns and half-crowns of Cromwell.

HENRICUS ROSAS REGNA JACOBUS. (Henry united the roses, James the kingdoms.)
On English and Scottish gold coins of James I (VI).

HONI SOIT QUI MAL Y PENSE. (Evil to him who evil thinks.) The Motto of the Order
of the Garter, first used on the Hereford (?) halfcrowns of Charles I. It also occurs on
the Garter Star in the centre of the reverse of the silver coins of Charles II, but being so
small it is usually illegible; it is more prominent on the coinage of George III.

ICH DIEN. (I serve.) Aberystwyth Furnace 2d, and Decimal 2p. The motto of The Prince
of Wales.

INIMICOS EJUS INDUAM CONFUSIONE. (As for his enemies I shall clothe them with
shame: *Psalm* 132, 18.) On shillings of Edward VI struck at Durham House, Strand.

JESUS AUTEM TRANSIENS PER MEDIUM ILLORUM IBAT. (But Jesus, passing
through the midst of them, went His way: *Luke iv. 30.)* The usual reverse legend on
English nobles, ryals and hammered sovereigns before James I; also on the very rare
Scottish noble of David II of Scotland and the unique Anglo-Gallic noble of Edward the
Black Prince.

JUSTITIA THRONUM FIRMAT. (Justice strengthens the throne.) On Charles I half-
groats and pennies and Scottish twenty-penny pieces.

LUCERNA PEDIBUS MEIS VERBUM EST. (Thy word is a lamp unto my feet: *Psalm
119, 105.)* Obverse legend on a rare half-sovereign of Edward VI struck at Durham
House, Strand.

MIRABILIA FECIT. (He made marvellously: *Psalm 97.1.*) On the Viking coins of (?) York.

NEMO ME IMPUNE LACESSIT. (No-one provokes me with impunity.) On the 1984
Scottish one pound. Motto of The Order of the Thistle.

NUMMORUM FAMULUS. (The servant of the coinage.) The legend on the edge of the
English tin coinage at the end of the seventeenth century.

O CRUX AVE SPES UNICA. (Hail! O Cross, our only hope.) On the reverse of all half-
angels.

PAX MISSA PER ORBEM. (Peace sent throughout the world.) The reverse legend of a
pattern farthing of Anne.

PAX QUÆRITUR BELLO. (Peace is sought by war.) The reverse legend of the
Cromwell broad.

PER CRUCEM TUAM SALVA NOS CHRISTE REDEMPTOR. (By Thy cross, save us,
O Christ, our Redeemer.) The normal reverse of English angels.

PLEIDIOL WYF I'M GWLAD. (True am I to my country.) Used on the 1985 Welsh one
pound. Taken from the Welsh National Anthem.

POST MORTEM PATRIS PRO FILIO. (After the death of the father for the son.) On
siege-pieces struck at Pontefract in 1648 (old style) after the execution of Charles I.

POSUI DEUM ADJUTOREM MEUM. (I have made God my Helper: *comp. Psalm* 54,
4.) Used on many English and Irish silver coins from Edward III until 1603. Altered to
POSUIMUS and NOSTRUM on the coins of Philip and Mary.

PROTECTOR LITERIS LITERÆ NUMMIS CORONA ET SALUS. (A protection to the
letters [on the face of the coin], the letters [on the edge] are a garland and a safeguard to
the coinage.) On the edge of the rare fifty-shilling piece of Cromwell.

QUÆ DEUS CONJUNXIT NEMO SEPARET. (What God hath joined together let no
man put asunder: *Matthew 19, 6.)* On the larger silver English and Scottish coins of
James I after he succeeded to the English throne.

REDDE CUIQUE QUOD SUUM EST. (Render to each that which is his own.) On a
Henry VIII type groat of Edward VI struck by Sir Martin Bowes at Durham House, Strand.

RELIGIO PROTESTANTIVM LEGES ANGLIÆ LIBERTAS PARLIAMENTI. (The
religion of the Protestants, the laws of England, the liberty of the Parliament.) This is
known as the 'Declaration' and refers to Charles I's declaration to the Privy Council at
Wellington, 19 September, 1642; it is found on many of his coins struck at the
provincial mints during the Civil War. Usually abbreviated to REL:PROT:LEG:
ANG:LIB:PAR:

ROSA SINE SPINA. (A rose without a thorn.) Found on some gold and small coins of
Henry VIII and later reigns.

RUTILANS ROSA SINE SPINA. (A dazzling rose without a thorn.) As last but on small
gold only.

SCUTUM FIDEI PROTEGET EUM or EAM. (The shield of faith shall protect him, or her.) On much of the gold of Edward VI and Elizabeth.

SIC VOS NON VOBIS (Thus we labour but not for ourselves). 1994 £2 Bank of England.

TALI DICATA SIGNO MENS FLUCTUARI NEQUIT. (Consecrated by such a sign the mind cannot waver: from a hymn by Prudentius written in the fourth century, entitled 'Hymnus ante Somnum'.) Only on the gold 'George noble' of Henry VIII.

TIMOR DOMINI FONS VITÆ. (The fear of the Lord is a fountain of life: *Proverbs, 14, 27.)* On many shillings of Edward VI.

TVAETVR VNITA DEVS. (May God guard these united, i.e. kingdoms.) On many English Scottish and Irish coins of James I.

VERITAS TEMPORIS FILIA. (Truth, the daughter of Time.) On English and Irish coins of Mary Tudor.

Some Royal Titles:

REX ANGL*orum*—King of the English.

REX SAXONIORVM OCCIDENTALIVM —King of the West Saxons.

DEI GRA*tia* REX *ANGL*iae ET FRANC*iae Domi*N*us HYB*erniae ET AQVIT*aniae—By the Grace of God, King of England and France, Lord of Ireland and Aquitaine.

D*ei GRAtia Magnae Britanniae, FRanciae ET Hiberniae REX Fidei Defensor BRunsviciensis ET Luneburgen-sis Dux, Sacri Romani Imperii Archi-THesaurarius ET ELector*=By the Grace of God, King of Great Britain, France and Ireland, Defender of the Faith, Duke of Brunswick and Luneburg, High Treasurer and Elector of the Holy Roman Empire.

BRITANNIARUM REX —King of the Britains (i.e. Britain and British territories overseas).

BRITT:OMN:REX:FID:DEF:IND:IMP: —King of all the Britains, Defender of the Faith, Emperor of India.

VIVAT REGINA ELIZABETHA — Long live Queen Elizabeth. On the 1996 £5 Queen's 70th birthday £5 crown.

APPENDIX III

NUMISMATIC CLUBS AND SOCIETIES

Coin News, The Searcher and *Treasure Hunting*, are the major monthly magazines covering numismatics. Many local numismatic societies and clubs in the British Isles are affiliated to the British Association of Numismatic Societies (BANS) which holds an annual Congress and an annual Conference (weekend meetings) with a range of speakers in convivial surroundings. Details and contacts for a club or society near can be found online, www.coinclubs.org.uk or by contacting the Hon. Secretary, Phyllis Stoddart, British Association of Numismatic Societies, c/o Dept. of Numismatics, Manchester Museum, Oxford Road, Manchester M13 9PL email: phyllis.stoddart@manchester.ac.uk.

The two principal learned societies are the Royal Numismatic Society (RNS), c/o Department of Coins and Medals, the British Museum, Great Russell Street, Bloomsbury, London WC1B 3DG, and the British Numismatic Society (BNS), c/o The Secretary, Peter Preston-Morley, c/o Dix, Noonan, Webb, 16 Bolton Street, London, W1J 8BQ, email: ppm@dnw.co.uk. Both these societies publish an annual journal. To find out more about membership, meetings and publications, for the RNS go to www.numismatics.org.uk and for the BNS, go to www.britnumsoc.org.uk

APPENDIX IV

MINTMARKS AND OTHER SYMBOLS ON ENGLISH COINS

A Mintmark (*mm.*), is a term borrowed from Roman and Greek numismatics where it showed the place of mintage; it was generally used on English coins to show where the legend began (a religious age preferred a cross for the purpose). Later, this mark, since the dating of coins was not usual, had a periodic significance, changing from time to time. Hence it was of a secret or 'privy' nature; other privy marks on a coin might be the code-mark of a particular workshop or workman. Thus a privy mark (including the *mintmark.*) might show when a coin was made, or who made it. In the use of precious metals this knowledge was necessary to guard against fraud and counterfeiting.

Mintmarks are sometimes termed 'initial marks' as they are normally placed at the commencement of the inscription. Some of the symbols chosen were personal badges of the ruling monarch, such as the rose and sun of York, or the boar's head of Richard III, the dragon of Henry Tudor or the thistle of James I; others are heraldic symbols or may allude to the mint master responsible for the coinage, e.g. the *mm.* bow used on the Durham House coins struck under John Bowes and the WS mark of William Sharrington of Bristol.

A table of mintmarks is given overleaf. Where mintmarks appear in the catalogue they are sometimes referred to only by the reference number, in order to save space, i.e. *mm. 28* (=mintmark Sun), *mm.28/74 (=mm.* Sun on obverse, *mm.* Coronet on reverse), *mm. 28/- (=mm.* Sun on obverse only).

1	Edward III, Cross 1 (Class B+C).	45	Slipped Trefoil, James I (1).	91A	Crowned Leopard's Head with collar (Edw. VI).
2	Edward III, broken Cross 1 (Class D).	46	Slipped Trefoil, James I (2).	92	Lion.
		47	Quatrefoil.	93	Lion rampant.
3	Edward III, Cross 2 (Class E)	48	Saltire.	94	Martlet.
4	Edward III, Cross 3 (Class G)	49	Pinecone.	95	Mascle.
5	Cross Potent (Edw. III Treaty)	50	Leaf (-mascle, Hen. VI).	96	Negro's Head.
		51	Leaf (-trefoil, Hen. VI).	97	Ostrich's Head.
6	Cross Pattée (Edw. III Post Treaty Rich. III).	52	Arrow.	98	P in brackets.
		53	Pheon.	99	Pall.
7	(a) Plain of Greek Cross.	54	A.	100	Pear.
	(b) Cross Moline.	55	Annulet.	101	Plume.
8	Cross Patonce.	56	Annulet-with-pellet.	102	Plume. Aberystwyth and Bristol.
9	Cross Fleuree.	57	Anchor.		
10	Cross Calvary (Cross on steps).	58	Anchor & B.	103	Plume. Oxford.
		59	Flower & B.	104	Plume. Shrewsbury.
11	Long Cross Fitchée.	60	Bell.	105	Lis.
12	Short Cross Fitchée.	61	Book.	106	Lis.
13	Restoration Cross (Hen. VI).	62	Boar's Head (early Richard III).	107	Portcullis.
14	Latin Cross.			108	Portcullis, Crowned.
15	Voided Cross (Henry VI).	63	Boar's Head (later Richard III).	109	Sceptre.
16	Saltire Cross.			110	Sunburst.
17	Cross and 4 pellets.	64	Boar's Head, Charles I.	111	Swan.
18	Pierced Cross.	65	Acorn (a) Hen. VIII	112	R in brackets.
19	Pierced Cross & pellet.		(b) Elizabeth.	113	Sword.
20	Pierced Cross & central pellet.	66	Bow.	114	T (Henry VIII).
		67	Br. (Bristol, Chas. I).	115	TC monogram.
21	Cross Crosslet.	68	Cardinal's Hat.	116	WS monogram.
22	Curved Star (rayant).	69	Castle (Henry VIII).	117	y or Y.
23	Star.	70	Castle with H.	118	Dragon (Henry VII).
24	Spur Rowel.	71	Castle (Chas. I).	119	(a) Triangle
25	Mullet.	72	Crescent (a) Henry VIII		(b) Triangle in Circle.
26	Pierced Mullet.		(b) Elizabeth.	120	Sun (Parliament).
27	Eglantine.	73	Pomegranate. (Mary; Henry VIII's is broader).	121	Uncertain mark.
28	Sun (Edw. IV).			122	Grapple.
29	Mullet (Henry V).	74	Coronet.	123	Tun.
30	Pansy.	75	Crown.	124	Woolpack.
31	Heraldic Cinquefoil (Edw. IV).	76	Crozier (a) Edw. III	125	Thistle.
			(b) Hen. VIII.	126	Figure 6 (Edw. VI).
32	Heraldic Cinquefoil (James I).	77	Ermine.	127	Floriated cross.
		78	Escallop (Hen. VII).	128	Lozenge.
33	Rose (Edw. IV).	79	Escallop (James I).	129	Billet.
34	Rosette (Edw. IV).	80	Eye (in legend Edw. IV).	130	Plume. Bridgnorth or late declaration
35	Rose (Chas. I).	81	Eye (Parliament).		
36	Catherine Wheel.	82	Radiate Eye (Hen. VII).	131	Two lions.
37	Cross in circle.	83	Gerb.	132	Clasped book.
38	Halved Sun (6 rays) & Rose.	84	Grapes.	133	Cross pommée.
39	Halved Sun (4 rays) & Rose.	85	Greyhound's Head.	134	Bugle.
40	Lis-upon-Half-Rose.	86	Hand.	135	Crowned T (Tournai, Hen VIII)
41	Lis-upon-Sun & Rose.	87	Harp.		
42	Lis-Rose dimidiated.	88	Heart.	136	An incurved pierced cross
43	Lis-issuant-from-Rose.	89	Helmet.		
44	Trefoil.	90	Key.		
		91	Leopard's Head.		

The reign listed after a mintmark indicates that from which the drawing is taken. A similar mm. may have been used in another reign and will be found in the chronological list at the beginning of each reign.